University of
Chester

This book is to be returned on or before the last date stamped below. Overdue charges will be incurred by the late return of books.

COMPARATIVE PSYCHOLOGY

An Evolutionary Analysis
of Animal Behavior

Edited by

M. Ray Denny
Michigan State University

JOHN WILEY & SONS
NEW YORK   CHICHESTER   BRISBANE   TORONTO

In Memory
of
Stanley C. Ratner
(1925-1975)

Library of Congress Cataloging in Publication Data:

Main entry under title:
Comparative psychology.

Includes index.
1. Animals, Habits and behavior of.   2. Psychology,
Comparative.   3. Evolution. I. Denny, Maurice Ray,
1918-

QL751.C65   574.5   79-21123
ISBN 0-471-70930-1

Printed in the United States of America

10 9 8 7 6 5 4 3 2 1

COMPARATIVE PSYCHOLOGY

An Evolutionary Analysis
of Animal Behavior

PREFACE

This text in comparative animal behavior is dedicated to the memory of Professory Stanley C. Ratner who had been planning, together with Ralph Levine and me, to write such a book just before his untimely death at the end of 1975. This edited book of contributed chapters takes the place of the original plan and holds to the original idea of an undergraduate text at the junior-senior level or as a beginning graduate text.

Most of the contributors to this book are former graduate students at Michigan State University who either received their Ph.D. or M.A. degrees under Stan Ratner's supervision or were strongly influenced by his teachings. And they were the ones to initiate the project. In addition, in this younger group of contributors, there are Jane Halonen who was a student of mine while teaching as a visiting professor at the University of Wisconsin-Milwaukee and Professor Dodd who was a colleague of Professor Weisman. There is also an older group who were colleagues at Michigan State or in graduate school with Stan at Indiana University.

Considerable effort was made to be comprehensive in covering the field of animal behavior. For example, although there is no chapter specifically devoted to the class of aggressive behavior, several other chapters—those on defense against predation, scent marking, applied animal psychology, parenting, and sexual behavior—treat various aspects of aggression.

Care has been taken to eliminate instances of gross overlap from chapter to chapter, but unavoidably in this sort of textbook there is some duplication of material. However, these well-spaced duplications in quite different contexts, according to good pedagogical principles, should improve the overall integration of the subject matter as well as facilitate the learning of certain points.

Special thanks go to Drs. Jerry Eyer, James Reynierse, Augustus Lumia, and Michael Figler for their encouragement and advice in this project.

M. Ray Denny
East Lansing, MI, 1979

CONTENTS

1

Introduction and Overview

M. Ray Denny
Michigan State University

This book represents a real adventure for the student — an unusual opportunity to learn many basic, interesting, and sometime, intricate facts about the behavior of hundreds of different animals. As human beings, we are naturally quite familiar with countless facets of human behavior, including how to classify much of our behavior and even how to predict behavior successfully on a number of occasions. However, when it comes to knowing about and understanding the behavior of other animals, most of us are woefully ignorant, and the common tendency is to conceptualize their behavior in terms of human characteristics or response classes. This sort of anthropomorphic view of animal behavior, as C. Lloyd Morgan warned comparative psychologists years ago in his Canon of Parsimony, can obscure both an appropriate classification of behavior and the identification of relevant independent variables. We hope that this text will help erase any residual anthropomorphism that the reader may harbor; but, perhaps more importantly, an objective view of much of animal behavior could also help in viewing human behavior more objectively and sensibly.

Countless aspects of behavior are touched on in this volume, but there are discernible patterns that make it possible to categorize many diverse behaviors into a limited number of response classes, thereby emphasizing the behavioral similarities and ties among animals. In addition, there are patterns that help identify certain behaviors as adaptive in the evolutionary sense and other behaviors as adaptive in the sense of being learned instrumental acts.

There are even practical advantages to be gained from this book. Behavioral management of a variety of animals is covered in several different chapters in varying degrees. Tortora's chapter, "Applied Animal Psychology," is obviously relevant, and Mountjoy's chapter, "An Historical Approach to Comparative Psychology," falls not too far behind despite the sound of the title.

Overview

Most chapters in this text take a rather neutral position toward theoretical issues and do not espouse a particular methodology, but there are a few conspicuous exceptions. In Part I, which discusses evolutionary and ecological matters, the chapter "Classical Conditioning and Evolution" by Weisman and Dodd clearly takes a cognitive view of learning and conditioning as well as an evolutionary stance. In the same section, Boice strongly and convincingly defends the thesis that domestication does not result in an inferior beast; and Levine champions the systems approach for studying problems in human ecology. In doing so Levine brings to fore a topical treatment that is rarely included in a book on animal behavior — an analysis of how humans fit into their ecological niche along side the rest of the animal kingdom.

In Part Two, which focuses on comparative analysis, some definite points of view are also advanced. Ratner presents his particular view of the comparative method, a conglomerate of ideas that have been distilled, organized, and revised from several of his published articles, chapters, and books. The method of comparative analysis for Ratner applies to any set of events characterized by diversity, not just to animal behavior. The comparative method consists of six sequential stages: (I) the search for *background information*, (II) the development of a *functional classification system* or taxonomy, (III) finding a powerful (valid and reliable) *research preparation* illustrative of a class, (IV) *identifying the variables* that affect the classes (of behavior), (V) *comparing* the classes with each other, and (VI) a *general theory* to integrate all of these comparisons and findings. As implied above, Ratner's comparative method involves comparing across classes of behavior much more than comparing across species or phyla. There are, at least eleven classes of behavior characteristic of most animals, and each of these classes, for example, typically has preconsummatory (appetitive) and postconsummatory components as well as a consummatory component.

The chapter by Zerbolio, which directly follows the one by Ratner, represents a rather elaborate attempt to use the method of comparative analysis at the advanced level of stage V, which specifically involves a comparison between response classes. Stage IV, which includes the comparison of behaviors between species, is also involved; the avoidance learning of goldfish is compared with that of the rat. The response classes compared in Zerbolio's analysis are two major types of learning, classical conditioning versus the instrumental learning of avoidance. In order to compare these two types of learning in the goldfish, Zerbolio and his associates conducted a series of interrelated experiments aimed at unraveling the question as to how goldfish learn to avoid in a shuttle box situation. Briefly, Zerbolio marshals strong evidence supporting the view that instrumental learning describes the fishes' behavior.

The research strategies that Zerbolio and his students employed are instructive, indicating how answers are arrived at through experimentation and how painstaking and gradual the process is. That is, Zerbolio's chapter has a much narrower scope than the other chapters and a much different mission. Instructors who want their students exposed to methodological thinking should welcome the inclusion of this chapter.

Part Three of the book is concerned with classes of behavior, although not exclusively. Classes of behavior among insects are briefly covered in the chapter on insect behavior by Hagaman in Part Two, and the class of migratory behavior is included in Chapter 4 by O'Kelly in Part One. Chapter 16, the initial chapter in Part Three, is a thorough treatment of sexual behavior, the starting point for all of us. All of the classes of behavior covered in this section are closely interrelated and combine to form the unique behavior repertoire of a species. Nevertheless, a conscious effort was made to put the most closely related classes of behavior next to each other when ordering the chapters. Part Three ends with the chapter on eating or feeding — what we all want to do to the very last — and that chapter ends with a message that could help make this possible.

Historical Considerations for a Comparative Psychology

This section is from a similar presentation in Chapter 1 of Denny and Ratner (1970) that was originally written by Professor Ratner; the general orientation stems from the writings of Kantor (1963). The selection represents a short history of comparative psychology that is more traditional than the unusual chapter by Mountjoy in Part Two.

The Naturalism of the Greeks

The first general treatise in comparative psychology was written by Aristotle. His analysis of behavior is summarized in two books, *De Anima* and *Parva Naturala* (Ross, 1942). *De Anima*, the more comparative of the two, is oriented around several of the objectives of comparative analysis that is covered by Ratner in Chapter 9 of this book. These objectives include the identification and classification of behavior, the postulation of relationships between behavior classes, and a consideration of the development of behavior within species. Aristotle anticipated in detail a number of major ideas regarding behavior, which fell into oblivion and were rediscovered many centuries later. For example, he postulated phylogenetic development, continuity between species, and a doctrine of five senses. Aristotle noted and described basic functions that arise from biological organization, such as nutrition, sensation, discrimination, appetite, and locomotion; and, finally, he proposed a doctrine of behavior modification (an elementary S-R theory).

The Rise of Dualism

The insights and formulations regarding behavior that culminated in Aristotle's work were set aside and virtually lost for many centuries. During these centuries another philosophical model dictated much of the thinking of scholars. This model, called *dualism*, was based on an assumption of two worlds — the psychic and the physical. During this period more attention was paid to defining the nature of the soul (the psychic world), than to exploring the natural characteristics of the body (the physical world).

Eventually the idea of two worlds (dualism) became considered a basic fact, although dualism is more properly considered an assumption. This trend toward dualism followed naturally from the domination by theology of most of the practical and scholarly aspects of life. In short, comparative psychology was not a "going concern" during this time, nor were any of the biological sciences.

Dualism in Disguise

The seventeenth century saw a shift in the style of thinking of scholars that had important implications for all biological and psychological inquiry. The shift is characterized as follows: "In the first place, there is an intensification of the sensitivity to *events* on the part of the thinkers of the period; in the second, these thinkers take definite account of the mechanical and other technological advancements evolved at the time" (Kantor, 1963, p. 360). Some of the outstanding figures involved in this shift were Hobbes, Descartes, Spinoza, and Leibnitz.

These men were dualists, but they began to attempt to naturalize the soul and make it a topic for scientific inquiry. They did not seriously question or reject the assumption of dualism, but worked within its framework. The transcedental soul became disguised in naturalistic, quantitative, or quasi-experimental theorizing. The talk shifted from the soul to the mind; and Descartes' separation of animals from humans in terms of two principles of functioning, mechanical versus rational, further facilitated the advance in biological inquiry of animals other than humans, even if humans were not included. About this time, Harvey was demonstrating the principles of circulation of blood in animals, and human anatomy was being studied from the examination of a human body that had become snagged in a river. The "dissection" was made by the action of the river's currents flowing over the body.

Dualism in Retreat

The scientific advances from the seventeenth to the twentieth centuries were almost breathtaking. These advances came in observation and analysis, and in methods and technology. For example, a classification, or taxonomy, of animal forms was available for Darwin's incisive theory of the mechanism associated with the origins and development of animal forms. Available surgical and recording techniques permitted the study of neural and muscular tissue of animals as shown in the work of Hall (1790-1857) and Flourens 1794-1867). These advances in the spirit of philosophical materialism furthered reformulations of dualism. Emphases on the mind gave way to emphases on the central nervous system and to organic theories of motivation, such as hormonal theories.

During this period many of the properties of the transcendental soul were simply attributed to organs and structures such as the hormones or the nervous system. Following Darwin, there was general espousal of the idea of *continuity of process* across all animal forms. The naturalization of the soul and the theory of evolution were specific forerunners of contemporary comparative psychology. Excerpts from the writings of several important figures of the time are included below to give the flavor of this work.

Charles Darwin (1809-1882) attempted a comprehensive review of behavior following the evolutionary model, a review described in his book, *Expression of the Emotions in Man and Animals*. Darwin stated, "I will begin by giving the three principles which appear to me to account for most of the expressions and gestures involuntarily used by man and the lower animals, under the influence of various emotions and sensations"

(1920, p. 27). Darwin then proceeded to describe specific movements, postures, and facial characteristics of a variety of species and to relate these movements and expressions to the "states of mind of the animal."

C. Lloyd Morgan, author of the famous Canon of Parsimony, dealt explicitly with animal behavior. He postulated a classification of behavior that included the categories of organic, conscious, instinctive, intelligent, social, and emotional behaviors. Morgan dealt with these behaviors in terms of the variable of the species.

Morgan used the abundant data that had been collected with regard to a number of animal forms and, like Aristotle, he even included material on the behavior of plants. In tune with the retreat from dualism, Morgan dealt with consciousness in only one chapter in which he said, "It is possible that all organic behavior is accompanied by consciousness. But there is no direct means of ascertaining whether it is so or not" (1908, p. 42). Morgan's further analysis of the concept of consciousness provides a particularly clear example of the type of thinking that was associated with the naturalization of the soul into a process of consciousness and into an equivalence with the central nervous system. He stated, "We seem to be led to the conclusion both from *a priori* considerations and from the results of observation, that effective consciousness is associated with the nervous system" (1908, p. 43). In order to prevent rampant misuse of concepts dealing with consciousness as they were applied to a variety of animal forms, the so-called Canon of Parsimony was stated by Morgan in his text, *Introduction to Comparative Psychology* (1894). Morgan's canon reads as follows: "In no case may we interpret an action as the outcome of the exercise of a higher psychical faculty, if it can be interpreted as the outcome of the exercise of one that stands lower in the psychological scale" (1894, p. 53). While this statement has continued to receive a great deal of attention in the construction of theories about animal behavior, one caution should be noted in particular: that the rules for judging the level of concept to be applied depends on knowing the *psychological scale of animals*. As a matter of fact, this scale is not yet known, unless it be taken as a simple equivalent of the evolutionary scale, which is not a simple linear scale.

George J. Romanes (1848-1894) is often described in a negative way because of his apparent devotion to the *anecdotal method*. But his text on comparative psychology, *Animal Intelligence*, is a serious inquiry into animal behavior. Romanes organized the text by animal groups (phyla), and he used all of the data he could obtain, much of this from popular sources, to inquire into the phenomena of "mind throughout the animal kingdom" (1912, p. 1). Romanes struggled in the introductory chapter with the problem of dualism, the body and mind of animals, but it was particularly difficult since he included the behavior of lower invertebrates. He came to the kind of conclusion that is not unfamiliar in recent work, making a rough equivalent between mental and neural. Romanes' error seems to be one of attempting to deal with complex behavioral episodes with molar concepts. For example, he notes a report of the death of a snake that had been separated from its original owners and then suggests that ". . . the probability rather points to the death of the animal having been accelerated by emotional shock. But then of course the question is an open one" (1912, p. 261). This incident was used by Romanes as an example of the development of associations (learned responses) on the part of reptiles. It was not, as his critics imply, that he was assuming the emotional life of reptiles to be the same as humans. However, the example illustrates Romanes' use of the anecdotal method.

At about the same time that the work of Morgan and Romanes was receiving attention in comparative psychology, a number of other outstanding scientists were observing and reporting the behavior of animals. Their contributions are still affecting current research and theory, and some of their work is noted in later chapters. Among these scientists were Pavlov, studies of conditioning; Watson, behavioristic theory in S-R terms; Yerkes, comparative studies of learning; Jennings, theory and study of behavior of invertebrates; Loeb, theory and study of behavior of invertebrates; Thorndike, theory and study of instrumental learning; and Lashley, neurology of learning.

The main emphasis of comparative psychology that is exemplified by the work of Morgan, Romanes, and Yerkes is characterized by their attempts to apply the theory of evolution., loosely conceived, to the behavior of animals. This work became the prototype of comparative psychology. In Chapter 9 we distinguish to some extent between the analysis of animal behavior in terms of evolution (ethology) and in terms of the comparative method.

We suggest that this section might acquire added meaning if it were read again upon completion of the book.

Behavior Genetics

Individual, strain, and species differences characterize the behavior of organisms. These effects stem from two sets of interrelated factors: short-term genetic factors (heredity) and long-term genetic factors (evolution or natural selection). The long-term effects are covered in the following chapter on adaptive behavior and to varying degrees in many other chapters throughout the book. Both sets of factors also account for the striking similarities of behavior among animals of the same species (conspecifics). For example, the species of an individual bird can be identified by hearing the song it sings or seeing the kind of nest it builds.

Behavior genetics and how its short-term effects can be assessed and experimentally manipulated are discussed in this chapter. Genetic effects on behavior are established by several research methods, most of which are considered here.

Selective Breeding

The method of selective breeding is a useful technique that involves breeding individuals that show a particular trait maximally or minimally. That is, individuals that show a particular pattern of behavior are bred with each other over a number of generations, until there is a generation that predictably shows the behavior in question. Tyron's famous experiment on breeding "maze-bright" and "maze-dull" rats, for example, used selective breeding. And these two strains, now called S_1 and S_2, respectively, are still in existence. Selective breeding of fruitflies for their reactions to light was also the method used by Hirsch and Boudreau (1958), discussed in Chapter 13.

Selective breeding is directional, changing the average level of a particular behavior by selecting phenotypes at one extreme or the other from the population average. The phenotype is the overt expression of the genotype but is determined by both genetic and environmental factors.

A special case of selective breeding is the procedure of inbreeding, for example, brother-sister mating. Here, phenotypic similarity is not necessarily involved, and the consequence of continued inbreeding can be loss of fitness in the inbred group. Nevertheless, when loss of fitness does *not* occur, the individuals of the inbred population become increasingly similar (a relatively pure strain of homozygous individuals develops).

Crossbreeding and Backcrossing

Crossbreeding involves mating individuals of two different strains and examining the behavior of the offspring, which are called hybrids. Such a cross permits us to refine our statements about the specific genetic factors that may be operating. Sometimes hybrid offspring show more of a behavior trait than either parent (*heterosis* or hybrid vigor); other times the offspring exhibit intermediate inheritance. For example, Bruell (1967) found that the hybrid offspring of two strains of mice had temperaments intermediate to the parents.

Backcrossing involves mating the offspring of the cross between two strains back to one or the other of the parents. The behavior of the back-bred offspring is then tested and evaluated. Sometimes the backcrossing indicates the extent to which the Mendelian ratio of the law of inheritance is operating.

Strain Comparisons

The comparison of behaviors of different strains of the same species differs from breeding studies in that the strains are already available from prior breeding. In many cases the selective breeding was for a structural rather than a behavioral characteristic, and the investigator's main problem is one of identifying the *behavioral* differences present among the strains. If differences in behavior occur in different strains, given that all individuals are raised in the same environment, these differences are presumed to have a genetic basis. The assumption about a similar environment may at times represent an oversimplification, however.

The results from strain comparisons can also be rather complex. For example, the strain differences in male guinea pigs indicate that inbred lines of males differ independently in frequency of mounting, rate of intromission, frequency of ejaculation, and latency of ejaculation. It appears that separate hereditary mechanisms determine various components of the male guinea pig's sexual behavior (Jakway, 1959).

With the overview and the brief review of history and behavior genetics completed, you are now ready to begin the quite-safe adventure of exploring comparative animal behavior.

Study Questions

1. What was the name of the book Aristotle wrote that contained material on comparative-animal behavior and what were some of the topics he addressed?

2. Define dualism and describe some of the effects this doctrine had on the development of behavioral science.

3. Who was Romanes and what was he noted for?

4. Describe briefly three methods used in behavior genetic research.

PART ONE

An Evolutionary and Ecological Perspective

2

Adaptive Behavior

John A. King

Department of Zoology
Michigan State University

Organic evolution, or the theory of evolution, refers to the fact that plants and animals change generation after generation. These evolutionary changes are the result of a reduction or increase in the frequencies of particular genes in a population. Such variations take place regularly or continually in most organisms, so one generation rarely has the same gene frequencies as the preceding one. Most evolutionary changes are usually too subtle to observe, mainly because they are obscured by the tremendous amount of genetic diversity present in any single generation. After all, no two individuals are exactly alike, unless they happen to share all the same genes. However, we readily recognize the effects of repeated changes in gene frequency when they accumulate in a population of familiar individuals. Even casual observers recognize differences between common species or subspecies, but not among less familiar organisms.

Evolution, or change in gene frequencies, depends on two factors — variation and selection — but evolution often requires a third factor — the isolation of a group of organisms — before recognizable species emerge (speciation). It is also possible for evolution to occur in the absence of selection as a result of random genetic changes from generation to generation (genetic drift); this is explained in the following paragraphs.

Variation in the physical structure, color, physiology, and behavior among individuals is readily apparent. This variation arises from three sources: mutation, gene recombination, and environmental acquisition. Mutations occur randomly in the germ plasm at a rate such that a gene fails to replicate itself perfectly during the generation of gametes, that is, of sperm and eggs, about once in 30,000 times. Since most vertebrates possess about 30,000 different genes, such a probability means that each gamete, or individual, is carrying, on the average, one new mutation. Mutation rates are accelerated by mutagens such as radiation, nitrous acid, and mustard gas, but for the most part germ plasm is protected against external factors. Most mutations are deleterious because they alter the genetic arrangement that has resulted from the selection of the best genetic material over thousands of generations. Moreover, individuals carry a number of genetic mutations that are usually hidden when combined with dominant genes.

Among sexually reproducing animals the genes of both parents are *recombined* in a random fashion at each generation, so each offspring is genetically unique. Although mutations are the only way new genes are created, most of the genetic variation is produced by recombination of parental genes at each generation. Therefore, such variation in conjunction with natural selection produces most evolutionary changes.

Genes control the way an organism develops, but the organism itself is constituted from nutrients provided by the environment, usually food. The type and amount of nutrients as well as other environmental conditions, such as temperature, oxygen, sound, and light, influence the action of the genes in producing an organism. Since most organisms do not grow and mature in exactly the same environment, they *acquire* characteristics unique to the environment in which they were raised. These acquired characteristics, unlike genes, are not passed on from one generation to another; thus, they have little effect upon evolution.

Selection is less apparent than variation and it took the insights of Charles Darwin to recognize its relevance to evolution. Natural selection is a devious and a compromising process that is complicated by its waxing and waning over time and in different environments. It is easy to understand but difficult to recognize and measure. Conceptually it means that the variation among individuals enables some individuals to produce more descendants than other individuals. Specifically, this ability refers to an individual's viability and to its capacity to produce fertile offspring. Some individuals, by virtue of their particular genetic combinations and the particular environment in which they are raised, are able to produce more fertile offspring than other individuals. Such differential fertility means that some individuals have a selective advantage over others. As this process of selection proceeds from generation to generation, gene frequencies change, with some genes becoming lost from a population and other genes becoming more abundant. The environment and the selection pressures it imposes change over time so that genetic combinations are continually changing to match those combinations most likely to promote survival and reproduction. Eventually these alterations produce individuals that no longer resemble either their distant ancestors or other individuals in different environments from which they have become spatially isolated.

Isolation in time or space is necessary before evolution can proceed far enough to produce distinct species, which are populations of organisms that can breed among themselves but are infertile with the organisms of other populations. Speciation results from reproductive isolation. In the absence of isolation, the interbreeding of individuals mixes their pool of genes and prevents any distinct differences (species differences) from appearing. Widely distributed species, like the fruit fly, house mouse, and humans, keep interbreeding throughout their ranges, which increases individual variation but not the formation of new species. Most other species of animals are limited in their distribution and are isolated sufficiently from other species that they cannot interbreed.

If a widely distributed species becomes separated by some barrier that prevents gene flow between isolated populations, the two populations evolve differently and become recognizable as distinct species. Then if the barrier that initially isolated the two populations disappears or if one or both of the new species evolves a way to cross the barrier, the two populations are reunited. When previously isolated populations of a once widespread species reunite, they can either interbreed freely and lose the distinctions that evolved between them or they may no longer be able to produce fertile offspring between them. When the latter happens, the amount of difference between them can vary to the extent that individuals of each population no longer recognize each other as possible mates to actual mating between populations and the production of viable, but infertile offspring, like the mule.

Any loss of fertility from interbreeding will be selected against, resulting in the evolution of behavioral, physiological, and morphological barriers to interbreeding. These secondary barriers replace the original spatial barriers and now enable many similar species to occupy the same geographical range. For example, most regions have several species of squirrels, mice, ducks, flies, beetles, and the like. Many of the distinct species are difficult to recognize without careful study, but each is unique in that it does not interbreed with any other species and occupies its own ecological niche. If two species occupy the same niche (i.e., have the same requirements for food, nests, and space), they will compete with each other until one of the species is excluded, evolves to occupy a somewhat different niche, or becomes extinct.

Although natural selection is almost always operating to some degree, it is possible for gene frequencies to change in the absence of selection, through random *genetic drift*. Genetic drift contributes little to evolution, except in small, quite isolated populations where a rare gene may easily become lost in the next generation. For example, a gene can be lost if the parents are capable of producing three genetically different offspring, but only have two offspring. The third offspring they failed to produce may have been the one with the rare gene that is now lost. There are many such ways in which genes can be lost or fixed randomly, but most changes in gene frequency are readily attributed to selection.

Adaptation

The differences in the relative success among individuals in leaving descendants are the basis for the concept of adaptation or an adaptive characteristic. An *adaptive character* may be defined as any character that increases the probability of the organism with that character leaving more descendants than an organism without it. If the character is behavioral, then an adaptive behavior confers a reproductive advantage to the animal exhibiting that behavior. Animals lacking that behavior are less successful in reproducing than those with it (Johnson and Hubbell, 1975).

Problem of Descendants

This simple definition of an adaptive behavior generates some problems. One problem is that the definition refers to reproduction or, actually, the ability to leave descendants, whose existence will be realized only in the future. During the life span of a given individual, it is usually possible to determine whether that individual reproduces and leaves offspring, but we can rarely determine the number of descendants beyond the second or third generation. We may also want to ask whether an infant's behavior is adaptive or not long before it reaches a reproductive age.

If we could look far enough into the future, we might find that some characters currently adaptive are no longer adaptive under different environmental conditions. This problem can be solved to a certain extent by examining ancestors rather than descendants. If animals with the character have many ancestors, it suggests that the character endowed those individuals with a reproductive advantage. For example, the presence of a backbone throughout the evolutionary history of vertebrates indicates that the backbone is an adaptive character. On the other hand, any character that appears for the first time in the current generation is regarded with suspicion until its adaptiveness is tested for temporal endurance.

Problem of Circularity

Although the problem of looking into the future (descendants) can partly be solved by looking into the past (ancestors), such a determination of adaptiveness suffers from circularity. A character that has endured through many generations of ancestors must be adaptive and the reason that it has lasted so long is because it is adaptive. That is, the character is adaptive because it exists and it exists because it is adaptive.

Such circularity is common in the reasoning of many students of behavior. For example, quail bathe in the sand in the laboratory and under "natural" circumstances. Since this is a frequently observed behavior, one assumes that it is adaptive; otherwise, they would not be doing it. Now that it has been declared adaptive, we can find out which birds are best adapted by examining the amount of sand bathing they exhibit. Presumably those that never sand bathe are not adapted. Observing a character in nature does not necessarily mean that it is adaptive because most animals exhibiting the character in nature will die, often before reproducing. The resolution to this dilemma is conceptually simple, but difficult to perform. One should examine the reproductive success of those individuals with and without the character. This resolution to the problem of identifying adaptive behavior will be examined later.

Problem of Optimality

Another problem in the analysis of adaptive characteristics involves the assessment of the character's value. Although many behaviors are adaptive, they may be more or less adaptive than another conflicting behavior, or the behavior may be adaptive at different times, in different circumstances, or at different intensities or frequencies. In other words, the adaptive value can vary from optimal, which leaves the most descendents possible, to suboptimal, which leaves fewer descendants. For example, it is adaptive to have offspring, but having too few or too many may interfere with leaving descendants. Too few offspring could result in the death of many of them before they become reproductively active, since most animals die before reaching reproduc-

tive maturity. Too many offspring could interfere with the parent's ability to care for them and the offspring's subsequent reproductive performance could suffer from lack of parental care. Each species has an optimal number of offspring. Students of animal behavior should attempt to determine not only if a behavioral character is adaptive, but also whether that character is optimal or suboptimal.

Problem of Beneficial Behavior

The fourth problem concerning the identification of an adaptive character is the distinction between a character that actually functions to produce more descendants and one that merely is beneficial to the animal (Williams, 1966). For example, the heart has the important function of pumping blood throughout the body. It is adapted for this function because most animals will die without a heart and cannot reproduce. In the process of pumping blood, the heart makes sounds that physicians can hear through a stethoscope and diagnose how well it is functioning. These sounds are very beneficial to the individual who has consulted a doctor and learns that certain treatments are necessary for survival. However, the heart is not adapted for making sounds.

Another example may be taken from animal behavior. Most mammals are capable of swimming whether they ever have occasion to swim or not. They swim by working their legs in the manner for which they were adapted: to walk or run. Under some circumstances, it may be beneficial to swim across a stream for food or to escape a predator or a flood. This ability to swim is not an adaptation, but simply a beneficial by-product of being able to run.

Now, it is possible that the ability to swim may confer a real adaptive advantage to the animal exhibiting this ability such that those individuals that swim leave more descendants than those that do not swim. If this advantage endures through many generations with only the best swimmers reproducing, swimming becomes an adaptation and, indeed, many animals are adapted to swim. The distinction is often difficult to make, but many types of behavior an animal exhibits are not adaptive even though they may be beneficial. Some behaviors are neither adaptative nor beneficial and may reduce the likelihood that the individual exhibiting them will leave descendants. A mouse, for example, that readily takes to swimming might easily be consumed by a large fish or turtle.

Function versus Mechanism

An adaptive character has the function of keeping the individual alive long enough to produce offspring that possess the same characteristics of viability and fertility. Often we assume a character has this function and proceed to examine its mechanism: What makes it work? If we are interested in the mechanism of sexual behavior, we assume its adaptive function is producing offspring, even if we do not examine how many offspring survive and reproduce. Animals deviant in their virility are often most useful in the study of how hormones or various stimuli induce sexual behavior. Most animal psychologists have studied learning in the rat in order to understand principles of learning, not in order to see how learning enables rats to leave more descendants. Students of animal behavior are advised to distinguish between function and mechanism in the objectives of their own studies as well as those of other investigators. If the objectives of a study are to determine the function of behavior, then one is concerned with adaptive behavior and should be knowledgeable about special techniques of study and interpretation of results. And if the study is about the mechanism of behavior, then one cannot draw conclusions about how the behavior functions. For example, an investigator who has found that testosterone, a male gonadal hormone, increases sexual mounting in the rat is

in no position to conclude that injections of testosterone make rats more adaptive. The increased propensity to mount could be maladaptive.

Procedures for the Study of Adaptive Behavior

One of the best ways to define a term or concept is to include in the definition the way it can be measured. This is often called an operational definition. Learning, for example, can be defined operationally as the decrease of errors over trials. Since the definition of adaptive behavior has created so many problems, perhaps the best way to understand it is by examining how it can be measured. Our measures are mere approximations, just like most watches are approximate measures of time. An absolute measure of adaptive behavior may be next to impossible to obtain (Lewontin, 1974). Nevertheless, an approximate measure is better than a simple declaration that the behavior is or is not adaptive.

Adaptation Experiments

Some tests for an adaptive character are so simple that we hardly need to perform them. Are breathing, eating, or drinking adaptive behaviors? A simple deprivation test quickly indicates that they are because animals cannot live long without exhibiting these behavior patterns. It may take a longer time to determine, but any bisexual animal that fails to exhibit sexual behavior will not leave any descendants.

Behavioral Modifications. We can logically extend our predictions about adaptive behavior further. Before a red-winged blackbird male can mate, it must have a territory (an area from which other blackbird males are excluded) to which prospective mates are attracted (no territory — no mate — no mating —no offspring — no descendants). A red-winged blackbird male cannot readily obtain a territory without exhibiting a special threat display called the "song-spread display." In this display, the male partially extends its wings, exposes its red epaulets, spreads its tail, and gives an "oak-a-lee" call, which is familiar to most residents of United States who leave their urban haunts in the spring. Thus, we can say that the song-spread display is adaptive because it enables a male to obtain a territory where it can attract a female with which it can mate and produce offspring.

Although most steps in this logic need not be rigorously tested, it was necessary to test the adaptive significance of the song-spread display before it could be included. This test was performed by blackening the red epaulets on the wings of males, devocalizing the birds, or both, and counting how many males so treated obtained territories as opposed to untreated birds [Peek, 1972 (see the following summarized study); Smith, 1972]. The advantage of the song-spread display, it was found, enables approximately 70 percent more birds with the display to obtain a territory than those birds without it.

A total of sixty-one red-winged blackbird males were trapped in their territories before, during, and after mating took place. Twenty-three birds were muted by removing a section of both hypoglossal nerves that innervate the syrinx, and eight birds were given sham operations. Seventeen other birds had their epaulets colored either black or white and thirteen served as controls. Of the twenty-one birds muted or colored during the premating period 71 percent left or lost their territories to other males, whereas only 10 percent of the birds treated during or after mating lost their territories. Red-winged blackbirds defend their territories at three levels: (1) with an advertising song that repels potential trespassers at a distance, (2) with song-spread displays that operate at intermediate distances particularly to males in neighboring territories, and (3) by

chase and attack. The first two levels are most critical early in the season when the males are establishing their territories.

Once a male red-wing has a territory and has mated, it will still exhibit the song-spread display. Is this an adaptive behavior? If males that already have territories have their epaulets painted and their voices silenced like those before they got territories, there is no particular advantage to the song-spread display. Birds without the capacity to exhibit the full song-spread display could still maintain a territory as well as those birds that exhibited the full display. In other words, a male with both territory and mates can maintain them without the full display, but needs the display to get them in the first place.

This last test does not exclude the possibility that males without the full display may spend more time and energy actually chasing out rival birds than those that can merely threaten rivals away with the display. If this were true, chasing and fighting activities could deprive a nondisplaying male from contributing its meager share to the care of the offspring. Only the female would be left to feed the young and this could be insufficient for their survival. Obviously it is easier to show that a behavior is adaptive than to demonstrate that it is not adaptive because, somewhere or sometime, it may be adaptive.

Changing the behavior, morphology, or physiology of animals in the field is quite difficult and may require long-term studies with uncertain results. In the red-winged blackbird, coloring the red epaulets is relatively simple, but this is a morphological alteration, not a behavioral one. In addition in the blackbirds, behavior was altered by field surgery on the vocal apparatus of birds. This was more difficult, and the behavior was changed indirectly by a structural modification.

Changing a specific behavior pattern directly could be done by depriving the animal of an opportunity to practice, for example, by keeping the red-wing in captivity, where it could not socialize with other birds. Animals have also been trained to perform or not to perform a given behavior in the field to see if that behavior influences their survival or reproductive outcomes. For example, many rats and mice, which consume or destroy large quantities of grains and seeds, can be trained to reject these foods by poisoning them with a sublethal dose of poison (Robbins, 1976). The rodents are made ill by the poison, which they associate with the particular seeds or grain; Thus they learn not to eat that food again. The effects of experimentally induced poisoning resemble the learning rodents do in avoiding naturally toxic food items. The adaptive significance of food avoidance learning has been observed in attempts to exterminate rodents by poisoning. Those that receive sublethal doses learn to avoid the poison and survive, whereas those that eat large quantities of the poisoned baits die.

Behavioral changes can also be accomplished by physiological intervention, such as by the injection of hormones that influence aggressive or sexual behavior. Such changes in behavior brought about by an increase or reduction in hormones can affect an animal's capacity to obtain mates and thus its ability to reproduce.

Experimentally Mimicking the Animal's Behavior. Other tests for the adaptive significance of a particular type of behavior can be accomplished by the experimenter performing an act normally undertaken by the animal. A good example of this is in egg shell removal in the nests of sea gulls (Tinbergen et al., 1962). Parent gulls almost invariably remove the eggshells from the nest after the gull chicks have hatched. Experimenters have postulated that this behavior of the parent gulls was adaptive because the broken shell and exposed white interiors of the normally camouflaged eggs attracted predators to the nest, where they ate the unguarded chicks or

unhatched eggs. It was very simple to test the vulnerability of nests with and without egg shells to predators by making artificial nests of both types. It was found that scavenging crows readily spotted the nest with broken eggshells and ate the remaining egg, but they rarely found nests without the shells. Eggshell removal by parents clearly increased the probability that their offspring would survive. In this type of experiment, the investigator substituted his behavior for that of the gulls, or actually left out a behavior that the gulls usually perform.

Adaptation experiments of all types are suitable measures of behavior that is presumed to be adaptive. They measure adaptation at only one stage in the process of surviving and reproducing, but they are definitely worthwhile approximations in the absence of our ability to assess future descendants. One can expect that other experiments like these will be carried out in the future and perhaps replace the comparative method of determining adaptive behavior, as described below.

The Comparative Method

The comparative method relies on ancestry, which is prone to the problem of circularity. That is, if the ancestors had the behavior and if it is still present in the current generation, then it must be adaptive, otherwise it would be lost over the course of generations. To some extent, this circularity can be avoided if one can predict which relatives will have or not have the behavior pattern in question. First, we must understand the comparative method.

Ancestry of an animal is established by phylogeny, that is, the evolutionary history of a species. Some species are more closely related to each other than they are to other species. Dogs and cats are more closely related than either is to rats or mice. Dogs are more closely related to coyotes and wolves than either is to cats. These relationships depend on common ancestry, with dogs, wolves, and coyotes having more ancesters in common than they have with cats. The determination of phylogenetic relationships is done by systematists, who examine evidence from fossil records, embryology, morphology, genetics, behavior, serum proteins, DNA, zoogeography, and any other area that may help in establishing relationships among recent species whose ancestry has been lost during the course of evolution. The basic rule in establishing relationships is that animals with more characters in common are more closely related than those with fewer characters. This is like saying that brothers and sisters have more common characteristics than cousins, because they share both grandparents with their siblings, whereas cousins share just the maternal or the paternal grandparents.

The comparative method traces a given behavior pattern through related species of animals. A behavioral character, like gnawing, has many ancestors among species of rodents and is consequently considered to be adaptive. Among rodents, only a few species, like squirrels, are adapted to climbing trees and climbing is less adaptive than gnawing. Indeed, many squirrels, like ground squirrels, do not usually climb trees, but have adaptations for digging. Many tree squirrels give a sharp, barklike call when warning or threatening other squirrels. This call is easy to locate by predators, but we say it is adaptive because tree squirrels can easily avoid a predator by running around a tree trunk. In contrast, many ground squirrels have a warning call that is a high-pitched, almost ventriloquistic trill. This high frequency, clear-toned call is difficult to locate and may be considered adaptive because ground squirrels cannot readily avoid predators when away from their burrows. They avoid detection by giving a hard-to-locate call.

This type of analysis of adaptive behavior is reasonable and often acceptable, despite its circularity. That is, ground squirrels have hard-to-locate calls because they must escape detection by predators and they escape detection by having a hard-to-locate call. The circularity can be broken, however, if one knows the feature that determined whether squirrels give easy or hard-to-locate calls. Here we predict that the significant variable is whether or not the squirrel can readily escape from a predator after it has been detected. If this is the variable that makes each type of call adaptive to either tree or ground squirrels, then we should be able to predict the type of call given by species of squirrels whose calls have not been studied. All we need to know is how readily the squirrel can escape after detection. Some species of squirrels live among rocks with lots of holes and crevices to dart into when a predator attacks. This situation more closely resembles that of tree squirrels with branches and trunks to hide in and dodge between than that of ground squirrels with widely scattered burrows. Rock squirrels would then be expected to have a barklike, easy-to-locate warning call. This hypothesis has not been thoroughly tested, but the common eastern chipmunk, which is a rock squirrel, does have a sharp, barklike call. Also, prairie dogs that never wander far from their numerous burrows have a barklike alarm call.

The problem with these predictions about adaptive behavior is that if the prediction is wrong, a post hoc explanation is usually found. For example, if a rock squirrel gave a hard-to-locate trill, we might explain this by describing that the rocks inhabited by this species of squirrel were scattered, without providing abundant escape holes and crevices.

A similar prediction from the comparative method would be that a positive correlation exists between the ventriloquistic quality of the warning call and the difficulty of escaping from a predator *after* being detected. Such correlations are useful, but not conclusive. An adaptation experiment would provide a better test of the basic hypothesis. An ideal experiment would be to make one group of ground squirrels give barks and another group give trills and check on the number of survivors after a period of time. The problem with this is that we do not know how to make a ground squirrel bark. Perhaps we could compare the difference in the number of warning barks given by a group of tree squirrels kept in a forest and another group kept in the open refuges. This adaptation experiment is not as satisfactory as changing the behavior, but it might demonstrate a relationship between warning calls and the ability to escape predators.

In summary, we have discussed two ways to test for adaptive behavior. The best test is the adaptation experiment, in which we examine the survival or reproductive abilities of two groups of animals: one with the behavior and one without. If the behavior cannot be modified by training, surgery, or physiological intervention, we may mimic the animals' behavior, as by removing egg shells, or we may alter some morphological feature related to the behavior, as in coloring the red epaulets on blackbird wings. The other test is derived from the comparative method, in which we attempt to predict which species of animal should exhibit the behavior on the basis of the ecology of that species and related species.

Levels of Adaptive Behavior

Behavior is classified in many different ways, but one useful classification depends upon its position in a hierarchy that extends from simple, observable movements and postures to highly abstract classes that are inferred or derived from these movements (Dawkins, 1976a). The terms used for such classification are less critical than the concepts they represent. The order from observable movements to abstract behaviors is *fixed action patterns, displays* and *instincts, resultant behavior*, and *abstractions derived from behavior*. This hierarchy can be subdivided, and categories can overlap, but the student of animal behavior is advised to recognize the level of behavior used in his or her analysis. These levels are described in detail in the following paragraphs.

Fixed Action Patterns

One of the principal contributions early ethologists made to the study of animal behavior was the identification and description of fixed action patterns (Eibl-Eibesfeldt, 1975; Moltz, 1965). Each species has a number of movements or postures that characterize it. The movements depend on the animal's morphology, particularly its musculature and skeleton. For example, the modes of locomotion or gaits are so characteristic of each species that they can often be identified by tracks left in the snow or sand. The bounding gait of a rabbit is readily distinguished from the trot of a fox or cat. Bipedal mammals, like kangaroos and some rodents, except humans and occasionally other primates, hop on two feet instead of walk. Birds can be identified at a distance when only the silhouette of their flight patterns can be seen. A large bird slowly flapping its wings readily distinguishes a crow from a soaring hawk. The flick of a tail, the scratch of the head, the rising of a feathered headcrest, the turning or bobbing of the head are as much a part of any animal as its structure. Vocalizations or calls made by insects, frogs, and birds are particularly species specific. Field entomologists, herpetologists, and ornithologists (students of insects, amphibians, and birds, respectively) readily recognize the number and variety of species that are calling or singing around them. These patterns can be readily observed; they are discrete units; they are relatively fixed by the structure or neurology of the species; and they are the basic components of complex sequences of behavior. The final section of this book on specific classes of behavior deals primarily with fixed action patterns.

The termed "fixed" applied to action patterns suggests that they are genetically fixed; that is, they are determined by genes. A great deal of controversy has taken place regarding the influence of genes on behavior and many of the arguments have been fruitless. However, if the genetics of behavior is to be examined, it is better to work with these fixed action patterns than at other levels of behavior because these basic units can often be genetically manipulated. One example of genetic manipulation of insect calls is the hybridization of two species of crickets that have different mating calls (Bentley and Hoy, 1974). The hybrid males have a different call than either parent species, and the hybrid females are more attracted to the hybrid males than they are to males of either parent species. The genetic recombination in the hybrids not only alters the male's transmission of the call, but also the female's reception of the call. Other action patterns become fixed through repeated practice or use, such as the fixed movements used in driving a car, walking, or even speaking. Squirrels have fixed patterns for gnawing through a net shell, but these develop only after considerable practice during their development.

Fixed action patterns are also useful for the study of other levels of behavior. For example, it is possible to use the abstract level of learning in order to determine if an animal can see color. An animal that can be trained to respond to one color and not another color has color vision. However, the training procedure may be so difficult for the animal that it fails to learn to discriminate colors it readily perceives. If a fixed action pattern is used instead of learning, the animal may exhibit the fixed action pattern when it sees the color. For example, an animal running toward a preferred color indicates that it has color vision. A male cardinal that attacks a red sock as a rival male, but not a gray sock, reveals its capacity to perceive color by the fixed action patterns of its attack. Most studies of learning relate to the use of fixed action patterns of locomotion, bar pressing, or licking rather than such complex patterns as putting sticks together to fetch food or pulling in strings with food at the end — patterns that require responses that are rarely emitted by the species being investigated.

Since fixed action patterns are usually necessary for finding food, shelter, and mates, they are generally considered adaptive. Although the adaptive significance of only a few action patterns have been adequately tested, a logical analysis is usually sufficient. If the mating call of a cricket departed significantly from that which was characteristic of its species, it would not attract mates and consequently leave no progeny. A squirrel that failed to gnaw through nut shells in a fixed pattern could very possibly starve to death.

Displays and Instincts

Displays and instincts are combinations of fixed action patterns often exhibited in stereotyped sequences. The order of the fixed action patterns may be altered, inverted, repeated, or terminated, but usually the order in the sequence is maintained. For example, the courtship display of the male red-winged blackbird consists of the following sequence of fixed action patterns: song-spread display, elevated wings, bows, symbolic nest-site selection and nest building, sexual chasing, wing quiver, and mounting. In the song-spread display, the male partially extends its wings, raises the red feathers of its epaulets, spreads its tail and gives the "oak-a-lee" call. This presumably attracts females and threatens potential male rivals. When the female approaches, the male drops to the ground, crawls among the marsh vegetation with elevated wings, and occasionally bows its head between its legs and pecks at vegetation. These acts are symbolic of nest-site selection and nest-building, although the nest is usually not built at that site.

Another sequence that may follow or precede the symbolic nest-site selection is sexual chasing in which the male chases the female around its territory or into adjoining territories. Soon after the male stops chasing, the female will settle near

Adaptive Behavior

him. After a few minutes, precopulatory behavior may begin with the male again dropping down to the floor of the marsh, with its wing tips fluttering and giving a whimpering call. When the female joins him, the male "with erected and sometimes violently-shaking epaulets, puffed-out feathers, lowered and spread tail, and lowered head, the male slowly, and often silently, walks stiffly towards the displaying female" (Nero, 1956, p. 32). He then mounts and copulation ensues. Although certain chains of this sequence are quite stereotyped, the sequence may be interrupted at any time, and some elements of it are repeated out of sequence, particularly the song-spread display. However, once the sequence has begun one can predict the likelihood of other patterns occurring in the sequence.

A complex sequence of fixed action patterns that occurs over a relatively long period of time is the food provisioning a mother sand wasp does for its larval offspring confined to a shallow burrow in the sand. The female first digs a burrow and then flies out and captures a caterpillar, which is immobilized by her sting. She carries the caterpillar to her burrow, lays an egg on it, closes the burrow with a plug of sand, and then repeats the sequence for another egg on another day. Soon she may have larval offspring of different ages, which she must feed in separate burrows, each requiring different amounts of food depending on their size. In feeding each, she remembers the location of the burrow, which cannot be detected by human observers, digs away the sand plug, inspects the larva, evaluates its size, plugs the burrow, and goes off and captures caterpillars of sufficient number to feed the larva for the day, bringing each caterpillar back individually. After provisioning one larva, she then goes on to another burrow with offspring, for whom she repeats the sequence.

The names applied to these sequences are less important to the animal behaviorist than recognizing them and being able to predict them. If we see a sand wasp unplug a burrow entrance and

go inside, we can recognize that she is probably inspecting her offspring and will soon emerge, fly off, and return with a caterpillar. Or if we see the song-spread display of a red-winged blackbird, we recognize this as a territorial display and can predict that another male is in the vicinity. These predictions are not absolute, but can be made within certain limits of confidence.

Sometimes the sequences include action patterns that appear unrelated to the activity in progress. This coupling of irrelevant activities is called *ritualization*. Animals incorporate action patterns derived from other activities, like feeding or escape, into, say, a courtship display and these irrelevant activities may help inform another individual about the intent or motivation of the performer. For example, black-headed gulls turn away from an opponent prior to escaping from an encounter. Turning away has been abbreviated to merely turning the head away. In a conflict situation, the head is often turned toward and then away from the opponent in rapid succession, as if the gull did not know what to do: escape or attack. Head wagging or flagging is also a part of courtship, where it appears out of place, but is actually an integral part of the courtship ritual.

Resultant Behavior

Behavior often produces results that can be observed and measured, like leaving footprints in the sand. The animal is not observed in the act, but the results of the act indicate that it was performed. If a bird's nest is discovered, we know a bird built it. We often use resultant behaviors for studying food and water consumption, nest building, and sometimes sexual behavior, which we know to have taken place when young are produced from a pair put together. Or, complicated pieces of apparatus are used to monitor various activities in the absence of the investigator. The well-equipped Skinner box, which provides an animal with a lever to press or a key to peck, automatically records the number and temporal sequence of the responses that the animal performed in obtaining food, water, or other reinforcer, even though the responding was not directly observed.

Resultant behaviors need not be adaptive themselves; but either they are, or they lead to adaptive behavior. For example, eating the right kinds of food is adaptive, so food consumption can be used to determine what types of food an animal selects to eat. By weighing or counting the amount of previously measured food left by the animal, we know its consumption without ever watching it eat. In contrast, lever pressing is not itself an adaptive response, but it resembles the activities most animals give prior to those that sustain life and insure reproduction, like stalking prey, climbing a tree for nuts or fruits, or simply walking to an area rich in nutrients.

Abstractions Derived from Behavior

Abstract concepts like learning, emotion, and motivation can be derived by definition and convention from overt behavior. An animal running a maze indicates that it has learned the shortest path to a goal by reducing the number of incorrect turns and the amount of time taken to reach the goal. Learning is abstracted from observing the motor patterns used in reaching the goal. Similarly, an animal's emotional state may be revealed to us when its fur rises on the back of its neck, when it freezes motionlessly in fixed posture, or runs wildly about. Motivation is inferred when an animal overcomes many obstacles in order to reach a goal or consistently avoids a noxious stimulus. It is not necessary to make these abstractions and label them learning, emotion, and motivation, but these concepts are useful substitutes for lengthy descriptions of motor patterns. Information is quite readily conveyed by saying, "a rat learned the maze in ten trials," rather than saying, "each time the rat ran through the maze the number of turns into blind

alleys was reduced until at the end of ten trials no further wrong turns were made." These abstractions also refer to behavioral characteristics of animals that are adaptive. A female sand wasp that readily learns the location of her burrow entrance after one orientation flight around it is exhibiting adaptive learning because the welfare of her progeny depends on it.

Our knowledge of the sensory capacities of animals is typically expressed in abstractions derived from overt behavior patterns. One exception is the use of electrophysiological recordings from the nervous system. Such recordings indicate that the animal's sensory organs and the nervous system are sensitive to the stimulus, but they do not reveal *how* the animal uses the stimulus. In order to determine if an auditory, visual, or olfactory stimulus is used by the animal in some adaptive way, we ask the animal to inform us by way of a behavioral response to the stimulus. For example, many animals visually pursue a moving stimulus that can be perceived. If we want to learn what is the weakest or smallest stimulus an animal can perceive, we watch its eye or head movements in pursuit of a large visual stimulus, preferably in a situation where only one visual stimulus is present. Then the stimulus, which may be a line, disk, or spot of light, is made smaller and smaller until the visual pursuit movements no longer occur. The value of the smallest effective stimulus is considered the lower visual threshold, even though a weaker stimulus may still give an electrical potential in the nervous system.

Another example can be taken from the response a fox gives to a high pitched tone, which resembles the squeak of its common prey, a mouse. A fox will prick up its ears, rotate them, and turn its head toward the source of this tone. With a gradual increase in frequency or pitch, the response will finally disappear (the tone is no longer heard). We would find that a fox can hear a much higher frequency than we can.

There are other methods that can be used in

arriving at abstractions about the perception, learning, emotion, and motivation of animals, but the above examples illustrate how behavior can inform us about characteristics of an animal that are not directly apparent. These characteristics can be adaptive if they lead to survival and successful reproduction. A fox must be able to hear the ultrasonic calls of mice if it depends on them for food. A rabbit may escape detection by a predator if it is frightened into a freezing posture. A rat than can learn the most direct path to food through walls, burrows, or tunnels has an adaptive advantage over one that may take a wrong turn and expose itself to predation. Sometimes we arrive at these abstractions by observing animals in the field, but repeated testing under controlled conditions usually requires laboratory experimentation. Most of the material described in this volume has been accumulated under such laboratory conditions.

Behavioral Strategies

Strategies are a series of behavior patterns used in solving some problem in the process of attaining a goal. They suggest a plan of action, but the "plan" need not be a conscious one (Barash, 1977). A squirrel harvesting nuts provides a useful example for distinguishing strategies from other levels of behavior. Squirrels eat nuts and bury them when they are abundant. The fixed action patterns involved are climbing a tree, biting off a nut, gnawing through its shell, and chewing it. If we discovered some nutshells on the ground with squirrel's tooth marks, these results could tell us that a squirrel ate the nuts. We could also abstract from these observations that the squirrel was motivated by hunger, that it preferred nuts to leaves, and that it could probably smell the nut through its shell.

There is more that we can learn about the squirrel's behavior, however, if we consider the entire process of how a squirrel goes about harvesting the nuts and storing them. The squirrel's problem is to get the nuts in an efficient manner and provide itself with food during periods of scarcity. It could wait for the nuts to drop to the ground and then bury them where they fell. This would leave the nuts exposed to insects, birds, and other mammals that might get to the nuts first. It could climb the tree, cut off a single nut, take it to a suitable site, and bury it. Or, it could climb the tree, cut off many nuts at one time, let them fall, and then go to the ground and bury them in different localities, where they are less likely to be found by other animals. The last solution is the strategy used by several species of squirrels when many nuts become ripe at the same time. It insures that the squirrel will obtain a good share of the nuts before other animals get them, and it saves the effort of repeatedly climbing the tree for single nuts. In late summer when the squirrel is hidden by leaves, one can often hear the cut-off nuts when they fall through the leaves and land on the ground. Squirrels that have adopted this strategy are apparently more successful in surviving and reproducing than those that have adopted less efficient foraging strategies.

The process or strategy an animal uses in solving problems resembles a game, which can be lost or won, with each move or deal having its costs (risks) and benefits. The object of the game is to leave as many descendants as possible. The costs are the energy expended, the risks taken by being exposed to predation, and the chances of losing some benefits to competitors. The benefits are primarily the energy gained through food and the reduction of risks involved in losing food to competitors or losing one's life to predators. The game of leaving the maximum number of descendants can be played by maximizing benefits, minimizing risks, or matching the likelihood of risks with gains. Some species solve all problems with one strategy, while others change strategies depending on the problem.

The feeding strategies used by squirrels in getting sunflower seeds from my bird feeder which is about 100 feet from the nearest tree illustrates several possible strategies. A squirrel can maximize its gains by crossing the lawn, which increases its risks to predation, or it can remain in the woods and minimize its risks, but it gains far less food. It can match the risk with the gain by running rapidly across the lawn, getting a mouthful of seeds, running back to the tree, and eating them there. Most squirrels in suburbia, because the neighborhood cats and dogs are not very efficient predators and involve few risks to the squirrels, tend to maximize their gains by settling at the bird feeder and eating for long periods of time.

Problem-solving strategies have been examined in the laboratory by giving a rat two levers to press for food. One lever may have a 70 percent payoff, that is, if the rat always presses that lever, it will get food 70 percent of the time. The other lever has a 30 percent payoff. The rat can either stay with the 70 percent lever for 100 percent of its presses or it can press the lever 70 percent of the time and press the 30 percent lever the remaining 30 percent of the time. Depending on how the probabilities are arranged, rats usually maximize, that is, stay with the highest payoff by always pressing the lever giving the higher percentage of rewards; whereas monkeys and people often match number of responses to each with the percentage of payoff. Although strategies can be examined for any problem solving behavior, the most thoroughly examined are those related to foraging and reproduction.

Foraging Strategies

These strategies have been described in the preceding examples, but one common distinction about such strategies often made by ecologists has not been mentioned. Species vary in their foraging along a continuum from specialist to generalist. Some birds, for example, specialize by eating only one or only a very few items, like the nectar consumed by hummingbirds or the cater-

pillars consumed by warblers. These specialists are highly efficient in obtaining their specialized diet; but, when the food is not available, they either die or move to areas where it is available. Hummingbirds and warblers are migrants that go to the tropics when nectar and insects are not available during northern winters. Other birds are generalists or jack-of-all-trades that can eat a variety of foods. Blue jays are generalists, consuming nuts, grains, insects, fruits, meat, suet, and scraps of bread. They readily find and eat new items of food, but they cannot perform any single food-getting act as well as the specialist can. The generalist blue jay and the seed-eating specialist cardinal both eat sunflower seeds when provided in bird feeders during the winter. Blue jays pick up a seed, fly to a nearby branch, put the seed between their toes, and hammer the shells open with their beaks. Sometimes the kernel falls before they can swallow it, and they fly down to retrieve it. In contrast, the cardinal sits on the tray, picks up a seed, crushes off the shell, and grinds the kernel to swallow it almost at the same time it reaches for a second seed. Differences in the amount of energy expended by the two species are considerable. Even the little goldfinch, which is also a seed-eating specialist, can eat big sunflower seeds more efficiently than the blue jay. But then, the blue jay can make up for this lost efficiency by flying to the suet rack to eat some suet, by hammering open an acorn, or by flying off with a crust of bread, none of which the cardinal does.

Each species of animal has its position along the specialist-generalist continuum, but individuals may shift during their life time or from season to season. Hummingbirds, for example, eat insects when they are young and only specialize on nectar as adults when relatively few insects are eaten. There also is a geographical correlation with foraging strategies, since specialists are more common in the tropics than in the temperate and northern regions. It has been suggested that foraging strategies are related to the predictability of the food resources. Where a certain type of food is highly predictable throughout the year, an animal can specialize on it, as in the tropics. Where food items are relatively unpredictable, generalist foraging strategies enable the animal to shift from one type of food to another.

Another environmental variable that seems to determine type of foraging strategy is the number of competitors for food. Where there are numerous competitors, those species specialized in foraging can more efficiently obtain food than the generalist. Thus, in the highly populated tropics, there are many different species specializing on particular types of food; whereas in northern regions where there are fewer competing species, most species are generalists.

Reproductive Strategies

Reproductive strategies are those patterns of behavior designed to produce the greatest number of descendants. They include age of initial mating, season of mating, frequency of mating, selection of mate or mates, mating systems, number and size of offspring, amount and type of parental care, and age at which the offspring are weaned or fledged. Species differ in their reproductive strategies, and sometimes closely related species diverge in many respects. For example, within the perch family, the darters are small, minnow-sized fish that live on the bottom of streams and lakes (Winn, 1958). The larger perch on the other hand, are social breeders with a school of both sexes passing over a spawning ground and depositing their eggs and milt on the sandy substrate of lakes. The eggs and fry are small and numerous with most of them dying or being eaten before maturity. The parents offer no care to their offspring. In contrast, some species of darters have reproductive strategies that include temporary pair formation, fewer eggs of larger size than the perch, and temporary nests for the eggs. Other species form permanent pairs,

establish a territory about the nest and lay one or two large eggs that are guarded and protected against marauders until the eggs have hatched and the fry are capable of surviving on their own.

This sequence of breeding strategies among contemporary species of perch and darters suggests an evolutionary pattern going from simple social breeding with numerous expendable eggs to complex patterns of mate selection, defended home sites, and extensive care of few offspring that survive to maturity. All of these species end up with approximately the same number of descendants, but the large perch puts its energy resources into producing numerous eggs of which only a few survive and the territorial darter invests its efforts in the care of a few young. Both extremes in this series of reproductive strategies are adaptive, but it is unlikely that any species could adopt a mixed strategy. A mixture of producing a large number of eggs and fry that require a lot of parental care would use more energy than the fish could afford and reproduction would be curtailed.

As with feeding strategies, attempts have been made to understand what factors determine a given reproductive strategy. There seems to be an evolutionary progression from investing energy into the production of numerous offspring to an investment of behavioral energy in the care of few offspring: a substitution of behavior for protoplasm. Since behavior is generally more readily modified by environmental changes than morphology or physiology, behavioral investments of energy enable a species to invade and occupy new environments or those that are rapidly changing. For example, the most advanced darters live in fast-flowing streams, where their eggs are deposited under rocks, which prevents them from being washed downstream. The social spawning perch could not invade such habitats without some modification of its reproductive strategy. The environment occupied and used by each species, therefore, appears to be an important factor in shaping reproductive strategies. (See Winn, 1958, summarized as follows).

> *The reproductive behavior and ecology of fourteen species of darters were examined in an effort to determine their evolution. The following results were obtained. Most species live in streams or shallow lake shores and migrate to and from their spawning grounds. There is an evolutionary trend in territorial defense from no territorial behavior to temporary territories around the nest and finally to permanent territories, which include areas not associated with reproduction. Sexual dimorphism increases with territorial defense, so that the nonterritorial perch shows little difference between the sexes, whereas highly territorial darters show sexual differences in size, color, and finshape. The spawning sites and position vary among the species, from horizontal spawning, through vertical positions on vegetation and rocks, to upside-down positions under overhanging rocks. The number and size of eggs is negatively correlated with parental care, territoriality, and sexual dimorphism among the species. Species considered to be evolutionarily primitive on the basis of their morphology are also most primitive in their behavior. Darters with specialized, narrowly adaptive behavior are the most recently evolved and inhabit streams with riffles or rapids that are produced by rocky rubble.*

Although reproductive strategies tend to be characteristic of a species, individuals of each sex may adopt a different strategy in the process of natural selection. Those individuals that leave the greatest number of descendants are favored by natural selection, which often brings about a different reproductive strategy for each sex. For example, males of many vertebrate species can have more young if they fertilize many females that raise their young to maturity. Thus, males

often have a strategy of polygyny, or promiscuity. The female strategy, which enables her to have more offspring, is to get the male to help care for the young, for two parents can feed more young than one parent. Thus, a female's most successful strategy is to withhold copulation until she is assured that the male will stay with her and help her raise a big family. Many females, particularly among species of birds, select a mate only after an elaborate courtship ritual that consumes so much of the male's energy and time that his chance of fertilizing other females are reduced and his best chances of leaving viable offspring is to stay with those he has already fathered. Since the optimal reproductive strategies often differ between the sexes, the sexual conflict endures throughout evolution, with each sex being selected for its capacity to produce the greatest number of descendants.

Sociobiology

The study of social behavior and organization of animals is correctly labeled sociobiology; however, it also has come to indicate a theoretical point of view. Sociobiology stresses how natural selection can influence complicated patterns of social behavior, which initially often appear to be incongruous with natural selection (Wilson, 1975). The most striking behavior that appears to refute natural selection is altruistic behavior, which typically means that an animal will sacrifice its reproductive potential for that of another animal.

Wynne-Edwards (1962) attempted to explain this apparent refutation of natural selection by proposing that selection operated on groups of animals rather than individuals as Darwinian concepts of selection required. Those social groups that adjusted their reproduction to the available food supply would survive, whereas those that reproduced without restriction soon overconsumed their food resources and became extinct. This meant that some individuals had to curtail their reproduction in order that certain other individuals, usually the dominant individuals, could reproduce. This sacrifice of reproductive potential, even when forced by dominant individuals, was considered the basis of all forms of altruistic behavior by Wynne-Edwards. The best examples of this loss of reproduction among some individuals for that of another are the social insects, which have one queen or reproductive female and numerous nonreproducing female workers.

The problem with the Wynne-Edwards thesis is that it fails to account for cheaters, which would reproduce when other group members curtail their reproduction. The cheaters or individuals that do not cooperate in curtailing their reproductive activities would leave the greatest number of descendants. After a few generations the population would consist primarily of cheaters because the self-sacrificing individuals lose whatever genetic factors contributed to their altruistic behavior by not leaving any descendants.

Another explanation of altruistic behavior in social insects and of the sacrifices parents make on behalf of their offspring is that these sacrifices take place among members of a family. An individual can afford to make some sacrifice if by doing so it insures the success of the genes it shares with its relatives. Each parent shares one half of its genes with its offspring and siblings also share one half of their genes on the average. Among social bees, wasps, and ants, sister workers share 75 percent of their genes as a result of a unique reproductive characteristic in these social insects, which is called haplodiploidy (Trivers and Hare, 1976).

Since, according to the theory of sociobiology, genes are the critical unit in natural selection, mathematical models can be created to account for complex social relationships. For example, when individuals share one half of their genes, as siblings do, then one sibling can exhibit altruistic behavior toward the other sibling when the recipient benefits by twice as much or better. In other words, the likelihood of leaving descendants with one's own genes is equal, whether each sibling has one offspring or one sibling has two offspring and the other sibling has none. The amount an individual can sacrifice on behalf of a relative is determined by the number of genes shared with that relative. Nieces and nephews share only one quarter of their genes on the average, so we can expect altruism to occur among these relatives only when one niece gains four times as much as the other niece or nephew loses. When the fitness of relatives is included with that of each individual, as above, we speak of *inclusive fitness*.

Most parents sacrifice very little in energy outlay in order to insure the perpetuation of their genes through their offspring. Offspring, however, are selected to demand as much parental sacrifice as they can get, because 50 percent of their genes are different from either parent and they are attempting to perpetuate their complement of genes. The offspring's strategy is to obtain as much care, attention, and energy from the parents as they can get in order to enable them to produce more offspring, which now bear only 25 percent of the grandparents' genes. Parents, on the other hand, are willing to sacrifice their future reproductive capacity by yielding to their offspring only until the offspring become independent or can be coerced into helping care for younger siblings. Among mammals, this sort of parent-offspring conflict is particularly pronounced at weaning and at the time of sexual maturity, with each generation, according to the tenets of sociobiology, acting to insure the maximum representation of its genes in the next generation.

Different strategies have also evolved to insure that each mate maximizes its fitness. Among sexually reproducing species, both sexes are obviously necessary to produce offspring. However, once the eggs have been fertilized, each sex can behave differently in order to produce the maximum number of descendants. At the time of conception, the female has usually invested more in the future offspring than the male by virtue of the difference in size between the egg and sperm. Among birds, the discrepancy is tremendous, but even among fish and mammals the egg is many thousand times larger than the sperm. A female must work harder to obtain the energy necessary to produce an egg than a male does to produce a sperm. This difference is parental investment in the offspring is often maintained until the young have matured sufficiently to become independent. Maternal care of offspring is more common than paternal care, but not always. The determining feature may be which parent has the greater opportunity to leave its offspring in care of the other parent. Among mammals, the female nurtures the young in her body, so the male can easily leave the female "holding the bag," so to speak. The male can continue to mate with other females as long as the female is left with the offspring, which she can nurture to maturity. This apparently is the reason polygyny is so common among mammals. A male can leave more of its genes in the next generation by mating with many females, as long as the female can and will care for the offspring alone.

Females of many species cannot raise the offspring alone; they need the help of the male. This is particularly true among birds. If a male songbird lets its mate feed the hungry brood, the young often starve. Neither mate profits from dead offspring. However, a male bird might take its chances by mating with many females because a few very energetic females might be able to raise his offspring. This apparently happens among red-winged blackbirds that live in marshes and fields where food is abundant. In contrast, the females of most bird species have a strategy that induces the males to hang around and share in the care of their offspring: they refuse to copulate. These females mate only with those males that indicate they will also invest in the care of their offspring. Males indicate this by

providing territories for their mates and by enduring long courtship periods before mating. Once a male has invested in a territory and in the long courtship of a single female, he is better off staying with his offspring and helping to raise them than to go off and fight for another territory and court another female. Approximately 90 percent of the species of birds are monogamous, whereas less than 10 percent of mammalian species are monogamous.

The ability to leave the offspring in care of the male often occurs among fish, which frequently exhibit paternal care. Male stickleback fish, for example, build nests into which they induce gravid females. The female swims through the nest and deposits her eggs just before the male, which follows and deposits his sperm. Not only has the male invested considerable effort in making the nest, but he is also left caring for the fertilized eggs, which must be aerated and protected from predators. In many species of fish, the fathers brood and protect their young, sometimes by holding them in their mouths.

With each sex attempting to achieve a maximum number of descendants, it is not surprising that their sexual strategies often come into conflict, while at the same time requiring cooperation from the sexual partner. The outcome of these sexual conflicts necessarily leads to successful reproduction for the species, but that success does not alter the severe struggle and even violence that may occur between the sexes as each sex attempts to attain its own genetic advantage. Usually where behavioral conflicts arise, like those between mates or those between parent and offspring, a dynamic equilibrium emerges, which is called the evolutionary stable strategy, or ESS (Maynard Smith, 1978). ESS means that natural selection keeps the various strategies employed by each individual at a stable level. Any departure from this level suffers being selected against, so that the original balance is maintained either among the number of different individuals exhibiting the different strategies or within an individual from time to time.

For example, in a monogamous breeding population, a few males may successfully cuckold the mates of "adulterous" females. These polygynous males leave their offspring in the care of the female and the faithful male. Since their offspring would be more numerous and bear more of the polygynous males' genes than the cuckolded male, one might expect that the species would soon become entirely polygynous. This does not happen, however, because as soon as most of the males behave polygynously, there are not enough cuckolded males to help raise the offspring of the freely mating male. Thus, it becomes advantageous for a male to become monogamous among a population of polygynous males. Such alterations in frequency of the two types of males usually does not take place because the number of each type of male becomes stablized during evolution. Perhaps a typically monogamous species can tolerate only 5 percent of the males to become polygynous before natural selection makes such behavior disadvantageous. Instead of achieving this stability through numbers of individuals, a similar stability could be reached if most males were polygynous in only 5 percent of its matings. The good father momentarily succumbs to the way of all flesh.

In sociobiology theory, since genes instead of the individual are the unit of selection, this means that the individual is little more than an instrument for the survival and maintenance of the gene. This concept is taken to the extreme in a delightful popular book entitled *The Selfish Gene* by Richard Dawkins. The author portrays the individual as a survival machine, fashioned by its genes, which endows the machine with properties that insure perpetuation of the genes throughout time. He generalizes this concept to any entity with the capacity of self-replication like the DNA of genes. The only other entity with the capacity of self-replication is an idea, or "meme," as Dawkins chooses to call it. Natural selection operates on memes (ideas) as well as genes. Memes may then proliferate, mutate, and become extinct independent of the individuals who have them. With natural selection operating on the only two self-replicating entities recognized, genes and memes, it is possible for them to reinforce each other as they do in parental love or to work against each other as they do in celibate priests.

Summary

Adaptive behavior is any behavior that fits or adjusts an animal to its environment, in a way that enables it to produce the maximum number of descendants. This definition encompasses several problems, including the difficulty of predicting future descendants, the ease of circular reasoning, the recognition of the difference between beneficial and adaptive behavior, and between mechanism and function. Solution to these problems include the fact that behavior can be tested for its current adaptiveness by the comparative method of examining ancestral behavior patterns that have persisted among many closely related species. This procedure should enable one to make predictions about the adaptive behavior of species not yet studied. Another test for adaptive behavior is the adaptation experiment, which contrasts the viability or fertility of individuals with and without a given behavior. The behavior itself can be manipulated in such experiments, but it is generally easier to alter some structure associated with the behavior or to mimic the behavior of the animal.

Adaptive behavior can be examined at many levels. Fixed action patterns are stereotyped movements or postures that are characteristic of the species. Sequences of fixed action patterns create displays, usually of threat or courtship, and series of acts often called instincts. In the absence of direct observations of behavior, it is possible to determine what the animal has done by the results of its behavior. From any or all of the preceding three levels of behavior, we can infer abstract behavioral characteristics of an animal such as perception, learning, motivation, and emotion. In addition, the strategy an animal uses in achieving the ultimate goal of leaving descendants can be examined by considering its costs (risks) and benefits. The immediate energy budget (cost-benefit ratios) can be ascertained from an animal's feeding strategies. Animals with surplus energy usually convert it to reproduction, which also involves different strategies of finding mates, producing offspring, and caring for them.

The social interactions primarily involved in feeding and reproductive strategies are the subject material of sociobiology, which attempts to explain social behavior by the process of natural selection. Although some patterns of social behavior, like altrustic behavior, initially appear to refute natural selection, these patterns readily fall within the laws of natural selection when genes are considered the unit of selection. Parents will sacrifice their lives for their offspring because the offspring are the means of perpetuating the parents' genes. Ideas or concepts resemble genes in many respects and are similarly altered by natural selection. Concepts used and adhered to by humans are often compatible with perpetration of the genes, as in the altruism parents exhibit toward their offspring.

Study Questions

1. Squirrels regularly bury nuts and it has long been proposed that this behavior is adaptive because the nuts can furnish a supply of food during the winter. Although this is a reasonable explanation, it has never been put to an experimental test. How would you design a field experiment to test this hypothesis?

2. Human behavior is usually compatible with biological demands, but many behaviors do not promote biological goals. Make a list of socially acceptable human behavior patterns that are not biologically adaptive. Can any part of this list be applied to animals other than human beings? To be specific, would you categorize foreign aid to developing nations as adaptive?

3. List some fixed action patterns in a household pet, like a dog or cat.

4. Evolution, by means of natural selection, tends to make behavior efficient, that is, the animal expends the least amount of energy or endures the least risk in the process of obtaining the greatest benefits (usually food, shelter, mates, etc.). Take an animal you are familiar with, describe its feeding behavior, and then propose how it might become more efficient, if natural selection acted on it alone.

3

Animal Distribution and Dispersal

Lawrence I. O'Kelly

Michigan State University

People have long speculated on the possibility of life existing on other planets of our solar system, and astrophysicists have assured us of the high probability that other parts of our universe have the right combination of circumstances to support life. Thus far, however, all we are sure of is that our planet Earth *is* a home for living organisms. From that long-ago time when the first chemical arrangement that we could call "living" emerged, life has evolved in time with our evolving planet. As the planet has aged it has created and destroyed innumerable physical settings to which living organisms have adapted. Geologists and paleontologists have provided us with the outline of the history of life on earth, showing us that oceans once rolled over areas that are now deserts, forests, or farmland; that lowland marshes have been lifted to mountain heights; that continents have drifted together or parted; that volcanic outflows have created great plateaus; and that all earthly features are dynamically changing. Yet in every place, save in the molten brew of liquid lava, there is life now and evidence of life in the past. As Krecker has so eloquently said:

The story of evolution has been the story of protoplasm's attempt to accommodate itself to its environment. It is as though in the beginning living material, protoplasm, was confronted with an environment which demanded obedience to its whims as the price of survival, and protoplasm, to live, has obeyed. It grovels in the slime as Amoeba, it flies free in the air as bird, it exists as a helpless parasite, it has risen to power as a man. Protoplasm has done everything, lived everywhere, assumed every conceivable form, has been humiliated and exalted, but it has lived (Krecker, 1934, pp. 574-575).

Definition and Range of Environments

A wide variety of environments, ranging from ocean depth to mountain summit, from bog to desert, supports some form of life adapted to its particular surroundings. The rich diversity of forms impressed young Charles Darwin as he carried out his duties as naturalist of the *H. M. S. Beagle* on its circumnavigational voyage of 1830-1831, leading him along the road to the theory of evolution. The adaptations are both *structural* and *behavioral*. These are not mutually exclusive categories, of course, since very frequently the behavior is a direct consequence of the structure, as the wings of birds make flight possible. In the most general sense, evolutionary selection, operating by genetic transmission, must be of structure, for it is only on structures that the genetic code can operate. Of significance for the psychologist is the fact that, even when the structural adaptation is not easily observable, the behavioral consequence usually is. Later on we will pursue this matter in a little more detail, but for now let us continue to consider the environment.

What is meant by "environment"? Your dictionary will tell you that it is: ". . . the aggregate of all the external conditions and influences affecting the life and development of an organism." Obviously, then, the environment for any given animal is defined by specifying the "aggregate of external conditions and influences" that surround the animal. Enumeration of environmental variables is relatively easy in some respects and very difficult in others. For example, temperature, moisture, and other weather and climatic variables, oxygen and other gaseous components, illumination, and other physical factors are quite easily measurable, as are most of their regular or irregular fluctuations. Other factors may give us some trouble, either because of the subtlety of their influences, as with trace amounts of necessary minerals or some nonvisible electromagnetic radiations or because we do not have the necessary knowledge of their importance, as with the small variations in odor or taste quality (which, as we will see later, are critically important to parts of the life cycle of some migratory fishes).

Of equal importance in describing an environment is an identification and description of the life forms sharing the space. Here the picture does become complex. Even Robinson Crusoe on his island coexisted with other animals of many species and with plants. As each organism is pursuing its own existence, it must not only share the physical features of the environment but must also adapt to other living individuals in the same space. A whole range of interrelationships predictably develop. Some resources that are shared may be present in limited amounts or segregated locations (such as watering holes on the African savannah), and *competition* for such resources may occur. Some forms secure their nutrients from other forms, and thus more or less complicated *food chains* develop. Some forms, over time, evolve cooperative modes of existence with other forms, as in *symbiosis*, or adapt themselves to unilateral support by another species, as in *parasitism*. The space may become divided into subspaces by members of a given species, and this may be manifested as *territoriality*.

Thus, if we really took seriously the task of describing the environment of an organism in both its physical and organic features, we would find that we have arrived at the fascinating and important field of study called *ecology*. Ecology is the branch of biology that synthesizes information and concepts from a wide range of physical, biological and behavioral sciences. Our study of animal behavior gains much from ecology and reciprocates by providing information and techniques to the ecologist. The basic vision of ecology has never been described better than in the words with which Darwin closed his *Origin of Species*:

It is interesting to contemplate a tangled bank, clothed with many plants of many kinds, with birds singing in the bushes, with various insects flitting about, and with worms crawling through the damp earth, and to reflect that these elaborately constructed forms, so different from each other, and dependent upon each other in so complex a manner, have all been produced by laws acting around us (Darwin, 1872, pp. 477-478).

Animal Distribution and Dispersal

Evolutionary Adaptation and Behavior

In broad terms, any organism may be said to be successful if it can live long enough to reproduce itself. The complex requirements of living systems must be met without failure if the individual is to survive to a reproductive age. Natural selection, operating on the genetically variable members of each generation of organisms, has produced an almost unimaginable number of species, each characterized by anatomical and functional features that fit it to a particular range of environmental variables in such a fashion that it may meet the varied requirements for maintenance of life. In the course of its long evolutionary history, life has managed to spread and survive successfully in almost all of the possible environments afforded by our planet. Examples are obvious: birds, mammals, and insects have developed wings for aerial existences; fish, insects, mammals, and a variety of other phyla have structures adapting them to aquatic existences; other forms have specialized in accommodating themselves to a varied range of terrestrial environments; still others have worked out the means of living in subterranean environments. The student of behavior observes the many ways in which adaptive structures create and regulate the functional relationships of organism to environment in the service of survival and reproduction. More specifically, we must determine how — and with what sensitivity — an animal receives peripheral stimulation, how it discriminates and analyzes the advantageous and threatening aspects of its surroundings, how it incorporates nutrients, how it moves in space, how it achieves reproduction, how it communicates with its own or other species, and how it shapes or transforms environmental features in its adaptive interest. All of these variables enter critically into determining the distribution and movements of each organism.

The Regulatory Theme

We have said that adaptations are the key to survival and evolution, and now we can ask further: What do adaptations actually do to make survival possible? Survival of the individual depends on establishment and maintenance of the complex physicochemical reactions that are necessary for life to continue. Additionally, adaptations must protect this energy machine from lethal extremes of environmental fluctuations. These functions of adaptation we can call the *regulatory* processes of the organism. Much of our basic insight in this critical area of biology we owe to Claude Bernard (1813 – 1878) who called attention to the complete dependence of body cells on an environment with minimal deviations from constant and correct conditions of many variables — chemical composition, concentration, temperature, acidity, and so on. For the single naked cell, few environments, save for certain marine situations, provide such constancy. Yet, as we know, multicellular organisms have successfully established themselves in environments that not only deviate from the correct conditions for cellular life, but also fluctuate grossly over time. Consider the human animal, whose cells depend on an environmental temperature of roughly 98F. Yet people live adequately in our "temperate" regions, where the temperature of the external surroundings may vary over a year from -60 to 110F. The concentrations of the body fluids bathing the cells must stay constant within rather narrow limits, yet some animals make do in arid deserts, while others live in waters either much less or much more concentrated than the optimal chemistry for their cells.

Bernard's consideration of this seeming paradox led him to distinguish an *internal* environment in direct contact with the body cells and protected by the skin from the *external* environment. The totality of the processes by means of which the internal environment is kept constant are usually referred to as *homeostasis,* or homostatic regulation. A large number of adaptive structures and their mechanisms are devoted to regulation of the parameters of the internal environment. For our purposes we distinguish two aspects of regulatory process: (1) *internal physiological* and (2) *external behavioral.* To make the distinction clear, consider body temperature maintenance. Internally, heat is produced by the chemical reactions of metabolic processes, aided by neural and hormonal mechanisms that augment heat gain or loss. Behaviorally, the animal can move to parts of its environment with more optimal temperatures, construct nests or shelters, or, as in the human, put on or take off protective clothing. Body fluid maintenance may be controlled internally through neurohumoral mechanisms that change the water and salt loss through kidney excretion. Behaviorally, the animal may move in its environment to sources of water and drink, or move to parts of its environment that minimize water loss. Much of the behavior of any animal is in the service of regulatory maintenance. It should be noted that the particular environmental location of an animal at any time is likely to be closely related to its regulatory problems and needs. Thus we can see that the distribution and dispersal of organisms is itself based on adaptive process.

Distribution

Imagine a four-dimensional map of the world, three of the dimensions being the spatial planes described by latitude, longitude, and altitude above and below the earth's surface, and the fourth being time. We could then indicate the loci in this space of each member of each species of plant and animal. Such a map, when completed, would accurately describe the *distribution* of organic life on earth. In this fashion, the millions and millions of species and the billions and billions of individuals, the total biomass of the planet, is spatially and temporally arranged. Biogeographers, ecologists, and taxonomists have

progressed far enough in describing this pattern of distribution (an endless task!!) to permit some principles and classificatory concepts to emerge.

For a beginning, at any place and time on our map, we can say that an individual or a species is either present or absent and can then seek to determine reasons for the absence. One attack strategy on this problem is diagrammed in Figure 3.1. It should be noted that behavioral factors in habitat selection also involve and do not

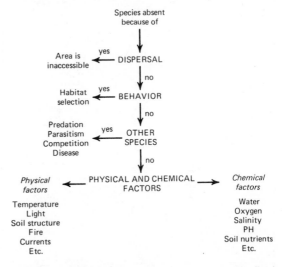

Figure 3.1. Methods of inquiry for explaining the distribution of organisms. [From Krebs, (1972), p. 16.]

exclude influences of physical and chemical factors or relations with other species. Important to our later consideration of migration is recognition that species presence or absence may be time-related, the species appearing in a given location at one time and in another location at some other time. In essence, what the inquiry outlined in Figure 3.1 does is enable us to match an animal to a total environment for which it is adapted. The importance of this matching is illustrated by what happens when a human or other transport agent introduces a species to an area in which it was not previously present. The most frequent outcome of such experiments is a failure of the species to survive. Many attempts to introduce game birds or fishes to a particular region for purposes of hunting recreation have failed to work out, as have similar experiments with transplanting vegetation. Less frequent, but more dramatic and socially significant, are the instances where the experiment works, where the environment *does* match the organism's requirements. The domestic sparrow and starling in North America (see Figure 3.2), the rabbit in Australia, the lamprey in the Great Lakes, and

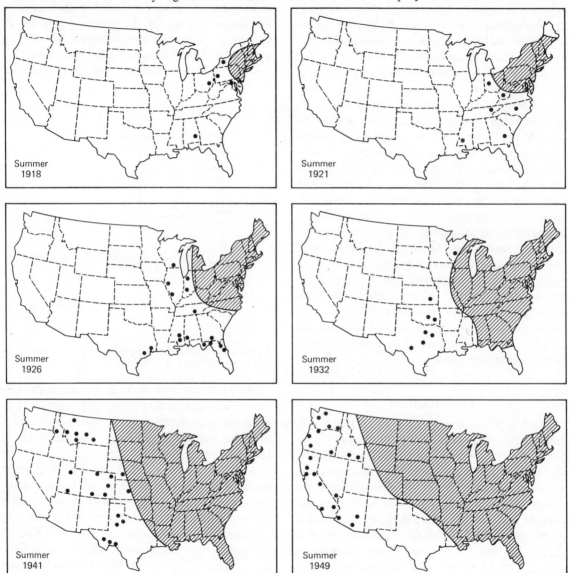

Figure 3.2. Westward expansion of the range of the starling. The shaded area shows the approximate breeding range for a given summer; dots indicate winter occurrences outside the breeding range for the same and two or three previous years. [From Kessel (1953), p. 64.]

An Evolutionary and Ecological Perspective

the water hyacinth in the southeastern United States are all regrettably successful in their new environments.

The example of successful introductions illustrates the point that, while species and habitat must match, not all suitable habitats will be occupied by all possible species suited to them. Figure 3.1 indicates that the most basic factor is *accessibility*. Barriers to dispersal are of many kinds; what constitutes an impediment is a function of the structural and behavioral capabilities of the animal. Most terrestrial animals find large bodies of water impassable, and conversely, aquatic animals are restricted by land masses. As most geological and geographical barriers change over time, so do dispersal possibilities. Land routes between Asia and North America, when existent, were traveled by many terrestrial species, including humans. Many of the differences between the flora and fauna of North and South America appear partially due to the shifting land bridges between these continents. Almost a new dimension in the explanation of distribution has emerged with the realization that the large land masses themselves have drifted and changed their relative position through the time span of organic life (see Figure 3.3). Freedom of movement, by bringing members of the same and diverse species together, makes possible the operation of other determining factors such as predation (see Chapter 21), parasitism, competition, and so on. Loss of freedom of movement by geological or other interference produces isolation of species. By restricting breeding possibilities consequent to this, evolutionary development is affected, as Darwin so acutely observed in his studies of the similarities and differences of South American mainland and Galapagos Island species.

The second major variable in the scheme of Figure 3.1 is *behavior* in relation to habitat selection. This is a recognition that organisms discriminate between various aspects of the environment. Discrimination depends directly on sensory capacity; a rather large amount of behavioral research has been invested in understanding the sensory capacities of animals. These data are of fundamental importance in our analysis of the role of habitat selection in distribution.

Let us take as an example the relationship between temperature and habitat selection in fish. Water temperature is an important, even critical, parameter of the aquatic environment. For fish, as for all cold-blooded animals, environmental temperature directly controls many metabolic processes. As Brett says:

Temperature sets lethal limits to life; it conditions the animal through acclimation to meet levels of temperature that would otherwise be intolerable; it governs the rate of development; it sets the limits of metabolic rate within which the

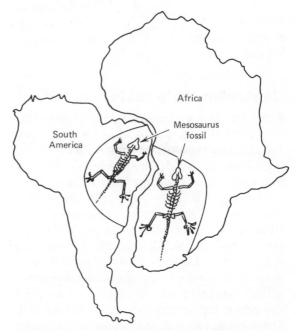

Figure 3.3. Continental drift. Fossils of *Mesosaurus*, a small freshwater reptile, are found in geologically similar deposits in parts of South America and Africa. During the Permian period, 250 million plus years ago, their environment was continuous. [From Hurlbut (1976), p. 22.]

Animal Distribution and Dispersal

animal is free to perform; and it acts as a directive factor resulting in the congregation of fish within given thermal ranges, or movements to new environmental conditions (Brett, 1956, p. 76).

Bull (1936) and Bardach (1956, 1957), using conditioned response techniques, showed that several species of fish were able to discriminate temperature increases of as little as 0.03C. Sullivan (1954) found that brook trout will orient to and maintain position in a narrow region of a temperature gradient. Similar findings have been reported for a wide variety of aquatic species.

In the limited space of this chapter we are not able to cite examples of the behavioral response to all of the physical and chemical features of the environment that go into determining distribution. Some of these variables and their behavioral relations are treated in other sections of this book, and any text in ecology will provide extended discussions of the determinants of habitat.

Population Variables in Distribution

Returning to our imaginary four-dimensional distributional map, with its dots for every individual of every species, we observe that the numbers of like individuals vary widely over the map, with each species being profusely represented in some places relative to other areas. Population factors are very important to all phases of distributional analysis as well as to the whole of evolutionary biology. Recall that the fundamental initial point in Darwin's theory of natural selection was the assumption that reproductive potential of organisms results in offspring in numbers that exceed the carrying capacity of their habitat. The resulting efforts of individuals within species and between species to survive to breeding age in an environment inadequate to support all provides the stage for the process of natural selection. For those competitors with "successful"

patterns of traits, such patterns are genetically transferred to the next generation. This basic view persists and has gained increased plausability as we have come to understand more of the genetic basis for individual variability among progeny, of the process of trait inheritance, and of the roles that populations play in the selective process. Analysis of the biochemistry of inheritance has been one of the outstanding achievements of twentieth-century science, and, when coupled with the substantial advances in population genetics, we can feel confident that evolutionary theory is on very firm ground.

Our concern here, however, is with the behavioral aspects of populations as they influence animal distribution. Any portion of the environment will support some maximal number of animals or plants of any given species. This *carrying capacity* usually is less than the *reproductive potential* of a species, creating the classical selective pressure described above, with its long-range evolutionary implications. A closer look at distribution, generation by generation, raises the question of how the populations are regulated. The primary variables determining the number of animals in a population are, of course, *births* as inputs and *deaths* as outputs. If birthrates exceed death rates the population increases, and an excess of mortality over births reduces the population. Regulation of populations, then, centers on factors that influence births and deaths.

Theoretically the regulatory process would hold a population constant at or slightly below the carrying capacity, but since the carrying capacity itself varies with climatic fluctuations and with interspecies competition (predation and parasitism), populations rarely maintain a stable equilibrium, but instead swing around some mean value more or less close to the carrying capacity. The amplitude of the deviations from the mean value may present either temporary or permanent dangers to the species; obviously, continued decline in numbers indicates a species facing extinction. Expansion of a population beyond resources predictably increases mortality, usually by starvation, and may also cause pressure for dispersal into new and less favorable habitats, perhaps displacing or posing new competitive factors for other species in the process. Adding complexity to the picture is the interdependence of life forms in the habitat community, particularly in its food chains. Expansion puts pressure on those species below and increases the food supply of those above the species in question, as when an increasing herbivore population overgrazes an area but also furnishes carnivorous predators with a more abundant food supply.

While a great deal of research has been devoted to the problem of population regulation, and many theories have been proposed, the question has not yet been satisfactorily resolved. It is very probable that different species solve the problem in different ways, and that no single regulatory mechanism operates in isolation. Theories may be divided into those that emphasize environmental circumstances and those that look to endogenous, organism-involved factors. The former may be independent of density of population, or density dependent; the latter are probably all density dependent. Price (1975) has suggested that the relative importance of the two factors is related to the distribution of animals within the range they inhabit, climatic or other environmental variables being limiting in the less favorable parts of the range and density-dependent factors being paramount in the more optimal parts of the range (see Figure 3.4; see also Birch, 1957).

Among the endogenous factors are the regulating aspects of behavior. As Wynne-Edwards (1962) has observed, the territorial behavior of birds interacts with available food supply to control population density. General activity levels of animals may be positively correlated with density, with the result that dispersal and migration take place, moving animals over a wider area. In the bug *Dysdercus fasciatus* crowding results in

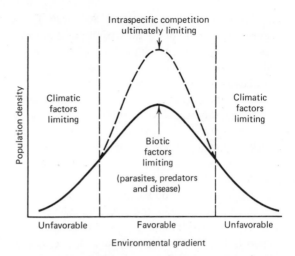

Figure 3.4. Hypothetical relationship between the major regulating factors on a species throughout its range. [Adapted from Price (1975), p. 182.]

smaller adults who show increased activity, as is the case also with the larvae of the noctuid moth *Spodoptera litteralis* (Hodjat, 1969, 1970). Other examples of this reaction to density will be given when we discuss migration.

Population control, to be effective, must result in changes in factors that add to or subtract from the population — that is, ultimately, to changes in reproductive and/or mortality rates. Density influences both of these factors in a complex interweaving of effects. A reduction in high-density populations is frequently accomplished by vectors acting to reduce or delay addition of recruits to the population. In the pike, *Esex lucius*, for example, the number of eggs deposited is inversely related to the biomass of spawning fish (Kipling and Frost, 1969). A number of birds show a similar relationship, usually mediated by differential food supplies at critical periods. In the Great Tit, *Parus major*, clutch size and hatching failure are both density dependent (Krebs, 1970). The Red Grouse, *Lagopus lagopus scoticus*, has a breeding success directly related to the quantity and quality of food in late winter via modification of clutch size, hatching success, and chick mortality (Jenkins, 1963; Jenkins, Watson, and Miller, 1963). Ashmole (1963, 1965) has argued that the small clutch size in oceanic birds — frequently only one egg is laid — is an evolutionary adaptation for reproductive success in populations highly competitive for food.

There are a number of striking egg-related reactions to increased density among insects. In *Locusta migratoria migratoriodes*, the migratory locust, crowding reduces the number of eggs from 1000 per female in isolated conditions to 300 per female in crowded conditions. The larvae from the crowded females, however, are larger and have better food reserves than those from the isolated females (Albrecht, Verdier, and Blackith, 1958). Females of surviving crowded larvae of the mosquito *Culex pipiens* lay a smaller number of eggs; additionally, third-instar larvae raised in overcrowded conditions produce a chemical factor that is highly toxic to younger larvae, slowing down their growth and development (Ikeshoji and Mulla, 1970a, 1970b).

While territorial behavior is examined in other chapters, we should note here that it is frequently hypothesized to be a mechanism in the self-regulation of populations. J. L. Brown (1969, p. 323), in a review of the literature, concluded that:

Although the hypothesis of population regulation through territorial behavior is a tempting one, too few critical studies on it have been done to conclude now that it is of widespread importance in limiting reproduction of avian populations; and in any case, such a limit will be determined not by territorial behavior alone, but by complex interactions between the environment, the number of birds competing for territories, and territorial behavior.

Brown's caution that regulation is not a single-factor mechanism is well taken. However, in a number of studies the role of territoriality seems to be critically important. In a series of studies of the red grouse (Watson, 1964, 1967; Watson and Jenkins, 1968; Watson and Miller,

1971) it was found that cocks with territories have better survival rates and better chances of breeding. Territorial behavior limits the population size and thus the breeding stock. Here, as in many other observations, it was noted that high density increases aggression in the vigorous defense of territory. Krebs (1970, 1971) demonstrated similar roles of territorial behavior in determining the breeding population density of the Great Tit (*Parus major*), as is also true of the following studies by Tompa (1962, 1964).

In this careful study of an island-isolated population of song sparrows, Tompa found that territories were established by males and accepted passively by females. The high number of unmated males without territory interfered with breeding activities, and in their competition with established males the unwanted males even induced territory desertion by the established male. The result was a high mortality (80 – 90 percent) of young birds, occurring mainly during the autumnal territorial season. Territorial competition, by interfering with reproduction and parental care of young, thus serves to hold the population of this species quite constant from year to year.

Territorial behavior may play much the same role in fishes. The ayu (*Ploceglossus altivelis*) a salmonlike fish living in Japanese rivers, grazes on diatoms and the algae of bottom stones. Eggs are laid in the autumn; and the young mature, spawn, and die the following autumn. The growing fish show strong territoriality, defending an area of about a square meter in places with abundant food. Fish without territories show schooling or solitary travelling in areas with less food (see Figure 3.5). Consequently the territorial fish show faster growth and a higher reproductive rate, and populations are maintained in balance with resources (Kawanabe, 1968). The summarized study below by Warren (1973) also illustrates population control in fish.

Warren analyzed the responses of the guppy to increased population densities. Male courtship behavior declined and agonistic or agressive behavior increased as density rose. Water from a high-density aquarium, when placed in a low-density tank, induced increased aggression and reduced courtship behavior. Perception of density is thus, in part at least, a function of the metabolic secretions of crowded fish. The overall consequence of these density-dependent responses is to establish a stable population proportional to the size of the living space.

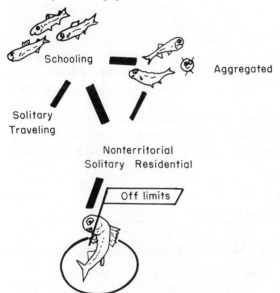

Figure 3.5. The social behaviour of the ayu shifts between the types indicated as a function of food availability and population density. The size of the bars is proportional to the frequency of behaviour shifts between the various modes. [From Kawanabe (1968), p. 246.]

Dispersal of Animals

Behavioral Aspects of Dispersal — Home Range and Territory

Thus far we have looked at circumstances that influence the gross distribution of animals about the world. Within the relatively fixed areas of distribution of animals there is also a great deal of movement to be observed. The movements of individual animals are the source of most of the research problems for the behavioral biologist. Collectively we call these movements in space over time *dispersal*, while the area in which the individual animal usually lives and moves is called *home range*. Among species showing social organization, the group can be regarded as a unit (as in herds of grazing animals, hives of bees, schools of fish, etc.). There are various degrees of overlapping in home range within species, and cyclical variations of population density can influence the degree of overlapping. Table 3.1 lists home range areas for a variety of mammalian species.

We have already considered the phenomenon of *territoriality* in connection with regulation of population density.

Here we are concerned with territories as they contribute to the movement patterns of individuals or groups. A *territory* may be defined behaviorally as an area that an animal defends from encroachment by other individuals of the same species (although in some cases the defense is against members of other species as well). In social animals the group may similarly resist trespass by members of another social unit. Territorial behavior is observed in a wide range of phyletic groups, appearing perhaps most frequently in birds, whose aerial mobility lends itself to more effective territorial surveillance and defense.

As we have previously seen, the distributional effect of territoriality is on the spacing of individuals or groups and thus works to determine the population density within an area. Since most areas are not homogeneous with respect to food and shelter, competition for favorable territory is usually present, and some individuals will have "better" locations than others, with a consequent impact on mating success and progeny mortality. In this way territoriality can be a factor in natural selection. A more immediate short-range effect of the territorial habit is elicitation of *competition* and *agonistic* or *aggressive* behavior, as the occupant of a favored location is obligated to defend against would-be displacers.

Territory defense may be interspecific or intraspecific. Because freshwater environments are relatively homogenous they offer few opportunities for specialization of species. As Larkin (1956) has suggested, freshwater fishes have a "relatively wide tolerance of habitat types, a flexibility of feeding habits, and in general share many resources of their environment with several other species of fishes." Territories in such an environment tend to be temporary and to shift with variation in food availability among members of whatever species share the same food preferences. In birds, however, territory is more generally maintained in an intraspecific fashion, with the territory being more stable and with minimal attention being paid to spatial transgressions by other species.

Several types of territoriality exist. The most common are connected with mating and nesting sites, which may be defended by one or both sexes. Since reproductive behavior is usually periodic or seasonal, territory establishment may reflect this; many birds, for example, establish territories during the mating season but move in flocks at other times. In more sedentary species with permanent living sites, territory is also more permanent, as in most colonial insects and many burrowing mammals.

While seasonal territoriality may be attributable primarily to reproductive factors, it necessarily will also involve foraging and feeding behavior, since usually the animal will gain most of its nutritive requirements within its defended territory. Consideration of feeding behavior in relation to time and space impresses us with the similarities between the concepts of home range and territory. We recognize that an animal has a territory when we see it defending the area against encroachment. Implicit is a fixed area exclusively occupied over an extended period of time. This state of affairs lies at one end of a con-

Table 3.1
Home Range Size of Some Mammals

Species	Extent of Home Range
Antelope *(Antilocapra americana)*	Daily feeding range up to 3 square miles
Big short-tailed shrew *(Blarina brevicauda)*	25-yard radius
Brown rat *(Rattus norvegicus)*	Depends on food availability; may move from human habitations in winter to fields in summer
Jackrabbit *(Lepus* spp.*)*	Density of 1 rabbit to 5–10 acres
Kangaroo mouse *(Napaeozapus insignis)*	Females, 1 in 6½ acres; males 1 in 9 acres; some overlap in ranges of individuals
Lemming mice *(Synatomys* spp.*)*	100 feet
Muskrat *(Ondatra zibethicus)*	Fixed housing; wanders over several miles in search of food or new housing area
Opossum *(Didelphis marsupialis)*	15 to 40 acres per individual
Pika *(Ochotona princeps)*	Usually forages within 100 feet of home nest
Porcupine *(Erethizon dorsatum)*	5 acres; some overlap between individuals
Raccoon *(Procyon lotor)*	10 acres
Red squirrel *(Temiasciurus* spp.*)*	½ to 1 acre
Striped skunk *(Mephitis mephitis)*	½ to 1 mile with some overlapping
Varying hare *(Lepus americanus)*	100 feet
Vole *(Microtus* spp.*)*	15 individuals per acre (low) to 250 per acre (high)

Adapted from Palmer, 1954.

An Evolutionary and Ecological Perspective

tinuum of distribution in space and time. At the other end would be an indiscriminate mingling of individuals. Between these two extremes lie most cases of spatial and temporal occupancy. For example, a predatory animal may have an overlapping foraging range with others of the same or different species, but will defend vigorously a specific kill. Thus, for a short period of time the animals occupy a specific spatial locus and will show the agonistic behavior that we identify with territoriality. Within the home range, then, there exist short-term territories, and the animal, within that time span, shows all of the characteristics of territorial behavior.

Directional factors in dispersal

As anyone who fishes knows, success depends on understanding where the fish are likely to be. As predators, people who fish learn to correlate physical features of the environment with the probable behavioral preferences of their prey. We have noted before the fact that, for any given species, there is an optimal combination of physical environmental parameters, and that, other things being equal, abundance of that species will be maximal where this optimum exists. How does any animal recognize and achieve its "best" environment? Let us analyze a part of the behavioral repertoire of a very complicated simple animal, the single-celled paramecium. It is a motile aquatic organism, swimming by means of patterned movements of its cilia — hairlike protoplasmic extrusions that beat back and forth like tiny oars. Its primary food is bacteria, and the paramecium forages through its environment searching out and grazing on these even smaller life forms. When the paramecium encounters obstacles to its movements, as Jennings (1906) has shown, it systematically carries out avoidance and escape maneuvers, as illustrated in Figure 3.6a. It also reacts actively to other factors of its environment, such as temperature gradients, as shown in Figure 3.6b. Clearly, as these two examples show, paramecia can *sense* obstacles

and temperature, and can control their movements on the basis of information received from stimulation. If temperature sensitivity did not exist, distribution and dispersal would be as random in a temperature gradient as it is in a medium with uniform temperature. This obvious fact is easily generalizable: *all active dispersion depends on the particular sensory capacities of the animal.* The adaptive relationship between the sensory equipment of an organism and its survival potential are equally apparent. Selective

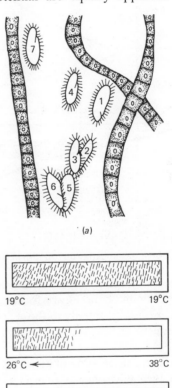

(a)

19°C   19°C

26°C ◄   38°C

10°C   ► 25°C

(b)

Figure 3.6. Directional behaviour in paramecia.
(a) Sequence of movements in avoidance of an obstacle.
(b) Dispersal in a temperature gradient.
[From Jennings (1906), p. 48, 71.]

Animal Distribution and Dispersal

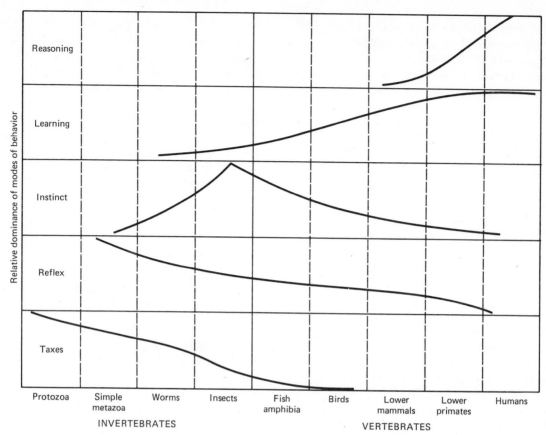

Figure 3.7. Changes in behaviour control in phylogeny. [From Dethier and Stellar (1961), p. 65.]

pressure leads to the evolution of those sensory capabilities minimally necessary for a particular species to *orient* differentially to those features of its environment critical to its maintenance and survival.

Analyzing the orientation of animals to salient aspects of their environment reveals a range of mechanisms that differ in some systematic fashion between phyla. The general types of behavior control as they appear across the phylogenetic scale are shown in Figure 3.7. In general it appears that the invertebrates orient through the relatively fixed and genetically determined mechanisms of *taxes*, *reflexes*, and *instincts*, and that the role of *learning* and "*reasoning*" is predominant in the vertebrates. In the pages to follow we

examine and give some examples of the part which taxes and instincts play in determining the directional orientation of animals in their various habitats. Reflexes seldom involve integrated movements of the whole animal and, while they may be components of more complex behavior, they are of minor importance to an understanding of dispersive behavior.

Taxes. The term *taxis* is used to designate the orientation of an animal with respect to a source of stimulation, and also the accompanying movement. The taxis may be *positive* — toward the stimulation, or *negative* — away from the stimulation. The term has been used inter-

An Evolutionary and Ecological Perspective

changeably with the word *tropism*, but modern usage reserves the latter term for the movements of parts of plants, such as roots growing downward, flowers turning with the sun, and so on. The oriented movement is designated by the type of stimulation that is involved: *phototaxis* — movement with respect to light; *geotaxis* — movement with respect to gravitational force; *thigmotaxis* — movement oriented around tactile stimuli; *rheotaxis* — movement with respect to water currents, and the like. The distributions of paramecia illustrated in Figure 3.7*b* may be considered examples of *thermotaxis*.

While the term taxis is frequently used to denote almost any reliable tendency in a particular species to orient in a particular fashion towards a stimulus source, there is frequently an assumption that the movement is "forced," that is, that the animal responds in an automatic fashion; and there is the further assumption that the response is determined by fixed arrangements of body structure. Common examples of the phenomenon are the attraction of some moths to lights, avoidance of light by cockroaches, upstream orientation of fish, and so on. The extent to which any particular animal is completely stimulus bound by its inferred taxic structure is still a matter of controversy, but the observational facts concerning reliable and predictable orientations are manifold. Taxic concepts are valuable aids in understanding the directional dispersal of many creatures in many situations. Knowledge that the cockroach is generally negatively phototaxic and positively thigmotaxic would lead one to predict that cockroaches would be found in dark places wedged into small cracks and crevices, as indeed they are.

The original conception of taxes as invariant consequences of the animal's genetically determined structure has received considerable modification. Many animals show reversible orientation directions. For example, the small crustacean, *Daphnia* spp., is basically negatively phototaxic, but reductions in light intensity cause a temporary reversal of orientation, and the animal will move in the direction of greater illumination (Clarke, 1932). Many insects show temperature-dependent reversals of phototaxis that become *negative* at higher temperatures, protecting the insect from the heat of midday (Jack and Williams, 1937). Taxes are good examples of readily observable behaviors whose underlying structures are not yet understood; but it is through those genetically determined structures that natural selection has operated to favor the taxic behavior.

Taxes are clear demonstrations of the role environmental differences play in animal dispersion. Even when the sign of the taxis changes, due to either internal or external variables, the end result is always a nonrandom distribution of animals in the environment.

Instinctive Behavior and Dispersal. We have already discussed, in other contexts, a variety of species-specific behaviors that are important in determining the distribution and dispersal of animals, particularly *territoriality*. The modern view of instinct retains the notion of genetic determination, recognizing that some determinants of even quite complex behavior are transmitted genetically in the species, and that the style and content of the behavior is thus *species specific*. However, there is also a recognition that "instinctive" behavior is not inflexible and invariant, nor is the behavior an autonomous part of the animal's behavioral repertoire. Instead, continuing investigation indicates that the genetic determination is subject to individual alterations by the circumstances in which the animal finds itself and by the retained effects of past experience in the expression of the behavior. As Tinbergen pointed out rather a long time ago (1951), instincts, on examination, show themselves to be hierarchically arranged groups of less complex behaviors, and these behaviors may be broken down into even smaller components. For example, if we consider *maternal care* as "instinctive" and examine the actual behavior manifested by any animal mother we may easily see that maternal care involves, for a given species, a large number of contributory subtasks. The mother laboratory rat makes a nest, gathers pups into the nest, grooms pups, keeps them warm by curling up around them, feeds them, and so on. Each part of the maternal behavior complex can be analyzed further into the component sensory-motor sequences that are involved. A more extended discussion of the role of instinct is available in the next chapter on animal migration.

Learning and Dispersal. The capacity of animals to retain the effects of past experience and to modify their behavior in the light of their memories seems to be particularly characteristic of vertebrates, but this capacity is not entirely absent in the invertebrate phyla. Many of the social insects are capable of memory storage, and they use it to regulate their dispersal movements. Consider the foraging activity of the honeybee (*Apis mellifera*). As it ranges around the vicinity of its home hive it may discover a concentration of flowers rich in nectar. After gathering a payload of this essential food it returns to the hive (the homing indicates a capacity to remember). Arriving at the hive, it communicates to its fellow workers basic information concerning the direction and distance of the newly found food source — information that must be remembered by the informant long enough to transmit it. Other workers remember the communication and increase their flight activity in the area located by the scout bee (von Frisch, 1967).

A somewhat similar demonstration of the utility of learning and memory is found in the ability of many animals to return to a specific location for reproductive behavior. Migratory birds will usually nest year after year in the same area and often in the identical nest site. Some fish, as the Pacific salmon, after an adulthood spent in the ocean, will return to the freshwater stream in which they were spawned several years before. Behavior of this sort is possible only if the animal retains critical memories of environmental features. Again, a more complete account is given in Chapter 4.

Study Questions

1. How do physical features of an environment interact with the structural and behavioral characteristics of an organism to determine distribution?

2. How does the study of animal distribution and dispersal contribute evidence for evaluating evolutionary theories?

3. Consider the common urban fauna of your own residence area, particularly its population of dogs and cats. What factors exist in your neighbourhood that determine the distribution of these pets? Similarly, what can you say about their dispersal within the neighborhood?

4. This chapter has presented an ecological viewpoint on animal distribution. In what way is behavioral research important for the ecological analysis of animal distributions?

5. If you were to write a paper on human distribution and dispersal, in what ways would it resemble this chapter? What additional variables would you have to consider?

4

Animal Migration

Lawrence I. O'Kelly
Michigan State University

In this chapter we look at the special case of animal movement called *migration*. Periodic mass movements of living creatures have attracted our attention and interest throughout recorded history and are represented in the myths of many peoples. From biblical tales to the historical account of the rescue of Mormon crops by locust-feeding seagulls, plagues of locusts sweeping over the land have had a terrifying reality through the ages. National television has covered the return of swallows to the mission of Capistrano. Sportsmen carefully regulate their vacation times to the spawning runs of the Pacific and Atlantic salmon. Tourists gasp over the tree-full clusters of monarch butterflies in their winter headquarters on the Monterey Peninsula. Even though misconceived, the "suicidal rush of the lemmings to the sea" has metaphorical usage throughout the world. There may be a tinge of sadness as the honking of geese high overhead in the autumn presages the coming of winter, while the return of robins to our lawns increases our thoughts of spring. The increased concern with the threatened extinction of the whales has made many people aware of their ocean-ranging migratory movements. Hunters know and follow the movements of elk, moose, and caribou from their summer to their winter ranges.

These are some of the better-known examples of migration, but they are only a very small fraction of the total migratory mass. Every phylum with motile animals has species that execute regular dispersive movements over distances that may vary from as short as that of the horse bot fly, whose larvae migrate from the region of the horse's nose and mouth into the intestinal tract, to the recored-achieving travels of the Arctic tern that regularly travels from the arctic regions of North America to Antartica and back again each year.

While many observations of migratory behavior have been made in all times and places by all peoples, serious biological studies of the phenomenon are a matter of the last 150 years. Much of the early data on migration was gathered by amateurs, most importantly by birdwatchers, insect collectors, hunters, and people who fish.

The study of migration has been supported and stimulated by the frequent economic value of the knowledge obtained. Prediction of the movement of insect pests may be of critical importance in crop protection; knowledge of the movements of food fishes, such as the herring, eel, salmon, cod, and tuna improve the success of the fishing industry. Recently we have seen how the acceptance of a plan for an oil pipeline across the Alaskan tundra depended on an environmental impact statement that required knowledge of the timing and routine of the caribou migration. As we find out more about these animal movements, however, we have become aware of a variety of very difficult explanatory problems, some of which we will touch on in this section. Migration has been and remains a challenge to the curious biologist.

Definition and Classification of Migration Movements

In the most general terms we can define migration as *the movement from one habitat to another that is a usual or integral part of the life cycle of the species concerned.* A useful synonym for migration, suggested by C. G. Johnson (1969), is *adaptive dispersal,* which reminds us of the utility of the movement and also eliminates those shifts of position that are accidental or random displacements from a habitat. While many migratory movements are "round trips" showing some kind of regular periodicity, in short-lived species the movements may be one-way, once-in-a-lifetime trips from one region to another. Thus, it is only natural that many ornithologists and mammalogists argue for the round-trip as being an essential criterion for migration, while many entomologists include (indeed concentrate on) one-way movement. In either case, however, the movement must be characteristic of the species and adaptively related to its overall life cycle. In this section we consider both types.

In addition to classifying migration as one way or two way, we can also distinguish migrations that are primarily *vertical* or *horizontal*. Among the examples of vertical migration we can cite are the movements of many mountain-dwelling animals from the higher elevations

where they feed in the milder summer months to lower elevations for winter residence. Many aquatic organisms also move from deeper to more shallow water, sometimes daily, probably under the control of illumination, and seasonally as a function of temperature. Figure 4.1 illustrates the movement of a small invertebrate, *Daphnia pulex*, in a mountain lake over a 24 hour period (Pennak, 1943). Vertical movements of zooplankton are important determiners of the depth at which many fish are to be found, as they follow their food up and down. We probably think more readily of examples of horizontal migration, as animals travel on, above, or in the earth or water from one locality to another. On the whole, flying and swimming organisms probably travel farther in their migrations than do animals that must crawl, walk, or run on the surface.

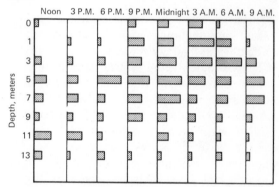

Figure 4.1. Diurnal migration of *Daphnia pulex* in Summit Lake, Colorado. The bars represent the number of animals found at the indicated depths at 3-hour intervals in the 24-hour period of observations. [From Pennak (1943), p. 406.]

Another basis for classifying migration is in terms of the basic physiological mechanisms and adaptations that are involved. There are three principal categories:

1. *Gametic*, relating to stages of the sexual cycle of the animal.

2. *Alimental*, relating to the search for food and water.

3. *Climatic*, relating to such environmental variables as temperature and humidity.

In the actual case, most migrations are caused by some degree of interrelationship among these three general factors. Later, as we consider the migrations of some species in detail, the respective roles of these variables will emerge.

An Instance of Migration and Some of the Problems it Presents.

Figure 4.2 outlines the breeding and winter ranges of the golden plover (*Pluvialis dominica*) and its northern and southern migration routes. In the course of a round trip this amazing traveler covers 16,000 or more miles! Even more remarkable is the fact that individual birds return each spring to almost exactly the same nesting spot from which they left the autumn before. The southward migration route is east or southeast from their summer range along the Arctic Ocean to Newfoundland and then south to southern Brazil, Uruguay and Argentina. In the spring these robin-sized birds take a quite different route, flying northwest to Central America, north up the Mississippi Valley, and across Canada. A proper appreciation of this journey has been expressed by A. A. Allen (1939, pp. 258-259):

The Golden Plover, A Gadabout

A single golden plover flew over heading northwest as if bound for Alaska, calling *to leeit* as he passed, and I thought of what a year, and what a journey he had before him. Somewhere between Churchill and Alaska he would stop for the summer and raise his family during the few short weeks of July and August. For less than two months would he know the anchorage of home and family before it would be time to start back, and by the first of September we might see him flying southeasterly over Churchill with others of his kind, headed for the great tidal flats of James Bay.

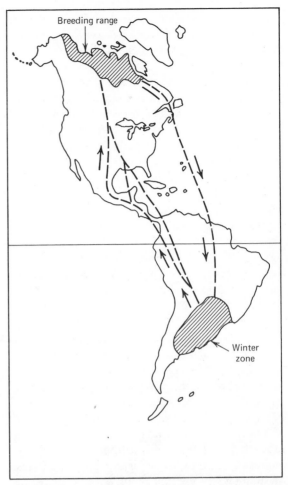

Figure 4.2. Distribution and migration of the golden plover. The adults migrate across northeastern Canada and then by a nonstop flight reach South America. In the spring they return by way of the Mississippi Valley. Their entire route is therefore in the form of a great ellipse with a major axis of 8000 miles and a minor axis of about 2000 miles. [After Lincoln (1939), p. 155.]

There he might play around for a week or more before undertaking the next lap of his journey to the berry-covered tundra of southern Labrador or the shrimp-strewn beaches of Nova Scotia. There he would feed and rest and store up energy for the 2,500 miles flight due South over the Atlantic for South America. High over the Bermudas and the Bahamas and over the mangrove-fringed coast of South America he would wing his tireless way until he could see below him the llanos of Venezuela, 150 miles inland, with grassy plains and mud-fringed estuaries.

There he could stop, feed and rest for perhaps a couple of weeks before starting off again — this time over the 1,500-mile forest of the Amazon heading for the pampas of Bolivia or Argentina. With shorter flights he might proceed into Patagonia, but the year is short and already he would sense the urge to turn about and start northward.

He would not, however, retrace his flight over the Amazon to Venezuela. Instead he would head northwestward over the Andes of Peru and across one corner of the Pacific for the high plateau of Guatemala. Then his course would lie due north across the Gulf of Mexico, never faltering, for Louisiana and the mouth of the Mississippi where in days gone by thousands of his kind were shot for the market.

Happily this practice is now forbidden by law, and by easy stages the golden plover can now proceed up the Mississippi Valley, arriving in the vicinity of St. Louis by the last of March or early April. There would be no rush then to the nesting grounds, for these would be ice bound for another two months, and in this interim the birds must change all their body feathers from the gray winter plumage to the variegated gold and black of summer. By the first of June, once again, he might be winging his way over Churchill; that is, provided he escaped the perils of the 12,000 miles over mountains and sea and successfully passed the barrage of gunners who have little thought save for the sport of marksmanship and the savory bit of breast muscle that propels those tireless wings.

The golden plover or any other migrant presents real challenges to the investigator who would explain their behavior. Looking at the matter logically, the understanding of animal migration depends on identifying and determining the causes of the following behavioral events:

1. Who does and who does not?
2. Initiation of Migratory movement — why does it start?
   (a.) Predisposing causes.
   (b.) Releasing circumstances
3. Route description — *from* where *to* where?
4. Orientation and navigation — how does it get there?
5. Site specificity — if a repeater, does it always come back to the same place?
6. Consummatory behavior — what does it do when it gets where it is going?

Who Does and Who Does Not?

Migration is generally thought to be species specific, some species being migratory and some nonmigratory. Among birds, for example, the robin (*Turdus morellis*) is uniformly migratory, while the English sparrow (*Passer domesticus*) stays in the same location the year around. But the distinction is not always so clear-cut within a species. Ducks and geese, popular symbols of migration though they are, sometimes will winter in their summer habitat, particularly if food is plentiful and the winter mild. Unlike the English sparrow, many other species of the *Passer* genus ordinarily migrate, but again some individuals may not. The reasons for the split are not always clear, but two sorts of factors are probably involved: (1) genetic strain differences and (2) an environment whose seasonal climatic changes are within the adaptive range of the nonmigrators. Thus, continuing field observations are necessary to establish the pattern of migration in each species and any subsequent changes in it.

Initiation of Migratory Movements

What starts the animal on its migration? At first glance we might think that seasonal migration would be initiated by the weather changes appropriate to the season. In some cases this may be true, as illustrated by the movement of elk herds from alpine summer grazing grounds as late fall snows begin. More frequently, however, as in most birds, the movement starts well before temperature change and while food is still plentiful — as if the migrants could look ahead and anticipate the future. Even less coordinated with weather factors are the migrations of salmon, who leave their ocean feeding ground after a number of years characteristic of their particular species, to find their way back to their natal stream. The return timing is not random, however. The spawning run of a given species to a particular river system occurs reliably at the same time of year. In birds whose wintering area is near the equator there are no day-length changes, nor are there seasonally reliable climatic changes to provide initiation cues. Obviously there is no simple or inclusive answer to our question, but we can indicate some of the possible causal circumstances, distinguishing between *predisposing* factors, which operate prior to migration, and *releasing* factors, which are the final triggers for movement.

Predisposing Factors

Earlier we distinguished three types of migration: gametic, alimental, and climatic. Each kind probably has its own set of predisposing factors, and we consider each separately.

Migrations that appear to be closely related to the *reproductive cycle* have been most carefully studied in birds, fish, and amphibia, all of which have at least some predisposing factors in common. Internally, cyclically reproducing animals undergo a complex series of glandular changes preparatory to mating. While there is some variation in detail from species to species, the basic process involves neurological and neurosecretory changes in the animal's brain (primarily in the hypothalmus), which initiate the releasing of gonadotropic hormones from the pituitary gland. These, in turn, stimulate the release of gonadal hormones and influence correlated changes in

the tissues of the gonads themselves as well as in other organs and structures.

In birds, at least, the circumstance most responsible for coordinating these internal processes with changes in the environment is the duration of light in the day-night cycle. These changes are detected, in still obscure fashion, by the hypothalamic areas concerned in secreting the pituitary releasing factors. Essential steps in the process are illustrated in Figure 4.3.

The metabolic changes during the premigratory period are important. The bird's migratory flights are usually long, and in overwater segments of the flight there is no opportunity to break for rest or feeding. Consequently energy must be stored before migration is initiated. As indicated in Figure 4.3, hypothalamic areas involved in feeding behavior are stimulated and fat stores are built up.

As the time for migration grows near, birds begin to show increased activity (*Zugenruhe*). This is most apparent if the birds are caged. An interesting aspect of this mounting restlessness in captive subjects is its directional orientation, the bird directing its activity to the side of the cage appropriate to the usual direction that its migratory flight would take. This tendency has provided the investigator with a useful technique for studying the role of environmental cues in orientation and navigation, since the surroundings of the caged bird can be independently manipulated.

Mating and rearing of young are normally the chief activities of birds in their summer habitat. During this period many birds establish territories in the immediate surroundings of their nest, and do not forage for food or engage in other activities in flocks. As the young mature, parental duties become lighter, and as the summer progresses toward autumn, territory defense becomes weaker and increased flocking is observed. These consequences of the maturation of the young are probably significant as predisposing factors for the initiation of fall migration.

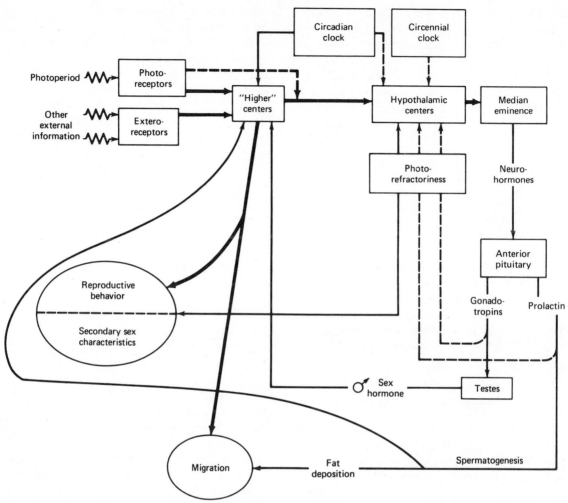

Figure 4.3. Schematic representation of the elements of the photoperiodic response system of the male white-crowned sparrow, *Zonotrichia leucophrys gambelii*. [From Farner (1970), p. 123.]

Releasing Factors

What actually triggers the migratory departure? Assuming that the animal has experienced the requisite predisposing physiological changes, the onset of migration itself probably depends on critical changes in environmental conditions, particularly on fluctuations of temperature, local food supply, favorable wind conditions, changes in patterns of precipitation and correlated changes in other features of the immediate biotic environment, such as plant foliage changes, migratory movements of other species, changes in patterns of predation, and the like. As was the case with the predisposing factors for migration, there is no single or easily identified releasing stimulus for the migration, each species having to be considered as a separate problem.

A rather common assumption among students of animal behavior is that there is a genetic, species-specific releasing mechanism for migration,

An Evolutionary and Ecological Perspective

whose releasing threshold will vary with the physiological state of the organism. As Dolnik and Blyumental (1967) have summarized the hypothesis,

The IRM (innate releasing mechanism) of migratory flight is influenced by three factors: internal metabolic conditions, external conditions affecting metabolism (food resources, weather) and social interaction. In other words, migration is regulated by the amount of fat reserves in the body, the availability of food in the environment, the weather, and the migratory behavior of flocks of the same species or other species. (P. 464.)

A well-known migratory phenomenon to people who live in the western coastal regions of southern California is the breeding migration of the grunion (*Leuresthes tenuis*). This small marine fish shows a curious pattern of reproductive behavior, as described by a long-time observer.

Three months during the year, usually March, April and May, on the second, third and fourth nights after the full moon, at full tide, great schools of them come out in the breakers, at the mouth and for half a mile on each side of where a small freshwater stream flows into the ocean, for the purpose of depositing their eggs or spawn in the sand. The water recedes and when the fish are not disturbed they wiggle tails down in the sand, as far out as the force of the water will carry them, both males and females — sometimes as many as eight or ten together — where the crust of the sand is broken. Sometimes only one female is found with just her head visible. Why they come out at night, which is usually from ten to one o'clock, and the run usually lasts three hours or longer, is a question. I have been observing them for thirty years and the time of their coming is so regular that during that time I have rarely missed them. [Letter of Mr. J. B. Joplin, quoted in Barnhart (1918, p. 181.)]

In the case of this fish it appears that either the moon phase itself, or the correlated tidal movements, furnish the appropriate releasing stimulus for the grunion's reproductive migration.

Route Description (from Where to Where?)

One of the basic research tasks in the study of migration is identification of the route taken from one residence to another. In the spring we see the robin and the red-winged blackbirds arrive, and in the fall they disappear. Where did they come from in April or May and where are they bound when they leave in October? Much of the literature of migration is concerned with questions of this kind. How can we go about finding the answers? One partial answer comes from reports of sightings in various localities. Bird-watchers are legion, and they are quite well organized, sharing their observations in a number of journals specifically devoted to publishing migrational information. If the robins are reported as gone from Michigan on some given date and are reported as present in Louisiana shortly thereafter, we can infer that their route took them from the northern to the southern state. En route sightings are also reported, giving us additional clues of their route.

Charting of flight routes of birds and insects presents some difficulties. Since they fly through the air, sometimes even less constrained by surface topography than a commercial air flight from Detroit to New Orleans, they are at liberty to take more or less variable routes toward their destination. Only slowly, through patient collection of thousands of individual bits of observational information over periods of many years, have the basic migrational routes been mapped.

A difficulty with simple reports of sightings is the uncertainty as to whether the animal seen by one observer in Michigan is the same individual seen later in Louisiana. This problem has been solved by giving the animal some distinctive individual identification or mark. The most frequently used technique with birds is *banding* or *ringing*. The bird is netted or otherwise captured, and a light metal or plastic band with a number stamped on it is attached to the bird's leg. The number is registered, along with data on species and date and locus of capture. Then, when the bird is captured elsewhere, the band will tell where it was previously. If the bird is found dead, the finder is encouraged to send the band to the central registry. By this procedure carried on over many years, much additional knowledge of the worldwide travel routes of birds has been accumulated. Similar procedures are followed with many migratory species of fish, butterflies, bats and other mammals, amphibians, and reptiles.

Another source of information is observational "traffic counts" taken during the migration months in spring and fall. Methods are various. Using a telescope aimed at the moon (see Nisbet, 1961, 1963 and Nisbet and Drury, 1969 for detailed accounts of the technique), one can count the number of birds passing through the visual field per minute or per hour. In recent years similar information has been gained by radar observations. [An excellent review of techniques and results is the book by Eastwood, *Radar Ornithology* (1967)]. On a more morbid note, counts are made of birds killed by striking obstacles to flight, such as tall buildings (the Washington Monument and the Empire State Building are frequent sources of such fatalities) or TV towers. Commercial fishermen, hunters, and seal trappers are asked to return tags recovered from their catches.

To illustrate the assembled information gathered by all of these techniques, we can now give some examples of migration paths. In North America, certain routes are followed by so many species in their north-south travels that we call them "flyways." The major flyways are shown in Figure 4.4. Figure 4.5 shows the paths followed

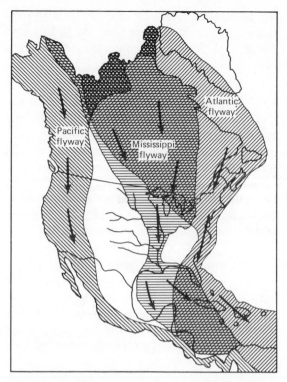

Figure 4.4. North America migratory flyways. [Adapted from Lincoln (1939).]

by many European species that winter in Africa.

A number of commercially important fish have been studied intensively, notably the Atlantic and Pacific salmon, the herring, the tunas, and the eels. As with birds there seem to be relatively circumscribed routes that are followed. In fish that migrate between the ocean and freshwater streams, the stream channels limit choices of route to a certain extent, but, as we will see, many of the fishes make nonrandom systematic choices when they come to a branching of the waterway in their upstream migration. Figure 4.6 shows the round trip route of a Pacific Salmon spawned in a tributary of the Skeena River in British Columbia. It should be observed that the adult salmon spends its allotted span of years in the North Pacific Ocean where salmon from streams in Asia, Canada, and the United States

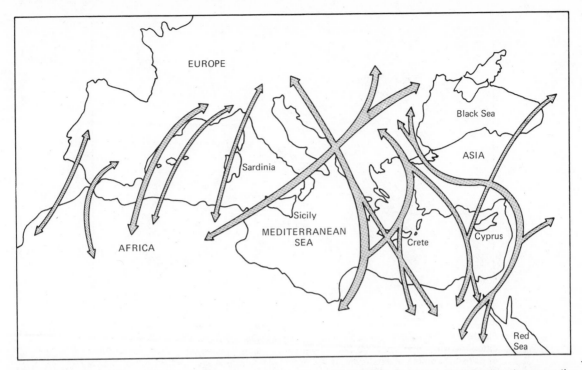

Figure 4.5. Some migration routes of birds between Europe and Africa. Note that some birds fly directly across the Mediterranean, but that other—primarily large soaring and gliding birds (hawks, cranes, eagles)—minimize open water traverses by detouring around by way of the straits of Gibraltar or Bosporus. [From Jarman (1970), pp. 36-37.]

apparently mingle, but when the spawning migration takes place each fish returns to the stream of its birth.

Similar dependable route data could be presented for any of the great majority of migrating animals, from butterflies to bats to whales. The most interesting feature of route selection is its dependability. While the illustrations given here have been of species that travel relatively great distances along topographically reliable paths, some migrations show a constancy that is not necessarily topographically fixed but, in a different fashion, is just as invariant. For example, many parasitic organisms, after hatching, must make contact with one or more hosts and then move, either actively or passively, over the surface or within the body of the host in order to complete their feeding and/or reproductive cycle. Ticks of the *Dermacenter* genus, such as

the dog tick *Dermacenter variabilis*, hatch on the ground as larvae and attach themselves to passing small animals (rats, voles, ground squirrels, etc.) where they feed and grow, undergoing developmental changes from six-legged to eight-legged forms, after which they drop to the ground and complete their transformation into adults. Then they attach themselves to larger animals (dogs, cats, people) where they feed and mate. Larvae of the ox warble fly (*Hypoderma bovis*) hatch from eggs that have been laid on the legs of cattle. The larvae then dig under the cow's skin and migrate to the back of the cow, where they continue feeding (while producing swellings in the host). Their larval development completed, they dig their way out of the cow's skin, and drop to the ground to pupate.

A somewhat similar, but even more complex, life cycle involving selective migratory routing, is

Animal Migration

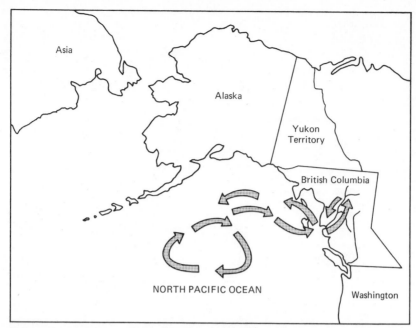

Figure 4.6. Migratory routes of Pacific salmon (*Oncorhynchus* spp.). We have indicated the route that would be taken by juvenile salmon spawned in the Skeena River of British Columbia downstream to the ocean. The circular area in the Gulf of Alaska sector of the North Pacific Ocean is the basic adult feeding ground where salmon from Asia and North America comingle for the two, three, or four years that elapse between their arrival and their return, each to its natal home stream to spawn and then die.

that of the rosy apple aphid *Dysaphis plantaginea*, which "overwinters on apple trees and passes the early summer there, then migrates to the narrow-leaved plantain as a secondary host, later migrating back to the apple tree" (Borror and Delong, 1971, p. 244). The life cycle is illustrated in Figure 4.7

One basic conclusion that can be drawn from contemplation of routes of migration is that they are definitely nonrandom and that they remain constant, both for individual animals that live long enough to repeat their migratory trips and for species across generations. The reasons for these consistencies are not well known. Genetic determination is obviously involved, and the genetic patterns are the result of a long natural selection process, in the course of which the poor and dangerous routes would be selected against.

As in most matters of animal behavior, we cannot rely solely on genetic causes. Behaviorally, a route implies a continuous process of interaction with the environment, requiring frequent discriminations and decisions concerning direction, speed, and other parameters of successful routing. Additionally, there can be a great deal of flexibility in route selection under abnormal circumstances. Thus, genetic factors do not operate blindly. A coordination of situational variables and underlying species specificities is necessary to insure successful migratory cycles.

Orientation and Navigation (Where to Go and How to Find Their Way?)

The most intriguing aspect of migration is the

An Evolutionary and Ecological Perspective

problem of how animals find their way from point of departure to destination. Most migratory trips are accomplished with little wasted energy and always by routes that involve the minimal elapsed time for the given animal, operating under the internal and environmental restraints peculiar to the traveler and the terrain and weather along the route. When one considers that some birds travel by night, some invertebrates burrow through the ground, and some fish travel in an almost featureless ocean, how do they find their way? We frequently hear of humans becoming hopelessly lost in forested wilderness areas or in the street maze of unfamiliar cities. What do these lower animals possess that we frequently do not?

Let us start by considering some authenticated miracles. You are no doubt familiar with the ability of pigeons to "home" after being carried many miles from their lofts. So efficient is the pigeon's homing that they have been used extensively in military service to carry messages in situations where field telephones or even radios are impractical. But pigeons are not unique in this ability. An ornithologist at the University of Michigan (Southern, 1959) captured a nesting purple martin (*Progne subis*) female in northern Michigan and transported it 234 miles south in a covered box to Ann Arbor, where he released the bird at 10:45 P.M. The next morning at 7:15 A.M. the bird was back in its nest! The sky that night was completely overcast with a double cloud layer, precluding any guidance cues from moon or stars. Repetition of the experiment with various distances of displacement were done with another fifteen purple martins. All returned successfully to their nests.

Another bird, Leach's petrel (*Oceanodroma leucorhoa*), has been tested extensively. Four birds taken from their breeding ground on Kent Island, New Brunswick in Canada, were transported across the Atlantic, 2980 miles, to Selsey Banks, England, where they were released. Two birds were back home in 13.7 days — mean speed

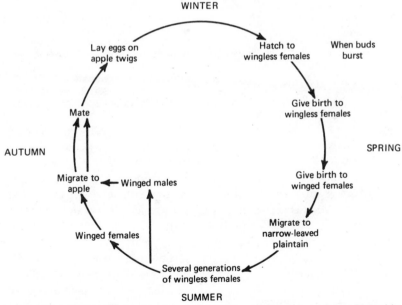

Figure 4.7. Diagram of the life cycle of the rosy apple aphid, *Dysaphis plantaginea* (Passerini). [From Borror and DeLong (1971), p. 245.

of 217 miles per day. The other two were slower (Billings, 1968).

Perhaps the most sensational example of birds overcoming the disadvantage of displacement is an experiment by Mewaldt (1964) with migratory sparrows (*Zonotrichia*). These birds regularly migrate from their breeding grounds in Alaska down the West Coast to winter quarters in central and southern California.

In the winter of 1961-1962 Mewaldt took some of these birds by aircraft to Baton Rouge, Louisiana, a distance of 1800 miles from San Jose, where he had captured them. The birds returned to San Jose the next winter (1962-1963). Mewaldt then transported the returnees to Laurel, Maryland, about 2300 miles from San Jose. Six of the twenty-two birds returned to San Jose and were recaptured in the winter of 1963-1964. Tag returns from birds that did not make it back to San Jose indicated that on release in Maryland they set course, not to California, but to their breeding-ground area in Alaska, as shown in Figure 4.8. Mewaldt concludes that small passerines of the genus Zonotrichia *have an innate ability to home, probably by means other than chance, and they can home as far as across the continent of North America. The type of returns observed implicate a mechanism which includes an ability to home from a geographic area beyond their experience.*

It must be recognized that the conclusion by Mewaldt that the birds have an "innate ability" is not a satisfactory explanation (as Mewaldt recognizes), although "learning a route" can be eliminated as an explanation in this case. Actually, as with most species specific behaviors, performance improves with familiarity or practice, as has been found for homing pigeons by Matthews (1963) and Wallraff (1959). We are certainly not sophisticated enough in chemical

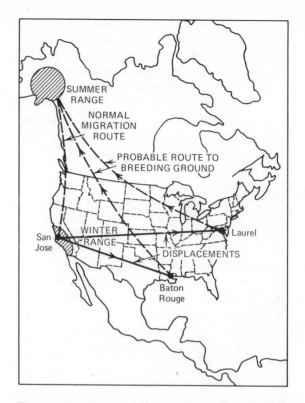

Figure 4.8. Migratory behavior of sparrows after displacement from winter quarters at San Jose, California, to either Baton Rouge, Louisiana, or Laurel, Maryland. Hypothesized postdisplacement flights to breeding grounds in Alaska are partially substantiated by recovery of tags from birds that died or were captured en route. Solid lines denote artificial transport, dotted lines probable bird flight. [Adapted from Mewaldt (1964), p. 941.]

genetics to look for an answer in the molecular properties of the genes, even if we were satisfied that the behavior is genetically influenced. What we can do is ask a simpler question: Given an animal with sense organs and nervous system of known sensitivity and range of function, what features of its environment are used as guideposts in its journeying? If we can achieve this sort of understanding, we will be in a better position for solving the more difficult problems of the genetically determined use of these guideposts.

Let us consider some of the possibilities that have been suggested.

Celestial Cues to Orientation and Navigation

Long before the compass was invented, people found their way over land and sea with the guidance of fixed and variable reference points in the sky. Descriptive phrases survive: "toward the land of the setting sun," a "lodestar", and so on. We have mentioned the *Zugenruhe* orientation of caged birds toward the side of their enclosure appropriate to the migratory direction. If the cage is shielded in such a fashion that the night sky cannot be seen, much of the preferential orientation disappears, and if the birds are housed in a planetarium, where the displayed "stars" can be placed in variable relationships to the cages, the birds will respond in a direction that is appropriate to that indicated by the stellar display, clearly indicating that they are able to use star patterns as guides (Mewaldt, Morton, and Brown, 1964). That the sun is also used in orientation was demonstrated by Kramer (1950), who found that starlings (*Sturnus vulgaris*) in cages that were open to the sky but excluded the horizon would correctly orient throughout the day, making remarkably good allowance for the movement of the sun across the sky. If the apparent direction of the sun was changed by reflecting mirrors, the birds would change the direction of their orientation accordingly.

Other groups of animals use stellar or solar cues in traveling and homing to specific destinations, including aquatic organisms whose vertical migration is entrained to the day-night cycle (see Figure 4.1) and the wolf spider (genus *Arctosa*) that generally lives on river banks or sandy beaches and forages in the nearby water. According to Papi and Tongiorgi (1963), these spiders consistently orient themselves in the shortest escape direction back to land, using the sun direction with requisite corrections for sun movement during the day. In laboratory-reared young, however, the escape orientation is always towards the north, irrespective of the direction that might be appropriate in their natural habitat. Presumably, the young wolf spider in its natural habitat learns to modify its innate orientational direction. In fact, Papi and Tongiorgi found that such learning did take place under the controlled conditions of the laboratory.

Other Terrestrial Forces as Possible Guidance Cues

Magnetic Fields. That birds can migrate under cloudy conditions that preclude celestial guidance has led to a search for other available cues. One pervasive and stable possibility is the earth's magnetic field. Human navigation by compass headings attests to the practicability of magnetic guidance. But do birds or other animals have built-in compasses? As far as we know, no specialized sensory structures sensitive to magnetic forces have evolved, but some secondary possibilities of detection seem possible. For example, the semicircular canals of the inner ear of birds do contain *otoliths,* tiny concretions suspended in the semicircular fluid. If the otoliths include magnetically sensitive substances in their composition, such as iron particles, their oscillations could be modified by the magnetic lines of force traversed by birds in flight. While much attention has been given to this possibility, the evidence is far from conclusive. Attempts to disrupt the homing of pigeons by harnessing them with strong magnets have met with varying results. A study by Van Riper and Kalmbach (1952) found no interference with homing accuracy, but more recent studies by Keeton (1971) and by Walcott and Green (1973) showed magnetic disruption of orientation. The directions birds travel do not seem to be altered by strong electromagnetic fields generated by radio or television towers, although many birds are killed each year by collision with them; and the possibility that the birds may become disoriented by their presence has not been refuted.

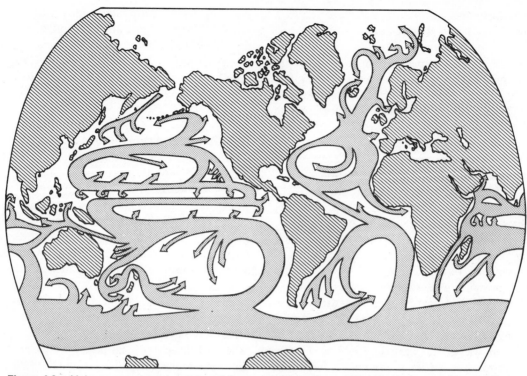

Figure 4.9. Major ocean current systems of the world. To some aquatic animals (e.g., eel larvae) these currents, like winds, provide transportation through passive drift; additionally, they may provide sensory cues for guidance. [From Idyll (1969), p. 118.]

The evidence is similarly tantalizing for other species. F. A. Brown, Jr. and co-workers (1960, 1962, 1964, 1971, 1975) and Ratner, 1976 found a magnetic influence on the responses of protozoa, planaria, and snails: Lindauer and Martin (1968) have similar results with the bee (*Apis melifera*); and Wehner and Labhart (1970) with the fly (*Drosophila melanogaster*). The orientation of other plants and animals in almost every phylum gives some evidence of sensitivity to magnetic effects. Hopefully, discovery of the means by which these forces are detected will give us a better understanding of their role in animal navigation.

Coriolis Effects. As a consequence of the fact that we live on a rotating earth, any object moving above the earth with a constant velocity will be deflected slightly from a straight path. This deflection is to the north in the northern hemisphere, and to the south in the southern. While the effect is negligible over very short distances, it is of significant magnitude in situations involving wind currents or long-distance flights. For migrating birds, in particular, it constitutes a navigational problem which, judging by the accuracy of their flights, they have successfully mastered. As was the case with possible magnetic influences, our problem is to understand how the animals senses this force pulling it toward a deviation from its flight path. Again, as with magnetism, the semicircular canals have been suggested as the possible detector system.

Ocean Currents and Prevailing Winds. Under the influence of the earth's rotation and planetary

An Evolutionary and Ecological Perspective

gravitational forces, there are consistent directional flows of air and water over the face of our plant. Figure 4.9 shows the oceanic currents. These forces play a crucial role in some migrations.

The eels (*Anguilla* spp.) have an interesting life history. While most of the species (14 out of 16) are found in the Indo-Pacific areas, the other 2 are found, as adults, in the streams of countries on both sides of the North Atlantic Ocean. The European species, *Anguilla anguilla*, and the North American species, *Anguilla rostrata*, are very similar, differing most markedly in the number of vertebra — the European species having a mean vertebral count of about 107, the American species a mean vertebral count of 115.

The respective life histories of *Anguilla* spp. are also similar. The adults, on reaching sexual maturity in freshwater streams, initiate a downstream migration to the ocean. Both American and European eels apparently make their way to the Sargasso Sea, and Atlantic basin in the area southeast of Bermuda, where they spawn and die. The young spend a rather long time in the ocean, where they go through two stages of development. In the initial stage the larvae, called *leptocephali*, drift with the Gulf Stream north and northeast. As they near their respective American or European coasts, they undergo a second metamorphosis, changing their appearance from the fragile, leaflike form of the leptocephali to something more eellike. In this stage they are called *elvers*. The elvers then enter freshwater streams and continue to grow and mature, reaching sexual maturity in 4 to 5 years. The European eels spend about 2.5 years as leptocephali, whereas the American eels mature into elvers in about 1 year. All of the migratory travels of the *Anguilla* species are with the great current circulation of the North Atlantic Ocean. The spawning journey of the adults carries them, whether they enter the ocean from the American or the European side, into the Sargasso Basin. The young are carried on a return journey by the same currents, whose general direction is shown in Figure 4.9.

Although the life cycle of the Pacific salmon is just the reverse of the eel's, ocean currents are of equal importance to them, carrying the young fish, after its ocean entry, into the great feeding area of the North Pacific, and later furnishing guidance cues for the adult's spawning return to its natal stream.

Wind currents are important to the flying migrants. Wind direction and velocity are most critical to insects, whose light weight lends itself to passive carriage and makes it difficult to fly into the wind. Thus we find that insect migrations are frequently directed by the prevailing winds. The African locus, *Schistocerca gregaria*, provides a good example. It breeds twice during the year, in northern areas of Africa from January to June and in southern areas from July to December. The locusts travel between these areas in vast swarms, so numerous that they appear as great sun-obscuring clouds. While the flight of the swarm is essentially continuous, individuals are constantly dropping to the ground, feeding briefly and then rejoining the swarm. The migratory movements are coordinated with the seasonal changes in direction of wind as well as with the onset of the rainless season.

Chemical Stimuli as Guidance Cues

All animals possess some means of receiving and discriminating differences in the chemical composition of their environment. The chemoreceptive capacities and the structures that make them possible differ from phylum to phylum, ranging from a general sensitivity mediated by cells more or less randomly distributed throughout the outer integument to specialized sensory organs of smell and taste localized in one region of the body. Chemical signals can guide the animal in specific directions towards particular destinations or instruct its withdrawal from a potentially dangerous region. Many species have the capacity to generate within their own bodies a variety of powerful chemical stimuli called *pheromones* that are reacted to in special ways by other members of the species (see Chapter 20). Pheromones serve a wide variety of communicative functions, signaling danger (alarm pheromones), sexual receptivity (sex pheromones), social communication (aggregation pheromones), and so on. Male moths are attracted over relatively long distances, even as long as a mile, by the sex pheromone of the female of their species; ants use chemical signals to discriminate workers of their own nest from strangers; many mammals mark their territorial boundaries with odoriferous urine. There is no doubt that chemical stimuli can exert powerful effects on directed behavior.

The role of chemical signals in migratory navigation has been analyzed in some detail in the Pacific salmon that returns from an adult life in the ocean to the river system in which it was hatched and from which, as a juvenile, it made its way to sea. There is a large body of evidence indicating that each fish can recognize the water from its natal stream, even when it is diluted by ocean water. Thus, the homing salmon, swimming in coastal waters, is attracted to the mouth of the river from which it entered the ocean years before. The discrimination is even more acute. As the fish ascends the appropriate river, it also avoids branching tributaries until it comes to the stream of its origin. This often requires a series of choices between branches, branches of branches, and so on, until the salmon reaches a location very close to the spot where it was hatched. Hasler (1966) has summarized the long series of research studies that led to our understanding of the salmon's homing behavior.

After it had been demonstrated that salmon can be trained to discriminate between odors from two different creeks (Hasler and Wisby, 1951), it was found that salmon with plugged olfactory passages were unable to home appropriately (Wisby and Hasler, 1954; Sato, Hiyama,

and Kajihara, 1966). The final step in this research was the demonstration by Hara and associates that the electroencephalographic reactions of the salmon, whose nasal passages were exposed to homestream water, were quite different from those that occurred when the passages were exposed to other waters. It appears, then, that the young fish becomes imprinted on the water in which it spent its earliest life, and that "on returning from the sea, the adult salmon retraced a trail of stimulatory factors, presumably the same ones that they were imprinted on as young fish on their seaward migration a few years previously" (Ueda, Hara, and Gorbman, 1967, p. 143). This conclusion gains support from studies in which fertilized eggs were transferred from the stream in which they were deposited to a distant stream for hatching. After hatching the fingerlings were marked and replaced in the stream in which they hatched. The marked fish returned as adults to the stream in which they hatched. None returned to the stream in which they were spawned (Donaldson and Allen, 1957).

In summary, animals find their way along migratory routes by using some combination of the cues afforded by their environment. It is clear that there have been a number of evolutionary specializations of sensory and neural structures that permit a species to take advantage of certain kinds of guidance stimuli. Finally, though the problems of orientation and navigation have been intensively studied for at least a hundred years, many fundamental parts of the problem remain unanswered.

Site Specificity (Does the Animal Always Go To the Same Place?)

There are far more studies of nest site specificity in birds. A large number of observations indicate that many birds nest year after year in the same area, and often at the same nest site. Werth (1947) showed that there is a strong trend for blackbirds and song thrushes to return to the vicinity of their birthplace and to establish nests. Rheinwald and Gutscher (1969) banded large numbers of house martins (*Delichon urbica*) between 1961 and 1968. Results from recapturing the birds indicated that more than 90 percent of the birds surviving return to breed in the same area. They calculated a "half-distance," which was the distance within which 50 percent of the surviving birds settled. For the house martins, this half-distance was about 75 meters (247.5 feet). For resettlement between one breeding year and another, the half-distance decreased to about 35 meters (115 feet), with about 7 percent of the returnees occupying the previously used nest. Somewhat similar results have been shown for the skylark (*Alaude arvensis* by Delius (1965) and for swallows (Davis, 1965). Among predatory birds, the golden eagle (*Aquila chrysectos canadensis*) uses the same nest site over a period of many years (Brown and Watson, 1964), and the peregrine falcon and gyrfalcon (*Falco peregrinus, F. rusticolus*) of Alaska return to the same cliffs each year, although they show more variability in sometimes alternating between two or more sites in the same approximate area (Cade, 1960).

Finally, the common tern (*Sterna hirundo*) was studied over a period of years by Austin (1949) and his conclusions apply rather generally to species showing nest-site tenacity. (1) Young birds tend to elect their natal colonies for first nestings. (2) Having once nested, terns tend to return from year to year to the sites of previous occupancy. (3) Attachment to a site increases with each additional occupancy, and with the increasing age of the individuals. (4) Provided ecological conditions remain propitious, individuals will nest from year to year within a few feet of formerly occupied sites. (5) If in any season birds renest in a second ternery, they tend to return in following years to the original site.

Thus, in addition to birds' using relatively consistent routes for migration, destinations themselves seem to be highly specific. The mechanics of site-specificity orientation are not known, but it is not implausible to suggest the same sort of early imprinting posited for the return of fish to the stream of hatch: the locus of return usually approximates place of hatching.

Consummatory Behavior (What Does the Animal Do When It Gets Where It's Going?)

This question brings us back to the basic adaptations served by migration. By far, the largest number of examples cited have been of animals concerned with reproductive functions. Adult salmon return from the ocean and swim up their freshwater streams to spawn . . . and die. Clearly the heroic journey with its navigational prescience and its challenges of swift currents, waterfalls, and predatory dangers has as its sole culmination the act of reproduction, which completes the individual's life cycle and insures the perpetuation of the species. As we have noted, the northward migration of birds through our hemisphere is synchronized with gonadal changes that prepare them for reproductive functions. Most birds travel in flocks during their migration, but when they reach their northern destination the flocks break up. Males establish territories and set about the earnest business of attracting mates, with more or less elaborate courtship behaviors. Nest sites are selected; nests are built (or refurbished); eggs are laid and incubated; the young are cared for as they grow toward independence. Similar stories could be told of the consummatory aspect of migratory efforts in many phyla.

In larger perspective we see that the whole migratory cycle is an elaborate set of adaptations for species survival. Over the evolutionary history of each migratory species the selective process, in the service of continued viability of the species, has perfected a synchronization between internal developmental changes and environmental events involving light-dark cycle, temperature, and other climatic changes.

In the case of the salmon, the story ends with spawning, but in other species life goes on. Birds spend their summer in activities centered on reproductive and parental activities, but as autumn approaches other factors influence behavior. The intimate family group breaks up as the young become capable of going it on their own. Territorial imperatives weaken, and gregarious flocking can be observed. Internally, gonadal involution has taken place, and other hormonal and metabolic changes can be detected. Again we find that these changes, both behavioral and physiological, are coordinated with seasonal changes in light-dark cycle and temperature. As the days shorten and night temperatures start dropping, the exodus toward the equator starts. Usually this takes place well in advance of any real shortage of food or dangerous changes in climatic factors, another example of advantageous evolutionary adaptation. However, even though there is no *immediate* compelling need to travel, the anticipatory initiation of migration can accurately be related to the need for food, as well as to the soon-to-be threatening changes in climatic factors.

In species other than birds, a single variable may be operative. The vertical migrations of elk and other herbivores between higher and lower levels of their mountain habitats are specifically coordinated with climatic circumstances. If there is an early spring, with faster snowmelt and earlier emergence of food plants, the drift to higher elevations takes place earlier; in the autumn the temporal pattern of snowfall and temperature determines the reverse journey to winter quarters. In the larger sense, however, there is synchronization of these movements with reproductive behavior. The elk's rutting season starts in late August or early September, and is essentially completed before the seasonal weather factors induce migration. As is true with many species, the mating season is adaptively

timed in such a way as to insure that the young will be born during favorable climatic conditions.

A Backward Look

From where the biological sciences now stand, we think we can perceive the overall adaptive nature of animal movements, and we have gained a few insights into underlying mechanisms. Many problems still exist, and much work remains to be done. There are large gaps in our knowledge of animal navigational techniques, although we know that some animals, in some situations, are guided by solar and stellar cues, by chemical gradients in the environment, by directional forces of wind and water current, by gravitational and magnetic forces, and, frequently, by simple perceptions of distinctive features of terrain that have been repeatedly experienced.

Unanswered is the basic question of how the animal develops the ability to use these cues. Juvenile birds of some species depart for the south at a different time than their parents and frequently follow different routes to winter quarters, although each route seems to be species-specific. How do the plausibly assumed genetic mechanisms translate themselves into the practical navigational use of sun azimuth, Coriolis forces, stellar configurations, or whatever aids the birds use? In a very real sense, all of the persistent problems that make psychology such a fascinating science are encountered in our attempts to understand migration. Thus it is understandable that people have so long been attracted to the study of this subject and that this interest will continue.

Study Questions

1. *Library project.* What can you find out about the migration of some species not particularly mentioned in this chapter? Possibilities that have been studied rather extensively

over the years are sea turtles, whales, bats, aphids, nematodes, lemmings, amphibious lizards, beetles, and many species of birds and mammals not cited in this chapter.

2. Why is the identification of species-specific migration as dependent on the genetic constitution of the species not by itself and adequate explanation of migratory phenomena?

3. What practical benefits to the human economy come from increasing our knowledge of animal migration?

4. What patterns of migration can you discern in the human species? Do any of the features emerge that we have discussed in connection with the migration of other animals?

5. What are the minimal physiological and psychological requirements an animal must meet if it is to be capable of accurate homing?

5

Classical Conditioning and Evolution [1,2]

R. G. Weisman and Peter W. D. Dodd

Queen's University, Kingston, Ontario

This chapter deals with the study of learning in animals. Traditionally it has been difficult to write about learning from a comparative point of view because the overwhelming majority of the research on animal learning has been conducted by experimental psychologists. The difference in approach between comparative and experimental psychologists can be simplified, perhaps oversimplified, to a single sentence. Experimental psychologists study animals to find out about learning while comparative psychologists study learning to find out about animals. Other scientists, physiological and applied psychologists, for example, also study learning processes, but their goals are different from those of the comparative psychologist.

When comparative psychologists have looked at learning it has been in relation to the species of the learner and the place of that species in phylogeny. Comparative psychologists have also

shown a special interest in learning in nondomesticated nonlaboratory species. These have been important research topics because comparative psychology is often considered to be the psychological branch of evolutionary biology (Hinde, 1970). Accordingly, evolutionary mechanisms and their products represent central organizing themes of a comparative psychology. Thus it is entirely appropriate that earlier textbooks of comparative psychology have been concerned with the generality of learning across species. A further concern in comparative psychology has been for differences between species resulting from selective pressures on learning.

The goal of the present chapter is to view classical conditioning as a product of evolutionary history. At this point in your reading in comparative psychology you will have already seen that the genetic determinants of species' physical structures and behavior patterns have been under considerable selection pressure throughout evolutionary history. This chapter simply extends the comparative and evolutionary viewpoint to the study of the behavior modification process, emphasizing that learning is subject to similar evolutionary pressures. We begin by

[1]We acknowledge our debt to the late Stanley Ratner for his contribution to the ideas elaborated in this chapter.

[2]We thank Andrea Wayne for her excellent sketches and Lee Paterson for her careful editorial assistance.

reviewing the complexities and organization of animals' innate behavior patterns. The units of innate behavior are important in the present context because innate behavior is surely what the learning processes modify (psychologists frequently define learning as a change in behavior). Here, learning is conceptualized as an associative mechanism that is sensitive to the relationships between events in time. This view points up similarities between learning and the sensory processes and holds that they are both subject to similar evolutionary pressures: Vision and hearing allow animals to acquire useful information about the world, so does learning.

The associative processes allow animals to learn about all manner of correlations between events, and we explore the important selective advantages such temporal associative processes generate. Finally we caution you not to expect "knowledge" to determine behavior directly. Tolman (1955) proposed principles of performance to account for the mapping of knowledge

into deeds. We do likewise, specifying the rules for such mapping. The need to understand the complex rules that intercede between cognition and behavior is nowhere clearer than in the comparative psychology of learning.

The early behaviorists did not allow animals to have any knowledge that was internal; an animal's learning was a change in its behavior. Through this chapter we illustrate, first, that animals do indeed acquire knowledge that does not affect behavior directly and, second, that the behavior changes that we observe are the product of a complex interaction among innate, species–specific behaviors, their releasing stimuli, and acquired knowledge about the relationships between environmental events.

A science that allows animals to have and acquire internal representations of events parallels a modern discipline that recognizes similar attributes in computers. Both psychology and information science provide mechanistic explanations couched in mentalistic terms. We present the methods and experimental evidence that allow clear inferences about the events and relationships animals are capable of representing internally. We call these complex central representations "schemata" ("schema" in the singular) because they are the innate, internal rules or structures that can categorize environmental events, store knowledge, and initiate and control innate sequences of behavior.

Innate Behavior

The ethologists proposed a dichotomy between instinctive behavior on one hand and everything else animals did on the other. As originally stated by Lorenz (1937) and elaborated by Tinbergen (1951) the distinction was made between consummatory acts said to be innate and appetitive behaviors that were not. Consummatory acts were to include only instinctive action patterns, while appetitive behavior was to include all manner of taxes, reflexes, and even conditioned responses. The distinction is not without charm. Indeed, many North American comparative psychologists and European ethologists have accepted this classification of the units of behavior.

We have found it useful to reexamine this classification of behavior in light of recent research and with an eye to some logical considerations. The new distinctions we propose are useful but hardly earthshaking. Our revised scheme includes three broad, descriptively named, mutually exclusive classes of behavior. These are orienting reactions, basic locomotor activities, and action patterns.

Orienting reactions, or taxes, locate objects or events in space, and maintain animals in a state of equilibrium with respect to some aspect of the environment. We are especially concerned with orienting reactions involved in localizing events in space. Consider the reactions of a dog hearing a strange sound, or smelling food; the dog's first reaction must serve to locate the event prior to approach or avoidance. Remember also that

specific orienting reactions will depend on the sense modality of reception as well as the event itself. A species with a highly developed visual system will orient to a wider range of visual stimuli than a species with a more limited visual system.

Orienting reactions are frequently precursors of the next class of behaviors, basic locomotion towards events of biological relevance. *Basic locomotor activities* are, of course, the particular behaviors that bring an animal from place to place. To the casual observer locomotor behaviors might appear to be quite variable. The careful systematic observer (e.g., Gray, 1968) is led to quite another conclusion — that the different phyla, genus, and species of animals have characteristic, highly specific locomotor patterns. These interesting and orderly locomotor patterns owe their variability to the anatomy and ecology of species and, of course, to the physical laws of mass and motion. Consider the locomotor activities of the horse and the cheetah shown in Figure 5.1. Notice that at a gallop the smaller cheetah has a stride five to six times the length of its body, while the horse's stride is less than four times the length of its body. Both animals are very fast at a gallop, but the cheetah is the faster, with speeds in excess of 60 miles per hour. However, the fleet cheetah seldom gallops for more

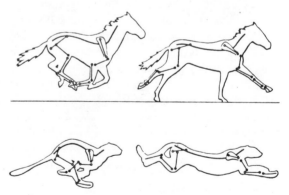

Figure 5.1. The galloping horse and cheetah, shown in positions of maximum flection and extension of the spine and maximum rotation of the scapula on the spine.

An Evolutionary and Ecological Perspective

than 1/4 mile while the slower horse can cover 4 miles in 8 minutes. The cheetah's instantaneous speed is a considerable natural advantage to a carnivorous hunter. The horse's endurance and still-impressive speed are advantages as much attributable to a human's selective breeding as to natural selection.

Action patterns, also called fixed action patterns, are the consummatory behaviors referred to as instinctive by Lorenz. It is generally agreed that action patterns are complex preprogrammed behavioral acts defined with reference to specific drive states, stimuli, and species. The release of each action pattern usually depends on the occurrence of its sign stimulus. The presentation of a sign stimulus releases an action pattern much as a key opens a lock. Sign stimuli are perceptual unconditional stimuli; to release an action pattern or behavior the sign stimulus must fit the innate schema for the releasing stimulus. A range of sensory stimuli may result in orienting reactions and locomotor activities but only the appropriate sign stimulus will release an action pattern.

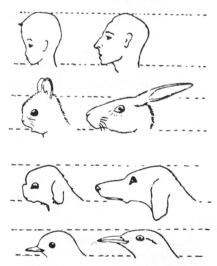

Figure 5.2. Sign stimuli that release parental reactions in humans. The left column shows a young human, dog, chick and rabbit; the adult profiles are in the right column.

Tinbergen (1951), for example, reported that the carnivorous water beetle, which has a complete visual system and undoubtedly can orient to and move toward visual stimuli, depends on a chemical stimulus to release the feeding action pattern. Similarly, a hen responds to the distress cries of a chick but not to the sight of a chick struggling to free itself (Tinbergen, 1951, p. 32).

Sign stimuli serve two roles, first to release an action pattern, and second to direct it. It is important to realize that for a given action pattern the releasing and direction stimuli are not necessarily the same, although in many instances they are. For butterflies in the *Pieris* and *Vanessa* species a scent is the sign stimulus that releases approach to a colored object, but the colored object directs the approach (Ilse, 1929, cited in Tinbergen 1951, p. 82). On the other hand, for nestling herring gulls the red patch on the parents' bill both releases and directs the young to peck the parents' beak to obtain regurgitated food.

Some human behavior may also be released by appropriate sign stimuli. Tinbergen (1951) reported, for example, that Lorenz had found that the profiles in the left column of Figure 5.2 elicited parental behaviors in humans while those in the right column did not. Tinbergen suggested that critical aspects of these sign stimuli for parental behavior are a short face in relation to a large forehead, protruding cheeks, and maladjusted limb movements. In the left column, of course, the profiles are of a young human, dog, chick and rabbit, while in the right column the adult profiles are presented.

Clearly the three classes of behavior are very closely linked in nature. The stimuli to which animals orient may also produce locomotor behavior and release or direct action patterns. Both orientation and locomotion require general status as behavioral classes because they are common to the broad range of complete behavior sequences yet quite separable from the specific action pattern seen in any particular behavior

Classical Conditioning and Evolution

sequence. Sequences of units may be seen to occur in just the order in which they were defined in an idealized instance of instinctive behavior, released by a biologically significant event, but in practice they can occur simultaneously or even alone. In general, orienting reactions steer locomotor behavior and action patterns, giving behavior a very purposive look.

The integration of orientation, locomotion, and action patterns can be illustrated from Leyhausen's (1973) descriptions of the way members of the cat family stalk and kill such prey as ground dwelling birds and small rodents. First, of course, is orientation to the location of the prey, a small, sometimes moving, furry animal. After orienting to the prey the cat may lie in wait, or orientation may give way immediately to the locomotor activities that bring the cat to the prey. A variety of locomotor activities can occur: chasing, stalking, running, a so-called "stalking run," and pouncing. The actual kill appears to be a two-part action pattern, with blows from the forepaw preceding a fatal nape bite that occurs only when the prey presents a vulnerable position or is quiescent after repeated blows. The cat's behavior is guided and directed throughout by stimuli provided by the behavior of the prey. Clearly not every kill will be identical; nevertheless, this seemingly very purposive behavior is comprised of an uninterrupted sequence of orientation, locomotion, and action pattern released and guided by the appropriate stimuli.

Some ethologists prefer to reserve the label innate for the fixed action pattern alone but it is easy to resist this restriction. All three units are " . . . innate in the sense that they are functions of the characteristics and the organizations of the animal's sensory, nervous, and muscular systems and are as much subject to genetic control as are structural features. It follows that in the course of evolution they have become adaptively moulded by selection in exactly the same way as has structure" (Ewer, 1968, p. 305). We would further suggest that oriented movements and action patterns are the very behavioral units the general associative processes have evolved to control. There are not learned and innate behaviors; there are only innate behaviors and learned modifications of innate behaviors (Denny and Ratner, 1970).

Instincts as Instrumental Acts

There is a logic within psychology suggesting that if an animal is behaving in such a way as to produce a beneficial consequence or ward off an aversive consequence, then it must be because the beast has learned the consequence of its efforts. Most theorists have classed all complex skeletal muscle activities that affect the environment as instances of instrumental learning. Evidence from comparative psychology makes it possible to deny the generality of this overgenerous definition of instrumental learning without denying the existence or the importance of the instrumental learning process itself. The cause of the confusion seems to be that the resemblence between highly organized innate skeletal behavior patterns and behavior under the control of instrumental learning is quite remarkable. Only recently have researchers begun to draw the conclusion that the former has been mistaken for the latter. The directedness of innate behavior somehow eluded most experimental psychologists, yet Lorenz (1939) seems to have understood the problem approximately forty years ago when he pointed out that taxes guide action patterns in innate behavior sequences with powerful adaptive consequences. It was in this context that Lorenz pointed out the evolutionary advantages of effective, purposive behavior.

More recently, Ewer (1968) has described instances of highly purposive-looking instrumental acts which, on closer examination, turn out to be innate control systems. One everyday example described by Ewer (1968, p. 7–8) involved a common house cat burying the feces of her young. If the feces were quite near the edge of the litter box when she sniffed them, then the cat made the usual scraping burying movements with her forepaws outside the box, accomplishing nothing. All that was needed to make her actions effective was a slight change in position, a simple enough behavior change, but instead she continued to scrape the floor. Someone watching a cat effectively burying feces might assume that this was a learned instrumental sequence reinforced, perhaps, by the removal of feces, their odor, or both. Yet, as is characteristic of these otherwise adaptive innate action patterns, " . . . when some slight alteration in the circumstances makes the normal pattern inappropriate and only a very minor adjustment is needed the animal obstinately persists in the old pattern" (Ewer, 1968, p. 9).

As we examine closely the behavior of animals, each category of survival activity, such as feeding, courting, fighting, and grooming, has associated with it a complement of adaptive, instrumental sequences of innate behavior. These activities share in common with all instrumental behavior, either learned or innate, (1) a goal event or "purpose," (2) an effect on that event, and (3) a common composition with respect to the innate orienting, locomotor, and action behaviors of the species. Clearly some of the adaptive behavior previously treated as the product of differential reinforcement contingencies (learning) seem instead to be the product of differential selection contingencies (evolution). The theory of the inheritance of purposive behavior is entirely plausible, and has been elaborated by J. A. King in Chapter 2. We simply remind you that animals use many genetically determined behaviors to alter or manipulate their environments in their day-to-day survival activities. There can be little argument that genotypes are selected by evolution when they favor increased fertility for the species. We may conclude, then, that behaviors, or at least their genetic determinants, are selected and inherited in much the same fasion as the genetic determinants of an animal's anatomical characteristics.

The Learning Processes in an Evolutionary Context

The effectiveness of innate behavior patterns has led many naturalists, and some psychologists as well, to suggest that learning, although perhaps common in psychological laboratory research, is rare in nature. You, too, may have wondered why, given innate instrumental acts, animals learn much of anything in nature. Across the remainder of this chapter we support by theory and by example the view that the processes that change behavior are a product of the same evolutionary forces as behavior itself. Most vertebrate animals' life histories include an all important role for learning. In some instances the survival function of an innate releasing mechanism is incomplete without classical conditioning; in other instances an innate action pattern only roughly approximates the skilled performance developed from it by instrumental learning.

Classical Conditioning

Most of you are familiar with Pavlov's classic experiments that demonstrated conditioning of salivation and gastric secretions in dogs to events originally incapable of eliciting such secretions. In a well-known example, Pavlov (1927) reported that salivation, normally elicited by food, could also be elicited by the sounding of a bell, provided that it was made to regularly precede the presentation of food to the dog. Pavlov provided labels for each event in the conditioning paradigm. The stimulus events are an originally neutral event, labeled the conditioned stimulus (CS), and an event of biological importance, labeled the unconditioned stimulus (US). In the salivary conditioning example the bell is the CS and the food is the US. The response events, salivation and gastric secretions, elicited by the US and by the CS, are labeled the unconditioned response (UR) and the conditioned response (CR), respectively.

The evolutionary significance of classical conditioning lies in the acquisition of the CR. The conditioning response is the large-as-life behavioral result of an animal's sequential-temporal analysis of events in its world. For many years only glandular and smooth muscle responses were considered to be appropriate products of classical conditioning by many textbook writers. But researchers from the time of Pavlov have observed and reported classical conditioning of motor acts. It now appears that the biological importance of conditioning is best understood with reference to the control of the units of innate motor behavior already described. These units are both instrumental, because they serve a specific function in animals' control of themselves and their environments, and adapted, because the form of specific units of behavior has been shaped and selected through evolution over generations to ensure the survival of the species. Classical conditioning of these complex adapted instrumental sequences of behavior places learning firmly in the evolutionary, and therefore the comparative, context. Conditioning involving innate action patterns from several behavior classes has been reported. We illustrate the process of classical conditioning with examples from such biologically important action classes as feeding, drinking, fighting, courting, and defensive behaviors.

Feeding and Drinking. Feeding behavior, not surprisingly, was the first behavior formally subject to classical conditioning in the laboratory. In the Russian work, animals have been rendered nearly immobile by a harness and stock. Accordingly, reports of motor reactions have never been a significant feature of the Russian work with dogs. Nonetheless, Pavlov (1927), Zener (1937), and others have noted head orientation to the CS, locomotor activity, and action patterns such as licking and tail wagging as well as salivation when dogs learn to associate a CS with food.

More recently, classical conditioning of feeding reactions has been studied extensively in the

pigeon. In these experiments the major emphasis has been on the pecking response. The procedure, often called autoshaping, correlates a localized visual stimulus with the presentation of grain to hungry pigeons over a series of trials. The visual stimulus is a light shining through a translucent paddle switch behind a circular opening on the wall of the chamber, usually above the feeder. The typical result of this training is that pigeons orient to and walk toward the visual CS, then peck it repeatedly. These pecking responses have been observed to bear a striking resemblance to the pigeon's normal feeding action pattern (Jenkins and Moore, 1973). Figure 5.3 shows a pigeon directing an eating peck at the visual CS. Notice in this dramatic instance of the conditioned feeding action pattern that the pigeon's beak is open and encloses the visual CS.

Figure 5.3. A pigeon's conditioned feeding action pattern. The beak is open and encloses the visual CS, a small illuminated dot on a much larger response key.

Drinking reactions have also been subject to classical conditioning. One of the authors (Weisman, 1964; 1965) developed a lick-conditioning method, for laboratory rats. Boice (1968) has used the method to study the conditioned drinking reactions of wild Norway rats and desert rodents. The usual finding has been that rodents will approach and lick at a site correlated with water during a visual or an auditory CS.

Pigeons, too, show conditioned drinking reac-

Figure 5.4. A pigeon's conditioned drinking action pattern. The tongue is extended toward the CS as if to "drink" it.

tions. Jenkins and Moore (1973) conducted some ingenious research in which one localized visual CS signaled water and a second visual CS signaled food. Figure 5.4 shows a pigeon oriented with its tongue extended toward the visual CS for water; birds also opened and closed their beaks rhythmically during the water CS. With few exceptions, the food CS evoked only feeding reactions and the water CS evoked only drinking reactions. Figure 5.5 shows that conditioned feeding reactions were somewhat more probable than conditioned drinking reactions during the initial six sessions of the experiment. In their

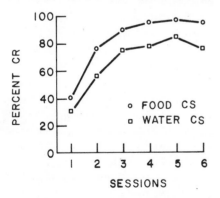

Figure 5.5. The percentage of trials with a keypeck response to a visual CS predicting food (circles) and water (squares) over the first six sessions of training.

other experiments Jenkins and Moore (1973) showed that the form of the response to the CS was clearly a function of the correlated reinforcer, and not a function of the deprivation state of the bird. For example, hungry pigeons emitted conditioned lick responses to a CS predicting water, and water deprived birds responded with eating movements to a CS predicting food.

Courting. Courting action patterns are studied much less frequently by psychologists than feeding or drinking, at least in infrahuman animals. However, it is now quite clear that stimuli correlated with the presentation of a mate to male birds will release the innate courting patterns typical of the species. While anecdotal evidence of such conditioning has existed for some time, Farris (1964, 1967) conducted the first laboratory study of classical conditioning of sexual behavior. Farris signaled the presentation of a female quail to male quail by sounding a buzzer over a series of trials. The buzzer came to release toe walking, neck and body tonus, feather puffing, and vocalization, all components of the male quail's courting sequence. Their reactions were most often directed at the location at which the female quail was presented. Figure 5.6 illustrates toe walking and feather puffing released by the buzzer CS in Farris' experiment. Farris also found that quail isolated after hatching showed normal courting after only a few weeks of normal social contact.

Rackham (1971) and Rackham and Moore[3] also classically conditioned courting behavior in birds. These investigators correlated visual CSs with presentation of a mate to male pigeons. As one might expect, the CS released typical courting action patterns often directed at the visual CS. Cooing, circling, and bowing, all elements in the innate action pattern, increased in frequency over

[3]D. W. Rackham and B. R. Moore. Personal communication concerning sexual conditioning in the pigeon, January 1977.

Figure 5.6. A conditioned sexual response in a male quail. The buzzer CS released toe walking and feather puffing before the female quail was presented.

90 trials of sexual conditioning conducted by Rackmam and Moore as shown in Figure 5.7.

In Figure 5.8 you will observe an instance of the pigeon's courting bow directed toward a visual CS contained in the stimulus box at the pigeon's feet. Instances of sexual conditioning in mammals are probably not rare, but have been little studied in the laboratory (Rackmam, 1966).

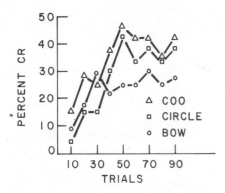

Figure 5.7. The percentage of trials containing the components of conditioned sexual responding in pigeons over 90 trials. The frequency of cooing, circling, and bowing are shown by the triangles, squares and circles, respectively.

Fighting. Fighting, like courting, gets short shrift in the conditioning laboratory. However, some evidence of the classical conditioning of aggressive behavior is available. In a provocative paragraph, Lorenz (1957) describes being attacked by jackdaws after first carrying about folded black bathing trunks that simulated a predator to the jackdaws. More formal evidence of the conditioning of fighting comes from the work of Thompson and Sturm (1965) with the Siamese fighting fish, *Betta splendens*. These investigators were able to condition four components of the aggressive display to a visual CS paired with a mirror image display of the fish itself. Other experiments by Adler and Hogan (1963), also appear to demonstrate classical conditioning of fighting in *Betta splendens*. Unfortunately, work with mammals has not shown rapid reliable classical conditioning of aggression (Vernon and Ulrich, 1966). We do not yet know whether this is because of interference by conditioned defensive reactions or because the studies have used electric shock rather than some other more "biologically familiar" releaser of aggression. We describe an interesting instance of the

An Evolutionary and Ecological Perspective

Figure 5.8. An example of a pigeons's courting bow to the visual CS contained in the box at the bird's feet.

Pavlovian control of fighting in birds later in this chapter as an example of the subtle nature of the rules governing performance in classical conditioning.

Defensive Behavior. The defensive reactions of animals are many and varied. Species specific defense reactions include vocalizations (e.g., alarm cries), suppression of other ongoing activities (e.g., flattening and freezing), as well as escape and withdrawal reactions (e.g., recoil and fleeing). These latter reactions often include negative taxes in which animals turn and orient away from the releaser.

Psychologists have shown considerable interest in the conditioning of defensive and emotional reactions in animals. More often than not, the experimental psychologist's interest has centered on the laboratory rat and electric shock as a Pavlovian US. This narrow base has provided much more knowledge about "associative processing" in conditioning, a topic discussed later, than about the evolutionary adaptedness of the conditioning of defensive behavior, the topic of current concern.

The most commonly studied classical defensive conditioning procedure is termed the conditioned emotional response, or conditioned suppression. In this procedure a CS, for example, a tone, precedes delivery of strong electric shock to rats over a series of trials. The tone is presented while the rat is engaged in some ongoing feeding or drinking-related behavior. The typical result is profound suppression of these eating and drinking reactions during the tone. Moreover, well-trained instrumental responses such as lever pressing (Estes and Skinner, 1941) and maze running (Leslie and Garrud, 1976) for food or water are easily disrupted and suppressed by the CS for shock. Rats subject to physical restraint during CS shock pairings also emit vocalizations during the CS (Davis and Hubbard, 1973).

A very special sort of learned suppression of eating and drinking, called bait shyness or conditioned taste aversion, has been the subject of considerable recent research (Revusky and Garcia, 1970). In laboratory studies, events correlated with illness produced by X rays, or poisons such as lithium chloride have been used as USs (see also Chapter 2, p. 16 and Chapters 14 and 22). Fluids with a range of novel flavors (e.g. saline, sweet, grape, and even peppermint) have served as CSs for thirsty rats. In bait-shyness experiments, with delays of even several hours between ingestion of the novel CS fluid and illness, a conditioned taste aversion is produced. When the delay between CS ingestion and illness is less than an hour, a profound taste aversion is conditioned. Also, rats often recoil from the taste of a CS associated with illness. On the other hand, for birds the relevant CSs may be visual not gustatory. Wilcoxon, Dragoin, and Kral (1971) compared aversion in rats and quail. Whereas the rats tended to avoid flavors, the quail avoided the colors associated with the illness-inducing agents.

Bait shyness has been observed in natural settings as well as the laboratory. Among the first noted examples was that birds will avoid eating insects resembling those that have made them sick. Brower (1969) describes this avoidance reaction in bluejays. Bluejays sometimes feed on Monarch butterflies. In the larval stage the insect feeds on milkweed, of the genus *Asclepias*, sev-

eral species of which contain a substance (cardiac glycosides) harmless to the larvae but emetic and sometimes lethal to birds and livestock. In the adult phase the butterfly contains a sufficient amount of the cardiac glycoside to cause a severe gastric upset to a bluejay ingesting it. Naive bluejays readily devour Monarch butterflies raised on nonpoisonous species of milkweed, but after one experience with the poisonous variety the bird will avoid all other Monarchs. Furthermore, in future, although the bird may sample the Monarch butterfly, it does so by tasting very small portions first. The bird, then, learns very rapidly not only to avoid the Monarch butterfly, but to be wary of other insects with a similar appearance and, indeed, to approach all new substances with some caution. As Brower says, the bird is transformed from a nondiscriminating gourmand to a gourmet in a single conditioning trial.

Recently Garcia and associates (1977) have described bait shyness in wolves, coyotes, and hawks. All three species occasionally hunt and kill sheep and lambs. However, after a single conditioning trial, initiated by consumption of a portion of lamb, wrapped in sheepskin and laced with lithium chloride, individuals of these species escape and withdraw from the sheep and lambs (see also Chapter 15.) Figure 5.9 shows a wolf submitting to a sheep after bait shyness conditioning in a fenced but otherwise natural setting.

A final, and rather different, example of a naturally occurring defensive behavior involves the flight reactions of certain herd animals to predators. These ungulates show innate fright and flight reactions on hearing a conspecific's alarm call but not to any attribute of the predator. The alarm call occurs long after it could be of much use to the victim. However, the alarm call releases a species-specific defense reaction of oriented fleeing in the herd. The correlation between the predator (CS) and the alarm call (US) results in conditioned fleeing from the predator CS by the entire herd.

An Evolutionary and Ecological Perspective

The Learned Release of Innate Behavior

The preceding examples should guide you to a fuller appreciation of the range of directed motor behaviors actively controlled by classical conditioning. We hope that you are impressed by the degree to which the CR in classical conditioning is an instrumental act consisting of orienting reactions, locomotor activities, and action patterns. Pavlovian control of feeding, drinking, courting, and defensive reactions has tremendous evolutionary consequences for survival of the species. Consider two examples: a species' food supply is measurably increased when its members can learn to locate and approach previous feeding sites, then begin feeding. Similarly, illness and death from poisoning are reduced when animals can learn to avoid substances correlated with prior sickness.

The learned release of innate behavior accomplished in classical conditioning has been seen by Denny and Ratner (1970), Moore (1973), and Hearst and Jenkins (1974) as a natural extension of the innate releasing mechanism. You may recall that innate releasing mechanisms function by matching perceptual representations of sign stimuli to genetically determined, species-specific, central schemata much as a key is matched to the tumblers of a lock. Of course, the evolutionary advantage of innate releasing schemata is that they insure the release of directed innate instrumental motor acts toward biologically suitable targets without the intervention of experience. There are at least two serious disadvantages to the innate releasing schema as the sole instigator of motor acts in animals. First, innate schemata are, by definition, insensitive to changes in the environment occurring within the space of an individual animal's lifetime. Thus innate central schemata are inflexible in that they are subject to change only between and not within generations. Second, a system of innate central schemata may be inefficient, requiring as

Figure 5.9. A wolf shown submitting to a sheep after eating poisoned meat in a bait-shyness conditioning experiment.

Classical Conditioning and Evolution

many schemata as sign stimuli. Animals might require as many innate schemata as there are predators, poisons and passions. In the analogy of the lock and key, an animal responsive only to sign stimuli that match innate schemata is like a house possessed of many doors, each door securely locked, and each lock accepting only a precision-made key.

Classical conditioning appears to be the evolutionary modification of a system of exclusively innate central releasing schemata. The evolutionary advantage is at least twofold. First, learned release allows more individual flexibility through the addition of new schemata within an animal's lifetime. Changes in the schema responsible for the release of an innate motor act are continuous as a result of classical conditioning. Second, an infinite array of innate central schemata is no longer required. Instead, a vast array of predators, poisons, and passions can be represented efficiently in modifiable central schemata. Thus, classical conditioning, returning to the lock and key metaphor, allows a large and changing selection of keys to open a smaller and stable set of locks. The open-ended schema learning possible in classical conditioning allows any novel taste to enter a poisoning schema thus releasing recoil, withdrawal, and escape. Similarly, visual and spatial features of any location can enter into a feeding schema thus releasing approach and eating.

Mechanisms of Classical Conditioning

In this section we treat some of the mechanisms considered responsible for the shift from innate release of behavior by sign stimuli to the learned release of behavior by CS in classical conditioning. Two distinct kinds of mechanisms must be discussed. First, one kind of mechanism is needed in order to represent the sequential relationships between the events occurring in classical conditioning. Without some such associative

mechanism, Farris' quail might have courted as much in the buzzer's absence as in its presence. Second, another kind of mechanism is needed in order to translate learned schemata into conditioned responses. The behavior or performance that is measured is the product of the associations the animal has made, and we must also describe the mechanisms that produce conditioned responses appropriate to the conditioned stimulus. For example, some performance mechanism must have ensured that courting rather than fighting or even copulation resulted from the learned schema of a buzzer sound and a female quail.

Associative Mechanisms

Modern learning theories must account for animals learning that the occurrences of two events are positively correlated, as in our prior examples, that the occurrences of other events are negatively correlated, and even, as we shall see of still other events, not correlated at all. Our review of this material will encourage you to view classical conditioning as, in part, a cognitive ability to analyze temporal relationships between events. Our cognitive learning hypothesis states that animals more or less automatically produce central representations which preserve the order of events in time. Also we suppose that these central representations of relationships, or associations, are formed whether the events themselves are biologically important or trivial.

Positive Conditioning. In the preceding sections we have provided examples of many classically conditioned complex motor acts. All were based on only one, rather simple, temporal arrangement of the CS and the US: the CS preceded the onset of the US on each conditioning trial. We call this kind of learning positive conditioning, and we do not need to review again the behavioral effects of positive conditioning when the US is a biologically relevant stimulus such as food, water, or a mate.

The cognitive view of association also requires that positive (and other) associations may be established when the US is replaced with a neutral stimulus. For evidence that animals can learn associations between essentially neutral stimuli one need only consult the often slighted literature of sensory preconditioning. In the sensory preconditioning experiment, the preconditioning phase correlates two motivationally trivial stimuli, say S_1 and S_2, usually in the literature a light and a tone, then the conditioning phase correlates S_2 with a reinforcer. Finally, during a test phase, S_1 is shown to control behavior conditioned to S_2. Of course, results obtained during the test phase should be compared against various controls to avoid mislabeling stimulus generalization, unlearned reactions, and the like as sensory preconditioning.

In a review of sensory preconditioning research Seidel (1959) concluded that the procedure generated small but reliable effects. Research conducted over the intervening 16 years (e.g., Prewitt, 1967; Rizley and Rescorla, 1972) has actively confirmed this conclusion. Three further conclusions seem justified. First, overt behavioral mediation of association between S_1 and S_2 can be rejected as an explanation of the phenomenon. There is evidence that animals have learned associations betwen stimuli emanating from the same sound source (Kendall and Thompson, 1960) and between a light and tone even when rats were paralyzed by curare (Cousins, Zamble, Tait, and Suboski, 1971). Second, motivationally powerful reinforcers are not necessary to associative learning as it occurs in the first phase of the sensory preconditioning. The main consequence of the preconditioning trials seems to be that animals construct central representations of the stimuli and the relationship between them. Third, since the association of neutral events (as in sensory preconditioning) is limited by the rapid intervention of habituation, animals may learn to ignore correlations between repeatedly presented neutral stimuli.

These conclusions certainly do not suggest that events of biological importance are necessary to each individual instance of learning. Consider the following analogy between learning and perception. Most biologists believe that the senses have evolved to serve highly adaptive functions, yet few biologists would claim that animals can only use their senses to perceive biologically important events. The visual system most probably evolved to warn us of predators and help us find food effectively, but it also allows us to detect dust on the furniture. Most psychologists believe that learning has evolved to serve highly adaptive functions as well, but some are reluctant to allow that animals can learn about relationships between biologically trival as well as important events. The view we suggest to you here is that learning, like perception, does not prejudge completely the biological importance of the knowledge it provides.

Negative Conditioning. If animals were affected by only positive contiguous relationships between events, as in positive conditioning, then perhaps only very simple associative processes might suffice to explain learned behavior. You are about to discover, however, that animals learn more and behave less than any simple associative theory ever insisted that they should. Historically, psychologists have tended to oversimplify their methods and theories in animal learning. Undoubtedly this tendency is a reaction against tender-minded anthropomorphic and anecdotal descriptions and explanations of animal behavior expressed in the early writings of Romanes (1912) and more recently in Walt Disney films.

When the CS predicts the absence of the US for some period of time we say that the CS and US are negatively correlated, and we term this sort of learning negative conditioning. The basic procedure, and its typical results, are demonstrated in some research concerned with the conditioned emotional response in rats (Rescorla,

1969). During several sessions Rescorla established a tone as a negative CS by arranging that brief but intense electric shocks occur occasionally in its absence, but never in its presence. In the absence of the tone there were 0.2 shocks per minute in one group, 0.05 per minute in the second group, and none in the control group. Then a flashing light was presented repeatedly, followed on each occasion by shock, establishing the flashing light as a positive CS. While the hungry rats pressed a lever to obtain food during a subsequent "test" session, the positive CS, the flashing light, was presented sometimes alone and sometimes simultanously with the negative CS, tone, but always without the US, shock. The results, shown in Figure 5.10 illustrate how negative CSs function opposite to positive CSs. The greater the negative correlation between the tone and shock (i.e., the higher the frequency of shock in the absence of the tone), the more effective the tone became as an inhibitor of the suppression elicited by the flashing light.

A CS negatively correlated with a US not only inhibits the effects of a positive CS, but it also resists positive conditioning. Rescorla found that a tone first negatively correlated with shock, as

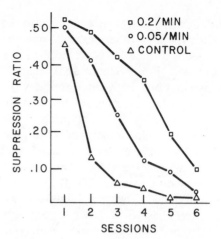

Figure 5.11. The acquisition of suppression to a tone positively correlated with shock. In prior training the absence of the tone had signaled 0.0 (triangles), 0.05 (circles), or 0.2 (squares) shocks per minute.

above, was retarded in the acquisition of conditioned suppression when positively correlated with shock in the second phase of the experiment. Figure 5.11 shows that the acquisition of conditioned suppression was markedly retarded by prior negative conditioning to the tone, indeed, the more negative the prior correlation with shock the more retarded was acquisition.

A third function of negative stimuli is the learned release of behaviors appropriate to the absence of an expected US. Denny and Adelman (1955) were among the first to suggest that the removal of a positive reinforcer elicited withdrawal. We have some examples of the releasing function of a negative stimulus. In pigeons, Rackham and Moore (1977) have recently observed an increase in advertising calls and in facing away from the visual CS negatively correlated with presentation of their mates. Hearst and Franklin (1977) report the acquisition of withdrawal from a visual CS negatively correlated with food; similarly, the removal of a stimulus correlated with food releases fighting directed at a second pigeon (Rilling and Caplan, 1973). Fighting is, of course, an important spe-

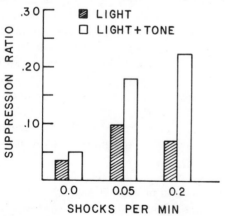

Figure 5.10. Suppression ratios to a light (shaded bars) and light-tone compound (open bars). In training the absence of the tone signaled 0.0, 0.05, or 0.2 shocks per minute, and the light was always followed by shock.

cies-specific behavior normally released by aversive events. Finally, Rescorla (1969) noticed that dogs presented with a negative CS for shock relaxed, panted, raised their tails and even sat down on the electric grid (cf. Denny and Weisman, 1964).

So it appears that stimuli negatively correlated with the US(1) inhibit behavior released by positive CSs,(2) acquire learned release functions through positive correlations with the US very slowly, and (3) release behaviors appropriate to the absence of the US.

Habituation and Learned Irrelevance. When the CS occurs alone, or does not reliably predict the occurrence of the US we say that the CS and US are uncorrelated. In this case, we term what animals learn about the CS-US relationship either habituation or learned irrelevance. The two mechanisms seem similar, but, as you will see, stem from slightly different sequences of environmental events.

Habituation is the gradual waning of an orienting reaction or an action pattern with repeated presentations of a stimulus. Habituation is the most widely observed learning phenomenon, seen in species from every phylum (Thorpe, 1956). In spite of this wide generality, habituation has been a sort of stepchild in the family of learning phenomena, somehow too simple and nonassociative to be considered a true relative of classical conditioning and instrumental learning. But recently, more emphasis has been placed on the central processing involved in habituation. According to this view, habituation involves learning to ignore a repeatedly presented event (Mackintosh, 1973) as well as the waning of responding to the event.

Habituation is an active selective result of learning to ignore events. First, consider the fact that not all stimuli habituate at the same rate. Orienting reactions to biologically trival stimuli (e.g., lights and tones) habituate after only a few minutes of exposure, but orienting reactions and action patterns released by biologically important sign stimuli (e.g., stimuli involved in defense

or care of the young) habituate slowly after hours or days of exposure if at all. Second, remember that habituated responses can recover immediately when the stimulus itself or the context changes even slightly. Recovery from habituation due to context change demonstrates considerable central processing of the habituated event after orienting reactions have waned.

In recent years psychologists have begun to study some quite exciting interactions between habituation and classical conditioning. Stated most generally the finding has been that prior habituation of a stimulus retards later classical conditioning with that stimulus. Mackintosh's (1973) experiment, using Weisman's conditioned drinking procedure for rats, illustrates the effects of two somewhat different ways to learn to ignore a stimulus on later classical conditioning. In the first stage of the experiment thirsty rats received several brief presentations of a tone in the CS-only group, several brief presentations of tone and of water at random with respect to one another in the CS-water group, or only simple exposure to the conditioning apparatus in the control group. Then all three groups had identical pairing of the tone, CS, and the water, US, in six classical sessions. As shown in Figure 5.12,

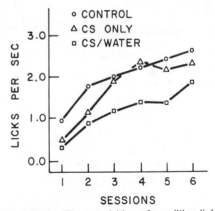

Figure 5.12. The acquisition of condition licking to a positive CS for water over six sessions. Previous training consisted of simple exposure to the conditioning apparatus (circles), CS presentations alone (triangles), or random CS and water presentations (squares).

Classical Conditioning and Evolution

the CS-only group was markedly retarded over the first two sessions and the CS-water group was retarded over all six sessions compared to the Control group in the acquisition of the conditioned drinking response.

We label the rather short-term retardation of conditioning shown by the CS-only group "CS habituation" and the much longer retardation of conditioning shown in the CS-water group "learned irrelevance." CS habituation results from learning to ignore a stimulus because the stimulus is not correlated with any environmental change. Learned irrelevance results from learning to ignore a stimulus during random presentation of that stimulus and a US because the stimulus is not correlated with the US, a specific environmental change. CS habituation is general to later association of the stimulus with any other stimulus, while learned irrelevance is specific to later association of the habituated CS with the habituated US. The effects of CS habituation are most impressive when conditioning is normally effective in a trial or two. For example, habituation of a flavor greatly reduces conditioned aversion to that flavor (Revusky and Bedarf, 1967). The effects of learned irrelevance might be judged more impressive when conditioning normally proceeds over several trials, as when feeding and drinking action patterns are subject to classical conditioning after random presentation of CS and US.

Finally, remember that CS habituation and learned irrelevance are quite different from conditioned inhibition. The first two refer to learning that stimuli are not related while the third refers to learning that stimuli are negatively related. Remember that both learning to ignore and to inhibit retard the acquisition of positive conditioning but you should now note that only learning to ignore retards later negative conditioning. That is, both CS habituation and learned irrelevance, but not learning to inhibit, will retard later learning about a negative correlation between CS and US.

Performance Mechanisms

The central issue of this section is just how knowledge concerning relationships between events is converted into performance, for the evolutionary importance of the impressive cognitive structure we have described must remain in the manner in which it affects behavior.

Learned Release. Psychologists have sought some singular mechanism capable of implementing any and all conditioned responses. One such suggested mechanism is stimulus substitution (Pavlov, 1927); that is, animals perform behaviors appropraite to the US during the CS. A second mechanism proposed by Tolman (1955) was expectation; the CS elicits the CR because animals expect the US. A third mechanism held responsible for behavior in conditioning is preparation (Kimble, 1961); the CS elicits behavior that prepares the animal for the US. Stimulus substitution, expectation, and preparation are three mechanisms traditionally proposed, each one as the singular performance rule for the conditioned response in positive conditioning. It is revealing that most learning theorists have never envisioned performance rules for negative conditioning, CS habituation, or learned irrelevance. Perhaps substitution, expectation, and preparation only describe various aspects of the learned release of innate behavior and are not mechanisms of performance. We want you to view learned release as one of the mechanisms for generating the CR in positive and negative conditioning. Recall that both negative and positive CSs can release innate behavior patterns: in pigeons a positive CS for food releases approach and feeding while a negative CS for food releases withdrawal and aggression.

Inhibition and Suppression. Although learned release is an important performance mechanism it is hardly the only performance rule. The inhibitory mechanism is a second important determinant of conditioned responses. Responses released by a US, or a positive CS, can be inhibited by a negative CS. Drinking released by a flashing light can be inhibited by a tone signaling the absence of water to the rat. A third performance mechanism perhaps related to inhibition is suppression. Remember that a CS positively correlated with shock suppressed lever pressing for food but a second CS negatively correlated with shock inhibited conditioned suppression. This is good evidence that suppression and inhibition are separate performance mechanisms since one mechanism, inhibition, can be used to reduce the effects of the other mechanism, suppression.

Retardation. Another mechanism, separable from learned release, inhibition, and suppression, is retardation. We have described three situations in which acquisition of CRs is delayed by prior learning about the CS or the US. Most notably CS habituation and learned irrelevance slow the later acquisition of either learned release or inhibition to a CS. Also, negative conditioning retards the later acquisition of learned release to the same CS. We have classified retardation of learning as a performance mechanism somewhat arbitrarily; it is probably better classified as a transfer of training phenomenon that affects both later learning and performance.

The evolutionary significance of the retardation of learning may seem obscure at first. However, it is well to remember that in the natural environment many events can be seen to precede an event of biological importance. Some of these events have valid positive correlations with the US but others do not. Among the events unlikely to acquire valid positive correlations with the US are those stimuli previously uncorrelated with the US. For example, when an animal becomes ill it may associate the illness with a meal taken over the past several hours. But which meal? Animals tend to associate illness with novel rather than familiar food. It is adaptive for animals to learn to associate illness with novel foods and ignore more familiar foods, since habitually

eaten foods are much less likely to be truly correlated with illness than novel foods. Retardation of acquisition to some familiar stimuli makes acquisition to other more novel stimuli more likely.

Natural Selection of the Conditioned Response

We cannot assert that learned release, inhibition, suppression, and retardation are the only mechanisms for mapping knowledge into deeds (classical conditioning). These particular mechanisms appear to account for much behavior change in conditioning but their origin is important too. To understand that origin we must return to the organizing principle of this chapter — the role of evolution in conditioning. Consider the following evolutionary propositions: first, most of the significant temporal sequences of events likely to occur in the experience of any contemporary member of a species have already occurred in the life history of its ancestors. Second, the behaviors resulting from these temporal sequences are the product of natural selection that has taken place over countless generations during the existence of the species; and the genetic determinants selected affect both the behaviors and the associative mechanisms on which the behaviors depend. Thus from this evolutionary view, the determinants of specific instances of learning and performance are in the evolutionary past and not necessarily in the present.

Some examples might make our evolutionary propositions clearer and a bit more concrete. First, consider that not all of the events in a bird's environment are equally likely to be correlated with food. Instead, localized visual stimuli are followed much more often than diffuse auditory stimuli by events that release the feeding reaction. Accordingly, over an evolutionary time span, natural selection has favored birds that rapidly made the correct associative analysis of the visual CS-food relationship, and then responded with approach and feeding. Birds that made the visual CS-food association slowly or reacted with less than rapid oriented locomotion toward the CS have simply been displaced over generations by the descendents of their more "able" conspecifics. It further seems reasonable to suppose that little, if any, selection for pigeons' conditioned feeding reactions to auditory CSs has occurred simply because food is only rarely correlated with sounds in the pigeons' natural environment.

Our second example involves conditioned bait shyness to events correlated with poisons. Rats and many other small mammals tend to eat in the dark but to chew and taste their food carefully. These animals also learn to avoid the taste of a food correlated with illness more rapidly than the sight of a food correlated with illness. Many birds are at least as dependent on visual as taste stimuli in feeding. Quail eat relatively tasteless whole grains and seeds that are ground up in their gizzards after ingestion. Significantly, these birds develop aversions to a visual CS at least as rapidly as to a taste CS correlated with illness. Natural selection has influenced the condition of *taste* CS-poison aversion in the rate and *visual* CS-poison aversion in the quail more rapidly than the converse, simply because, over generations, rats and quail have been most frequently exposed to taste-CS and visual-CS poison correlations, respectively.

A restatement of our evolutionary propositions may further your understanding. Conditioned feeding patterns and learned food aversions are reactions to correlations between events occurring again and again in the life history of a species. Animals have been confronted with these and many other similar learning situations for countless generations. The mechanisms of association and of performance in these frequently occurring learning situations have undergone relentless selection, generation after generation, to produce the most adaptive form of the conditioned response. It follows, however, that correlations between events that rarely occur in nature may not be associated as rapidly or release as highly integrated adaptive behavior patterns. Seligman (1970) has suggested that by natural selection animals are more prepared to make some associations than others. This view is, of course, similar to our own — although we believe that the form of the conditioned response is also under strong selection pressure.

Summary

The central theme of this chapter has been the role of evolution in the selection of innate behaviors and associative processes. Innate behaviors consist of three classes, (1) orienting reactions, which locate objects or events in space, (2) basic locomotor activities, which move animals from place to place, and (3) action patterns, which are the consummatory behaviors released by sign stimuli. Sequences of behavior from all three classes often give behavior a very purposive appearance. It is reasonable to suppose that the genetic determinants of these behaviors were selected by evolution because they led to increased fertility for the species.

We have treated learning, and in particular, classical conditioning, as a mechanism that allows innate behavior sequences to come under the control of a wide variety of environmental stimuli. Classical conditioning correlates a previously neutral event, the CS, with a biologically significant event, the US. The unconditioned response, the UR, is the response to the US, while the conditioned response, the CR, is the acquired response to the CS. Classical conditioning involves at least two mechanisms, one cognitive and one behavioral. The left column of Table 5.1 lists the cognitive or associative mechanisms that depend on the relationship between the CS and the US. In positive conditioning the onset of the CS predicts the onset of the US, in negative conditioning the onset of the CS predicts the absence of the US, and in habituation and learned irrelevance the occurrence of the CS and the US are entirely independent. Of course, knowledge of the relationship between events does not necessarily produce behavior, so in the right column of Table 5.1 are listed the behavioral or performance mechanisms that map knowledge into deeds. Learned release is a mechanism for generating the CR after positive or negative conditioning, suppression is the reduction of a behavior through positive or negative conditioning, inhibition is a reduction of release and suppression by negative conditioning, and retardation is a delay in the acquisition of new associations and performances when a new correlation between events conflicts with prior correlations involving the same events. This final mechanism, retardation, represents the effect of prior learning on later learning and performance.

Note that the performance mechanisms do not necessarily derive from particular associative mechanisms. Indeed, the antecedent conditions for given performance mechanisms provide the subject matter for a considerable amount of contemporary research in learning not reviewed in this chapter.

Finally, we have argued that associative and performance mechanisms have been under much the same evolutionary pressures as the anatomical characteristics. The origins of associative and performance characteristics of present day animals, no less than anatomical characteristics, lie in the evolutionary history of the species.

Study Questions

1. Identify and describe briefly the basic types of innate behavior.
2. How does classical conditioning seem to be related to innate behavior?
3. Describe the mechanisms presumably involved in classical conditioning.
4. What is the relation between classical conditioning and habituation?
5. What are performance mechanisms?
6. What is the authors' argument about natural selection and the mechanisms of conditioning?

Table 5.1
Mechanisms of Classical Conditioning

Associative Mechanisms	Performance Mechanisms
Positive conditioning	Learned release
Habituation	Suppression
Learned irrelevance	Inhibition
Negative conditioning	Retardation

Classical Conditioning and Evolution

6

Domestication and Degeneracy

Robert Boice

SUNY-Albany

Most comparative psychology is based on research with domesticated animals. Yet comparative psychologists have generally ignored the study of domestication. It is mentioned, as a rule, only in the midst of concerns that domestication has produced degenerate animals unfit for meaningful research.

There is a quandary here. The same researchers who insist on empirical evidence in their own specialized study of behavior have been content to speculate about the effects of domestication on behavior. In fact, domestication is a researchable phenomenon. When the behaviors of our domestic animals are actually compared to those of wild animals, the effects of domestication appear to be surprisingly positive.

Defining Domestication

Intuitively, domestication means a change from wildness to tameness. When we talk of something or someone being domesticated we usually mean that it is civilized, manageable, and perhaps even trained. Technically, domestication means the *controlled breeding* of animals *over generations*, usually in *captivity* (Ratner and Boice, 1975).

Dogs are probably the best and oldest examples of what domestication can accomplish. They were domesticated from wolves some 10,000 years ago, even before our ancestors began domesticating plants (agriculture), beasts of burden, and eventually themselves. The incredible variety of dogs reflects the different motives of their domesticators who have shaped them into breeds as diverse as whippets, bulldogs, and Chihuahuas. Domesticators have accomplished these ends by selectively breeding for desired characteristics in appearance and behavior.

Domestication is not an all-or-none event; instead it is more a matter of location on a continuum. The *continuum* runs from wildness to domesticity. An animal is domesticated to the extent that it has undergone *removal from natural selection pressures* (e.g., predation, starvation, and competition for mates and shelter) over generations. The transition from wildness to domesticity is effected by changes in *early experience and genetics*. So it is that park pigeons (who are provisioned with food but who do not generally live in cages or live entirely free from predators) are partially domesticated and laboratory rats (who rarely fend for themselves) are more completely domesticated.

Relevance of Domestication

For the moment, research on domestication seems most useful in quieting anxieties about the overuse of domestic animals in comparative psychology. Beyond that, it offers a rich potential for insights about effects of genetics and early experience on behavior (e.g., Price, 1976). Domestication can, for example, provide an instructive model of evolution. Darwin's study of domestication was germinal to what he called the principle of selection; his breeding experiments with his beloved pigeons provided clues as to how evolution can produce changes in appearance and behavior. Domestication had at last made the leap from the folk knowledge of farmers to the uncommon knowledge of scientists.

Notions of Degeneracy and Overuse

Criticisms of degeneracy and overuse have been directed most extensively at comparative psychology's favorite research preparation, the domestic rat. These criticisms can be seen clearly in the classic papers of four prestigious authors; taken together, the papers represent a theme based more on appeal to emotion than to fact.

Calvin P. Stone (1932) is the first of these. His article includes a replication of earlier research by Yerkes (1913) on the savageness and wildness of wild and laboratory rats. Stone's article was also the first report since the earliest studies of rat learning (Small, 1901) of an attempt to compare the maze learning of wild and domestic rats. Stone found just what Small had found. His wild

rats crouched or ran frantically while domestic rats, of course, evidenced a nice learning rate. Nonetheless, both investigators concluded that *if* the wild rats could have been induced to cooperate, they would have shown a greater learning ability than their domestic counterparts. Both Small and Stone helped perpetuate the belief in degeneracy by subscribing to the notion that wild animals that fend for themselves must be more clever and intelligent than laboratory rats living in the luxury of captivity.

The second classic paper is by Curt P. Richter (1949). He is an important pioneer in the study of domestication in rats (Richter, 1968) and in a variety of innovative areas including biological rhythms (Kolb, 1967). His message about domestication is mainly one of degeneracy, even in supposing that it extends to civilization in humans (Richter, 1959). In the 1949 paper, Richter chronicles the development of the Norway rat into the first animal domesticated strictly for laboratory research. His signal contribution in this area was showing that domestication has brought a decrease in adrenal gland sizes and an increase in gonad sizes. Accordingly, he assures us, it is reasonable to picture the domestic rat as less aggressive and more sexual than its wild counterpart. Rather than viewing this as a positive result for animals shaped to live in laboratories, Richter concludes that laboratory rats have been selected for defective equipment. The problem, he claimed, was that domestication worked to eliminate the fiercest, most alert rats of the original wild stocks: "Hence would result the increase and perhaps even the predominance of the progeny of the weaker, milder, 'better adjusted' individual (p. 44)." Richter's implication was that domestication produced animals that could not survive in the wild.

The third classic paper, "The Snark Was a Boojum," has been so influential that it merits abstracting here. Its author, Frank A. Beach is one of comparative psychology's most important leaders in research on hormones and reproductive behaviors. His autobiography (1974) is a reminder that he is one of psychology's most fascinating authors (Boice, 1977c).

The title is from Lewis Carroll's poem, "The Hunting of the Snark." Therein, the quarry, a Snark, turns out to be a rare variety known as a Boojum. This causes the Baker to vanish. Beach uses Lewis Carroll to make a point about comparative psychology; in searching for animal behavior (the Snark) we have unfortunately found the albino rat (a Boojum). This has caused comparative psychology to vanish. His graphs showing the historical decline of non-rats in comparative articles have been reprinted and lionized in a variety of publications. So too has the cartoon showing the white rat as a large Pied Piper leading mesmerized psychologists to a watery end. Beach's point about albino rats was one of overuse. His secondary message was that rats are not ideal for the study of special problems; e.g., domestic sheep are better subjects for the study of the development of gregarious habits.

Although Beach did not speak to the issue of degeneracy, he left the powerful suggestion that use of the domestic rat should be accompanied by a sense of guilt. Indeed, it appears that this has been the result for many psychologists who, nonetheless, continue to run rats.

The fourth article, also summarized, is a contemporary classic that incorporates the most persuasive ideas of degeneracy and overuse (Lockard, 1968). Its effect is widespread in encouraging a view of albino rats as degenerate and as unsuitable for comparative research.

Lockard begins much in the style of Richter in reconstructing the vague history of domestic rats. He continues in that same style in pessimistically concluding that under domestication the . . . "behaviors essential to survival in the wild are no longer kept in peak condition (p. 737)." The answer to the question posed in the title is quickly apparent; according to Lockard . . . "It is at least a waste of time, if not outright folly, to experiment upon the degenerate remains of what is available intact in other animals (p. 739)." Here is a claim for degeneracy of the strongest sort. Lockard argues that domestic rats are degenerate in sensory, emotional, and natural behavior systems. He concludes that domestic rats are poorer learners than wild rats. And he leaves the message that laboratory rats are "schmoos" with little or no relevance to natural animals.

The tradition of belief in degeneracy under domestication is much more extensive than these four papers, but each represents a key component in the belief system. C. P. Stone was prototypical in assuming that wild rats, because they survive by their wits, must be more intelligent than domestic rats. Curt Richter was influential in supposing that the increasing docility of domestic rats was tantamount to weakness and dullness. Frank Beach merely echoed a recurring concern about the misdirection of evolutionary ideals (Boice, 1977a) with the albino rat as the scapegoat. Finally, R. B. Lockard combined all those traditions in making dramatic claims for decadence and overuse. He depicted the domestic rat as degenerate in learning and as an unnatural animal that has been misguidedly overused in learning research.

Evidence for Degeneracy and Overuse

It may well be that Beach was right about overuse of white rats, at least in encouraging the use of a broader variety of animal preparations. But if psychologists are to heed the call to abandonment as urged by Lockard, perhaps it should be on the basis of actual evidence for degeneracy and unnaturalness.

To date, there is no substantial evidence for behavioral degeneracy in domestic rats (e.g., Boice, 1973). Backing for the belief in degeneracy seems to come from subjective judgments about domestic animals as less attractive than animals that survive the rigors of life in the wild. Eibl-Eibesfeldt (1975), for example, emphasizes the short legs and wings of barnyard fowl in comparison to wild fowl. This kind of judgment, of course, ignores the desirability of these characteristics to domesticators who value animals with less potential to escape captivity and with more potential to produce meat.

Support for the degeneracy belief also seems to arise in imagining what probably happens to behaviors that go unused. The idea of disuse is simple: If domestic animals stop using formerly adaptive behaviors (e.g., burrowing) then those behaviors must be lost to the animals. Even though there is scant evidence that this is true, it nonetheless has popular appeal.

Overall, the attractiveness of degeneracy notions is probably tied to a persistent belief that civilization and unnatural procedures such as domestication bring a kind of decadence. Contrast this with the lasting appeal of ideas like the noble savage of Rousseau. There too the appeal is to emotion, not fact — certainly not to the likelihood that many of us would actually prefer a return to nature.

This picture of a traditional belief in degeneracy was the inspiration for my research on domestication. Much of the rest of this chapter is an autobiographical account of a decade of experimentation on domestication and degeneracy.[1] It shows how a research program can grow through successes and criticisms. The emphasis is in the adventure of ideas and in answering questions with experiments.

First Stage: Practicality

Inspirations

My inspiration came in time of need. I was at the awkward stage of searching for a dissertation topic, anxious that I might never conjure up an original, researchable idea. It came from a fellow student, D. J. Zerbolio, in a graduate seminar. He stated the degeneracy notion so clearly and damningly that I rushed off to the library after class. To my delight, I discovered that there was no solid research showing behavioral degeneracy in domestication. I had found my research topic.

Whatever else I might have needed as an incentive came with the almost overwhelming warnings about the sheer impracticality of this problem. They centered around the prospect of my using wild rats in laboratory comparisons with domestic rats. The first warnings came from well-intentioned zoologists who justifiably could not envision a psychologist persisting in trapping wild animals or in managing them in the laboratory.

Even stronger cautions were implanted in the literature on wild rats. The picture was clear: here were creatures difficult to trap in any numbers or with any dispatch; here were beasts likely

[1]This chapter is dedicated to the late Stanley C. Ratner. He, along with M. Ray Denny, patiently directed my graduate education at Michigan State University. It was an atmosphere of encouragement and freedom. To Professor Ratner, in particular, I owe the inspiration to pursue unconventional ideas with unconventional animals — as long as it is fun.

to be vicious and diseased; here were pests uninclined to cooperate in any laboratory endeavor, especially breeding (Boice, 1971b). There were also the troublesome articles by Small and by Stone, suggesting that wild rats might simply refuse to cooperate in the sorts of learning tasks employed by psychologists.

Fortunately for me, none of these turned out to be a problem. The real significance of these warnings was in motivating me to attempt something that appeared difficult.

Trapping and Sampling

I knew nothing about trapping so I simply set out for a place where people reported having seen lots of rats. I began in a landfill, on a moonless night, somewhat apprehensive and armed with a single Havahart trap.

It was a fortuitous choice. Landfills are a recent development for rats — and for trappers. These modern dumping grounds are unique in that the trash is bulldozed daily and often mixed with fill-dirt. Here was a critical difference from the apparently more stable habitats where my predecessors had trapped; landfills are unstable and rats living there cannot survive by avoiding strange objects or human ordors.

In the unstable landfill where I began these researches I was able to trap rats in a matter of minutes. Often I had to run off other rats who continued to try to gain entrance after the trap door had been triggered shut. Years later, one of my graduate students, Carroll Hughes, devised an even easier method of collecting by using materials already in the dump. An appliance carton was placed on its side, some of the more desirable garbage was thrown inside, a long rope was attached to the top edge, and we waited until some 50 to 100 rats were inside before pulling the box upright. Whichever way we trapped them, rats from landfills proved to be disease free and easy to use in the laboratory.

When I tried trapping in other, more stable habitats such as apartment houses, packing plants, and feed lots, wild rats were indeed difficult to capture. Moreover, these rats from stable habitats proved to be as impractical to cage or breed as the literature suggested.

The difference between rats from unstable (i.e., landfills) and stable habitats appears to be a matter of sampling. Samples from landfills seem to represent the whole population but rats from stable habitats represent a very limited sample of their populations. The rats trapped in stable habitats appear to be the social losers; that is, they are the rats who are denied access to central sources of food, who live in peripheral, deteriorating burrows (Calhoun, 1962), and who are most subject to predation and trapping (Thiessen, 1966). In hundreds of hours of observations of rats in their natural habitats, I learned to identify these socially submissive rats by their scar-marked backs and tails. Their scars come from being nipped while turning and fleeing from another rat in a social encounter. It turned out that while scar-marked rats constituted a minority of the samples from landfills, they comprised a majority of the samples from stable habitats.

What was the significance of determining that samples of rats from landfills were representative of the wild population? It meant that I had the good fortune to begin with samples of wild rats that did not pose the problems of scarred wild rats. I later found evidence that scarred wild rats are prone to disease, emotionality, and uncooperativeness in the laboratory.

As I began my research with wild rats, I decided to devote considerable time to collecting evidence on the difference between samples from unstable and stable habitats. Here, I suspected, was a clue into the pessimistic reports of predecessors who had worked with wild rats. My goal in this unanticipated diversion was concerned with practicality; I hoped to demonstrate that representative samples of wild rats were suitable for research purposes.

Scar Marking and Behavior

My initial concern was with the apparent link between social status and scar marking. A variety of laboratory tests showed that scar-marked rats tend to be submissive to unscarred rats in competitive and spontaneous encounters (e.g., Boice, 1972).

I also found that scarred rats behaved differently in regard to reproduction. In contrast to unscarred captives, scarred wild rats characteristically showed poor breeding success, small litters, and poor maternal care. Table 6.1 summarizes one of the studies in which unscarred rats reproduced at a level comparable to laboratory rats.

There was a clear suggestion in these studies that scarred captives were more emotionally reactive. Accordingly, there was a clear indication that my unscarred captives from landfills were *not* highly emotional. A few of them could be handled with no more difficulty than domestic rats with equivalent raising.

One idea for an experiment came in rereading one of Richter's articles on domestication (Richter and Mosier, 1954). Many of his wild rats drank excessive amounts of water, presumably because of their large adrenals; excessive water intake is often considered an index of emotionality. I suspected that scarred wild rats would be the individuals consuming large amounts of water.

Figure 6.1 shows the water intake of 50 domestic rats, 50 unscarred wild rats, and 50 scarred wild rats (Boice, 1971a). At the end of the first 50 days in captivity the scarred rats were still drinking excessively. The unscarred rats, in

Table 6.1
Reproductive Success of 10 Unscarred Pairs and 10 Scarred Pairs of Wild-Caught Norway Rats (1968)

Pair Number	Capture Date	Pairing Date	Date of Litter	Litter Size	Percent Raised to Weaning
1	1/18	1/25	2/28	7	100
2	1/18	1/25	2/28	9	100
3	3/1	3/8	-	-	-
4	3/1[b]	3/8	3/8	10	100
5	4/26	5/4	6/1	5	100
6	4/26[b]	5/4	-	-	-
7	7/15	7/22	9/3	11	100
8	7/15	7/22	10/15	6	100
9	9/3[b]	9/10	9/3	5	100
10	9/3	9/10	12/12	9	100
1[a]	1/18	1/25	-	-	-
2[a]	1/18[b]	1/25	2/2	3	0
3[a]	3/1	3/8[c]	-	-	-
4[a]	3/1	3/8	4/13	7	0
5[a]	4/26	5/4	5/27	4	100
6[a]	4/26[b]	5/4	5/9	9	66
7[a]	7/15	7/22[c]	-	-	-
8[a]	7/15	7/22	-	-	-
9[a]	9/3[b]	9/10	9/6	4	0
10[a]	9/3	9/10[c]	-	-	-

From R. Boice, 1972.   b Pregnant when trapped.
a Scar marked.   c Male was subsequently killed.

contrast, had an intake that dropped to the level of the domestic rats; thus, once a representative sample of wild rats adjusts to captivity, water intake is equivalent to that of domestic rats. It appears, once again, that the low social status captives are highly emotional animals that so impressed previous investigators.

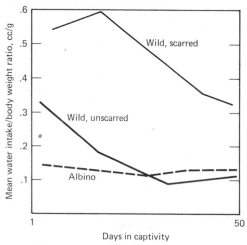

6.1. Mean water intake (expressed as a ratio of cc water/g body weight) in 50 days following capture in wild and domestic rats.

Basic Learning Comparisons

My basic mission in beginning this research on domestication was in finding ways of comparing learning in wild and laboratory rats. I began by devising ways to handle and transfer wild rats with a minimum of upset to subject or experimenter. So, for example, handling boxes that could be slipped into the rats' cages proved more efficient that actual handling (Boice, 1971b). It would be no surprise to a circus animal trainer that many of my wild rats came to cooperate in these transfers by calmly walking into the handling box and then into the apparatus. Habituation occurs in both wild rats and their human handlers.

My first comparative study of learning in wild and domestic rats employed a simple task in which thirsty rats learned to anticipate drops of

water (Boice, 1966; 1968). I measured their licking (UCR) in response to water (UCS) — and, as conditioning occurred, I measured licking in anticipation to the water drop (CR) as elicited by a signal light (CS). Classical conditioning seemed a good place to begin because it is a learning task in which subjects are likely to cooperate because little effort is required.

The subjects were wild rats and domestic rats born and raised in the laboratory. Even the wild rats begin licking at the occasional small drops within minutes and it was quickly apparent they would cooperate in learning. Figure 6.2 shows the pattern of learning the conditioned response over hundreds of trials including repeated extinctions and reacquisitions.

Overall, the response style of the wild rats was more inhibitory than that of the domestic rats; the domestic rats appeared to be the better learners. Perhaps the only expert who might have predicted this result was Tinbergen. He had argued (1965) that selection procedures in the laboratory favor rats that are cooperative in learning tasks.

There were two important findings in that initial research. One was the demonstration that experimentation could supplant speculation about the performance of wild rats. The other was the suggestion that domestic rats may be better learners than wild rats.

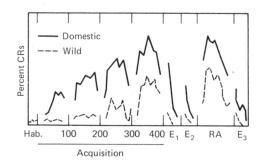

6.2. Conditioned licking (CRs) measured over nine daily sessions beginning with habituation, four sessions (100 trials each) of acquisition, two sessions of extinction (E_1, E_2), a session of reacquisition (RA), and another extinction (E_3).

This initial success led to a variety of other simple comparisons in laboratory tasks, especially in shuttleboxes (Boice, Denny, and Evans, 1967); I still believed that wild rats would have to be somehow coerced into cooperating. In a shuttlebox, individual rats must respond, by running, to avoid or escape a foot shock. Learning was measured in terms of how quickly and how consistently the rats made avoidance responses by running before the shock began.

The results were similar to those in the study of conditioned licking. Wild rats in the shuttlebox showed inflexible response styles and they learned the avoidance task more slowly and less completely than did domestic rats. This general result was true for wild rats that were newly captured, in captivity for three months, or born and raised in the laboratory (Boice, 1970b).

These were the first successful comparisons of wild and domestic rats in conventional learning situations. Here, at last, was evidence about the supposed fall in learning ability during domestication. Instead of demonstrating a fall, the experiments suggested that domestication somehow facilitates learning ability. Not surprisingly, the critics were unconvinced. How could I assume that my wild rats had performed up to par so long as there they were not fully at ease in the laboratory?

Second Stage: Attempts at Maximizing the Wild Rats' Performance

Quietude and Mazes

Critics were quite directive in getting me to resurrect the old maze used by Stone (1932). Their guess was that it would most likely be in a maze that wild rats would evince their superior learning skills. There may be a good insight in remembering that rats in the wild navigate in complex pathways and burrows. Indeed, this was the rationale of early maze users who . . . "generally conceded that the rat is preeminent among animals of his ability to thread a labyrinth" (Hubbert, 1915, pp. 4–5). One defender of degeneracy even told me that because wild rats are more natural animals than domestic rats, a natural learning task such as maze running would produce evidence of superiority in wild rats.

The problem was discovering why Small and Stone had both failed to get the cooperation of wild rats in their mazes. My students and I began with a question about sampling. We found that unscarred wild rats performed reasonably well in a complex maze whereas scarred wild rats did not.

We also discovered the importance of quietude. When we replicated the Stone experiment we modified both apparatus and procedure to reduce emotional reactivity in the wild subjects. These included changing the goal box door so that it did not catch the rat's tail; eliminating Stone's buzzer, which announced the rat's entrance into the goal box; and devising ways to observe the subjects unobtrusively.

When we used representative samples of wild rats, we found that nearly all of them performed well and learned to a standard criterion. Nonetheless, domestic rats were clearly superior in learning this maze. (Bamber and Boice, 1972). It may be that the performance styles of the wild and laboratory rats can tell us something about the effects of domestication in promoting better learning. This is a task where early trials take as long as 30 minutes. During the lulls where rats were making little progress toward the goal box, the wild rats sat, groomed, and apparently slept. The domestic rats, in contrast, were typically busy exploring during lulls. Very likely, curiosity and exploration facilitate maze learning.

Sophistication and Simplicity

Another approach to maximizing wild rat performance came in recalling Harry Harlow's

(1949) classic researches on learning to learn. He showed that primates become labwise with experience in experiments and as a result can solve new tasks with surprising quickness. If a comparable kind of sophistication could be acquired by rats, then this might be a way to facilitate the performance of wild rats (Hughes and Boice, 1973).

We used wild and domestic rats who had a history of successful training over the preceding four months. Rats who first had become extremely sophisticated in bar pressing for food pellets were switched to a new learning task.

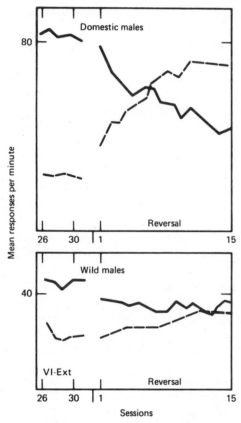

6.3. Mean S+ (dotted line after reversal) and S- (solid line after reversal) response rates of bar pressing in 15 sessions of discrimination reversal. (Abbreviation: VI-EXT = variable interval, extinction.)

They then learned to run (or shuttle) in anticipation of foot shock. At the outset of shuttlebox training, the usual arrangement was employed where rats were forced to run in two directions. In this two-way task, sophistication had no apparent effect. Domestic rats continued to show superior performance. When, however, we simplified the task to require only one-way running there was an apparent effect of sophistication so that wild rats performed as well as (but not better than) domestic rats.

The upshot was to encourage our critics. If the addition of sophistication and a simple task brought wild rats to equivalency with domestics, why not suppose that additional facilitators would push wild rats to a level above the domestic rats? At that point we initiated the difficult experiments we knew would eventually be demanded. It was time to study the effects of calming wild rats by manipulating their early experience.

We began doing this with the bemused realization that we were, in fact, trying to facilitate the performance of wild rats by increasing their domesticity.

Habituation and Handling

One of the first projects in early experience involved handling wild rats until they were docile. Properly done, this is tedious research. It was my good fortune to have a graduate student willing to do this in an effort to change my thinking on domestication. Richard Millar came to my laboratory as an irreversibly imprinted Skinnerian, certain that genetics cannot affect learning. Thus, he assumed that my findings of differences in the complex learning skills of domestic and wild rats could be explained by their prior experience or by my inadequate methodologies. His dissertation (Millar, 1975) was an extraordinarily extensive and fair examination of operant learning in rats handled until tame and trained until sophisticated. The result was the most decisive

An Evolutionary and Ecological Perspective

indication of superior learning in domestic rats yet published.

Handling and taming the wild rats in a lengthy regimen (beginning at 50 days of age, daily for 9 weeks before training began) had no effect on learning. Overall, the wild rats performed at lower response rates and with less efficiency than domestic rats. Figure 6.3 shows the result of the most critical learning situation from a long series of tasks. It is a discrimination reversal task where the rats were required to change response preference to the cue that had previously signaled absence of reward. Thus, S- became S+, and vice-versa.

Before the reversal, both kinds of rats were discriminating in favor of S+, although domestics were doing so more effectively. After the reversal of cues, domestic rats readjusted much more quickly and effectively than the wild rats. Even after the seventh session under reversed cues, the wild rats showed no clear discrimination. It appears that domestic rats not only learned more quickly but that they were also more flexible with their responses once learning was established.

Cross Fostering and Early Enrichment

Many people had asked if raising wild rats with domestic mothers would be a good facilitator. By 1973 I had found a student with the skills and patience to attempt a proper study of cross fostering. Carroll Hughes and I decided to attempt to maximize the benefits of early experience in wild rats by cross fostering wild babies with domestic mothers and then exposing the same infants to two other supposedly facilitative experiences. His dissertation (Hughes, 1975) was a factorial study of cross fostering, early enrichment, and preweaning handling.

All three factors are presumed to reduce emotionality in rats. Early enrichment (of increased perceptual and motor experiences) in particular is thought to facilitate learning. In this extensive

test we decided on a bit of a shortcut. Instead of trying to measure the effects of these early experience variables in a learning task, Hughes tested the emotional reactivity of the rats as youngsters and as adults. Further tests in learning situations would come if the results in emotional reactivity seemed promising.

Our greatest optimism for finding a facilitator was with cross fostering. The results of raising wild rats with domestic mothers were, however, negligible. There was also no clear effect of raising domestic babies with wild mothers. Cross fostering proved to be a difficult and disappointing manipulation.

The second variable, early enrichment, had only marginal effects in reducing the emotionality of wild rats. It seems clear that the greater emotionality of wild rats has a genetic basis that is not readily affected by these kinds of early experience.

Of all the early experience factors tested by Hughes, only handling had lasting effects into adulthood. This was not surprising in view of research showing that handling wild rats makes them less reactive to human handlers (Galef, 1970). Indeed, Millar had found much the same thing with his docile wild rats; Millar did not, however, find evidence that docile rats were better performers than unhandled wild rats.

Overall, Hughes' dissertation indicated that we can expect little improvement in learning by wild rats even when they are given the combined benefits of experiences such as cross fostering and early enrichment. In a sense, he concluded by telling the critics that domestication of the Norway rat cannot be abbreviated into one generation of emotional reeducation.

Overview of Evidence on Domestication and Learning

What had begun as curiosity about the practicality of testing for possible effects of degeneracy grew into a rather lengthy defense of the laboratory rat. In no instance was there evidence of a fall in the learning ability of domestic rats. Even with years of patient attempts to facilitate the performance of wild rats, my students and I could not find the crafty wiles that nature had supposedly implanted in rats.

The real closure in this series of experiments came in publishing a review paper on the evidence for domestication and degeneracy (Boice, 1973 and summarized below). It was, in particular, a response to the degeneracy claims of Lockard (1968).

The premise of this paper is that the traditional belief in degeneracy flourishes because psychologists know little about domestication. Some understanding comes in appreciating its mechanisms: Domestication usually begins with captivity, an event that in itself initiates major changes in behavior including multiple breeding seasons. Selection is a factor since only a few species seem ideal for domestication in the first place. Successful progenitors in captivity are probably high in factors including sociality (i.e., they aggregate without fighting), promiscuity, subjugation (especially to human captors), and tamebility. Once breeding is underway, genetic selection works in at least three powerful ways; inbreeding (between closely related animals), genetic drift (from the wild population), and artificial selection (for desired characteristics such as docility). Research on domestication in Norway rats is presented in several categories; none of the research areas shows support for behavioral degeneracy. Physiology — the only clear effects are in the smaller adrenals of domestic rats. In spite of Richter's insistence that this change is tantamount to degeneracy, recent experiments do not indicate obvious behavioral effects of these small adrenals, certainly not in eliminating any wild type behaviors in domestic rats. Laboratorization — there is an increase in fertility of domestic
over wild rats although the change may not be as dramatic as had been believed. There is also a clear increase in docility under domestication with evidence that the change has roots in genetics and can be altered with brain lesions. Sociality — domestic rats, compared to wild rats, tolerate greater crowding without fighting and are less likely to show severe aggression when they do fight. This change appears to be a function of higher thresholds for intense aggression in domestic rats; when in competition with wild rats they can show all the variety and intensity of wild type behaviors including hissing, threat posturing, and wounding. Plasticity — domestic rats show greater flexibility of behavior in learning situations than their wild counterparts; there is no evidence, in a variety of experiments, that domestication has produced a fall in learning ability. The conclusions of this review are that: (1) Domestication is a legitimate research topic in comparative psychology. (2) Domestication is not necessarily equivalent to degeneracy. (3) Domestication is an adaptive fitness for animals living under captive and research conditions. (4) Domestic rats may be good research models for domestic humans!

By the time this review paper appeared in print it was apparent that it would be only partially successful in quieting the critics. True, most of the old claims for degeneracy were countered with research on wild and domestic rats. But comparative psychologists, myself included, were asking new questions (Boice, 1976b). Why, we now asked, was it fair to require wild rats to learn things that apparently are not important in nature (Boice, 1977d)?

Third Stage: Ecological Relevance

There were a number of good reasons for asking

questions about the ecological relevance of laboratory experiments. In the course of trying so many tests of learning in wild rats, it was inevitable to begin wondering what kinds of learning were important for rats outside the laboratory. My own transition in thinking about ecological relevance began with simple experiments on other species.

So, for example, I became interested in showing that traditional notions of intellectual inferiority of amphibians would be undone with changes in procedures that made ecological sense (Boice, 1970a). The traditional subjects had been leopard frogs. They had been required to learn a shuttlebox task even though they are not active hunters in nature; little wonder that these animals do not learn well when anticipatory locomotion is required. Common toads, on the other hand, are active hunters and did learn the shuttlebox task fairly well. Thus it may make sense to match the learning task to the natural style of the animal under consideration.

The larger push for my interest in ecological relevance, though, came from the impetus of other writers whose influence has been revolutionary. Notable among these is Martin E. P. Seligman whose paper on the generality of the laws of learning is summarized as follows (1970). He goes straight to the point:

"After all, when in the real world do rats encounter levers which they learn to press in order to eat, and when do our pet dogs ever come across metronomes whose clicking signals meat powder (p. 406)?" Seligman's message is that we should rediscover why psychologists began studying such unnatural behaviors as bar pressing in the first place. It was because they assumed that an unnatural task learned in an unnatural surround (e.g., Skinner box) would produce more general laws of behavior than would tasks with ecological relevance. This assumption included the belief that all animal learning is essentially the same and that choice of a particular response of reinforcer is a matter of indifference. In other words, any stimulus is as likely to be associated with one response as any other; the animal or the situation do not matter much. Seligman counters this traditional disinterest in nature by showing that animals are naturally prepared to learn some tasks easily and contraprepared to learn others. Oddly enough, psychologists have often preferred to study learning for which animals are contraprepared, probably because the learning (e.g., rats learning to avoid shock by bar pressing) is so very gradual. If animals are required to learn something that is clearly adaptive in nature, learning may occur in a few trials or less. Rats, for example, appear to be prepared to associate tastes with illness/malaise even over a delay of many hours, sometimes in a single trial. Seligman is arguing, rather convincingly, that the old premise of equivalence of associability is wrong. The evidence already available suggests that animals do have a continuum of preparedness for learning. Thus, he argues that laws of learning are not general but are quite specific to the particular physiological and cognitive mechanisms of a species.

The gist of papers such as Seligman's is easily translated into a question of ecological relevance for comparisons of learning in wild and domestic rats: What *do* wild rats learn in nature; what would they be especially well prepared to learn in the laboratory?

Circadian Flexibility

One clue came in observing wild rats in various landfills where each population had different activity cycles depending upon the regular appearance of food and/or of humans with guns. Changing daily (circadian) rhythms in response to natural contingencies appeared to be a natural kind of learning for Norway rats.

As a laboratory analog of that natural learning, I compared wild and domestic rats in a test where changing contingencies favored a change in circadian rhythms (Boice, 1973). Individual wild and domestic rats were housed in operant chambers where they lived continuously for 50 days. Food was freely available but all drinking water had to be earned in small drops by bar pressing. During the first 15 days water was available on easy terms at FR 1 (i.e., a ratio of one bar press per drop of water). Both wild and domestic rats began earning water in the first day and both showed regular circadian rhythms of bar pressing during the dark half of the day. Rats, whether domestic or wild, are normally nocturnal.

The test of learning came in changing contingencies so that daytime responding (during the nonpreferred half of the day) was much more efficient than nocturnal bar pressing. Terms during the day remained easy (FR 1) but terms at night became difficult (FR 16). Domestic rats were far more inclined to shift to daytime responding than wild rats; wild rats persisted in their old circadian rhythms even at great expense in bar pressing more for less water (and while showing obvious signs of thirst). Even in this task with apparent ecological relevance, wild rats once again showed less behavioral flexibility than their domestic counterparts.

Burrowing and Feralization

My interest in finding a learning task with ecological relevance finally grew into a more general curiosity about the behavior of rats outside the laboratory. I began to wonder what domestic rats would do if placed back into a natural setting. Some old cues were reinstated as I discovered the challenge of another area with a lot of speculation and few facts.

Nothing of any substance had been published about the abilities of domestic rats to assume feral life. It was not even clear if they would still construct burrows. Nonetheless, degeneracy theorists assumed that a hundred years of pampered living in the laboratory must have produced domestic rats unfit for outdoor life. This logic, not surprisingly, includes the assumption that hundreds of generations of living in wire cages must have brought the disappearance of burrowing behaviors. Skinner's (1966) notion of "phylogenic extinction" made the point very nicely: he supposed that the "relaxed contingencies" of domestication bring the demise of previously "serviceable habits" such as burrowing.

I decided to begin by placing domestic rats in a large outdoor pen. In doing so I hoped to gather information on several questions: (1) Would albino rats be hardy enough to live outside in the extremes of Missouri weather? (2) Would this feralization (i.e., reversing the domestication process) produce an increase of wild type behaviors in domestic rats? (3) Would albino rats still dig complex burrow systems of the sort that wild rats dig? The answer was clearly positive in all three cases (Boice, 1977b).

Once the outdoor pen had been made escape proof, I installed five pairs of young adult albino rats. Not knowing if they would burrow, I had built five wooden nest boxes with drain tile entranceways. The nest boxes were buried in the ground and covered against rain. As a precaution against severe weather, the experiments were initiated in late summer; this and other precautions turned out to be unnecessary.

The pioneer rats began digging burrows within hours. All ten of these albinos and their offspring lived through a severe winter with no apparent ill effects. In fact, they fared better than a control group of albinos that stayed in the laboratory for winter. Albino rats continued to survive in the outdoor pen for 2 years and over several generations. For the most part, these animals died only at a very advanced age. One of the interesting results in this regard was that this well-fed group maintained a constant population size of around fifty. Perhaps these rats used burrow and pathway systems to maintain spacing and thus controlled population density.

Evidence for effects of feralization came with the first generation born outdoors. Albino rats raised for a single generation in burrows showed marked increases in wild-type behaviors, especially in emotional reactivity. This is a finding with great potential for reevaluating the effects of raising laboratory rodents in open cages (Daly, 1973). More recent research under laboratory conditions shows that laboratory rodents can be feralized (i.e., undomesticated) to some extent by raising them in dark, quiet burrows (Boice, 1976a, b; Clark and Galef, 1977).

An important result was the simple demonstration that albino rats can resume most of the rigors of outdoor life with no apparent difficulty. We have since found that domestic rats raised in burrows can later fare nicely in natural situations without an enclosure to ward off predators; this is yet another counter to the persistent criticisms of the albino rat as a degenerate, unnatural animal.

Burrowing behaviors by albino rats provided the most quantifiable evidence against degeneracy notions. Beyond the qualitative observations that domestic rats constructed and lived in burrows, it was a simple matter to map and measure their burrows. Burrows of these albinos and of wild rats living in similar situations were essentially identical. Similarities were found in size of entrance holes, lengths and diameters of tunnels, configurations of tunnel systems, and the proportions of the nest cavity. Here was surprisingly strong evidence that domestication and disuse have not changed the burrowing propensities of laboratory rats.

As a further comparison of burrowing by wild and domestic rats, I devised ways of studying it in the laboratory. It took some 2 years of trial and error to discover practical digging chambers that permitted observation. In the end I modeled them after the ant farms I had enjoyed as a child. Once I had conjured a successful recipe for a dirt mixture (that encouraged digging without collapse of the tunnels), there were few difficulties in inducing wild and domestic rats to burrow in the laboratory. Figure 6.4 shows the configuration of a burrow dug within a few days. Even in these constricted chambers, rats dug burrows that were "correct" in almost every aspect. This is one of few clear indications in comparative research to date that it is possible to bring a natural behavior into the laboratory with a minimum of distortion.

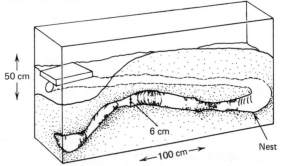

6.4. A typical burrow system in captivity showing the nest cavity at the end of the first tunnel segment.

The advantage of this laboratory arrangement came in testing for the kinds of variables of interest to psychologists. One of these was early experience; burrowing for both wild and domestic rats continued to be identical and unchanged even when they had been raised in burrows. Burrowing was also unaffected by sex, maternal state, or age (except for fat old males).

Summary

It is now slightly more than 10 years since that original inspiration to study the possible effects of domestication in behavioral degeneracy. The result has been an unanticipated investment in disproving claims of degeneracy and in defending the domestic rat against a strong tradition of criticism. It has proved to be much more fun than I would have guessed from what I have read about research (Boice, 1977a).

Some of my persistence owes to the good fortune I had in finding an area rich in speculation and poor in research. The tradition of speculation and criticism was characterized in four papers denigrating domestic rats an unintelligent (Stone, 1932), weak (Richter, 1949), overused (Beach, 1950), and as degenerate schmoos (Lockard, 1968). Some more of that persistence came with the unplanned successes in trapping, maintaining, and breeding wild rats in the laboratory. There was no way of knowing in advance that I would stumble onto the critical differences in samples of wild rats taken from stable and unstable habitats.

In the long run, it was the criticisms of degeneracy advocates that kept me trying new aspects of research. They were a positive influence.

My earliest comparisons of learning in wild and domestic rats proved to be correct prototypes of differences in performance. They showed wild rats to be inflexible, rigid performers who did not learn as quickly or as thoroughly as did domestic rats. Nowhere was there an indication that domestication has produced a decline in the intellectual abilities of laboratory rats. Instead, it appears that domestication has produced rats with improved plasticity and educability.

Critics were instrumental in shaping a second phase of comparisons in which numerous attempts were made to maximize the performance of the more emotionally reactive wild rats. Overall, manipulations such as handling to docility, training to sophistication, and cross fostering wild rats with domestic mothers did not improve the performance of wild rats in complex learning tasks. Only when the learning situation was simplified to require a direct, stereotyped response did the wild rats perform as well as domestic rats.

The original problem of collecting evidence about domestication came to closure in the review paper, abstracted above (Boice, 1973). But, just when the critics seemed to be quieting, new kinds of questions were asked. Suddenly, comparative psychologists began wondering about the ecological relevance of the learning tasks arbitrarily imposed in the laboratory. One of the most influential movers in this revolution is Seligman (1970). In this new context, it became appropriate to criticize my tests of learning in wild rats because they seemed to have little to do with what rats learn in nature.

Although my attempts to study degeneracy in an ecologically relevant way are only preliminary, two kinds of approaches appear to be productive. One includes comparative tests in the laboratory where the learning requirements are clearly analogous to what wild rats learn in nature. In the comparison described above, wild rats were not as flexible as domestic rats in shifting circadian rhythms to meet changes in reward patterns. Even with ecologically relevant tasks, the wild rats continued to perform below the level of domestics. Instead of supposing that domestication brings a degeneracy in intelligence we might better conclude that it somehow facilitates curiosity, exploration, and the flexibility leading to an increase in learning ability (Boice, 1977d).

The second direction to emerge from the new emphasis on ecological relevance has been the most exciting. It involved studying the feralization (i.e., undomestication) of domestic rats taken outside the laboratory. The emphasis continued to be very much concerned with assumptions of degeneracy. Once again, the old speculations were not supported with research. Domestic rats, after hundreds of generations of protected living in wire cages, were immediately able to construct burrows and pathways just like those of wild rats. Moreover, these supposedly decadent albino rats were hardy in outdoor living in all extremes of Missouri weather.

In the final analysis, questions of degeneracy proved to be much broader and more productive than I had anticipated. Consider, for example, the potentials for research with domestic rats kept in an outdoor pen. Dynamics of social behavior appear outdoors that would go unseen in laboratory cages or chambers. Maintenance is far simpler and less expensive than in the laboratory. Picture then, if you can, an even more dramatic feralization than might occur in the albino rat; what would happen to the civilized comparative psychologist who gives up laboratory study for the rigors and discomforts of outdoor observations?

Study Questions

1. Why do many people have an inclination to view domestication as a degenerative process?

2. In what ways is the domestication process akin to civilization in humans? Would you expect parallel results?

3. What would the advantages/disadvantages have been of planning the research program on domestication in advance rather than letting it follow a course dictated by criticisms and accidents?

4. What evidence is there that the laboratory rat is an unnatural, degenerate animal for psychological research? How might such a question be reformulated to have a constructive influence on comparative psychology?

5. How do the studies on burrowing behaviors speak to the traditional assumptions of degeneracy in domesticated rats? How does the study of feralization relate to the study of domestication?

7

Human Behavioral Ecology

Ralph L. Levine

Michigan State University

Editor's Note. Over the years, both Ratner and I have firmly maintained that any treatment of comparative animal behavior should include human behavior as part of the subject matter. Without adequate reference to human behavior the comparative picture is incomplete, and humans are misleadingly excluded from the animal kingdom and the ecological system.

In this chapter Levine is trying to make several important points that are usually not noted:

(1) Behavior (e.g., predator-prey relations, sexual behavior, distribution of animals in space) plays a critical role in ecological systems; and humans, as a part of nature, are an integral part of these systems. Human behavior at critical points needs to be related to the behavior of other animals.

(2) As is true of the rest of the book, this chapter emphasizes the functions of certain behaviors and does so for humans from an ecological perspective.

(3) A systems point of view is taken in this chapter as the best way to demonstrate and understand our role in the structure of nature, especially as our behavior ties in with the energy chain. Recreational flow and population density represent examples of energy systems that involve the behavior of human beings.

Unlike many of the other chapters in this book, which stress the comparative behavior of species, this chapter views behavior more from a systems perspective, treating the interaction of human behavior with plant and animal communities. Our main emphasis is in understanding environmental influences on human populations and how human behavior in turn changes the environment. We do this by introducing the elements of systems thinking and then by showing how the systems approach relates to several classes of behavior within the area of human behavioral ecology.

Systems

The study of how human populations affect their natural environments falls within the domain of many disciplines: human ecology, geography, environmental economics, and ecological psychology, to name a few. What appears to be common among these fields is the notion that there is an interaction between the environment and the individual. The assumption of interaction is itself an example of systems thinking. To put it simply, a *system is a collection of components or units* which, when coupled, form an organization or structure. Systems thinking deals with understanding the dynamics or behavior of the total system as well as its subparts over time (Karnopp and Rosenberg, 1975). There are three major characteristics of systems: (1) components or basic units make up the subparts of the system, (2) the parts are coupled to form a particular structure or organization, and (3) the behavior of the system may change over time.

Mass-Energy and Control Systems

In systems where the theory has been applied successfully, mostly in the engineering sciences, people working in the field have distinguished between mass-energy processes and control processes. Although the distinction is sometimes rather arbitrary, energy processes in general deal with (1) concentration of energy, as in a battery, a power plant, or a waterfall and (2) a flow of concentrated material in space and time. Control systems, on the other hand, deal with information processes such as sensing changes in the environment and making policy rules that regulate the flow of energy. Obviously the two types of systems go hand in hand, but it often proves important to separate them conceptually for the study of human behavior involved with recreational activity, land management decisions, and pollution control.

Mass-Energy Systems. This type of system can be observed whenever materials flow from one point in space to another. For example, consider solar heating units in systems terms. The system is composed of a power source (the sun), solar collectors, a heat storage unit, and other components that make up the solar heating system. The engineer characterizes the process as an energy system and attempts to predict its capacity to heat the house or building under different climatic conditions and to estimate the cost of building and maintaining the system in time.

Another example of a mass energy system, this time from the field of ecology, involves the flow of materials throughout a food chain. For example, in Hudson Bay, eider ducks feed on the shelled animals there. The females convert much of their biomass into making eggs, which may be food for other species, such as herring gulls and jaegars, that prey on eider duck eggs. This is primarily an energy system characterized by the concentration and flow of materials in time.

If one takes a broad view of the concept of energy, then energy systems are also found in the field of economics. Here the flow of money and the conversion of materials into goods and services characterize our economic system as a generalized energy process. The allocation of funds, policy decisions, and the regulation of the flows of moneys in our economy also represents a control system. But the point is that some aspects of human behavior can be characterized as energy processes and analyzed accordingly.

Control or Information Systems

Control systems process information and control the flow of energy throughout the system. It should be stressed that control systems do take energy.

As a matter of fact Odum (1971) and Odum and Odum (1976) have suggested that energy that is associated with control or information processes may be more important than was previous thought. Their holistic theory (Odum and Odum, 1976) of the role of energy in ecosystems states that, if one counts the energy that goes into the development and maintenance of information systems as well as the energy expended to control a process, then the energy embedded in these processes may not be trivial at all. If their assumption about the unifying role of energy in all types of systems is correct, then in particular our separation of mass-energy and control (information) should be considered only as a temporary conceptual device to learn more about systems.

Negative and Positive Feedback. One of the more basic characteristics of a control system is the presence of feedback. In a system that has feedback, if X affects Y, then the change in Y in turn will feed back to modify X. For example, the sociologist David Heise (1975), in describing a model of career development, suggests that productivity and accomplishments (variable X), such as scientific achievement, lead to increased status or prestige (variable Y). However, as status goes up, the person may become increasingly concerned with committee meetings, lecture tours, review panels, and so on that cut into research time, so that both the quality and quantity of scientific contributions goes down. Thus, X affects Y, and Y in turn affects X to form a feedback loop between the two variables.

In this example, the control system exhibited *negative* feedback. There are indeed many examples of this type of control system. For example, one's thermostat is set so that, if the house is too cold, the furnace goes on, and if the house warms up to a certain set point, the furnace goes off again. In stable negative feedback systems, positive changes are offset by negative changes in such a way that eventually the system reaches a state of equilibrium.

Another type of feedback system involves *positive* feedback. Here an increase in X increases Y, which increases X again. Examples, of positive feedback systems are economic inflationary spirals and learning situations in which correct responses are reinforced. If a rat goes to the correct side of a maze (X), it is reinforced by getting food (Y) since a reinforcement increases the probability of going to the correct side, then as Y increases, so does X, and the animal learns the maze.

Feedforward Techniques. Almost all systems that are of interest involve positive or negative

feedback loops. Such systems are called cybernetic systems. One class of cybernetic systems incorporates a different principle of control known as "feedforward techniques." This is a type of control system that involves forcasting the state of the system at some future date because knowing the future state is critical for making *current* decisions. An illustration can be found in modern pest management control systems. Here, for example, a pest management program might be set up to rid an entire region of some pest, such as the cereal leaf beetle, which devastates wheat crops. If one introduces biological controls that prey on the beetles, it is important to time the introduction of the predator species at the proper moment. Part of the problem lies in the fact that weather conditions determine the effectiveness of the biological control. It is necessary to forecast the weather conditions before they happen; if the forecasts suggests optimal conditions, then one begins to introduce the biological control into the system. Thus one *feeds forward* in an attempt to coordinate and control the system, updating one's forecast, of course, as the actual weather conditions occur.

The main difference between feedforward and feedback control is that in feedback systems, one has to wait for some event to happen before reacting. For example, two countries, A and B, may have relatively stable relations, until suddenly A will do something, such as threaten B's fishing fleet. Once this event occurs, B will react by doing something to make A angry. This in turn causes A to do something, and so forth.

Feedforward techniques are associated with design and planning functions. An example of the difference between feedback and feedforward systems can be found in the area of pollution control. Suppose company X has been dumping a toxic product into a large lake for a number of years. Biologists, concerned about the damage to animals and plants in the lake as well as damage to the human population coming in contact with the pollutants, find that in order to force the company to desist from polluting the lake it is necessary to demonstrate conclusively that the pollutants have already affected the plants and animals in the lake. This is a feedback system, because one has *to wait for the event to occur before action is taken*. On the other hand, suppose the biologists can demonstrate that, once damage can be detected, it will be too late to save the lake. They can show that the damage will be totally irreparable and will occur if pollution continues at the same rate. Feeding such a forecast forward, one then changes the system by attempting to modify the company's practice of dumping its waste products in the lake. In this illustration, feedforward techniques are used because feedback processes are too slow and the stakes are too high.

It must be added that feedforward techniques are relatively new and somewhat controversial, for in a country where there are a number of different factions and value systems, the concept of planning and long-term forecasting is not well accepted or understood. Feedback appears to be the most useful method for obtaining changes in the system, as we note later when we attempt to relate human ecological concerns with the problem of technological change under dwindling energy resources.

Coupling Mass-Energy and Control Systems

The field of psychology traditionally has specialized in studying information and decision processes rather than mass energy systems. Psychologists study intelligence, probe sensory and perceptual processes, and have become experts on how individuals learn. All of these behavioral classes deal with the handling and storage of information. On the other hand, workers in biological sciences, such as field biologists and ecologists, have been concerned primarily with mass-energy systems. Studies of predator-prey behavior and reproduction, while certainly dealing with a number of interesting control mechanisms, have primarily been viewed from the mass-energy point of view.

Actually both types of systems go hand in hand. To make this clear, consider the following (tongue in cheek) example: Sputdunk U suffered a great setback in its football program several years ago when it was caught in several flagrant violations of recruitment rules. The university lost both players and coaches as well as some of its prestige. In order to build up the team in a minimum of time, someone had a brilliant idea. They trained a college-age elephant to play fullback. There is nothing in the rule book that says that college football players have to be human. They hired a comparative psychologist to train the elephant to take the ball, and, with the words "tut, tut," run toward the goal posts.

The team was very successful (see Figure 7.1). There were a few problems of controlling the animal, however. The elephant sometimes failed to recognize its own teammates and would on occasion step on them by accident instead of the opposing squad; also the sports department kept losing goal posts. In any event, the Sputdunk team climbed back into national prominence until other teams replaced their human players with college-age elephants.

This illustrates the coupling of mass-energy and control systems. The elephant, as represented by its mass, is an essential part of an energy system; indeed as the animal moves forward knocking down the opposing team and officials one intuitively senses the energy system in action. However, such acts as placing the ball in its trunk, giving the "tut, tut," and carefully guiding the elephant towards the end zone can be characterized as part of the control system.

A less facetious example of systems' involving both energy and control aspects comes from the field of comparative behavior. Denny and Ratner (1970) have suggested a taxonomy of consummatory behavior that includes such classes of behavior as drinking, nesting, care of the body surface, and the like. A slight modification of

Fig. 7.1. An illustration of an energy system on the rampage. (Drawing by Elizabeth Gordon.)

their list of response classes can be found in Table 7.1. Although each class may be primarily concerned with either energy processes or control processes, nevertheless both types of systems are apparent in any general class of consummatory behavior. Fighting among conspecifics for instance, takes energy and has the effect of spreading individuals out in time and space in territorial species. Fighting is also controlled by a system of variables. For example, the sequence of

Table 7.1
Classes of Consummatory Behavior from the Energy and Control Point of View

Class of Behavior	Energy Component	Control or Signal Component
1. Resting	Restoration due to fatigue	Pacing oneself
2. Contacting	Searching in time and space	Communication of one's presence
3. Elimination	Recycling of minerals and organic matter	Toilet training
4. Drinking	Maintenance of normal cellular functioning	Avoiding salt water
5. Feeding	Transforming protein to amino acids	Joining Weight Watchers
6. Care of body surface	Sunbathing	Using suntan oil
7. Fighting	Deployment of troops in time and space	Camouflaging tanks and troops
8. Sexual behavior	Having a baby	Using family planning

After Denny and Ratner, 1970.

An Evolutionary and Ecological Perspective

displays exhibited by the parties involved or certain neurohormonal correlates increase or decrease the amount of observed fighting. Although the Denny-Ratner taxonomy of behavior is primarily concerned with relatively simple, stereotyped behavior, many of these categories also apply to some extent to human behavior, even though human behavior seems at times more complex, or at least less predictable.

Human Behavioral Ecology with Respect To Natural Systems

System concepts, such as feedback and feedforward techniques, can be important in understanding how human populations relate to nature. Let us start by representing the conceptual relationships between natural ecosystems found on land and human activities such as agriculture, manufacturing, and recreational behavior. Figure 7.2 shows such a relationship. The so-called "natural system" deals with the relations between plants and animal populations. Going back to some previously discussed ideas, one might think of the energy component as being represented by the storage of energy, bound up in protoplasm, and transformed throughout the food chain. In addition, minerals are flowing through the system.

There are also control elements associated with the natural system. For example, animals have evolved to have some degree of control over the distribution of their numbers by means of various behavioral subsystems, such as territoriality. In general, species adapt to changing environments by "moving" closer to conditions that increase the likelihood of long-term survival. In most cases this is not really a conscious process at all. It is primarily occurring by means of evolutionary mechanisms and in some species by means of other short-term processes, such as learning, habituation, and imprinting.

The second component of the total system (Figure 7.2) is the human support system. This is composed of three subparts: agricultural, indus-

trial, and populational activities. The arrows indicate the direction of energy flow as represented by goods, materials, and food for the human population. In addition, a fourth component deals with the conversion of certain energy forms to usable energy, such as electrical energy and the refinement of fossil fuels to run engines.

Energy conversion is obviously quite important. In order for the human support system to function properly, vast amounts of energy must be expended to overcome the effects of other processes. For example, in agriculture, the farmer who plants one crop has to fight a never-ending battle against the natural process of succession, which will occur over time if the farmer leaves the field alone. A great amount of energy must be expended each year to "fight back the weeds," so to speak.

Finally, the last portion of the system represented in Figure 7.2 concerns the control of the human support system. The components are primarily political and social institutions. Their purpose is to monitor the state of the life-support system and to control the flow of goods and materials throughout this second component. Although the control system is composed of institutions, such as political bodies, religious groups, governmental agencies, and the like, the mechanisms these institutions use to monitor and control the human life-support system are social in nature — based on beliefs, attitudes, values, and the behavior of people in these groups. As we will see later in this chapter, when discussing present and future problems of energy resources or use of land, one has to understand the psychological principles of human motivation and thinking in order to change behavior with respect to conservation of energy resources and cleaning up the environment.

Now every good system is more than just a mere collection of components. A necessary ingredient is the coupling, or interrelationships, among the components. In the system represented in Figure 7.2, for example, raw materials,

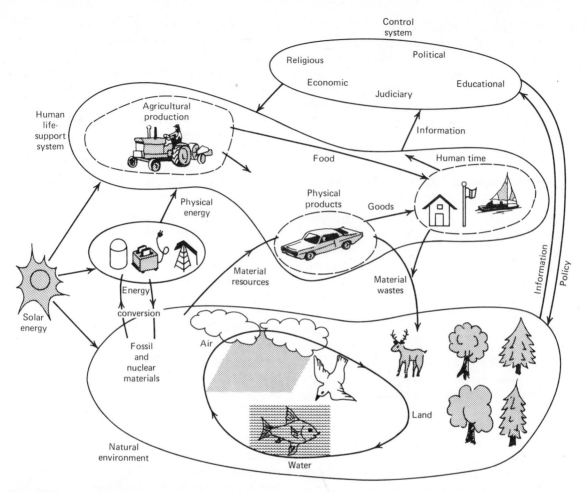

Figure 7.2. Total natural system composed of the natural environment, the human life support system, and a human control system that controls the production of agriculture and the production of durable goods used by human populations. [After Koenig and Edens (1976).]

and fossil fuels are taken into the human life-support system and converted into energy and other material products. Waste materials are given off to the air and land, and of course if the wastes are too highly concentrated, pollution results.

There are also feedback loops between the control system and the human life-support system. These take into account the state of the latter component and include decision processes that take the form of implementation of eco-nomic and political policies. Presumably planning and other feedforward techniques come into play at this stage to prevent dangerous and extreme fluctuations in the economy.

An Alternative Systems Model. Up until now we have presented the relationship between human and natural environment as if there were one and only one correct representation. But in fact, alternative formulations are possible and can lead to very different sets of human values

An Evolutionary and Ecological Perspective

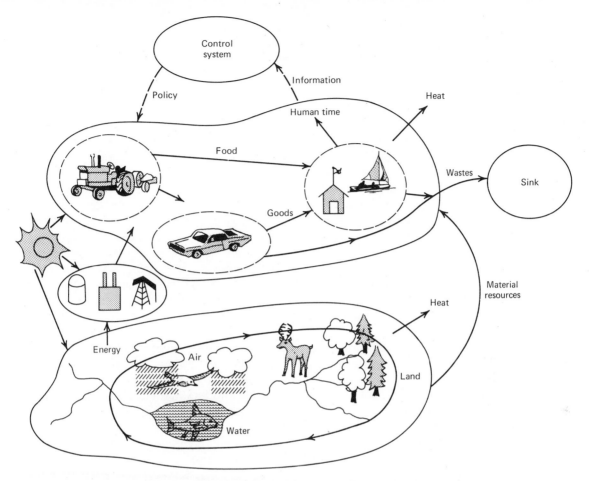

Figure 7.3. An alternative model of the total system. In this model resources are taken from the natural environment and processed; the wastes are conceived as being dumped into a pollutable sink, having no connection to the natural environmental subsystem.

and future actions. Conceptual differences can be important to societies. For example, what comes to mind is the *throughput* model that differs somewhat from our original formulation (Figure 7.2). The throughput model can be seen in Figure 7.3. In this type of conceptual formulation, materials and energy are taken into the life-support system, processed, changed, consumed, and finally thrown away. Note that the natural resources component is divided into two mutually exclusive parts, a source for raw materials and a sink for unwanted waste products. In

terms of the economic aspect of the life-support system, as long as our resources appear to be plentiful, one pays most attention to the state of the economy by monitoring flow rates, as indexed by the gross national product (GNP). Indeed the GNP has been considered as being very important in measuring the perceived international power of a nation. Shinn (1969) found, for example that perceived international power was a function of a nation's GNP and the size of its population.

Perhaps the major difference between Figures

7.2 and 7.3 is the absence of a feedback loop from the sink to the source of materials and energy in the throughput model. Dolan (1969) has described the economic implications of adopting one model over the other. From an environmental cost point of view, the lack of a connection between the source and sink leads to the assumption that pollution should not be figured into the costs of production. In the past, the cost of pollution has usually been borne by someone else, like the townspeople down the river; thus those costs were considered external to the company's manufacturing costs.

Today people appear to be more sensitive or least aware of the model presented in Figure 7.2, which is a variation of the good ship earth model (Boulding, 1970). Currently, state and federal laws are being passed, which in effect bring the cost of pollution back to the manufacturer and the consumer. Although this does not make sense from the point of view of the throughput model, it does follow in a system in which there is a finite amount of natural resources and it is known that many of the byproducts of the manufacturing process cannot be recycled by the natural environmental system to be available again as raw materials for future use.

Illustrations of Mass-Energy Processes in Human Ecology

The Need for Multidisciplinary Research

In the next three sections, we examine several current areas of research in behavioral ecology: population density, recreational behavior, and human predator-prey relations. One gets the feeling from the complexities of Figure 7.2 that it would take a team of specialists to do good research in the field, for the total system requires a knowledge of biology, physics, systems theory, political science, sociology, and psychology to understand fully the workings of the system. One of the major problems inherent in human beha-

vioral ecology is that it is basically multidisciplinary in nature, and very little is known about being successful in working together (Sherif and Sherif, 1969).

A case in point occurred when the chapter author first began working with a group of wildlife biologists connected with a state regulatory agency. I had written a preliminary proposal concerning how hunters utilize the habitat, especially around areas where trees have been recently cut down to increase vegetation and cover for wildlife. Following the comparative method (Denny and Ratner, 1970), I generated a tentative taxonomy of behavior and included among a long list of behavioral classes, urination and defecation. My proposal was presented at an informal meeting and was immediately rejected. One of the chief research biologists felt very strongly that he could not present the proposal to his superiors if it included those two categories of behavior. It was not so much the principle of the right to privacy that bothered him. He believed that urination and defecation had no relevance to hunting behavior and his superiors would laugh him out of the room.

As a psychologist I believed that urination and defecation certainly play a role in the outdoors experience and could have psychological meaning. I was however concerned about some of the privacy issues, even on public land, and went along with their demand to drop those classes of behavior from consideration. Now during the deer season, one of the biologists and I had the task of interviewing hunters in the field concerning the effects of clearcutting (of forests) on their hunting practices. We came over a hill and found a deer camp near the road. The people in the camp had stretched a sign with the name of their camp across the road between two trees. A picture of the sign can be found in Figure 7.4. This brought a faint smile to my lips when I remembered the proposal meeting.

To continue, we interviewed one of the hunters who had come into the camp for coffee. It

Figure 7.4. The name of a deer camp. (Photo by Ralph Levine.)

seemed that his family had camped for more than 20 years in the same place. He kept talking for more than 15 minutes about the two unmentionable human behavioral categories and how he and his family kept getting tired of having to go in the woods. Therefore, they built a *heated* outhouse on public land for the use of the deer camp, the snowmobilers during the winter, and the summer campers.

Now it is hard to tell whether this was typical of deer hunters, although I would like to think so. When you are out camping in late November and eating beans every day, urination and especially defecation can be important. I think the main point is that, in many cases, biologists and social scientists have been trained to be sensitive to completely different domains of knowledge. It takes a long time to communicate. If Figure 7.2 represents the true relationship between human systems and our natural environment, there will have to be changes in the way we conduct research and communicate our results.

Population Density and Crowding

One of the major components of the human life-support system is the human population itself, which includes the activities of people living in concentrations of cities and towns. The distribution of human populations is an important factor in obtaining stable relationships between the natural environment and the human life-support system. If you were to fly over a region of the United States, you would see that the landscape is partitioned into large blocks of farmland interrupted by urban areas. These urban areas contain high concentrations of people. The distribution as well as the movement of people in time and space can be considered from a mass-energy systems point of view, just as the concentration and flow of goods and materials can be analyzed in a monetary system. When the distribution of people appears to be concentrated in massive urban centers, the primary systems question of interest to us concerns the psychological and physical effects of high population density on the "human component" of the urban system.

Animal Studies of Population Density. For years ecologists have been aware of the potential importance of population density as a variable in determining the size of animal populations. Indeed, as the size of the population goes up, the availability of food and other resources usually goes down. This has the effect of regulating the population in terms of birthrates, deathrates, and the rate of migration to other areas. Animal behaviorists also have described mechanisms, such as territoriality, which appear to affect the distribution of individuals over the landscape. Territoriality, although more difficult to define for human populations, nevertheless appears to be a viable concept that recently has been the focus of study by human ethologists, anthropologists, and environmental psychologists (Ardrey, 1966; Edney, 1974).

Numerous laboratory studies have been performed to determine the behavioral effects of increased population density when other mechanisms such as territoriality breakdown. Calhoun (1962, 1973) found that when rodents were allowed to reproduce in a population cage, reproduction eventually went down, cannibalism and aggression went up, and normal social behavior disintegrated. In general, there is a vast accumulation of evidence from animal studies to show that high densities are harmful to nonhuman animals (Thiessen and Rogers, 1961), and few biologists would disagree with that conclusion.

From a theoretical point of view, ecologists have assumed that each population has a certain *carrying capacity* that is a function, for example, of the location and availability of food and land resources. Presumably as the population density inches its way toward the carrying capacity, mechanisms like migration that regulate the population number come into play. In the laboratory studies, the experiments were performed with extremely high densities, far exceeding the carrying capacity of the rats in the laboratory environment. Currently, however, Calhoun (1976) has initiated a new line of research to increase the carrying capacity and perhaps even prevent pathologies by means of organizing the animals into social subgroups (communication networks) that require the experimental subjects to learn

relatively complex tasks to obtain water. This new, more creatively structured environment may help the animals to "cope" with extremely high densities.

Human Dimensions of Population Density. In the area of comparative psychology, a standard research procedure is to obtain an animal model or "behavioral preparation," to use Ratner's terminology (Ratner and Denny, 1964). In the study of the effects of high population density, this was done by using mice or rats. Rodents were selected because they have relatively short gestation periods, are easy to manage, have a physiology similar to humans, and so on. The interest in population density studies stems from basically two kinds of motivation: (1) an interest in the evolutionary and ecological principles that could be learned about animals in high-density conditions, and (2) an interest in applying the findings to human populations. It is the latter topic that is of more interest here. The study of human population density, launched originally with a knowledge of the results of animal studies, is interesting and somewhat full of surprises.

In such research, one of the first questions one can ask is about the nature of population density for human populations. The simplest definition is that population density is the number of people per unit of area. This is an example of an "extrinsic" or aggregate definition of density. To a certain extent, such a definition may be misleading. For example, on a worldwide basis, the United States in 1970 had a density of 57 people per square mile (Day and Day, 1973). This figure of course appears to be very small, and does not take nonhabitable land into account. Day and Day (1973) point out that many dense areas of the United States, such as New York State and the East Coast, are comparable to European countries such as France, Denmark, and Greece (see Table 7.2). The data here have been organized by matching countries and United States land units on the basis of equivalent areas. For

Table 7.2

Areas and Population Densities of Selected European Countries and Contiguous American States of Equivalent Size

Country or area	Area including inland waters, in square miles	Population Density (persons per square mile)
New York, Pennsylvania, Ohio, Indiana, Illinois	228.8	246
France	211.2	240
Massachusetts, Rhode Island, Connecticut	14.4	659
Switzerland	15.9	394
Denmark	16.6	296
New York	49.6	363
Greece	50.9	175

From Day and Day, 1973.

example, New York State and Greece are about the same area, but New York has about twice the density.

Measures of Intrinsic Density. Another approach to defining population density is to look *intrinsically* within large land areas by measuring the number of people within a small geographic unit, such as an apartment or a room. The intrinsic measure of density may or may not be comparable to the extrinsic measure of density at a regional level. For example, although you may live in a fairly dense area of the city, you may be only sharing an apartment with one other person. Of course, it may be true that, for certain short periods of the day, one is subjected to high densities in the street. However, even these high densities may not be typical of the number of people found in one's "life space" on a 24-hour basis.

Crime and Density. The results of the animal studies clearly show that population density is highly correlated with fighting and other aggressive behaviors. Given these unambiguous findings, workers in the field first assumed the same thing would be true for human populations as well. One might look at the rampant increase in the incidence of mugging, gang wars, rapes, and other aggressive acts in the cities and conclude that density per se is a prime cause of this social pathology. Yet, density, whether extrinsically or intrinsically defined, may not be a major contributor to crime.

In an attempt to answer this question, Freedman, Heshka, and Levy (1974) studied the relationship between density and general crime rates in a large number of metropolitan areas. Their results showed that density had no influence on crime rates as long as one controlled for factors such as socioeconomic status and education. The lack of relationship was even more obvious in predicting rates of aggressive crimes such as assault, rape, and robbery. Similar trends have been found in other studies (e.g., Pressman and Carol, 1971).

The Physiological Effects of Human Intrinsic Densities. A recent correlational study by D'Atri (1975) on inmates in three correctional institutions showed that inmates who were housed alone, had lower mean systolic and diastolic blood pressures than inmates living in dormitories. D'Atri suggested that density per se was not the main factor in this relationship. Instead he suggested that inmates living in a group

Human Behavioral Ecology

situation are in a much more threatening environment, one that includes fights over territories, arguments with guards, homosexual rape, and other aggressive acts. Thus D'Atri suggests that violence prone human relations helped generate the physiological stress represented by higher blood pressure. Whether density per se generated social pathologies was not answered in D'Atri's study. In some populations, increased density could possibly lead to good human relations and thus no increase in blood pressures.

Population Density and Cognitive Functioning. Although the data do not unambiguously show a direct link between population density and either crime or high blood pressure, one might expect that large numbers of people packed within an area would affect cognitive functions such as learning or decision making. Saegert, Mackintosh, and West (1975) conducted two studies in public places, a shoe department in a downtown store and a large railroad station, and found that under low density conditions people could learn incidental facts about their environment, whereas this was not always true when the environment was full of people. Presumably people have to deal with problems of information overload in crowded situations and have to adopt strategies for overcoming such negative effects (see also Milgram, 1970). Under high-density conditions, some people appear to have a less accurate and less detailed picture of their environment. Saegert et al. suggest that one cannot rule out the possibility that high-density conditions produce a general stress condition that may decrease performance. In other words, the negative effects of high-density conditions could be due either to stimulus overload or to stress or, in all probability, to both factors.

Experimental Manipulations of Density

Recently there has been a number of controlled experiments studying the effect of room density on learning, acts of aggression, changes in social

relationships, and attitudes toward the experiment. Although there are a few exceptions, in general male groups appear to be adversely affected by high-density conditions while female groups appear to be affected more positively (Freedman, Levy, Buchanan, and Price, 1972; and Ross, Layton, Erickson, and Schopler, 1973). The study by Freedman et al. on Crowding and Human Aggressiveness is summarized as follows:

Several experiments on the effects of density were performed. In one experiment, groups of four all male or all female subjects of high school age were put in either a small or a large room for several hours. The groups first spent time getting to know each other and then participated in more structured discussions. They next played a labyrinth game in pairs so that coordination between pairs of players was necessary. Finally they played a competitive game that was a variation of the prisoner's dilemma game where choices could be reliably scored as either competitive or cooperative in nature. The major findings of this study were that density had no overall effect. However, in the prisoner's dilemma game, there was an interaction between sex and the size of the room as to the mean number of competitive choices. The interaction is seen in the diagram on top of next page.

Density and the Design of Buildings. One of the problems frequently found in large urban apartment houses is that apartment dwellers experience feelings of alienation and fear concerning their safety. Concerned with the design of high-rise apartments, Freedman (1975) has suggested designing buildings to maximize the interaction among a small cluster of apartment dwellers. Presumably such interactions would increase mutual sharing of responsibilities and confidences, which would decrease the tendency of people to isolate themselves in their apartments. Freed-

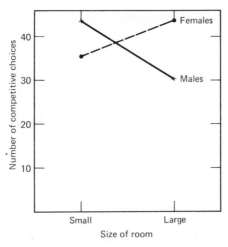

man would like to see apartment houses designed so that every floor was broken up into suites or clusters of apartments with each cluster having its own work area and childrens' play area as well as its own elevator. The common work and play areas would presumably foster maximal interaction so that people would get to know each other and feel responsible for each others property, safety, and well-being. The benefits of such an arrangement appear to be borne out by a recent study of dormitory design, as undertaken by Baum, Harpin and Valins (1975) and summarized briefly below.

> *Students living in rooms along a corridor as opposed to living in suites have less consensus of opinions and disclose fewer of their confidences with others. In addition, corridor residents are more likely to feel that their floor is crowded than suite residents. Finally, corridor residents are less likely to participate in local residential groups than students living in suites.*

Density-Intensity versus Matching Theories. It seems clear that high population density among human beings does not automatically generate negative effects. Several attempts at understanding what happens here has led to the formulation of a theoretical framework. Desor (1972) and Rapoport (1975) suggest that people first go through a process of matching the density of the environment to their past experience with environments. If there is a large discrepancy between the currently perceived density and the "standard" situation, the person may feel that the place is either too crowded or too isolated, depending on the direction of the discrepancy. In either case, the discrepancy could lead to a decrement in performance. The idea here is that crowding is a *perceptual judgment*, which is different from population density; density refers simply to the external conditions that initiate this matching process (see also Stokols, 1972; Moos, 1976).

Freedman (1975) on the other hand, has formulated what he calls a "density-intensity" theory of crowding, which may be somewhat incompatible with the notion of matching. He hypothesizes that high densities multiply with the effects of performing particular tasks, regardless of whether the effect is positive or negative in direction. For example, if one does not enjoy waiting in lines, high-density conditions would make one feel even more uncomfortable. But if one enjoys cocktail parties, then as people get packed into the room one's enjoyment would increase.

Of the two theoretical approaches, the matching theory appears to be the more general and more viable. The density-intensity theory states that there is a monotonic relationship between population density and the intensity of the reaction. What this means is that as the population increases, the effect on behavior, whether positive or negative, increases in intensity. The matching hypothesis, which introduces a perceptual element between the environment and behavioral output, specifies an optimal level of population density for any given situation. Deviations from a perceived range of normal density lead to both arousal and appropriate cognitive strategies for coping with informational overload (see Moos, 1976). Although, in many situations the two theories predict the same results, there are a number of situations in which only the matching theory seems plausible.

Density in a Systems Perspective. From the evidence thus far presented on the effects of population density on human behavior, it looks as if the relationship between density and behavioral output is extremely complex. The picture of results for nonhuman animals does not carry over completely to human populations. This is one of the pitfalls of a comparative psychology that rests upon the use of animal models. However, it would be somewhat hasty to attempt at this time to generalize the results of these human density experiments to the typical high population density urban environment, for there are too many differences between the two situations. At the aggregate level, for example, high concentrations of people in the urban situation increase the likelihood of polluting the environment. This effect of density could feed back to the population, making living and working in cities unpleasant and unhealthful to say the least. On the other hand, in the human experiments, although density was carefully manipulated, pollution and noise were kept to a minimum. The rooms were usually well ventilated and generally comfortable from the subject's point of view; this is different from being in the city during the hot summer.

With high concentrations of persons, there are tremendous strains on the feeding and servicing of those numbers. Here is where one discovers that urban systems have an important energy component to them. Energy is needed to transport food and vital necessities to the population. Later, we consider the effects of large concentrations of people on energy use. Also, from the control aspect, large populations are frequently divided into numerous semiautonomous political units such as cities and townships. The lack of coordination among various parts of an urban region makes control of pollution and the solution of other regional problems very difficult.

Recreational Behavior

Systems Concepts

In the last section we discussed the effects of population density on behavior, without treating its more dynamic aspects. An example of a dynamic system is recreational behavior, which involves movement of individuals in time and space and thus represents another aspect of human ecology. Although some may argue that recreation is not as basic as, say, migration patterns of human groups in search of food and shelter, outdoor recreation has become extremely popular in the United States with the availability of increased leisure time and with the public's increased interest in outdoor activities. It is important to study this class of behavior from the point of view of both energy and control.

In any populated area, one can find thousands of people taking to the roads at the start of the weekend. They go by buses, cars, trucks, mobile homes, airplanes, and so on, frequently pulling long trailers filled with some combination of dune buggies, boats, bicycles, sleds, and snowmobiles. The movement in time and space can be represented as a mass-energy system. Moreover, much of outdoor recreation today in the United States appears to be energy dependent, for it takes a great deal of energy to produce and operate the cars and other vehicles that transport the people and their machines to a given recreational spot.

A Taxonomy of Recreational Land. There are many factors that control the usage of a land for recreational purposes. However, before discussing the elements of control, it might be best to describe how land itself can be classified by its recreational characteristics. A relatively comprehensive taxonomy was used in a survey of recreation by the Outdoor Recreation Resources Review Commission reported to the U.S. Congress in 1962 (see Hurst, 1972). Six basic types of recreational areas were specified.

1. High-density recreational land.
2. General outdoor recreational land.
3. Natural Environmental areas.
4. Unique natural areas.
5. Primitive areas.
6. Historical and cultural sites.

Each of these broad classes of recreational land appears to be associated with specific user groups. Naturally in primitive areas one would usually find so-called "backwoods" types who probably read *Backpacker Magazine* and are very much aware of the latest outdoor equipment. These people enjoy the benefits of relatively low population areas that have minimal road access. They are also prepared to bear the cost of a low population density, such as lack of medical facilities.

Other types of recreational areas have more than one user group associated with it. For example, the population of high-density water recreational areas might be composed of passive participants (pleasure drivers, sightseers, etc.), water-oriented recreationist (sailing, boating), and active participants (picnicking, bicycling, and horseback riding). This diversity may generate problems for recreational managers because of the conflict among recreational types in the use of the land.

Motivational Aspects of Recreation. The idea of having more than one type of recreation at a site can be looked at at the motivational level as well. For example, Deal and Halbert (1971) studied the attitudes and motivations of individuals using a national recreational area in Delaware. In general, a total of 449 park visitors filled out their questionnaire. The results indicated that there was a small number of factors that describe the attitudes of the recreationists. They dealt with (1) feelings about nature and peace of mind one finds in the outdoors, (2) the social aspects of being in the park, (3) the physical activity and accomplishment in hiking and doing things in the park, (4) being away from one's home environment.

These were the primary factors emerging from their study, although other factors were discovered. More importantly Deal and Halbert (1971) were able to distinguish several types of people coming into the park, including those who were (1) primarily sociable people who wanted to get away from home and relax, (2) those who were nature lovers attracted by the natural beauty of the park, and (3) those backpackers who found the physical activity reinforcing and were attracted to the potential privacy and solitude that the park had to offer. In addition, the perceptions of population densities might be quite different for each recreational type. In all probability the social type of person depends on large numbers of people, while the backpacker might feel too crowded with just a few people on the trail (Hendee, 1969; Hendee and Potter, 1971).

The findings of the Deal and Halbert study (1971) are interesting in another way. The results show that people go to outdoor recreational facilities for two main reasons: to avoid conditions at home, at least temporarily, and to partake of certain attractive features at the recreational site. Some persons are "pushed" away from home and others are primarily "pulled" toward the park. Actually, Deal and Halbert found that most recreationists appear to be motivated by a combination of push and pull factors.

Models of Recreational Choice. Numerous attempts have been made to understand the variables that determine recreational choice and usage. A key approach to modeling recreation usage is the so-called "gravity model technique" (Cesario, 1969), which was developed many years ago by geographers interested originally in the spatial behavior of consumers in cities (Reilly, 1931; Huff, 1963). This approach rests on the assumption that populations are concentrated in certain locations and can be represented as discrete "masses," almost in a physical sense. In some ways the gravity model parallels our approach to energy systems, and it was derived to predict the use of a specific set of recreational sites. However, this approach for predicting recreational choice is not concerned with why people or groups go to particular spots; the gravity model predicts aggregate usage only.

What does the gravity model look like? First of all, the distance between the "masses" (population centers) and other characteristics of points on the map become important variables in determining recreational flow or the interchange between cities. One of the simplest examples of a gravity model is provided by Abler, Adams, and Gould (1971). If we let I_{ij} be the amount of interchange between the jth origin, usually some population center, and the ith resort area, then a simple gravity model can be represented by the following equation:

$$I_{ij} = \frac{a\, M_j^b}{D_{ij}^c}$$

M = the population density of the origin
D = the distance between the origin and the recreational site
a = the scale constant
b and c = the weights associated with M and D, respectively

It can be seen in the equation (given that b and c equal 1) that the amount of usage is proportional to the population density of the origin and inversely proportional to the distance between the two points on the landscape. This is about the simplest version of the gravity model.

There have been a variety of extensions of the basic model to include the attractiveness of the particular recreational site (Ellis and Van Doren, 1966). In addition others have also enlarged the list of variables and the general form of the equations. For example, in 1970 an extension of the basic model was proposed in a study prepared

for the Committee on Tourism and Recreation in Ontario that took into consideration such things as the general income of the people at the origin of the recreational visit and alternative opportunities for other recreational activities. Most of these attempts to refine the usage model have been at the aggregate level. However, recently Levine, Boling, and Higgs (1973, 1975) have developed a framework that first considers the individual's perceptions of the recreational environment and then attempts to predict aggregate usage of a set of recreational sites. Their model primarily stresses the attractive features of the recreational site and has omitted from consideration any motivational factors associated with conditions in the home situation.

Much of the work on the perception of crowding is relevant to recreational behavior. Levine et al. (1973), in developing their model, suggest that one's interest in going to a location for various recreational purposes may be an inverted U-shaped function of population density in reaction site; that is, an intermediate density level is most attractive. This assumption comes very close to the basic ideas underlying the matching theory of population density (Moos, 1976) as described in the previous section.

Human Predator-Prey Behavior

The third illustration of human mass-energy system deals with hunting behavior in the United States. To a certain extent hunting can be considered both from the point of view of recreation and as an activity used in wildlife management. During the fall, as the leaves turn color, the countryside is deluged by large groups of hunters, carrying shotguns, bows and arrows, rifles, and even replicas of flintlocks. The history of hunting and predator-prey relations in other than human species are covered elsewhere in this book. However, there appears to be very little known about modern-day hunters and the hunting behavior of inhabitants of large industrialized countries like the United States. Work is just beginning in this area.

Sport hunting, as an illustration of a process, should be of interest to behavioral ecologists and environmental psychologists. As a hunter myself and as a researcher of this predator-prey process, there are personal reasons for discussing hunting behavior. First, since so many people have an emotional investment in the activity, there is a need to study the process in more detail from the social science point of view. Second, hunting in the United States is a controversial topic filled with emotion and misinformation; the facts about sport hunting need airing. Third, although sport hunting is frequently associated with both rural populations and urban blue-collar workers, very few industrial psychologists and even fewer academic social scientists care to study the phenomenon; and, I might add, from my experience even find it distasteful. This antagonism toward the behavior of so many blue-collar workers is most unfortunate, for the opportunity to hunt and engage in other kinds of outdoor recreation, rather than doing a good job, may be a prime motivator for working in industry (Bass and Bass, 1976). Perhaps for this population, outdoor recreation could have more payoff for labor relations than any possible job enrichment program.

Hunting Behavior

What are hunters like and why do they hunt? First, there are at least two or three major categories that hunters fall into in the United States. There are those who hunt for sport, who usually eat what they kill and follow a traditional set of principles, such as the principle of fair chase, which states that the prey species must be given every opportunity to hide and escape. Then there are those who hunt either (1) to supplement other sources of food and maintain their families or (2) for profit. Nonsport hunting is usually associated with illegal kill. These hunters do not follow the principle of fair chase, using any method that maximizes their chance of getting the animal.

Although the illegal kill rate could have profound implications for appropriate management of animal populations, there are too many technical and measurement problems involved to cover illegal hunting in detail. On the other hand, there is a growing interest in understanding the nature of sport hunting and that is now our concern. Let us begin by reviewing the behavioral components of hunting; Laughlin (1968) suggests that the typical hunting sequence is first learned as a child. Out in the field, the hunting sequence is likely to go through the following phases: scanning the environment, stalking, immobilizing, and retrieving the prey. The sequence, of course, may not be completely fixed and may never be completed.

The total hunting sequence is similar to one described by Denny and Ratner (1970) for consummatory behavior. The first phase of a consummatory sequence involves orientation and anticipatory actions, and, when applied to hunting behavior, phase 1 would include preparation for the hunt, looking at magazines, checking out equipment in sporting goods stores, looking over maps, and talking about hunting with friends. As the hunting season begins, getting to the hunting site, picking a camp and talking to others at the location comes into play. All these factors play a role in the hunting process even before a shot is fired.

The next phase is consummatory in nature. The primary component of this phase is sensing signs of the prey species, such as seeing deer tracks and hearing shots, and ending with killing the prey. Finally there is a postconsummatory period, if and when the prey is killed. This may include gutting the animal to prevent spoilage and, in the case of deer, hanging the animal on a buck pole for all to see.

Motivation for Hunting. The sequence just described suggests something about the motivation of certain types of hunters, because, for many individuals, the sequence rarely goes to completion. For example, in the state of Michigan, where deer hunting is extremely popular among hunters, the probability of getting a deer on public land is relatively low. In other parts of the country, the likelihood of getting a deer may be higher or lower. In Michigan it is approximately 10 percent for modern firearm deer hunters (Hawn, 1976) and considerably lower for bow hunters. One might ask why then do hunters come back year after year if their chances of killing a deer are so low. Perhaps the answer is that hunters and other outdoors recreationists report that seeing signs of deer per se is extremely rewarding (Langenau, Levine, Jamsen, and Lange, 1975). Killing may not be a necessary condition for hunter satisfaction.

There is also a strong social element in hunting that should not be discounted. For example, Copp (1975), in a study on why hunters like to hunt, found that many duck hunters would deliberately attempt to congregate even though they knew that this would decrease their chances of getting ducks. From a social point of view, it should be emphasized that hunters frequently stay in deer camps during most of the deer hunting season, which may last for 16 days or so. According to hunting lore, deer camps provide enjoyment and satisfaction even when most of the hunters in the camp fail to get a deer.

The study by Copp (1975) is abstracted as follows:

A 3-year study of the motivation and behavior of duck and goose hunters using the Delevan National Wildlife Refuge was undertaken. Most hunters chose a location that had a very low probability of success. They tended to cluster together in what was known as the "firing line." This particular location was chosen because of its proximity to the parking lot and its popularity with other hunters, rather than upon a knowledge of the birds'

flight patterns. With respect to population density and aggression, it was found that squabbles over specific sites rarely occurred in crowded areas, but occurred rather frequently in less densely populated hunting areas. The results of a questionnaire seemed to show that these hunters went hunting to escape home conditions and to release certain tensions. Information from interviews, amplifying this point, showed that many hunters received a heightened sense of arousal from hunting, almost a peak experience for forgetting the cares of job, school, and family and concentrating on sights, sounds, tactual contacts, and smells. Finally, successful hunters often felt addicted to hunting, for they let this activity permeate most other aspects of their lives.

Finally, hunting may provide an opportunity for the bond between father and youngster to become stronger. Fathers frequently teach their children about hunting and about nature in general. Most hunters were introduced to hunting long before adulthood (Klessig, 1970; Schole, Glover, Sjogren, and Decker, 1973). The satisfaction of modeling after one's father may have lasting consequences for future hunts and attitudes toward hunting.

There are numerous descriptions of the personality characteristics of hunters (see Hendee and Potter, 1976). Brown (1975) studied the motivations and characteristics of Colorado deer hunters and found the following factors important among hunters in this location:

1. Opportunity to use one's skills in hunting.
2. The suspense of waiting to see a deer and the thrill of seeing signs of deer.
3. The ease of the hunt.
4. Killing and eating the game.
5. In-group contact and companionship.
6. Being well equipped.
7. Having a chance to relax.

8. Being outdoors, getting exercise, and seeing wildlife.

Some of these factors appear similar to those found by Deal and Halbert (1971) as reasons for going to a national park, as mentioned earlier. The results of Brown's study indicate that one can pick out at least ten types of hunters, each one emphasizing different patterns of the eight factors listed above.

Antihunting Groups. Other studies have compared the beliefs and characteristics of hunters with antihunters. Shaw (1975) found that hunter and antihunter groups had about the same amount of biological knowledge but differed philosophically with respect to the morality of killing animals for sport. But this was not exactly what Pomerantz (1977) found in a study of 2362 Michigan schoolchildren representing seventh through twelfth graders. In this population, hunters scored significantly higher on a test of ecological knowledge than did antihunters. Moreover, hunters claimed that they spend more time driving and hiking to look for wildlife than do antihunters.

Hunting from a Systems Perspective: The Control Components

Now let us consider hunting from a broader perspective than just the hunter's. Figure 7.5 shows some of the components of an extended predator-prey system as well as the connections between components, all of which is discussed at length below.

1. Regulatory Agencies
Consider a population of animals such as deer and the regulatory agencies involved. The number of deer in a given area is monitored from time to time by a state or federal agency. The natural resources agency determines the general condition of the herd and implements certain policies concerning the nature of the hunting season, such as its length, where one can hunt, and which types of deer can be taken. The

agency also monitors each year's harvest rate and uses this rate together with knowledge of the severity of the winter and other factors to modify its rules for the next year. Thus it uses both feedback and feedforward techniques to regulate the size and condition of the herd. In addition, agencies usually have systematic programs of wildlife management to provide a good habitat for the animals, stabilizing the herd's location.

2. The Legislature
In addition, one finds that state or federal legislative bodies play significant roles in controlling the total system. Legislatures control the financing of conservation and of research programs dealing with wildlife managment. In many cases they set up the rules as well as the fee structure for hunters.

3. Commercial Interest
Hunting definitely has commercial benefits associated with it. Figure 7.5 shows the flow of dollars from the hunters to those who provide goods and services to the hunters.

4. Antihunting Groups
During the past few years there has been an increased amount of organized resistance to hunting and hunter groups. The general attitudes and beliefs of antihunting groups will influence legislators, regulatory agencies, and finally the hunters themselves.

5. Hunter Groups
There is a clear relationship between the regulatory agency and the hunter groups. First of all, hunter fees help pay for much of the wildlife research programs and for purchasing public lands. The hunters themselves frequently influence the legislature by using the same kind of organized pressure the antihunter groups use. In addition, in recent years hunters have influenced policy decisions of the regulatory agencies by withholding fees and by way of their answers to questionnaires.

6. Landowners
A lot of hunting is done on private lands. Thus

owners aid in regulating the spatial distribution of hunters. When prey populations go up in an area, endangering the crops, farmers frequently express their needs and wishes to the regulatory agency and to the legislature.

7. The Prey Species

The final component of this system is the prey species itself. The prey's presence influences the satisfaction of the hunting group. Their numbers are controlled by hunting pressures, environ-

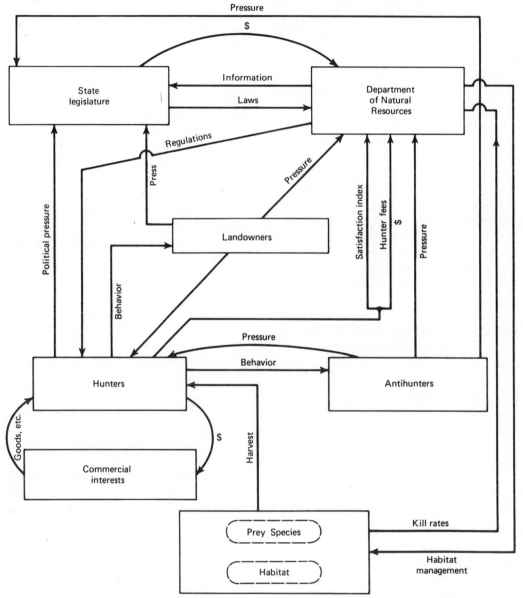

Figure 7.5. A human predator-prey system.

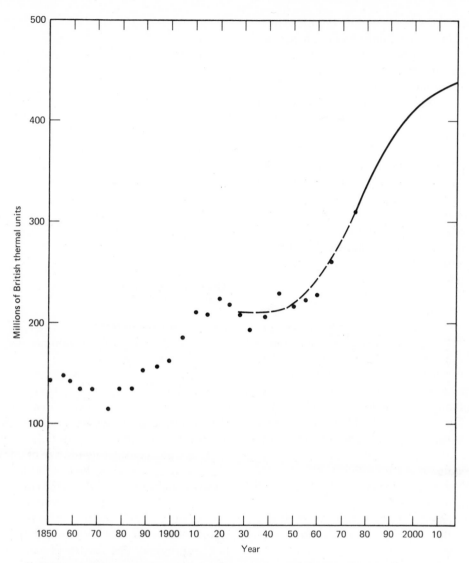

Figure 7.6. Per capita energy consumption in the United States from 1850 to 1970 with projects to the year 2010. [After Fisher (1974).]

mental conditions, and the quality of the habitat, which can be somewhat controlled by the regulatory agency.

The Systems Dynamics

This is a description of the system in larger perspective. Every hunting season the system becomes alive and dynamic. Millions of hunters converge on the woods, money is passed back and forth in gas stations, hotels, motels, and restaurants. The natural resources agencies try to keep track of the number, the location, and the general health of the herd or prey population. Some farmers are writing "cow" on their livestock, others are going hunting on their own land; some are letting hunters onto their land and others are posting it. The legislators are either ignoring the hunting season, going hunting, or going antihunting. With hunting in full swing, the prey species appears to be scattered to the wind only to bounce back in about equal numbers the next year.

Energy Sources and Environmental Values

In this chapter, we have investigated several examples of systems associated with human ecology — the effects of changes in population density, recreational behavior, and human predator-prey relations. Each system has been looked at from the energy and control aspects. In this section, we discuss the role of energy in the functioning of the human life-support system.

In 1977 the United States came out of a bitter cold spell that at least gently shook the foundations of industry in the midwest (especially Ohio) and the Northeast. Suddenly the country lacked the available natural gas resources that fulfill the energy requirements of industry as well as our homes. Although in some cases this can be regarded as a temporary problem, perhaps the writing is on the wall. In the next few years, our energy resources are in danger of being used up at an accelerated rate, and what happened in the winter of 1976–1977 may only be a small reminder of this fact.

There are many uses of energy: for industry, homes, agriculture, maintaining cities and towns, and transporting people, goods, and services. Moreover much of our modern materials like plastics are oil based. Let us look at some of the facts concerning the scarcity of energy resources. Figure 7.6 shows the per capita energy consumption in the United States from 1850 to 1970 as well as future projections (Fisher, 1974). One can see that the curve is flat until 1900 and has risen almost exponentially for the last 70 years. It should be obvious that, barring some new breakthrough in fusion power or other energy technol-

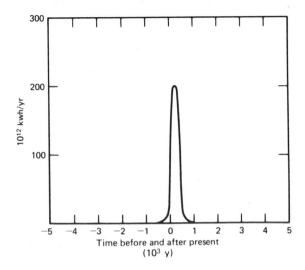

Figure 7.7. Fossil-fuel exploitation with respect to time. (After Hubbert (1971).)

nology, our consumption of energy will by necessity level off, given a finite amount of coal, gas, and other fossil fuels.

Figure 7.7 dramatically indicates our use of fossil fuels over time. The surveys of our natural resources indicate extremely rapid exploitation of known reserves which will lead to depletion in the near future. Another factor that is not always obvious when considering the size of our remaining natural resources is the cost of getting those reserves out of the ground. As the concentrations of minerals and fossil fuels become more dispersed, the cost of extracting them rises very rapidly. In the 1850s, when gold was first discovered in California, all one needed to go gold mining, was a pick, a pan, a map, and a rifle, but this is obviously not the case now.

In the area of oil exploration, we have now reached the point where, in order to get some of our offshore oil, the oil companies must merge their financial resources to carry out a major operation led by engineers, geophysicists, and other specialists. If you refer back to Figure 7.7, it is possible to see that by the year 2000, less than 25 years from now, there probably will not be very much oil left in the United States and what oil there is will be very costly to pump out of the ground. The costs, of course, will be passed on to the consumer.

Assessing Future Technology.   Energy is a central and underlying theme when exploring the ramifications of increased population density, recreational behavior, and even human predator-prey systems. With a change in the energy picture, the distribution of people on the landscape may change drastically, and recreational behavior for one, may be modified to compensate for the lack of energy resources.

If the linkage between our natural resources and the human life-support system is so finely tuned, then it seems reasonable to begin to pay attention to the tradeoffs generated by maintaining a world full of people, an industrial technology, and a vigorous agricultural activity pattern. In recent years, techniques to assess social impact have been developed at a rapid rate to track the social and psychological effects of various alternative environmental changes (Wolf, 1975). In addition, we have been provided with a picture of the future with respect to technological advancement. Montgomery (1975) for example, suggests that one can look at four dimensions of change that can occur whenever a new technology comes into being. The first dimension deals with society's goals to provide material goods and services, which relate to the functioning of what he calls the human life-support system. The second dimension deals with the quality of the physical environment — air, water, soil, and plant and animal life or the natural biological system. As the quality of material goods goes up, in many cases the quality of the environment declines providing a tradeoff. Thus when a superhighway is built, the natural environment usually changes, and land for the highway is taken away from farming.

But the picture is more complicated than this. As Montgomery suggests, there are at least two social psychological dimensions to consider: the dimension of equity or justice and the dimension of personal fulfillment in the psychological or esthetic sense. Thus, for example, if the industrial section of a town has to shut down because it is polluting both the air and the local water supply, then, although the town may look better (a question of esthetics) and be more healthful, manufacturing stops and many townspeople are out of work (a question of equity or justice).

The Role of Values in Human Ecology.   For the moment, let us assume that the four dimensions (human goals), (1) providing goods and services, (2) maintaining good quality of the environment, (3) fulfillment of psychological and esthetic needs, and (4) maintaining a just society, are useful enough to assess our human life support system in the face of finite resources. The big problem is the weighting of these dimensions rather than the identification of the goals, for the priority we place on each of these dimensions reflects our *value system*, which varies from group to group. The weighting of values has been accomplished recently by Rokeach (1974), a social psychologist, and his method may be relevant to assigning priorities to land use and other areas of resource development.

Briefly, values deal with what Kluckhohn (1951) labeled "the conception of the desirable." Rokeach (1968, 1974) has pointed out that values are stable and enduring. He suggests that there are terminal values that deal with endstates of existence, such as a sense of accomplishment, inner harmony, a world of beauty, and so forth. In addition there are modes of conduct that are *instrumental values*. These deal with ethical and moral behavior on the one hand and competence of performance on the other hand.

In regard to Montgomery's four dimensions, we might want to assume that terminal values help determine the weighting of each dimension when making an environmental decision, while many of the instrumental values deal with behaving in a just and equitable way. It is unfortunate that very little is known about the relationship between values and environmental decision making; there is a great need for research here. As a matter of fact, one would be hard pressed to find research studies on values and decision making in general; most of the empirical studies on values look for differences in values between groups (Feather, 1975).

There is, however, in the field of education, a group of people who have developed a way of making people examine their values more carefully to see how their values enter into decision making. The method used is called "values clarification" and was originally developed by Raths (1966). Although the technique has been widely applied in school systems around the country, there has been little effort to evaluate the effects of the program (see Stewart, 1975 for additional comments). In general, the method attempts to help people focus on their value system and to use it consistently in making decisions, as in choosing a career.

Although value clarification techniques look promising, there is no guarantee that the people's values can be changed in time to prevent the depletion of natural resources and the eventual breakdown of the life-support system. In fact, Raths (1966) explicitly states that the value clarification movement is concerned with the valuing process rather than with what people value; the movement is not in the business of changing values.

Although we are just beginning to find out about the nature of values and how to change them, there are two time-worn methods of changing values that appear possible. First, we can try to change values by legislation, by compliance to the law. Second, we can let the system run its course without strong governmental regulation of values. With reference to legislating the changing of values in a democratic country, it should be emphasized that a whole set of processes come into play when people are told what to do. When subjects perceive that certain freedoms are being threatened they become motivated to protect their freedom (Brehm, 1966; Wicklund, 1974). This is called "reactance." The same seems true of automobile makers whenthey were required to meet auto emission standards. They fought it tooth and nail, by going to court, delaying, and lobbying in Congress.

With the second way, changes come about a bit more naturally. Recent research on technological change has uncovered some of the mechanisms underlying the acceptance of new or old technologies. One illustration of these mechanisms relates to the use of railroads from 1890 to the present (Hamblin Jacobsen, and Miller, 1973). During the early period, 1890 to about 1920, there was an exponential rise in the use of trains, perhaps because of a lack of competing modes of transportation. From 1920 to the Great Depression there was a rapid drop in use, perhaps due to the fact that automobiles were less costly and more reliable than before. Then there was another increase during World War II, followed by a postwar decline when cars became available once more.

The major principle is that different technologies go in and out of vogue depending on the *natural* reinforcements involved. Another example comes to mind. In many game areas of Michigan, regulations about using the area can be found tacked to a tree. In most cases it is impossible to read the regulations because the sign has been riddled with bullets and buckshot. Moreover, even when one can find an intact sign, it is virtually impossible to understand the regulations. The wording is in "legalese." In actual fact, many of the behaviors observed at game areas appear to be controlled by what is there in the environment. If one does not want rabbit hunters near cross country skiiers, one can modify the habitat and cover to make certain areas more attractive to one group than the other. In general, people may be more inclined to comply to nature's wishes than to a set of rules and regulations written on some tree.

Playing with Mother Nature. There are dangers and risks involved in letting the system run its own course. First, one is at the mercy of environmental and external events. By this I mean that one hopes for a set of minor disasters to occur instead of the whole system going into a nosedive. The gasoline shortage of a few years ago and the shortage of natural gas in the winter of 1977 are examples of minor disasters. In the winter of 1977 the state of Ohio was shaken by the effects of the bitter cold: factories had to suspend production due to the lack of energy, schools could not be heated, government came to a standstill, and industry began thinking of locating elsewhere. Still this was far from being a major disaster.

A second related problem in letting the system run its course in order to change values is that people appear to have a short memory for minor disasters. Presumably, people do not perceive these shortages as symptoms of real resource depletion. Currently, for example, American automobile manufacturers find that larger cars are still selling. Do people want their last fling at owning the "big bomb" or does this reflect the general disbelief that the price of gas will go up much higher?

Summary

In the beginning of this chapter you learned about the difference between feedback and feedforward mechanisms. In order to change to a stable way of life that does not exhaust our resources, we must go from the feedback situation — which is essentially a short-term, "knee jerk" reaction to, say, what is perceived as a temporary shortage — to the adoption of a new set of values. Such values place a premium on conservation and on careful resource planning.

In conclusion, all we can reasonably hope for is a series of fairly minor disasters, like recent natural gas and oil shortages. Although these are hard for us to take and many of us will suffer the effects of such shortages, it appears that we of the energy-consuming nations must be bombarded at frequent intervals by the effects of these shortages to make us aware of the dependency of our life-support system on our natural environment and of how tenuous this relationship is.

Study Questions

1. Define the concept of a system. What are three major characteristics of any system? Consider the characters Tom and Jerry, and try to remember a cartoon in which they appeared together. Put them into system framework. Try to apply the three major characteristics of a system to a Tom-and-Jerry movie. What do you think Tom is like without Jerry and Jerry is like without Tom?

2. What is the difference between mass-energy and control systems? Define positive and negative feedback. How does feedback differ from feedforward techniques?

3. Consider Figure 7.2. What are the connecting links between the natural ecosystem and the human life-support system? Describe how institutional control systems can regulate the flow of economic goods produced by society. How does the government control the natural system?

4. What are the major differences between the throughput model and the model presented in Figure 7.2?

5. What is the difference between intrinsic and extrinsic measures of population density?

6. What is the distinction between high population density and crowdedness?

7. What are some of the reasons for people going to parks and other outdoor recreational facilities?

8. Denny and Ratner (1970) describe three stages of any so-called "consummatory"

behavior: orientation, consummatory, and postconsummatory stages. How does their analysis relate to hunting behavior?

9. Consider the density-intensity theory of crowding. Can the density-intensity theory explain Copp's findings that showed that duck hunters tend to cluster together in groups, rather than utilize the area more randomly? Can the density-intensity theory explain why hunters in more densely populated hunting areas had a lower number of squabbles over hunting sites than those hunters choosing to stay in less populated areas of the wildlife preserve?

10. Define the notion of values. Let us play a little game. Suppose the majority of the world's population considered (1) a comfortable life, (2) a sense of accomplishment, and (3) pleasure as life's most important values. Montgomery has suggested that all human goals can be divided into four categories: provision of material goods, environmental quality, a just world, and having the opportunity for fulfillment. What is the relationship between values (1) to (3) above and these categories of human goals? Given the above value system, which of Montgomery's human goals would be weighted more heavily by the majority of the world's population? Go one more step and predict what would happen to our future natural resources.

11. Suppose the following set of values were considered most important: equality, a world at peace, and self-respect. Go through the same steps as before to see the potential relationship between values and human goals, as well as between values and future use of the environment.

PART TWO

A Comparative Analysis

8

An Historical Approach to Comparative Psychology

Paul T. Mountjoy

Western Michigan University

Scientific progress is measured by the establishment of continuities that indicate order and regularity among phenomena that previously appeared to be a bewildering variety of discrete events. Organic events have been analyzed into the most diverse set of categories known to the scientist. Consider that there are only 92 naturally occurring inorganic elements and about 3000 mineral species, whereas it is estimated that there are between 2 million and 4 million living organic species and at least 15 to 16 million extinct ones. For example, there are about 250,000 living species of beetle alone. That is diversity with a vengeance. Since each organic species is defined by its set of hereditary structures, and these structures are important determiners of behavior, we see that the possible diversity in behavior is potentially bewildering.

The solution to this problem, of course, is to reclassify behaviors into categories on the basis of the function of those behaviors. Thus each class of functionally similar responses can include the behaviors of many different species. Many of the chapters in this book discuss a particular class of such behaviors, for example, parenting, feeding, sexual behavior, predator defense, and so on. This chapter describes the broad sweep of our interest in animal behavior, or comparative psychology. Note that as the chapter-title implies, this chapter is *not* so much a history of comparative psychology as it is a discussion of the history of thought that is relevant to comparative psychology. As such, this historical report has a strong applied perspective.

Hypotheses

All scientific work is guided by hypotheses, and historical work is no exception. Our hypotheses are as follows. (1) There is an historical continuum of scientific work in comparative psychology from the earliest known documents up to the present. (Today's scientists owe a debt to their predecessors.) (2) There is continuity between the everyday behaviors of the nonscientist and the highly technical behavior of the scientist. (3) There are continuua of (a) biological adaptivity and (b) behavioral selection by the environment over a wide variety of species ranging from the invertebrates to *homo sapiens*. (4) The study of the history of animal behavior interacts with the study of modern comparative psychology so that each is better understood in the light of the knowledge cast by the other.

With reference to the fourth and last hypothesis, we emphasize many fascinating accounts of behaviors that can no longer be experimentally observed — ranging from those prohibited by our ethical standards (e.g., certain aggressive behaviors in and toward human beings) to those no longer in existence (e.g., the behavior of the dodo). Yet, current behavioral principles help us classify and understand those historical observations. In addition, the historical record suggests research that should be carried out in today's experimental laboratory.

Basic Definitions

Modern behavioral scientists have reached a consensus concerning the general classification of those variables that determine a behavioral event. It is generally agreed that any observed response is a function (or an outcome of the combination) of three broad classes of variables. These are not listed in order of importance since all three are of equal importance in determining the occurrence of an event.

1. *The phylogenetic (species) history of the organism.* By this we mean that each individual organism is representative of a species, and each species is the outcome of a process of biological evolution that has extended over a period of approximately 3 billion years. During this evolutionary process, the environment has selected both structures (Darwin, 1859) and tendencies to perform certain responses (Skinner, 1966, 1975). We have already indicated that structures are important determiners of behavior, and the modern comparative psychologist is involved with investigation of this variable. Behaviors so determined that are typical of a species are called species-specific responses. Gross structural changes that are *not* genetically determined also affect behavior but are ignored in this presentation.

2. *The ontogenetic (individual) history of the organism.* Each individual organism undergoes a unique series of interactions with the environment during its lifetime. The environmental consequences that result from these interactions (loosely termed reinforcements and punishments) shape tendencies to respond to certain aspects of the environment in specific manners. This is sometimes called learning history, and we frequently use that term in this chapter.

3. *The stimulus situation.* The environmental circumstances surrounding organisms are in a continual state of flux. As these stimulus situations change, so do the responses of the organism.

For many centuries it was unquestioned that in addition to these three classes of factors there was a fourth factor, a spiritualistic factor. The historical origins of the notion that psychologists dealt with a spiritual entity, and the reasons why behavioral psychologists have discarded that notion, are presented in detail by Kantor (1963, 1969). It is not merely a coincidence that Kantor was the first modern psychologist to organize the three factors of phylogenetic evolution, ontogenetic evolution, and stimulus situation into a comprehensive and coherent system of psychology (Kantor, 1924, 1926, 1957). He was able to do so in large part by his careful study of the history of psychology itself (Kantor, 1964).

Prehistory

History is generally regarded as beginning when people first recorded events in writing, while all prior events are considered to be prehistoric. We accept that convention, and this section is based on archaeological evidence (with support from anthropological data regarding presently existing preliterate peoples).

Hunting Technology

The hunter is the comparative psychologist par excellence. All of the interactions of the predator with its prey require that the predatory species predict and control the species-specific responses of the prey. Hunters of whatever species do not hunt at random; their efforts are usually directed toward a specified species, and the strategy and tactics followed by the predator are appropriate for the particular species that is being sought. Whether we consider falcons, coyotes, or humans as our example, observation will reveal that their hunting behaviors are not random but are directed toward an appropriate habitat for the prey whose capture is expected. The falcon circles high above the marshes that shelter ducks. The coyote leaves the hills containing its den to seek mice in the meadow. Humans also direct their steps toward the habitats that shelter whatever prey they seek.

There is an enormous amount of evidence to indicate that prehistoric peoples were extremely efficient in the prediction and control of the behavior of the species upon which they subsisted (Cornwall, 1968). The Olduvai Gorge Bed I (the oldest layer, at least 1 to 1.5 million years old) reveals that our remote ancestors consumed small organisms such as lizards and reptiles as well as juvenile and aged representatives of larger species. More that 1 million years later, in the upper Palaeolithic there is evidence of increased ability to predict and control the behavior of prey species. A site dating to about 15,000 or 20,000 B.C. has been excavated at Solutré, France. At this spot, herds of wild horses were driven over a cliff for a period of many years. Clearly, persistent exploitation of this single species over a considerable time span indicates an ability to predict and control certain behaviors of the horse.

The efficiency of our predecessors as carnivores is attested to by the proposal of Martin and Wright (1967) that the five mammoth kill sites excavated in North America (as well as other archaeological evidence) support the hypothesis that the extinctions of over twenty-four genera in the late Pleistocene were the result of human hunting pressures. More recently Moisimann and Martin (1975) have developed computer simulations that are compatible with the proposal that the mammoth, mastodon, camel, horse, ground sloth, and others, became extinct in North America as a direct consequence of human predation.

Even in the twentieth century there exist primitive and preliterate tribes whose way of life has remained relatively unchanged for many centuries. An excellent example is the polar Eskimo. Nelson (1969) sought out hunters of acknowledged ability in order to accompany them into the field and observe their highly skilled performances. Nelson reported that the Eskimo knew the preferred habitats of varied species and concentrated their efforts in these areas. The Eskimo also presented stimuli that attracted prey species toward the hunter. Seals were lured by scratching the surface of the sea ice, while birds were similarly induced to approach by skillful mimicry of their calls. For centuries the Eskimo has hunted and killed the bowhead whale with primitive weapons. The introduction of modern weapons, however, has not appreciably changed their techniques (Graves, 1976; Kristof, 1973). Since the bowhead may grow to a length of 50 feet, and is hunted from a 21-foot sealskin boat, our admiration for the courage and skill displayed by the Eskimo is unbounded.

From the preceding examples of hunting technology it should be clear that the hunter regularly predicts the behavior of the sought for species in terms of behaviors that are typical of that species (species-specific behaviors). At times the hunter also will manipulate the stimulus situation in order to attract prey. The attraction of an animal by stimulus presentation represents a shift from simple prediction to actual control of behavior. One last example must suffice.

The residents of Tonga capture the octopus by means of a lure entitled the *makafeke*. A stone, ground into the shape of a cone, is the basic component. To this is lashed a long stick, and at right angles to that are similarly lashed two cross pieces, decorated with tassels. On top of the cone are attached two cowrie shells (a species of mollusk). The color of these cowrie shells is selected carefully as it determines whether the lure will be effective at high or low tide (and the hunter has two *makafekes*, one for each tidal condition). Suspended from a cord the *makafeke* is skillfully vibrated close to the bottom until an octopus seizes the lure, at which time the lure is retrieved, with the octopus clinging to it. Apparently, no other lure will entice the octopus to leave its lair (Ruhen, 1966).

Domestication

We will confine ourselves to a general consideration of the knowledge of animal behavior that the human being must have in order for domestication to occur. The human captor must appreciate the nature of species-specific behavioral tendencies or else domestication is impossible. For example, any stimuli that would provoke attack responses toward the human captor must be withheld, and the stimulus conditions that lead to copulation, successful rearing of offspring, and so on must be provided.

Domestication represents efforts to manipulate the learning history of species other than our own. One can presume that at a bare minimum the human captor repeatedly approached the captive, and thus tendencies by the captive to attack or flee declined to some degree. With animals that were frequently handled, the degree of tameness would increase as a function of the amount and frequency of handling. (habituation). Finally, the captor could systematically manipulate environmental cues and consequences so that the behavior of the captive species came under almost complete control. The evidence for systematic manipulation of the learning history of animals, however, is presented most clearly in documents. Thus we now enter the period of written history.

The Cuneiform Texts

Along the fertile banks of the Tigris and Euph-

rates rivers in Asia the domestication of both plants and animals was successfully accomplished quite early. The inhabitants (the Sumerians) utilized the plentiful clay both as building material and as a substance on which to write. Over 5000 years ago (prior to 3000 B.C.) the Sumerians began to inscribe marks on pieces of clay (tablets) and by 3000 B.C. had developed a phonetic system of writing. Because the writing instrument (a reed) produced a triangular (wedge shaped) mark in the clay, this system is called cuneiform (wedge shaped) writing.

The Plant and Animal Lists

The Sumerian vocabulary which described animals was quite extensive. Tablets have been found which evidently served as textbooks in botany and zoology, and which listed hundreds of different plants and animals. For example, more than 100 different birds and over 50 kinds of fish were listed (Kramer, 1956, 1963). These lists may be regarded as the beginning of systematic zoology.

The Horse Training Manuals

The earliest known documents devoted completely to the management of animals are cuneiform tablets dating from the fourteenth century B.C. Five tablets that described the daily procedures for training horses to pull war chariots are the most famous of these. Their author was a horseman named Kikkuli, and he presented in detail a completely rational and empirical set of procedures to acclimatize horses and to produce animals that would be capable of pulling the heavy war chariots of the period at high speeds for long distances, as well as responding to the charioteer's commands. Translations of the tablets into German have been completed by Potratz (1938) and Kammenhuber (1961).

The high state of animal training in Sumer may be inferred from Salonen's (1955) work on the vocabulary related to the management of asses, horses, mules, hinnies, oxen, camels, and elephants. We mention only a few of the specialized items Salonen discusses: yokes, bits, reins, whips, spurs, and devices designed to protect the animal's hooves. In addition, there was a specialized vocabulary related to grooming, feeding, exercising, as well as to veterinarian medicine. It is evident that the Sumerians were well versed in predicting and controlling the behavior of most of the species of domesticated animals, which constitute the majority of the domesticated animals of today.

Classical Antiquity

We consider the period from the fifth century B.C. to the fifth century A.D. as that of classical antiquity. Thus in this section we discuss events that occurred between the flowering of Athens under Pericles during the fifth century B.C. and the fall of Rome to various barbarian invaders in the late fifth century A.D., or a period of roughly 1000 years.

Greece

A contemporary of Socrates, the Athenian General Xenophon (ca. 430–355 B.C.) produced two books that dealt extensively with the behaviors of various species of animal. In one (*Cynegeticus* or *About Hunting*) he considered those behaviors that are largely a function of the phylogenetic history of the organism, while in the other (*Hippike* or *About Horsemanship*) he discussed the manner in which the horseman could produce desired behavioral outcomes by manipulating the learning history of the horse.

The *Cynegeticus* is a practical work, devoted to the procedures to be followed by the hunter in the successful pursuit of game. A readily available translation is that of Hull (1964). Xenophon (fourth century B.C.) presented detailed descriptions of the behaviors of the subjects of the

chase, such as the hare, deer, and wild pig. He discussed the differences in behavior to be expected at different seasons of the year (during the rut, for example) and by different sex and age groups as well. Among the behaviors accurately depicted are the tendencies of some animals to "freeze" and thus escape detection by predators (including the human hunter) by becoming immobile, and how the hunter could use this behavioral propensity to capture game. Xenophon also described certain behaviors that served as indicators of the imminent performance of a behavioral sequence. A compelling example is his instruction to the hunter to watch the eyes of a wild boar at bay. A certain eye movement indicated that the boar would charge. This prediction was an absolute necessity to the hunter since the social mores of that time and place dictated that the boar be killed with a spear while the hunter was dismounted.

The *Hippike* is also a practical work (Anderson, 1961), and Xenophon devoted considerable space to matters of feeding, watering, stable, construction, etc., even as do modern books on the horse. In addition, in a manner that again is similar to modern works on the horse, he discussed the manner in which environmental cues and contingencies can be arranged so as to produce a particular learning history and thus a targeted behavioral outcome. That is, he described how repeated pairings of stimuli with responses can produce a functional relationship between those stimuli and responses. Indeed, Xenophon may be regarded as the source of the concept that the stimulus is at first irrelevant to the animal ("neutral" in conditioning terminology) and acquires its functional relationship to the response solely as a consequence of its pairing with that response quite independently of the phylogenetic history of the organism concerned. At any rate, Xenophon is, to our knowledge, the first person to speak of the conditioning process in an abstract manner.

Greek interest in hunting continued high even

while Rome was conquering Greece. Arrianus [flourished (fl.) second century] called himself the younger Xenophon and some 500 years after the original produced his own *Cynegeticus*. This work reflects the changes in hunting technology that had occurred during the passage of half a millennium.

At the height of Greek power and influence the Greek General Ptolemy I (ca. 367–283 B.C.) became the ruler of Egypt. His son, Ptolemy II (309–246 B.C.), ascended the throne of Egypt in 283 B.C. and immediately began a collection of exotic animals that may be regarded as a prototype of the modern zoological collection. In 280 or 279 B.C. Ptolemy II held an enormous triumphal procession or pageant at Alexandria, of which descriptions have been preserved. It appears that Ptolemy exhibited all or almost all of the animals from his collection in the pageant, as the procession included the following: twenty-five chariots, each drawn by four Indian elephants; twelve teams of saiga antelope, seven teams of oryx, and fifteen teams of hartebeests, each drawing a chariot. In addition, the procession contained one white female bear, one African rhinoceros, one giraffe, four lynxes, and many cages of parrots, peacocks, guineafowl, and pheasants. Ordinary domestic animals were also represented, including sixty pairs of goats (each pair drawing a chariot), pack camels, three breeds of sheep, twenty-six zebus, and 2,400 dogs.

The maintenance of exotic species requires remarkable biological expertise, and the difficulty of breaking exotic species to harness is testified to by Caton (1877). Ptolemy, of course, was surrounded by experts such as the elephant trainers he had imported from India. The point is that the expertise necessary to manage and to maintain a wide variety of animal species had been developed well over 2000 years ago.

Rome

As the power and glory of Greece fell, that of Rome rose. Although there was geographical, temporal, and cultural overlap, we regard them as separate societies. However, a very convenient source for both cultures is Toynbee (1973), and unless otherwise noted we have referred to that work.

The Romans followed the paths laid out by Xenophon and Arrianus. On the one hand there were works devoted to hunting; among these is the *Cynegeticus* of Oppian of Corycus (fl. second century). Oppian of Corycus (fl. second century) also produced a work describing fishing, the *Halietica*. The use of the artificial fly for catching fish was developed in Roman times (Radcliffe, 1921), and those who are skilled in the use of the artificial fly are the aristocracy of twentieth-century anglers.

The Romans were an intensely practical people who are frequently characterized as engineers rather than scientists. Thus, they developed to new heights the skills required to manage and train animals for draft and riding. Acutely aware of the role of phylogenetic history as a factor in behavior they carefully bred animals for desired traits, following earnestly in the footsteps of their Greek predecessors. Stud farms were established for the express purpose of breeding horses for draft, racing, and military uses. The breeding of mules for draft and pack purposes was seriously pursued and perfected since the mule combined the stamina of the ass with the docility of the horse. Note that mules are the sterile offspring that result from crossing male asses with female horses.

Cavalry was an important aspect of the Roman army, and the use of the horse for war required careful training over a lengthy period. The mounted cavalry of this period did not possess the stirrup. This meant that the rider was not only a superb horseman but also possessed a well-trained mount that was extremely responsive to the pressure cues of the horseman's legs. Although the Romans (like the Greeks) used a bit and reins, some representations of Roman horsemen depict horses being ridden without bridles. Today exceptionally skilled horsemen sometimes train a horse to the point at which it may even be jumped without a bridle, guided completely by leg pressure, and without stirrups. It is possible that the Romans had mastered this highly advanced riding and training technique.

The importance of continual training for the cavalry horse is attested to by the results of excavations of Roman military camps. A prominent feature was an enclosed riding arena in which training could be carried out regardless of the weather.

The use of the elephant for warfare in Western Europe reached a peak in Roman times, and we therefore describe it here. When Alexander the Great invaded India the native kings used military elephants against his armies. Later, Alexander's General Ptolemy and his descendants imported Indian elephants and their trainers to Egypt and also captured and trained the native African elephants for warfare. From the Ptolemys the Carthaginians learned how to train elephants, and some of their military successes against the Romans were at least in part due to the presence of elephants in the Carthaginian armies. However, the Romans soon acquired war elephants and the skills necessary to train the beasts for use in warfare so that advantage was lost to the Carthaginians.

The ancient Indian literature on the training of elephants has been translated by Edgerton (1931). Briefly, once the captured elephant was tame enough to be ridden the mahout (keeper and driver) began to use a process of negative reinforcement to guide the elephant. A painful prick of the elephant goad was applied to the beast's side, and removed if the elephant moved away from that stimulation. The negative reinforcement (removal of the aversive pricking) was paired with a previously neutral stimulus on the same side. That is, the mahout pressed the big toe of his left foot against the right side of the elephant while prodding the left side with the goad. If the elephant turned right the goad was removed (negative reinforcement). In time the pressure of the big toe alone would serve to turn the elephant. Similar processes were followed for other responses.

Even the stern Romans found time for diversion, and at least the wealthy ones enjoyed talking birds. Most of the species that can be trained to mimic human speech were known and trained during this period. In Roman literature, parrots, crows, ravens, pies, starlings, and blackbirds were frequently described as having been taught to talk. During this period, the goldfinch was trained to manipulate objects with its feet and beak, and goldfinches have been trained in a similar manner in the nineteenth century (Browne, 1850). It is evident that the Romans were exceptionally clever at discovering behaviors that were within the capabilities of a variety of species and then providing the sort of learning history necessary to produce those repertoires.

The Medieval Era

The extent of the medieval era varies from writer to writer. For our purposes, we define it as extending from the fall of Rome in the latter part of the fifth century to the invention of the printing press about 1450. The justification for this is simply that immediately after the fall of Rome, the documents that pertained to comparative psychology (indeed, all scientific writings) became stereotyped works that were primarily religious in emphasis. These documents preserved some of the knowledge that had been acquired by the Greeks and Romans, but only very gradually did people begin once again to be guided by the nature of events rather than by religious considerations. When the printing press was introduced, the peoples of Western Europe had begun once more to be oriented toward events in a manner similar to that of their Greek and Roman predecessors (Kantor, 1963, 1969).

It is an unfortunate fact that the medieval period is a difficult one in which to conduct library research. Many of the important works of classical antiquity have been translated into modern languages and are readily available in recent editions. However, the majority of medieval sources remain in Latin and are available only as individual manuscripts in specialized library collections, often in Europe. Some facsimile editions are available and we list three that repay examination. The unique Vatican manuscript of the Emperor Frederick II (Friedrich II, Holy Roman Emperor, 1250) is remarkable for the illustrations that adorn its pages. Among the especially interesting paintings are flight patterns of birds, renditions of agonistic display, and the mobbing of an owl by passerines. The Baillie-Grohmans have published a facsimile of *The Master of Game* (Edward, 2nd Duke of York, 1406). Hands (1975) has made *The Book of St. Albans* readily available. In terms of strict chronology *The Book* is not medieval (having been printed in 1486) but since it is basically a compilation from various medieval manuscript sources, we include it at this point. In addition, although it is a popular rather than a scholarly work, we suggest the student will find Brusewitz (1969) interesting as he describes many aspects of medieval hunting technology.

The student who wishes to understand falconry should examine modern works before consulting the treatise of Frederick II. Two modern books of extreme clarity are those of Beebe (1976) and Beebe and Webster (1964). Either of these will repay study, although Beebe (1976) reflects the legal and ecological changes that have affected birds of prey and falconers since 1964.

The Medieval Bestiaries

In medieval times, when personal salvation was the overwhelming concern of everyone, even animal behavior was perverted to religious ends. A medieval bestiary is a collection of descriptions of the biological structures and the behaviors of various species of animals. The animals were usually presented in alphabetical order, although sometimes they were grouped in other fashion.

The bestiary was derived from prior Greek and Roman works on natural history with distortions that resulted from the fact that these documents were merely copied without the benefit of actual observation of the species described there. The basic function of the bestiary was to extend the zoological metaphors contained in the *Bible* in order to elaborate Christian morality. So we find such statements as lion cubs are born dead, but on the third day the lioness licks them and they come to life, even as our Lord rose from the sepulcher, etc. The bestiaries were extremely popular, and were available in all European languages by the ninth century. White (1954) has translated a twelfth century Latin bestiary, and in his appendix presents a history of this literary tradition.

Bizarre and unbelievable as it may seem, the influence of these rather juvenile works extends to the present day. First, the quasi-alphabetical arrangement of the beasts and their illustrations are to be seen in modern books designed to teach the alphabet to children. Next, the myths contained in them live on, as in our speaking of crocodile tears. The crocodile shed tears of "remorse" after devouring a human, but, since it lacked a soul, these were false tears that did not result from guilt. Finally, they were a stimulus to the development of systematic zoology. The earliest works of systematic zoology (e.g., Topsell, 1658) drew heavily from the medieval bestiaries rather than reporting actual observations, and listed beasts alphabetically.

The Hunting and Falconry Books

Fortunately, some attention was directed toward actual events during this low period of investiga-

Table 8.1
Chronology of Selected Medieval and Later Hunting and Falconry Books

The Hunting Tradition	Books that Combine Both Traditions	The Falconry Tradition
	The Noble Art of Hunting Turberville, 1576 *The Book of St. Albans* Berners, 1486	
		Prince Edward's Book (late version, 1450–1475)
The Master of Game Edward of Norwich, 1406 *The Book of Hunting* Gaston III, 1387–1391	*Tristram* 1400–1425	
	Book of Birds and Hunting 1350–1375 *The Book of King Modus and Queen Ratio* 1325–1375	
The Art of Hunting Twiti, 1300–1325		
		The Art of Hunting with Birds Frederick II, 1250 *Prince Edward's Book* (early version, 1175–1200) *William the Falconer* 1125–1150 *King Dancus* (date unknown)

tion. The tradition of hunting books of the type written by Xenophon, Arrianus, and Oppian did not die (although it nearly did). Except where otherwise indicated, the material of this section draws from Hands (1975). All known medieval books of the chase are of relatively late date, that is, fall into the second half of the medieval era.

In Table 8.1 we present a chronologically and topically arranged list of some of the more important hunting and falconry manuscripts of the medieval period, as well as indicating the first two important printed books on hunting in the English language. We have divided these works into those that are devoted basically to falconry, those that discussed other forms of hunting (but largely excluded falconry, and those that discussed both topics with about equal emphasis.

The left-hand column of Table 8.1 contains three works. The earliest, Twiti's *The Art of*

Hunting, is a manuscript written in French, which influenced Gaston III. From the preface we know that Gaston (who wrote in French) composed this book between 1387 and his death in a hunting accident in 1391. *The Master of Game* (Edward, 2nd Duke of York, 1406) is a translation of Gaston into English, with some added chapters that described specific conditions in England as contrasted to France. Edward carried out his translation while imprisoned for his part in a treasonous plot against the-then King of England. All three works described the habits of animals of the chase and the manner in which the hunter could exploit his knowledge of animal behavior in order to be a successful hunter (Baillie-Grohman, 1919).

The right-hand column contains the earliest known medieval falconry treatise, *King Dancus*. The first book that can be dated with any certainty is *William the Falconer*, which was written in the reign of Rober II (King of Sicily, 1130 – 1154). About either the early or late versions of *Prince Edward's Book*, little can be said except that the anonymous authors reflected the development of falconry from the twelfth through the fifteenth centuries. Frederick II wrote what is probably the most important existing book on falconry, and we discuss it in detail shortly.

The center column lists two early French works, and the early English verse treatise, *Tristram*. The upper two items are English printed works. *The Book of St. Albans* is the first book devoted to hunting to be printed in English. Turberville's *The Noble Art of Hunting* is basically a translation and expansion of *The Book of St. Albans* and Turberville published it in the reign of Queen Elizabeth I. Thus, Table 8.1 indicates the manner in which medieval books on hunting and falconry evolved from the mysterious *King Dancus* to the well-documented Turberville. In general, the later works drew on earlier ones, and added and changed materials as the social and ecological conditions that influenced hunting changed over time.

These works were all serious manuals of instruction and contained detailed descriptions of how the hunter could use behavioral tendencies of various species to bag the prey successfully. The value of these books to the hunter may be estimated from the fact that the first printed book in the English language that was devoted completely to hunting drew on all of them.

The Art of Hunting with Birds

Falconry began in Persia, probably about 4000 years ago, and diffused slowly throughout much of Asia. The Mohammedan conquest of Sicily introduced falconry to Western Europe in an indirect manner. That is, the reconquest of Sicily by the Christians in the eleventh century exposed Western Europeans to falconry for the first time. We have summarized the early manuscripts in Table 8.1 and an oriental falconry scene is depicted in Figure 8.1. The falconry books combined descriptions of the behavioral tendencies of the prey to be hunted by falcons with descriptions of the procedures to be followed in capturing, training, and managing falcons.

De Arte Venandi cum Avibus is the single most important book on comparative psychology until the nineteenth century. The title (literally translated it is *The Art of Hunting with Birds*) fails to suggest the wealth of biological and behavioral information that it contains. Its author, Fredrick II, Holy Roman Emperor, King of Sicily and Jerusalem, (1194 – 1250), was regarded in his own time as "the wonder of the world" and even a cursory survey of his accomplishments indicates the basis for this admiration. We mention only that Frederick II was a successful crusader (as is indicated by his title King of Jerusalem), was literate in six languages at a time when most noblemen were illiterate, and attempted to replace the feudal system of rule with a governmental structure that resembled modern methods of management and administration. For our purposes the important aspect of this many-faceted genius is that his book on falconry (Frederick II, Holy Roman Emperor, 1250) was based on direct observations, and whenever observations came into conflict with the doctrines of others, Frederick chose to accept the observations. In a refreshing manner, the Emperor repeatedly points out instances in which his own observations refute the writings of his predecessors. It is not too farfetched to regard him as an experimental scientist since he conducted research on whether vultures found carrion by vision or by smell (a problem still investigated in the twentieth century). There is even a tale that he investigated the effects of sleep and exercise on digestion by disembowelling condemned criminals following these designated activities. He rejected the fable that geese were born of barnacles and argued instead that geese simply nested in a region as yet unknown because it lay far to the north of the inhabited regions of Europe.

Frederick's keen interest in zoological matters is evident not only from his own writings but from the fact that he commissioned Giordeno Ruffo to prepare a treatise on veterinary medicine. This first such manual in Western Europe was translated into many languages and remained popular for centuries. In addition, the Emperor maintained a menagerie that is reminiscent of that of Ptolemy II. Among the specimens was the first elephant seen in Europe since Roman times. There were hunting cheetahs, panthers, lions, camels, monkeys, and even a giraffe, as well as many species of the birds to which he

Figure 8.1. Oriental falconry in ancient times.

was so devoted, and most of these traveled with him wherever he went. When his duties required that he visit Germany, a significant segment of his entourage crossed the Alps in his company (Haskins, 1967).

The Art of Hunting with Birds (Frederick II, Holy Roman Emperor, 1250) consists of six books. The first of these contains a wealth of information regarding the anatomy and physiology of birds as well as consideration of such behaviors as feeding, reproduction and care of the young, migration, and selection of habitats. The remaining five books (about 75 per cent of the treatise) are devoted to the behaviors of birds of prey, their quarry, and their human captors (Mountjoy, Bos, Duncan, and Verplank, 1969).

The Emperor knew well the importance of the phylogenetic history of the animals with which he dealt. He determined which species of falcon to use for a particular species of prey by evaluating the species-specific behaviors of both his falcons and the proposed quarry. For example, the gerfalcon was suitable for attacking cranes (Book IV), the saker falcon was used for herons (Book V), and the peregrine was reserved for waterfowl (Book VI). Figure 8.2 illustrates one manner in which falcons were transported to a site where game could be found.

Frederick was a master at the manipulation of stimulus situations in order to produce the specific learning history necessary for his purposes. There were causes for behavior, and the skilled falconer knew those causes and exactly how to use them in order to control the behaviors of his falcons. This is exemplified in his discussion of teaching the peregrine to "wait on." (To wait on is to circle high above the falconer, waiting for the game to be flushed.) In Book VI, the Emperor discusses eight behaviors that the falcon may exhibit instead of "waiting on", plus the precise stimulus the falconer must present in order to terminate each of these unwanted responses and produce waiting on (Mountjoy, 1976).

A significant proportion of the operations of the modern animal psychologist was exploited by Frederick in training falcons. Food deprivation was manipulated in order to obtain the state of motivation necessary for the falcon to attack game. Following a successful kill the quarry was removed and the falcon fed only a small piece of meat so that the level of motivation was maintained. Stimulus control and reinforcement of the target response were developed by the processes of fading and shaping. For example, the falcon first learned to hop from its perch onto the falconer's gloved fist. Then the distance separating the falcon from the falconer was gradually increased to require one wing beat, then several wing beats, and so on, until the falcon could be recalled from a distance of several hundred yards (shaping). Generalization of the response to a variety of environments was accomplished by carrying out the training in a wide variety of environments, but the stimulus changes were made, or faded, in very small steps (a procedure that has not been improved upon to this day).

It is truly remarkable that at a time in which so little attention was paid to investigation of events (after all, all knowledge was thought to be contained in the *Bible*), the Emperor could produce a work that was both empirical and rational. Here, by "empirical" we mean based on observation of events, and by "rational" we mean that when he was unable to observe he maintained that in principle it was possible to observe — but that the observation had not yet been accomplished. Remember the barnacle geese!

The cultural conditions that led to the rebirth of scientific activity have been discussed in detail by Kantor (1963, 1969). Briefly we may mention that the return to the study of events rather than relying on authoritative texts was due in part to increased contacts between Western Europe and other cultures. Frederick II is an excellent example of this process as he traveled widely and carried on extensive correspondence with such Mohammedan rulers as the Sultan of Egypt.

Figure 8.2. The falconer of years past.

Science Reborn

The invention of printing from movable type was a potent stimulus for the rebirth of observation. Printing not only made the books of the ancients readily available, it also enabled individuals to disseminate their own writings more cheaply and easily than ever before. Two consequences followed. First, more students were exposed to ancient treatises and noted discrepancies between the written word and actual events. Second, students were encouraged by the ease of dissemination of their own writings to produce new treatises which more accurately described events.

Voyages of Discovery

The medieval bestiary contained many fabulous beasts such as the phoenix and the unicorn. These were all said to dwell some place far away. The voyages of discovery (Hakluyt, 1589) revealed no phoenixes or unicorns, but they did reveal a bewildering variety of new (previously unknown) plants and animals. Some account had to be taken of these discoveries; they had to be organized within the system of knowledge.

The Encyclopaedists

To be sure, encyclopedias have a long history, the earliest probably being that of Pliny in the first century A.D. The tradition continued through the medieval period, but it was largely a matter of copying from Pliny. However, the accumulation of new factual knowledge led to an upsurge of activity in the compilation of these additional materials into encyclopedias in the seventeenth century. During the medieval period there was about one new encyclopedia each century. In the seventeenth century alone over twelve encyclopedias were published in various European languages. Much of the content of all these works from Pliny onward was an account of the structures and behaviors of animals.

Hunting Technology

In this later era, medieval hunting technology was elaborated and adapted to the changing environment. Markham (1621) summarized the techniques that had evolved for the capture of birds of all sorts. Among the important aspects of his book, for our purposes, is his discussion of how the fowler could exploit the tendency of passerines to mob predators in order to attract quarry to his traps, nets, and snares. Another interesting point is his description of the lark mirror. This device is of unknown origin and antiquity; it had been used for centuries and was well known before Markham described it.

The lark mirror consisted of a small cylinder to the perimeter of which were attached small pieces of mirror. The cylinder was counterbored in the center of the circular section so that it could be placed on a vertical axle and rotated by means of strings operated by someone concealed in a blind. Later ones had spring activated rotation (Brusewitz, 1969). At sunrise, during the fall migration, the lark mirror was deadly since it was apparently irresistible in its attraction of larks. The mirror continued in use into the nineteenth century even though nets were replaced by shotguns.

Around 1614 Wolfgang Birkner was appointed court painter to Duke Casimir of Saxony (reigned 1586 – 1633). Early in 1639 Birkner began what is known as the *Younger Hunting Book* which was probably completed about 1649. Lindner (1969) has published an exquisite facsimile edition (with commentary) of the thirty-nine paintings that compose the work. The paintings are of special value to the historian as plates 12 and 13 depict the medieval ritual of dressing out ("grolloching") of the game. Of particular interest to the psychologist is the recording of the ceremonial "partnership feast" of the hounds (called the "curée" in medieval French and English hunting books).

The curée is an interesting example of behavioral management. Traditionally hounds were food deprived before the hunt. After the quarry had been bagged and grolloched the hide was placed on the ground, flesh side uppermost. The entrails were chopped up, mixed with blood and bread, and spread on the skin. Then the hounds were fed on the hide. The resemblance to the modern operations of deprivation, stimulus control, and reinforcement is obvious.

Animal Training

Late in the sixteenth century a showman named Banks exhibited a trained horse named Morocco. Little is known of either Banks or Morocco; however, in 1594 Shakespeare alluded to the horse in *Love's Labour's Lost*. Scanty contemporary records indicate that Morocco could count the number of spots on a pair of dice after they had been rolled and could even "read the mind" of a member of the audience. How could this be? As you may imagine, a trick was involved — and a good deal of skill in training animals as well. First the trick, then the training procedure.

The trick required that Banks be informed of the target response. For example, if the number of shillings in an individual's pocket were to be "counted, then said individual was requested to whisper that fact into Banks' ear (ostensibly to prevent the horse from overhearing). Once Banks possessed that information, Morocco would paw the ground the proper number of times. An early seventeenth-century author known only as "Sa: Rid" (1612) described the signaling system in this manner.

. . . and marke the eye of the horse is alwaies upon his master, and as his master moves so goes he or stands still . . . then the horse paws with his foote whiles the master stands stone still: then when his master sees hee hath pawed so many as the first dice showes itselfe, then he lifts up his shoulders and stirres a little . . . and note that the horse will pawe an hundred times together, untill he sees his master stirre: and note also that nothing can be done, but his master must first know, and then his master knowing, the horse is ruled by him by signes.

And, 5 years prior to Sa: Rid's exposé, Markham (1607) had described in exquisite detail how to train a horse to duplicate the feats of Banks' Morocco, and even to surpass those feats. Although Markham did not use modern termi-

nology, he is sufficiently descriptive that we may easily translate his procedures into those of contemporary psychologists, as follows. The horse was deprived of food and water for a specified period (and the deprivation level could be increased by lengthening that period). Food was used as the primary reinforcer for the target response. Since only the trainer (and no one else) ever fed or watered the horse, the trainer became a cue for the administration of those primary reinforcers and hence a prepotent cue; that is, the horse observed the trainer very closely in preference to observing other stimuli. We might say that the trainer became a combined food and water magazine. Thus, the actions of the trainer, for example, caresses, became potent secondary reinforcers since they frequently were paired with food and water. Markham described the training of a horse to pick up a glove from the ground and hand it to the master in a manner which we can recognize as a backward chaining procedure. In other words, the horse was first reinforced for dropping the glove into the trainer's hand, then required to hold it before dropping it, then to pick the glove up from the ground.

Markham also described the use of fading to teach the horse to paw the ground ("count") until signaled to desist. First, the trainer taught the horse to cease pawing when a large arm movement occurred. Then the magnitude of the arm movement cue was attenuated (faded) to a degree that the audience no longer discriminated as movement, but the cue still controlled the horse's behavior. This procedure may well have been more useful in mystifying an audience than Banks' trick of standing still until the desired count was reached, as Markham could act in a more natural manner.

The Duck Decoy

By the sixteenth century a unique system of animal behavior technology was in operation in the

Netherlands. Hans Bol published an engraving depicting the duck decoy at Amsterdam in 1582 (Baillie-Grohman, 1919). It is not known how early the decoy had been developed, but clearly such a complex behavioral technology would have required an appreciable period of evolution. It is known, however, that Charles II of England imported Dutch experts to construct and operate a decoy near London in 1665 (Gallwey, 1886). It appears that the peak of popularity of the duck decoy occurred in the eighteenth century, and that various cultural and ecological factors resulted in a decline in the use of the technology in the nineteenth century. However, at least one decoy was still in operation in England between the two world wars of this twentieth century.

What is a duck decoy? The origin of the term sheds some light on this matter as the Dutch word was *endekooy* or literally the duck cage. The duck decoy, then, was a trap for capturing ducks. The feature of most interest to us is that aspect of its operation that exploited the tendency for flocks of various avian species to mob predators. Mobbing may be defined as orientation toward and display of agonistic behavior to a predator. Summaries of modern experimental investigations of mobbing are found in Hinde (1970) and Thorpe (1956). These reports are limited to the passerine birds, and we have been unable to find any discussion of mobbing by waterfowl in the contemporary literature. Yet Gallwey (1886) reported numerous instances of ducks' mobbing predators. Incidentally, from time to time geese and swans were captured in decoys, and hence we assume they also mob predators.

A duck decoy consisted of a small pond covering two to four acres, from which extended several shallow, curving canals. A duck's-eye view of how these canals appeared where they connected to the pond is seen in Figure 8.3. A small dog, somewhat resembling a fox, is visible on the bank. The operator of the decoy (the decoyman) controlled the dog's movements so that as the ducks entered the canal the dog advanced down the bank, and thus the ducks were lured further and further into the canal. The screens of rushes concealed the decoyman so long as he was in front of the ducks and were designed so that once the operator appeared behind the ducks (between them and the pond) he was visible. The ducks then flushed and were guided by the overhead arch of netting into the tunnel net. Once that had happened, the decoyman removed them one by one and wrung their necks. This final act is depicted in Figure 8.4.

The interest of the modern comparative psychologist in the mobbing behavior of birds has been confined to the passerines and to scientific questions rather than the practical concern of the decoyman in obtaining food. Nevertheless, by 1886 Gallwey had reported most of the aspects of mobbing which have since been described by modern scientists. Hinde (1970) and Thorpe (1956) have discussed the weakening of the mobbing response with repeated elicitation in terms of an habituation effect. Gallwey did not use our modern vocabulary, but he clearly described a similar phenomenon. Hinde elicited mobbing with a stoat and a model of a dog. Gallwey reported that he had successfully decoyed ducks with a cat, ferret, rabbit, stoat, and even a monkey (although the behavioral management of all except the dog was a problem). Andrews studied the calls of mobbing passerines (Hinde, 1970), and Gallwey described the calls of ducks when they followed the decoy dog down the canal.

We have been unable to find a modern comparative psychologist who mentions the duck decoy or the mobbing reaction of waterfowl. That seems to be a pity as Gallwey reported field observations (and even some quasi-experiments) that could have justified laboratory experimentation more than half a century before modern researchers turned to the phenomenon. The mobbing reaction of waterfowl is still completely neglected as a research topic today, reflecting

Figure 8.3. Duck decoy in action. The dog can be seen running along the decoy pipe.

ignorance about the historical existence of the duck decoy and its significance for comparative psychology.

Systematic Biology

The organization of plants and animals into the categories of phyla, classes, orders, families, genera, and species was largely achieved during the eighteenth century. This accomplishment was accompanied by a gradual realization that fossils represented the surviving traces of long-dead plants and animals. These achievements set the stage for the theory of evolution by Darwin (1859) in the succeeding century. Evolutionary theory is an essential aspect of modern comparative psychology, and every chapter in this book testifies to its importance for the comparative psychologist, but we must not forget that the

endpoint of this scientific evolution began in Sumer over 5000 years ago with the plant and animal lists.

The Nineteenth Century

The Industrial Revolution

One criterion for the industrial revolution is the replacement of animals by steam as a major source of energy. The Romans had harnessed animals to a vertical axle that the beast rotated as it walked in a circle. The rotary movement had been used to grind grain, and the like. In the medieval era, similar animal powered devices were used to drain mines (Agricola, 1556). James Watt's firm made steam engines available for mine drainage beginning in 1775. Gradually steam was adapted to other uses and slowly it

A Comparative Analysis

Figure 8.4. Decoyman taking fowl from tail end of net.

displaced the animals that had for so long been relied on as a source of energy. In the nineteenth century the railroad supplanted the horse as the preferred method of overland transportation in the United States. However, historical developments are complex, and as the railroads became the major agent for moving goods and people over long distances, the use of the horse also increased. Americans became enamored of the horse, not simply because it could go where railroads had not yet ventured but also because the horse remained the best available method for short distance hauling of small amounts of merchandise or small groups of people. That situa-

tion did not change until the development of the automobile in the twentieth century. In this last quarter of the twentieth century we have almost forgotten that less than 100 years ago most Americans were in daily and intimate contact with horses. Everyone knew how to ride horseback; everyone knew how to harness a horse to a conveyance and drive the animal. The skills involved in the behavioral management of horses were not only a matter of practicality but a source of pride in accomplishment as well. We modern Americans can gain some appreciation of what a life dependent upon animals was like from Mitchell (1971).

An Historical Approach to Comparative Psychology

The Bee Space

Throughout recorded history, humans have practiced apiculture, or beekeeping. Probably the ancestral protohumanoids robbed wild bee nests as do so many other animals. It has seriously been proposed that the honeybee was the first domesticated animal (at any rate, it is the only domesticated invertebrate). From the earliest times until the mid-nineteenth century apiculture was wasteful and inefficient because of the inadequate beehives then in use. Wicker baskets, clay pots, and other variants were tried to no avail. The harvest of the honey killed many bees and destroyed the honeycombs since the combs had to be cut out of the container. As might be expected, the bees took umbrage at this outrageous behavior on the part of the beekeeper, and another unfortunate aspect of the harvest was a bee-stung beekeeper.

This was the problem. Honeybees filled all available space with honeycombs. When apiculturists attempted to provide frames that could be removed once they had been filled with comb, the bees glued those frames to the hive with propolis! Propolis is a very efficient glue, a resinous substance with which bees fill and seal

Figure 8.5. The staples between the honeycomb frames provide the bee space. A careful examination of the figure makes it clear.

A Comparative Analysis

every crack in the hive. As one eminent apiculturist put the matter: "As Nature abhors a vacuum, so bees seem to abhor a crack or crevice" (Root, 1901). To be sure, a boiling solution of water and lye, or live steam, will remove propolis, but such drastic treatment has many undesirable side effects on hives, combs, honey, bees, and human skin.

During the late eighteenth and early nineteenth century an unbelievable number of ingenious schemes of hive construction were tested. Nothing worked until Lorenzo L. Langstroth (1810 – 1895), a Congregational minister, educator, and amateur beekeeper, carried out a series of experiments and discovered an amazing behavioral principle. As seems to be the case with so many great ideas, the concept was extremely simple. A rectangular frame 17 5/8 inches wide and 9 1/8 inches high was constructed with the top frame member extending about an inch beyond the side members. The hive was built with an inside width of 18 1/8 inches. Thus, when the frame was hung vertically inside the hive by the extended tips of the top cross member, there was exactly 1/4 inch of space between the outside of the frame and the inside of the hive. This miraculous quarter of an inch is the bee space. It is too small for the bee to construct comb, and so large that the bee does not attempt to fill it with propolis. It is just right for the bee to crawl through, a cozy quarter of an inch. Figure 8.5 illustrates how a properly constructed frame, and strategically placed staples, preserve the bee space within a hive. Langstroth received a patent for the first successful movable frame hive on October 5, 1852.

We regard the discovery of the bee space as an important point in the history of comparative psychology. For millenia humans had used the biological fact that bees make honey. In the middle of the nineteenth century Langstroth discovered a behavioral propensity, a reaction to a stimulus situation, which could be exploited to improve the yield of honey as well as to increase the ease and efficiency of harvesting honey. Obviously, the time and energy bees devoted to building combs could be better spent in making honey. Langstroth's invention allowed just that to be done, for the combs could be drained of honey and replaced in the hive. In addition, his invention preserved the population of the hive and prevented the beekeeper from being stung.

Masturbation in Horse and Human

The nineteenth century is frequently called the Victorian period, and we moderns tend to laugh about the degree of sexual repression that was practiced at that time. To those who lived under those repressive conditions sexuality was no laughing matter, it was deadly serious because it was widely believed that any sexual behavior in excess of that minimal amount necessary to perpetuate the species resulted in a wide variety of organic and mental diseases. For example, epilepsy, schizophrenia, and mental retardation were attributed to excessive sexual activity. Given this state of affairs an enormous amount of time and energy was devoted to the suppression of "the secret vice" of masturbation. Indeed, so widespread was the conviction that serious effects followed masturbation that even horse breeders attempted to prevent their stallions from indulging in "the secret vice." (Incidentally, horses do appear to masturbate almost as much as primates.)

We have found that during the late nineteenth and early twentieth centuries the United States patent Office issued at least thirty-four patents for devices designed to prevent masturbation by stallions and for an additional fifteen mechanisms that were claimed to discourage sexual activity by human beings (Mountjoy, 1974).

Although the belief that masturbation causes illness is false, we must point out the behavioral sophistication of some of these antimasturbatory devices and the degree to which they were based on sound observation of sexual activity. The penises of both horses and humans are vascular-muscular in nature. That is, unlike the fibroelastic penises of most mammals they increase in diameter as well as lengthening when they become erect. The Victorian repressors of sexual activity noted correctly that ejaculation required an erect penis and that a ring that exerted pressure on the penis as it enlarged in diameter would reflexively prevent erection; hence ejaculation by masturbation could not occur. The application of an automatic response prevention device in two species of similar biological structure and similar behavioral propensity must be regarded as a stroke of genius, no matter how much we may deplore the repression of sexual activity from the standpoint of our position in history. The principle of pressure on the penis to prevent ejaculation has also been used by Masters and Johnson (1970) in a therapeutic procedure designed to increase sexual enjoyment by preventing premature ejaculation. Hence we should remember that scientific knowledge can be used for either good or evil. It is, in the final analysis, a matter of cultural values.

Learned Animals

We have already discussed Banks' Morocco, Sa: Rid's exposé of Banks, and Markham's exposition of how to train horses to perform miraculous feats. Entrepreneurs have continued to amaze audiences with their learned or educated animals into the twentieth century. The following excerpt illustrates the ignorance of the majority of nineteenth century scientists of behavioral principles. Its author was Nathaniel Southgate Shaler (1895), Dean of the Lawrence Scientific School of Harvard University.

The . . . [pig] . . . had been trained by a peasant . . . who made his living by instructing animals for show purposes . . .

A score of cards were placed upon the ground, each bearing a numeral or the name of some distinguished person. These cards were in perfect disorder. I was allowed, indeed repeatedly, to change their position and mix them up as I pleased. The pig was then told to pick out the name of Abraham Lincoln and bring it to his master. This he readily did. He was asked in what year Lincoln was assassinated. He slowly but without correction brought one by one the appropriate numerals and put them on the ground in due order. Half a dozen other questions concerning names and dates were answered in a similar way. Each success was rewarded with a grain of corn . . .

It seemed clear that the master of this learned pig did not guide the movement of the animal by other indications than words . . .

The above-described exhibition made it plain to me that the pig can be taught to understand a certain amount of human speech and to associate memories with phrases substantially as we do ourselves.

Shaler's gullibility is not an isolated or unusual state of affairs, for no rational explanation of these apparently miraculous behavioral feats was available in the *scientific* literature before Pfungst's early twentieth century description of his research with the horse of Mr. von Osten, the famous Clever Hans. Nevertheless, in addition to Markham's discussion of the procedures to follow in training a horse to perform amazing tricks, a similar detailed presentation of the procedures necessary to produce an educated pig had been available for 90 years before Shaler published his account.

Pinchbeck (1805), the author of the first book on conjuring to be published in the United States (*The Expositor: Or Many Mysteries Unravelled*)[1] described the day-by-day procedures to be followed in order to train a pig to appear to respond to questions stated in English, and even appar-

[1]We thank Mr. Leonard N. Beck, Curator, Special Collections in the Rare Book Division of The Library of Congress and his staff for allowing, and assisting us in, the examination of *The Expositor* and other rare volumes.

A Comparative Analysis

ently to "read the mind" of a member of the audience. The early training of the pig was a backward chaining procedure; that is, a card was placed in the pig's mouth and the pig was reinforced with food for dropping the card into the trainer's hand (a highly probable behavior). Additional components of the response chain were then sequentially added prior to the reinforced response of placing the card in the trainer's hand. First the animal was taught to pick up the card from the floor and then place it in the hand of the trainer. Next the pig was trained to select one card from among several cards on the floor. This was simplicity itself as the trainer had established stimulus control of the response of picking up the single card by always presenting a cue-stimulus as the animal grasped the card in its mouth. To complete the training, the cue was presented only when the pig's snout was oriented toward or pointing at a specific card in the display. Only if the pig picked up that particular card was it reinforced. The signal or cue was then faded (decreased in magnitude) so that the audience could no longer discriminate its presence, but the signal in its attenuated form still controlled the behavior of the pig. Symbols were placed on the cards in order to bamboozle the human audience.

It was not until the early part of the twentieth century that Pfungst (1911) described to a scientific audience how Mr. von Osten had inadvertently trained Clever Hans to respond to minute postural cues so that the horse appeared to give intelligent answers to complex questions. We have pointed out that the principles used to train animals and baffle audiences had been in print since 1607. Surely there could be no better argument for doing historical research on animal behavior.

The Immobility Reaction

This volume is a memorial to our late colleague, Professor Stanley C. Ratner, and it seems only fitting that we discuss the history of thought concerning a behavioral class to which he devoted much research time and contributed significant understanding. We use the label of immobility reaction, although various authors prefer other terms,[2] for this label does not appear to presuppose any particular theory. We also use a somewhat broader definition of that reaction than do many modern psychologists since we define it as any reaction to the approach of a predator other than fight or flight (rather than restricting it to an immobility reaction to seizure by a predator). We argue that extension of the definition may result in increased understanding of that reaction by relating it to other behavior classes, per Ratner's comparative method.

Predators, including human beings, are frequently confounded by the immobility reaction of their intended prey. A recent study of the duck-fox interaction shows that ducks that become immobile have a higher probability of escape from the fox that seized him than do birds that continued to struggle after being seized (Sargeant and Eberhardt, 1975).

The human being is one predator that developed responses to the immobility of prey to increase the probability of successful predation. By the fourth century B.C., Xenophon had described the tendency of young fawns and adult hares to remain immobile in a human's presence, and he discussed how the hunter could use that behavioral tendency to bag quarry. When the animal is visible, modern hunters refer to such behaviors as "freezing." Otherwise, they refer to the animals as "holding tight" (Zutz, 1977). They also refer to the cessation of struggle, that sometimes occurs when an animal is seized, by various terms such as "playing possum." In the twentieth

[2]As this chapter was undergoing final revision the Special Issue of *The Psychological Record* devoted to the immobility reaction appeared (Crawford and Prestrude, 1976). We decided not to revise this section to include that material, but instead urge the student to read that Special Issue. Or, refer to the Tonic Immobility section in Chapter 21.

century, the immobility reaction was recognized by Ratner for what it indeed is — basically, a reaction to predators. And for centuries, the ultimate predator — man — has exploited the immobility reaction to further his own predatory activities.

Presumably the immobility reaction has been selected by the environment because it contributes to survival. Even predators display this reaction. This fact should not surprise us for most predators are concurrently the prey of other predators. Larger falcons kill and eat smaller falcons, and falcons exhibit the immobility reaction. For untold centuries, falconers have exploited this behavior to transport falcons without injury. As soon as a wild falcon was captured by the medieval falconer, it was placed in a "sock" that secured the wings firmly against the body. The birds then ceased struggling and could be easily transported from the site of capture to home base (Frederick II, 1250; Friedrich II, 1250).

Even human beings, when mauled by a predator, display the immobility reaction, as the following quotation illustrates. The narrator is the nineteenth century African explorer and missionary, Dr. David Livingston, and he described his reaction in these words when seized by a wounded lion.

Growling horribly in my ear, he shook me as a terrier does a rat. The shock produced a stupor, similar to that which seems to be felt by a mouse after the first shake of the cat. It caused a sort of dreaminess, in which there was no sense of pain or feeling of terror, though quite conscious of all that was happening. It was like what patients partially under the influence of chloroform describe, who see all the operations, but feel not the knife. This singular process was not the result of any mental process. The shake annihilated fear, and allowed no sense of horror in looking round at the beast. (Greenwood, 1865, pp. 100 – 101).

Note that Livingston was severely injured (an artificial shoulder joint had to be constructed) but escaped with his life. (Greenwood, 1865, p. 101).

Other human beings have reported their reactions when seized by a large predator. Taylor (1955) describes the absence of pain when being mauled by a leopard, and Legault (1976) reports that the polar bear that was biting him left to attack another man who was moving, as was the case with Livingston's lion. Legault also reports that, after he had been flown to a hospital, the pain of stitching his wounds was more severe than that of the bite of the bear.

How can this reaction of immobility be adaptive? It appears that a struggling victim stimulates additional attack by the predator. The victim who does not struggle no longer elicits attack. Hence, there is an opportunity to escape (as Sargeant and Eberhardt have demonstrated); both Livingston and Legault were dropped by the predator in order to attack another person *who was moving*, and hence elicited attack.

We note that human beings who live to tell the tale of severe injury by a large predatory animal universally report feelings of unreality, detachment, and an absence of pain. It appears possible that only human beings who become immobile survive such attacks. If that is true, it would indicate the survival value of the immobility reaction. Indeed, the U.S. Forestry Service advises anyone who believes attack by a large predator is imminent to lie down and become immobile as this simple act reduces the probability of attack.

However, the environment which selects behaviors that increase the probability of escape for prey animals must also select behaviors that increase the probability of successful predation by predators. There are many stories in the literature of the nineteenth century of predators that produced immobility in their prey by means of prolonged eye contact.[3] And even that coin has another side. Some prey-species suddenly display eyelike spots and escape while the would-be predator is immobilized!

It is our conviction that a combination of historical studies and modern field and laboratory research will gradually untangle the complexities of the immobility reaction across species. Historical studies should suggest variables to be investigated in the field and laboratory, and these investigations should result in increased understanding of the behavior of all animal species. And, after all, that is the goal of comparative psychology.

Conclusion

We stated at the beginning of this chapter that historical work is guided by hypotheses, just as is any other research. It is now time to decide whether our four hypotheses have been supported by the historical records we have described.

1. There is an historical continuum of scientific work in comparative psychology from the earliest known documents up to the present. Numerous examples selected from the historical record support this hypothesis. Both mobbing and the immobility reaction were discussed for several hundreds of years before modern scientific comparative psychology began.

2. There is continuity between the everyday behavior of the nonscientist and the highly technical behavior of the scientist. Nonscientists described behaviors accurately long before they were studied by scientists. An excellent example is the process of conditioning as discussed by Xenophon, Markham, and others. However, we also noted that during the medieval period there was excessive reliance on texts rather than upon observation.

[3]We have not analyzed these anecdotes, and they may be unreliable, but they abound in the nineteenth century literature of hunters and explorers.

3. There are continuua of (a) biological adaptivity and (b) behavioral selection by the environment, over a wide variety of species ranging from the invertebrates to humankind itself. Limitations of space have prevented as full a discussion of this hypothesis as we would have liked. However, the treatment of the immobility reaction has illustrated the validity of this hypothesis in as much detail as is possible under the circumstances, and material presented in several other chapters in this text provides ample support for the hypothesis.

4. The study of the history of animal behavior interacts with the study of modern comparative psychology so that each is better understood in the light of the knowledge cast by the other. We indicated how historical descriptions of behavior could suggest field and laboratory investigations, as in the study of immobility reactions. In addition, we can argue that only those who understand modern comparative psychology can know what behaviors were really being described in the historical documents. Thus we conclude that historical and modern studies do interact to the mutual benefit of the historian and today's psychologist.

The student who has read this chapter carefully will, of course, be able to provide support for these four hypotheses beyond that which we have presented in our concluding remarks (see the Study Questions).

Study Questions

1. Explain what is meant by the phylogenetic (species) history of an organism. (That is, give a general definition and one or more examples.)

2. Explain what is meant by the ontogenetic (individual) history of an organism. (That is, give a general definition and one or more examples.)

3. What evidence was presented to support the hypothesis that there is an historical continuum of scientific work from the earliest known documents up to the present?

4. What evidence was presented to support the hypothesis that there is continuity between the everyday behavior of the nonscientist and the highly technical behavior of the scientist?

5. What evidence was presented to support the hypothesis that there are continuua of (a) biological adaptivity and (b) behavioral selection by the environment over a wide variety of species?

6. What evidence was presented to support the hypothesis that the study of the history of animal behavior interacts with the study of modern comparative psychology so that each is better understood in the light of the knowledge cast by the other?

9

The Comparative Method

Stanley C. Ratner
Michigan State University

Many areas of scientific and scholarly study contain a branch called *comparative*. There are comparative fields in anatomy, embryology, political science, economics, geography, sociology (anthropology), literature, religion, and psychology. On the surface, these areas share very little except for the name *comparative*. But closer examination reveals that they have a common characteristic.

When Is an Area of Study Comparative?

According to this chapter, an area is comparative whenever the subject matter has diversity, that is, when the events or processes under study have variety in form, structure, or function. In psychology, behavior and all of the factors that relate to behavior show diversity. If one multiplies the different things that organisms do by the differences among organisms, one can appreciate something of the diversity of behavior. It is also obvious that literature, anatomy, political process, and so forth have diversity.

The question arises as to how to handle diversity. The traditional answer in psychology and other behavioral areas over the past half century has been to imitate the biology that followed the theory of evolution. Thus, biology has had both obvious and subtle influences on comparative psychology. My view is that these influences are valuable but that they constitute only one feature of comparative psychology. An examination of biology and other areas suggests that a special method, the *comparative method*, is involved when studying content that is diverse. And it should be stressed that the application of this method was a necessary precursor to the development of the theory of evolution.

This chapter deals with the comparative method and other ingredients that combine to produce comparative psychology. A working definition of comparative psychology is as follows: *comparative psychology involves the analysis of behavior of organisms, including man, by means of the comparative method*. In the broadest sense, then, it is assumed that, when comparative psychology is fully developed, it is general psychology. You will see, as the comparative method is described, that explicit comparison comes into comparative psychology only after preliminary stages are completed. In this book, the authors pay attention to the preliminary stages and make a number of broad comparisons among behaviors. Specifically, the relations between innate behaviors, between learned and innate behaviors, and among a number of types of learned behaviors are described or analyzed.

But before the comparative method is examined, I want to identify myself as a comparative psychologist whose formal opportunity to work in comparative psychology came when I joined the faculty of Michigan State University and became responsible for this rather uncrowded area of study. A year of research and study with zoologists at Cambridge University and other continental centers made me understand something of the style of zoology and the meaning that zoologists attached to comparative study. Thus, I began to understand that the study of behavior by zoologists had a different theoretical perspective than the study of behavior by comparative psychologists. My first attempt to organize this understanding appeared in *Comparative Psychology* (Ratner and Denny, 1964). Since the time when Denny and I began to work together to identify, describe, and use a comparative psychology, the idea that it is not merely a restatement of the theory of evolution as it relates to behavior of organisms has come to the fore. The rest of this chapter amplifies and illustrates these ideas and helps move us, I believe, toward a bona fide comparative psychology.

Animal Behavior

The study of animal behavior, one of the oldest areas of biological study, constitutes the first ingredient of comparative psychology. This area traditionally excludes humans, so that information about human behavior must come from other sources. This exclusion is unfortunate because humans are then put into a unique category, with special and often mystical theories used to characterize human behavior. Investigators of animal behavior have made many contributions that are important for comparative psychology, and recently zoologists who specialize in animal behavior are extending their analyses to humans (Lorenz, 1965; Tinbergen, 1974).

Reasons for Studying Animal Behavior

Ratner and Denny (1964) identify four main reasons for the study of animal behavior: (1) interest in the animal itself (which is *not* elaborated on below), (2) relevance of animal behavior for the theory of evolution (i.e., ethology), (3) interest in the animal as an economic element, and (4) interest in one species as a model for others. Thus, the resources available to the comparative psychologist is almost limitless.

Animal Behavior and the Theory of Evolution. The largest number of theoretical contributions comes from zoologists, many of whom call themselves *ethologists*. Ethology is the study of habits or behavior, a definition equally as appropriate for the subject matter of psychology; however, ethology refers to a particular approach that is strongly influenced by the theories and methods of zoology. The ethologists are concerned with classification of behavior, evolutionary theory, and the study of the animal in its natural habitat (the field method). They pay close attention to what the animal is doing and try to explain why. The emphasis on evolutionary theory means that ethology is a comparative discipline that is concerned with the concepts of *natural selection, selection pressure, and adaptation* — ideas common to zoologists, yet often foreign to psychologist (but self-consciously treated and exploited in this book).

Although zoologists have not related the theory of evolution to behavior as much as they have to structural data, because behavior leaves no direct fossils, they have been concerned with the two-way relationship between behavior and evolution. As ethologists Hinde and Tinbergen (1958) have pointed out: "Species-specific behavior is in part the product of evolutionary process.

Likewise, the behavior of a species must influence the course of its evolution (p. 25)".

Animal Behavior and Its Economic Consequences.   The behaviors of many animals are of great economic consequence — in some cases positive and in other cases negative. The training and use of Seeing Eye dogs, watchdogs, and horses suggest a few of the positive uses, while certain aspects of the behavior of blackbirds, crows, pigeons, mosquitoes, rabbits, and the like, have negative economic consequences for many people. Intensive study and understanding of the behavior of this latter group is needed in order to reduce their negative effects (see also Chapters 13 and 15).

The Use of Animal Models.   Psychologists commonly study the behavior of one species as a model of how other organisms behave. Thousands of psychologists and their students investigate the behavior of laboratory rats, pigeons, schoolchildren, and monkeys, focusing on the animal as a model of a behaving organism. One unfortunate factor associated with the use of an animal as a model is that the investigator frequently knows very little about the model-species that he or she is using. So, for example, information about the biology and living habits of the model is often unknown to investigators. Kenk (1967), a biologist who specializes in the study of the flatworm, has described some of the difficulties that investigators of learning in planaria have encountered when using supply-house information about worms. The problems include identification of the species, relating the living and laboratory conditions to the species' requirements, and recognizing limits to the generality of the experimental findings. Similar problems can arise if the model is a rat or child when the researcher knows little more about the model than its name and that he or she wants it to be a model-species. The motto of the comparative psychologist is, "Know your animal."

On the positive side, it is emphasized that psychologists have learned a great deal about learning from the intensive study of the behavior of rats. The data in Skinner's Behavior of Organisms (1938) are based on the study of no more than ten rats; and appreciation of the large and subtle effects of schedules of reinforcement, to mention but one of many areas, is based on studies of the rat and the pigeon

Concepts Related To the Study of Animal Behavior

Theoretical concepts specifically related to the behavior of infrahumans are relatively well developed, as, for example, the concept of *instinct*. Analyses of behavior published at the beginning of this century often referred to "instinct," which at that time meant an inherited pattern of behavior more complex than a reflex. However, uncritical use of the concept led to its downfall.

Recent Instinct Theory.   Recent redefinition and reconsideration of the concept of instinct have led many contemporary workers, particularly the ethologists, back to its use. According to Tinbergen (1951), for example, the concept of instinct refers to complex patterns of behavior that are (1) unlearned, (2) specific to particular species, (3) triggered by particular stimuli, and (4) more difficult to elicit after repeated elicitations. The fighting behavior of male stickleback fish is considered an instinct in this sense, occurring when the male sees the red belly of another male stickleback during the mating and nesting seasons. Tinbergen found that the fighting pattern may be "released" by any red-bellied object shaped like a fish that is close to the nesting site. A "releaser," in this case the red underside to an object, is often called a *sign* stimulus.

The principles used in tying and casting flies for trout fishing constitute an informal use of the notion that certain sign stimuli or releasers may be used to elicit the feeding response in fish. That is, when anglers are tying flies, they do not duplicate the insect in detail; they only imitate those aspects of the insect that they suspect are the releasers for the feeding response of the fish.

The concept of instinctive behavior involves a set of interlocking concepts that are still undergoing development by investigators like Tinbergen (1951), Thorpe (1956), and Lorenz (1957). One novel aspect of the present formulation of instinct is the concept of "fixed-action patterns," stereotyped responses that animals make during an instinctive sequence of behavior (as described in Chapters 2 and 5). Nest building, courting rituals, fighting patterns, and other such complex behaviors have been analyzed in terms of releasers and fixed-action patterns. An ethological analysis describes these behavior patterns, or consummatory acts such as nest building and copulating, without reference to the animal's working toward a goal of having a nest or producing young. Instead, it is assumed that a response is elicited when an appropriate releaser is present. The releaser-response sequence means that a response typically brings about a releaser, which elicits the next response in the sequence, which leads to the next releaser and so forth throughout the chain. In such instances, the chain of S-R units is not learned, as it is in the case of development of a chain in the Skinner box; instead, the chain is instinctual. However, just because a behavior chain is an instinct does not mean that the analysis of the behavior stops there. One must still determine the conditions under which the chain occurs, identifying the sign stimuli or releasers, for example. Instincts are *not* disembodied responses that occur in a vacuum. They are tied to stimuli, and only very rarely are internal stimuli powerful enough to evoke an instinct without external stimulus support.

An early study by Jean Henri Fabre (see Chapter 13), as excerpted from a book by H. G. Wells and associates (1934) and as summarized as follows, illustrates how an instinctual chain operates.

In its first year of life, without ever having had an opportunity to learn to do so, the female Sphex wasp exhibits a complex pattern of behavior after laying her eggs in a burrow. She leaves the burrow and searches over a wide territory for a cricket, which, when found, is stung and paralyzed and brought back to the burrow. The cricket is left outside, at the threshold of the burrow, while the wasp goes inside. Soon the wasp emerges from the burrow and drags the cricket inside to her eggs. Then the female wasp leaves the burrow, sealing it shut and leaving the cricket as food for her young when they hatch.

Fabré discovered that, if he picked up the cricket while the female was inside the burrow and moved it a short distance away, the wasp would find the cricket and drop it at the threshold again before going back inside the burrow. Fabré moved the cricket away from the entrance to the burrow about forty times, and each time the wasp would drop the cricket at the entrance, never bypassing this link in the chain by dragging the cricket directly into the burrow. The wasp's behavior indicated that when such an instinctive chain is interrupted it must go to completion in the order prescribed; in many other instances, however, instinctive behavior is not so rigid or unmodifiable.

Classes of Animal Behavior. Scott (1958) has proposed a set of concepts to describe animal behavior. His system is oriented around an assumption that has guided the thinking of zoologists since the time of Charles Darwin — that behavior is "adaptive" (see Chapter 2). Scott identifies the following types of adaptive behavior: ingestive behavior, shelter seeking, agonistic behavior (fighting), sexual behavior, caregiving behavior (particularly to the young), eliminative behavior, allelomimetic behavior (responding in the same way as other animals that are in close proximity), and investigative behavior. Many of these response classes are part of the classification scheme for comparative analysis, as described in this chapter.

Concepts Applied To Behavior of Invertebrates.
A detailed system to classify the behavior of invertebrates has been proposed by Fraenkel and Gunn (1961). Their system is devised to "deal with the orientation of animals, the directions in which they walk or swim, and the reasons why particular directions are selected (p. 5)." An assumption underlying this descriptive system is that orienting reactions of animals are unlearned. The reactions of moths to flame or other sources of light is one such example of an unlearned orienting response. Fraenkel and Gunn attempted to devise a system that was applicable to quite different invertebrates from the amoeba through the insects. Thus, the descriptive system is relatively complex, but very useful for analyzing the behavior of many species. It may even be applied to the behavior of vertebrates, though little research along these lines has been undertaken.

Three classes of orienting reactions are identified: *kineses, taxes*, and *compass* reactions. Each class can be further subdivided, but such details are minimized here.

A *kinetic reaction* is one in which the animal moves in an *undirected manner* in response to some stimulus. When stimulation is terminated, or when the movements have led the animal to another set of stimuli that does not elicit kinetic reactions, then the undirected movements stop. An example of kinesis is the reaction of a paramecium to an increase in thermal stimulation. If its water medium is heated, the animal becomes more active and eventually stops when it has moved into a cooler area. Such a reaction is called a thermokinesis. In general, organisms with undifferentiated receptors show kinetic reactions.

(A *tactic reaction*, or taxis, was fully described in Chapter 3, and the reader may choose to skip to the last sentence of this paragraph.) A taxis is a response in which an animal moves in a *directed manner* toward or away from some stimulus. Thus, taxes are classified as positive (movement toward) or negative (movement away). In the case of a positive tactic response, the animal moves along a gradient of stimulation toward the source. Obviously then, the tactic reactions require rather highly developed receptors that are sensitive to the intensity of stimulation. For example, earthworms show negative tactic responses to light. If the stimulus is presented only briefly, then withdrawal is momentary. As in the case of kinetic reactions, the name of the source of stimulation is often included in the description of the taxis. So, for example, the behavior of the earthworm is called a negative phototactic reaction. (Such a phototaxis is exploited in the following chapter in a comparative analysis of learning in goldfish.) Other sources of stimulation that are associated with *directed movements*, both positive and negative, are chemical gradients (chemo-taxes), water pressure gradients (rheotaxes), body contact gradients (thigmotaxes), and gradients of gravitational pull (geotaxes). A complication in the analysis of orienting reactions comes from the fact that the reactions interact so that reaction to one gradient may be affected by the reaction to another (Ratner and VanDeventer, 1965).

Compass reactions, also called *transverse orientations*, are directed reactions in which the animal moves or adjusts itself so as to be at some fixed angle in relation to the direction of the gradient of stimulation. The most familiar examples of compass reactions involve the orientation of insects, such as ants and bees, to photic radiation. These animals often move about by temporarily navigating a path that is at some fixed angle from the direction of sunlight. Thus, for example, a bee may repeatedly orient from a source of food to the hive using a heading in relation to the angle of the sunlight. Such reactions require a receptor made up of a number of sensitive elements that are pointed in different directions — as in the eye of the insect. Transverse orientations are also made in response to gravitational fields. In this case an animal maintains some fixed orientation to the earth's gravitational field. Unlike other compass reactions, gravitational reactions are not movements toward some source, but rather are ways of maintaining the body's orientation.

The Concept of Learning: Modification of Innate Behavior. There is an interesting and important question related to innate behavior. To what extent can such behavior be modified in the lifetime of an animal? Can innate orienting and instinctive behaviors be changed? A basic view of learning it that it involves changing innate behaviors. Skinner (1938), for example, conceived of two kinds of learning. One, a modification of reflexes and smooth-muscle responses, was called *respondent learning*. The other, a modification of emitted movements and skeletal responses was called *operant learning*. Both types may be viewed as the modification of innate behavior processes. Denny and Ratner (1970) also make the assumption that learning involves the modification of innate behavior. (See also Chapter 5.)

General Experimental Psychology

The second component of comparative psychology involves contributions from general experimental psychology. Since comparative psychology is part of the subject matter of psychology, it must emphasize psychological rather than zoological processes and theories. This distinction has been missed by ethologists like Konrad Lorenz (1950), who stated: "An American journal masquerades under the title of *Comparative Psychology* although . . . no really comparative paper has ever really been published in it (p. 240)." Lorenz seems to mean that no research has been published that flows directly from the theory of evolution, which is

the central theory in comparative biology. Lorenz is correct in criticizing some of the weak uses of the theory of evolution that some psychologists have made. But these studies do not constitute the main theme of comparative psychology. They can be considered as weak examples of the application of evolutionary theory, frequently involving capricious comparisons — studies in which the behaviors of two different animals are compared because they are close at hand. An example of capricious comparison is running rats and chickens in a T maze. Since we already know that these animals differ in evolution and in many other ways, a comparison of their behaviors in the T maze tells us nothing about evolution and very little else.

General experimental techniques have strong positive characteristics and some perplexing limitations as they are used in comparative psychology. The limitations come primarily from the attitudes and style of experimental psychologists. From the point of view of the comparative psychologists, practically anything that moves the emphasis of the research away from the animal and its behavior toward the apparatus and the investigator's concepts is considered negative. All research is bound to some extent by the concepts and apparatus of the investigator, but failure to know the animal and its general behavior makes an experimental study of little use for the purposes of comparative analysis.

Contributions from General Experimental Psychology

The characteristics of general experimental psychology that coordinate positively with comparative psychology are many and varied. Two of the general contributions involve the methodology of experimental psychology and analysis in terms of stimulus and response. Specific contributions involve content from the studies of learning, perception, and physiological psychology.

The experimental method, particularly as

used in the laboratory, is a key contribution and an obvious one. Statistical procedures also contribute to comparative analysis as do the psychophysical methods for establishing stimulus thresholds and the like.

The stimulus-response language of behaviorists is not a necessary part of general experimental psychology, but it is closely associated with the experimental study of behavior from the time of John B. Watson and Ivan Pavlov. As Ratner and Denny (1964) point out, S-R concepts are particularly useful in comparative psychology because the concepts used by ethologists to describe orienting and other innate behaviors constitute a language that is roughly equivalent to the concepts of stimulus and response. So, for example, psychologists who study learning speak of unconditioned stimuli and unconditioned responses; ethologists speak of releasing stimuli and fixed action patterns. One can readily coordinate these two vocabularies when employing the comparative method.

As for content, virtually every topic that general experimeneal psychologists have studied has invaluable relevance for comparative psychology. But as discussed in Chapter 8, many of the facts about animal behavior, including facts about learning, were not discovered by experimental psychologists. For example, elephants were being trained for several thousand years by elaborate conditioning and instrumental learning techniques. These ancient methods are still being used in India, as the following report by Hallet (1968), an amateur observer, indicates.

. . . calves were then roped or netted, brought to the station, tethered to trees, and accustomed to the sight, sound, smell, and manner of men over a 10-month training period: Their *cornacs* talked to them, sang traditional Hindu songs, and plied them with sugar cane . . . The songs were all-important. Emotional as they are, elephants show extreme sensitivity to music. Circus elephahts sway in time to marches, trumpet excitedly when trumpets blow, and fall asleep during symphonies (p. 84).

The Comparative Method

The final ingredient of comparative psychology is the use of the comparative method. The approach is called the *Stages Method*. This method evolved from my reviewing the history of biology preceding the development of the theory of evolution and from reading the writings of a number of comparative psychologists like C. P. Stone (1951), R. H. Waters (1960), and M. E. Bitterman (1960) who have been seriously concerned with the question of the nature of comparative psychology.

Table 9.1 shows the six stages of comparative analysis and examples of the comparative psychologist's activities at each stage. These stages are sequential, but developments within one stage allow reanalysis in preceding and subsequent stages. One can think of comparative psychology as developing by "successive approximations." We start at stage I (Background Information), which then permits the first systematic attempt at classifying behavior (stage II). Systematic classification stresses the importance of having a more or less complete collection of background information and sets the stage for the development of powerful research preparations. The analysis continues with continual sharpening of activities at all stages, as each stage is developed. So, for example, the development of a powerful research preparation makes it possible to determine with precision the variables that affect a particular class of behavior.

No single stage is particularly unfamiliar when considered individually, but the stages provide a rather powerful analytic method when combined. In biology, for example, it appears that the comparative method, although unrecognized, slowly moved investigators from observing in the field to classification activities and finally to the development of the theory of evolution.

Table 9.1
Stages of Comparative Analysis and Sample Activities

Stage	Function	Sample Activity
I	Background and perspective	Review formal and informal sources
II	Classification of behavior	Determine major classes of behavior
III	Research preparations	Find clear examples of each class of behavior
IV	Variables	Use preparations to find effects of variables
V	Relations and comparisons	Show relations among behavior classes across species
VI	General theory	Postulate general mechanisms relative to behavior of organisms

The Stages

The first four stages are considered to be *preparatory stages* that precede specific comparisons. Stages V and VI are the ones that involve comparison and general theory.

Stage I: Background Information. One of the most conspicuous characteristics of biology, the queen of comparative studies, is the breadth and depth of background information that Darwin and others had available. For well over a thousand years, gentlemen scientists, naturalists, professional biologists, explorers, and the like, had walked through the woods or in other ways viewed the biological scene and written about it. The life histories of hundreds of species of birds, mammals, and other creatures were carefully reported. In much the same way, information on the behavior of organisms must be collected as the first stage of the comparative method in psychology. Background information gives the investigator a broad appreciation for the events that interest him or her, together with ideas about the important characteristics that can be used in classifying these events.

The point about acquiring background information is not unique to comparative analysis; every research study involves a search of the literature. But in the comparative method the search must come early in the inquiry and use both *formal* and *informal* sources of information. Both types of sources are needed for *breadth* and *perspective*. Remember that the final goal of this method is general theory. Breadth and perspective at the early stages fit this goal. In addition, a thorough search of background information increases the chance that the inquiry is valid. Professor M. E. Bitterman, for example, reported to me that he spent more than two years preparing to do research with sea crabs. The rule of the thumb is: "If in doubt, get information."

Charles Darwin's reflections in his autobiography on the developmental course of the theory of evolution illustrate the use of background information. Darwin reported:

After my return to England it appeared to me that . . . by collecting all facts which bear in any way on the variation of animals and plants under domestication and nature, some light might perhaps be thrown on the whole subject. My first notebook was opened in July, 1837. I worked on true Baconian principles, and without any theory collected facts on a wholesale scale, more especially with respect to domesticated productions, by printed inquiries, by conversation with skillful breeders and gardeners, and by extensive reading. When I see the list of books of all kinds which I read and abstracted, including whole series of Journals and Transactions, I am surprised at my industry.

For the comparative psychologist one of the primary sources of background information comes from the area of *animal behavior*. The field of animal behavior has formal sources (journals and professional books) and informal sources that include naturalists, animal breeders, hunters, and animal management personnel. *Biological Abstracts*, available in most libraries, is well indexed both for behavior classes and species.

While psychologists are typically conscientious about searching formal sources for background material about human behavior, they seem to make little use of informal sources. Alcoholics Anonymous and the Christian Science Church, for example, deal with thousands of adult humans in ways that bear a relation to clinical and social psychology. The great southern preachers seem to be experts at persuasion. The psychologist who wants to get some breadth and perspective on human behavior might profit from contact with these informal sources.

Stage II: Behavior Classification. After an investigator has some appreciation for the breadth and general characteristics of the behaviors of organisms, he or she is ready to sort behaviors into classes. This is a difficult and elusive task, but biologists and chemists, for example, had a similar task and eventually achieved success. The classification, or taxonomy, of behavior, may yield tentative results because the classification system undergoes change as background information accrues and later stages of analysis are improved.

The importance of classification of behavior can be seen in a number of ways. First, consider the state of chemistry if chemists did not know what elements they had in their test tubes. Consider also the difficulty of doing zoological work with sea animals if zoologists only had the three classes: sea animal, land animal, and air animal. The zoologist might indiscriminately and unknowingly mix fish with lobsters and shrimp. The "error" in such research would be very large.

It is difficult to imagine biology without an adequate taxonomy of animal forms, and chemistry without a periodic table. But such conditions did exist for a long time while these sciences were working through the preparatory stages of comparative analysis. While chemists and biologists have been successful, comparative psychologists have not yet provided us with an adequate classification of behavior. Denny and Ratner (1970) have presented a tentative classification that draws heavily on concepts from animal behavior. They describe major types of behavior that are considered to be innate: appetitive (orienting) behaviors, consummatory behaviors, and postconsummatory behaviors. *Appetitive*, or *preconsummatory, behaviors* involve actions that precede and move an organism toward consummatory behaviors. Examples are courting, searching for food, and freezing when an unfamiliar noise occurs. *Consummatory behaviors* involve the vital activities of organisms such as copulating, feeding, reacting to predators, and caring for the body surface. Consummatory activities are rigidly stereotyped in form in many species. However, this stereotypy is decreased to some extent in a number of domesticated species, including humans. *Postconsummatory behaviors*, such as scratching the earth after eliminating, are only relatively stereotyped and follow immediately after consummatory behaviors. Their main function is to move the organism to the next appetitive-consummatory-postconsummatory sequence.

Table 9.2 presents the list of consummatory behaviors and examples of each. In reviewing the list you will see that not all animals show all of these behaviors in an obvious way. Nesting and caring for the young are minimal in some species, fighting is minimal in others, and so forth. This is a characteristic of animals and their behavior and is not a negative recommendation for the classification system. The list in Table 9.2 is heavily loaded with behaviors that characterize the activities of infrahumans and may omit a number of behaviors that characterize humans. For example, how should we classify the activities that are involved in writing a chapter such as this

Table 9.2
Taxonomy of Consummatory Behaviors and Related Biological Processes Arranged in Order of Behavioral Development in High Vertebrates[a]

Behavior class	Biological system	Example
Resting	Recuperative	Sleeping
Contacting	Arousal	Visual following
Eliminating	Eliminative	Urinating
Drinking	Ingestive	Sucking
Feeding	Ingestive	Pecking
Care of body surface	Skin sensitivity	Grooming
Predator defenses	Defensive	Immobility reaction
Fighting	Defensive	Biting
Sexual behavior	Reproductive	Ejaculating
Nesting	Reproductive	Fur pulling
Care of the young	Reproductive	Retrieving

one? Can we subsume such human behavior within the present system of classification or should other categories be added? Perhaps writing about a topic and displaying this writing might be considered a highly evolved form of establishing and marking a territory that leads to avoidance and deference from competitors. The concept of territorial marking is used by analogy in this case, but careful analysis of both human and infrahuman territorial behavior may show that the concept is appropriate once the later stages of comparative study are advanced. On the other hand, we may have to add new categories that reflect unique human behaviors, even if these occur for only a small part of the population.

One of the ideas behind the classification of behavior as shown in Table 9.2 is that it permits a psychologist to describe the behavior of the individual organism in these terms. We can say that a rat is showing the appetitive and consummatory components of feeding or resting. We can also apply this scheme to human behavior. When young men are in the presence of females, much of the behavior of these young men can be described as courting, the appetitive component associated with attracting females for copulation. The men may strut, flex arms, and engage in man-to-man sparring, much as the young males of other species do.

Denny and Ratner (1970) see the process of learning as representing the modification of certain features of innate behavior. One common example of modification of innate behavior in rats involves changing the appetitive component of feeding and the typical reactions to predators (in threatening situations) to a learned sequence of instrumental behavior. In a T maze, for instance, the rat gradually learns to run faster and more unerringly to the arm of the maze containing food. In this case, a chain of appetitive responses associated with feeding and exploring are established, and some of the rat's responses to threat are reduced or eliminated through *habituation.*

Procedures for classifying events are relatively complex, often unfamiliar to psychologists, or not directly applicable to psychology. Jensen (1967), a comparative psychologist, has described a method for classification which has been mainly applied to types of learning in invertebrates. The basic premise of this system, called *polythetic taxonomy,* is that things are grouped together "by overall similarity, i.e., by the presence of a sizeable number of the many characteristics typical of the group (p. 45)." Based on work by Sokal and Sneath (1963), this scheme contrasts with the older procedure of classification by *monothetic similarity.* In monothetic classification, events are grouped together if they share one important characteristic. Jensen believes that the use of monothetic classification has led to the controversy about whether or not lower organisms learn. In other words, a number of different criteria may need to be satisfied before the process of learning can be inferred.

A second important consideration in classification involves the use of *functional classification* as opposed to *structural classification*. This means identifying classes and putting events together based on "what is happening" or "what they do" rather than putting them together on the basis of "sharing some static or structural feature." An example of functional classification comes from Skinner (1938) who classified neutral stimuli as S^Ds, S^Δs, or S^rs based on how an animal responded to the stimuli, rather than the physical properties of the stimuli.

The classification that is suggested in Table 9.2 attempts to use polythetic, functional principles. Other characteristics and requirements of classification are illustrated by Bitterman's discussion of types of learning (1960).

Stage III: Research Preparations. As previously mentioned, not all classes of behavior are shown with clarity by all animals under all conditions. In other words, the study of a class of behavior requires a situation (preparation) in which the process shows itself clearly. The third stage of comparative analysis deals with the discovery and characterization of *research preparations* that have sufficient clarity to permit study of the class of behavior identified in stage II. Research preparations can be thought of as "good examples" or "archetypes," but these labels do not express the full sense of powerful research preparations.

The tradition of comparative study, as seen in biology and chemistry, includes the search for clear examples of classes of events and processes. Zoologists, for example, continue to seek preparations for research that have properties that are clearly characteristic of a particular phylum or class within a phylum. The phylum Annelida (segmented worms) and the class Oligochaete has many members, some of which show the features of this calss more clearly than others. The familiar research preparation for this class is the earthworm, *Lumbricus terrestris*. Other species within this class are not as suitable as research preparations. Similarly, physiologists use the giant axon (nerve) of the squid as the appropriate structural preparation for studying aspects of nerve physiology. The axon is long, large in diameter, relatively accessible, readily procured; and most important, it is true neural tissue. So the tradition of comparative analysis clearly suggests that one of the stages of the comparative method in psychology should be the search for powerful research preparations.

We can consider an anthropologist to be a comparative sociologist, and, when we do, the reasons that anthropologists go to "strange places" make more sense. They may be collecting background information, but a lot of this has already been done. Instead, the anthropologist may be using a research preparation that has obvious characteristics of the particular social process that is of interest to him or her, such as a particular type of kinship system.

Although self-conscious attention to research preparations is not an integral part of psychological research, psychologists already have some research preparations that are coordinated with the narrow spectrum classifications that they use. There are research preparations for the two main types of learning. The use of the maze and the lever-pressing apparatus with food reward for hungry laboratory rats constitute preparations for the study of instrumental learning; the salivation to meat powder and the eyelid-closing procedures used with dogs and humans, respectively, constitute research preparations for the study of classical conditioning.

Powerful research preparations have a number of characteristics that are reflected in the use of the giant axon of the squid for the study of neural activity: (1) research preparations represent the response class or process in a *valid* way, (2) they yield *reliable* information about the response class under consideration, (3) they offer a very *clear* example of the process under study, and (4) the preparations are *convenient*. An evaluation of these characteristics of a research preparation is difficult in psychology, but concern with the question of powerful preparations should make it easier to reach later stages of analysis.

Webb et al., (1966) has described some of the details for establishing the validity and reliability of preparations, including methods for standardizing procedures. Ratner (1968) has examined the reliability of a preparation for studying learning by planaria; the results of this analysis were disappointing since the reliability of performance was very low. Wilson and Collins (1967) studied the reliability of observers who scored the responses involved in planarian learning and found that the observers agreed with one another in scoring behavior on a single trial, but from Ratner's data we know that the animals are erratic from trial to trial. There is the further question of whether the behavior changes that the planaria show can be considered valid examples of learning (Jensen, 1967).

To say that a powerful research preparation shows the process clearly means that it is maximally conspicuous and unconfounded by other processes. The laboratory rat, and especially the albino rat, makes a weak preparation for the study of visual factors in learning, for vision is poor in comparison with olfaction. In a powerful research preparation, visual factors should predominate, as they would in a preparation that used birds as the test animal. So within the past few years, investigators who are interested in the stimulus control of learned responses through visual cues use pigeons, and those who are interested in maze learning or shock-avoidance learning use rats.

Preparations for comparative psychology involve more than the test animal itself, although we frequently refer to the preparation in terms of the test animal. A preparation includes *the animal, the test situation, the procedures for measurement,* and *the antecedent conditions.* Weakness at any of these points reduces the value of the preparation. The best research preparations are not necessarily the simplest; that is, a process that appears simple often has other processes bound with it, so that the process under study may be obscured and difficult to isolate. It is partly for this reason that the study of learning with single-celled organisms is a weak preparation. Such animals feed, reproduce, and make orienting responses that mask learning, assuming that it occurs.

A good research preparation, including animal and apparatus, for studying a variety of behavior is described as follows.[1]

*As early as 1917, Baldwin constructed semi-natural habitat for the purpose of studying the daily activity of earthworms in their burrows. Their apparatus, which has been profitably used by several investigators besides ourselves, consists of two glass sheets about 20 by 15 inches held 1/4 inch apart by grooved pieces of wood. Soil is packed into the space between the glass plates and the worm or worms are introduced into the apparatus where they eventually establish a burrow system that is visible through the glass. Using such a habitat, Baldwin found activity to peak in the common earthworm (*Lumbricus terrestris*) from 6 P.M. to midnight. Evans (1947) found that* Allolobophora calignosa *constructed interconnecting burrows near the surface with U-shaped entrances and suggested that the several deep burrows served as retreats in the event of adverse environmental conditions. Khalaf and Ghabbour (1964) repli-*

[1]From an unpublished document by S. C. Ratner and L. E. Gardner on the behavior of earthworms.

cated Evans' findings using A. calignosa *found in Egypt, and concluded that the different ecological conditions of Egypt did not affect burrowing behavior.*

Roots (1956), who also used the semi-natural habitat, found that some species of earthworm, such as terrestris, *uniformly avoid habitats immersed in water and choose moist air-filled soil, whereas some individuals of other species, such as* calignosa, *were always found in the water-filled soil.*

Gardner and Ratner (1970), who explored several behavior classes of L. terrestris *in the seminatural environment by observing the worms over a 4-week period, found the mechanics of the burrowing process were similar for all of worms: Within 12 hours they started the burrow at a depression or irregularity in the soil. The worms then ate their way through the soil, depositing the piling around the perimeter of the burrow entrance. After the worms reached a depth of 15 to 20 centimeters, they ceased to deposit pilings at the surface and began "plastering" the sides of the burrow instead. On about the twelfth day the worms started to rework the pilings at the burrow entrances; that is, they dragged pieces of sphagnum moss, twine, and cellophane paper, which were on a shelf by the burrow entrance, and worked them into the moistened pilings. When completed, these pilings, or burrow crowns, were about 4 centimeters high and resembled tufts of dry grass. Presumably this structure functions to conceal the burrow, to impede water drainage, and to provide extended foraging area while the worm's posterior remains in the burrow.*

From these observations, four stages in the establishment of a burrow system were identified: initiation of burrowing, burrowing, food collection, crowning, and resting. These stages, or broad behavior classes, subsumed a number of specific stimulus-response units. For example, the initiation stage included

lack of body contact on the open surface as an elicitor of movement, a surface irregularity as the stimulus for insertion of the prostomium into the depression, and increasing body contact as a stimulus for continued burrowing.

One instance of mating behavior was observed in the 4-week period — one that suggested the possibility of "courting behavior" in L. terrestris. *The rather complicated "courting" sequence lasted for about 15 minutes and was followed by a 3-hour copulation session.*

The use of the seminatural habitat has allowed investigators to study many behaviors that occur in the normal environment but are not observable from the surface. This apparatus could well be used in the investigation of behavior processes ordinarily studied on the surface, as in classical conditioning and habituation, for example.

Stage IV: Variables. Armed with a powerful research preparation, the investigator is now ready to identify the variables and interactions among the variables that affect the behavior in question. This constitutes the conventional activity of experimental psychology. In a comparative study, a number of variables almost automatically suggest themselves: age of the animal, sex, and species. Results related to these variables convey information about the *generality of the behavior.* A behavior that is exhibited across age, both sexes, and a variety of species is obviously general. Other important variables to study include temporal conditions: intertrial interval, stimulus duration, interstimulus interval, and duration of shock and nonshock intervals.

Notice that at this stage of comparative analysis the contributions of general experimental psychology are substantial. Notice also that a powerful research preparation makes it possible to detect the effects of variables in a clear, unconfounded way. If little is known about the behavior process, the investigator may need to use *field*, or naturalistic, studies to get some hints about the types of variables that affect the behavior. This is frequently done by ethologists to good use (Hinde and Tinbergen, 1958; Klopfer and Hailman, 1967). I have used the field method at several points in the study of predator defenses that have been called animal hypnosis or tonic immobility (Ratner, 1967).

Stage V: Comparisons and Relations. One of the more fully developed examples of comparison in psychology comes from the narrow spectrum classification of types of learning as developed by Hilgard and Marquis (1940). In a similar vein Kimble (1961) compared instrumental and classical learning. In this analysis he assumed that the classification of types of learning was valid and that powerful research preparations had been used to identify variables and effects. Chapter 10 by Zerbolio represents an extensive exercise in working out Stage V of the comparative method, specifically with reference to these two categories of learning.

I have had the opportunity to do an exercise in comparative analysis that moved from the preparatory stages, I to IV, to stage V (Ratner, 1967). In this case, I was concerned with a large and unorganized mass of naturalistic and experimental material that has been called "animal hypnosis." Previous attempts to deal with this material had started at stage V, although this was not clearly recognized by those concerned. Pavlov, the father of classical conditioning, related animal hypnosis to inhibitory neural processes in 1927; Gilman and Marcuse (1949) related it to fear; and Volgyesi (1966) related it to human hypnosis.

The approach I took for this narrow-spectrum comparative problem involved all five stages of comparative analysis. I started by reviewing both formal and informal sources of background information on animals that became immobile, including material from general experimental psychology. At stage V, I concluded that the

behaviors that were called animal hypnosis were related to the class of behaviors we called *predator defenses* and are best described as *immobility displays*. The response called animal hypnosis represents one of the kinds of displays animals make when predators attack them — when the distance between prey and predator reaches zero (see also Chapters 8 and 21.)

Another example of stage V is pointing out that most, if not all, consummatory responses also have preconsummatory as well as postconsummatory components.

Stage VI: General Theory. The final stage of comparative analysis involves postulation of the general mechanisms that integrate what we know about the behavior of organisms. In chemistry this took the form of atomic theory and in biology it took the form of the theory of evolution. Earlier attempts at general theory had occurred in both biology and chemistry; such theories were approximations to the later and more adequate ones, as work at different stages led to modifications of the theories, illustrating the continuous interplay among the stages of analysis.

Psychology certainly has no shortage of theories: psychoanalytic theory, generalized forms of learning theory, information processing theory, and physiological theories. The general mechanisms that are proposed by these theories, such as pleasure-pain principles, S-R reinforcement principles, or DNA-RNA principles, often have precursors in earlier general theories that were based on very slim support. Aristotle, for example, proposed a classification of memory into short-term and long-term memory, plus a general theory to relate these processes. The classification may be useful, but Aristotle's theory is inadequate.

It is my premise that a general theory in comparative psychology will develop from a conscientious application of the six stages of comparative analysis to the content and ideas of animal behavior and general experimental psychology. Such a theory will help integrate what we know about the diversity of behavior of organisms much as the theory of evolution has helped us understand the diversity of animal forms.

Study Questions

1. Distinguish between kinesis and taxis.

2. List and briefly describe all stages of the method of comparative analysis.

3. What is a good research preparation and what does it include?

4. List the eleven classes of behavior common to most, if not all, animals.

5. What components of behavior are shared by each of these classes?

10

An Application of the Comparative Method: Is Conditioned Avoidance a Classical or Instrumental Process in Goldfish?

Dominic J. Zerbolio, Jr.

University of Missouri — St. Louis

Editor's Note.   *As pointed out in the Introduction, Zerbolio's chapter has a different mission than the other chapters in this book. It attempts to present the "nitty gritty" involved in making a comparative analysis and shows that such research can be a time consuming, though rewarding, effort. The chapter illustrates in detail what Ratner was globally concerned about in Chapter 9. Instructors with a methodological bent should be particularly interested in having their students study this chapter.*

Since 1960 when Horner, Longo, and Biterman (1960, 1961) introduced an avoidance shuttlebox for fish, a substantial amount of research on shuttle avoidance with goldfish has been completed by several investigators. A major question in regard to this research, especially in the context of Ratner's comparative method, is whether the goldfish learns to avoid by way of a classically conditioned or instrumentally learned response. Commonly used subjects, like rats and dogs, learn avoidance instrumentally, that is, because the shock is terminated or kept from occurring by occurrences of the learned response. But does the goldfish learn this way? This chapter discusses these learning processes and the control procedures needed to identify them, and attempts to answer this question as well as possible through reference to a number of recent research studies.

The Apparatus

The typical shuttlebox used with goldfish is shown in Figure 10.1. It is an oblong plastic box, about 12 inches long, 4 to 5 inches wide, and 4 to 5 inches high. The box is divided into two end compartments by an insert, usually called a hurdle, which restricts the water depth in the center to about 3/4 of an inch. The hurdle, with 45° sloping sides, has a flat top about 3 inches long, and when the fish crosses the hurdle it must pass through the two photobeams located at the ends of the flat top of the hurdle. This size box easily accommodates fish about 2 inches long. The conditioned stimulus (CS), or warning signal, has

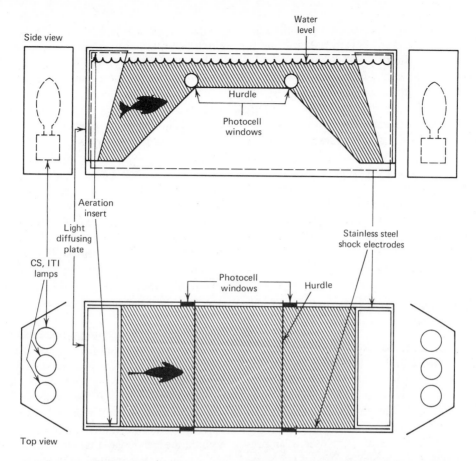

Figure 10.1 A stylized drawing of a shuttlebox for goldfish. The shaded area is open to the animal. The photo-cells are used to detect the subject's movement and position. The lamps provide the illumination or color-change stimuli, and the stainless steel plates deliver the US.

usually been a small light bulb (or bulbs) located at the ends of the box. A translucent diffusing plate covers the bulbs to provide even lighting over the inside ends. The unconditioned stimulus (US) is electric shock, delivered through conductive material affixed to the interior sides of the box. In Figure 10.1, stainless steel plates are shown. The experimenter cannot turn on shock as in a rat apparatus, for even small durations of continuous shock will tetanize a fish. Thus, the typical procedure calls for pulsed shock (e.g., 200 milliseconds on, 800 milliseconds off). Additionally, Figure 10.1 shows three light bulbs at the end

of each compartment. These bulbs can be of different color and/or illumination (wattage) which, with appropriate programing, can provide the experimenter with a variety of CS and intertrial interval (ITI) conditions.

A Typical Avoidance Trial

A typical active avoidance trial proceeds as follows. The CS is turned on for a period of time prior to the presentation of the US (the CS interval). If the CS interval elapses without the fish's shuttling (swimming from the end it is on at trial onset through the photobeams on top of the hurdle to the other side), the US is initiated. Usually the US will elicit a shuttling response, but this is not always true, especially in the early phases of training. When a subject shuttles during the CS interval prior to US onset, it is called an avoidance. If a subject tarries until after the US starts, it is called an escape. Usually there is a limit on the number of shocks administered to a subject on any one trial. If the US period elapses without the subjects shuttling, it is a nonresponse trial. Of course, this does not mean that the fish has not responded, but just that, of the responses it made, none had served to transport it across the hurdle on that trial.

The Two-Factor Explanation of Avoidance Learning

The generally accepted explanation of how a subject learns to avoid by shuttling during the CS interval is called the two-factor theory of avoidance. Let us look at this explanation in detail. During the initial phases of training and before the subject has learned to respond in the CS interval, the CS and US are paired or presented together. This pairing of CS and US is not because the experimenter planned it that way, but because the subject, by failing to respond during the CS interval, allows it to occur. As a result of the CS-US pairing, the subject acquires a fear response to the previously neutral CS. Conditioning of fear to the CS by virtue of its being classically paired with the US is the first factor of the theory.

In addition to acquiring a fear response to the CS, the subject also learns how to escape from the US. When the subject shuttles during the US, the US is immediately terminated; and the shuttle-escape response is thereby reinforced. Because of the way the stimulus events are programmed, if an escape response occurs during the CS interval, it terminates the CS and pre-

vents the occurrence of the US for that trial. Such an anticipatory response is called an avoidance. Thus escape from the US can be viewed as the prototype for the avoidance response.

When the subject makes an avoidance response, terminating the CS, the fear originally elicited by the CS is presumably reduced. This reduction in fear is the second factor in the two-factor theory — the one that reinforces avoidance responding. Thus an avoidance response can be viewed as an escape from the fear-provoking CS.

In the typical avoidance-learning procedure, escape from the CS is similar, if not identical, to the escape response from the US. From the perspective of the animal and two-factory theory, an avoidance does not prevent the occurrence of the US but terminates the CS, and calling it an avoidance response is, in this sense, a misnomer. The criterion for labeling a response is the point in time when the response occurs. If the response occurs during the CS interval prior to US onset, it is called "avoidance"; but theoretically it is an escape from the CS. If the response occurs after the US onset, it is an escape from the US; but regardless of the name, neither response is an avoidance response that is reinforced by the omission of a stimulus that has yet to occur. [From another point of view, for example, Denny's relaxation theory (1971), this is not the case. The omission of the US brings about relief or relaxation, which is the reinforcing state of affairs.]

Why Goldfish?

Using the conditioned avoidance procedure and the apparatus described, investigators have discovered a good deal about learning in goldfish. Acquisition performance is related to US intensity (Bintz, 1971); US power or duration X intensity (Zerbolio and Wickstra, 1975); the intertrial interval (Pinckney, 1966); locus of CS (Gallon, 1974; Zerbolio and Wickstra, 1976a); trial distribution (Wickstra and Zerbolio, 1976; Zerbolio, 1976); and color changes in the CS (Zerbolio and Wickstra, 1976b), to name a few. The last item is interesting because goldfish are sensitive to color (Yager, 1968), whereas most laboratory animals used by behaviorists, with the exception of birds and apes, are not. In addition, goldfish are poikilothermic or cold blooded: this fact has great potential value in studies concerned with the biochemistry of learning and memory formation (Rozin, 1968). Whereas attempts to change the temperature of the central nervous system (CNS) of warm-blooded animals or homoiotherms, except in the very young, will result in a comatose state or death, goldfish can and do tolerate surprisingly wide ranges of temperature, as several studies have shown (Prosser and Nagai, 1968; Riege and Cherkin, 1971: Zerbolio, 1973). Changing the CNS metabolic rate by simply changing the temperature of the environment is an attractive procedure. But, like any other procedure, it is important to understand what the subject is doing or learning under nominal or control conditions before conclusions about the effects of various other conditions are contemplated. This is especially true if the experimenter hopes to generalize his or her findings to account for behavior in other species.

Are Goldfish Different?

Before the problem of how goldfish learn an avoidance response is tackled — whether they are basically different from homoiotherms in this type of learning — the two basic learning processes will be described. Although a large number of differences have been suggested historically to distinguish between classical (Pavlovian) conditioning and instrumental learning, most of them, through extensive research, have been eliminated. There is one critical difference — the consequence of the animal's response.

In the active instrumental procedure, which was outlined earlier in the chapter, the presenta- tion of the US is contingent on the subject's response. Specifically, a subject is shocked if and only if it does not make the appropriate response. If a subject does make the appropriate response, which in this case is shuttling during the CS interval, the CS is terminated and no shock occurs. The animal can control both CS duration and the frequency of shock by its response.

In the classical procedure, described in every introductory text, the CS and US are repeatedly paired. On each trial, regardless of what the animal does or does not do, the CS and US are presented. Obviously the classical procedure does not allow the subject to control the CS duration or the frequency of shocks; the duration of the CS and the presentation of the US are completely independent of the subject's response. Learning occurring under the classical procedure is thought to be simpler than under the instrumental procedure because, in the classical procedure, the subject does not have to acquire any "knowledge" of the consequences of its response in regard to terminating the CS or US.

The Problem

While comparing the classical with the instrumental procedures in an active avoidance situation with the goldfish, Woodard and Bitterman (1971, 1973) found that their instrumentally trained animals did not respond during the CS interval significantly above the levels shown by classically trained subjects. This finding prompted Mackintosh (1974) to say "that goldfish would swim from one compartment of a shuttlebox to another just as readily when shocks were unavoidable (classically trained) as when a swimming response resulted in the omission of shock (instrumentally trained)". In their original work, Woodard and Bitterman (1973) stated, "It seems, then, that all of our data on avoidance conditioning in goldfish can be accounted for without reference to a process of instrumental learning," and "Whether there is anything like instrumental avoidance learning in goldfish remains, therefore, to be demonstrated." (p. 128).

One implication of their results is that goldfish learn to respond during the CS interval without acquiring any "knowledge" of the consequences of their response. Only a few responses studied in the laboratory have failed to show additional learning when an instrumental avoidance contingency has been used (toe twitch in humans, Turner and Solomon, 1962; nictitating membrane response in rabbits, Gormezano, 1965). In the main, the instrumental training procedure augments CS response performance over that shown by the classical training procedure. What is surprising about Woodard and Bitterman's (1973) finding is that a motor response as complex as shuttle avoidance is not amenable to augmentation by an instrumental procedure. But there may be an alternative explanation for their results. In order to follow through on this lead, one must first understand the process by which evidence for "learning" is gathered and how alternative interpretations of the "learned" effects are eliminated.

Requirements for Concluding a Response Has Been Learned

Kimble (1967) states that "the standard procedure for producing a classically conditioned response (CR), or a response in the CS-interval, involves pairing CS and US at some fixed relationship in time." But, as Kimble points out, how is one to know if the presentation of the CS alone, the US alone, or random pairings of CS and US might not produce very similar if not identical effects? One important operation required to demonstrate learning is to run control procedures whose sole function is to rule out or eliminate alternative explanations for the phenomenon observed. The most commonly run control group is a group in which the CS and US

are presented *unpaired*, frequently called a pseudoconditioning control (Kimble, 1961 and 1967). The usual assumption is that the pseudoconditioning control represents everything that other controls might do. But again, as Kimble points out, this assumption may not be sound. Indeed, current work by Rescorla (1967) suggests that, in the pseudoconditioning procedure, the CS may come to stand for the absence of the US, as suggested earlier by Pavlov (1927) and Mowrer (1960) (see also Chapter 5).

In order to conclude that learning is occurring in the experimental group, one must compare the performance curves of all control procedures with the experimental (true learning) procedure. The set of curves in Figure 10.2 is idealized, but shows how the experimenter would compare performances under different procedures to rule out alternative explanations for the conclusion that learning occurred in the experimental group. Initially, let us assume that all curves presented in Figure 10.2 represent responses that occur during the CS interval over blocks of trials. Note that, if the instrumental procedure is being run, a CS-interval response is an avoidance response and would both terminate the CS and prevent the occurrence of the US. This is not necessarily so for the other procedures, but the responses shown are all from the CS interval, or its equivalent in time, although such responses may not be in any way related to the US or avoidance.

Instrumental Procedure

In the instrumental procedure (see Figure 10.2), the CS and US are paired, but a response during the CS interval (avoidance) terminates the CS and prevents the occurrence of the US. This is called an *active* avoidance procedure because an active response is required during the CS interval to prevent the occurrence of the US. If learning occurs with this procedure, there should be a progressive increase in the number of CS intervals in which at least one response occurs. Note that the

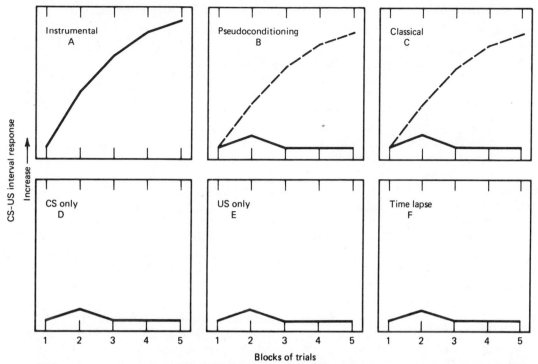

Figure 10.2 A stylized drawing representing the expected performances of homoiotherms trained under various learning and control procedures. Shown is the mean number of CS-intervals where at least one response occurred. The solid lines show the expected performances needed to conclude that the learning was instrumental, and the dashed lines represent what would be anomalous performances for homoiotherms. Panels A, B, C are the traditional groups run [Kimble, (1967)] and the panels D, E, and F the additional controls recommended by Jensen (1961).

plot indicates the number of CS intervals in which there is at least one response, not the frequency of responses in the CS interval per se. A subject may respond (shuttle) more than once in the CS interval, but only the initial response in any CS interval counts as an avoidance. The curve in Figure 10.2*a* is a typical negatively accelerated learning curve.

Pseudoconditioning Procedure

In the pseudoconditioning procedure (see Figure 10.2*b*), the same number of CS and US presentations are administered as in the instrumental procedure, but the CSs and USs are randomly presented, usually with the constraint that they

are never paired. Figure 10.2*b* (solid line) shows the frequency of CS intervals over blocks of trials in which at least one shuttle response occurs. In this procedure the CS period is identical in length to the CS interval of the instrumental procedure but, of course, is not followed by the US; and a CS interval response does not result in the omission of the unpaired US. As Figure 10.2*b* shows, a slight rise followed by a return to essentially a zero level is the expected performance curve. If, for instance, there were an increase in CS responding comparable to the instrumental procedure (Figure 10.2*b*, dashed line) this would mean that the paired presentation of CS and US is not necessary to produce increased CS responding over trials.

Classical Procedure

In the classical procedure for the shuttle box situation (see Figure 10.2c), the CS and US are presented in exactly the same way as in the instrumental procedure, but the subject's response does not terminate the CS or prevent the US. The US occurs at the end of the CS interval, no matter what the animal does. Obviously we can still measure the incidence of responding during the CS interval in exactly the same way as if a response did prevent the US. The normal expectation, based on work with dogs, rats, and other homoiothermic animals, is that for a response like the shuttle response, which is more an operant than a respondent response, there would be a slight rise in CS interval response rate followed by a return to baseline (Figure 10.2c, solid line), very much like that expected for the pseudoconditioning procedure (Figure 10.2b, solid line). If the curve resulting from the classical procedure were to show the negatively accelerated shape similar to the instrumental curve (Figure 10.2c, dashed line), this would imply, given that the pseudoconditioning curve is flat, that the CS-US pairing is necessary, but that the response-contingent termination of the CS and omission of the US (avoidance) is not necessary to produce an increase in response rate during the CS interval.

The procedures above are the commonly used ones, but, as Jensen (1961) points out, the experimenter should run three other control groups in addition to the pseudoconditioning control procedure: a CS only, a US only, and a group with *only* a lapse of time for the period consumed by the conditioning procedure. Ordinarily, these additional controls are assumed to be superfluous; for the pseudoconditioning procedure is thought to account for everything these other groups would do (Kimble, 1967). The details of these procedures are as follows:

CS-Only Procedure

In this procedure (see Figure 10.2d), the CS is presented for a period of time equivalent to the CS interval of the instrumental procedures, but the US never occurs. The number of trials in which a CS interval response occurs is plotted over trial blocks and appears in Figure 10.2d, and the typical expectation is a fairly flat performance curve (Figure 10.2d) very similar to the pseudoconditioning curve (Figure 10.2b, solid line).

US-Only Procedure

In the US-only procedure (see Figure 10.2e), the response measure is the same as it has been in the CS interval for either the classical or instrumental procedures, except there is no CS. If we were to run either the classical or instrumental procedures with the CS light turned off, we would have a US-only procedure. The unsignaled 10-second period prior to the US is temporally comparable to the CS period of the other procedures, and the incidence of response in this pre-US period is the measure of response we use for the US-only procedure.

The US-only procedure can be run with either a "classical" US or an "instrumental" US. In the first case, a response in the pre-US interval does not affect the US presentation, which is comparable to the classical procedure. In the second case, a response in the pre-US period prevents the US for that "trial," which is similar to the instrumental procedure. The "instrumental" US-only procedure is, on the surface, similar to procedures using unsignaled shock such as in Sidman avoidance in which each response postpones the shock for a specified interval. But in the Sidman technique, the time between shocks (without responding) is fixed and carefully controlled. In the "instrumental" US-only procedure, the time between shocks is a variable time period, like the time between trials in the instrumental or classical procedures. In both the "classical" and "instrumental" US-only case, however, the expected responses rate in the pre-US interval is flat and, as shown in Figure 10.2e, comparable to the pseudoconditioning curve (Figure 10.2b, solid line).

Time-Lapse Procedure

In the time-lapse procedure (see Figure 10.2f), the animal is simply placed in the experimental apparatus for the same time period as are the other subjects, but no stimuli, CS or US, are administered. However, the subject's response rate in the blank CS period is measured. Thus, the rate of CS interval responding over trials is measured in exactly the same way as in the other procedures, but of course no stimuli are presented. The CS interval response rate is again expected to be relatively flat, as shown in Figure 10.2f, and is similar to results with the pseudoconditioning procedure.

The six graphs in Figure 10.2 summarize what would be expected to occur under the procedures outlined. Woodard and Bitterman (1973) found no significant difference between the goldfish run under the instrumental and classical conditioning procedures, obtaining results comparable to Figure 10.2a and the dashed line of Figure 10.2c, a finding which we have replicated in our laboratory several times. Following the law of parsimony, Woodard and Bitterman (1973) concluded that all of their avoidance conditioning data could be accounted for without reference to an instrumental learning process.

But what appears to be the most parsimonious explanation may not always be the correct one, especially in the face of new data. An alternative explanation of the phenomenon reported by Woodard and Bitterman (1973) lies in comparing what goldfish do under seldomly used control conditions with the typical expectations for homoiotherm data, for example, for rats.

Experiment 1

In this experiment, all goldfish were run twenty trials a day for 5 consecutive days. The CS was the onset of a 7.5-watt blue light and the US was a 7.5-volt A.C. shock of 200 millisecond duration. The intertrial interval period (ITI) was dark. All groups had ten subjects and were treated identically except for the training procedures. Two experimental groups were run, a true "instrumental" and a true "classical" procedure. True instrumental means that both the termination of the CS and omission of the US were controlled by the subject's response; responding during the 10-second CS interval terminated the CS and brought about the omission of the US on that trial. True classical means that CS duration and US presentation were controlled strictly by the clock and were not affected by any response. In addition, there was a pseudoconditioning group in which the CS and US were never paired and responses had no effect on the CS or US.

Now I must digress for a few lines. In the Pavlovian or classical situation, the CS interval for the conditiong of many responses (e.g., eyeblink) is about 0.5 second. Because of this very short CS duration, the question of response-contingent CS termination does not usually arise in most classical conditioning studies. In the present case, however, with a much longer CS duration (10 seconds), would the response termination of the CS have different effects than a procedure in which the CS duration is not response-contingent? Henceforth, when duration of the CS is *contingent* on response this condition is abbreviated as (CSc), and when CS duration is *not* response contingent the abbreviation is (CSnc). The question of response contingency for CS duration can, with slight modification in procedure, be applied to the instrumental, classical, and pseudoconditioning procedures equally well.

To examine the CS contingency question, separate instrumental, classical, and pseudoconditioning groups were run with CS termination contingent (CSc) on response and CS termina-

An Application of the Comparative Method

tion not contingent (CSnc) on response (conditions for the US remained the same and defined instrumental, classical, and pseudoconditioning) for these modified groups. Additionally, in line with Jensen's (1961) suggestion, controls with CS-only, US-only, and time-lapse procedures were run. In the CS-only condition, one group was CSc and one was CSnc. US contingent (USc) and US noncontingent (USnc) were also run under the US-only condition. Since no stimuli were programmed for the time-lapse procedure, only a single group was run. The results for all these groups appear in Figure 10.3.

Keeping in mind Figure 10.2, which depicts the expected results of these procedures for homoiotherms, note that in Figure 10.3 the instrumental groups show a negatively accelerated learning curve, as do the classical groups. However, the true classical group (CSnc) shows significantly slower acquisition than the modified classical group (CSc). The two pseudoconditioning groups are right down where they ought to be according to the expectations of Figure 10.2. Statistically, all groups except the pseudoconditioning groups and the US-only, USnc group show improved performance with training. Since the classical and instrumental groups show a high degree of "learning," it seems reasonable to conclude, as Woodard and Bitterman (1973) did, that the US contingency (instrumental condition) is not necessary to produce high "avoidance" performance rates in goldfish. Obviously, these animals "learn" to move from one end of the shuttlebox to the other whether or not the US is prevented from occurring by their response. This is the parsimonious conclusion.

But, before we go any further, let us take a look at the performances of the three additional controls, CS only, US only, and time-lapse. Instead of being similar to the pseudoconditioning group, as would be expected and as shown in Figure 10.2, these groups *all* show statistically significant increases in CS interval responding over blocks of trials; and this occurs even with

no stimuli at all in the time-lapse groups. Another point is that the CSnc, CS-only group, in which the *light stays* on the full 10 seconds, shows significantly better "learning(?)" performance than the CSc, CS-only group, in which the light goes off with the response. For a complete comparison, all of the data are plotted on a common axis in Figure 10.4.

In Figure 10.4, notice that three groups, the true instrumental, the modified instrumental, (CSnc) and the modified classical (CSc) group have the best overall performances. The true classical group is high, but surprisingly close to the CSnc, CS-only group. The top three groups all have at least one instrumentally controlled stimulus, either the US is response contingent, the CS is response contingent, or both are response contingent. Inspection of the inset at the top of Figure 10.4 shows the same order of performance, except that the CSnc, CS-only performance tends to be superior to the true classical group, although this difference is not statistically reliable. When the performance of the true classical group is compared with the performance of the CSnc, CS-only control, it is very hard to conclude that any kind of learning is taking place in the true classical group; this is true even though the performance curve for the classical group is negatively accelerated and looks like a typical learning curve.

An explanation for these results may come from findings by Zerbolio and Wickstra (1976b) and Zerbolio (1976), who concluded that goldfish become dark adapted during the darkened ITI used when the CS is the onset of light, and that the sudden onset of CS illumination produces a negative phototaxis (retreat from light). One can assume further that pairing an aversive US with the already negatively phototactic CS would increase the negative phototaxis. Thus, one can argue that the reason the top four groups were similar is because all of them had in common sudden illumination from the CS, which on some trials at least had been paired with the

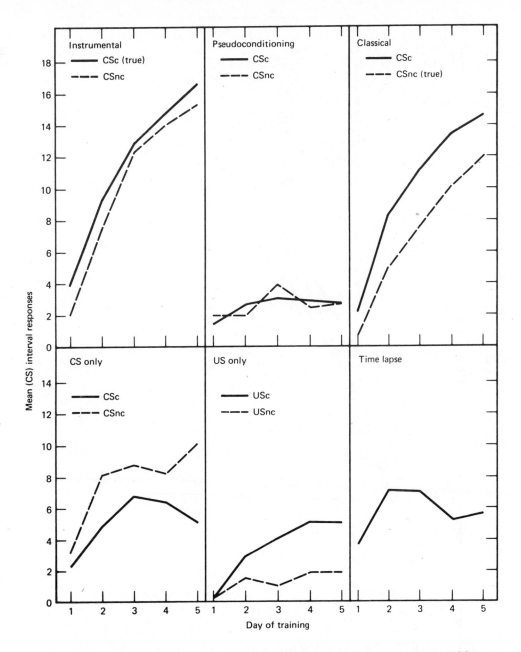

Figure 10.3 Shown are the data from experiment 1 in terms of the mean number of CS intervals or analogous unsignaled time periods in which at least one shuttle response occurred. Performances for both the traditional groups [Kimble, (1967)] and additional control groups [Jensen, (1961)] are presented. In the true instrumental procedure, both termination of the CS (CSc) and omission of the US were response-contingent, and in the true classical procedure neither CS termination nor US omission was response-contingent.

An Application of the Comparative Method

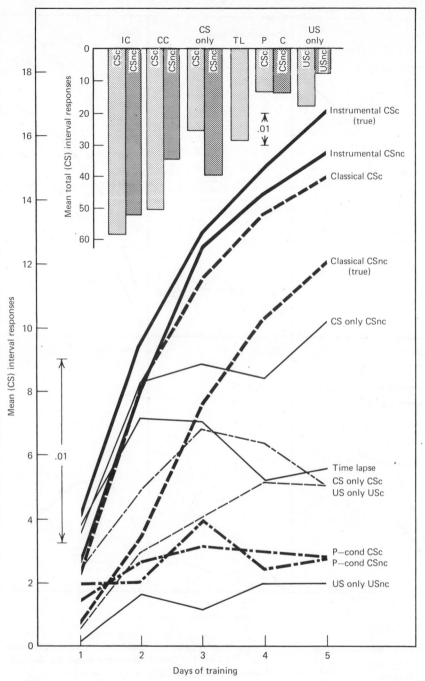

Figure 10.4 The groups plotted in Figure 10.3 on separate axes are shown plotted on a common axis. The bold lines represent the traditional instrumental, classical, and pseudoconditioning procedures and their CS contingency variants. The lighter lines represent the additional controls suggested by Jensen. A .01 significance interval for point comparison is delineated at the left inner margin. In addition, the total number of CS-interval or analogous-interval responses over 5 days of training for all groups appears as an inset at the top of the figure. A .01 significance interval is also shown for these data.

US, augmenting the negative phototaxis.

Presumably, the reason the true classical group had the poorest performance of any of these four groups is that it is the only procedure in which the subject can be punished for responding during the time the CS is on. That is, if a true classical animal responds late in the CS interval, or responds more than once, then the occurrence of the US could be adventitiously punishing that response and reducing the frequency of its occurrence. The adventitious punishment of a response *during the CS* is much less likely in the other three groups since the response either terminates the CS or prevents the US on that trial.

The argument that assumes for the fish that the critical experimental event is the onset of a shock-augmented negatively phototactic light and not the training procedure demands experimental examination. Such an experimental test is one in which color vision in goldfish becomes an important consideration. For a CS to be effective it must be a distinctive change. If we were running a typical experimental animal such as a rat, we would be reduced to a change in illumination level as the CS. But goldfish respond equally well to a color-change CS (Zerbolio, 1976). By using an illuminated ITI with color change for the CS, we can eliminate the conditions that produce the negative phototaxis. The fish will not dark adapt during the illuminated ITI, and there will be no sudden increase in illumination with CS onset, which presumably will eliminate the phototaxis effect.

Experiment 2

The entire set of procedures of Experiment 1 was replicated in Experiment 2 with new animals, with the exception that a green light illuminated the ITI period and the CS was a color change to a blue light. The data appear in Figure 10.5.

The first thing to note in Figure 10.5 is that subjects in all of the control conditions suggested by Jensen (1961) were generally responding at higher levels than when these same procedures were run without illumination during the ITI. A comparison of the lower three figures of Figure 10.5 with the same panels of Figure 10.3 clearly shows this. Such a finding is consistent with the negative phototaxis interpretation of the results of Experiment 1. As in Experiment 1, all of the Jensen control conditions except the US-only USnc group showed statistically significant "learning (?)" effects, even though there was only one stimulus (CS *or* US) or no manipulated stimulus at all (time lapse) in these control conditions.

In the top three panels of Figure 10.5, it can be seen that making the CS non contingent (CSnc) significantly lowered instrumental performance below that of the "true" instrumental group. Note also that the noncontingent CS (CSnc), or true classical, procedure yielded markedly lower performance than the modified classical procedure with a contingent CS (CSc). In fact, visual inspection shows that performance in the true classical procedure was at or below the level of the pseudoconditioning groups. Statistically, the two pseudoconditioning groups — the US-only USnc group and the true classical group — did not show significant increase in performance (learning?) over days of training. A clearer comparison of the relative performances of these groups is shown in Figure 10.6 in which all groups are plotted on the same axis. As is obvious from Figure 10.6, the use of an illuminated ITI markedly reduced the performance level of the true classical procedure.

Note that the true instrumental groups showed substantial learning, better than any other paired stimulus procedure, but at the end of 5 days they had only just begun to perform above the level of some of the control groups, specifically the CS-only, CSnc and time-lapse groups. The effect of the response-contingent CS is clearly shown in that the CSc, or instrumental CS, procedure yielded higher performance than

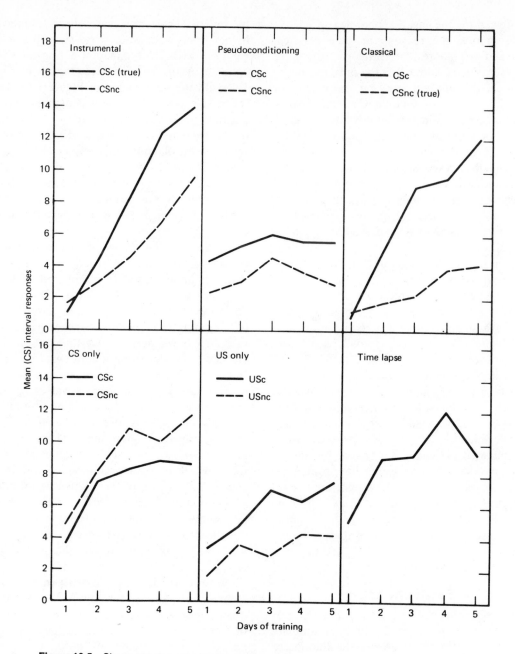

Figure 10.5 Shown are the data from experiment 2 in terms of the mean number of CS intervals or analogous unsignalled time periods in which at least one shuttle response occurred. The goldfish were run with an illuminated ITI and a color-change CS. Data for both the traditional groups and additional control groups are shown.

A Comparative Analysis

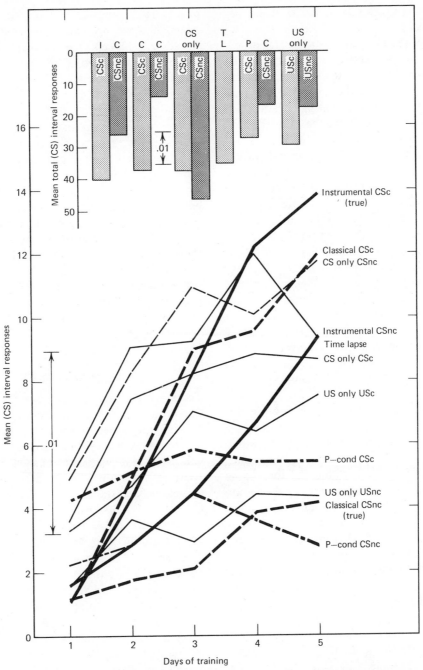

Figure 10.6 The groups plotted in Figure 10.5 on separate axes are shown plotted on a common axis. The bold lines represent the traditional instrumental, classical, and pseudoconditioning procedures and their CS contingency variants. The lighter lines represent the additional controls suggested by Jensen. A .01 significance interval for point comparison is present at the left inner margin. The total number of CS-interval or analogous-interval responses over 5 days of training for all groups also appears as an inset at the top of the figure. A .01 significance interval is also shown for these data.

the CSnc procedure for both the instrumental and classical groups.

In addition, the modified instrumental procedure with a noncontingent CS (CSnc) showed much poorer performance than the true instrumental procedure, and the modified classical procedure with a response-contingent CS (CSc) showed much better performance than the true classical procedure.

On the basis of these data, one can rather clearly conclude that both the US contingency (instrument versus classical variable) and the CS contingency (CSc versus CSnc variable) have strong, predictable effects on performance. In fact, the classical procedure, stripped of an illumination-induced phototaxis and stripped of an instrumental CS, did not show statistically significant learning. Inspection of Figure 10.6 (top inset) indicates that performance in the true classical group was no better than the poorest of all other groups in total "avoidances." Thus it is not appropriate to conclude that goldfish learn to swim from one compartment to another regardless of whether or not their responses prevent the occurrence of shock.

Nevertheless, as is clear from inspecting the top inset of Figure 10.6, the true instrumental procedure is not superior to some of the other control groups. In total avoidances, the CSnc, CS-only; the CSc; CS-only, and the time-lapse groups all show roughly equivalent total "avoidance" rates, although it is obvious that, since none of these groups had a US, none of them had anything to avoid. A legitimate question arises. Are any of the so-called "learning" groups learning at all or are they just returning to the very high operant rate of "avoidance" displayed by the control groups? The performance characteristic that makes this question difficult to answer is that active avoidance requires subjects to learn to shuttle during the CS interval in order to avoid shock. If subjects normally respond at a very high rate, as these data show, it is very difficult to demonstrate that the instrumental

procedure for active avoidance has significantly augmented the normally high response rate. If the control subjects responded at very low levels, as would be expected of homoiotherms (see Figure 10.2), this problem would not arise. But since goldfish respond at very high levels during the nonshock control procedures, we can exploit this fact by running them in an avoidance procedure that requires them to reduce their CS interval response rate instead of increasing it. This procedure is called passive avoidance and is one in which a response during the CS interval is punished. Thus learning is indicated by a clear reduction in rate of responding during the CS interval rather than in an increase. Since goldfish show very high response rates under control conditions (see Figures 10.3 and 10.5), there is sufficient room for a reduction in CS interval responding to show itself with a passive avoidance procedure. Experiment 3 deals with the acquisition of passive avoidance in goldfish.

Experiment 3

There are two ways to arrange the administration of the US in a passive avoidance procedure. The essential aspect of each is to punish the subject for making a response during the CS interval. The first way, designated here as the "passive" procedure, is to administer the US immediately on the occurrence of response in the CS interval. Obviously the passive procedure involves zero delay between response and US administration. The second way, designated the "punishment" procedure, is to punish any response(or responses) that occur in the CS interval with a single US administration at the end of the interval. The "punishment" procedure, used by Woodard and Bitterman (1973), imposes a variable interval of delay between the subject's response and US administration. One would expect the delayed reinforcement procedure (punishment) to yield slower learning than a no-delay (passive) procedure. Since a subject in the

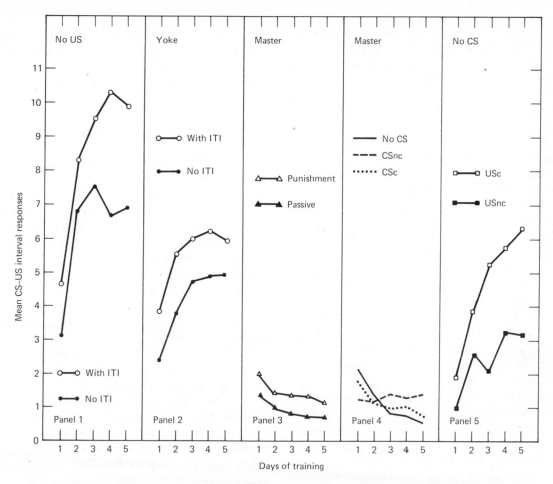

Figure 10.7 The data from experiment 3: the mean number of CS intervals or analogous time periods in which at least one shuttle-response occurred 5 days of training for the master punishment and master passive groups, and for the yoked controls with punishment and passive combined. With ITI means with *illuminated* ITI; no ITI means a *dark* ITI. The combined no US (CS only and time lapse) groups and the combined no CS (US only) groups from experiment 1 (with a dark ITI) and experiment 2 (with an illuminated ITI) are shown in panels 1 and 5, respectively. Panels 1 and 5 are presented for comparison purposes only. In comparing the results of Figure 10.7 with earlier figures, note that the y axis is a different scale.

punishment procedure can receive a maximum of only one US per trial, the passive procedure also was limited to one US per trial, but the US was administered immediately on the first response.

In addition, since significant differences due to the CS contingency and ITI illumination manipulations were found in Experiments 1 and 2, these conditions were added to Experiment 3.

Thus, twelve groups, two procedures (passive or punishment) by three CS conditions (CSc, CSnc, or NoCS) by two ITI illumination conditions (with ITI illumination or no ITI illumination) were run. Each subject in each of the twelve conditions was also run with a "yoked control." In the yoking procedure, there were two shuttle-boxes with a fish in each. The boxes were connected to a control apparatus in such a way that

An Application of the Comparative Method

the responses of only one fish controlled the stimuli that were administered simultaneously to both of them. Thus, the controlling or master fish determined the duration of the CS and/or the frequency of the US administered. The yoked fish received exactly the same pattern (frequency and/or duration) of CS and/or US as the master fish, but none of its responses controlled any of the stimulus events imposed on it. Of course, the frequency of CS interval responses in the yoked subject could still be measured.

If the frequency, duration, and patterning of CS and/or US, without reference to response consequences, govern the behavior of the goldfish, then we would expect the master and yoked fish to behave very similarly. If, however, response-contingent control of the stimuli is the important condition, then the master subject would be expected to behave very differently from its yoked control. The significant differences found between the twelve master groups and the twelve yoked controls are shown in Figure 10.7.

Both the passive and delayed punishment procedures produced acquisition of a passive avoidance response, as is evident from inspection of panels 3 and 4 of Figure 10.7. Panel 3 shows, as expected, that the passive procedure (upper curve) produced a significantly lower CS interval response rate than the punishment procedure (delayed punishment); that is, the immediate punishment yielded superior acquisition performance. In panel 4, it can be seen that passive avoidance took place under all CS conditions including the no-CS group. The amount of suppression of the shuttling response can be gauged by comparing panel 3 with the response rate exhibited by the yoked controls (panel 2). The difference between the master and yoked animals' performance is very large, highly reliable statistically, and the most crucial finding in Experiment 3 since it demonstrates the importance of the passive response contingency.

For the sake of additional comparisons, the data of the combined no-US and US-only groups from Experiments 1 and 2 (taken from Figures 10.3 and 10.5) are presented in panel 1 and panel 5 of Figure 10.7. When we compare panel 2 with panel 1, we see that the few shocks the yoked controls suffered did take their toll in response suppression. But this suppression was nothing like the level of response inhibition shown by the master fish, which clearly showed the importance of the shock-contingency on the acquisition of a passive avoidance response. Simply shocking a fish does not, by itself, produce response suppression like that shown by the master fish. This can be seen by comparing the performance of the US-only groups (Panel 5) from Experiments 1 and 2 with the performance of the master fish. Notice also that only the master fish have a decreasing performance curve rather than a negatively accelerated increasing response curve (see especially panels 3 and 5 of Figure 10.7). Finally, note that both the performance of the yoked controls and the no-US groups (CS-only and time-lapse groups from the previous experiments) were clearly affected by the level of ITI illumination (panels 1 and 2 of Figure 10.7).

In other words, goldfish can acquire a passive avoidance response when the US is administered either with a zero delay following the response (passive) or with a variable time delay following the response (punishment). With either of these procedures, the number of CS interval with responses shows a marked decline in comparison to yoked controls, no-US controls, or US-only controls. Obviously, the response contingency or instrumental nature of US administration is crucial for a learned decline in CS interval-shuttle rate.

But the data of Experiment 3 pose a further question. Note, as previously mentioned, that the master no-CS groups acquired the passive avoidance response at least as quickly as the master CSc and CSnc groups (Figure 10.7, panel 4). These results suggest that, although the passive avoidance contingency was sufficient to produce

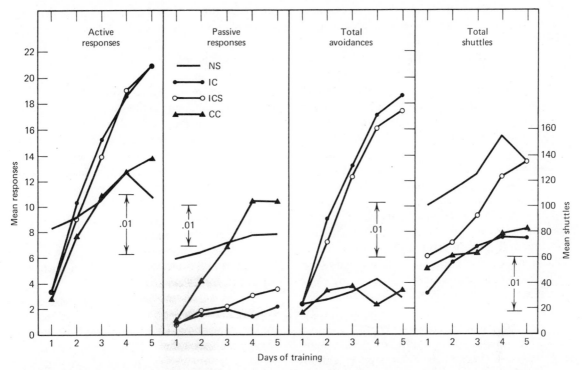

Figure 10.8 The mean number of CS intervals in which at least one shuttle response occurred per trial for active (first panel) and passive (second panel) conditions in the classical (CC), instrumental (IC), instrumental shock-equated (ICS), and no US (NS) groups. The third panel shows the net total avoidances (active-passive) above a random baseline (thirty) for all groups. The fourth panel shows the shuttle rate for all groups. Each panel has a .01 significance interval incorporated in it.

the acquisition of response inhibition, the inhibition was not specific to the CS. In other words, if the fish simply learned to stop responding altogether rather than just during the CS interval, the results would be the same. Indeed, the results as a whole can be readily interpreted in terms of generalized response inhibition.

If, however, goldfish could learn to inhibit the response under one stimulus (passive avoidance) and shuttle under a second stimulus condition (active avoidance), this would provide evidence of stimulus-specific learning. In other words, if half of the trials in the shuttlebox required an active response to CS_1 and half required a passive response to CS_2, would the fish learn to make the appropriate response under each CS

condition? Bagné (1974), for example, has shown that this is easy for a rat to learn. Experiment 4 is an attempt to answer this question.

Experiment 4

In this last experiment (Zerbolio and Wickstra, 1976c), subjects were run sixty trials a day, thirty with the CS being light onset on the same side of the box as the fish and requiring an active response to avoid shock, and thirty trials with the CS being light onset on the side of the box opposite to the fish and requiring passive avoidance, or no response. Two instrumental groups and one classical conditioning group were run. Subjects in the classical group (CC) were shocked on every trial whereas those in the conventional instrumental groups (IC) were not. Thus classically trained subjects received more shocks than instrumentally trained subjects. To equate for number of shocks received, a second instrumental group was run in such a way that if a response was correct on a trial (i.e., active when it should be active and passive when it should be passive), the US was postponed until the middle of the ITI. Thus, this instrumental shock-equated group (ICS) received the same number of shocks as the classical group. A no-Shock (NS), or CS-only, group was also run.

The results of Experiment 4 appear in Figure 10.8. In the first panel of Figure 10.8, the two instrumental groups (IC and ICS) show a smooth, negatively accelerated learning curve for active avoidance responses, but so does the classical (CC) group although the performance level reached is lower. Note that this similarity between the instrumental and classical groups, not unexpectedly, is comparable to the data from Experiment 1 (Figure 10.3) for similar conditions. And, not unexpectedly, because of the possibility of negative phototaxis, the no-shock group (CS only) had a high level of "active avoidance." In the first panel of Figure 10.8, note that on the initial day of training the US suppressed the active avoidance response rate for IC, ICS, and CC groups below that of the no-shock group, but that this effect was quite temporary.

The passive avoidance responses are presented in the second panel of Figure 10.8. As expected, the response rate during the CS interval on passive avoidance trials is low for the two IC groups but for both the no-shock and classical groups comparable to their "active avoidance" levels.

If the negative phototaxis effect described in Experiment 1 were controlling the CS interval-response rate of the classical group in Experiment 4, one would expect the classical group to respond appropriately both when the CS is on the same side of the box as the fish (leave or actively avoid) and when the CS is on the opposite side (stay away from or passively avoid). If the classical group had tended to do this, its performance to some extent would have looked like the acquisition of "discriminated avoidance." There is some slight evidence for such a phototaxis effect in the classical group in the data based on total discriminated avoidances, labeled total avoidances in the third panel of Figure 10.8.

To understand the data in this panel, consider a subject that shuttled on every trial; it would successfully avoid on all active trials (+30) but fail to avoid on all passive trials (-30) for a net score of zero-discriminated (total) avoidance. If, on the other hand, a subject were quiet on all trials, it would successfully avoid on all passive trials but fail to avoid on all active trials, again for a net score of zero-discriminated (total) avoidances. Thus, a score of zero in panel 3 could indicate thirty avoidances, but zero-discriminated responses. If a subject tended to avoid discriminatively, it would have a score above the zero-total baseline. The data in panel 3 of Figure 10.8 indicate a slightly greater than zero effect in both the CC and NS groups. Although the difference from the zero baseline is not statistically significant, the fact that these two groups were above zero suggests that the same phototactic effect that presumably occurred in the classical conditioning group in Experiment 1 was operating in Experiment 4. Note that both instrumental groups (ICS and IC) showed high rates of discriminated avoidance. The instrumental procedure, or US contingency, clearly enhanced the acquisition of avoidance performance. Furthermore, the fact that the instrumental subjects responded discriminatively indicates that the responding was controlled by the specific CS's used on active and passive trials.

In comparing the results of the instrumental and classical procedures in Experiment 4, one can argue, and rightly so, that there is no classical procedure comparable to the instrumental passive avoidance procedure. But, if one assumes that goldfish do not learn via an instrumental process but only via a classical process, it is hard to see what difference this makes. In fact, if the acquisition of avoidance only occurred via a classical process, the instrumental animals should acquire the response by the same process as the classical animals and ought to perform the same. That the instrumentally trained subjects avoided discriminatively, following the stimulus-specific response contingencies, whereas the classically trained fish did not, strongly implies that goldfish learn to avoid via the instrumental process.

A Summing Up of the Argument

In sum, then, let us review the data of these experiments to see how they bear on the question of how goldfish acquire avoidance responses. When there was a dark ITI and a sudden increase in illumination as a CS, the results of Experiment 1 show that the classical and instrumental procedures produced comparably high, negatively accelerated performance curves consistent with a homoiotherm learning expectation. By contrast, the pseudoconditioning procedure yielded low and relatively flat performance. On the basis of these data alone, one might be tempted to conclude that the learning is based on a classical conditioning process — which is considered simpler than the instrumental process. But Experiment 1 contained a few surprises. The nontraditional controls, specifically the CS-only, USc, US-only, and time-lapse procedures, did not look at all like the pseudo-conditioning results, suggesting that the basis for responding in all groups was not well understood. Earlier work by Wickstra and Zerbolio (1976b) and Zerbolio (1976) indicated that a shock-augmented negative phototaxis is present in shuttlebox avoidance with goldfish when the CS is a light; perhaps at least part of the failure to find large

differences between the classical and instrumental groups could be due to a phototaxis effect. Experiment 1, by having a dark ITI and sudden onset of illumination provided the right sort of conditions to produce such a phototaxis effect; thus Experiment 2 was designed to eliminate the phototaxis by using an illuminated ITI and a color-change CS.

In Experiment 2, the true instrumental group again showed high, negatively accelerated performance typical of learning, whereas the true classical procedure showed performance at or below the levels of all other groups. This was in striking contrast to the results of Experiment 1. Furthermore, the CS contingency produced a similar effect: The modified instrumental procedure with a classical CS but instrumental US yielded a substantially lower level of performance than the true Instrumental procedure; and the Modified Classical procedure with an instrumental CS but classical US showed a substantially higher performance level than the true classical procedure. The performance of the pseudoconditioning groups was still low and flat and at the same nonlearning performance level as the true classical procedure (without the negative phototaxis effect).

The contrasting results of Experiments 1 and 2 strongly support the interpretation that the high performance levels shown by both the classical and instrumental groups in Experiment 1 were due to shock-augmented phototaxis: for the fish in the tank in Experiment 1, the critical factor was the sudden onset of light, not the consequences of its response. The US (shock) served mainly to potentiate the normally occurring negative phototaxis.

A question this interpretation poses is, why in Experiment 1 were the true classical subjects lower in performance than the other stimulus-paired groups? A possible explanation is that only the true classical group of Experiment 1 could be punished for responding *while* the CS was occurring. If, in the "true" classical procedure, a subject tarried until the very end of the CS-US interval to respond, the US would occur and adventitiously punish the shuttling response. None of the other paired stimulus groups would have a response punished *during* the CS because the response would either produce the omission of the US (both instrumental groups) or produce the termination of the CS (modified classical group). Thus, it seems that Experiment 1 does not involve an unambiguous comparison between instrumental and classical procedures.

Experiment 2, on the other hand, involved a comparison of the instrumental and classical procedures without the confounding effect of phototaxis; and here the instrumental procedure yielded markedly superior shuttle avoidance behavior. However, even though the performance of the pseudoconditioning groups in Experiment 2 was low and relatively flat, as expected, the nontraditional control procedures (CS-only, US-only, and time-lapse groups) again showed unexpectedly high and negatively accelerated performance rates. In fact, the CS-only, CSnc group was superior overall. Given the high performance levels of the CS-only, CSnc and time-lapse controls, it is questionable whether the true instrumental groups' performance represents learning. Instead, its high level of performance could simply be a return to the high baseline, or control rate, following early suppression of this rate by the US.

It is difficult to answer this question directly because the no-shock controls responded at such a high rate throughout. The answer lay in conducting an experiment, as in Experiment 3, in which the fish had to acquire a passive avoidance response; here successful avoidance meant a lower CS-interval response rate than shown by the control conditions.

Experiment 3 definitely showed that goldfish learn to avoid passively. Since the passive avoidance subjects were clearly lower in performance rate than the yoked controls and lower even than the US-only subjects of Experiments 1 and 2, it is

highly probable that this superiority was due to the instrumental contingency which made possible the omission of the US. This argument is strengthened by the fact that the acquisition of passive avoidance was a function of the delay of reinforcement gradient (*passive*, or immediate shock, was superior to punishment, or delayed shock). The finding that goldfish are capable of acquiring passive avoidance also lends credibility to the contention that the reason the true classical group in Experiment 1 was somewhat lower in shuttling performance than the other stimulus-paired groups was because of being adventitiously punished for responding *during* the CS period. However, although goldfish seemed to be sensitive to the instrumental passive avoidance procedure, the finding that the no-CS group performed as well as or better than the CS groups brought the stimulus specificity of control into question.

Experiment 4 attempted to answer the stimulus-specificity question by having the goldfish jointly acquire an active avoidance response to one CS and a passive avoidance response to a second CS. In this experiment, the instrumentally trained subjects learned to avoid discriminatively, and the classically trained subjects did not differ significantly in the performance from a no-CS control. While one might argue that the classical group was not able to acquire a discrimination because they could not be passively trained, this does not obviate the fact that the classical and instrumental groups responded quite differently, implying that their shuttling was controlled by different processes.

Taken in conjunction with the results of the other three experiments, the parsimonious interpretation of the results of Experiment 4 is that the instrumentally trained subjects truly acquired a stimulus-specific passive/active discrimination, whereas the classically trained subjects responded indiscriminately, as did the no-shock (CS-only) controls. Collectively the results of the four experiments indicate that goldfish learn instrumentally in shock-avoidance situations. Once "learning" in the classical group in Experiment 1 is ruled out by the negative phototaxis explanation, the rest of the shuttle-avoidance data uniformly require an explanation in terms of an instrumental process.

The data also pose several other interesting questions. For instance, why does the pseudoconditioning procedure produce such relatively low and flat response curves whereas the no-US controls do not? Preliminary evidence from our laboratory indicates that with the pseudoconditioning procedure goldfish learn to shuttle more in the 10-second period just prior to the US than in the 10-second CS period, suggesting that goldfish learn to discriminate between a CS that is explicitly unpaired with shock and the 10-second part of the ITI that precedes the US. This finding supports Rescorla's (1967) contention that, in the unpaired pseudoconditioning procedure the CS signals a "safe" time and that this procedure may not constitute an appropriate control for conditioning studies. Our finding of a higher response rate in CS-only and time-lapse controls than in the pseudoconditioning controls is in keeping with such an interpretation because without a US there is no shock or danger period and, therefore, no "safe" period.

Another curious finding relates to the fact that the US was a single 200-millisecond shock in all the work presented here. We have tried to train rats to learn a wheel-turn avoidance response using a single 200-millisecond US, but without success, Zerbolio, Reynierse, Weisman, and Denny (1967), on the other hand, had no trouble establishing this response in rats when the US was terminated by the rat's response. Although rats show maintenance of an avoidance response with a 200-millisecond shock *once it is acquired,* they do not originally learn to avoid with such a brief US. One explaination for the rats' failure to learn with a short US is that the brief US does not allow sufficient time to acquire an escape response. Without the acquisition of an escape

response, there is no prototype or basis for an avoidance response. Thus, the avoidance response, if one views it originally as an anticipatory escape response occurring during the CS, never really occurs in the rat and thus cannot be instrumentally reinforced.

Yet, goldfish do very well with a short shock pulse shuttle-avoidance procedure. A likely explanation of the fact that goldfish learn to shuttle with a 200-millisecond US is that, since they have a very high baseline shuttle rate, the probability of a response occurring during the CS period is high; and once shuttling occurs during the CS interval, the instrumental consequence of CS termination and US omission reinforces the avoidance response just as if it were originally elicited as an anticipatory escape response. What is important about this characteristic behavior pattern in goldfish is that it doesn't require the classical conditioning of fear to account for the initial escape from the CS. The initial high normal response rate is sufficient. But the finding that CS termination augments performances for both the classical and instrumental procedures in Experiment 2 supports the notion that something like fear reduction occurs with CS termination. This indirect evidence for the presence of fear may be the only evidence of classical conditioning in these experiments.

Conclusion

Overall, then, the present data indicate that goldfish, contrary to earlier reports, do learn an avoidance response via an instrumental process. Also, the pseudoconditioning control procedure, at least for the goldfish, does *not* represent everything that the CS-only, US-only, and time-lapse control procedures represent. The budding experimenter would do well to keep this in mind. Since these control procedures produce behaviors different from what one would expect from homoiotherm data, it would be wise to heed Jensen's (1961) advice: whenever examining a new or infrequently used experimental animal, run all

An Application of the Comparative Method

the control procedures, not just the pseudoconditioning procedure. In fact, this is good advice when doing research with any animal.

The moral is simple. A fish is not a rat. It is simply good experimental procedure to check out all the relevant control behaviors of the experimental animal before drawing conclusions about one's results. While recommendations for using additional controls will require more time and effort on the part of the experimenter, the end result will be to reduce the amount of confusion and noise in published results and to enhance our understanding of the learning process in all animals.

Study Questions

1. Describe the problem addressed in this chapter. Include its origins.

2. What are the main differences in behavior and physiology between goldfish and rats?

3. Summarize the experimental results and the main conclusion from these results.

4. List all the control procedures used in the four experiments. Name the psychologist who recommended the three rarely used procedures.

5. Try to think of another shuttle-avoidance experiment with goldfish, possibly a follow-up of the experiment described in this chapter or one that will help answer one of the questions raised near the end of this chapter.

11

Brain Function: Comparative Analysis of Problems in Physiological Psychology

Donald G. Stein

Clark University
University of Massachusetts Medical Center

No one knows for certain when humans first became interested in understanding behavior, but there is little doubt that they were concerned about it long before the dawn of recorded history. Archeological studies of the late Paleolithic and Neolithic periods have revealed that human skulls, with or without fractures, sometimes have round, oval, or square portions removed. This practice was apparently widespread since such skulls have been found in Europe, the British Isles, Africa, and even America (Gurjian, 1973). These holes were made while the person was still alive, and this is known by the fact that the edges of the bone are smooth and show signs of healing. In some cases, individuals apparently had multiple operations with some degree of healing after each trephination. Trephination (the drilling of a hole in the skull) is practiced in much the same form today as it was in Paleolithic times. That the act occurred during these early times implies the existence then of some form of organized society with certain rules and regulations and belief in certain concepts of treatment or religious ideology (Gurjian, 1973 p. 4). Thus, even before people were able to write, they left us with a record of their ideas about disease and, to a certain extent, their ideas about the nature of behavior.

Today, one might be tempted to take for granted the notion that the brain is critically involved in the control of our mental and bodily functions, and it might come as a surprise to learn that this idea has not always been as popular or as acceptable as it is now. Some of the greatest philosophers in Athenian Greece, such as Aristotle, thought that the heart was the seat of all rational activity and that the brain served only to cool the passions and the vital spirits of the body. In ancient Egypt, physicians thought the liver to be the seat of the soul, and while most vital organs such as the heart, stomach and liver, were preserved and buried with the corpse, the brain was withdrawn through the nose and discarded.

Although by the middle ages Western scholars had grown to realize the central importance of the brain, the seat of rational and spiritual activity was thought to exist not in the brain tissue itself, but in the four "cells" encased by the tissue; we know these cells today as the cerebral ventricles. The brain itself was seen as a vase that held the animal spirits circulating within the ventricles that were so necessary ("vital") for all aspects of rational life (Figure 11.1). Even through the sixteenth, and early parts of the seventeenth centuries, controversy raged as to whether the heart or the brain was the repository of rational thoughts and behaviors. This uncertainty as to which of the two was most critical is reflected in the following couplet by Shakespeare.

"Tell me, where is fancy bred, Or in the heart, or in the Head? How begot, how nourished? Reply, reply." Merchant of Venice, III, 2.

Comparative-physiological experimentation is now thought to have begun in the second century A.D. when the Greek Physician, Galen, created lesions in the frontal portions of the brain in baby pigs in an attempt to determine what such trauma might produce. His findings have been lost to history, but Galen's influence was to assume great importance during the centuries that followed, and especially during that period now known as the Middle Ages. Ecclesiastic authorities in this period claimed not only the Bible as their authority but also Galen and Aristotle. No deviation from these sources was permitted; there were no other facts than those reported by these authorities. Indeed, anyone daring to perform anatomical studies, even in animals, was ridiculed or, worse, subjected to very harsh penalties, such as burning at the stake.

Because of these severe penalties, many of the early ideas concerning the functions of the bodily organs, including the brain, had to derive from secret studies on pigs, oxen, sheep, and dogs. Many of the observations that were made

were incorrect, especially those concerning the nature of people since there was really no possibility of anatomical investigation in humans. Galenic doctrine, as developed by church authorities, became codified into dogma in spite of the fact that Galen had often contradicted himself and never had done any dissections of the human body, limiting his investigations to the pig or ox. Throughout the Middle Ages, it was incorrectly assumed that Galen was describing the anatomy of people and, when contradictions were found, they were not taken to indicate that he (or Church authorities) could be wrong, but instead that the structure of people's bodies had changed since his time, perhaps due to the tighter clothing so popular during the Middle Ages! In any case, during this dark period people seemed to be more concerned with saving their souls than in understanding the functions of their bodies.

Empirical techniques probably were not employed in conducting animal research until the beginning of the seventeenth century. Rene Descartés, the French philosopher and mathematician, played an important part in this development by convincing the church that people's souls were not perturbed by examinations of the machinery of the body. This notion made it possible for seventeenth century investigators to examine more carefully the relationship between anatomical structure and function in humans, which then led rapidly to a comparative study of *all* aspects of bodily function, including that of the brain.

But it was not until the early part of the nineteenth century that major steps were taken to understand how nerve conduction worked. And systematic analyses of brain function and behavior, whose first steps were in the clinic and not the laboratory, were not attempted until the middle and late 1800s.

There were many contributors to the new science of "natural physiology" in this period. Perhaps the best known were Gall and Spurzheim,

Figure 11.1 A speculative drawing of where the various psychological functions of human beings were located, according to a view held during the Middle Ages. [From Edwin Clarke and Kenneth Dewhurst, *Illustrated History of Brain Function*, University of California Press, Berkeley, (1972).]

Brain Function: Comparative Analysis of Problems in Physiological Psychology who helped create the field we know today as phrenology. Gall and Spurzheim proposed that psychological functions could be localized in the cortical (surface) tissue of the brain, and that specific neural areas were responsible for particular behavioral acts or functions. The functions of the different cortical areas were assessed by measuring the size of bumps on the heads of gifted and retarded individuals (or criminals). If the individual were a gifted artist, a phrenologist would infer that the enlarged area was the zone that determined artistic ability (Figure 11.2).

Although Gall and Spurzheim were wrong in most, if not all, of their assumptions, their work stimulated considerable attention in the medical and scientific community. Subsequently, more systematic investigations of brain functions, based on clinical observation of patients suffering from brain injuries, were conducted. Here, neurologists such as Pierre Broca and Marc Dax, among others, made important, pioneering observations that language functions could be disrupted by damage to the left hemisphere of the brain, in particular the left temporal area. These observations led to laboratory studies of the relationship between brain function and structure that guide our thinking today.

Much can be learned from clinical observations of patients who have had the misfortune to suffer traumatic injury to the brain (stroke, accidents, etc.). Patients with head injuries often manifest behavioral symptoms or syndromes, that are associated with damage to a specific area. For example, parietal lobe damage often causes severe impairments in spatial orientation, while temporal lobe injury in the left hemisphere often results in loss of language. Consistent clinical observations of this type naturally led scientists concerned with brain mechanisms to ask whether experimentally induced damage in localized areas of the brain would reveal the functions of those areas. Of course, ethical consideration precluded performing such operations on humans. Consequently, researchers resorted to using animal species as experimental subjects. Thus, a comparative physiological psychology was developed. Almost all current empirical research on the relationship between brain and behavior is performed on various species, ranging from the sea hare to the rhesus monkey.

Reasons for a Comparative Approach to Brain Functions:

One might ask the following questions. "Why bother with comparative investigation in physiological psychology?" "Why not simply concentrate on a single animal species that is close in complexity to humans, such as the monkey?" "Can anything be learned about brain function in primates and humans by examining neurons in the sea slug, or the rabbit, or the cat?" Actually, much of what is known about neural activity does not come from the study of complex organisms such as the primate, but rather from animals with relatively simple nervous systems. Indeed, the squid was used in most of the initial work on the conduction of nervous impulses. This organism has very large and durable nerves, so that investigators were able to place electrodes directly inside its axon for recording nerve signals. In addition, physiologists could alter the chemicals assumed responsible for the initiation and transmission of nerve impulses, and then examine all of the possible effects of these changes on signal transmission. In fact, A. L. Hodgkin and A. F. Huxley, who shared the Nobel prize for their discoveries on nervous transmission, remarked:

It is arguable that the introduction of the squid giant nerve fiber by J.Z. Young in 1936 did more for axonology than any other single advance during the last forty years. Indeed a distinguished neurophysiologist remarked recently at a congress dinner (not, I thought, with the utmost tact), "It's the squid that really ought to be given

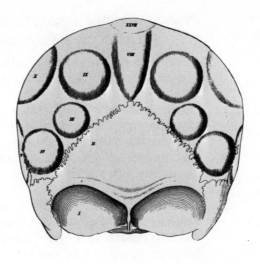

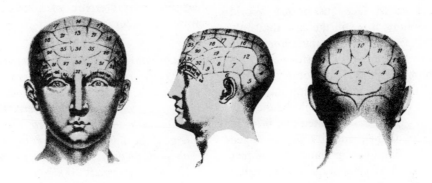

Figure 11.2 The Phrenologist view of psychological characteristics as a function of areas of the head. [From Clarke and Dewhurst, (1972).]

Brain Function: Comparative Analysis of Problems in Physiological Psychology

195

the Nobel Prize." (Ratner's emphasis on the importance of a good research preparation, p. 163 is reinforced here).

Once a basic understanding of nervous conduction had been worked out in simpler systems, researchers could ask whether the same principles of organization and function held for different and more complex species. Thanks to the development of electronics permitting precise recording of very small electrical and chemical changes at the neuronal level, the techniques developed in working with the squid and other invertebrates were applied to more complex nervous systems. As a result, the *general* principles of nervous conduction were found to be very similar in all species.

In the study of the physiological bases of learning, memory, and other behavioral phenomena, scientists are still confronted with many of the same technical and theoretical problems that neurophysiologists faced just prior to World War II. Fortunately, it is still the case that only very limited experimental manupulation of the human nervous system can be performed. Most research on human beings is done only when it is demonstrated that such manipulation has direct benefits for the subject, such as might be the case when a patient's brain is stimulated just prior to surgery in order to help localize the damaged area for removal. That is, stimulation techniques are sometimes used by neurosurgeons to localize diseased regions of the brain and to determine which areas remain healthy, by noting the patient's verbal response to the electrical stimulus. While useful information can be obtained under these circumstances, note that, for the most part, one is examining a sick person with a diseased brain. Consequently, any generalizations to normal function in healthy subjects must be made with great caution.

Problems with Animal Experiments in Physiological Psychology

Direct intervention in healthy animals is one way to explore brain function. However, it has to be recognized that the intervention itself (for example, introducing a chemical into the brain, or stimulating a given area) may have not only drastic consequences for the particular area under investigation, but also for areas physically adjacent to, or even far removed from, the site under study.

Comparative analysis of brain-behavior relationships is also important because there is evidence to indicate that, while similarities among brain structures in rats, monkeys, and humans do exist, the behavioral and physiological effects of CNS manipulation of anatomically analogous structures are not necessarily the same across species. For example, in a recent paper Bitterman (1975) has reported that "phenomena of learning characteristic of some animals fail entirely to occur in others."

Bitterman notes that, after training with a preferred reward, laboratory rats will not work as effectively for a less favored reward than control animals that were trained initially with the less favored reinforcement (e.g., if the animals prefer wet mash, they will not perform as well for sunflower seeds, which are less preferred). While this "depression effect" is seen in laboratory rats, analogous experiments in the goldfish conducted by Bitterman yielded totally different results. Fish were trained to strike at a target and tested in three different groups; one was given four worms for each correct response, another forty worms, and the third group was shifted from forty worms per correct response to four. Bitterman found that the shifted group was entirely unaffected by the shift from a preferred to a less preferred reward, thus indicating that the depression or negative contrast effect seen in laboratory rats probably does not occur in the goldfish. These findings suggest that the reward mechanisms underlying learning in rats and goldfish may be different due to the possibility that the nervous systems of these two types of creatures process information about reward in different ways (See also Chapter 10).

Differences in learning between genus and species are one important reason why it is necessary to conduct comparative analyses to elucidate the general principles of behavior and the physiological processes underlying it. Unfortunately, the comparative approach is rarely employed. Most laboratories are not prepared to handle a wide variety of animals and are not particularly interested in developing, as did Thorndike at the beginning of the century, the tests or tasks necessary to evaluate performance that would be equivalent for chickens, rats, dogs, and cats, to name a few. Also, the convention among experimenters, which dictates the type of animals available for research and permits investigators to repeat each others' findings, sometimes poses a problem. At present, the great majority of experiments designed to examine the neural bases of behavior are conducted on the albino rat because it is still relatively cheap and accessible to almost all laboratories. However, even different strains of these "standard" animals can show remarkable differences in both behavior and anatomy in laboratory settings across the country.

Comparative Analysis of Brain Lesions and Performance in Vertebrates

Late nineteenth and early twentieth-century investigators were more interested in comparative analysis of brain function than those today. One of the pioneers of the comparative approach

was David Ferrier, who worked at King's College, London, in the 1800s. Ferrier and Pierre Flourens, a contemporary from Paris, were among the first to make lesions in different brain regions in a variety of species, including fish, frogs, rabbits, pigeons, dogs, cats, and monkeys. Their experiments were the first truly comparative studies of the role of different parts of the nervous system in the control of behavior. Ferrier initiated the research by ablating cerebellar tissue in different species and then studied the effects of his surgery on the ability of his subjects to right themselves, maintain posture, and walk, jump, or fly. He reported that effects of total cerebellum removals were greater for birds than for toads or fishes. Pigeons, in contrast to monkeys, were eventually able to recover from this extensive cerebellar damage. In conducting later experiments on the cerebral hemispheres, Ferrier demonstrated that total removal of the cerebral hemisphere: "operates differently in different classes or orders of animals, insofar as relates to their motor stability and powers of response to external stimulation. In the fish, frog, and pigeon the removal of the hemispheres exercises little or no appreciable effect on the faculties of standing upright or locomotion. Under the influence of stimulation from without, these animals swim, jump, fly with as much vigor, apparently, and precision, as before. In the rabbit, the destruction of the hemispheres, while greatly impairing the mobility of the forelimbs, does not render equilibration impossible or destroy the the power of coordinated movements of locomotion in response to appropriate external stimuli. In the dog, however, the removal of the hemispheres renders the animal completely prostrate and unable to stand or walk." Ferrier concluded by stating that the independent organization of lower centers is thus seen to vary as we ascend or descend the animal scale.

Ferrier was not only one of the first comparative psychologists to provide detailed observations on the effects of brain lesions in homologous areas of different species, but he was also one of the first to develop the technique of electrically stimulating the exposed brain in healthy animals to determine the behavioral consequences. Although his elecrical stimulation procedure is frequently used by present day investigators, Ferrier's systematic comparative approach to the study of brain-behavior relationships is rarely employed.

Shepard Franz and Karl Lashley, working in this country in the early 1900s, were two of the leaders in the development of modern physiological psychology. Using soldiers with head injuries or the ablation of cortical tissue in the rat as techniques for determining the relationship between structure and function, these workers came to the conclusion that localization of function in specific structures of the brain might, at best, be limited to certain stages of development in the life of the animal. In fact, after about 30 years of continued research on the problem of localization of function, in which he tried to find a specific, critical locus for memory storage, Lashley, at the end of his career said: "I sometimes feel, in reviewing the evidence on the localization of the memory trace, that the necessary conclusion is that learning is just not possible (1960)". Lashley based his somewhat pessimistic statement on his inability to observe complete elimination of any given cognitive function after destruction of various brain structures in the rat. However, most of his findings were based on experiments in the laboratory rat, which at that time had only recently been introduced as a subject for learning experiments (Small in 1901, working at Clark University). Although they proposed many excellent ideas, the techniques of Franz and Lashley were not as sensitive as those now available.

Present-day Approaches to the Study of Brain Functions

Many contemporary researchers have tended to ignore the findings of Franz and Lashley and have concentrated instead on the search for neural "centers" or specific "systems" that control or are responsible for each type of behavior they choose to investigate. For example, the hypothalamus is seen as the center for motivated and agonistic behavior, while the hippocampus is sometimes characterized as a center for the initial formation of the engram (memory trace) in the central nervous system. Very few investigators have had the time, inclination, or funds to evaluate the effects of brain lesions in a natural, or "field," setting where the results of their experimental treatments might have far different consequences for the animals' behavior. Thus, a lesion that might disrupt a rat's performance in a T-maze might have no dramatic effects in a field setting. Conversely, lesions of the visual cortex could be fatal to the animal's survival in a natural environment (consider its ability to spot predators quickly).

In a recent review, R. L. Isaacson (1976) discusses some of the problems arising from attempts to evaluate the effects of brain damage on learning and memory. His anaysis can be interpreted to indicate the importance of comparative investigation of the kind used by Ferrier, Thorndike, and others at the turn of the century. Such an analysis of behavior would emphasize that in *any* experimental paradigm, certain independent variables do not remain constant in their effects across species. Thus, a comparative psychologist, in designing an experiment on learning capacity, would ask whether an incentive or motive for learning appropriate to one species or genus has the same effect in a quite different species. In a very real sense, it may be suggested that a brain-damaged animal may represent, with respect to its behavioral and perceptual capacity, a different species or class than its intact counterpart. Consider, for example, animals given lesions of the brainstem region called the hypothalamus. Such animals show dramatic differences in their response to incentives such as food and water. A rat with lateral hypothalamic lesions will only eat highly preferred foods, such as chocolate chip cookies, and will starve to death even though less palatable food is available at all times. A summary of Isaacson's review follows.

When examining memory and learning, it is necessary to motivate the experimental animals adequately in order to determine how much is remembered. If the lesion that is made affects the animal's motivation or incentive to perform, impaired performance will be observed following the brain damage, but the altered behavior might not *be due to the perturbance of the memory process* per se. *The experimental brain lesions could alter the animal's metabolic processes (hippocampal and hypothalamic lesions modify liver glycogen levels), which could change the animal's response to various kinds of incentives, including food, or even aversive stimuli such as electrical shock. Brain damage can also alter, distort, or destroy the perception of the environment, and such changes can easily be mistaken for changes in memory capacity. Thus, a cortical lesion can modify the sense of taste or smell and such sensory modification could be expected to reflect significant changes in performance on a learned task. The animal's memory might be fine, but its tendency to approach (or avoid) previously relevant stimuli could be changed by altering its sensory acuity or level of motivation.*

Isaacson's analysis of problems facing investigators interested in the relationship between brain damage and memory can be taken to serve as a useful model for a comparative inquiry into the relationship between neural mechanisms and behavior. If meaningful generalization about such relationships is to be made, an awareness of species differences *and* similarities in response to

direct manipulation of the central nervous system is of primary importance.

One of the few recent systematic, comparative analyses of the effects of brain damage on memory has been undertaken by Beritoff (1972) and his co-workers in the Soviet Union. Since the 1930s, his laboratory has been making a detailed study of memory in many species of vertebrates from fish to monkeys. In Beritoff's experimental setup, animals are shown food at a distance before it is placed behind an opaque obstacle. In other instances, animals receive painful electrical stimulation when they approach certain areas of their test chamber. At certain intervals after their initial experience, the animals are returned to the testing chamber and their behavior observed. If they started directly toward the food when released from confinement or immediately avoided the place where they had been shocked, Beritoff concluded that the animals had a memory of their previous experiences even though these experiences were based on a single exposure to the test situation.

Beritoff observed some interesting phenomena in the various species studied. For example, fish (*Carassius auratus*) could remember the location of food no longer than 8 to 10 seconds. For shock, the maximal delay was from 10 to 12 seconds; if the fish were removed for longer periods of time, they repeatedly swam into the area in which they had received shock. After forebrain ablation, a delay of 4 seconds was sufficient to disrupt memory of food location.

The results obtained with marsh turtles were considerably different. Delays of up to 2 to 2.5 minutes did *not* disrupt memory for location of food. Memory for noxious stimulation could withstand a delay interval of from 4 to 5 minutes; after that the turtles would return to the same place in which they had been shocked. After forebrain ablation, the turtles were only able to remember where they had obtained food if the delay interval was no longer than 15 to 30 seconds; and, for avoidance of noxious stimulation, the maximal delay was 20 to 25 seconds. These data can be taken to indicate that a severe impairment resulted from the surgery.

In chickens and pigeons, delays of from 8 to 10 minutes did *not* disrupt memory of where food was located, and memory of noxious stimulation was present up to *one month* after the experience. In such birds, lesions of the hyperstriatum and cortex drastically impaired memory for location of food; the animals did very poorly if the delays exceeded 15 seconds. When both cortex and hyperstriatum were ablated, memory was totally lost.

In cats and dogs, memory for location of food was present after lapses of 20 to 30 minutes and "emotional" memory of the noxious stimulus persisted for weeks. Following neocortical ablations, "image" memory for location disappeared completely although some emotional memory was retained.

From these observations, Beritoff concluded that there is a gradual development of image memory from fish to monkeys (see also Chapter 14). At lower stages of evolutionary development (fish and reptiles) only short-term memory is evident. Birds seem to be the first category of animals to show evidence of long-term memory.

In each of the species studied, memory for spatial imagery was disrupted by lesions of the forebrain. Evidently, the neocortex becomes important in mediating memories as it develops. In the monkey, lesions of the dorsolateral surface of the frontal cortex, particularly in the principal sulcus, disrupt delayed alternation (DA) and delayed response performance (DR). On the DA task, the monkey retrieves a food reward, which is placed under one of two identical placques placed in front of it. To continue to receive reward, the animal must alternate from one placque to the other after a suitable intertrial delay.

In DR, the monkey is permitted to observe which foodwell is baited, and then, after a certain delay, it is allowed to retrieve the reward. Both tasks depend on what Beritoff would call

"image memory" and both are disrupted by bilateral, single stage lesions of the principal sulcus. The comparative analysis of different species of animals given forebrain or cortical lesions can be taken to show the emerging importance of these structures in the mediation of memory in *vertebrates*. Interestingly enough, although all of the species studied were impaired after brain damage, the consequences of the lesions were greater for those species with the more highly evolved brains. Thus, cats, dogs, and monkeys showed complete loss of image memory after brain damage, while fish, reptiles and birds with forebrain lesions were still able to respond, but at a markedly reduced level of efficiency.

Encephalization of Function and Comparative Analysis

In comparative studies of the type we just discussed, it is tempting to interpret the data as supporting the notion that functions are increasingly encephalized as one "ascends" the evolutionary scale. Encephalization means that "there is an evolutionary process in which the forebrain progressively takes over functions which, in more primitive forms, are organized in levels (structures) below that of the cerebrum" (Weiskrantz, 1961).

The concept of progressive encephalization of function has been criticized on several grounds that are particularly relevant to those concerned with *comparative* analyses of brain-behavior relationships. First, when comparisons are made between species subjected to brain damage, one should ask the following: Do the tests used to examine the presence or lack of deficit have the same meaning for the different types of animals? As Weiskrantz has pointed out in a hypothetical reversal of the types of learning apparatus typically used with rat and monkey:

. . ."to what extent is a monkey tested in a water maze or jumping stand equivalent to a rat reaching for a banana with a long stick or dismantling a puzzle box?"

Second, differences in brain structure between different species may be such that brain damage may alter CNS organization to a much greater extent in one species than in another — that is, structures may not necessarily be homologous (see end of page for definition) with respect to function. Weiskrantz also suggests that an increase in cortical development not only leads to an increase in the complexity of behavior, but may also lead to progressive change in functions with advancing phylogenetic status. Thus, parallels between structure-function relationships in simple and complex organisms may not always be appropriate for conceptualizing neural mechanisms underlying behavior across species. Indeed, in some cases, brain structures are more complex in "lower" animals than in man. Weiskrantz (1961, p. 39) cites the anatomist Van Bonin, who said:

"It is customary to consider man as the proud and finished product of an evolutionary line starting from rather imperfect forms and gradually approaching human standards by increasing differentiation. It needs no more than a glance at photographs of the striate cortex (a part of the visual system of the brain) to see that lamination of the striate area is more elaborate in tarsius than in the monkeys, and more elaborate in the monkeys than in apes or man."

Supporting Van Bonin's idea is Clarke and Penman's finding (1934) that the lateral geniculate nucleus (a subcortical brain area implicated in visual information processing) of the rhesus macaca shows greater differentiation into laminae than is true of humans.

More recently, Hodos and Campbell (1969) have strongly criticized the notion of a *scala naturae* (phylogenetic scale) in which man represents the high point of evolutionary development. These authors claim that classification according to a heirarchy in which the relative positions of animals are organized as "higher" or "lower" with respect to humans (and each other) is inaccurate. How, they ask, would one determine whether a porpoise is higher (on the scale) than a cat? Hodos and Campbell suggest that:

"while a hierarchical classification can provide interesting information about relative performance and relative degrees of structural differentiation, it tells us nothing about evolutionary development since it is unrelated to specific evolutionary lineages. Thus, to say that amphibians represent a higher degree of evolutionary development than teleost fish is practically without meaning since they have each followed independent courses of evolution. Moreover, one can find characteristics in which teleosts exceed amphibians as well as vice versa."

Comparing the behavior of different species or classes of animals in their normal state or after CNS manipulation is a perfectly legitimate endeavor and is the only way to understand important similarities in the behavior of diverse organisms. However, Hodos and Campbell stress that comparative psychologists, neuroanatomists, and physiologists have failed to recognize the important principle that there are diverse sources of similarity (both morphological and behavioral) among various organisms.

Only one of these sources is inheritance from common ancestors and is usually referred to as "homology." Conversely, similarities may also be due to the independent evolution of similar characteristics by more or less closely related forms. Similarity that is not due to inheritance from a common ancestor is referred to as "homoplasy." Homoplasy is a generic term, which includes such forms of similarity as parallelism, convergence, analogy, mimicry and the like. When nonhomologous structures serve similar *functions*, whether or not they are similar in appearance, they are referred to as "analogous." Thus, the hands of a racoon and a human are homologous as anterior appendages and homoplastic in their particular appearance as hands. They are not homologous as hands since they were evolved independently of each other. Finally, they are analogous in their functions as prehensile organs.

With respect to brain functions, one can observe analogous behaviors in different species that are mediated by nonhomologous structures differing in complexity, morphology and perhaps importance for the animals's adaptability to the environment. Only a careful, comparative analysis of the means-end relationships that animals use to resolve problems in their environment with, or without brain damage, can elucidate the neural mechanisms which subserve their behavior (see Laurence and Stein, 1978, for discussion of this problem). In contemporary physiological psychology, the tendency is to use a few strains of laboratory rats, a few different strains of mice, and sometimes, the rhesus monkey (see above). The rhesus has become the primate of choice because initially it was most easily obtained, but also because "standardized" tests of its behavior has been developed and used by the community of investigators fortunate to have monkeys available for their brain research. As a result, surgical procedures, histology, anatomy, and other techniques could also be standardized, and the same general considerations have applied to those working with the albino rat as well.

Mayr (1968, cited in Hodos and Campbell, 1969) has described the situation as follows: "When the learning psychologist (or physiological psychologist, etc.) speaks of THE RAT or THE MONKEY, or the racist speaks of THE NEGRO, this is typological thinking." Hodos and Campbell point out that "the typological approach carries with it the implication that the particular species being investigated is a generalized representative of the entire order, or class, when in fact that species may be highly specialized and *not at all representative* (italics mine, p. 348)."

In the next section of this chapter, the reader will see that there are important differences in behavior and physiology within the same class of animals. Strain differences often limit the degree to which one can generalize about the neural mechanisms underlying behaviors such as nest building, mating, response to fearful stimuli, and learning.

Genetic Factors Influencing Learning and Memory

Suppose an investigator is asked to determine whether a certain new drug improves memory. Not enough is known about the substance to administer it to humans, so the next best approach would be to test the experimental compound in laboratory rats under carefully controlled conditions. (I will use a hypothetical drug that improves memory as an example, but think of the recent controversy engendered over the question of whether saccharine is safe for humans because it produced tumors in one strain of rat.)

To begin, select a group of rats or mice designated to receive the drug (several groups, each receiving a different dose, would be even better) and give another group a control injection of just the solution in which the drug is dissolved. [Ideally, one should be ignorant of which substance (drug or control) any given animal receives.] As a good scientist, make certain that all other variables (e.g., handling, feeding etc.), *except* for the administration of the memory-facilitating drug, are held constant across groups. After the animals are trained on each task, they are given an injection of Compound "X" or the control solution, and then all of the animals are retested at a later time. Suppose that the experimental group shows highly significant improvement in retention on all of the tasks compared to animals receiving the control injection. Can you conclude that this new drug improves memory? A series of experiments performed by Daniel Bovet and his colleagues (1969) might prove helpful in answering this question.

These investigators were interested in testing the hypothesis that learning can be enhanced by increasing activity in the cholinergic arousal systems of the brain (acetylcholine in the brain is considered to be an excitatory neurotransmitter) by giving animals potent stimulants. Bovet et al. first showed that nicotine administered to rats improved "elementary" forms of learning and

was probably a stimulant of the arousal system. On the basis of this finding, the experimenters injected 0.5 milligrams per kilograms of nicotine into nine different inbred strains of mice and trained the animals to make a conditioned avoidance response in a simple shuttlebox (see Chapter 10). Their results showed that the various strains attained quite different performance levels in the same test situation and that there were important differences in the effects of nicotine in the various strains. Nicotine facilitated learning

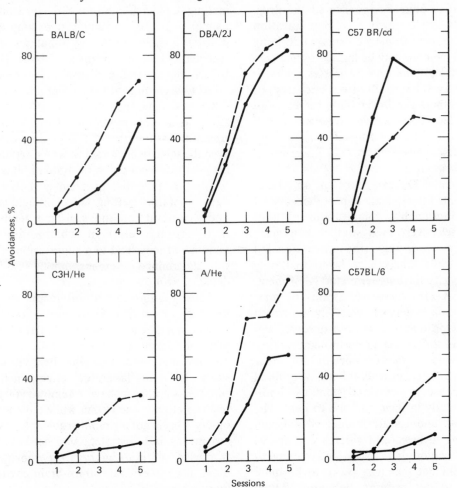

Figure 11.3 Effects of nicotine (0.5 mg/kg) on avoidance conditioning of six inbred strains of mice. Dotted lines, nicotine-injected groups; solid lines, control groups. [From Bovet et al. (1969).]

Brain Function: Comparative Analysis of Problems in Physiological Psychology in six out of nine of the strains while the same dose impaired performance in two of the strains tested. Figure 11.3 graphically represents some of these data. In general, nicotine facilitated learning in those strains of mice that generally showed low levels of performance in the non-drugged state, which probably tells us something about the function of nicotine in the CNS.

In any event, the experiments by Bovet et al. indicate that a so-called memory facilitating compound can have different effects depending on the strain of animal administered the drug. The findings suggest that any generalization regarding the neural mechanisms underlying learning and memory may be limited by the possibility that the physiological processes responsible for memory storage differ from one strain of mouse to another. The Bovet study serves as an example of how comparative investigation can reveal strain differences in drug effects. There are probably class, genus, and species differences in drug effects, as well.

More recently, Duncan, Grossen, and Hunt (1971) attempted to replicate in part the Bovet et al. results. Presumably, some strains of mice have been selectively bred so that they have short-term memory (e.g., the strain labeled C3H/HeJ), while others have been bred only with the capacity for long-term storage of memory (e.g.,DBA/2J). These two strains of mice were tested on a battery of aversively motivated tasks, and Duncan and co-workers observed significant strain differences in performance. They concluded, however, that the mice did not differ on memory capacity: instead, the strains differed in their response to stress and stimulus conditions, particularly in their response to light. The Duncan et al. findings are reminders of Isaacson's warning to beware of variables in an experimental situation that are not always immediately apparent but that may prove to be quite significant in determining behavior. Thus, changes in performance attributed to differences in memory storage capacity were shown to be due to the animal's ability to cope with stress and to the peculiar response of one of the mouse strains to the presence of a light as a conditioned stimulus in the test situation. If comparative testing had *not* been carried out in this experiment, it would have been easy for the researchers to draw the wrong conclusions about memory processes.

A failure to carry out a comparative analysis in testing the effects of drugs or lesions on memory storage can sometimes lead to both practical and theoretical difficulties. For example, some investigators have questioned the possibility that memory storage capacity can be improved by posttrial injection of neural stimulants and have reported failure to confirm the facilitation effect. In arriving at this conclusion, the researchers failed to account for the fact that they had used a different strain of rats than those used to demonstrate facilitation of memory. There is no *a priori* reason to assume that the same dose of drug or even the same behavioral test would replicate earlier results when a different strain of rat is used.

Another potential problem is that the standard laboratory setting (small individual cages under constant conditions of light, temperature, diet, activity, etc.) in which animals are maintained may lead to a suppression of genetically determined differences among strains (Henderson, 1970).

Thus, a failure to find differences in response to drugs or other CNS manipulation between strains, might *not* be due to similarity of treatment effects on all animals, or to unity of the mechanisms mediating the behaviors under study. The same laboratory environment might suppress or alter behavior (emotionality, food-seeking, etc.) in one strain, while enhancing it in others. This is not a simple problem to resolve by any means, but this interaction needs to be confronted if one is to improve experimental paradigms used to evaluate strain-brain-environment interactions.

In drug or environmental manipulation studies dealing with strain differences and behavior, it is sometimes argued that the effects observed are due primarily to variability in the *rate* or speed of information processing in the central nervous system. For example, the *mechanisms of* memory consolidation (i.e., the hypothetical process by which short-term memory traces are converted into long-term structural memories or "engrams") are assumed to be the same from one strain to another. Any differences that exist are in the rate of information processing or degree of arousal produced by the administration of stimulant drugs. Differences in the biochemistry of the brain area that is assumed to mediate memory in the strains under study may produce either disruption or facilitation when a particular drug in administered. A study by Izquierdo and associates (1972) illustrates this point. They examined the biochemistry of the hippocampus in rats with a poor, inborn learning ability.

> Rats with a low ability to learn conditioned avoidance responses in a shuttlebox were inbred over five or six generations to produce animals that performed poorly in both a shuttlebox and Lasley III maze situation. Izquierdo hypothesized that during learning, the hippocampus is particularly active and necessary for stimulus recognition and inhibition of inappropriate responses. Correlated with this functional activity is a change in release of potassium (K^+), an ion which plays a very important role in conduction of the nerve impulse. The release of potassium appears to be necessary for the synthesis of proteins and RNA, both of which are required for the hippocampus to process information during the learning. It has been shown that drugs which facilitate learning, such as nicotine and amphetamine, act to increase neural activity in the hippocampus and also increase the levels of RNA in this structure.
>
> In genetically bred slow learners, Izquierdo and his colleagues were able to demonstrate that potassium release is lower

during hippocampal stimulation than in rats that learn more rapidly. When the hippocampus was submitted to 25 minutes of a suitable afferent stimulation (by direct implantation of electrodes into the structure), "high performance" rats featured an increase in RNA concentration while "poor learners" showed none.

These series of experiments by Izquierdo and his colleagues show that strain dependent differences in learning ability are mediated by biochemical factors that vary according to whether the animals are selectively bred for speed and accuracy of learning.

Karczmar and Scudder (1967) performed similar experiments on different genera and strains of field mice. The mice they examined occupy different ecological niches and vary markedly in behavior and rate of maturation. *Microtus*, for example, is a grassland creature, herbivorous and quite fearless; *Anychomys* is adapted to desert life and, depending on food conditions, is omnivorous or herbivorous. As mentioned before, there are significant differences among strains of mice on various learning tasks. *Mus musculus* learn avoidance and many other tasks well, while *Microtus* are unable to do so. *Peromyscus* and *Onychomys* show improved maze performance with training but are unable to learn to avoid.

As in the Bovet et al. study, the mice studied by Karczmar and Scudder show dramatic variation in exploratory response and activity in response to acute or chronic injections of a neural stimulant (methamphetamine): some strains exhibit no drug effect at all; others show increased activity; and some display a marked decrease in response. And, at the biochemical level of analysis, Karczmar and Scudder found significant differences between the different strains in levels of brain catecholamines (another type of neurotransmitter found in the CNS).

These differences are evident in Figure 11.4,

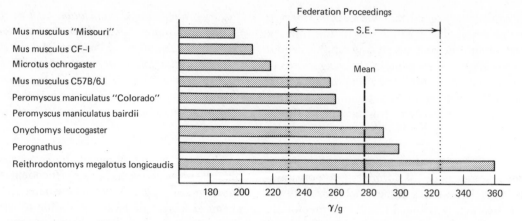

Figure 11.4 Total brain levels of biogenic amine for six genera and several strains of mice. Each barograph represents, in micrograms per gram, wet brain weight, combined values of scrotonin, dopa, dopamine, norepinephrine, and epinephrine. Generally, the levels of the various bioamines run parallel in the various strains and genera. [From Clark and Dewhurst (1972).]

which shows total brain levels of biogenic amines in six genera and several strain of mice. Here, the extreme values (*Mus musculus* versus *Reithrodontomys*) indicate that there can be a threefold difference in brain amine levels between groups; and it is certainly reasonable to assume that these strain-dependent concentrations of neurotransmitters would affect the animals' reactions to drugs and their consequent behavior. If one wants to talk about brain amines and learning in "the mouse," which mouse would be most appropriate to refer to?

Anatomical Considerations

Biochemical differences among different strains of the *same* genus are paralleled by morphological or anatomical variations in the structure of the central nervous system. Under such circumstances, the *consequences* of brain damage might be very different from one strain of animal to another. If the results of lesions vary among strains, the *function*, as well as the output of brain structures (in terms of levels of neurotransmitters), might vary from strain to strain. If this were the case, then generalizations concerning the function of the hippocampus, the frontal

lobes, the visual cortex, or *any* structure in the brain, for that matter, would be very limited.

With respect to gross anatomical differences among strains of mice, Wimer, Wimer, and Roderick (1969) were able to demonstrate that there are significant differences between strains in total brain volume, as well as in absolute and relative size of the hippocampus and frontal cortices. The same authors (1971) subsequently showed that the *ratio* of hippocampal volume to forebrain volume was positively correlated with passive avoidance conditioning and that relative volume of the neocortex was negatively correlated with open field activity. In other words, animals with larger hippocampi learned passive avoidance better than mice with a smaller hippocampal structure.

If naturally occurring variations in anatomical structure influence performance, what effects would removal of structures in different strains have on performance? Meyer, Yutzey, and Meyer (personal communication) trained albino (Wistar strain) and hooded (Long-Evans-strain rats) to perform a black-white discrimination. There were no strain differences in original learning, but albino rats relearned the habit more slowly than hooded rats after a bilateral removal of posterior visual cortex. The two strains did not differ on measures of reactivity, postoperative weight gain, and mortality. Since both strains initially learned equally well, the deficit following surgery in the Wistar albinos must have been due to differences in the capacity of the "residual visual mechanism" to mediate recovery. Thus, the organization of the visual system (and perhaps functional organization of the CNS) may vary from one closely related strain to another, at least as far as the response to traumatic injury is concerned.

Summary

If we are to gain a detailed understanding of the physiological mechanisms related to human behavior, data gained from experimentation on animals are necessary. At the same time, we must be aware of the great differences in neural organization and behavioral responsiveness that may exist between animals differing in genus, species, and even strain. The difficulties involved in interpreting these differences cannot be underestimated, but the situation is far from hopeless. By comparing across broad classes of animals and determining similarities and differences in the way nervous systems relate to behavior, we can derive the general principles underlying all

neural activity. In this way, we may construct educated, although possibly tentative, hypotheses concerning how our own distinct nervous systems organize and, in turn, are organized by our environment.

Study Questions

1. What are the advantages of a comparative approach to the study of brain functioning?
2. What are some of the problems attached to experimenting with different animals in the area of physiological psychology?
3. Who was the first person to do bona fide comparative research in brain-behavior relationships? What was one of the main conclusions he arrived at from his research?
4. Summarize Isaacson's main point on doing research on neural mechanisms and behavior with animals.
5. Who is Beritoff and what has he descovered about animal memory?
6. Distinguish between homologous and analogous structures and relate this distinction to the analysis of behavior in different species.
7. What can you say about strain differences in learning and the biochemistry of the organism?

12

Habituation From A Comparative Perspective

Bruce C. Leibrecht and Henry R. Askew

U.S. Army Medical Research and Development Command,
Fort Detrick, MD.
Morna Valley School
Ibiza, Spain

In its constant struggle to cope with the daily business of living, each member of the animal kingdom must be able to adapt to a complex and changing environment. In response to these unique and changing demands, a variety of mechanisms for modifying behavior has evolved. One of these basic mechanisms is habituation, generally defined as a reduction in response strength due to repeated stimulation (Harris, 1943).

In the natural world, stimuli commonly occur on a repeated basis. Animals encounter leaves of a tree rustling in the wind, birds singing, the odors of the burrows, and the like many times a day. These repetitive stimuli may occur irregularly or predictably and intermittently or continuously; for example, the sounds of a flowing brook or a waterfall are likely to be continuous. When these stimuli tend not to convey any special biological significance (e.g., danger, food, shelter), the responses that they initially elicit typically wane and may disappear altogether.

This decrement in response strength is the basic characteristic of habituation, and it should be noted that the elimination of unneeded responses is as important to the welfare of the animal as the acquisition of new patterns of behavior.

Let us consider a deer grazing at the edge of a meadow as dawn arrives. A woodpecker in a nearby tree raps sharply as it searches for food. The deer quickly raises its head, ears erect and alert, eyes gazing apprehensively, muscles tense in preparation for flight. It has, of course, stopped feeding. After thoroughly inspecting the surroundings for signs of danger and finding none, the deer slowly lowers its head and resumes grazing. Again the woodpecker raps, and again the deer assumes an alert stance. But this time the pause is shorter, and feeding resumes in earnest. By the third or fourth series of raps, the deer merely raises its head momentarily before resuming its meal. Finally, when several more intrusions by the woodpecker have passed, the deer no longer ceases grazing or raises its head but shows only the slightest flick of its ears as the woodpecker continues its own search for food. A complete disruption of feeding gradually has given way to only slight evidence of responding. Were the deer to persist with the full-blown alerting response each time the rapping occured, it might have little time left for feeding. On the other hand, failure to attend to potentially dangerous stimuli might make the deer's meal its last one.

The *adaptive value of habituation* appears to result from the animal's eliminating responses to frequently occurring, "biologically irrelevant" stimuli while maintaining responsiveness to potentially significant stimuli. A large number of stimuli impinge on the typical organism at any given time. Each one may have potential significance, but some more than others. The shadow of a hawk, for example, is more critical to the foraging ground squirrel than the rustling of leaves in a tree. Concomitantly, the animal is quite limited in how many stimuli it can respond to at once. It must focus on only a few stimuli at a time, ignoring those of little significance. If nonproductive responses were to occur, they could compete with vital activities such as feeding or fleeing, or they could cause the animal to waste energy. Not surprisingly, then, selection pressures have led to the evolution of mechanisms, including habituation, whereby the animal can focus its attention and energy on critical aspects of the environment. Habituation thus serves two major functions: *focus of attention* and *economy of activity*. Such a viewpoint is generally accepted among major theorists who have considered the topic (e.g., Lorenz, 1965).

The Experimental Study of Habituation

In the laboratory, investigations of habituation proceed under controlled conditions. Work by Clark (1960) represents a good example of laboratory studies of habituation.

Marine worms of two species, Nereis pelagica *and* Nereis diversicolor, *were maintained in aquaria and exposed to shadows, sudden light changes, or mechanical vibrations. The worms' defensive withdrawal reflex was measured as stimuli were presented regularly at 1-minute intervals. Nearly all the worms of both species reacted to the first stimulus of a series and then reacted sporadically to subsequent stimuli until responding ceased altogether. Typical habituation curves are presented in Figure 12.1. The degree to which a stimulus might warn of an approaching predator, (i.e., its biological significance) influenced the rate of habituation to the various stimuli. The greater the biological significance of the stimulus, the slower was habituation: complete habituation failed to occur within sixty-five trials for mechanical vibration combined with a sudden decrease in light intensity, but habituation occurred within twenty trials for a simple moving shadow.*

The definition of habituation most commonly used is the one by Thorpe (1963, p.61). He defines it as "the relatively permanent waning of a response as a result of repeated stimulation which is not followed by any kind of reinforcement. It is specific to the stimulus." There are three key features to this definition: (1) relative permanence, (2) stimulus specificity, and (3) lack of reinforcement.

The criterion of relative permanence suggests that habituation is characterized by relatively long-term retention. But just how long is "relatively permanent?" There are few clear-cut guidelines available for making this decision. Hinde (1970) has discussed the wide variation in recovery times found in the literature and concluded that there is no precise dividing line between "short-term" and "long-term" response decrements, especially when comparing different species. Similarly, Thompson and Spencer (1966)

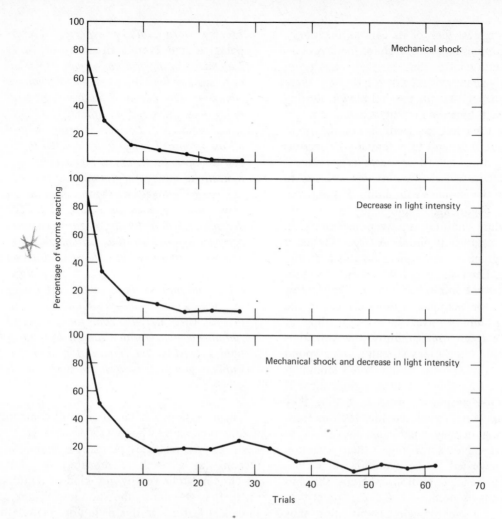

Fig. 12.1 Habituation of marine worms (*Nereis pelagica*) to mechanical shock, to sudden decrease in light intensity, and to a combination of both stimuli presented simultaneously. [Adapted from Clark (1960).]

argue that recovery times are influenced by so many factors that differentiating between long-term and short-term categories is, at best, arbitrary. Although valid, these points do not negate the definitional role of relative permanence in separating habituation from strictly transient phenomena.

Stimulus specificity refers to the notion that habituation is specific to the training stimulus. However, specificity is not an all-or-none phenomenon. To the extent that two stimuli are similar, habituation to one stimulus does generalize to the other. The important point is that habituation is a selective rather than a generalized decrement in response strength.

The requirement that neither positive nor negative reinforcement follow the elicited response rules out the possibility that any decrement due to habituation will be overshadowed by the incremental effect of reinforcement. Also,

A Comparative Analysis

this requirement makes it possible to distinguish habituation from classical and operant conditioning. These two conditioning precedures involve the repetition of stimuli, and here response strength can also decline. Conditioning paradigms that show a decrease in response strength include passive avoidance, conditioned suppression, punishment, and experimental extinction.

Essential Elements in a Study of Habituation

The basic habituation procedure consists of repeatedly presenting a stimulus to an animal and measuring some aspect of the elicited behavior after each stimulus presentation. The following sets of variables need to be considered when investigating the phenomenon of habituation.

The Animal. The species (and possibly the subspecies or strain), sex, and age influence habituation under certain conditions (Brookshire and Rieser, 1967; Glickman and Hartz, 1964; Masur, 1972; Valle, 1971). Other potentially important factors include the animal's past history, sensory capabilities, neuroanatomical organization, state of health, plus knowledge about the animals' natural habitat.

The Response. The only restriction here is that the response be unlearned (Thorpe, 1963). The response can be overt or covert and simple or complex. The level of analysis can be behavioral (e.g., head movement), physiological (e.g., heart rate), neurophysiological (e.g., neural activity), or biochemical (e.g., hormone levels). Multiple behaviors or levels of analysis can be studied simultaneously. While the majority of studies look at only one aspect of behavior, a better picture can generally be obtained by looking at several aspects at once (Wyers et al., 1973). The following summary (Figler, 1972) nicely illustrates the use of multiple behaviors in a study of male Siamese fighting fish. Here habituation of

threat display is studied as a function of the strength of the eliciting stimulus.

Four different stimuli — a responsive ("unhabituated") male Betta, *an unresponsive ("habituated") male* Betta, *a red male* Betta *silhouette ("Cutout"), and a mirror — were used to elicit the male Siamese fighting fish's threat display. Several components of this display pattern were quantified: frequency and duration of gill cover erection, frequency and duration of medial fin erection, and frequency of air gulping. The stimuli were presented continuously for 40 minutes in each of two daily sessions. Only duration of gill cover and fin erection decreased systematically within sessions (Figure 12.2). The gill cover and fin erection measures were highly correlated. For all five measures, the responsive male was the strongest elicitor, followed by the mirror, unresponsive male, and silhouette.*

The most common measure of response in habituation research is *frequency of occurrence*. When only one response can occur during a trial, frequency is occasionally converted into the percentage of animals responding, as was the case in Clark's summarized study. Another commonly used measure is *response strength*, generally expressed as amplitude or intensity. *Response duration* is occasionally used (e.g., Leibrecht and Askew, 1969), and *latency* is used very infrequently.

The response measures mentioned so far are all *direct* measures of habituation effects. From these we can derive *indirect*, second-order measures. The simplest of these expresses response strength as a percentage of some control or reference level, but the most common second-order measure attempts to quantify *rate of habituation*. Three different indexes of rate have been aptly summarized by Hinde (1970): (1) the time or number of trials required for the response to disappear or reach a stable level; (2) the *absolute*

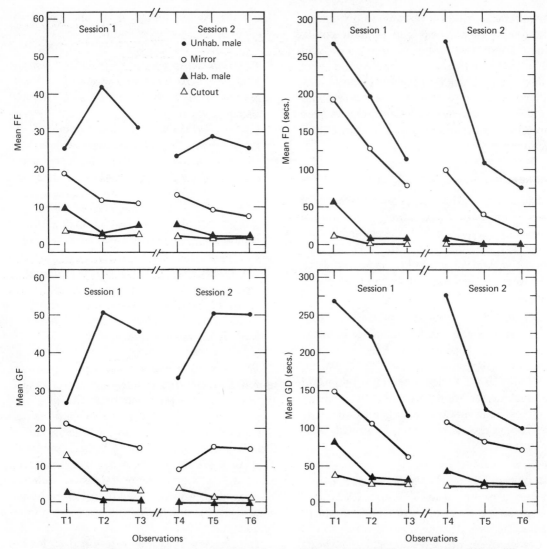

Fig. 12.2 Habituation of four components of the threat display of male Siamese fighting fish to different stimuli. GF = frequency of gill cover erection; GD = duration of gill cover erection; FF = freqency of fin erection; FD = duration of fin erection. [Adapted from Figler (1972).]

amount of response decrement in a given time or number of trials, and (3) the *relative* amount of response decrement in a given time or number of trials. Indirect measures are especially valuable for comparing several different groups or conditions along common dimensions.

The Stimulus. While not every response has a clearly identifiable stimulus, such a stimulus is essential when studying habituation. A wide variety of stimuli has been used in studies of habituation — visual, auditory, vestibular, tactile, and so on. While discrete stimuli of brief duration offer certain advantages in terms of control, prolonged presentations have been used frequently. And sense organs have been bypassed by using direct electrical innervation of neural tissue (Thompson and Spencer, 1966).

Every aspect of a situation that can impinge on an animal's senses is in a very real sense a potential stimulus, whether or not it has a direct or contingent relationship with a selected response. We can identify a host of stimuli for every situation that might well influence an animal's behavior, in addition to the particular eliciting stimulus. These additional stimuli have been called "concurrent stimuli" by Denny and Ratner (1970), who point out that they can occur in either an intermittent or constant fashion. Examples include extraneous sounds (talking, air conditioner, noisy equipment, etc.), visual features (e.g., ambient lights, blinking lights on equipment, movements of the experimenter), tactile stimulation (handling of the animal, physical restraint devices, etc.), and so on. The concept of concurrent stimuli makes it possible to understand an aspect of an animal's behavior that does not conform to expectations. Leibrecht and Kemmerer (1974) have reported that different behaviors of the chinchilla vary in their sensitivity to constant concurrent stimulation, and this is reflected in their rate of habituation. In general, concurrent stimuli can (1) indirectly influence habituation by affecting the animal's state of arousal (Groves and Thompson, 1970; Leibrecht and Kemmerer, 1974), (2) facilitate habituation by eliciting competing responses, or (3) retard habituation by eliciting responses compatible with the response being habituated (Denny and Ratner, 1970). Later in this chapter concurrent stimuli are used to help analyze a special aspect of habituation — dishabituation.

Stimulus Repetition. In most laboratory studies of habituation, the stimulus is repeated in quite regular fashion. The physical features of the stimulus and the rate of presentation are held more or less constant. A single presentation of the stimulus is called a *trial*. The time separating successive trials is called the *intertrial interval*, frequently abbreviated as *ITI* ; but sometimes it is called the *interstimulus interval*. The ITI may vary widely from one study to another, but normally ranges from a few seconds to several minutes. It may be of a fixed or variable duration. Trials are normally organized in a group known as a *session*, and blocks of sessions may be presented at a given *intersession* interval.

What Habituation Is Not

Response decrement can result from a variety of processes, only one of which is called habituation. Our main concern is with the types of response decrement that do *not* represent learning, for these are the easiest to confuse with genuine habituation. This category includes sensory adaption, effector fatigue, motivational changes, and biorhythms. All of these are fully reversible and the first two are generally considered to involve peripheral rather than central nervous system mechanisms (the evidence for habituation as a central process is quite convincing). Two other sources of response decrement, generally irreversible, also deserve brief discussion — maturation and trauma.

Sensory Adaptation

Adaptation refers to decreased responsiveness of the sense organ that occurs during prolonged or rapid stimulation. This phenomenon is usually quite shortlived, although there is considerable variability across different sensory modalities. Typical recovery times range from several seconds to 30 minutes (Kling and Riggs, 1971). In studies of habituation, several procedures can be used to rule out or test for sensory adaptation effects. The most straightforward procedure consists of repeating the eliciting stimulus at an ITI sufficiently long to allow sensory adaptation effects to dissipate (e.g., 10 minutes). Because such long ITIs are usually impractical, an alternative procedure is more commonly used. This involves testing for retention of the decrement following an interval sufficient for complete recovery of sensory adaptation effects. If test stimuli show little recovery of responsiveness after, say, 60 minutes, we can be confident that the decrement was not produced to any large extent by sensory adaptation. A third procedure is the dishabituation test. If, after waning of the response, presentation of a novel stimulus causes the next presentation of the standard stimulus to elicit a response (dishabituation), we have solid evidence that the receptor organ is still functionally responsive and thus that adaptation cannot account for the observed decrement in response. Hinde (1970) and Goodman and Weinberger (1973) discuss additional procedures for assessing sensory adaptation effects.

Effector Fatigue

By effector fatigue we mean decreased responsiveness of the effector mechanism, which includes the muscle system involved in the response plus the neuroeffector junction (Thompson and Spencer, 1966). Effector fatigue is most likely to occur with high rates of stimulus repetition or with continuous stimulation. In assessing fatigue effects, the general approach is to test whether the response that has waned is still capable of occurring, usually by substituting a new stimulus for the old eliciting stimulus. Failure of the response to occur to the new stimulus does not demonstrate effector fatigue produced the decrement, but occurence of the response does eliminate fatigue as the basis for the decrement. In applying this test it is wise to minimize the similarity between the old and the new stimulus in order to minimize generalization of habituation. For example, a tactile or auditory stimulus could be appropriately substituted for a photic stimulus. Most of the procedures used for evaluating sensory adaptation can also be used for ruling out fatigue effects.

Motivational Changes

Habituation-like response decrements can be produced by changes in the motivational state of the organism (e.g., by reduction in hunger or thirst). Changes in responding due to motivational factors are the result of changes in internal physiological conditions, including hormone levels, rather than of experiential factors that we usually associate with learning. Thus, Hinde (1970) argues that cases of decrement that follow a "consummatory response" (e.g., eating, drinking, and copulation) do not constitute habituation. In experiments on habituation we can minimize the potential influence of motivational factors by precluding reinforcement from the test session and by holding *all* conditions constant across days.

Biorhythms

A universal characteristic of biological phenomena is the occurrence of rhythms or cycles of varying duration. Eating, sleeping, locomotion, body temperature, heart rate, and so on all show distinct rhythmic fluctuations (increments and decrements). The duration of these cycles may be in minutes, hours, days, or even months. One of the most common is the circadian rhythm, with a cycle of approximately 24 hours. Goodman and Weinberger (1973) have amply pointed out how periodicities of short duration may influence the course of habituation, at least in amphibians. However, periodicities on the order of 6 to 24 hours can also interact with the typical habituation experiment. If a series of stimuli is presented during the descending phase of a behavioral cycle, any progressive decrement in responding could be due to the rhythm itself rather than habituation. Davis and Sollberger (1971) have reported that the startle response in rats shows circadian threshold fluctuations, and they point out how these changes could confound the results of habituation studies. We can guard against spurious conclusions due to bio-rhythms by gathering adequate *baseline information* on the responses in question. Both *spontaneous* and *stimulated* baseline data are required. The latter data are obtained by presenting the test stimulus at relatively long intervals (e.g., every 2 to 4 hours). Both types of data are then used to correct or adjust the habituation curves obtained in the same or other animals. While baseline data cost the experimenter additional time and effort, they are indispensable in the systematic study of habituation. Ratner (1970) offers a good discussion of the importance of baseline observations in studies of habituation.

Maturational Changes

Decremental changes in behavior that can be attributed to growth, maturation, or aging clearly cannot be considered habituation. Such changes are most likely to occur in (1) long-term studies of habituation where sessions may be spaced across several days, or weeks, and (2) studies using young animals as subjects. Behavioral changes in this category are most often irreversible or permanent. As a check for maturational effects in habituation studies, we can test for recovery (reversibility) of the decrement. We can also include control groups that do not receive the stimulus in the early sessions but do receive it in the later sessions. If, in the later sessions, the control animals exhibit the same response levels as the experimental animals, any decrement shown from the early sessions by the experimental animals would not likely be due to experimentally produced habituation.

Trauma and Disease

Trauma that produces tissue damage can result from accidental injury, surgery, blood transfusion, hemorrhage, hypoxia, and so on. The term has also been used to refer to receptor damage caused by intense stimulation (Goodman and Weinberger, 1973). It is clear that response decrements due to temporary or permanent tissue damage or to illness-related functional changes do not constitute habituation. Since the majority of the effects in this category are irreversible, a good first step in checking for them is to test for reversibility by a spontaneous recovery test. Lack of recovery is solid evidence in favor of a trauma interpretation, but the occurrence of recovery does not necessarily rule out trauma. Additional procedures include using control groups (e.g., sham surgery controls) and replicating suspicious findings with new animals. Finally, neurological evaluation procedures may be of value in assessing traumatic injury.

Characteristics of Habituation

Habituation exhibits a number of characteristic features. With minor modifications, the set of characteristics proposed by Thompson and Spencer (1966), which focuses on stimulus and training variables, guides the following discussion.

Negative Exponential Response Decrement

As the number of trials increases, the average strength of the response decreases progressively as a decelerating or negative exponential function; that is, the decrement occurs rapidly at first then more and more slowly (see Figure 12.1). Many habituated responses cease to occur entirely (e.g., Gardner, 1968), while others never seem to reach a zero level (e.g., Leibrecht and Askew, 1969).

Group or *average* curves usually decline smoothly, though some curves show a considerable number of fluctuations (Leibrecht and Kemmerer, 1974; Morrell and Morrell, 1962). However, *individual* habituation curves commonly show marked fluctuations (Hinde, 1970), and there are substantial individual differences in rate of habituation for the same preparation. In fact, Denny and Ratner (1970) consider the occurrence of *individual differences* a general characteristic of habituation. Gardner (1968), for example, observed that individual earthworms required between 2 and 72 trials for their withdrawal response to vibration to disappear, while the same individuals required between 12 and 197 trials for the hooking response to disappear. These individual differences were very stable across 8 days.

Although the frequency of the response does generally decline with stimulus repetition, it is often the case that *not all measures of response show a decline*. Leibrecht and Askew (1969), studying the head-shake response in rats to a puff of air in the ear, found that frequency, latency, and interresponse time all underwent changes consistent with habituation, but duration and several other measures of the response failed to change at all. Similarly, Figler (1972) observed that during waning of the threat display of the male Siamese fighting fish, gill cover erection and fin erection both decreased in duration but not in frequency.

While the response selected for study may decrease during habituation trials, other responses or behaviors may simultaneously increase in strength. Gardner (1968) noted that, as the earthworm's withdrawal response to vibration habituated, feeding responses increased in frequency. And Russell (1967), who studied responses of guppies (*Lebistes reticulatus*) to a shadow stimulus, reported that nonjerk responses increased in frequency as jerk responses decreased across trials.

Spontaneous Recovery and Retention

When the eliciting stimulus is discontinued, the strength of the habituated response increases (recovers) spontaneously over time. This is analogous to a decay or forgetting process and differentiates habituation from various irreversible processes, such as maturation and trauma effects. A typical recovery curve can be seen in

Figure 12.3. The decelerating shape of this curve is characteristic of the recovery of habituated responses. That is, recovery occurs rapidly at first, gradually slowing as complete recovery or some intermediate level is approached. The time required for complete recovery varies greatly, ranging generally from a few minutes (especially

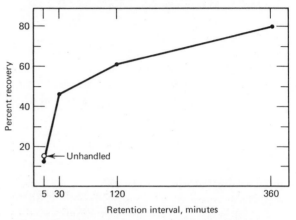

Fig. 12.3 Recovery of the habituated head-shake response of rats. "Unhandled" = control animals. [From Leibrecht and Askew (1969).]

for simpler organisms; see Hinde, 1970) to several weeks (e.g., Brown, 1965). As Hinde (1970) and Peeke and Peeke (1973) point out, part of this variability may be due to procedural differences in stimulus intensity, length of ITI, and the like. Peeke and Peeke tentatively conclude that recovery occurs more slowly the more complete the habituation. Time for recovery, as suggested by Ratner (1970) and Hinde (1970), also seems to be determined by the nature of the responses.

The reverse of recovery from habituation is the concept of *retention* of habituation; what has not yet recovered is obviously still retained. If, for example, an habituated response undergoes 60 percent recovery after 24 hours, we can say that 40 percent of the original habituation is retained. We measure retention in two major ways. The easiest method is to measure the response on a single trial at the end of the retention interval and compute an absolute or relative retention score. This procedure focuses on initial responsiveness. The second, and more comprehensive, approach is to administer an additional session identical to the original habituation session following the retention interval. When this approach is followed, retention is indicated if habituation is faster following the retention interval than it was originally. This "savings" effect may occur even if initial responsiveness seems to indicate full recovery. The phenomenon of more rapid habituation in later sessions has been labeled *potentiation of habituation* by Thompson and Spencer (1966).

Stimulus Frequency Effects

One of the major variables which influence habituation is stimulus frequency or rate of stimulation (Denny and Ratner, 1970; Thompson and Spencer, 1966). The usual effect is for higher rates of stimulation to produce faster and greater habituation (e.g., Askew, 1970; Prechtl, 1958), as can be seen in Figure 12.4. However, the situa-

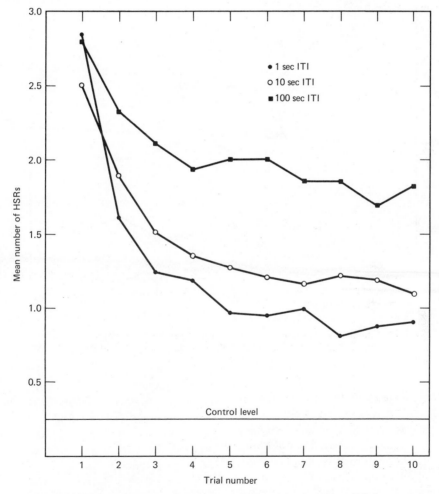

Fig. 12.4 Effects of stimulus frequency on habituation of rats' head-shake response to air-puff in ear. [From Askew (1970).]

Habituation From A Comparative Perspective

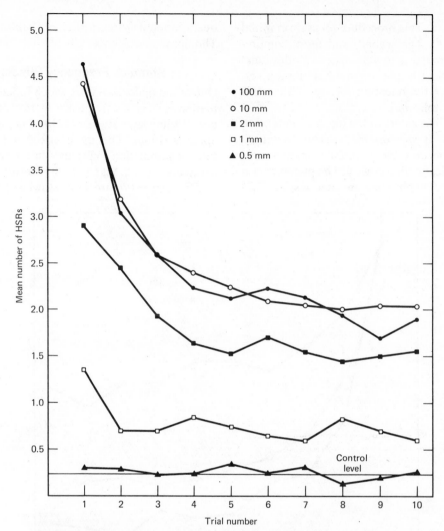

Fig. 12.5 Effects of stimulus intensity measured in millimeters (mm) drop of column of mercury on habituation of rats' head-shake response to air-puff in ear. [From Askew (1970).]

tion is more complicated than this. In a review of the literature, Askew (1970) concluded that shorter ITIs produce lower terminal response levels *or* faster habituation, but usually not both. Furthermore, the habituation of human neonatal cardiac acceleration to sound is not affected by stimulus frequency (Bartoshuk, 1962), and Davis (1970a,b) obtained contrary results when study-

ing the habituation of the startle response in rats. Using separate training and test series, Davis found greater habituation after a longer ITI, although the habituation curves during the training session showed the typical ITI effects. This illustrates that different conclusions can be reached depending on the procedural approach followed. In short, it seems that habituation occuring within a single session is directly related to rate of stimulus presentation, while habituation across days is inversely related to presentation rate.

The variability of the ITI can also affect habituation. A common finding is that *fixed* ITIs produce faster and/or greater habituation than *variable* ITIs (Fox, 1964). Such results have been reported by Davis (1970a) and others. However, opposite results were obtained by Pendergrass and Kimmel (1968); and Simons et al. (1966) found no difference between fixed and variable schedules.

The general conclusion we can reach on the basis of the data is that stimulus frequency effects are inconsistent. Thus, it is dangerous to make assumptions about a given experimental situation without an empirical assessment. It is possible that other procedural or organismic variables interact with stimulus frequency to produce this somewhat complicated pattern of results.

Stimulus Intensity Effects

It is generally held that weaker stimuli produce faster and/or greater habituation than stronger stimuli (Thompson and Spencer, 1966). This is especially true for *direct* response measures — higher intensities typically produce higher initial and terminal responses levels (Askew, 1970; Uno and Grings, 1965). However, as Askew (1970) points out, *indirect* measures indicate that stimulus intensity has mixed effects on amount and rate of habituation. In line with such findings, Peeke and Peeke (1973, p. 67) conclude "the relationship between stimulus intensity and rate of waning is not simple and universal even when method of assessment is held constant." Finally, when weaker stimuli are found to yield faster habituation, Askew (1970) and Hinde (1970) argue that the effect is often an artifact of the weaker initial response strength associated with weaker stimuli. This is illustrated in Figure 12.5.

Thus, here again it seems wise for the investigator to evaluate the effects of stimulus intensity in each experimental situation used to study habituation.

Stimulus Generalization

After habituation to stimulus A, presentation of a new stimulus (stimulus B) that would normally elicit the response at full strength may yield a decreased response. When this happens, we say that the habituation to stimulus A *generalizes* to stimulus B. For example, Geer (1969) found that habituation of the galvanic skin response in humans to a 1000-Hertz tone generalized completely to a 1010-Hertz tone, but not at all to an 1100-Hertz tone. The converse of stimulus generalization is *stimulus specificity*: in the example from Geer (1969), habituation of the galvanic skin response to a tone exhibited a fairly high degree of specificity. Generalization can be tested along stimulus dimensions of frequency, hue, intensity or amplitude, spatial location, duration, and even changes in a normally fixed ITI, in pattern structure or sequence, and in sensory modality. Graham (1973) provides a particularly good discussion of generalization of habituation, based exclusively on orienting response research.

Dishabituation

Dishabituation refers to the reinstatement of an habituated response following the presentation of an extraneous stimulus. The procedure here consists of habituating response X to stimulus A, presenting stimulus B, and then measuring response X to stimulus A again. This is somewhat similar to the procedure for testing for stimulus generalization, but the focus is on responsiveness to the original stimulus, not the "intruding" stimulus. Indeed, the procedures for dishabituation and generalization may easily be combined within a single experiment. Whereas in generalization testing stimulus B *must* be an effective elicitor of response X, no such requirement applies to the dishabituation test. Often stimulus B involves a different sensory modality than stimulus A. As mentioned earlier, the dishabituation test is a useful procedure for ruling out both sensory adaptation and effector fatigue.

The bulk of the literature indicates that most responses which habituate can also be dishabituated (cf. Thompson and Spencer, 1966). Gardner (1968), for example, observed that gently squeezing earthworms with tweezers dishabituated the withdrawal-hooking response to vibration in 100 percent of the animals. Often the effects of the dishabituating stimulus are relatively short-lived, lasting only a few trials or a few minutes. However, a few investigators have tried and failed to find dishabituation even when relatively strong dishabituatory stimuli such as an electric shock were used (e.g., Fried et al., 1966; Wickens et al., 1966).

The nature of the dishabituation process has received a good deal of attention, and three general viewpoints have been espoused. The older view was to regard dishabituation as the neutralization, or reversal, of habituation (Humphrey, 1933). A second and more popular approach considers the phenomenon to be an independent and temporary process of sensitization (Groves and Thompson, 1970). Finally, Ratner (1970) analyzes dishabituation as a special case associated with concurrent stimulation. According to this position, concurrent stimuli can produce dishabituation by eliciting responses compatible with the habituating response or can facilitate habituation by eliciting competing responses. This interpretation is especially useful in explaining failures to find dishabituation.

Thompson and Spencer (1966) argue that *habituation of dishabituation* is a basic characteristic of the process of habituation. However, very little research has been directed at this effect. Where it has been shown to occur (e.g., Zimny and Schwabe, 1966), there is little reason to consider it more than a special case of habituation

(Hinde, 1970), rather than an additional general characteristic of habituation processes.

Below-Zero Habituation

According to Thompson and Spencer (1966), when habituation training is continued after the response stabilizes or disappears, slower spontaneous recovery results. Conceptually this represents a kind of overtraining phenomenon, and Gardner (1968) refers to it as "overhabituation." However, very few studies have dealt with this phenomenon, and the available results are contradictory (Gardner, 1968). A thorough evaluation of overhabituation in different experimental situations, with emphasis on multiple response measures, would be of great interest.

Conclusions

The results discussed in this section may have seemed confusing at times, but this is a genuine reflection of reality. Contradictory findings from a broad range of species, stimulus-response systems, and experimental procedures are more or less expected. The "characteristics" we have listed are features commonly, but *not necessarily*, found in the various experimental situations used for studying habituation. Specific experimental findings depend on the response measures and experimental procedures employed.

The Dynamic Nature of Habituation

So far, we have conveniently conceptualized habituation as the simple waning of a response or behavior pattern. This notion is reinforced in the literature by calling habituation the *simplest* form of learning (Thorpe, 1963) and by focusing, as most studies do, on a single stimulus-response system. However, this simplified account fails to do full justice to the concept of habituation. For one thing, individual behaviors rarely occur in isolation, and, for another, the experimental situation nearly always involves a complex, multi-faceted stimulus array, even though we typically focus on a single eliciting stimulus.

Ratner (1970) has called attention to the dynamic nature of habituation by emphasizing that the phenomenon characteristically involves *changes in response topography*; that is, *qualitative* as well as quantitative changes in behavior occur during habituation. Consider Gardner's (1968) study of earthworms; the initial withdrawal-hooking response to vibration gradually gave way to a simple hooking response, while feeding activity and locomotion gradually increased. The latter two behaviors represent *competing responses* in the sense that they compete with and thereby reduce the probability of the habituating responses. Additional examples of topographic changes during habituation are discussed by Wyers et al. (1973) and Peeke and Peeke (1973). Habituation is thus seen as far more than the passive waning of a response; it also seems to involve active competition between responses and the emergence of new sequences of behavior. As Wyers et al. (1973) note, such qualitative changes in the organization of behavior imply a modification in the central mechanisms responsible for integrating behavior.

Hinde (1970) mentions evidence of the complex nature of habituation in discussing the chaffinch's mobbing response to predators. Hinde observed a number of incremental and decremental effects that appeared to operate simultaneously. Short-term, intermediate-term, and long-term *incremental* processes were found to interact with short-term and long-term *decremental* processes, arguing against the notion of habituation as a passive, unitary process.

Habituation and Learning

Nearly all investigators who have studied habituation classify it as a type of learning (Denny and Ratner, 1970; Harris, 1943; Humphrey, 1933; Thompson and Spencer, 1966; Thorpe, 1963). It certainly fits the following common definition of learning: a relatively permanent modification of behavior that occurs through responding to a stimulus situation.

Similarity between Habituation and Learning

Petrinovich (1973) has carefully compared learning and habituation, concluding that both phenomena exhibit many of the same characteristics. His analysis is presented here in summary form:

1. The negative exponential shape of the typical habituation curve is mirrored in the *negative exponential acquisition* curve commonly found in various types of learning experiments. Learning occurs quickly at first, then more and more slowly as trials progress.

2. The *spontaneous recovery* which characterizes habituation is analogous to *forgetting* as seen in learning. Both of these processes follow a negatively accelerated course as a function of time.

3. *Retention* (relative permanence) is characteristic of both learning and habituation by definition. This phenomenon is often studied as *memory* in learning experiments. Also, *potentiation*, or faster acquisition with successive training sessions, is typically encountered in studies of learning (e.g., savings scores in relearning experiments).

4. Below-zero habituation, or *overhabituation*, has its analogue in the learning situation in the form of *overlearning*.

5. *Stimulus generalization* is one of the most pervasive characteristics of learning as well as habituation. A response conditioned to one stimulus will generalize to similar stimuli. The *stimulus specificity* seen with habituation is studied very commonly as *stimulus discrimination* in learning experiments.

6. Analogous to *dishabituation* is the phenomenon of *disinhibition*, usually found in the context of extinction training.

7. The *stimulus frequency effects* usually found in habituation studies can also be found with learning of certain tasks and with extinction of conditioned responses. When learning proceeds more rapidly with longer ITIs, this could often be due to the fact that habituation to the CS and US or the like needs to be minimized to promote efficient learning of the target response (Denny and Ratner, 1970).

8. The *stimulus intensity effects* typically associated with habituation (stronger stimuli produce slower and/or less habituation) do not apply to learning. In fact, learning is usually faster with stronger stimuli. This difference may be related to the fact that habituation weakens stimulus-response associations, whereas learning usually strengthens them.

Petrinovich (1973, p. 144) sums up the evidence by stating, "It seems fair to conclude, with Thorpe, that habituation is probably a basic form of learning."

Habituation in Other Types of Learning

Many studies of learning involve habituation, either by coincidence or by design, which can exert a substantial influence on the course of the learned response. Frequently, habituation training precedes reinforced or final training in order to reduce or eliminate competing responses such as emotionality or exploration.

Preconditioning Adaptation. As Ratner (1970) notes, most studies of animal learning include an initial habituation phase to allow each animal to adapt, or "get used to," the equipment and procedures to be used. During this phase the animal is exposed to handling, restraint (especially common in classical conditioning), test chamber, display panels, and various other features of the experimental situation. All of these features constitute distracting stimuli and can have a disruptive influence on the animal's behavior upon first exposure. In the case of preconditioning adaptation, the experimenter is rarely concerned with habituation per se, but with setting the stage for the training to follow. Consequently, the animal's responses to a particular stimulus are not measured and no habituation curve is plotted. In short, preconditioning adaptation is usually seen as a nuisance — necessary, but bothersome. Preconditioning adaptation, together with procedures that minimize habituation effects to the critical US and CS, such as spacing of trials and short CS presentations, rather clearly facilitate classical conditioning (Denny and Ratner, 1970; Hupka, Massero, and Moore, 1968).

Latent Inhibition. Familiarity with the CS in the standard classical conditioning procedure has been rather thoroughly investigated (e.g., Siegel, 1969). The usual procedure is to present the CS by itself in repeated fashion (habituation training) prior to pairing the CS with the unconditioned stimulus. When this is done, conditioning is retarded or inhibited. Because the apparent inhibition shows up *after* the habituation trials, this phenomenon has been called "latent inhibition" (Lubow, 1973). Here we have another instance where habituation seems to interact with and influence learning.

Comparative Aspects: Response Differences

Classes of Behavior that Habituate

Are all behaviors subject to habituation? We can answer this question by examining the general classes of behavior proposed by Denny and Ratner (1970). Nearly all of the general classes have been shown to habituate in at least one study. These classes include: *exploration* or contacting, including the orienting response (Fowler, 1965; Lynn, 1966); *predator defense* (Hinde, 1954; Rodgers et al., 1963); *aggression* or fighting (Peeke and Peeke, 1973; Ulrich and Azrin,

1962); *feeding*, including preycatching (Lipsitt and Kaye, 1965; Peeke and Peeke, 1972); *sexual behavior*, including courtship and copulation (Barrass, 1961); *care of the young (Noirot, 1964); care of the body surface* (Askew et al, 1969; Kimble and Ray, 1965); and *elimination* (Valle, 1971). In addition to these categories, a handful of simple reflexes has been studied, including flexor reflexes (Thompson and Spencer, 1966), the startle reflex (Davis, 1970a), and nystagmus reflexes (Guedry, 1965). The only general class of behaviors that has not been used in an habituation experiment is *resting*. Thus, the range of behaviors subject to habituation is very broad indeed.

Simple Reflexes Versus Complex Behavior Sequences

A number of major investigators have suggested that the nature of the behavior influences the course of habituation (e.g., Hinde, 1970; Ratner, 1970). In reviewing the relevant data on this issue we consider only studies that have examined two or more behaviors simultaneously or sequentially in the same animals.

Simple Reflexes. Lehner (1941) observed that the rat's tail flexion reflex habituated in half as many trials as its startle response, while the patellar reflex failed to habituate at all. The same investigator reported that in humans the abdominal reflex habituates with moderate speed, while no habituation is seen with the biceps or pupillary reflexes. After obtaining similar results with rats, Prosser and Hunter (1936) suggested that polysynaptic reflexes (possessing at least one internuncial neuron) are capable of habituating while monosynaptic reflexes are not.

A functional approach to differentiating reflexes has been taken by Kozak and Westerman (1966). They conclude that orienting, startle, searching, and body-cleaning reflexes are all habituating responses. On the other hand, postural and alimentary reflexes do not habituate.

They view habituating responses as "positive feedback" reflexes whose motor acts tend to increase afferent input. Conversely, nonhabituating responses are seen as "negative feedback" reflexes, decreasing afferent input. Interestingly, habituating responses are alleged to be easily conditioned using classical conditioning techniques. Kimmel (1973) has endorsed and extended this view, which is consistent with the findings of Lehner (1941) and Prosser and Hunter (1936). In the broad view, however, it may be more realistic to consider different reflexes as varying in speed of habituation along a continuum, rather than habituating or not habituating.

Complex Behavior Sequences. Complex sequences of behavior involve several components organized in serial order and often terminating in consummatory activity. Initial orientation is usually followed by approach, then by some form of physical contact with a goal object. In studying the prey catching behavior of toads, Precht and Freytag (1958) found that the initial orientation toward the prey waned much more slowly than the "approach" or the "jump." Similarly, Rodgers et al. (1963) reported that the goldfish's orienting and alerting responses waned less rapidly than the defensive tailflip response. Similar patterns have been observed in care of the young responses in mice (Noirot, 1964), courtship of hymenoptera (Barrass, 1961, summarized below), and prey-catching behavior of spiders (Szlep, 1964). Such results have led Hinde (1970) to conclude that the earlier, orienting components of a sequence habituate more slowly than the terminal or consummatory components. Essentially the same conclusion was reached by Peeke and Peeke (1973) and Wyers et al. (1973). An opposite conclusion was reached by Ratner (1970) but was based on relatively isolated responses in different species. Therefore, we can provisionally conclude that in complex behavior sequences the orienting or alerting components are the most resistant to habituation. (Here, we are not referring to the readily learned appetitive components of classical and instrumental conditioning — they have a more intermediate status.

The courtship pattern of the minute male chalcid wasp Mormoniella vitri pennis (Walker), *involves a complex sequence of behaviors: turning and chasing the female; mounting; up and down movements of male's head during copulation, organized in repeated head series; and postcopulatory courtship. In this study by Barrass, this pattern was elicited by both receptive and nonreceptive females. Response measures included turns and chases, attempts to mount, mounts, duration of courtship, and number of head series per courtship. Exposure to successive females led to a more or less orderly waning of responses, head series waning first, followed by mounting, and then by attempted mounting. Turning and chasing rarely disappeared. These findings indicate that earlier, orienting behaviors are the slowest to habituate.*

Methodological Pitfalls

Several students of behavior (e.g., Ratner, 1970) have attempted to determine response differences in habituation by comparing responses studied in separate investigations. For example, habituation of the rat's startle response as studied by Davis (1970a) might be compared with habituation of the rat's head-shake response, studied by Askew et al. (1969). We encounter many problems in following this approach. Even when the same species is used, stimulus intensity and frequency, instrumentation, number of trials, response measures, ambient light and noise, and a host of other variables may differ between studies. Occasional investigators use natural stimuli, but most use some sort of artificial stimulus. Some investigators study two or more different behaviors simultaneously, while others study one at a time in sequential fashion.

And even if the same species is used in two separate studies, there are still likely to be differences in subspecies, rearing history, age, nutrition, and other organismic factors. In short, any attempt to compare different responses in independent experiments is fraught with pitfalls.

Experimental Approach for Comparisons Across Responses

When comparing habituation across responses, it is advisable to study the various responses simultaneously with the same stimulus in the same animal. For example, Gardner (1968) measured both the withdrawal and hooking responses of earthworms to the same vibratory stimulus. In cases where it is necessary to study behaviors one by one, stimulus duration, intensity, and frequency should all be constant or comparable across the different phases, as should handling, restraint, concurrent stimuli, and any other feature.

Analysis of Selection Pressures. How are we to interpret any response differences found in habituation? Rozin and Kalat (1971) have argued that a given learning process represents an *adaptive specialization*, shaped by natural selection. They emphasize the importance of considering each learning mechanism in the context of the selection pressures which gave rise to it (See also Chapter 5). According to this approach, it is critical to relate the animal's behavior to its natural history and the ecological requirements involved. Petrinovich (1973) has recommended such an approach in studying habituation.

Accordingly, habituation can be viewed not so much as a *general* characteristic of behavior, but rather as a type of special adaptive function built into each stimulus-response system by separate but somewhat similar selection pressures. From this viewpoint, certain behaviors in some species may be too critical for survival to remain habituated for very long, or habituation may need to be specific to a narrow range of stimuli. Thus, differences in selection pressures may account for response differences in habituation.

Conclusions

This section has focused on the response, without regard to the eliciting stimulus. However, as Peeke and Peeke (1973) imply, the more relevant unit of analysis may be the stimulus-response system. Many responses can be elicited by several different stimuli, and the course of habituation may be influenced by the nature of the stimulus as well as the response.

The evidence described should leave us with an awareness of potential response differences in habituation, especially when we distinguish between simple reflexes and complex sequences of behavior. Such information is important to the comparative psychologist, but, unfortunately, the published research has only scratched the surface. A particularly valuable approach for additional research might be to consider response differences in the context of specific selection pressures acting on individual stimulus-response systems.

Comparative Aspects: Species Differences

Comparisons Across Phyla

All of the major characteristics of habituation have been observed at least sporadically throughout the animal kingdom, with the possible exceptions of potentiation and below-zero habituation in simpler organisms. Harris (1943), Eisenstein and Peretz (1973), Thorpe (1963), and Wyers et al. (1973) have reviewed the literature from all phyletic levels. One provisional conclusion that emerges from these studies is that arranging organisms on a rough continuum from simplest to most complex does *not* shed much light on phylogeny and habituation. Considera-

tion of ecological requirements and associated selection pressures seems to be more important than morphologic complexity of the organism.

Even so, it is self-evident that, as morphologic complexity increases, behavioral complexity also increases. In other words, as sensory, motor, and neural integrative capabilities become more complex, the array of effective stimuli and responses expands accordingly. And two major characteristics of habituation show promise of differentiating between phyletic levels — spontaneous recovery and potentiation.

Spontaneous Recovery.   Several investigators reviewing the literature have concluded that the recovery of habituated responses proceeds more rapidly among simpler organisms (Harris, 1943; Hinde, 1970). In protozoa, at the simplest level, complete recovery of the contraction response requires on the order of a few hours (Applewhite and Morowitz, 1966; Wood, 1970). Similarly, among the coelenterates contraction responses of *Hydra* recover completely within 3 to 4 hours (Rushforth, 1965). While these values overlap the shortest recovery times found at more complex levels, it is generally true that *maximum* observed recovery times increase as morphologic complexity increases. As Hinde (1970) points out, habituation of certain behaviors in more complex organisms can be permanent, or nearly so.

Potentiation.   Wyers et al. (1973) suggest that potentiation, or faster habituation on successive sessions, may be the most useful parameter when comparing across phlya. Potentiation has not been observed in protozoa such as *Spirostomum* (Applewhite and Morowitz, 1966; Kinastowski, 1963), whereas in platyhelminthes (flatworms) and annelids (segmented worms) potentiation is well established (Westerman, 1963; Gardner, 1968). On the basis of these and related data Wyers et al. (1973) suggest that potentiation requires bilateral symmetry and a nervous system with an anterior ganglion. We hasten to note that more research is needed to document the proposed relationship between phyletic status and potentiation of habituation.

Comparisons Among Related Species

It is informative to examine those studies that have directly compared closely related species, for even here there are differences in habituation. Evans (1969) studied the withdrawal response of three closely related marine worms — *Nereis pelagica, Nereis diversicolor*, and *Platynereis dumerilii*. He found marked differences between these species in the rate of habituation. In an investigation of locomotor exploratory behavior in seven species of rodents, Glickman and Hartz (1964) observed differences in the *absolute* rate of habituation. Chinchillas habituated most rapidly, and guinea pigs most slowly. However, there were large differences between species in the overall levels of locomotion and consequently there were no species differences in the *relative* rate of habituation. Hughes (1969) observed that exploratory behaviors (locomotion, rearing, and sniffing) habituated in mice and rats, but not in hamsters. Exploratory behavior was also examined by Brookshire and Rieser (1967) in three strains of mice. They obtained differences in the rate of within-session and across-session habituation.

These results illustrate that we need not cross major phyletic boundaries in order to observe substantial species differences in habituation.

Methodological Pitfalls

Studying different species forces us to contend with a host of *organismic factors*. Sensory capabilities and behavioral repertoires vary widely across phyletic levels, reflecting differences in morphology and complexity of the nervous system. Some animals are nocturnal, others diurnal; some are aquatic, others terrestrial. We must be careful even when dealing with species we consider very similar (e.g., guinea pig and hamster). The further apart the species, the more caution

we need to exercise (consider the earthworm versus the frog). In addition, all of the *procedural problems* discussed earlier apply equally seriously here.

Experimental Approach for Comparisons Across Species

In spite of the formidable difficulties involved, it is possible to design relatively sound studies for comparing habituation in different species. The critical step is selecting a stimulus-response system that is comparable for the species being studied. Homologous behaviors comparable in both function and structure are ideal, but these may be lacking when species are dissimilar. If lacking, the best strategy is to seek classes of behavior that are comparable in function if not in structural basis. Orienting, defensive, and feeding behaviors are especially useful here. The eliciting stimuli should be comparable, ideally involving the same sensory system in each species; and stimulus intensity should be adjusted so as to provide approximately the same eliciting effectiveness. Needless to say, all other procedural details should be as similar as possible, which means having a thorough familiarity with the species being studied, including knowledge of their natural habitats.

Conclusions

From single-celled protozoa (Applewhite and Morowitz, 1966) to humans (Lynn, 1966), habituation occurs throughout the animal kingdom. There is some evidence suggesting that selected characteristics of habituation differentiate between phyletic levels, although the differences are not as profound as we might expect. When all is said and done, we know relatively little about species differences in habituation.

The finding of differences between related species points to a need to examine habituation within the perspective of each species' natural ecological requirements. Evans (1969) and Clark (1960), for example, found that differences in the rate of habituation among closely related species of marine worms appeared to be related to the ecological significance of the stimuli. If habituation is viewed as having been shaped by adaptive selection pressures, then we would expect a given stimulus-response system to exhibit habituation, recovery, generalization, and other habituatory features only to the extent that specific selection pressures operated in the species' evolutionary past. Eventually, such an approach might help explain much of the apparently random variability seen in the habituation literature.

Habituation as a Comparative Tool

To the comparative psychologist habituation offers several features that make it a valuable research tool. (1) As one of the major mechanisms by which the animal adjusts to its complex and changing environment, it has considerable biological importance in an animal's life. (2) The phenomenon occurs throughout the animal kingdom and therefore can be studied in the simplest as well as the most complex organisms. It does not require the presence of an organized nervous system. (3) Habituation is *procedurally* the simplest paradigm in which learning can be studied. It is generally less time consuming and entails fewer interpretation problems. (4) It offers an ample number of well-defined characteristics for comparing different species and stimulus-response systems, providing a detailed, quantitative approach for comparative studies. (5) Its study can help in understanding other aspects of behavior. Thompson and Spencer (1966) point out that habituation is especially useful in studying neurophysiological mechanisms of behavior, and Askew and Kurtz (1974) found aspects of habituation of the abdominal rotation response in pupae of *Tenebrio molitor* helpful in analyzing the adaptive functions of this behavior.

The comparative study of habituation could follow a *between-species* or a *within-species* approach. A *between-species* approach would involve comparing the characteristics of habituation of one behavior (or behavior *class*) in different species. A *within-species* approach would involve comparing the characteristics of habituation of different behaviors in a single species. A variation of the latter approach would be to compare habituation of a given behavior when elicited by different stimuli. Combining both the between- and within-species approaches simultaneously would provide a particularly powerful, although time consuming, strategy. Regardless of the approach chosen, it would appear worthwhile to analyze any similarities and differences found in terms of specific selection pressures that have acted on the different species in their natural habitats.

In habituation, then, the student of comparative psychology has a powerful ally. Through comparative studies of habituation we stand to broaden considerably our knowledge about the evolution of learning mechanisms.

Summary

1. Habituation is defined as "the relatively permanent waning of a response as a result of repeated stimulation which is not followed by any kind of reinforcement" (Thorpe, 1963).

2. The four essential elements in a habituation paradigm are: (a) the animal, with its associated organismic factors; (b) the unlearned response, which can be quantified by both direct and indirect measures; (c) the eliciting stimulus, which is differentiated from concurrent stimuli; (d) stimulus repetition.

3. Direct response measures include frequency, strength (amount, amplitude, or intensity), duration, and latency. Indirect response measures include conversion of frequency to percent of control or baseline level, time or trials to reach a stable level, absolute decrement, and relative decrement.

4. The adaptive value of habituation is that it focuses attention on significant stimuli and makes for economy of activity.

5. Both general and specific considerations point to habituation as a type of learning.

6. Nonlearning processes, which may be confused with habituation, include sensory adaptation, effector fatigue, motivational changes, biorhythms, maturation, and trauma. There are specific procedures for testing for or eliminating these processes in habituation experiments.

7. The more common characteristics of habituation include: (a) negative exponential response decrement; (b) spontaneous recovery, retention, and potentiation; (c) faster habituation with shorter ITIs; (d) faster habituation with weaker stimuli; (e) stimulus generalization; (f) dishabituation; (g) below-zero habituation. A given preparation may not show all of these characteristics, and the direction of certain of the effects may depend on the response measures and experimental procedures employed.

8. Detailed analysis reveals that habituation appears to be a dynamic, complex process involving active competition between responses and the emergence of new sequences of behavior. Multiple incremental and decremental processes may interact to produce apparently simple cases of habituation.

9. Habituation can substantially influence the course of learning, as in preconditioning adaptation and latent inhibition experiments.

10. Differences in habituation of various reflexes have been related to the presence or absence of internuncial neurons and to the positive or negative feedback nature of the reflex.

11. In complex sequences of behavior, the early orienting components generally habituate more slowly than the terminal or consummatory components.

12. Of the major characteristics of habituation, spontaneous recovery and potentiation show promise of differentiating phyletic levels. In general, retention of habituation increases with morphologic complexity.

13. In interpreting both response differences and species differences in habituation, it may be important to examine the selection pressures operating in the animals' natural environment.

14. Habituation is a useful research tool for comparative psychologists because of (a) biological significance, (b) broad phyletic generality, (c) procedural simplicity, (d) multiple characteristics suited to quantitative comparison, and (e) usefulness in studying other aspects of behavior.

15. In addition to the sources mentioned frequently throughout the chapter, it should be noted that Leibrecht (1972, 1974) has published two extensive bibliographies of research on habituation and that Peeke and Herz (1973) have edited a two-volume work on habituation.

Study Questions

1. Cite an example of each of the two major adaptive functions of habituation. Try to think of your own examples.

2. Discuss the attributes of habituation and distinguish habituation from similar inhibitory phenomena.

3. Discuss the main independent variables that determine the course of habituation.

4. Discuss the similarity between habituation and learning and the role habituation often plays in traditional learning situations.

5. According to comparative data, what

components of a complex behavior sequence are most resistant to habituation?

6. What are the major conclusions one can make when comparing species and plyla on the process of habituation?

7. What are some of the difficulties involved in making such comparisons?

13

Insect Behavior: Using the Cricket as a Comparative Baseline

Thomas E. Hagaman

Departments of Psychology and Entomology
Michigan State University

This chapter illustrates a microcosm of animal behavior, representing in miniature the organization, emphases, ideas, and comparative methodology of this book — attempting to do for the insect what the book attempts to do for the animal kingdom.

Historically, the study of invertebrate behavior, including the study of insects, has had a definite impact on the development of psychology as a discipline. In the nineteenth century, J. Henri Fabré conducted extensive investigations of instinctive behavior in insects that foreshadowed the work of this century. Fabré was, in the words of his correspondent Charles Darwin, an "incomparable observer." Fabré was interested in recording behavior as it occurred, preferably in the field. His work deserves our attention because of his incisive observations, the elegantly simple experimental procedures he used to interrogate his subjects, and the delightful prose in which he described his work.

Fabré's observations led him to believe that, once activated, an instinctive sequence of behav-

ior must be followed to its conclusion with very little variation. An example may be found in Teale (1949);

Because one thing has been done, a second thing must inevitably be done to complete the first or to prepare the way for its completion, and the two acts depend so closely upon each other that the performing of the first entails that of the second, even when, owing to casual circumstances, the second has become not only inopportune but sometimes actually opposed to the insect's interests (p. 61).

Fabré's work is full of examples of what he called the "ignorance of instinct." This refers to situations in which normally adaptive behavior becomes grotesquely maladaptive due to the insects' inability to respond to situations in a flexible manner. He described how a hunting wasp captures and feeds honeybees to its larvae. After capturing a bee, the wasp typically eats the pollen and nectar of the foraging bee before taking it to her larvae. If the wasp herself is captured during the consummatory stage of her feeding behavior she is unable to respond appropriately to the new situation. Again, Teale (1949) gives us an example from Fabré:

I have seen the wasp, with her prey, seized by the Mantis: the bandit was rifled by another bandit. And here is an awful detail: while the Mantis held her transfixed under the point of the double saw and was already munching her belly, the Wasp continued to lick the honey of her Bee, unable to relinquish the delicious food even amid the terrors of death (p. 57).

Subsequent research has demonstrated that insect behavior is not quite as inflexible as Fabré believed, but his basic findings remain valid. The example given above hints at the operation of some very powerful principles of behavior in insects and introduces a number of concerns shared by many modern researchers.

But it should also be emphasized that Fabré described behavior in global or holistic terms, rarely attempting a detailed analysis of the phenomena under observation. At that time, unlike today, "instinct" was used as an explanatory concept; labeling something an instinct was considered sufficient explanation of the observed event.

More recent work in behavioral origins and organization began with Lorenz's hydraulic model of behavior (Lorenz, 1937). Baerends (1976) pursued a number of methodological and theoretical issues relevant to behavioral organization including the problem of plasticity versus rigidity in insect behavior. Much current research in this area takes the form of identifying the elements of behavior to be found in a given functional class such as feeding or sexual behavior and determining a set of conditional probabilities for transition between behavioral elements. Baker and Carde (1978) reported an extensive set of experiments illustrating the inter-

active nature of sexual behavior in the oriental fruit moth and identifying the order in which the elements of sexual behavior occur.

After an apparently ordered set of behavioral elements is identified, another type of research can begin. Questions can be asked about the nature of this "sequence". What happens if this set of behaviors is disrupted? There are a number of possibilities. The insect may perseverate at the point at which disruption occurs. For example, Steiner (1962) studied the consummatory component of provisioning behavior in a hunting wasp, *Liris nigra*, that preys on crickets. This wasp typically immobilizes her prey by stinging it in each of four ganglia with the subesophageal ganglion in the head being the last to be stung. Steiner found that if a wasp was presented with a decapitated cricket, the wasp would make the first three stings normally, but then would continue to search for the site of the remaining ganglion for an hour or more.

When a sequence is disrupted the insect may return to the first element and begin again. Howse (1975) has reported an observation by Fabré on another hunting wasp that preys on crickets. This wasp habitually carries its prey to the entrance to its burrow, enters and inspects the burrow, returns to the surface, and drags the cricket into the burrow by its antennae. Fabré moved the cricket away from the hole while the wasp was inspecting the burrow. The wasp responded by moving the cricket back to its original position at the entrance to the hole and then reentered its burrow for another inspection. Fabré repeated this little experiment about forty times before he, not the wasp, gave up (see also Chapter 9).

An insect may move back one or more elements but not necessarily all the way back to the beginning of the sequence. Baxter (1977) studied sexual behavior in the domestic cricket. The male of this species shows three major components of sexual behavior, the calling song, mating song, and copulation. If males were interrupted during the mating song, they usually started again with the mating song, but some started back at the calling song.

These examples illustrate the types of questions that are being asked and some rather simple procedures being used. The analysis of behavioral organization can be carried much further than description and simple element to element transition probabilities. McFarland (1971, 1974) has attempted to apply the methods of systems analysis, decision theory, and computer science to the analysis of behavior.

Early in the twentieth century, the zoologists Jennings and Loeb, who studied the behavior of single-celled organisms as well as insects, exerted considerable influence on psychology, particularly the behavioristic school. Jensen (1962), in his foreword to a new edition of Jenning's *Behavior of Lower Organisms*, has described an interesting anecdote in relation to the development of behaviorism. According to Jensen, John B. Watson, generally recognized as the founder of behaviorism, early in his career and in a book review he wrote, strongly criticized Jennings for defining perception and other phenomena in terms of objective behavior. Watson also objected to Jenning's advocating a basic continuity between lower and higher organisms. Seven years later, after studying under Loeb at the University of Chicago and moving to Johns Hopkins University where Jennings was Professor of Zoology, Watson (1914) had completely reversed his mentalistic position, as reflected in the following passage:

Psychology as the behaviorist views it is a purely objective experimental branch of natural science. . . . The behaviorist attempts to give a unitary scheme of animal response. He recognizes no dividing line between man and brute (p. 1).

The study of invertebrate behavior was important to Watson and the rise of behaviorism, and we still have much to learn from such study.

Behavioral Research on Insects and Reasons for It

Extensive knowledge about behavior across all representative species is a prerequisite for the development of comparative psychology. Insects provide a fabulous range of species (several hundred thousand have been described, three times as many as are found in the rest of the animal kingdom) and a comparable range of behaviors. It is no accident that the burgeoning science of sociobiology (see Chapter 2) — the study of the evolution of social behavior — had its origins in the study of the evolution of the great variety of social behaviors found in insects (Wilson, 1971, 1975).

But variety is only one reason for studying insects. Because we are often overwhelmed by the complexity of behavior, we view the study of "lower organisms" as attractive. We assume that understanding the behavior of simpler organisms will aid in understanding more complex animals, and this search for simpler animal models of behavior has led a number of ethologists and psychologists to the insect. In this connection, Denny and Ratner (1970) have emphasized the importance of the research preparation — that combination of species, apparatus, and methodology that combines with a hypothesis to produce informative research.

Insects as subjects also offer a number of practical advantages. Large numbers of many different species can be easily and inexpensively maintained in the laboratory in a minimum of space. All of the classes of behavior found in other animals can be observed in insects, and insects are excellent for the study of behavior genetics and the organization of behavior.

In addition, the study of insects offers ample opportunity for combined laboratory and field-work on the same animal. Psychologists have traditionally focused on laboratory research, which places emphasis on precision and control, while animal behaviorists with an ethological orientation have pointed out the importance of doing research in more natural settings. They are willing to sacrifice some of the control and comfort of the laboratory in exchange for the ecological validity of field research. And in field research it is possible to apply a basic principle known to generations of naturalists; that is, to allow nature to take care of animal maintenance chores in order to free time for observation.

In the final analysis, scientists have been interested in insect behavior because of its intrinsic fascination. For these researchers, the exploration of an alien but intimate world has been very rewarding.

Consider, for example, the chain of stimulus-response events involved in the feeding behavior of the female mosquito. A female mosquito resting in the grass responds to the disturbance produced by any large animal moving through the undergrowth by rising and beginning her aerial search. A mosquito that is airborne searches by flying across the wind until it meets a stream of warm, moist, air with a high carbon dioxide content. The mosquito enters this stream and flies upwind, turning back into the stream if she leaves the main concentration of cues. Eventually she finds the source of the cues associated with approach, and biting ensues. The stimuli associated with approach, landing, and feeding-site selection vary with the species of mosquito. Gillet (1971) has found that some African species prefer the knees of humans whereas others prefer noses. Although some mosquitoes do hunt at species-specific heights, preference for a certain feeding location, is not based on height in this case, because the favored site is chosen even if the experimenter is naked and lying prone. Given the combination of stimuli to which the mosquito is able to respond, it is not surprising that people have had such difficulty in avoiding these insects.

How Much Can We Generalize from One Species to Another?

Once we have obtained a broad perspective from the study of a variety of groups of animals how can we use this information to develop a general theory of behavior? The first difficulty that must be faced is the problem of cross-species generalization. What does knowledge about behavior in one species tell us about the behavior of another species? This issue is especially important to the insect behaviorist.

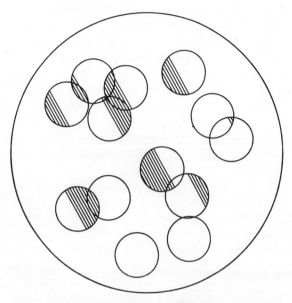

Figure 13.1 Generalization of behavioral principles across species.

It may be useful to think about behavior in terms of the diagram shown in Figure 13.1. The large circle represents all that there is to know potentially about behavior in general. The smaller circles enclosed by the larger one correspond to all there is to be known about the behavior of each individual species. Look at the cluster of circles in the upper left area of the large circle. Imagine that each circle represents knowledge about the behavior of a single primate species. Note that some of these circles overlap. According to our model, the overlap suggests that knowledge about a given behavior in one species may be directly applied or generalized to prediction about that behavior in the adjacent species. For example, we have found that some kinds of learning-extinction phenomena, such as illustrated by the principle of partial reinforcement, have very similar characteristics in a variety of species.

As you look further, note that many circles have no overlap. This means that we cannot gratuitously generalize between these species. We can illustrate this point with a concrete example. Knowledge about the feeding behavior of a certain species of grasshopper may tell us something about the feeding behavior of a closely related species of grasshopper, but it tells us nothing directly about feeding behavior in humans. Unfortunately, American comparative psychology went through a period in which making this kind of capricious comparison was fairly common. See Warden (1927) for a history of comparative psychology.

Each time we wish to generalize from one species to another or find a model of a particular behavior it is necessary to validate that comparison. For example, researchers concerned with vision have found that cats' eyes are similar to human eyes. So cats are widely used as models of human vision, but considerable research was required to justify this generalization. The cockroach happens to have a giant neuron that has evolved to conduct a limited amount of information very rapidly. The large size of these neurons and their similarity to nerve tissue in many species allows physiologists to use them as models in the study of neural conduction.

Now look at the shaded areas in Figure 13.1. These areas represent the extent of our present knowledge about the behavior of these species. Notice that most of the diagram is empty, just like the *terra incognita* of early mapmakers.

If, in many cases, we cannot generalize directly from one species to another, of what use

is our broad knowledge of behavior ? Look again at the large circle and at the small amount of shaded or mapped territory. The more we know about the behavior of individual species, the more we know about behavior in general. The more we understand behavior in general, the better equipped we will be to make testable prediction about the behavior of any individual species. In a truly comparative psychology, all species are of equal interest and importance because they all show behavioral adaptations that have evolved in response to basic needs common to all animals. This may seem to be an elementary point and, once considered, not at all difficult to understand. Yet it is remarkable how frequently misunderstandings arise in this area.

How Research on Insect Behavior Fits a Broad Perspective

Behavior Genetics. This field is currently of great interest and insects are specially favored as subjects for research. In an early study, Hirsch and Boudreau (1958) measured individual differences in orientation to light in fruit flies. A mass screening technique was used to obtain a group that showed a strong positive orientation to light and a group that showed weak positive orientation to light. These two groups were reared in isolation and additional selection pressure was applied for twenty-nine generations. At this point, the two strains differed greatly in light orientation. The strong light orientation group showed 80 percent approach responses to light as compared to 20 percent in the low orientation group. This was a clear demonstration of genetic control of behavior and of the possibility of rapid behavioral evolution.

Ewing (1963) used similar procedures to Hirsch and Boudreau in attempts to select for "spontaneous activity" in Drosophila melanogaster. His first attempt, using a mass screening technique produced what at first appeared to be strain differences in activity, but on closer analysis, he found that he had produced a strain of flies that was intolerant of and moved away from other flies, thus appearing to be more active. A second attempt in which flies were tested individually in an apparatus resembling a tube composed of a series of funnels again appeared to have produced one strain of active flies and another strain of inactive flies. Nevertheless, a closer analysis indicated that the difference was not one of activity. Ewing had actually produced a strain of "claustrophobic" flies that appeared to be inactive because they avoided the narrow ends of the funnels that led to other compartments in the tube. Although such research demonstrates genetic control of behavior, it mainly shows how much caution is necessary in identifying the behavior that is really under genetic control in a given experiment.

In field studies, Leonard (1974) has described fairly rapid selection for a specific behavior in female gypsy moths. These insects were introduced into eastern areas of the United States in the middle nineteenth century and, by the 1920s, had spread north to southern Quebec and New Brunswick, where their advance was apparently limited by the extreme cold temperatures of northern winters that killed their eggs. As evidence for evolutionary changes in response to the cold temperatures, Leonard mentioned changes in the chemistry of the eggs that give them an increased chance for survival at low temperatues. But this is not the only difference between northern and southern members of the species. There has also been selection for different behaviors. Moths in northern areas lay their eggs on tree trunks like their more southern relatives, but the northern moths lay their eggs closer to the ground, thereby increasing the probability that the eggs will be protected from extreme cold by an insulating layer of snow.

Behavior genetics continues to be a productive area of research through which the effects of selection pressures on behavior may be discovered and explicated. We are becoming increasingly aware of the intimate interaction between genetics and learning.

Learning. Recently, animal behaviorists have studied learning in insects, while early investigators, like Fabré, who frequently described instinctive behavior in insects in terms of "wisdom," rarely mentioned the possibility of learning and flexibility in the behavioral repertoire of these animals. In fact, fierce arguments have been waged over the question of "intelligence" in insects. Learning has traditionally been viewed as a function of the brain, and Howse (1975) has pointed out that most biologists prior to the twentieth century were "loath to admit that insects possess brains." Indeed, he continued:

one criterion of Linnaeus' definition of the Insecta was the lack of a brain. The behavior of decapitated insects made this easy to believe. The great eighteenth century naturalist, Buffon, wrote: "the. . .horsefly will live, run, may even copulate, after being deprived of its head (p. 359)."

We now know that insects do have brains, but that the insect brain does not always serve the central guiding function that it does in other animals. The mosquito and the praying mantis, for example, copulate more readily *after* losing their heads, and, thus, their brains. Truman (1971) reported that pupa of *Hyalophora cecropic*, without a brain, can perform the sequence of behavior required to emerge from its cocoon.

Alloway (1972) and Howse (1975) have reviewed experiments demonstrating that isolated ganglia in decapitated insects are capable of learning a simple conditioned response. They point out, however, that memory is usually better in insects that have their brains and ganglia still connected. These findings again illustrate the importance of studying insects on their own terms, recognizing the possibility that qualitative as well as quantitative differences may exist between major groups of organisms. This is yet another example of the care that must be taken in cross-species generalization.

The basic fact that insects are capable of learning is well documented. Tinbergen (1968) studied hunting wasps that dig burrows in which they store and lay eggs on paralyzed prey. These wasps learn the positions of landmarks in order to be able to return to their burrows with prey. Von Frisch (1953) and other students of bee behavior have used the bees' learned orientation to cues surrounding a food source in order to study their visual and chemical sensory systems.

The difference in learning ability that separates insects from other animals seems to be not only quantitative but also qualitative. There are situations in which insects seem "prewired" to learn limited or specific things in a specific situation and are unable to adapt to "unnatural" changes imposed by experimenters.

For example, Tinbergen (1968) has reported work done by Baerends and Baerends with *Ammophila campestris*, the sand wasp. They found that the female wasp digs a burrow with a chamber at the bottom, which is large enough for the larva and some caterpillars. Then she covers the entrance to the burrow with bits of earth and debris and flies off in search of prey. She usually returns on foot dragging a caterpillar and goes directly to the burrow, drops the caterpillar, opens the entrance, and descends into the burrow. She then returns to the surface for her prey, drags it down to the chamber, and deposits an egg on the caterpillar. Finally the wasp leaves the burrow and seals the entrance. She will return in a few days to inspect the stock of provisions (the "inspection visit") and to bring one to four more caterpillars if the larva has consumed the available stock. A few days later, this procedure is repeated once more after which the burrow is tightly sealed with pebbles, bits of wood, and

earth, which the wasp packs in using her head or a pebble as a hammer. The larva then pupates and, later, emerges as an adult.

The behavior described above requires complex learning. The wasp must be able to respond to the contents of the nest after a single inspection visit and retain the information obtained for a variable period of time. In some cases the hunt actually occurs on the day following the inspection visit. Still, the wasp brings the correct number of caterpillars to feed the larva until her next visit. This behavior becomes even more remarkable when we realize that each *Ammophila* cares for two or three nests simultaneously and that each larva is at a different stage of development.

Although the female sand wasp is able to learn specific things in a complex situation, this learning is severely limited to specific situations. Baerends and Baerends studied these limitations by constructing artificial nests so that they could observe and modify the contents of the burrows. Then they conducted a series of experiments designed to explore the extent of the wasps' adaptability. They found that when all caterpillars were removed from a nest *before* the wasp inspected it she would later bring more than the normal number of caterpillars. If extra caterpillars were placed in the nest *before* the wasp inspected it, no additional prey were brought. The wasp also responded to the size of the larvae. Inserting a larger larva in the nest *before* the inspection resulted in an increase in the amount of prey provided by the wasp. The wasp was able to respond appropriately to a given stimulus situation and retain that information for several hours while behaving differently at other nests.

A similar set of experiments was conducted altering the burrow contents *after* the inspection visit. These manipulations did not affect the wasps' behavior. On the inspection visit, if a wasp found a large hungry larva and no food, she would return several times with prey, even if several caterpillars had been placed in the burrow by the investigators in the period between the inspection visit and the first provisioning visit. The results were similar if a well-stocked larder was experimentally depleted *after* the inspection visit. No additional caterpillars were brought by the wasp to make up for the loss. If a wasp found a larva on the inspection visit and, in the intervening period the investigators replaced this larva with a pupa (which requires no food), she still delivered the amount of food required by the larva.

Experiments such as this confirm Fabré's observations to some extent. Insect behavior has aspects of rigidity. But they also reveal that insects can learn fairly complex tasks. In these particular experiments, learning was observed to occur in a highly limited fashion. The point of this discussion focuses on insects' potentials for learning complicated behaviors, qualified by the fact that these potentials are qualitatively different from our perceptions of learning. In insects, we see a complex interaction between instinct and learning in that the insect is "instinctively set" to encode and process complex, but precisely limited, bits of information.

Classes of Behavior

This section illustrates the diversity of insect behavior and acts as a guide to authoritative and readable sources of additional information. For each of the eleven classes of behavior several examples from different species are presented. In addition, to provide continuity and a comparative baseline, information on one selected species, the house cricket, is included for each class of behavior. The house, or domestic, cricket (*Acheta domesticus*) was introduced into the United States from Europe. It is most familiar as the small grey cricket commonly sold in bait and pet shops. This insect has a fascinating behavioral repertoire. It is a good animal to study in the laboratory because it adapts well and reproduces readily in captivity and because the laboratory does not represent a major distortion

of its natural habitat, mostly refuse piles and basements.

Feeding and Drinking Behavior

Insects eat almost everywhere and almost anything. The annual loss in the United States due to the feeding behavior of insects has been estimated at about $5 billion (Borror, Delong, and Triplehorn, 1976). Nevertheless, these authors have emphasized that the value of the services provided by beneficial insects is far greater than the loss caused by harmful species.

Many insects have mouth parts that serve both the functions of feeding and drinking; thus these two classes of behavior are combined. The feeding-drinking behavior of the mosquito as described in the introduction is a good example of combined functions.

Many insects have a valuable ecological function in the breakdown and disposal of biological waste. Without these scavengers, such material as dead trees, carrion, and dung would simply accumulate. Dung bettles and burying beetles dispose of dead animals and animal waste products. A host of insects including termites and carpenter ants feed on dead trees.

Numerous insects eat other insects, as predators or as parasites. Most people recognize the praying mantis that sits quietly on a leafy branch until another insect passes by and then suddenly strikes out with enlarged and powerful forelegs. Gardeners consider this insect to be highly beneficial and collect or buy mantid egg cases to ensure a plentiful supply of mantids. These predators do capture and eat many insects that come to feed on the garden plants. Unfortunately, they also eat other mantids as well as the bees that pollinate the plants.

Perhaps the most complete analysis of this behavior class in an insect has been conducted by V. G. Dethier (1962, 1976) on the blow fly. His books are especially worth reading because Dethier does more than provide substantive information about feeding and drinking. By sharing his impressions about how ideas develop, how experiments and apparatus are designed, and how mistakes are made and corrected, he provides a comprehensive view of what research and researchers are really like. An illustration of his approach to research is provided in the following passage (Dethier, 1962).

Between the fly and the biologist, however, there is a language barrier that makes getting direct answers to questions difficult. With a human subject it is only necessary to ask: what color is this? does that hurt? are you hungry? The human subject may, or course, lie; the fly cannot. However, to elicit information from him it is necessary to resort to all kinds of trickery and legerdemain. This means pittings one's brain against that of the fly — a risk some people are unwilling to assume. But then, experimentation is only for the adventuresome, for the dreamers, for the brave.

The first fruitful experimental approach to this problem began less than fifty years ago with a very shrewd observation; namely, that flies (and bees and butterflies) walked about in their food and constantly stuck out their tongues. The next time you dine with a fly (and modern sanitary practice has not greatly diminished the opportunities), observe his behavior when he gavots across the top of the custard pie. His proboscis, which is normally carried retracted into his head like the landing gear of an airplane, will be lowered, and like a miniature vacuum cleaner he will suck in food. For a striking demonstration of this, mix some sugared water and food coloring and paint a sheet of paper. The first fly to find it will leave a beautiful trail of lip prints, hardly the kind suitable for lipstick ads but nonetheless instructive.

The brilliant idea conceived by the biologists who first speculated on why some insects paraded around in their food was that they tasted with their feet. In retrospect it is the simplest thing in the world to test this idea. It also makes a fine parlor trick for even the most blasé gathering.

The first step is to provide a fly with a handle since Nature failed to do so. Procure a stick about the size of a lead pencil. (A lead pencil will do nicely. . .) Dip one end repeatedly into candle wax or paraffin until a flysized gob accumulates. Next anaesthetize a fly. The least messy method is to deposit him in the freezing compartment of a refrigerator for several minutes. Then, working very rapidly, place him backside down on the wax and seal his wings onto it with a hot needle.

Now for the experimental proof. Lower the fly gently over a saucer of water until his feet just touch. Chances are he is thirsty. If so, he will lower his proboscis as soon as his feet touch and will suck avidly. When thirst has been allayed, the proboscis will be retracted compactly into the head. This is a neat arrangement because a permanently extended proboscis might flop about uncomfortably during flight or be trod upon while walking.

Next, lower the fly into a saucer of sugared water. In a fraction of a second the proboscis is flicked out again. Put him back into water (this is the control), and the proboscis is retracted. Water, in; sugar out. The performance continues almost indefinitely. Who can doubt that the fly can taste with his feet(pp. 23-25)?

The flys' proboscis response can be used to investigate many questions about this animal's sense of taste. Dethier found that a very hungry fly is ten million times more sensitive to sugar than are humans.

The house cricket is omnivorous and thrives in the laboratory on a diet of chicken mash. It "tastes" and manipulates food particles with a complex set of mouthparts. A very close relative of this species causes considerable damage to stored grain in India and Pakistan. These crickets are cannibalistic; if a researcher forgets to feed them they will eat each other.

Contacting or Exploratory Behavior

Insects do not play or explore like mammals. Nonetheless, if we watch carefully we may observe something that *looks* like exploration. In deciding whether insects really explore their environment, we are forced to define what we mean by exploration. A careful analysis of what looks like exploration may give us some insight into the evolution and functional significance of this behavior class.

Dingle (1965) studied alternation behavior in bugs (Heteroptera) and Wilson and Fowler (1976) studied the same behavior in the cockroach. A typical alternation experiment involves allowing an animal to move through a T-maze or a series of multiple T-mazes that offer a succession of two-way choice points. Alternation occurs when an animal chooses a left turn after making a right turn or vice versa or a new path over a path that has already been explored. This behavior is usually explained as a positive response to change and constitutes a basic element of exploratory behavior. Dingle and Wilson and Fowler reported alternation behavior in the insects they studied, and their results are compatible with a response to change theory of exploration. Dingle suggested that a "delayed compensatory response" in which an insect tends to turn left after a right turn, and right after a left turn, could be part of a general orientation system that would prevent random movements. Exploration at this very basic level may have functional importance when combined with other classes of behavior, such as feeding.

One may speculate that exploration evolved in conjunction with preconsummatory components of feeding behavior. Most organisms, including insects, increase their general activity in response to food deprivation. This usually increases the probability that they will find food. However, purely aimless activity is not an optimal strategy for locating food. This observation leads us to ask about how an insect could improve its chances of finding food. We will return to this question after considering some general ideas about exploration.

While most of the theoretical work on exploration is based on mammals, there seem to be certain common characteristics of this class of behavior in most species: A novel or complex stimulus elicits approach, and this attraction is usually shortlived. Dember (1956) has proposed a theory of exploration in which an organism at a given point in time is considered to be at a certain adaptation level with respect to perceptual novelty and complexity. According to this theory, slight deviation — especially increases in novelty and complexity as compared to the adaptation level — are reinforcing or rewarding. Extreme deviations — especially increases from the adaptation level — are punishing or noxious.

Such a model of exploration suggests that moderately novel stimuli are explored and highly novel stimuli are avoided. Extending our comparative analysis to insects may provide some clues as to how exploration as a behavior class could have evolved. Imagine an insect that lives in a burrow or crevice and forages for food in a circumscribed area surrounding the shelter. There could be certain selective advantages for the insect to avoid familiar objects (those previously tasted and found lacking) and to approach something moderately novel, such as a windblown seed. Extremely novel stimuli, on the other hand, could represent a hungry, active predator. It would thus be appropriate for the insect to respond to these very novel stimuli with antipredator, or avoidance, behavior.

The house cricket is rather like the hypothetical insect described above. Placement of a novel, nonfood object (such as a screw) in the home terrarium of five or ten crickets will elicit a brief period of approach and contact followed by no further contact above a chance level. This example of the crickets' brief approach and contact with a moderately novel stimulus is compatible with the hypothesis that exploration could be related to preconsummatory components of feeding behavior.

Sexual Behavior

This is another class in which, like feeding, insects excel. Sexual behavior in insects is diverse (See also Chapter 16). Dragonflies often fly in tandem while copulating as do so-called "love-bugs," a species of march fly that occurs in huge swarms in the Gulf states. Some insects, such as many beetles, copulate in a more conventional fashion except that copulation may last for an hour or more. Many male insects, such as the house cricket, extrude a spermatophore or packet containing sperm and transfer this case to the female. Males of more primitive insects such as some bristletails (Thysanura) simply drop the spermatophore on the ground where it is later picked up by the female. In springtails (Collembola) the males deposit small hardened droplets of sperm on stalks that are attached to the substratum. A single male may deposit a hundred or more of these miniature spermatophores. The female wanders into this forest of spermatophores and the structures burst when they come in contact with the female's moist vulva and the sperm enter her vagina (Wigglesworth, 1974). Many adult insects, such as the gypsy moth and the mayfly, literally live to mate. They do not exhibit feeding behavior as adults.

In our earlier discussion of instinctive behavior we saw the manner in which an insect typically runs off an ordered set of behaviors. Sexual behavior often involves similar interactive sequences of behavior. An individual emits a stimulus that elicits a specific response from a member of the opposite sex; this response serves as the stimulus that elicits a second response from the first individual. This process continues until the interactive sequence has been completed. A concrete example of this type of interactive behavior is presented below.

Khalifa (1949) identified and studied the major components of sexual behavior in the house cricket. First, the male produces the calling song, which although softer, is similar to the familiar calling songs of field crickets. The female responds to this song by approaching the male. When she is within a few centimeters of the male, he switches to his mating song, characterized by an increase in the frequency of chirping, a lowered body posture, and side-to-side swaying. Either the receptive female actively mounts the male or the male backs under the female, forcing her to mount. The male arches its back so that the tip of its abdomen, from which its spermatophore is suspended, is raised to contact the tip of the female's abdomen. The consumatory stage of this sexual behavior sequence involves transfer of the spermatophore from the male to the female. Figure 13.2 shows a mating pair of crickets in the immediate postconsummatory stage. The female has just received the spermatophore and the male is preparing to crawl out from underneath her. After copulation, the male "watches" the female with his antennae touching her for up to an hour (an example of postconsummatory behavior per Ratner).

If one of the stimuli above is altered or omitted, the dual sequence may be broken. Young and Stephen (1970) found that exposing male house crickets to sublethal doses of some common pesticides causes them to produce abnormal calling songs. When this happens, the changed calling song fails to elicit approach in females. Similarly, in normal crickets, if a male produces a calling song but no female approaches, he does not proceed to the mating song. Thus we see that if any stimulus in the double chain of behavior is omitted the sequence may be interrupted.

No review of sexual behavior in insects would be complete without extensive information about the important role that olfaction plays in the lives of these animals. The use of substances called "pheromones" are common in insects, including moths. Typically, an individual emits a pheromone that elicits a specific response in

Figure 13.2 The Postconsummatory component of sexual behavior in the domestic cricket.

another member of the same species. Phero-mones are common to the sexual behavior repertoire as described in detail in Chapter 20, and an example of applied research on the use of sex pheromones in pest control is presented at the end of this chapter.

Insect Behavior: Using the Cricket as a Comparative Baseline

Grooming Behavior

Care-of-the-body-surface (COBS) is as important and as common to insects as it is to other groups of animals. Self-grooming often results in the insect's assuming some very awkward appearing postures. Having a rigid exoskeleton can provide some very real problems to the grooming insect.

Wilson (1971), in his review of grooming in social insects, points out that mutual grooming may occur and is an efficient strategy for care-of-the-body-surface. Many social insects such as bees, termites, and ants use mutual grooming and feeding to spread a variety of pheromones throughout the colony. Ants use this system for the dispersal of their colony odor, and the importance of this colony odor will be dealt with in the section on fighting behavior.

The communication dances of bees (von Frisch, 1953) are well known. Most of these dances are related to feeding behavior but one dance solicits grooming. As Wilson (1971) has described it:

The worker shakes her body rapidly back and forth and from side to side, while attempting to comb her thoracic hairs with her middle legs. Often, but not always, this behavior induces a nearby worker to approach and employ her mandibles to groom the hairy coat on the petiole and base of the wings. These are the parts which a bee is unable to clean herself. . .(p.271).

Crickets perform complex grooming movements and the insect is seen to assume odd postures. Time-lapse photography (one frame per minute taken by the author) reveals that over a 24-hour period one or two 30-minute periods of extensive grooming occur.

Fighting Behavior

The fighting between "armies" of ants has fascinated both naturalists and moral philosophers. Some of the more dramatic conflicts can be observed on the sidewalks and in the yards of the eastern United States where the pavement ant, *Tetramorium Caespitum*, is common. These battles may represent territorial conflicts. Although intense combat may continue for hours, Wilson (1971) has pointed out that the actual damage inflicted is minimal. Fighting among large groups of ants is also common in the tropics, especially when one species is moving into an area and displacing another species.

Nestmate recognition is necessary before aggression against an outsider is possible. The recognition process can be readily observed, and, once again a chemical stimulus plays a major role. Ants coming into a colony are met by other ants and antennal contact is briefly made before the insects continue on their way. That such casual contact conveys essential information is evident when we have the opportunity to observe what happens to an invading individual from another colony. The intruder, depending on the species involved, may be accepted, but receive little or no food; may receive a more intense investigation; or, as is most common (Wilson, 1971), be attacked and driven away or killed.

House crickets do not actually fight other crickets. In fact, the absence of within-species fighting behavior is interesting. Whereas these insects have an extremely well-developed set of antipredator behaviors, none of these seem to be used during conflicts with a member of the same species. These insects are occasionally cannibalistic, and sometimes it is possible to observe one cricket actively chewing on another. It is striking that the cricket being attacked does not attempt to fight off its attacker, but, instead, wanders aimlessly about dragging the aggressor along behind.

Nesting Behavior

In this class we again have an opportunity to see the diversity and complexity of insect behavior.

Karl von Frisch (1974) has written a delightful book called *Animal Architecture*. Although this book is not limited to insects, von Frisch relates how bees are capable of orienting their combs by the earth's magnetic field and many other unusual aspects of insect nesting behavior. He tells of termites that build huge nests, some of which are shaped like thin slabs with the thin edge toward the sun to reduce heating effects; some have chimneys or towers; while others have umbrellas that keep out the rain. Von Frisch described the nesting behavior of an ant as follows:

In the crowns of trees in tropical southern Asia, one occasionally comes across the round or oval leaf nests of a reddish, fairly large species of the genus *Oecophylla*. They consist of living, undetached leaves held together by a dense silky web. . . For zoologists, these nests were once a major puzzle because ants possess no spinning glands. Admittedly, their larvae have spinning glands and, in many species, spin cocoons of silk strands before they pupate like silkworms and many other caterpillars. But this fact alone could not solve the problem because ant larvae are helpless grubs tended by the workers in the depth of the nest, and it would be impossible for them to crawl to the surface and join the leaves together with threads. Working on the assumption that the ants would reveal their secret if they could be induced to come out to repair a damage deliberately inflicted on their dwelling, a brave naturalist once climbed up into the crown of a tree and made a slit into such a leaf nest. He had to be brave because he knew that these ants vehemently attack intruders and seek to drive them away with painful bites and squirts of corrosive poison. In this case they tried in vain, and his bravery was rewarded, for soon a group of ants came along and took up a position on one side of the tear. Attaching themselves firmly with the sharp end claws of their six legs, they seized the other with their mandibles and carefully tried to pull it closer by moving their legs, one after the other, further back. It was a strange sight. While the gap gradually got smaller by their joint efforts, other workers appeared and carefully cut away the ragged ends of the torn web with their mandibles. They carried them to an exposed part of the nest and, opening their jaws wide, let them be carried away by the wind. Where the distance between the two edges was too great, other ants were seized to form a living bridge across the gap. What happened next was even more astounding. A group of workers, each carrying a full-grown larva, emerged from the depths of the nest. Where the two edges had been pulled together sufficiently, they went to work pressing the mouths of the larvae (which were thus compelled to act as live shuttles) against the leaf surface on one side, then on the other, and, by squeezing them with their mandibles, made them discharge some of their glandular secretions. . . In this manner the two edges of the tear in the nest cover were stitched together again with the silken threads produced by the larvae. This use by the ants of their own larvae as both spindle and shuttle is probably the most remarkable example among the few instances of the use of tools by animals (see Figure 17.1).

Some field crickets are somewhat territorial and live in crevices and burrows whereas the mole cricket digs burrows like its namesake. However, our model species, the house cricket, does not show any specialization in the class of nesting behavior.

Parenting or Care-of-the-Young Behavior

Care-of-the-young behavior is highly developed in social insects. In fact, the gradual development of this class of behavior is intimately related to the evolution of social behavior. This subject is reviewed in detail in *The Insect Societies* (Wilson, 1971). Species presently exist that represent all points on a continuum of social behavior, from completely solitary to very social. An analysis of care-of-the-young behavior must inevitably become an analysis of social behavior. The scope of this chapter does not permit an adequate summary of Wilson's work (see Chapter 2). In addition to *The Insect Societies*, his more recent book, *Sociobiology* (1975) presents a broadly comparative look at the evolution of social behavior in the entire animal kingdom.

An extensive description of the sand wasp caring for her larvae was presented above as an example of the complex interaction between instinct and learning in insects. In contrast, the only interaction a house cricket has with its young has been mentioned in the section on feeding behavior.

Defensive or Antipredator Behavior

Most of us are familiar with at least some type of antipredator behavior in insects. You are doubtless aware of the rapid response of the cockroach or the house fly to the descending shoe or flyswatter. Insect eyes are well adapted to the detection of movement; and the cockroach, for example, has giant neurons adapted for extremely rapid conduction of limited amounts of information, which generally results in a rapid exit. In fact, the reaction time of the fly to the flyswatter is 0.1 seconds — much faster than approximately 0.18 seconds in humans to a visual stimulus.

Insects show at least as much variety in their antipredator behavior as is found in any other order. Many insects are camouflaged by coloring, markings, and shape and resemble everything from bark, leaves, and twigs to bird droppings. Although an insect may perfectly resemble a loose piece of bark, its behavior remains crucially important. For the camouflage to be effective, the insect must orient toward and come to rest on bark — not on a stone or on the side of a white house. Stinging insects take a more active role in their defense, as most people

are aware. Stinging in some species is accompanied by the release of a pheromone that elicits approach and attack by other members of the same species. Some grasshoppers secrete repellent substances when disturbed, while many beetles emit unpleasant odors. The bombadier beetle accurately sprays a repellent from its anus and can fire up to twenty rounds over a short time period (Wigglesworth, 1972). Rohrmann (1977) has reported some remarkable camouflage systems in tropical mantids. Some immature mantids not only appear to have a flower growing on their backs, but they change color to match the background. These mantids feed on insects that are attracted to flowering plants, so their floral mimicry is functional for both antipredator and feeding behaviors.

The Cricket. This section concludes with a detailed look at the antipredator behavior of the house cricket. Laboratory research conducted by the author has revealed that *A. Domesticus* shows a variety of behaviors in response to a rat (an ecologically valid predator). Table 13.1 presents these antipredator behaviors together with the eliciting stimuli found to be associated with them.

Autotomy, as defined in Table 13.1, is the reflex separation of a hind leg. Brousse-Gaury (1958) has described the structures, muscles, and nerve impulses involved in autotomy in the cricket and reported autotomy to be "capricious and irregular." Brousse-Gaury was unable to make any statements about possible eliciting stimuli for this response.

"Thigmotaxis" is simply orientation toward cracks and crevices to maximize contact with surfaces. "Freezing" is an upright posture with no leg or body movement. Frequently the antennae are moved to a raised position and held there for the duration of the freeze. "Hopping" and "struggling" are self-explanatory. A "captive freeze" occurs after about 3 seconds of struggling. If, at this point, the cricket is released, it actively moves away. An "immobility reaction" (see Chapter 21), as distinguished from freezing, is elicited by contact and inversion. If at this point, the cricket is released, it remains ventral side up and immobile for at least 3 seconds, but usually for many more seconds.

Sequential Analysis.   Once the behaviors associated with response to a predator have been classified, questions can be asked about the sequencing of the behaviors: (1) Are the behaviors emitted in response to specific stimuli? (2) Is there a specific sequence factor involved? These questions can be answered by presenting the stimuli in Table 13.1 at different points in the normal antipredator sequence.

My doctoral research on sequence effects in the antipredator behavior of the house cricket (Hagaman, 1977), which is summarized below, attempts to answer these questions.

The experimental results supported the hypothesis that a given eliciting stimulus is maximally effective only at its appropriate position in the sequence. Sudden capture, before any other components of the behavior sequence had been emitted, elicited autotomy in 12 out of 48 (25 percent) of the crickets

tested. Sudden capture never elicited autotomy in 144 crickets exposed to this stimulus at later points in the sequence. On the other hand, inversion elicited immobility in 46 out of 48 insects (median duration = 60 seconds) when most of the earlier behavior components had been "run off." When inversion was presented prematurely at the beginning of the sequence, immobility was elicited in only 31 out of 45 cases (69 percent), and the median duration of immobility was reduced to 13 seconds. These results are compatible with a model of behavior in which the previous responses of an insect play an interactive role with external stimuli in determining the next response of the insect.

Applied Research on Insect Behavior

Currently, there is a good deal of interest in the "natural" control of insect pests. Methods of control include the introduction and management of predators, parasites, and insect diseases as well as the use of sex pheromones in a variety of ways. In any method, extensive knowledge about the behavior of the pests to be controlled is a prerequisite for a successful program.

Cardé (1976), who has reviewed the history of

Table 13.1

Behaviors and Eliciting Stimuli

Behavior	Stimulus
Autotomy	Sudden capture
Thigmotaxis	Vibration
Freeze	Vibration
Hop	Very close proximity of predator
Struggle	Capture
Captive freeze	Continued contact with predator
Immobility reaction	Contact and inversion

Figure 13.3 Gypsy moth flying in a wind tunnel.

current status and the use of pheromones in the control of moth pests, indicates that one of the first techniques developed was the use of pheromones to monitor populations of pest species. Traps are baited with a synthetic pheromone, and the number of males captured is used to estimate the size of the local population. Such data are used to determine whether conventional pesticides should be applied. This practice has resulted in a reduction in the quantity of pesticides used. When the population is low, there is no need to apply pesticides. And the effectiveness of pesticides has been enhanced by timing their use with periods in the insects' life cycle when they are most vulnerable to a given pesticide.

Another use of synthetic pheromones involves an attempt to attract and capture enough males to reduce significantly the reproducing population of a species. The success of this technique has been limited by a variety of factors. One of these is our incomplete knowledge of the chemistry of pheromone systems and of the behavioral responses to them. For example, Cardé, Baker,

A Comparative Analysis

and Roelofs (1975) found that, in the oriental fruit moth, two components of the pheromone are involved in eliciting flight orientation toward the chemical source from a distance whereas a third component elicits landing and close approach.

A third possible use of sex pheromones in population control could involve the disruption of male orientation to females by permeating the area with a synthetic pheromone. Here again, knowledge of the precise behavioral roles of the pheromone components is needed. Pheromone research is well established and greater use of these substances in pest management programs is quite promising. For example, the gypsy moth is an introduced pest species that in the larval stage does extensive damage to oak foliage particularly in the eastern United States. The female "calls" or emits a pheromone and the male orients to this pheromone. Many aspects of this insect have been studies because its economic importance, including male behavior in response to female sex pheromone. Detailed knowledge of the behavior of this insect is important in the development and testing of synthetic pheromones for use in the types of control procedures outlined above.

Analytical techniques currently available in the chemistry laboratory are not adequate to determine whether or not a given synthetic pheromone is identical to the natural substance. It is at this point that the applied animal behaviorist assists in developing bioassays in which the insect's behavior is used as the final measure of synthetic pheromone effectiveness.

Bioassays for sex pheromone activity using wing fanning (a common element of sexual behavior in moths) and walking approach are common. However, upwind zigzag flight is a critical element of pheromone orientation. This element evaded laboratory researchers until Kennedy and Marsh (1974) developed a sustained-flight wind tunnel. The essential elements of such a tunnel include fans for controlling wind speed and a moving floor, which capitalize on the fact that the male gypsy moth use optomotor feedback to adjust its flight speed in response to visual cues from the substratum when its flight is oriented to a pheromone plume (the pheromone plume is an aerial track beginning at a point source and trailing downwind in a diffuse, conical shape). Thus, by controlling visual cues, the experimenter can "fly" a male at a given point, move it forward, or move it backward. The following study by Cardé and Hagaman (1979) on the responses of the gypsy in a wind tunnel to air-borne pheromones extends this analysis.

A 1.4 x -0.8 x 2.8 meter tunnel with a striped endless belt under the clear plexiglass floor was used to provide visual cues. With this apparatus the early components of sexual behavior (e.g., wing fanning), as well as flight characteristics such as speed and duration were studied. With the addition of videotape equipment, details of the zigzag flight pattern such as deviation from the center of the plume and the frequency with which the moth crosses the center of the plume were also measured. All of these dependent variables were found to be differentially responsive to dosage and the particular synthetic pheromone being tested, which made it possible to identify the best pheromone for the purpose intended.

Figure 13.3 shows a moth in flight in the wind tunnel. The receptors for the pheromone are on the large V-shaped antennae. This photograph also illustrates the degree of fine control possible in manipulating the moth's flight. With the lenses used to obtain this picture the moth had to be flown into a "window" less than 1 centimeter wide in order to have most of the moth in focus. This was achieved without major difficulty. It is also interesting that once the moth was established in a stable plume-oriented flight it was very resistant to interruption. Many moths contin-

ued to fly even when they were in extremely bright photographic lights, strobe lights, and smoke plumes. This illustrates yet another principle of animal behavior: behavior is most difficult to interrupt when the animal is approaching the consummatory stage of a given class of behavior.

Study Questions

1. Many psychology students limit themselves to the *Psychological Abstracts* when doing review papers and class projects. Go to your library and explore the *Biological Abstracts, Zoological Record,* and *Animal Behavior Abstracts*. Try to find behavioral information on selected species. Try to find information on selected classes of behavior.

2. While at the library, find and browse through five of the references mentioned in this chapter. These are some of the most interesting and substantive sources for information in this area.

3. Describe the main characteristics of instinctive behavior in insects and relate these characteristics to the role of incoming stimulation.

4. Compare the sexual behavior of the cricket with that of other representative insect species.

5. Go out and watch insects. If it is winter, find a cockroach. Note the insect's behavior once per minute for a period of an hour or more. You will find yourself asking interesting and relevant questions. How far does an ant or bee travel from its nest or hive on foraging trips? How does a cockroach find your crackers? How could you use this information to your benefit?

14

Complex Behavior: Traditional Comparative Psychology

M. Ray Denny

Michigan State University

Editors Note. *This chapter is very much like one of a similar title that I wrote for a graduate text called Comparative Psychology (Denny and Ratner, 1970). Although revised here for an advanced undergraduate audience, this chapter has only been updated and added to in places where this was deemed especially important. (For example, the concept of span has been introduced to help integrate the various finding about complex behavior.) Thus the instructor may elect to spend more time supplementing this chapter with outside material for updating purposes than would be the case for any other chapter, and the instructor could very well welcome the opportunity to do so.*

The main thesis of this chapter is that complex behavior refers for the most part to behavior that is jointly controlled by two or more relevant stimuli (Bachelder and Denny, 1977 a and b). This means that in complex behavior the target response cannot occur, at least consistently, unless the organism uses all of the necessary or conjuctively relevant cues. This idea is mostly clearly illustrated by the immediate memory span test commonly used in standard tests of intelligence for human beings. Let us say that the examiner orally presents the following sequence of digits at a standard rate to the subject: 9-3-6-5-8-1. The subject's task is to reply immediately with the same string of digits in exactly the same order. To do this the subject must have paid attention to every one of the presented digits. All stimuli (the 9 in the first position, *and* the 3 in the second position, *and* the 6 in the third position, *and* so on) must have been processed for the target response to occur. That is, all digits in each position are *conjunctively* relevant for eliciting the response 9-3-6-5-8-1. In such a test an individual who can consistently repeat correctly any string of six digits is said to have a span of at least six, and the task in turn can be considered to have a complexity of six.

Complexity equals the numbers of conjunctively relevant stimuli needed to elicit the target response; these stimuli can occur simultaneously or over a brief period of time and, depending on the nature of the target response, they can be held in immediate memory or be presented concurrently. When the response can be broken down into subresponses, as in the immediate memory or digit span test, then the only way one can know that all digits in the stimulus string were fully processed is when they are all responded to correctly in memory. Only if processed can the stimuli be remembered, as for example in repeating complicated instructions given to you. However, if the target response is discrete and unitary, as in choosing one alternative over another or in estimating the number of randomly arranged dots presented for a brief period of time (span-of-attention task), then the target response can occur in the presence of the controlling stumili and still be determined by more than one stimulus. Memory is not necessarily involved.

For any situation in which the elicitation of the target response requires the more or less simultaneous operation of two or more different stimuli, Bachelder and Denny (1977, a and b) have invoked traditional stimulus-response terminology and specified that such a response is under *complex stimulus control*. This label extends the rather common notion of span to areas of performance that are not ordinarily considered spanlike phenomena. For example, a simple two-choice discrimination task can be performed by always approaching the positive cue or by always avoiding the negative cue; that is, only one cue can control the target response, or the animal needs only a span of one to perform the task. So, for example, we find that all vertebrates, many invertebrates, and profoundly retarded human beings can learn simple discriminations. But having a span of two, which simultaneously permits both approach to the positive cue and avoidance of the negative cue, makes the task much easier and seems to be the preferred way of learning whenever this is possible (Zanich and Fowler, 1975)

A conditional discrimination, on the other hand, *requires* a span of at least two and is consistently much harder to learn for an animal like a rat than a simple discrimination. In a typical conditional discrimination situation, the subject must learn something like the following: select the square figure rather than the circle when both are on a red background and select the circle rather than the square when both figures are on a blue background. The correct figure is conditional on the background present. At a minimum, the subject must respond to both the background cue and the figure cue that is positive for that background. Thus, the conditional discrimination is more complex than the simple discrimination and seemingly beyond the capacity of many forms of animal life.

Wherever possible the various kinds of complex behavior described in this chapter will be analyzed in terms of complex stimulus control, or span.

Complex Mazes and Cue Utilization

When a maze consists of a series of choice points, it is considered complex. According to the present analysis such a maze represents a complex task because *two* different sets of cues are conjunctively relevant at each choice point — the external cues in the alley and the response-produced, *internal* aftereffects from responses earlier in the chain. Both sets of cues are needed to specify each correct choice-point response.

The learning of a complex maze is characterized by several interesting features. When a maze has approximately the same difficulty throughout its extent, it is usually learned by animals other than a human being in a roughly backward order, the errors first eliminated being nearest the goal and those last eliminated nearest the start. This is particularly true when an error consists of taking a longer instead of a shorter path to the goal rather than when an error means entering a dead-end blind or cul de sac (unpublished research by J. F. Shepard). That is, learning most clearly proceeds in a backward order when approach to the goal is the main sequence of responses being learned. To the extent that maze learning, involves the avoidance of dead-end blinds it tends to be learned in rats, also found by Shepard, in a more or less all-over-at-once fashion, complicating the backward order of maze learning. That is, all blinds appear to be equally aversive.

The backward learning of a complex maze is presumably mediated by the step by step backward chaining of approach responses to the goal object along the true pathway, with the first established link in the chain being direct approach to the goal box (Denny, 1971).

In human beings, complex mazes are typically learned in a sequential order that is characteristic of any serial learning task in the human that requires a number of trials to complete — typically a sequence in which the number of items presented exceeds the learner's span. Whenever events occur in a constant order, the initial portion of the behavioral sequence is learned first, then the final portion, while the central portion is learned last (the serial position effect). The fact that the serial position effect describes human maze learning indicates that the way human beings learn mazes is probably different from the way other animals learn them. This is true for at least two reasons. First, human beings tend to use language to aid in learning (verbal mediators) throughout the length of the maze; second, the final goal region typically lacks any real importance for human subjects for they are not striving to obtain a meal or the like. Thus, from the very first trial human beings are verbally oriented to be correct at every choice point and hardly more so at the final choice than at the others. Consequently, they start learning the first part of the maze right from the start, and the bow-shaped serial position effect just mentioned describes their progress over trials. The serial order effect also operates to a slight extent among other animals in complex mazes with cul de sacs, further complicating the backward order effect in their maze learning and showing that internal cues as well as external cues are necessary for correct responding.

A complex maze is learned proportionately much faster than a single unit is learned; for example, 10 units are learned in much fewer than 100 trials if 1 unit is learned in 10. This is as true for the chicken as it is for the rat (Warden and Hamilton, 1929; Warden and Reiss, 1941). It is probably true for at least two reasons: (1) after a few trials, learning proceeds in all units on each trial; (2) the tendency to alternate or explore different directions is partially satisfied in the complex maze because the true path, as in a *multiple* T-maze, can point in any one of four different directions and varies from choice point to choice point. In contrast, the alternation tendency is satisfied in a *single-unit* T-maze only when the animal makes an error. Thus, performance in the complex maze is not as disrupted by the exploratory tendency as in a single-unit maze.

One of the best established and more important principles concerning complex maze learning is that an animal uses whatever cues are available to it in learning the maze. Eliminating the cues of an entire sense modality, either by surgical means or by indirect experimental manipulation, has practically no deleterious effect on complex maze learning; even eliminating two avenues of stimulation still permits learning to occur, although eliminating three avenues, for example, by making a rat deaf, blind, and anosmic (unable to smell), virtually prevents learning.

Vision, if available, is the cue most often used by rats and even by some species of ants (genus Formica). Such ants can learn mazes nearly as complex as those learned by rats (Schneirla, 1929). The saliency or importance of visual cues is indicated in a number of ways. For instance, elevated (open alley) mazes that provide a wealth of visual cues are learned faster than enclosed mazes and also mediate better positive transfer effects when the original route to the goal is no longer

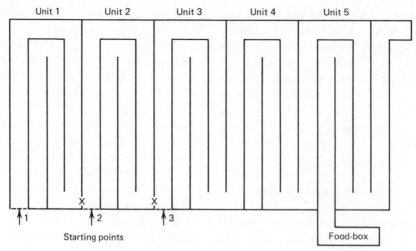

Figure 14.1 The unit maze used by Curtis. The arrows indicate different starting points which may be used. The sections marked *X* are removable. They are inserted only when the latter part of the maze is used.

available but an alternative route is, the animal takes the path that points toward the goal (so-called insight or reasoning effects).

In the early stages of complex-maze learning kinesthesis plays a much smaller role than other cues because it is not a constant stimulus (and only a stimulus that bears a relatively constant relationship with a particular response can become a cue for that response). Kinesthesis varies from trial to trial at each choice point early in learning because the animal responds in a variable way, making a variety of errors and different kinds of errors across trials. The early ineffectiveness of the kinesthetic cue explains why the rat that is blind and deaf, as well as anosmic, is unable to learn. Once the maze habit is well established, however, the kinesthetic stimuli just preceding each correct choice-point response are constant and can then serve as the sole set of cues for the maze habit. Thus, in terms of a span analysis, the behavior is under somewhat less complex control than earlier, although a pattern of kinesthesis can still be considered complex. Evidence for the exclusive use of kinesthetic cues in well-learned complex mazes comes from a variety of studies by Hunter (1940), Shepard (1929, 1931, unpublished), and Spragg (1933).

In demonstrating learning and performance on the basis of kinesthesis, Shepard used what he called a unit-alike maze (see Figure 14.1). This maze was an extended chain of identical units all of which were accessible from the same long corridor like the compartments of a European train. He started the animal in different units on different trials but always kept the food reward a constant number of units from the start unit, say, three units away (the animals were always running in the same direction so that the kinesthetic pattern or rhythm was constant). Rats were typically able to learn such response with kinesthesis as the only obvious cue. Shepard's work on the kinesthetic cue in the unit-alike maze has been essentially replicated and confirmed in an unpublished study by Denny, Thomas, and Elliott. By using a visual "crutch-cue" in the initial stages of training they found that an 85 to 90 percent level of correct response could be achieved in most rats when they were trained to enter the third unit of a maze, regardless of starting position. A crutch-cue in this case means that the entrance to the

A Comparative Analysis

252

third unit away was specified by a ¾-inch square of black tape stuck to the floor just at the threshold of the correct unit. When a 90 percent level of responding was achieved, the piece of tape (crutch-cue) was eliminated and after a slight drop in performance the rats quickly reattained the 85 to 90 percent performance level. When the order in which the units were run was reversed, creating quite a different pattern of kinesthesis, performance fell to a chance level and remained there. Thus, it seems clear that the rats were not in any abstract or symbolic sense counting to three.

In the process of studying kinesthetic cues, Shepard also discovered another subtle cue that the rat can use, which he called a "floor-cue." This cue was found by carrying out the following manipulations: Instead of the location of the food reward being varied from trial to trial, the food was always placed in the same unit, and the animal was started at varying number of identical units away from the identical goal unit. Such a procedure eliminated any possibility of kinesthesis serving as a cue and posed the problem of what cue was operating (odor of food was controlled for). Under these conditions many rats learned the food location even when the walls and the immediate floors of all units were continuously interchanged, eliminating all possibility of visual cues operating. Not until the subfloor structures were also manipulated or interchanged did these rats fail to learn. The available evidence seemed to indicate that the floor-cue is mediated auditorially as the animal walks across the floor. Many rats show remarkable sensitivity to this cue, but this subtle cue is virtually undetected by humans.

Delayed Reaction Studies

Delayed response refers to the ability to respond correctly in the absence of the critical external cue a short while after it has been removed. The animal is first trained to respond appropriately to a particular cue or stimulus in order to obtain the incentive (indirect method). For primates with well-developed perceptual orientation, this initial training procedure is often unnecessary (direct method): here the animal is shown where the incentive is by obviously placing the lure under a particular container (which can be identified by a position cue, color cue, or form cue). After the cue-approach association has been established by the indirect method, the cue is momentarily presented and the animal is permitted to respond after a certain passage of time, including zero delays. In the case of the direct method, used primarily with primates and dogs, the incentive simply is hidden and the animal permitted to respond later. The occurrence of the appropriate response after removal of the cue or hiding of the lure and after the delay interval has elapsed is called a delayed response.

The ability of nonhuman animals to delay a response, that is, to bridge the time gap between cue and response, was once thought to be evidence of symbolic (representative) behavior. But there is a simpler explanation that seem to fit the data better. In essence, the explanation consists of viewing the maximum delay possible in delayed response as the time it takes to forget after one learning trial. The response to be delayed, or learned in one trial, is minimally elicited, either by the lure or the appropriate cue, in the form of an orienting response. Thus, the orienting response is weakly conditioned to the stimuli that prevail on that trial. After the delay, the cue for eliciting the delayed response is complex. It consists of the specific stimuli produced by making the orienting response plus the particular external stimuli to which the animal last oriented itself. In short, two different sets of stimuli are conjointly relevant for making the target response. Thus it follows that a span of at least two is required for executing a delayed response. But so long as the interval remains short, the effect of one learning trial is sufficient to mediate a correct response. However, as the delay interval increases, more and more of the response-produced stimuli undergo change, and the stimuli of the last trial become indistinguishable from those of prior trials; thus the animal can no longer delay successfully.

This interpretation receives support from the fact that the more nearly the animal is allowed to complete the instrumental response prior to the introduction of the delay the longer it can delay successfully. A well-trained rat that is just permitted to orient to the cue can typically delay a response for 3 to 4 seconds (Hunter, 1912) but it can delay as much as 45 seconds if permitted to run up toward the cue before the delay is introduced (Honzik, 1931). In Honzik's experiment the differential stimulation is more profound with a more complete response, and the learning is better according to elicitation theory, because, learning is brought about by relevant responding (Denny and Adelman, 1955). The following experiments done by Blake, Meyer, and Meyer (1966) also support the one-trial learning interpretation of delayed response.

Four experiments were carried out with rhesus monkeys, with and without frontal lesions, to evaluate the impairment in classic spatial delayed response that the frontal subject typically exhibits. Under some conditions of the study the monkey itself discovered the cue-reward relation rather than being shown what this was by the experimenter. It was found that frontal subjects can perform a delayed response as well as normal subjects when the frontal subjects' own predelay response of picking up objects over the foodwells revealed the cue-reward relation (subject was unrewarded on half of these discovery trials because a clear plastic barrier covered the bait half the time). A delay test followed each trial, and the response was reinforced if the choice was correct. Note: One implication of these data is that the frontal animal does not ordinarily make an incipient approach response when the experimenter puts the bait under an object. However, when the subject is required to make an approach response through the use of discovery trials, one-trial learning occurs and delayed responding becomes possible. To explain their results, the investigators stated, "making the response guarantees attending to the cue-reward relation," which is functionally or behaviorally identical to the interpretation offered in the text above.

Further support for a one-trial conditioning interpretation of delayed responding comes from studies of the effect of deprivation level and incentive magnitude on the success of delayed response. In the elicitation framework, the main role of both incentive magnitude and deprivation level in learning is to help specify the appropriate response (Denny and Ratner, 1971). Obviously, if learning is going to occur in one trial, per the delayed response problem, the response must be nicely specified. Therefore, on would predict that increasing the value of the incentive or increasing the deprivation level should facilitate delayed responding. The data on this point are strongly confirmatory. Gibbons delay significantly better when preferred food is the incentive than when nonpreferred food is used. They also perform better for a nonpreferred incentive when food deprivation is increased (Berkson, 1962). The apparent clincher, however, is a study by Gross (1963) using both normal and brain-operated monkeys in which performance on spatial-delayed response and spatial-delayed alternation was compared at both high and low deprivation levels. In the delayed alternation situation, the monkey was presented with two stimulus plaques from which to choose, with a delay of 3 to 5 seconds between the choice-response and the next stimulus presentation. The animal was reinforced (i.e., received a raisin) each time after it had alternated its response from trial to trial. In the delayed alternation situation the bait (raisin) was presented *after* the correct response had been made and therefore could not directly specify the correct response, whereas in regular delayed response, the bait is the US or specifier of an incipient correct response. Gross' results clearly indicated that increased deprivation improved delayed-response performance in all animals but had no effect on delayed-alternation performance. That is, high deprivation level facilitated performance when it participated in the specification of the UR (incipient approach to baited object), but did not aid performance when it could not enter into response specification.

Different species vary considerably in the amount of time they can delay a response, given roughly comparable experimental situations. This fact may reflect several things: (1) differences in one-trial learning ability, (2) whether or not the incentive can be used as the cue (a monkey sees fine detail better than a rat), (3) general activity level of the animals (a rat is more active than a turtle), (4) differences in span, and (5) how responsive the organism is to external stimulus changes. For example, the fact that the mentally retarded children can delay for less time than normal children of the same MA (mental age) could reflect the greater distractability of the retarded child to external stimuli (Pascal et al., 1951). Among the higher primates (chimpanzee, gorilla, orangutan), the experimental data seem to indicate only minor differences in delayed-response performance and no appreciable difference in performance on the patterned-string problem, a complex perceptual-motor task (Fischer and Kitchener, 1965). Such a similarity in performance is quite in keeping with our ignorance as to which species, if any, is more primitive.

From Meyers, McQuiston, and Miles (1962), Berkson (1962), and Michels and Brown (1959) we can rank order various species in delayed-response performance. The rhesus monkey excels, followed by gibbon, marmoset, raccoon, and cat in that order. This ordering must be qualified by whether or not the experimental situations were strictly comparable or provided the appropriate set of variables for each species studied.

The variable of language can be virtually excluded from human performance in delayed response by using the multiple delayed-response technique. When this is done, an adult chimpanzee, performs as well as adult human beings and better than 7- to 9-year-old children (Tinkelpaugh, 1932). In the multiple delayed-response situation there are, say, thirty-two identical containers arranged in pairs and located haphazardly at different places in a large room. One member of each pair is baited as the subject watches, and afterward the subject is permitted to respond to each of the pairs in turn. Due to the large number of pairs in unspecified places, verbalizing that the lure is on the right or on the left is of no aid to a human subject. Since the human being cannot verbally rehearse during the delay period, he or she has only one learning trial for the location of all the lures, as is always the case with infrahuman organisms. Thus the performances of the chimpanzee and human are roughly equivalent (the human being is not automatically superior to other animals; the basis must be specified).

Double Alternation Problem

Another behavioral phenomenon that has been used to infer symbolic behavior in lower animals is the double-alternation problem in a temporal maze. But, as was true with delayed response, the behavior can be analyzed in terms of learning responses to complex cues. The temporal maze is shown in Figure 14.2. In this piece of apparatus the animal is called on to make successive responses at the very same choice point. The only cue for differential responding is the preceding pattern of internal, response-produced stimuli. If the animal is confronted with the problem of a simple alternation of left and right turns (LRLR), there is a distinctive proprioceptive stimulus for each response. Just having turned left provides the cue for a right turn, and just having turned right is the cue for a left turn. Most mammals, including mice and rats, can readily learn the simple-alternation problem. But when the cue is made more complex by using a double-alternation pattern (LLRR), rats typically fail to learn, though some success with rats in a temporal maze has been reported (Diamond, 1967). Other mamals such as cats, dogs, and raccoons seem quite capable of learning a LLRR problem. Since, however, these animals fail to learn a longer sequence than LLRR, it is gratuitous to assume that a symbolic process is operating here. (A symbolic process would allow an indefinite sequence of correct responding.)

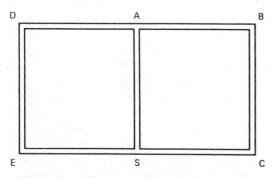

Figure 14.2 Diagram of the temporal maze. The pathways consist of elevated poles. The animal is required to run two right circuits (S—A—B—C—S) and two left circuits (S—A—D—E—S) in succession after which it is rewarded. During the training the direction of the animal's progress is controlled by blocking off the incorrect route.

For the learner, two main difficulties arise with the double-alternation problem. (1) The cues for the correct response are not produced by the immediately prior response, but by the previous *two* responses (there are *two* jointly relevant sources of stimulation). In the double-alternation problem this also means that there are two distinctly different stimulus patterns for the same correct response: For example, the cue for turning right is (a) having just completed two left responses or (b) just having turned right after having turned left (the cue for each right turn response varies with the context or is even more complex than having two relevant components). Thus double-alternation performances requires at least a span of two and probably somewhat more. (2) As if this were not complicated enough, solution of the double-alternation problem also requires the consistent production of each response in the LLRR sequence so that consistent kinesthetic stimuli, no matter how complex, can prevail at the choice point each time the subject arrives there. In this connection, experimenters often help the animal by inserting a barrier in the wrong alley to shorten any errors made. Thus the animal is kept on the track as much as possible. Evidence to support such a kinesthetic chaining hypothesis has been found by Diamond (1967).

Presumably simple alternation, double alternation, delayed response, and unit-alike mazes all require the use of perseverative kinesthetic cues, but these learning problems differ in the complexity and salience of the cues available. For the rat, which cannot delay a response as long as the dog or raccoon, the kinesthetic cues do not seem to last as long as they do for other mammals. The maximum for the rat appears to be about 45 seconds (Perkins, 1947; Honzik, 1931). In the double-alternation problem, considerable time can elapse between making a response and arriving at the choice point one or two responses later. Consequently the rat could be specially handicapped in learning the doublel-alternation problem whereas if the time between successive responses were kept short, the rat should be able to solve the double-alternation problem. Such an interpretation is in keeping with the fact that a rat can learn to press two adjacent levers in a Skinner box in a double-alternation pattern (Schlosberg and Katz, 1943).

"Insightful" Problem Solving

An initial point to be made here is that the studies that seem to support the notion of "insight" or "reasoning" in other animals all employ open-field situations in which visual cues abound and the animal's solution response can be elicited by distal (distant) stimuli. When studies investigating the possibility of solving comparable problems in enclosed mazes or in a homogeneous surround have been conducted, the animals uniformly fail to perform insightfully (Graziano, 1956; Grice 1948; McNamara, Long, and Wike, 1956; Tolman and Honzik, 1930; Wolfe and Spragg, 1934). It is not an uncommon observation in maze experiments to see a fairly well-trained rat prematurely jump out of the experimenter's hand and run across the top of a shallow, complex maze directly to the goal box. Such behavior has been labeled insightful. But it is possible to consider such behavior as neither "insightful" nor contradictory to a careful stimulus-response analysis. The best-learned response of the animal is to approach the visual stimuli associated with the goal region, including the extramaze cues. In fact, the chain or sequence can be said to begin with the learning of this response (Denny, 1971). Thus it is no surprise that the rat shows appropriate approach responding (positive transfer) when so permitted. In addition, this behavior indicates that it is inappropriate in the initial stages of maze learning to classify the animal's learning as a series of right and left turns, for such a classification implies that the animal's responses are guided primarily by kinesthesis. Only in the latter stages of learning does kinesthesis also control maze behavior. Direct approach to the goal ("insight") is guided by visual cues and is quite predictable after learning to these cues has occurred.

Furthermore, even in open-field situations an animal as high in the phylogenetic scale as the chimpanzee fails to show "insight" in a situation which rigorously controls and defines "insight-ful" behavior (Razran, 1961). In the final analysis, many studies that purport to show "reasoning" in nonhuman animals seem to be slightly complicated delayed-response problems with delays that the animal in question can handle. And Schiller (1957), who was himself an early proponent of insight in animals, has impressively pointed out that the behavior that has been referred to as insightful in the chimpanzee is behavior that is dominant in their original behavioral repertoire. Without lures, chimpanzees stack boxes when boxes are available and poke sticks together when such sticks are about.

Nevertheless, recent research on Maier's three-table "reasoning" problem (Maier, 1929) has provided further evidence that the rat is capable of feats that seem rather difficult to explain. The three-table problem involves an elevated structure consisting of three open platforms (tables), equidistant apart, that are connected to each other by three open, equilateral runways intersecting at a central choice point (see Figure 14.3). The walls of the room behind the tables are distinctively different from each other, and the presence or absence of a food cup on any table is hidden from view at the choice point by a shield placed at the entrance to each table. The typical procedure consists of permitting a food-deprived rat to explore all three tables thoroughly (15 minutes each day), with food absent from this stage of the experiment. Then the rat is placed on one of the tables and permitted to eat wet mash from a food cup there for, say, 3 minutes. After this eating experience, the rat is picked up and placed on one of the *other* two tables to see if it will select the arm at the choice point that leads to the table containing the food (a test trial). Over days, or test trials, all tables are used equally often as initial feeding points and starting points, eliminating the possibility of learning to turn in a particular direction or to approach a particular table consistently.

Over test days, the rat typically performs correctly about 90 percent of the time, which is

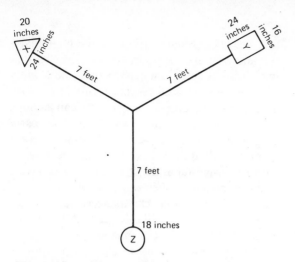

20 inches
24 inches
7 feet
7 feet
24 inches
16 inches

7 feet

18 inches

Z

Figure 14.3 Maier's three-table problem.

interpreted to mean that the rat has demonstrated reasoning (defined by Maier as the result of combining two *independent* experiences). Experience 1 is exploring all three tables and connecting runways. Experience 2 is finding food on one of the tables prior to test. Considerable evidence exists that successful performance requires the daily exposure to experience 1 in addition to experience 2 (Stahl and Ellen, 1974). If the rat were simply approaching the table and location where it last ate, experience 1 would seem to be unnecessary. A rat could presumably approach the table where it last ate, as a sort of delayed response behavior, without the initial exploration having occurred.

It is possible, however, to account for the importance of the exploration experience without invoking the concept of reasoning. The concept of habituation can also be used to explain the effect. Equivalent exposure to all three tables and connecting alleys during the exploration period just preceding the feeding and testing stage means that any tendency to approach a table because of recent feeding there would *not* be counteracted by a stronger tendency to explore either one of the other two alleys. In other words, the initial exploration period presumably satisfies the general tendency to explore and lets the tendency to approach the place

where feeding occurred to predominate. Otherwise, the tendency to explore an alternative alley could predominate.

Such an analysis rules out reasoning or anything like it in the rats' solution to the Maier three-table problem and represents a straightforward, parsimonious interpretation of the phenomenon. In fact, Stahl and Ellen (1973) found that rats with septal lesions whose exploratory behavior increases markedly failed to "reason," nicely supporting this analysis.

None of this implies that nonhuman animals do not solve problems; they in fact do. When other animals solve problems, it typically appears to be a trial-and-error procedure, which is usually the way in which human beings solve problems. However, the presence of language, long spans, and the diversity of prior experience in humans can make a mammoth difference in behavior. The double-alternation problem, for example, become trivially easy when one can verbalize "twice to the right, twice to the left." Any rudimentary representative behavior possessed by other animals in quite ineffectual by comparison. This does not imply that language represents an entirely new process; the role language plays seems quite understandable in stimulus-response terms. In fact, an excellent case can be made against the use of such concepts as "reasoning" and "insight" even at the human level. One definite value of studying the behavior of other animals is to view ourselves more objectively. A typical problem solving situation is illustrated in the following summary:

Patterned-strings problems are typically defined by presenting a subject with various configurations of two or more strings, one of which has a conspicuous reward attached at one end. The task is to select the string with the attached reward regardless of the pattern formed by the strings.

Past investigations of patterned-strings problems have been conducted mostly with monkeys (Harlow and Settlage, 1934; Warden, Koch, and Fjeld,) chimpanzees (Finch, 1942), and lowland gorillas (Riesen, Greenberg, Granston and Fantz, 1932). Some work with dogs and cats has been reported (Richardson, 1932; Trueblood and Smith, 1934), but this research did not conclusively demonstrate discrimination of different string patterns by these carnivores. However, more recently, Michels, Pustek, and Johnson (1961) showed that raccoons can solve moderately complex string patterns if a sufficient number of trials are presented.

In a study by King and Witt's (1966), four rock squirrels learned a series of paralled patterns; however, only one subject was able to learn the entire sequence including crossed (X) and pseudocrossed ( )> <) string patterns. On an intermixed series of crosses and pseudocrosses, this particular subject could not perform effeciently on both problems simultaneously, whereas the raccoon can do this.

Learning Set

When an animal is given a long series of different problems, it shows progressive improvement until it finally may be able to learn a new problem in one trial. This "learning how to learn" phenomenon was first demonstrated by Harlow (1949), who called it learning set. Harlow gave eight monkeys 344 object-discrimination problems (344 different pairs of distinctive stumili such as "dime store" objects and solid geometrical figures). The monkeys received fifty trials on each of the first 32 problems and about nine trials on each of the remaining problems. After 256 problems, performance on the second trial of a new problem was 97 percent correct.

In the past few years it has been demonstrated that rather marked differences in ability to form learning sets exist among species of primates, as well as across the mammalian class. Among the primates the chimpanzee, gorilla, and rhesus monkey are at the top and the marmoset at the bottom, with other species ranging in between, in much the order that phylogeny might predict. Simple discrimination learning does not ordinarily yield these ladderlike differences. Thus learning set has been entertained as a comparative psychology measuring stick of degree of intellectual development.

One possible interpretation of learning set, in keeping with the present theoretical approach, is in terms of complex cue utilization. The first assumption that needs to be made in this interpretation is that the perceptual discrimination between the to-be-discriminated stimuli requires little or no learning (a natural discrimination exists — the animal immediately sees the "ash tray and sponge" as different). This means that the large number of trials initially taken in learning a discrimination problem is due largely to the special methodology of the discrimination learning experiment, not to any inherent difficulty in perceiving stimulus differences. When an animal is given a long series of problems to learn, it is then in a position to solve the method, so to speak. Reinforcements and nonreinforcements, as such, then become the most relevant cues in the learning situation. They are the only cues that remain constant across problems, and with a large number of problems there is a sufficient number of trials to mediate learning of the method of a discrimination experiment. In other words, the animal gradually learns that, when an object is reinforced, it continues to be reinforced (to select it consistently) and that, when an object is nonreinforced, the *other* object is to be selected. In the jargon of the experimental investigator, the animal learns a "win, stay – lose, shift" strategy. Adult human beings already know that this is typically the way things are, based on their wide experience with two-choice situations and the usual meaning of "right" and "wrong." Thus they typically "learn" a simple discrimination by the second trial on the very first problem, staying with the one selected on the first trial if correct and shifting to the other stimulus if the first one selected was incorrect. A young child, on the other hand, probably does not know this strategy very well and shows the development of "learning set" at a rate which is comparable to the chimpanzee (Kaufman and Peterson, 1958).

A learning set problem, *at a minimum*, has a complexity of two; the subject must respond to the reinforcement or nonreinforcement event *and* the object selected in order to respond appropriately on the next trial. But learning to use reinforcements and nonreinforcements as cues should definitely be facilitated by attending to *both* object-stimuli. This way, the strategy of staying with the positive stimulus and shifting away from the negative cue should be learned unambiguously on the early trials of a new problem. For example, if a subject shifted to the other object-stimulus after a nonreinforcement but did not attend to the stimulus shifted from (only to the stimulus selected), the shift strategy would be learned very slowly or not at all. Very recent data on monkeys show that the number and duration of eye fixations for the patterns to be discriminated increase as learning set develops and level off when performance does, indicating optimal use of *both* object-stimuli to solve the problem (Schrier and Povar, 1978). Thus only animals with a span of three or greater would be expected to perform well on learning set problems, as the available data indicate.

To the extent that learning the strategy of a discrimination experiment is involved in learning any kind of discrimination problem, a higher span could help. That profoundly retarded children, presumably with spans of one or two, have great difficulty learning simple discriminations (House and Zeaman, 1958) is consistent with this notion. According to the analysis presented above, the use of learning set problems to measure the "intellectual" level of species in the animal kingdom is a reasonable procedure. The following experiment conducted by Leonard,

Schneider, and Gross (1966) on learning set and delayed-response in tree shrews is relevant here.

Three tree shrews (Tupaia glis) showed no interproblem improvement in 800 six-trial object-discrimination problems (e.g., a soap dish, versus a ball for one problem). Although all subjects then learned a series of object discriminations in which they were trained to criterion on each, only one shrew showed any interproblem improvement on this series. When the shrews were returned to 50 six-trial problems, performance was superior to that in the original 800 problems, but no further inter-problem learning was evident. Five shrews were also tested on a series of delayed-response problems. On both learning set and delayed-response tasks, peformance was clearly inferior to that previously reported for straight discrimination problems (A shrew's span is probably quite limited).

Oddity Learning, Complex and Conditional Discriminations, and "Concept" Formation

An interesting experimental technique in the area of complex behavior that has been exploited in the Wisconsin Primate Laboratory is the oddity problem. Two different pairs of identical stimuli are used, but only three stimuli are presented on any one trial. Let us say the two pairs of stimuli are identical wooden blocks and identical doorbells. On a particular trial two doorbells and one block are presented. Here, the block is singly represented, or odd, and its choice is reinforced. On another trial the doorbell may be odd and the one to select. Each stimulus is odd equally often over trials, and the odd one occurs in all three positions equally often; thus position and object quality are irrelevant. To solve the problem an animal must attend to each of the identical stimuli to see that they are the same and to the third stimulus to see that it is different before it can correctly choose the one that is different. That is, all *three* stimuli are jointly relevant for making the target response. Thus the oddity problem requires a span of three for solution. Such a task seems to be too difficult for a rat to learn. There are no unambiguous data published that support such learning in the rat, and extensive unpublished investigations carried out by Elizabeth Gordon and the author in 1978 using very gradual fading and shaping procedures failed to reveal true oddity learning in the rat.

Adult nonhuman primates have no particular difficulty with oddity problems, suggesting that they have a span at least of three, while subprimates either fail the problem or encounter considerable difficulty. In fact, given a series of oddity problems, some monkeys develop learning sets to the point where one-trial oddity learning occurs; and complicating the problem further can still yield learning in primates. For example, rhesus monkeys can be trained to respond to the odd color when presented on a light background, and to the odd form when presented on a dark background. Such a problem has at least a stimulus complexity or span requirement of four: The monkey must look at the *background* plus all *three* stimuli to see which ones are the same and which one is different along the *relevant* dimension. It is interesting to note that the typical moderately to mildly retarded human being has a span of about three or four, and it is doubtful if any nonhuman animal could learn a problem more complex than this so-called Weigl principle oddity problem.[1] Oddity learning in children, adults, and seniles (Strong, 1966) and the role of cue dominance in oddity learning (Draper, 1965) are summarized as follows.

[1]It appears that the immediate memory span for the bottle-nosed dolphin is at least four (Thompson and Herman, 1977), and the data show many similarities to the data for humans on equivalent tests. Given the dolphin's general level of behavior, this finding is consonant with a span analysis.

One hundred thirteen humans from the age of 3 years to hospitalized senile patients were run on identical one-trial, two-position oddity problems used previously with cats, racoons, monkeys and chimpanzees. The youngest child to learn was 3 years, 4 months of age (a minimal span of three is presumably needed to solve the problem, which some children of this age have). Sixty-four percent of the 6-year-olds learned (span increases with age until about 16 years; most 6-year-olds would have at least a span of three), while all 12-year-olds and college students reached criterion performance within the second day. Some seniles learned the problem, but showed atypical, insightlike learning curves.

The use of oddity problems with humans indicates that 6-year-old children tend to learn oddity in the same manner as nonhuman primates. While children require fewer trials, the distributions almost overlap when the fastest nonhuman is compared with the slowest human, suggesting differences in performance are quantitive, not qualitative.

Six rhesus monkeys were tested on 350 oddity problems that differed in color, form, size, or a combination of these. Oddity learning only occurred when the odd object differed in color from the two identical stimuli. Combining cues resulted in no increase in discriminability. These results support previous findings (Warren, 1953) that color is a dominant cue for monkeys. Note: Very similar results on cue saliency and cue combination have been obtained by Fidura (1966) using Japanese quail in complex discriminations involving three simultaneous dimensions: color, form, and pattern. When the dominant color cue was irrelevant and either form or pattern was relevant, learning was markedly retarded; but when color was relevant, the presence of irrelevant form and pattern cues made learning no more difficult than if they were absent.

Nonhuman primates also excel in concept formation problems in which the relevant stimulus is presented in a multitude of ways and contexts, although cats, dogs, and rats also appear, in a more limited way, to be capable of such learning. Upon appropriate signal, sophisticated rhesus monkey have learned to select all red, but otherwise differentiated, objects from a mixed group of red and blue objects, on a different signal to select all blue objects, and on neither signal to inhibit all responses (Weinstein, 1945). Here, a span of two seems to be the minimum required to do the problem (signal plus relevant color), but also inhibiting the choice of the *wrong color* should clearly facilitate performance (which would require a span of three). This so-called concept formation experiment is really a conditional discrimination with a large number of complicating irrelevant cues present. High proficiency was attained in this experiment even though size, number, form, brightness, and satuation of the stimulus objects varied from trial to trial.

There is no necessary implication here that "concept" formation in nonhuman animals involves symbolization. In fact, when adult human subjects sort stimuli in a concept learning experiment, they typically sort correctly before they are able to identify (verbalize) the concept or principle on which the sorting is based. In other words, the human and nonhuman may learn the task in much the same way despite the amount of verbalizing, often irrelevant, that the human subject may engage in during the learning situation. Rohles and Devine (1966) explored the concept of middleness in visual displays presented to the chimpanzee and found that a chimp can select the middle object from as many as seventeen objects when three, five, seven, nine, eleven, thirteen, fifteen, or seventeen objects are used in a random presentation. But nearly 2000 trials were required to reach criterion for seventeen objects. They also found that the chimp was not visually bisecting the display, for it could solve the problem when the middle object was

numerically, but not spatially, in the middle. There was also good evidence that the chimpanzee was learning many individual patterns rather than "middleness." Kelleher (1958) also found in one of the concept formation problems that he used with chimpanzees that the patterns were learned separately rather than through the formation of a concept.

Imagery, Long CS-US Delays, and Self-Concept

Recent research with nonhuman animals rather clearly suggests that they possess images — probably in all sense departments. Some investigators call these indirectly observed effects *memories*, but it is difficult to conceptualize what a memory for an animal without language would be if it is not an image (overt running responses in a sleeping dog may very well indicate a series of images, or dreaming).

In the rat, the clearest evidence for imagery is the fact that rats show patterning when runs down an alley are reinforced and nonreinforced on alternate days. Patterning means that the rat learns to run significantly faster on reinforced days than on the intervening nonreinforced days. Such patterning with one trial per day only occurs when the food reward or incentive is large, the nonreward confinement duration is long, and the start box and end box are highly similar (Jobe, Mellgren, Feinberg, Littlejohn and Rigby, 1977). When an animal's running time in such a situation reflects the simple alternation of reinforcement and nonreinforcement, this means that what happened on the previous trial is serving as a cue for the current response: a prior reinforcement serves as a cue to inhibit performance on the next trial, and a prior nonreinforcement elicits increased responding on the next trial. Patterning, of course, readily occurs when trials are massed, and here the aftereffects of the previous trial can cue the running on the following trial. But when trials come once a day, it is inconceivable that stimulus aftereffects are operative. With one trial per day when the rat is put in the start box, it must remember, or have an image of, what happened in the end box on the previous day and respond accordingly.

That patterning only occurs when start and end boxes are alike strongly supports this interpretation. The image of the prior end-box event is elicited in the start box as a cue for slow or fast running down the alley only if the two boxes are alike (reinstatement of end-box cues). Plus it makes sense that a good image of both reinforcement and nonreinforcement would require a large incentive (patterning occurs with a small incentive, but only when trials are relatively massed).

Long-delay Learning

As soon as we assume that animals other than man can have images, it becomes possible to explain the occurrence of learning with long CS-US intervals, as described for taste aversion conditioning in Chapters 5, 15, and 22, and possibly for long delays of reinforcement (Lett, 1973). Taste aversion conditioning (see pp. 426–427) has the following special characteristics (Riley and Baril, 1976), and all of them, as I hope to show, are consistent with an interpretation in terms of imagery. (1) Very long CS-US intervals, even as long as a day, yield conditioning, (2) Considerable learning takes place in one trial, (3) Especially when the CS-US interval is long, the Garcia effect holds for species like the rat: a taste or olfactory stimulus is a good CS when the aversive US is a toxic substance that causes illness but a poor CS if the aversive US is electric shock; and, vice versa, a visual or auditory stimulus is a poor CS for a toxic US but a good CS when the US is shock. For the visually oriented bird, however, a visual stimulus is an excellent CS for taste aversion conditioning, (4) So-called backward conditioning can occur, (5) The taste CS must be relatively novel for good condition-

ing to occur, (6) Reconditioning an aversion to a taste-CS after extinction of this aversion is poor or nonexistent (Danguir and Nicolaidis, 1977).

The interpretation proceeds as follows. After ingesting and tasting the CS substance for a number of minutes, the subject typically eats nothing until made ill by an injection of the toxic US. The gastronomical upset presumably elicits images of recent gastronomical events (probably salient events for most animals), which would *include* gustatory images of the taste CS (point 3 above). Thus the image CS would actually be contiguous with the UR, or nausea, and good conditioning would be expected (point 1 above). Also the image could be elicited a number of times while the subject is ill, actually resulting in more than a single conditioning trial for one pairing of CS and US (point 2 above). This same sort of notion also handles point 4 above: long-lasting nausea would mostly follow the CS solution with which the rat was intubated following injection of the toxic US (that is, forward conditioning rather than backward conditioning actually prevails).

A visual or auditory CS for a rat is *not* closely associated with gastronomical events, and thus visual or auditory images would *not* be elicited by nausea and therefore could *not* mediate aversive conditioning with a long CS-US interval (point 3 above). Moreover, a visual-auditory CS *can* mediate aversive conditioning for a US that produces nausea if the CS-US interval is conventionally short. For a bird that constantly searches for food visually, it would seem reasonable for a bird to have an image of any novel visual stimulus that preceded nausea — even by several hours — and thus show good aversive conditioning to such a visual CS (point 3 again).

To be most effective as a CS the gustatory image must be uniquely elicited by the nausea, and for this to occur the CS must be novel. Such a distinctive stimulus would *not* be conditioned to competing responses and would be distinctive enough to be remembered hours later when the illness occurred (point 5 above). Finally, if the true CS is an image and the aversive reaction to the generalized taste-CS were extinguished, then the backward association between nausea and gustatory image would also undergo countercon-ditioning (or extinction). Thus the gustatory image would *not* be elicited by nausea during reconditioning trials; and reconditioning, with the actual CS (the gustatory image) absent, would be very poor or nonexistent (point 6 above). In ordinary reconditioning situations the CS is definitely present and reconditioning is typically rapid.

Self-concept

Recent work by Gallup (1977) on mirror image stimulation of chimpanzees suggests that humans might not be alone in the possession of a self-concept. The self-concept represents a spatial and temporal integration of a very complex input of stimuli and could be thought of as an integrated bundle of images.

Upon first exposure to a mirror, a chimpanzee sees facial features it has never seen before. Such a stimulus reliably elicits behaviors that are like those elicited by an unfamiliar conspecific, including vocalizations and threat displays plus apparent attempts to find the three-dimensional counterpart to the stimulus. During the first two days of exposure to a full-length mirror, chimps engage predominantly in such other-directed behavior, but by the third and fourth day they begin to engage in self-directed behavior, using the mirror to view areas normally inaccessible to vision (e.g., in picking food from between the teeth).

In Gallup's study, the chimps were exposed to a mirror for 10 days. Following this, each chimp was anesthetized and the mirror removed. At that time a bright red, odorless, nonirritating spot was painted on one eyebrow and one ear of each animal. When the animals were fully recovered, a baseline of the number of times either spot was touched was taken. The mirror was then reintroduced, and the frequency of contact with the spots was found to be twenty-five times greater than baseline. A group of control chimpanzees that were naive to the mirror and similarly marked only touched the spots in the presence of the mirror with a frequency that approximated the experimental group's baseline.

These findings are especially impressive when it is realized that monkeys (rhesus, java, and stumptail macaques), as well as gibbons (a more primitive ape), show no evidence of self-recognition. Self-recognition has only been demonstrated in the chimpanzee, orangutan, and human. This is true even though monkeys can be trained to manipulate objects using mirrors and to reorient themselves to gain access to food from its reflection (Brown, McDowell, and Robinson, 1965).

Because it seems impossible to recognize oneself without a self-concept, Gallup's findings strongly suggest the presence of such a set of images in the champanzee. Monkeys, on the other hand, respond to features of themselves as the result of visual or tactual feedback as *not* fundamentally different from the objects in the environment (Gallup, 1977).

The importance of the self-concept in humans is reflected in the fact that pair-bonds, whether or not they are officially married, tend to look alike (Plomin, DeFries, and Roberts, 1977). Unpublished research by Charles Johnson and the author indicates that about 70 percent of a large, unselected group of married couples of a wide age range are lookalikes, even with attractiveness controlled. According to the present author, "love" is a mutual identification process that is clearly facilitated by similarity of appearance. Everyone likes himself or herself and thus finds it easy to like a physical counterpart. This is a "fun" hypothesis to check whenever there are mates to compare as to likeness of head shape, noses, mouths, eyes, complexion, posture, stature, and so on.

Language in the Chimpanzee

Because of TV, newspaper, magazine, and introductory textbook coverage the accomplishments of chimpanzee Washoe with sign language (Gardner and Gardner, 1971), of Lana with computer language (Rumbaugh, 1977), and of Sarah with the arrangement of plastic symbols (Premack, 1976) are almost commonplace. Consequently, I shall emphasize some of the more remarkable accomplishments of Lana to show how similar the chimpanzee's language structures can be to that of the human being. That is, it is now quite clear that human beings are not the only organism that can use a set of arbitrary signs in a symbolic fashion and creatively generate new combinations of signs according to a set of rules, or syntax. Language no longer separates humans qualitatively from the rest of the animal kingdom; the separation is better viewed as quantitative.

To help convince the skeptic let us examine some of the things Lana has done. On Lana's computer keyboard there are combinations of nine different design elements with background color signifying grammatical class. The keyboard contains four 5 x 5 matrices of these lexigrams. A projector, computer readouts in English, and an automatic dispensing device for a variety of incentives complete the picture. After considerable training in learning to make a variety of requests, including the name of a particular object, by punching the appropriate keys, Lana was able to ask for the names of objects she did not know. For example, Lana did not know the name for the object *box*, and called it a "can" and a "bowl" in order to get the M & M's in it. When this ploy was unsuccessful, she asked, "Tim give Lana name of this." Tim replied "Box name of this," and Lana replied "? Tim give Lana this box." A similar event occurred when Lana did not know the name of the fruit *orange*. Lana finally asked "? Tim give apple which is orange." Similarly, she called a cucumber a "banana which is green" and orange soda a "Coke which is orange."

In one session in which Tim purposely would not comply with Lana's requests (she finally settled for cabbage instead of the requested chow), Lana refused to "talk" with Tim for over an hour. And when water was substituted for the requested item, Lana said "Water in milk" and "? You move water out-of machine." Previously, "out-of" had only been used with reference to moving herself out of her room.

In another instance, when trying to get the "reluctant" Tim to honor her requests, Lana requested "? You move bowl behind room" ("behind room" meant load food dispenser). There were two bowls present and Tim asked "? What bowl". Lana soon replied "? You move bowl which is green." This answer was correct but Tim did not comply, which initiated a novel combination for Lana when she said "? You move *bowl* of chow." Previously, only the word "piece" had been used to modify "chow."

Some Concluding Remarks

The view that comparative psychology is truly general psychology holds up well in the context of the findings on complex behavior. One of the most obvious conclusions from the research findings reviewed is that a great number of species of the animal kingdom are qualitatively similar with respect to basic learning processes and many aspects of complex behavior. This similarity is especially striking throughout the class of mammals. More or less the same sort of conclusion has been reached by Warren (1965), even though he has been earnestly searching for specific qualitative differences among various species of mammals. Warren also indicates that quantitative differences are often not striking and that considerable overlap among species, because of large individual differences within a species, is the rule. At least this is the case when performance is measured by the tools and methods which we now employ.

However, sizable *quantitative* differences (speed of learning, dependence on favorable experimental conditions, etc.) do exist at the level of complex behavior. And to the extent that quantitative differences in span seem to exist across species and longer spans mediate complex behaviors, it might be argued that qualitative differences also exist across species. For example, only higher primates are capable of doing the Weigl oddity problem, and rats cannot learn an oddity problem while higher mammals can. Both the quantitative and qualitative differences in performance suggest an interaction between phyletic level and the variable of stimulus complexity (e.g., Gossette, 1967). The interaction closely parallels the interaction found for levels of human intelligence and task complexity across both retarded and normal individuals (Bachelder and Denny, 1977a and b; Denny, 1964) and the similar interaction for task difficulty found in "mentally deficient or phenylketonuric" rats when compared with normal rats (Schalock and Klopfer, 1967).

This interaction says that performance differences only emerge as a function of intelligence or phyletic level if the task is difficult, and more so the more difficult the task. If a difficult task can be made easy by breaking it down into its simplest components, we consistently find that less intelligent individuals can perform adequately. By such techniques, severely and even profoundly retarded individuals can be taught to read words, write their names, assemble bicycle brakes, and pronounce polysyllabic "jawbreakers" like hippopotamus.

Study Question

1. When is behavior complex?
2. Describe the role cues play in complex maze learning and what happens when the cues are removed.
3. Explain delayed response in a way that does not assume the operation of symbolic activity.
4. What can you say about "reasoning" in animals other than man?
5. What makes you think that other animals have imagery?
6. Discuss the evidence for language learning and the presence of a self-concept in the chimpanzee.

15

Applied Animal Psychology: The Practical Implications of Comparative Analysis

Daniel F. Tortora

Jersey City State College

This chapter describes a field of psychology that does not really exist. To my knowledge, there is currently no textbook, seminar, or course entitled Applied Animal Psychology. There is no psychology graduate program that attempts to train applied animal psychologists; there is no license one can obtain in this country or any other country that will certify the credentials of an applied animal psychologist; there is no journal or division of the American Psychological Association dealing with applied animal psychology.

However, there are about two dozen psychologists in this country who have been applying the knowledge of animal behavior, animal learning and motivation, physiological psychology, and behavior modification to significant animal behavior problems. Most of these professionals are Ph.D. level psychologists trained in one or more of the academic specialties just mentioned.

It could be said that this "field" does exist, but on an embryonic or infant level — in the incipient stage of growing and maturing. Whether or not this potential will materialize depends to a certain extent on whether the psychological community realizes that the knowledge gained in the application of basic behavior principles to the solution of animal behavior problems can advance our basic knowledge of behavior.

Animal Behavior Problems

Inasmuch as applied animal psychologists endeavor to solve animal behavior problems, our first concern is to analyze the nature of these problems. In a very broad sense, a behavior problem exists whenever the species-typical or learned behavior of an animal does not fit the demands of the environment that it inhabits. This broad definition includes animals and situations as diverse as the gazelle and other species of prey that do not attend to the stimuli predictive of the presence of predators; mallard ducks failing to migrate south for the winter; migrating lemmings that periodically swarm through Scandinavian towns, drowning in great numbers in attempting to cross large bodies of water; periodic overpopulation of rodents and rabbits in Australia and California; birds flying into skyscrapers; polar bears terrorizing Manitoba townspeople; attacks on people by packs of stray dogs; pacing and other aberrant behaviors of captive zoo animals; elimination, feeding, sexual problems, and so on in domestic farm animals including tail biting and cannibalism in pigs; innumerable behavior problems of pet dogs and cats (to be discussed in detail later) as well as problems stemming from the use of animals in military, industrial, or recreational settings.

Obviously, an applied animal psychologist could not be concerned with all of these problems. Some naturally occurring maladaptive behavior patterns in wild animals are solved by the process of natural selection. The inattentive gazelle will soon be removed from the gene pool by an attentive predator. The tardy mallard may not survive the winter. These problems are recurrent in nature and may be a function of the genetic variability within the species. This variability, as discussed in Chapter 2, is necessary for the ultimate survival of the species (Mayr, 1970) even though it results in the demise of a few selected members.

But consider problems such as these:

1. Herds of African elephants, in time of famine and drought, will debark and uproot trees destroying entire forests. This destroys the habitat for years, imperiling the survival of great numbers of elephants as well as other species that inhabit the forest. These elephants will also devastate the crops of the native farmers imperiling the natives' survival (Hamilton and Hamilton 1975).

2. Each year there are a small number of grizzly bear attacks on hikers walking the back trails of national forests. These attacks are usually unprovoked, in as much as the hikers do not intentionally attempt to antagonize the 800 pound bear blocking their path. Approximately 80 per cent of the attacks result in death or serious injury (Schneider, 1977).

3. Each year flocks of blackbirds fly south for the winter, roosting in the millions, in states like Arkansas, Louisana, and Kentucky. The enormous density of these birds threatens crops, may spread disease through their dropping, and may result in the extinction of the species if the local human inhabitants have their way.

4. In the United States, at least one person in every 183 is bitten by a dog every year (A. M. Beck, personal communication 1977). The incidence of reported dog bites in New York city averaged about 27,699 per year from 1950 to 1965. Within the last 12 years reported dog bites in New York City have risen 50 per cent, 37,896 in 1970 (Harris et al., 1974) and approximately 40,000 in 1977 (Beck, 1977). Similar statistics can be found for other large urban cities.

Practically all of these examples of behavior problems refer to species-typical behavior patterns that, due to their intensity or frequency, have become problems of major concern to the public. A common link is that humans are typically involved as a direct or indirect causative agent. The destroying of forests by herds of elephants is partially caused by restricting the range of these animals to national parks. Grizzly and brown bear attacks on humans are encouraged by the food and refuse left by visitors to the parks and by the habituation of the bear's fear response through repeated exposure to humans. The blackbirds congregate in large groups on the only available trees left standing. The increased incidence of dog bites is partially attributable to the increasing number of large aggressive breeds being purchased by urban dwellers for protection. These problems become "important" when they affect our livelihood, existence, or well-being.

The Roots of Applied Animal Psychology

In view of the enormous range of behavior problems potentially confronting the applied animal psychologist, it could be instructive to see what problems have been addressed. Basically, there are two classes of problems that have received some attention: utilitarian problems and interactional problems.

Utilitarian problems are the oldest form of animal behavior problems and stem from the economic or military exploitation of animals. Consider prehistoric humans as predators. Their prey usually possessed great strength, speed, and keen distance sensors that evolved especially to reduce predation. Close in to the prey, the early human had to contend with an impressive array of horns, claws, hooves, and teeth. Given the prey's physical assets, it appears almost impossible that man, the puny predator, could have been very successful. However, the human being was one of the most successful predators.

The early human's success was based on an accumulated knowledge of the behavior of the prey. Mountjoy documents this point extensively in Chapter 8, suggesting that the ancients were in reality the first comparative psychologists. To some extent they were, but the activities of ancient humans are probably better described as applied animal psychology. Comparative psychology developed when humans had the luxury of engaging in purely academic pursuits.

Interactional problems, which will be dealt with at great length later, stemmed from the domestication of many different animals. Taming and training animals placed humans in intimate and prolonged contact with them. This interaction betweeen human beings and other animals created new sets of animal behavior problems.

Recent History of Applied Animal Psychology

Twenty-six years ago the field of applied animal psychology was christened by Marian and Keller Breland (1951) in the *American Psychologist*. They considered their work to be an "excellent example of how the findings of 'pure' research" concerning animal behavior and animal learning "could be put to practical use" (p. 202). They envisioned and succeeded in establishing a behavioral factory — in their words, "a flourishing and expanding business concerned with the mass production of conditioned operant behavior in animals" by applying "systematic behavior theory."

The consumers of their conditioned operants were mostly advertisers who used animal displays to attract attention to their product. For example, to advertise chicken feed for General Mills Inc., they created a display of performing chickens. One chicken was trained to play a small piano, while another performed a "tap dance" in costume and shoes, and still another "laid" wooden eggs on demand (Breland and Breland, 1951).

From their meager beginnings in 1947, they expanded, creating exhibits for zoos, natural history museums, department store windows, fairs, trade conventions, tourist attractions, television shows, and commercials. By 1966 they had managed to condition "over eight thousand animals representing more than 60 species including everything from alligators to zebras" [reindeers, cockatoos, pigs, cows, sheep, rabbits, dogs, whales and porpoises, many species of birds, and monkeys (Breland and Breland, 1966)]:

The Brelands' main contribution to psychology is a concept they called "instinctive drift" (Breland and Breland 1961). Simply stated, this means "learned behavior drifts (in topography) toward instinctive behavior" when the two behaviors share a common motivational system. For example, when they tried to train a raccoon to place a coin in a metal container for food reward, the raccoon persisted in rubbing the coin in its hands and dipping the coin in and out of the container as if washing it. This washing sequence impeded the learning of the operant and caused the raccoon to delays, reinforcement but for minutes. Usually one would expect an animal to stop performing behavior that delays reinforcement but since washing is part of a species-typical behavior sequence used by raccoons before ingesting food this did not happen.

Another area of application of animal behavior principles is the military use of animals. It has been pointed out that this use of animals has a very long history. The military still trains guard dogs; in addition, the military trains whales, porpoises, and seals to retrieve sunken objects. But, interestingly enough, it was B. F. Skinner (1960) who brought this military application to a high art or perhaps to the ultimate absurdity. In 1940, he, along with others including Keller Breland, proposed to train pigeons to guide missiles.

This may sound like a crackpot idea but it had merit. During World War II there existed an air-to-ground missile called the "Pelican." The problem was that the guidance system took up most of the available cargo space, leaving no room for explosives. Skinner's solution was to place a trained pigeon in the nose of the missile. The pigeon was trained to peck at the silhouette of the target. When the pigeon pecked the silhouette when it was in the center of the display (i.e., on the cross hairs) no course correction was made. However, when the pigeon pecked the silhouette when it was off center a servomechanism made the appropriate course correction and returned the silhouette to the center. The net effect was that the pigeon steered the missile. By combining three trained pigeons in the nose cone they were able to increase the reliability and accuracy of the system substantially. One expert looking at the performance graphs of the pigeon system exclaimed, "This is better than radar!" (Skinner, 1960, p. 33). Although the concept of an animal guidance system was vindicated by the pigeon's performance data, the project was terminated. As Skinner said, "The spectacle of a living pigeon carrying out its assignment, no matter how beautifully, simply reminded the

committee of how utterly fantastic our proposal was" (Skinner, 1960, p. 34).

Two other projects involving trained pigeons deserve mention. Both of them used pigeons as quality control inspectors on assembly lines. One project used pigeons to inspect and discard defective gelatin drug-capsules (Verhave, 1966). The pharmaceutical firm used large, complex machines to make and fill the capsules with a precise quantity of drugs. Defective capsules could jam the machine, wasting countless working hours in repair and necessitating human capsule inspectors. Verhave reasoned that inspecting capsules visually was a dehumanizing job better relegated to a pigeon than a person. To accomplish this he trained pigeons to discriminate defective capsules presented one at a time behind a display window. The pigeons were rewarded with grain for pecking the display window when a defective capsule was exhibited. When a good capsule was displayed the pigeon was trained to peck an opaque changeover key that brought the next capsule into view for inspection. The procedure allowed for rapid indentification of defective capsule and worked very well. Individual birds could be brought to an error frequency of 1 error in 100 inspections. If two birds were hooked in series so both had to "agree," the error frequency could be as low as 1 out of 10,000 inspections.

Cummings (1966) used almost the identical procedure to train pigeons to inspect and discard defective electronic parts. An electronics firm had installed a machine that would accept component parts on one end and then assemble them into finished products that emerged from the other end. It was far more accurate and rapid then the usual human assembly line. The problem was that the deviant parts would stick in the machine's throat, so to speak, jamming it. This resulted in the same sort of problem the pharmaceutical firm had. Cummings was able to train his pigeons to a level of 98 per cent accuracy at an inspection rate of 1000 parts per hour.

Like Skinner's project, both of these ventures were abruptly terminated when it appeared that they were successful and feasible. Thus, when the project had to be taken seriously, the ultimate decision makers seriously considered the possibility that there would be repercussions such as bad publicity and problems with labor unions and balked at the idea. Undertakings that exploit animal behavior may represent the ultimate affront to human workers. First machines take over some of their tasks; then pigeons take over the remaining tasks, do a better job, and work long hours for pigeon feed.

Interactional Problems

Interactional problems are created when humans and other animal's interact. Unlike some of the utilitarian problems, the solutions to these problems may hold the most promise for the future. For one thing, solving interactional problems may improve the human condition rather than appearing to detract from it as do some of the utilitarian examples.

Ecological Problems

There are two types of interactional problems. One type is related to behavioral ecology; examples of this type of problem were described earlier when reference was made to elephant's debarking trees and blackbirds' congregating in small areas. The gist of these problems is that humans have altered the environment in such a way that the behavior of the affected animal has become a nuisance or hazard to humans. This area of applied animal psychology is relatively unexplored, and it represents an opportunity for psychologists to become involved in areas that are traditionally left to the zoologist and natural resource persons.

An example of a behavioral solution to an ecological animal behavior problem comes from the work of Garcia and associates on condi-tioned taste aversions. In 1967, Garcia and Koelling demonstrated that laboratory rats readily learn to avoid food or sweetened water adulterated with chemicals that cause illness (see also Chapters 2, 5, 14 and 22). Many animals learn this association rapidly, often within one trial (Revusky and Bedarf, 1967) and even with long intervals between eating and onset of illness (Garcia, Erwin, Koelling, 1966); in addition the association is very resistant to extinction Garcia Mcgowan and Guean, 1972). Such information provides a potential behavioral solution to a problem of sheep farmers in the southwest. These farmers' flocks are periodically plagued by predation from coyotes. The farmers' solution has been to poison and shoot these animals, threatening the survival of coyotes and any other species that happened to eat the poisoned meat.

Garcia's solution (Gustavson, Garcia, Hawkins, and Russiniak 1974; Garcia, Rusiniak, and Brett 1977) was to place dead sheep laced with the nausea-inducing chemical, lithium chloride, in the field for the coyotes to eat. The chemical has no permanent harmful effects; however, the coyotes learn to associate the eating of sheep with illness, resulting in the coyotes' complete avoidance of the sheep. Such a technique could be used rather generally to reduce sheep predation by coyotes.

Animal Clinical Psychology

The second type of interactional problem occurs when a human is in prolonged and intimate contact with another species. The most common are pet behavior problems involving a dog or cat. Tuber, Hothersall, and Voith (1974) and Hamilton and Robbins (1975) were the first psychologists to address the topic of behavior problems with pets, which they call "Animal Clinical Psychology." Animal clinical psychology refers to the diagnosis and treatment of behaviors that animals exhibit that constitute a problem for the interacting human being. These animals typically

Figure 15.1 Therapist psychoanalyzing the dreams of his client, Fido, says, ''Ah, so you believe that your owners didn't understand you.''

have some economic or emotional importance to humans. To date, behavior problems in dogs appear to make up the majority of cases that have been treated by psychologists.

Placing the modifier "animal" in front of "clinical psychology" is likely to conjure up some queer images, especially when the animal is a dog. An obvious image is a dog lying on a leather couch with the psychologist sitting behind it interpreting every bark (Figure 15.1). Of course, this is incorrect. However, this image leaves the reader with a number of questions. Can a dog's behavior be abnormal? How do you diagnose a dog's behavior problems? How is it possible to treat these problems? What psychological methods of the clinic are appropriate for our canine comrades?

A partial answer to these questions is that animal clinical psychologists share a common goal with ordinary clinical psychologists: the reduction or removal of behavior problems and the misery that goes along with them. The animal clinician may even use interview techniques, per-

fected by humanistic clinical psychologists, when interacting with distraught clients (dog owners), that is, techniques such as accurate empathy (Egan, 1975) and reflecting (Rogers, 1961). However, the animal clinician is typically rather different from the ordinary clinician. His perspective, theoretical orientation, basic knowledge, and diagnostic and treatment techniques have their origins in the academic fields of animal behavior, animal learning and motivation, comparative and physiological psychology, and canid and felid ethology. Thus animal clinical psychologists are behavioristic in their orientation and eclectic in applying knowledge from several different disciplines of experimental psychology. This eclecticism has the effect of forcing the integration of material from these diverse fields, which may have the advantage of generating new knowledge and new research questions, as suggested in outline form at the end of this chapter. For now we focus on the activities of an animal clinical psychologist.

A Comparative Analysis

Types of Problem Encountered

The diversity of problems confronted by the "therapist" far exceeds anything encountered in the laboratory. For example, one recent case of mine concerned Sebastian, a 4-year-old male miniature poodle: it barked continuously when the mother and daughter conversed or ate; attacked the daughter's leg with its teeth and forelegs, holding on for up to 10 minutes; guarded and consumed inedible objects and its own waste; chewed its front paws until they bled; guarded its front paws, holding and carrying away a paw in its mouth when approached; continuously barked at its water dish, consuming large quantities of water as well as occasionally spilling and drinking the liquid detergent; urinated at random; roamed the house during the night barking and growling; and, on at least one occasion, defecated near the ear of the 15-year-old daughter in the middle of the night.

The owners' attempts to solve these problems invariably resulted in an intensification of the problems. For example, the problem of the dog's barking continuously for food when they ate got worse because they unintentionally reinforced the dog for this behavior by feeding it when it barked. Initially, the dog was satisfied by a single morsel of food. However, as the dog grew, so did its appetite; the dog therefore had to be continually fed from the table to prevent the racket that could ensue if it were ignored. As a labor-saving scheme, the owners started giving the dog larger chunks of food, allowing them greater uninterrupted time to consume their own meal. As a result, the dog began to eat more rapidly, returning to the table for more food when it was finished. If ignored, the dog would jump into the owners' laps and growl in their faces, a behavior impossible to ignore. In response to this the owners began an eating race with their dog in an attempt to finish their meal before their ravenous pet finished its meal. Of course, they would invariably lose the race. The next trick the own-

ers tried was to eat surreptitiously, stealing into the kitchen when they believed the dog was asleep. The dog appeared to become more alert, intently watching the movements of its owners. Finally, the owners tried literally "eating on the run." They would dash to the kitchen, grab some food, and attempt to escape the clutches of their dog, who was in hot pursuit. The problem got so bad that they ended up eating all their meals at restaurants. A detailed analysis of all of Sebastian's problems is beyond the scope of this chapter and is presented elsewhere (Tortora, 1977). However, this listing indicates the potential complexity of an animal behavior problem.

To make sense of the complexity of the problems confronting the applied animal psychologist, the first two stages of Ratner's comparative method were followed (see Chapter 9). The first stage (i.e., the gathering of background information) is relatively easy to accomplish for dogs but more difficult for cats. The ethology of wolves and dogs has been extensively studied (Fox, 1975; Scott and Fuller, 1965; and Beck, 1973), and the reader should consult Fox (1971) for a detailed description of canine behaviors and displays. Unfortunately, the ethology of the free-roaming domestic cat has not been studied as extensively (Leyhausen, 1965, 1973). This lack of basic scientific information is surprising given the fact that the cat has been a domesticated companion of humans for some 10,000 years.

The Behavior Problem Matrix

The second stage of Ratner's comparative method (i.e., the creation of a classification scheme) was accomplished by combining Denny and Ratner's (1970) classification of consummatory behaviors with the conceptualization of behavior problems by Kanfer and Phillips (1970) as employed for doing behavior therapy with humans.

Table 15.1 represents such a classification scheme, a list of twelve consummatory behaviors and across the top of the table three ways of conceptualizing a behavior problem. As one of these ways, *response excess* obviously refers to behaviors that occur too frequently, for too long, or too vigorously, *response deficit* refers to just the opposite, and *inappropriate stimulus control* refers to a behavior occurring or not occurring when it is inappropriate. Filling in all these cells creates a matrix that satisfactorily classifies many, if not most, behavior problems for dogs and cats.

This matrix represents at least a first approximation to the classification of pet behavior problems. No presumption is made concerning completeness of the system, which can only be determined by its use. The only presumption is that it appears to have value in eliciting information from the client about the entire range of behavior patterns exhibited by the pet. In many cases, use of the matrix indicates that there are problems in behavior classes that the owner has not been aware of or has ignored. Often, as well, information gained by discussing the entire behavioral repertoire of the pet directly suggests methods of treatment.

For example, using the matrix has helped to distinguish at least three functionally distinct types of biting in dogs: "predatory-biting," "dominance-biting," and "fear-biting." They are distinguishable by a variety of criteria that are summarized in Tables 15.2 and 15.3. Across the top of Table 15.2 is a classification of sequential orginzation for species-typical behavior patterns from appetitive patterns through consummatory (Craig, 1918) to postconsummatory patterns (Denny and Ratner, 1970); see Chapter 9 for a complete description of this scheme.

Predatory Biting

Predatory biting refers to a behavior sequence of orienting, stalking, and lunging at the bite object, followed by tenaciously holding the bite object in the mouth while vigorously shaking the head from side to side. This is similar to the predatory feeding sequence of wild dogs and wolves (Scott and Fuller, 1965). It is not surprising, then, that food reinforcement associated with any part of the sequence tends to increase the probability of predatory biting.

In addition, therapeutic techniques like time out (TO), differential reinforcement of other behavior (DRO), extinction, and contingent punishment, all of which are normally successful in reducing the probability of a particular behavior, either have no effect on predatory biting or exacerbate the problem. Presumably, the explanation of this paradoxical state of affairs resides in the interaction between the species-typical predatory behavior of canids and the behavioral consequences involved in the techniques listed above. Take extinction and TO for example. Both of these procedures involve the removal of external reward for the behavior, which usually brings about a decrease in the probability of that behavior. There are at least three explanations for the failure of these procedures to reduce predatory biting: (1) biting, being a consummatory behavior, is not susceptible to modification (Denny and Ratner, 1970); (2) the biting is at the end of a predatory sequence and is thus self-reinforcing (Denny, 1971; Guthrie, 1952; Premack, 1965); (3) predatory biting is not susceptible to extinction due presumedly to natural selection for high resistance to extinction. All these arguments make evolutionary sense and are not mutually exclusive. The predatory success rate of juvenile wild canids is very low. An animal that would extinguish rapidly would stop hunting and consequently die of starvation. Selection pressure would thus be in the direction of very high resistance to extinction.

A similar argument can be made for punishment, the delivery of painful stimuli contingent on biting. It is likely that during capture the prey delivers many painful bites or blows to the predator. A predator that would be easily intimidated by these punishments would be at a selective disadvantage.

Table 15.1

Problem Behavior Matrix

Behavior Class	Problem Response Excess (too much Behavior)	Problem Response Deficit (too little Behavior)	Problem Inappropriate Stimulus Control (wrong Behavior)
Feeding	Hyperphagia; excessive eating or excessively rapid eating leading to vomiting; hiding food	Anorexia; eating deficit leading to inanation, also food preferences leading to deficiency	Pica: eating of nonnutritional substances such as paint, hair, waste
Drinking	Polydipsia; excessive drinking or excessive rate of drinking (stress induced)	Adipsia: deficit in rate or quantity of fluid consumption	Unusual gustatory preferences for certain dangerous liquids; drinking from toilet and "alcoholism"
Sexual	Hypersexuality; heightened sexual arousal in the presence of minimal eliciting stimuli; excessive courtship	Impotence: failure in lordosis for female; improper positioning for male; diminished sexual activity; abbreviated courtship	Masturbation: sexual behavior directed at humans and other species; mounting female inappropriately
Fighting	Conspecific dominance problems; between owner and pet (guarding objects; dominance attack)	Lack of protectiveness when necessary; excessive submissive behavior interfering with other behavior (submissive micturition)	Guarding objects or places from members of family; attacking strangers, *overprotectiveness* without control
Fear	Fear biting: excessive fear reaction to normally fear producing objects; uncontrolability	Lack of appropriate fear to dangerous objects	Phobias: thunderstorms; noises; being alone; enclosed places; open spaces
Eliminating	Encopresis and enuresis: involuntary defecation and urination; excessive micturition during walk	Overcontrol of defecation and urination due to excessive punitive training, "takes to long to go"	Soiling problems in home; litter box problems
Exploring	Puppy behavior in adult dogs; excessive chewing and mouthing objects; getting into things; distractability	Inattentive to environmental stimuli	Lack of fear of dangerous objects; attention to irrelevant cues
Care of body surface	Excessive hair chewing or scratching leading to damage of integument; excessive care seeking	Incomplete grooming practices	Clawing objects in home; conditioned scratching
Care of young	Failure to wean	Failure to groom or feed young; attacking, killing eating young	Adopting objects or other species as young
Resting	Apparent lazy dog	Hyperkenisis; excitability	Resting on couch or table when not allowed; unusual sleep cycles
Operant	Bizarre behavior rituals; barking and whining	Lack of obedience; no owner control over behavior	Failure to differentiate commands; failure to generalize commands
Nesting	Guarding objects or places; hoarding objects and or food in nest	Failure to build or establish maternal nest	Nest site in inconvient place

Table 15.2

Summary of the Behavior Sequence of Three Forms of Biting

Types of Biting	Appetitive	Behavior Sequence Consummatory	Postconsummatory
"Predatory"	Appetitive components occurred in the following sequence. (1) Orienting: dogs appeared to search for, stare at and visually follow the object of the bite (2) Stalking: dogs would slowly approach the object of the bite, lowering its body close to the ground and creeping forward (3) Lunging: rapid movement of the bite object elicited rapid running towards and leaping at the bite object, followed by the bite	(1) Grasping and holding with the mouth (2) Shaking head from side to side	(1) The bite was usually terminated by forcefully detaching the dog's mouth from the bite object (2) The likelihood of another predatory-bite sequence remains high for up to an hour after detachment
"Dominance"	(1) Facial expressions and body postures displaying dominance (i.e., head up, ears erect, puckered lips, direct eye contact with bite object, erect body and tail, standing over and jumping on bite object).	(1) Grasping and holding with the mouth (2) Shaking head from side to side (3) Bite force decreased by submissive behavior of the bite object	(1) The bite was usually terminated by the dog upon submissive behavior of the bite object (2) The likelihood of another dominance bite is a function of the behavior of the bite object
"Fear"	(1) Facial expressions and body postures of submission, (i.e., head down, ears back, submissive smile, no eye contact, lowered body and tail, rolling over on back). (2) Releasing stimulus: a movement previously associated with punishment	(1) Very abbreviated bite, no holding (2) Snaps in air without contact with bite object	(1) The bite is self-terminating (2) It is generally followed by escape, withdrawal and submissive postures and expressions

Thus, in order to modify predatory biting, one must take an indirect approach. An effective method is to countercondition an early or appetitive component, such as stalking, with a withdrawal response.

Dominance Biting

Dominance biting refers to biting incorporated into appetitive and postconsummatory patterns that frequently occurs during the social interaction of two or more dogs. Schematic diagrams of a dog's facial expressions and body posture displaying dominance and submission are presented in Figures 15.2 and 15.3, respectively.

Methods effective in modifying dominance biting differ from those for predatory biting. However, they are logically related to the species-typical social behavior of canids. For example, contingent food reinforcement can now be used to modify the probability of both dominant

Table 15.3

Relative Effectiveness of Various Procedures for Modifying Three Forms of Biting

Procedures	Predatory	Types of Biting Dominance	Fear
Reinforcement for biting	Increases biting	Increases biting	Decreases biting
DRO	No effect	No effect	Systematic desensitization of fear decreases biting
Time out	No effect	No effect	No effect
Extinction of biting	No effect	Partially effective—when external reward for biting exists	No effect
Contingent punishment	Increases biting	(1) Decreases biting of punisher (2) Increases biting of others	Increases biting
Noncontingent punishment	Increases biting	(1) Decreases biting of punisher (2) Increases biting of others	Increases biting
Enforced submission	Increases biting	(1) Decreases biting of enforcer (2) Increases biting of others	Increases biting
Habituation	No effect or increases biting	Mixed effects	Decreases biting
Dominance training	No effect	Increases biting	Decreases biting
Submissiveness training	No effect	Decreases biting	No effect or decreases biting
Counterconditioning of stalking	Decreases biting	Not relevant	Not relevant

ₐ **DRO=differential reinforcement of other behavior.**
ᵦ **Enforced submission=forceably pushing the dog over on its back and holding it there.**
c **Habituation=repeatedly eliciting biting with no consquences.**
d **Dominance training=reinforcement for dominance postures and facial expressions.**
e **Submissiveness training=reinforcement for submissive postures and facial expressions.**

and submissive postures or facial expressions. Modification of each of these postures and expressions alters the probability of biting. Increasing submissiveness *decreases* the probability of biting and increasing dominance *increases* the probability of biting. These effects are in keeping with the observation that wild wolves and dogs use dominance postures to guard their food from other members of the pack and use submissive postures to obtain food from more dominant animals.

Other methods such as contingent punishment and enforced submission (i.e., forcing the dog down into a submissive posture) can have multiple effects: (1) it may reduce the probability of biting toward the enforcer but increase the probability of biting individuals dissimilar to the enforcer, (2) the punishment, if painful, can cause pain-elicited aggression (Azrin et al., 1964), (3) if the enforcer's attempts to forcefully impose submission are unsuccessful, biting will increase.

Fear Biting

Fear biting refers to biting occurring while an animal is performing submissive displays (Figures 15.2 and 15.3). It usually is caused by associating the owner or some aspect of the owner with pain received from repeated beatings. In most cases, systematic desensitization (Wolpe, 1958, 1969) of the fear along a stimulus hierarchy of the owner's having progressively more and more physical contact with the animal alleviates the biting. Physical punishment administered to the dog is part of the etiology of the problem and its use typically results in an increase in biting.

Causal Analysis of the Problem

After clients have specified the behavior problem that concerns them, the next step is to perform a causal analysis of the problem. This step is similar to Ratner's third stage of the comparative method (Chapter 9), that is, investigating all the relevant variables, both independent and dependent.

This causal analysis is facilitated by using a different arrangement of Kanfer and Phillips' (1970), S-O-R-K-C equation, namely, the acronym R-O-C-KS. This acronym stands for a causal chain consisting of (1) a detailed description of the problem behavior or the topography

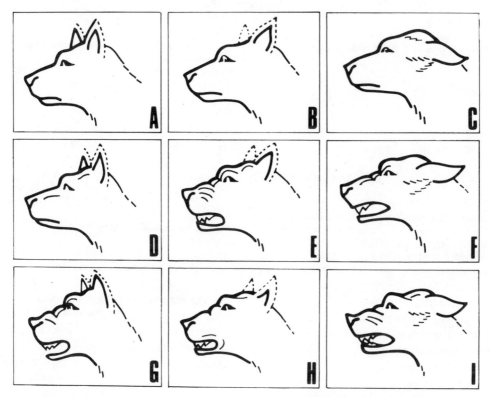

Figure 15.2 Facial expressions of the dog signalling dominance and submission (fear). Increasingly more dominant expressions are shown from top to bottom. Increasingly more submissive expressions are shown from left to right.

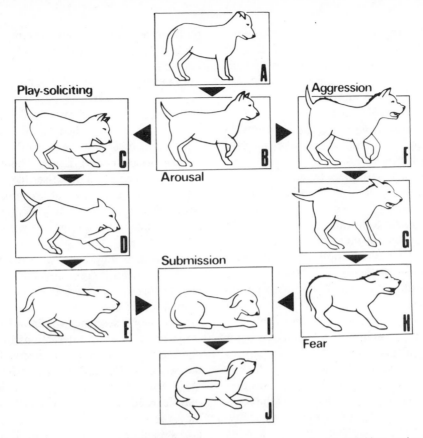

Figure 15.3 Body postures expressing aggression, fear, arousal, play soliciting, and submission.

of the response (R), and any other behaviors that might be associated with it; (2) organismic variables (0) that may relate to the behavior problem; (3) consequences of a response (C) that maintain or exacerbate the behavior problem, (4) contingencies (K) concerned with stimuli, responses, and consequences, and (5) stimulus (S) as an important antecedent condition. Information obtained using this behavioral equation may point directly to treatment techniques by indicating the variables controlling the problem behavior. However, the equation is not applied in a straightforward sequential manner since all behavior problems involve a nexus of interrelated variables. The job of the applied animal psychologist is to untangle this network of variables.

R: Response

The first step in diagnosing a pet behavior problem involves obtaining a clear unambiguous description of the response. In practice, this may be more difficult than it sounds. First, many clients feel guilty about the problem or uncomfortable about talking to a psychologist and beat around the bush.

A second impediment relates to the clients' use of vague, ill-defined, interpretative terminology when describing the complaint. A typical tendency of many clients is to focus on the "meaning" of the behavior, selecting information that supports their interpretation. The challenge here is to reinforce the client's behavioral descriptions selectively with attention, while

Applied Animal Psychology: The Practical Implications of Comparative Analysis obviously ignoring interpretative statements. Other techniques involve verbal modeling of behavioral descriptions by the "therapist." This is accomplished by reflecting back what the client has said, focusing on descriptions of observable behavior.

A third problem relates to the relationship between the initial complaint and the animal's entire behavioral repertoire. For example, is the complaint initially described by the client the only problem, the main problem, or irrelevant to the "real" problem? This question can be answered by going over each and every behavioral class in the behavior problem matrix, obtaining a behavioral description of each problem. This is done whether or not the clients have indicated that they have a problem with a particular class of behavior.

As mentioned earlier, information so gathered can indicate that a pet has other "problems". For example, the main complaint of one pair of clients was that the dog would attempt to bite strangers. They initially said they had no other troubles with the dog. When describing the feeding pattern they said that their dog ate normally. When asked if they could take food or a bone away from it, they said, "We cannot get near him if he is eating or has a bone. He growls and acts very ferocious, we just leave him alone. Isn't that normal?"

O: Organismic Variables

Organismic variables are those variables that are intrinsic to the organism. They involve questions concerning the effects of species, breed, sex, hormones, central and autonomic nervous system damage, circadian rhythms, illness and disease, and the like on an animal behavior problem. Many chapters in this text deal with laboratory studies of these variables as they affect behavior classes and behavioral processes such as habituation, classical and operant conditioning, and memory; and these effects need to be examined in natural settings as well as in

problem settings with pets. It is important for the applied animal psychologist to be aware of the main effects of these variables and processes, and the reader is advised to consult the appropriate chapters in this text.

Another aspect of organismic variables that has remained unstudied until recently is the interaction of certain behavioral processes with certain organismic variables. There are at least two ways behavioral processes like classical conditioning and instrumental learning can interact with the organism as a variable. There are intraorganism and interorganism interactions.

Intraorganism Interactions. Intraorganism interactions mean that for any one organism behavioral processes may be differentially effective in modifying different behavior classes or parts of the behavioral sequence within any one behavior class. Intraorganism interactions have been recognized for years and are nicely illustrated by the work of Edward L. Thorndike (1913). In 1898, Thorndike studied the behavior of cats as they learned to escape various boxes in which they were placed. Thorndike used a variety of boxes each equipped with a different escape mechanism (i.e., a wire loop, a button, a string suspended inside or outside the box, a food pedal, or a latch, etc.). Operating the appropriate mechanism opened the door of the puzzle box allowing the cat to escape the box and eat some food outside of the box. As one might expect Thorndike found that time to escape gradually decreased over trials. This led him to postulate the well-known law of effect, that is, that pleasurable events tend to "stamp in" S-R associations they follow and annoying events tend to "stamp out" S-R associations they follow.

A lesser known result of Thorndike's research provides evidence for an intraorganism interaction. When he placed his cats in box Z, one with nothing to manipulate for escape, and required the cats to lick their fur or scratch themselves to escape, Thorndike found that the cats had a great deal of trouble learning these operants. And when these responses were acquired, they were unstable, readily extinguishable, and tended to degenerate to a mere vestige of a lick or scratch over trials. Thorndike postulated that there might be "an absence of preparation in the nervous system for the connection between these particular acts and definite sense impressions (such as the interior of the box) . . . causing the difficulty in forming the associations" (Thorndike, 1898, p. 6-28).

This notion of preparedness of associations has been recently discussed by Seligman (1970, 1975) and Seligman and Hager (1972). Basically this position is that the association between certain stimuli and responses for particular reinforcers or consequences may be more or less prepared by the genetic endowment of the organism, allowing some associations to be readily formed while others are formed with great difficulty. Numerous studies that shed light on the concept of preparedness have been summarized by Hinde and Stevenson-Hinde (1973).

Such constraints on the formation of associations are obviously important when trying to treat pet behavior problems with conditioning techniques. For instance, a strict contiguity position would predict that the individual delivering a painful aversive stimulus (e.g., beating) would become the conditioned aversive or fear-provoking stimulus, eliciting submission or withdrawal and possibly aggression in the pet. However the association between the individual (CS) who delivers the aversive stimulus (US) and the conditioned response (CR) is not always a simple function of CS-US contiguity since other variables like the family dominance hierarchy appear to determine what CR will become associated with which family member.

Illustrating this point is a phenomenon reminiscent of "displacement of aggression" (Freud, 1909) that has been observed in eleven separate pet-problem cases. The salient features involve (1) a "dominance hierarchy" in the family in which the dog is at or near the top (alpha) position, (2) forceful imposition of a submissive posture or punishment on the dog by the most dominant member of the household, and (3) the dog's directing an aggressive attack (growling, biting) at an individual other than the one imposing the submission or punishment. The target of aggression is usually the family member who is closest to the dog's position in the hierarchy but less dominant than the dog. This occurs even when this family member has *never* been present when the dog was punished.

Consider the case of a 6-month-old male cocker spaniel owned by a young couple. The dog would roll over on its back and submissively urinate when approached by the husband or other males but bark and growl at the wife and other females. During the first therapy session, the wife was instructed to approach the dog as the "therapist" was petting it (petting simulates "standing over," a canine dominance posture (Fox, 1971). The dog growled and lunged at the wife necessitating forceful restraint (pushing the dog on its back and holding it in that position). During restraint the dog continuously stared at the wife, following her with his gaze as she moved about the room. When released the dog attempted to bite her. At no time during the restraint did the dog attempt to bite the "therapist"; when the "therapist's" hand was presented to the dog it would submissively lick it.

Displaced aggression has been observed in a variety of sexually mature male dogs (a toy poodle, Yorkshire terriers, a Kerry blue, a Dalmatian, a standard poodle, a Chow, a Great Pyrenees, and a bull mastiff). The object of the displaced aggression and the nature of the aversive stimulus (electric shock, hitting, loud noises, or enforced submission) varied, but the phenomenon of displacement was invariant. Thus the dog, as well as other social animals, may present an excellent preparation for the study of the interaction of social variables and aversive conditioning.

Interorganism Interactions. An interorganism interaction refers to the interaction between animal type (i.e., species, strain, breed, or sex) and the processes of learning. There is a weak and strong form of this concept. In its weak form one could postulate that all learning principles are manifest in all organisms but to varying degrees. In its strong form one could postulate that each species has its unique way of learning and acquiring information. Until recently, learning theorists (Hull, 1952; Skinner, 1953; Spence, 1956) have more or less assumed that the processes of learning are generalizable across species. Thus, except for a few details about response and sensory capabilities, it was assumed that learning in the albino rat was similar to learning in the pigeon, porpoise, dog, cat, human and so on. This continuity assumption has never been seriously challenged by empirical research.

The answer to the problem probably lies intermediate to the continuity and interaction positions. One can observe similarities between the course of classical conditioning of gill retraction in the limpid or sea slug, the nictitating membrane of the rabbit, salivation in the dog, and the eye blink in the human being (Brookshire, 1970). One can also observe similarities in the operant conditioning of the rat, pigeon, monkey, dog, and human (Brookshire, 1970). However, one is also able to observe dissimilarities from the standard learning paradigms in the imprinting of birds (Bateson, 1973), the learning of species-typical bird songs (Thorpe, 1961), and homing in pigeons (Matthews, 1963). A more complete answer will require research on learning that involves a greater range of behavior classes and a greater range of species than is currently the case.

C: Consequences

Many of the behavior problems encountered with pets involve long sequences of behavior with an intricate network of reinforcers in operation. The therapist faces two main challenges.

The easiest one to overcome is to observe the problem in its natural setting and accurately describe the behavioral chain of events. Doing this may tell one how to alter the sequence of events that are maintaining the problem in the first place. The more difficult task is to determine how the behavioral chain was constructed. Often information about the etiology of the problem is unnecessary for solving the problem itself, but in most cases such information reveals the subtleness of the crucial reinforcers, and how the problem learning has progressed, perhaps pointing to procedures to be investigated experimentally.

A commonly observed determinant of behavior problems is the client's use of "distractors," typically feeding the animal or engaging it in some new behavior as a means of "stopping" the behavior problem. These distraction techniques have a number of effects that constitute a "behavioral trap" (Platt, 1973). First, they immediately terminate the ongoing problem behavior pattern since a successful distraction technique always involves the elicitation of a behavior higher on the animals response hierarchy then the problem behavior itself. Second, a distraction technique, because it involves a high probability response, positively reinforces the problem behavior (Denny, 1971, Premack, 1965), increasing the probability of its occurrence. Third, the immediate termination of the aversive problem behavior negatively reinforces the clients' continued use of the distraction technique, completing the behavioral trap. Thus the owners unintentionally reinforce their dog for misbehaving and the dog reinforces the owners' use of the distraction technique by momentarily stopping the misbehavior. The owners of Sebastian, the dog described previously, would distract their dog with dog biscuits, or by showing the dog its leash signaling a walk when it performed each of the problem behaviors. The behavioral trap is part of the etiology of almost all of the problem cases observed to date and presents an interesting analogy to interpersonal problems in humans.

K: Contingency

The concept of contingency refers to the type of scheduled relationship between various behavioral events: stimulus (S), response (R), and consequences (C). The essence of the concept is the probability of occurrence of one event given the occurrence of another event. For example, continuous positive reinforcement (CRF), involves a contingency in which every response is followed by a reward, whereas 50 per cent partial reinforcement (PR) means rewarding only 50 per cent of the responses. Shaping, or the method of successive approximations, refers to a contingency that changes as the animal gradually acquires a criterion response. When the animal performs a requisite response the response criterion for reinforcement is increased, that is, the contingency changes. For example, to shape a dog to jump over a fence, one starts with a low fence and then progressively increases the height of the fence when the animal masters the previous level.

Laboratory studies have been concerned with only some of all possible contingencies beween S, R, and C, but have generated what appear to be basic "laws" of learning. For example, partial reinforcement is generally considered to produce greater resistance to extinction then continuous reinforcement. It is important for the applied animal psychologist to be aware of the "laws" of learning and also to be on guard, for they may not hold universally when dealing with real-world behavior problems.

The complexity of contngencies involved in most pet behavior problems offers a rich source of material for testing the efficacy of standard laboratory procedures and basic "laws" of learning. In most cases this complexity far exceeds anything studied in the laboratory, forcing the applied animal psychologist to speculate on how these various "laws" or procedures interact. The application of laboratory generated procedures and "laws" to the elimination of pet behavior problems raises theoretical questions about the continuity of learning processes across species and across behaviors within one species.

S: The Stimulus Complex

The stimulus complex controlling most problem behavior is just that — complex. The basic question is to identify the stimuli that are controlling the problem behavior. Identifying the stimulus may suggest treatment techniques such as counterconditioning or the reinforcement of a new response. For example, systematic desensitization, a counterconditioning technique, is commonly used to eliminate fears and phobias in humans (Wolpe, 1958, 1969). The rationale for this procedure is based on principles of classical conditioning and interference learning or competition. The assumption is that fears and phobias are acquired by the association of some neutral (innocuous) event with a painful or traumatic experience via classical conditioning. Consequently one reduces or eliminates the phobia by associating the feared object or event with behaviors that are incompatible with or antagonistic to fear, such as relaxation (Wolpe, 1958), sexual behavior (Wolpe, 1969), assertive behavior (Lazarus, 1971; Wolpe and Lazarus, 1966), or eating (Jones, 1924). In practice, this is accomplished by presenting the feared object or event at such a low intensity that little fear is elicited while simultaneously eliciting behaviors that are incompatible with fear. When the fear is extinguished at the low intensity levels, the intensity of the feared stimulus is increased and counterconditioned at this new level. The goal is to present the original fear stimulus at full intensity without eliciting a fear response.

The success of this procedure depends on identifying the feared stimulus and the dimension along which it varies. The logic here is identical to the logic the ethologist uses to identify the effective stimulus (releaser) controlling a fixed action pattern (Eibl-Eisbesfeldt, 1975). In many cases this procedure involves the use of models that simulates various characteristics of the stimulus complex. By systematically stripping away and manipulating parts of the stimulus complex and noting the animals reaction to the modified model, one is eventually able to specify the controlling stimulus. For example, Tinbergen (1951) was able to determine the releasing stimulus for attack in male sticklebacks. The fish will attack any male stickleback entering its territory (Tinbergen, 1951). A model of this fish can vary in size and shape and still elicit attack as long as it has a red underside. Neither a perfectly constructed model of a stickleback with all the appropriate fish characteristics but without a red belly nor an inverted (red-backed) model will elicit attack. Thus it is clear that the controlling stimulus for attack is a red underside.

An application of this "reduction to the basic stimulus" is illustrated by the analysis of a phobia in a 3½-year-old male dachshund. The dog would bark and refuse to enter elevators, showing signs of extreme fear, such as body trembling and whimpering when forced to enter. However, it would readily run up and down the five flights of stairs to go for a walk. The problem was acute because the owner, an elderly woman, could not negotiate the stairs the two to three times a day necessary to take the dog for a walk. This state of affairs ultimately resulted in defecation and urination problems in the apartment as well as fear biting because the dog was repeatedly beaten for eliminating in the apartment by the elderly woman's oldest son when he visited. The son's "good intentioned" punishments had one effect, the classical conditioning of fear to his presence and the generalization of this fear to other males.

The successful treatment of the dog's fear of the son and other males was a simple operant variation of systematic desensitization, using distance from the dog of an approaching male as the stimulus dimension. The competing response included the dog eating strips of swiss cheese, his favorite delicacy, which the dog received contin-

gent on quiet, nonaggressive behavior in the presence of a male.

What remained was fear of and refusal to enter the elevator. Initially this was conceptualized as a fear of enclosed spaces. However, the dog showed no apparent fear when confined in other small spaces such as an empty closet or cardboard boxes that varied in size from 6 x 3 x 3 feet to 2 x 1 x 1 feet. In order to determine the stimuli controlling the elevator phobia, the stimulus conditions in the elevator were systematically manipulated and data recorded. Figure 15.4 presents the initial data on the number of times the animal balked at entering the elevator during the 5 days of baseline recording and 4 days treatment. During baseline and treatment, the dog was brought to the elevator at 8:00 a.m., 12:00 p.m., and 5:00 p.m. and encouraged to enter. The number of balks, defined as vigorously withdrawing from the open elevator door, was recorded each day.

There were two main candidates for stimulus control: (1) those stimuli in the internal environment of the dog such as changes in heart rate and blood pressure and those related to hunger, thirst, hormones, drugs or illness and (2) those stimuli in the external environment such as lights, sounds, the blowing of the elevator fan, the elevator operator, etc.

As can be seen from Figure 15.4, the balking at the entrance to the elevator appeared to vary unsystematically with time of day and day of the week. This seemed to exclude any cyclical changes in the internal and external environment. What was left was some stimulus change in or near the elevator. Yet balking was not affected by the presence or absence of any of the previously mentioned external stimuli. However, it was noticed that the dog balked when the elevator was not perfectly lined up with the floor. This height discrepancy caused a slight widening of the space between the elevator and the floor of about one-half inch. When a small piece of carpeting was placed over the threshold of the ele-

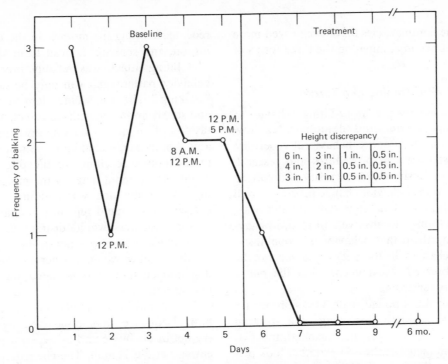

Figure 15.4 The treatment of an elevator phobia in a dachshund. The numbers beside the baseline data points indicate the time of day when the phobic reaction was exhibited. The figures in the box indicate the height discrepancy between the elevator and the floor on each of the three trials per day of treatment.

vator door, obscuring the space, the dog entered the elevator readily. The final test was to place transparent and opaque vinyl covers alternately over the threshold of the elevator. This served to hold tactual stimuli constant while manipulating visual cues. The dog balked with the transparent cover but crossed the threshold with the opaque cover. Thus it was determined that the dog was afraid of the sight of the small space between the elevator and floor. This made sense due to the proximity of the dog to the ground and because the dog on occasion had caught its nails in this space.

The solution was effected with the cooperation of the elevator operator. During the quiet of the afternoon, he consented to adjust the elevator so that there was 6-inch height discrepancy between the floor and the elevator. This did not change the width of space between the two levels but it forced the dog to leap up in order to enter the elevator, a behavior that was frequently performed without fear when ascending the stairs. The dog readily performed this leap into the elevator and was rewarded. The height discrepancy was reduced in stages over the next 4 days in the following steps: 6, 4, 2, 1 and ½ inch. Within 2 days the leaping response completely replaced balking (see Figure 15.4). This case study shows that, without adequate indentification of the controlling stimuli, an appropriate treatment procedure could not have been devised.

Solutions to Biting Problems

Earlier in this chapter, three functionally distinct types of biting in dogs were described: "predatory" biting, "dominance" biting, and "fear" biting. Tables 15.2 and 15.3 summarize their differences. The following cases demonstrate some of the contingencies that have proved more or less effective in eliminating the three forms of biting.

The Taming of a Terrier

This case concerns predatory-biting behavior in a Yorkshire terrier and demonstrates how observing the pet's entire behavioral repertoire can suggest treatment procedures and research ideas. It also illustrates the necessity of involving the clients in the behavior change process as well as the collection of baseline data. In this way, clients are trained to observe and record behavior, showing them that behavior is probabilistic and how changes in the pet's behavior can be reliably observed. Most clients find the entire process very rewarding.

A 2-year old, 4-pound male Yorkshire terrier belonged to a family consisting of a working woman in her late fifties, her husband and two daughters in their twenties. The mother took primary responsibility for feeding, grooming, walking, and playing with the dog. Most of the time the dog was friendly and tractable. However, about two or three times per week the dog would attack the mother. These attacks started when the dog was about 6 months of age and had increased progressively both in frequency and intensity, culminating in three serious bites to the mother's arm and hand over the 2-week period prior to my being contacted. The dog had never attempted to bite any other member of the family.

It was first determined, from the mother's report, that the attack consisted of the dog's repeatedly biting the mother on the hand, holding on, and shaking its head from side to side. The biting attack was reliably preceded by a behavior pattern that can only be described as "stalking." The dog would stare at the mother and slowly approach with ears erect, walking in a fashion of an animal stalking prey. In this state, any stimulation, including movements of people in the house, reaching for the dog, or noises, could elicit a rapid lunge at the mother and biting. When the dog was stalking the mother, everyone else would remain stationary and one of the daughters would distract the dog with food. If the mother was not in the dog's sight, a family member would tell her to hide until the dog stopped stalking or someone was successful in distracting the dog.

The stimuli that reliably elicited the stalking-biting sequence were discovered by observing the pet in the home and by experimentally presenting various stimuli. The clients reported that stalking-biting followed ringing noises produced by the telephone, doorbell, or kitchen timer. These stimuli, as well as a kazoo, clicker, handclap, cap pistol, cowbell, and small dinner bell, were presented independently in the presence of the terrier. The order of presentation was randomized and each stimulus was presented five times over a 2-day period. Table 15.4 presents the probability of stalking as a function of type of stimulus. It is important to note that ringing noises, particularly the telephone and doorbell, were invariably followed by a large amount of activity by the family as all members rushed to respond to the stimuli. By simulating this activity

Table 15.4
Probability of Stalking as a Function of Type of Eliciting Stimulus

Type of Stimulus	Probability of Stalking (%)
Nonringing noises (i.e., kazoo clicker, handclap, cap pistol)	10
Kitchen timer and small dinner bell	40
Doorbell	60
Telephone and cowbell	85
Family commotion	100

A Comparative Analysis

(i.e., asking the family members to run around the house yelling, "I'll get it"), it was found that this activity elicited mother stalking 100 percent of the time. Of course, during all simulations the mother wore protective clothing.

Analysis of the consequences and contingencies involved in this behavior problem revealed two possible conditioning events: (1) the classical conditioning of ringing noises (CS) to the stalking (CR) elicited by family commotion (US) and (2) the operant reinforcement of stalking by contingent food reward. As a first treatment procedure, the dog was placed on simultaneous operant and classical extinction schedule. Operant extinction involved eliminating potential reinforcers by instructing the family on how *not* to reinforce stalking by attention, food, or any other distraction technique. Classical extinction involved the repeated presentation of the ringing noises (CSs) without the subsequent commotion (US). The family members were taught to respond to ringing noises slowly (i.e., wait for at least five rings before an appointed family member would calmly answer the phone or doorbell). The telephone, doorbell, and cowbell were each rung at least five times per day with the dog tethered to prevent injury to the mother. One of the daughters was made responsible for recording the incidence of stalking, lunging at the mother, etc., while the other daughter presented the stimuli. Figure 15.5 presents the results of the treatment. By the fifth day of extinction, there was 10 percent decrease in elicited stalking. On the sixth day of treatment, the clients delivered three contingent punishments (hitting the dog on the nose with a rolled-up newspaper when it stalked). This procedure resulted in an increase in stalking, which persisted to the next day. From days 8 to 12 a combined time-out (TO) and differential reinforcement for nonstalking behavior (DRO) schedule was tried. This included reinforcement with food and attention when the dog was not stalking and immediate isolation in an empty kitchen cabinet (24 x 24 x 18 in.) for 2 to 30 min-

utes (duration of TO was dependent on clients' whims) when it did stalk. There was a small decrease in the frequency of stalking during this period (see Figure 15.5), but the decrease was not sufficient to reinforce the clients' behavior.

On the thirteenth day, the TO procedure was discontinued, the DRO schedule was maintained, and a counterconditioning procedure instituted. It was observed that when the dog was pulled on a leash it would pull in the opposite direction supplying a reliable withdrawal response that could be paired with the stimuli that elicited stalking. This procedure was as follows: first, the mother, dressed in protective clothing, gently pulled the dog by the leash toward her. When the dog resisted her pull, she was instructed to shout "Go away" and continue pulling the dog toward her. At the same time the daughters were told to ring bells and stimulate the usual high activity. The noise and activity potentiated the vigor of the dog's withdrawal response. At what appeared to be the peak intensity of the withdrawal response, the mother was instructed to release the dog, shouting "Go away." Two such counterconditioning sessions were run per day on days 13 and 14. This resulted in an immediate and permanent cessation of stalking and biting for at least 6 months after treatment (see Figure 15.5). The dog still had a tendency to bite when excited but now ran and hid under the daughter's bed rather than stalking the mother when ringing noises were heard. The dog came out only when calmed down, and was immediately reinforced with attention.

"Predatory" biting has also been observed in other Yorkshire terriers, a male Kerry blue, a female German shepherd, a male giant schnauzer, a 30-pound mixed breed, and a miniature poodle. These cases have the following common characteristics: (1) the bite is always preceded by a stalking, chasing, and then lunging component, (2) the bite involves grasping and holding with the mouth and shaking the head from side to

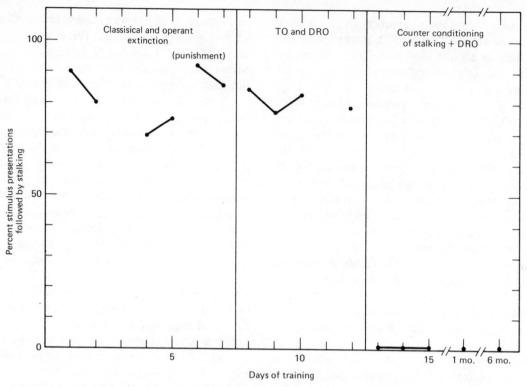

Figure 15.5 The treatment of mother stalking and predatory biting in a Yorkshire terrier.

side, often necessitating prying the mouth open. For example, two female Yorkshire terriers from the same household would bite each other and hold on so tightly that the animals had to be immersed in a tub of cold water to release their grip, (3) predatory biting is increased by contingent and noncontingent food reward and may form the basis of attack training, (4) DRO has mixed and not very powerful effects as a treatment procedure, (5) TO and extinction are also generally ineffective, (6) contingent and noncontingent punishment (hitting, electric shock, or loud noise) increase the probability of biting, (7) counterconditioning the stalking component with a withdrawal response is effective in eliminating biting (worked in seven out of eight cases; failure with a giant male schnauzer was caused by the inability to find any stimulus that elicited withdrawal).

Submissiveness Training in a Bull Mastiff

This case involves a cluster of behaviors often seen in large dogs, that is, "dominance" patterns such as guarding objects, people, and food; jumping up on people; and biting. The clients, a young couple, reported that their 18-month old, 190-pound male bull mastiff exhibited excessive dominance by biting, jumping on, and "standing over" other dogs, children, and adults, and guarding its territory, objects, and food. The dog started exhibiting these behavior patterns at about the age of 11 months. In response to the dog's dominance, the husband (a former college wrestler) started wrestling the dog, throwing it over on its back and holding it in that position by the throat. This technique was successful in eliminating any display of dominance toward the husband but led to an increase in dominance behavior toward the wife, in the form of growling

A Comparative Analysis

and attempted mounts. The husband's response to this displaced dominance was again to wrestle the dog to the ground and hold it down. This resulted in a reduction of dominance behavior directed at both of them but an increase in barking and growling at passersby, people entering the house, and neighborhood dogs. This increase in dominance towards others was highlighted by attacks on neighbors on three occasions.

The first attack was toward a 10-year-old boy who had played with the dog since it was a puppy. The boy bent over to pet the dog and it "pinned" the boy to the ground. The second attack was toward a 19-year-old male jogger running by the house. The dog uprooted a large wooden hitching post to which it was chained and leaped on the jogger and dragged him back to the house by the arm. The last and most serious attack occurred when a neighbor walked his dog past the 20 x 20 x 5 foot enclosure the clients had built for their dog. The dog made repeated attempts to escape the enclosure, eventually did so, and tracked down the neighbor who was by this time three blocks away. It then bit the neighbor on the hand and leg, necessitating eleven stitches. This last attack placed the clients in serious financial difficulties, particularly since the neighbor was a lawyer, and prompted them to seek help.

Changing the behavior of a large dog that is aggressive toward strangers is complicated by the fact that the therapist is also a stranger to the dog. It was decided that the owners would interact with the dog while the therapist gave advice. The appropriate treatment procedure turned out to be "submissiveness training." Basically, this technique is a shaping procedure along a gradient of progressively more submissive behavior patterns. For the first 5 days, the clients recorded baseline data on the number of times the dog barked or growled at passersby. This was done by confining the dog in the enclosure from 3 to 4 p.m., recording the number of passersby and the dog's behavior toward them. The clients were instructed to allow the dog to bark for 1 minute before commanding the dog to be quiet with the word "quiet" and then to record whether the dog stopped barking within 3 seconds of the command. Figure 15.6 shows that during the baseline phase there was a high probability of barking and growling and a low probability of calming down on command.

On the sixth day, submissiveness training was started. This involved reinforcing the dog with attention or dry dog chow when it produced facial expressions of submission to the verbal command "quiet." These expressions include ears back, no eye contact, and submissive grin (Fox, 1971) (see Figure 15.2c) and were readily elicited by the husband's presence. As control was gained over facial expressions, more submissive body postures were included in the criterion for reinforcement (see Figure 15.3) until the sixteenth day when the final posture was acquired. This final posture consisted of the dog's rolling over on its back, exposing the inguinal area and allowing the clients to hold it by the neck, all to the command "quiet." At this point in training, there was a precipitous decline in the amount of barking and growling at passersby, which continued to decrease until the twenty-fifth day when the procedure was discontinued (see Figure 15.7). A 6-month follow-up indicated that the clients had continued the procedure, somewhat haphazardly, and that the dog's "aggressive" behavior toward other dogs or strangers entering the house had also greatly decreased. The dog also became much easier to handle on a leash.

Cases that can be unambiguously classified as dominance biting have the following common characteristics: (1) the bite is always preceded by facial expressions and body postures of dominance and threat display, (2) the intensity of the bite is an inverse function of the amount of submissiveness exhibited by whomever is being bitten, (3) the eliciting stimulus is usually some behavior of the person being bitten that simulates a dominance posture in dogs [e.g., "stand-

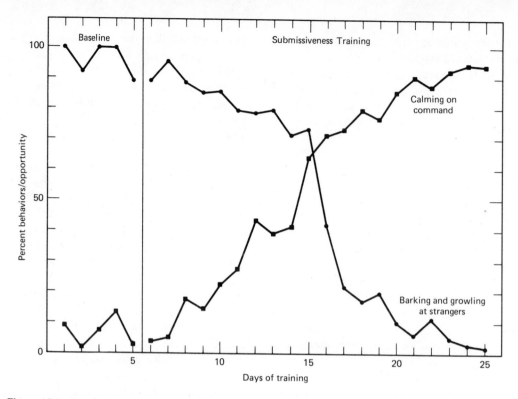

Figure 15.6 The treatment of dominance biting in a bull mastiff.

ing over" (Fox, 1971) in which a dominant animal places its front paws on the back of the submissive animal is stimulated every time a human bends over and pets the head or back of a dog], (4) reduction of dominance by rewarding submissive postures with food and attention results in a lowered probability of biting in all cases, (5) TO is ineffective, (6) extinction procedures can be effective if an external reinforcer can be identified and thus eliminated, (7) contingent punishment and enforced submission (e.g., wrestling dog to the ground) reduce the probability of biting the enforcer but increase the probability of biting individuals dissimilar to the enforcer and (8) if the punishment causes pain-elicited aggression (Azrin et al., 1964) or if the enforcer's attempt to impose submission are unsuccessful, biting will increase.

Fear Guarding in a German Shepherd

This case involved comparatively innocuous but quite common problems with a 2-year old, 65-pound female German shepherd. The dog would jump on anyone entering the house and would also steal and guard various objects. The guarding consisted of crouching over an object while under the dining room table and growling and "snapping" at anyone who approached. Here snapping refers to the consummatory component of biting, but one that is directed away from people. There were no problems with other behavior classes.

Even though guarding objects is typically clustered with dominance problems, the history of the guarding problem and the behaviors before and during guarding indicated that guarding in this case was also a "fear" related prob-

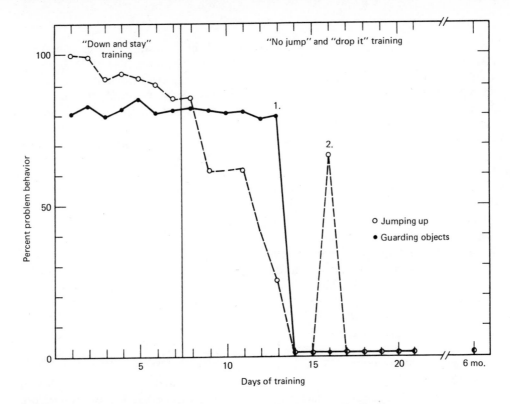

Figure 15.7 The treatment of fear guarding and jumping in a German shepherd.

lem. The dog had been beaten repeatedly as a puppy when it stole objects. Thus, when the dog stole an object it would "submissively" guard; that is, it assumed submissive postures and expressions while at the same time growling at people approaching the table. The dog had never bitten anyone but would occasionally snap if someone attempted to pet it or reach for the guarded object. The snap was always followed by a rapid and submissive retreat (i.e., the dog would crawl away).

Biting motivated by fear alone can be rather easily and reliably reduced by systematic desensitization as described by Tuber et al. (1974). In this case, because dominance was also a problem, counterconditioning was added to the treatment of both jumping and guarding. During this first phase, the owners were also instructed as to how to train their dog to lie down and stay on

command. "Staying down" was reinforced with attention and dog biscuits until the dog stayed down on command for one minute. At this point in training, "Down" and "Stay" was not paired with people entering or leaving the house.

Figure 15.7 presents the data collected during other periods than the training period for both phases of the treatment. Apparently training just on "Down" and "Stay" generalized to the stimuli present when people entered the house, for there was a 20 percent decrease in jumping under such conditions. There was no change in guarding behavior during the first phase of training.

During the second phase, "No jump" and "Drop it" training was started. The "No jump" training involved explicit pairing of the "Down" and "Stay" commands with people entering the house. This was done by giving the dog the

"Down" command 1 second before a person entered. The individual that entered the house reinforced the dog with attention and food for remaining in that position for 5 seconds. At least five trials per day were given. The criterion for reinforcement was then progressively increased until the dog remained down for at least 1 minute before it was reinforced. It is evident from Figure 15.7 that there was a progressive decline in jumping up on people at times other then the training period. On days 14 and 15 jumping up on people was completely eliminated. After the "cure," when people entered the house, the dog would run up to the front door and lie down. On day 16, relatives who were not familiar with the training routine but fond of the dog, visited. They encouraged the dog to jump on them, reinforcing this behavior with attention. The results of this naturally occurring return to baseline conditions are evident, but the dog's behavior was again exemplary as soon as the training regime was resumed (see Figure 15.7).

The "Drop it" training consisted of placing an object in the dog's mouth, commanding it to "Drop it" and reinforcing compliance with attention and food. A stimulus hierarchy of chewability of objects was used to facilitate this training. At first, highly unchewable objects (a metal spoon, screwdriver, pliers, ash tray,) and the like were placed in the dog's mouth. The dog's normal response to having these items placed in its mouth was to drop the item. As verbal control was gained with these items, more chewable items were used, culminating in items such as chewing toys and bones made of rawhide. The "Drop it" training was performed in a variety of locations around the house, excluding under the dining room table where the guarding occurred. There was a small but consistent decrease in the percentage of guarding during this period. Beginning on day 14, the "Drop it" command was used when the dog was guarding objects under the table. If the item was a chew toy or bone the dog was told to "Drop it," reinforced for doing

so, and the item was returned to her. If the item was something else, it was simply removed and the dog was given a bone or chew toy to chew as a reinforcement. Guarding stoped completely on day 15 and had not recurred up to 6 months after training.

Cases that can be described only as fear biting have the following common characteristics: (1) the bite or snap is preceded by postures and facial expressions of submission, (2) the bite snap is usually abbreviated and is generally followed by escape and withdrawal when possible, (3) the most effective treatment technique is systematic desensitization, (4) contingent and noncontingent punishment are part of the etiology of the problem, and the problem is exacerbated when punishment is used.

Implications and Conclusions

Applied animal psychology, with respect to scientific knowledge, is a two-way street. Working with behavior problems in animals can be a source of new knowledge as well an as opportunity to apply what we already know. One of the more important implications to be drawn from the material in this chapter is that there is a real scientific advantage to be gained when ideas obtained from treating animal behavior problems are returned to the laboratory for elaboration and further investigation.

The advantage is threefold. (1) New research questions are generated and old ones refined (2) Data are collected from the field that could not be collected in the laboratory (3) Animal behavior problems may serve as a model for the diagnosis and treatment of human psychopathology.

A direct outgrowth of a careful analysis of most animal behavior problems is the generation of new research questions or refinements. These problems represent a network of interacting variables, behavior, and behavioral processes. This state of affairs forces the applied animal psychologist to consider these interactions and ask how information from diverse field of experimental psychology that impinge on the behavior problem can be used and integrated. Contrast this with the laboratory scientist who has the "advantage" of studying one variable, one behavior, and one process at a time. This "advantage" allows for the elucidation of the main effects of any one variable but at the same time obscures the questions of interaction and integration.

Research questions are also generated because of gaps in the current body of knowledge about animal behavior and learning. For example, when attempting to modify a particular problem behavior in an animal, one is faced with the question of how this modification procedure will affect the entire organism. Such a consideration brings us to the relatively unstudied question of how behaviors interact — the nature of response generalization when one or more behaviors is modified.

Another gap concerns our lack of knowledge about the normative behavior of various species. At present, the only comprehensive study of behavior genetics of various breeds of dogs has been conducted by Scott and Fuller (1965), who lament that their interpretations of the findings from 15 years of study were hampered by a lack of diversity in environments and tasks used when the animals were tested. Field studies have been conducted on the wild counterparts of cats and dog [lions (Schaller, 1972); tigers Schaller, 1967); wolves (Fox, 1970, 1971); foxes (Fox, 1970, 1971, 1975); and coyotes (Fox, 1970, 1971, 1975)], but studies collecting normative behavioral data on common pets outside the laboratory are rare (e.g., Beck, 1973; Leyhausen, 1965, 1973). Perhaps the study of pet behavior problems could provide an opportunity for investigating a larger variety of organisms and behavior classes in a greater range of environments than is currently the case. Data accumulated from many practitioners over time could establish behavioral norms for different species and breeds in a variety of environmental settings.

A third class of research questions concerns constraints on the principles of learning as were discussed earlier in this chapter under intra and interorganism interactions. The point here is that as soon as you step out of the learning laboratory you find out when, how, and where "general learning principles" do and do not apply.

The second scientific advantage, collecting data that would otherwise be impossible to collect, means that experimental psychologists who study animal learning and motivation now have a "field" where naturally occurring animal learning can be observed. If taken advantage of, information from this sort of field could be returned to the laboratory to refine the questions we ask and stimulate new questions.

The general public is also interested in and supportive of applied animal psychology, which means that information can be obtained about animals without extensive laboratory facilities or the use of techniques that upset organized pet owners and animal lovers. In other words, psychologists just might be able to learn a great deal about animals by helping them rather than appearing to harm them.

The third scientific advantage, the possibility of creating animal analogues of human psychopathology, dates back to Pavlov's (1927) initial observation of experimental neurosis in the laboratory dog. Since then there have been numerous attempts to create animal analogues (e.g., Masserman, 1943; Seligman and Maier, 1967; Wolpe, 1958) in the laboratory. All of these attempts involved the creation of an artifical approach-avoidance conflict or a noncontingent relationship between responding and aversive consequences (Seligman, 1975). These manipulations usually resulted in deterioration of previously learned discriminations (Gnatt, 1944; Karn, 1938, 1940; Pavlov, 1927) or a failure to acquire escape-avoidance behavior (Seligman and Maier, 1967) or approach habits (Masserman, 1943; Wolpe, 1958). The results of such experiments have been interpreted as analogues of human depression (Seligman, 1975) or anxiety (Wolpe, 1958), and treatment techniques have been generated that appear useful in the therapist's office as well as the laboratory (Seligman, 1975; Wolpe, 1969).

As already demonstrated, the usual behavioral pathologies exhibited by pets in the home are considerably richer in diversity of behavior classes and complexity of etiology than laboratory-generated problems. The analysis of naturally occurring animal behavior problems may serve as a "blueprint" for the creation of animal analogues of human psychopathology in the laboratory. Without these blueprints it would tax the imagination of the most creative researchers to generate some of the "pathologies" observed.

A quote from the modern founders of applied animal psychology is prophetic of the promise of this field for human clinical psychology:

In understanding the basic business of living in which animals are engaged, the psychologists of the future will be investigating much broader and more significant problems. He (she) will take responsibility for understanding, explaining, and in many cases, control of their entire range of behavior. He (she) will be responsible for accounting for everyday behavior and not be entitled to dismiss certain problems because they do not fit into a certain theoretical system. He (she) can expect, by basing this knowledge on a firm understanding of the basic fundamental problems of animal life, to tie in with significant problems of human life. The old divisions between clinical psychology, for example, and animal experimenters, will tend to break down as the animal experimenters have something of true significance to tell the clinician. In short, there is a bold new world awaiting the animal psychologists of the future. It has been there all the time — all we need to do is look at it (Breland and Breland, 1966, p. 118).

Let us hope the future of applied animal psychology matches its promise. Without much doubt, to do so it must emphasize its scientific side. "Publish or perish" seems too harsh, but perhaps "Publish and prosper", as a discipline that is, could be our motto.

Study Questions

1. List six representative examples of an animal behavior problem.
2. What were the Brelands' main contributions to the area of applied animal psychology?
3. What are the three main ways to conceptualize a behavior problem for any class of behavior?
4. Name three types of biting behavior in dogs.
5. What does the acronym R-O-C-K-S stand for in the analysis of a pet behavior problem?
6. Why did the dog refuse to enter the elevator and how was this balking behavior modified?
7. How is submissiveness identified in an otherwise dominant dog and what is one way to train such a dog to be more submissive?
8. What are some gaps in our knowledge of animal behavior and learning that especially need to be researched?

PART THREE

Some Major Classes of Behavior

16

Sexual Behavior: Courtship and Mating

Howard E. Farris

Western Michigan University

Robert E. Otis

Ripon College

Background Information: Types of Reproduction

There are two general types of reproduction in the animal kingdom, asexual and sexual. Each type generates a unique set of problems that must be solved by behavioral and physiological processes for the species to survive. The critical difference between them is whether or not the offspring is genetically different from its parents.

Asexual Reproduction

Asexual reproduction involves the generation of offspring from the division of the parent's body into fragmented parts (Gardiner, 1972). There are several forms of asexual reproduction, including binary and multiple fission, budding, and parthenogenesis. In binary fission an animal simply divides into two fairly equal parts (e.g., in paramecium), and in multiple fission the animal divides into many equal parts (e.g., in some planaria). Budding occurs when the parent gener-

ates smaller organisms by splitting off parts of themselves (e.g., sponges, hydra); these small parts then grow into a new individual. Parthenogenesis involves the offsprings' being generated from the adult female gametes (sex cells) without fertilization by the male. For example, honeybees produce males (drones) by parthenogenesis but produce new females (workers) by sexual reproduction, exhibiting two forms of reproduction within the same organism (Michener, 1974). Although asexual reproduction is primarily restricted to invertebrates, there are exceptions to this rule in fishes, amphibians, and lizards (Uzzell, 1970). Still other organisms (e.g., aphids) exhibit a different type of reproduction during different stages of growth, or during different generations. But regardless of the form of asexual reproduction, the offspring generated are exact duplicates of the parents. Such species are destined for sameness in a world of constantly changing environments.

Sexual Reproduction

Sexual reproduction involves the union of two gametes (sex cells containing one-half of the parents' chromosomes), one from an adult female (the egg) and one from an adult male (the sperm). This union, called fertilization, can occur either externally or internally. Each "way" presents a different set of problems for the animals involved.

In external fertilization, gametes from the male come into contact with those from the female at a site outside of the female's own body. There are several forms of external fertilization in the animal kingdom, spawning being a common one (Gardiner, 1972; Hyman, 1940). In spawning, the female gametes are generally shed or "dumped" prior to or simultaneous with the dropping of the male gametes, as is common in fish and frogs.

Internal fertilization occurs inside the female's body. The male gametes are placed inside the female through specialized anatomical structures (e.g., cloacae in birds and reptiles; penis and vagina in mammals) usually at a time when the female is prepared for the reproductive process to begin (called estrus in mammals).

Nearly all vertebrates and some invertebrates are sexual in mode of reproduction. In most cases, males and females are sexually unique (dioecious), with each possessing different reproductive organs throughout their life span. In hermaphroditism, however, one animal has both the male and female reproductive organs. Hermaphroditism is common in invertebrates (e.g., tapeworms and earthworms) but rare in vertebrates, apparently being restricted to fish like the black bass (Ghiselin, 1969). Hermaphrodites generally exchange sperm with each other through internal fertilization.

Some hermaphroditic organisms change from one sex to another, a condition called protandry in which individuals produce male and female gametes at different stages in their lives (Gardi-ner, 1972). The American oyster produces sperm the first year, eggs the following year, and alternates sperm and egg production in regular annual cycles. Some popular aquarium fish (e.g., swordtails and bettas) may also change sex.

Advantages of Sexual Reproduction. Offspring generated from sexual reproduction inherit half of their genetic makeup from the female, the other half from the male. Thus they are a new and unique combination of genetic material from that of their parents. It is this variability of genetic makeup (genotype) that is acted on by natural selection, perpetuating reproductively successful combinations and eliminating those not so successful. That there are varying genotypes increases the likelihood that the offspring will succeed when changing habitats, sometimes even remarkably so. Sexual reproduction thus provides advantages to the individual as well as to the species as a whole (Alcock, 1975).

Problems Raised by Sexual Reproduction. Sexual reproduction raises problems that are not found with asexual reproduction, mainly that two adults, one male and one female, must approach each other very closely in order for fertilization to occur. Tinbergen (1953) characterized this problem when he noted that "being touched means being captured." The problems of physical contact must be solved through the coordination of behavioral and physiological processes in both partners. The problems are met sequentially as the partners get closer and closer to each other.

Specifically, the sexually reproducing animals must (1) locate and attract potential mates, (2) identify the attracted mate as being appropriate as to sex, species, and sexual receptivity, (3) ward off potential sources of interference from predators and others of the same species, (4) inhibit aggressive tendencies while violating territorial or "individual" space, (5) coordinate physiological processes ("sexual responsiveness") in both partners, (6) perform adequate behaviors to accomplish fertilization (either external or internal), (7) functionally remove themselves from the fertilization task so as to facilitate readiness for subsequent behaviors, and (8) maintain the pair bond, in some cases beyond the breeding season. Not all species are concerned with all of these problems, but all species are presented with some combination of them, those peculiar to their species. The behaviors through which species accomplish these tasks are called courtship, spawning, and copulation. The emphasis throughout the remainder of this chapter is on the analysis of courtship, spawning, and copulation in a variety of animals.

Courtship as a Behavior Class

Courtship Defined

Courtship is the communication between the male and female of a species that coordinates behavioral and physiological processes leading to fertilization. Courtship can be characterized as a chain of behavioral interactions with each link involving synchronized presentations of stimuli (Eibl-Eibesfeldt, 1975; Tinbergen, 1951). One *member of the pair* provides a stimulus (e.g., visual display, vocal call) which elicits behavior in the *second member*; the stimuli *produced* from this behavior in turn elicit appropriate behavior from the first member, and so on, *back and forth*, until the fertilization process begins or the chain is broken.

Courtship sequences are generally of two types (Morris, 1970a). One type involves a single continuous sequence of behavior, beginning when mates find each other (pair-bond formation), passing through synchronized courtship behaviors, and ending with fertilization. In a second type of courtship, the behaviors leading to pair-bond formation may be separated in time from the synchronized movements of the courtship displays. This spacing suggests the possibility of a functional division between mate attraction and synchronized prespawning or precopulatory behavior.

Courtship behaviors are rather fixed or uniform in character in all members of a species, creating a situation in which the chain of interaction can be broken at any point if one partner fails to produce the appropriate signal (species-specific behavior), thus tending to restrict reproductive behavior to only members of the same species. This restriction, called reproductive isolation, is beneficial to both individuals and species in that it prevents wasting time and energy, as well as presents random hybridization.

Variability in sexual responsiveness is a key feature of sexual behavior in most animals. Sexual partners are not invariably responsive to all courtship signals emitted by potential mates, and duration and frequency of courtship behaviors may vary considerably among individuals of the same species.

Courtship Chains in External Fertilization

For those species that reproduce sexually by external fertilization, courtship usually involves a chain of coordinated behaviors that culminate in the deposition of sperm and eggs at the same geographical site. As noted earlier, this process is called spawning. The spawning behavior of the three-spined stickleback fish is an unusually good example of courtship chaining (see Figures 16.1 and 16.2; Tinbergen, 1951). After establishing a territory and constructing a tunnel-shaped nest, the male stickleback "broadcasts" its sexual receptivity by swimming close to the water surface in a zigzag manner whenever a gravid female (laden with eggs) enters its territory. Other males entering the territory are attacked and driven off. Males are identified by their red bellies, the normal breeding (nuptial) coloration in male sticklebacks (Pelkwijk and Tinbergen, 1937). The belly of the female is silver. Gravid females respond to the male's zigzag dance by assuming a passive, oblique, head-upward pos-

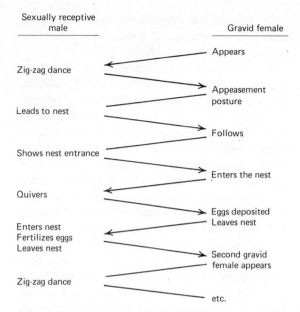

Sexually receptive male		Gravid female
		Appears
Zig-zag dance		
		Appeasement posture
Leads to nest		
		Follows
Shows nest entrance		
		Enters the nest
Quivers		
		Eggs deposited
Enters nest		Leaves nest
Fertilizes eggs		
Leaves nest		Second gravid
		female appears
Zig-zag dance		
		etc.

Figure 16.1. Idealized courtship sequence in the three-spined stickleback *Gasterosteus aculeatus*. (Modified from Tinbergen, 1951.)

ture. This posture serves to "appease" or inhibit further aggression from the male, who subsequently alternates its zigzag dance with repeated swims to the nest area. This behavior is called leading. If the female follows, the male "shows" her the nest by lying on its side and pointing its snout into the nest. The female may then respond by entering the nest. If this happens, the male stimulates egg laying by trembling or quivering its head against the female's tail. When laying is completed, the female then leaves the nest out the other side; the male enters, fertilizes the eggs and also leaves the nest, thus completing the reproductive behavior chain with this female. The courtship sequence may continue with three or four more females or until the nest is about full of fertilized eggs. This is an idealized picture of the complete sequence, omitting most of the less frequent response components (Wilz, 1970), but the sequence illustrates well the chain characteristics of courtship in which external fertilization is involved.

External fertilization is, however, a highly wasteful process. In many aquatic animals the deposition of eggs and sperm in open waters results in the loss of countless numbers of gametes. Many animals compensate for this ultimate loss by generating millions of eggs and sperm, thus increasing the odds that fertilization will take place. Courtship ceremonies increase the chances of fertilization occurring by ensuring that two mates will spawn in close proximity to one another at the same time.

Courtship Chains in Internal Fertilization

Internal fertilization is more efficient, however. Here, courtship involves coordinated responses of two sexual partners, which culminate in copulation, creating the new problem of making body contact. This problem is solved through courtship behaviors.

Figure 16.2. The sequential courtship display of the three-spined stickleback, the male (top left) attracts the female (top right) with the zig-zag dance and then leads her down to his nest. After the female enters the nest (lower right drawing) the male stimulates her to spawn by "quivering" behind her. (From Tinbergen, 1951.)

Some Major Classes of Behavior

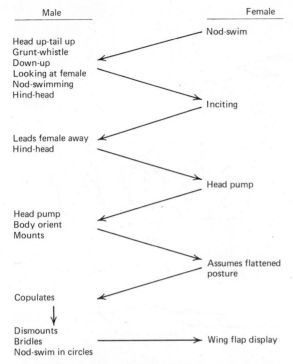

Male		Female
		Nod-swim
Head up-tail up		
Grunt-whistle		
Down-up		
Looking at female		
Nod-swimming		
Hind-head		
		Inciting
Leads female away		
Hind-head		
		Head pump
Head pump		
Body orient		
Mounts		
		Assumes flattened posture
Copulates		
Dismounts		
Bridles		Wing flap display
Nod-swim in circles		

Figure 16.3. Idealized sequence of courtship display in the mallard duck.

The colorful courtship sequence of the mallard duck (*Anas platyrhynchos*) provides an excellent illustration of chaining for internal fertilization (Figures 16.3 and 16.4; Johnsgard, 1965; Lorenz, 1971). Mallard courtship displays can be witnessed from late summer to early spring. These displays establish the pair bond as well as synchronize behaviors leading to copulation and fertilization in the spring. These displays occur, for the most part, on water and in social groups. The "courtship flight," is one exception where several drakes chase a single unmated female duck in the air.

Many of the female's early displays appear to be directed at singling out individual males. She accomplishes this by rapidly nod-swimming into and around groups of males. Nod-swimming by the female serves to stimulate courtship display in males, though it is not an essential stimulus for

such displays since all-male groups have been observed to give courtship displays in the absence of females (Weidmann and Darley, 1971).

Male courtship displays are generally synchronized group displays that focus on the behavioral presence of the female. As shown in figures 16.3 and 16.4 the male courtship display typically consists of the grunt-whistle, the head-up-tail-up, and down-up display. Other displays include the sequential combination of the head-up-tail-up, looking at the female, nod-swimming and the hind-head display occurring in rapid order (Weidmann and Darley, 1971).

As courtship proceeds, prospective consort pairs become noticeable by their close proximity to one another. Frequently the male leads the female while exhibiting the hind-head display. The female, in turn, often gives the incitement display. Here the female presumably "incites" the mate to attack other males (Lorenz, 1971). All these movements isolate the pair away from the rest of the group.

If the courtship continues, both partners enter into a mutual head-pumping ceremony, which is usually begun by the female. Eventually the male swims around and aligns its body along the same axis as the female's (body orient). The drake mounts her and maintains support by grabbing the feathers on the back of her head with his bill. Treading ensues, with the female being forced into a flattened position very low in the water. Eventually the cloacae of the two birds contact each other (called the "cloacal kiss") and the male's sperm is released into the female.

Immediately after dismounting the male pulls its head and neck backwards toward its rear without elevating the head. This postcopulatory display is called bridling. Bridling is followed immediately by a nod-swim, which carries him around the female in a complete circle. The female raises up in a wing-flap display during this time.

As in the earlier description of the stickleback,

(a)

(b)　(c)

(d)　(e)

(f)　(g)

(h)　(i)

Figure 16.4. Courtship displays in the mallard: (A) nod-swim in female, (B) grunt-whistle, (C) Head-up tail-up, (D) Down-up, (E) Nod-swim by male, (F) inciting, (G) Hind-head, (H) Head-pumping, (I) Bridling (A, F, G, H, I from Lorenz, 1971, and B, C, D, E from Bastock, 1967.)

this is an idealized picture of courtship behavior, in this instance involving a species that fertilizes internally. In actuality there is considerable variability in courtship behavior in both sequence and specific displays. For example, nod-swimming is not always the first behavior observed in the chain. Furthermore, some displays were omitted from this illustration as were frequent repetitions of certain components of the chain.

Mallard courtship reveals the complexity to which courtship behavior can develop. We will see that this complexity can be better understood by first examining the general types of courtship ceremonies that exist, second by noting the various kinds of mating systems that exist, and finally by looking at the components of courtship according to the functions they serve.

Types of Courtship Displays

Three general classes of courtship behaviors can be recognized according to the degree of involvement by the two partners: solo, mutual, and lek displays.

In solo courtship, one mate (usually the male) gives a solo display while the other mate (usually the female) remains passive. For example, the male jumping spider does a spectacular dance in front of his quiescent female mate (Crane, 1949). A more common sight is the courtship display of some pigeons. The males may spread their tails wide, fluff their throat feathers, and give a highly conspicuous "cooing" dance in front of their passive mates.

In mutual displays, both adults are active during courtship, at times behaving in an identical synchronous, mirrorlike fashion during all or part of the ceremony. Spectacular examples of these mutual displays can be seen in city parks in the spring when pairs of mute swans show synchronous head and neck displays (Figure 16.5).

An interesting situation may arise with mutual courtship displays. Since both sexes display identically, two males or two females may court each other up to the point where mounting is attempted. At this point the chain is usually broken since successful mounting requires different behaviors from each partner (e.g., mute swan).

A third type of courtship pattern is the lek display, in which the males of some species band together in social groups to present communal displays to females. When land areas are used solely for such display they are called leks or arenas (Wilson, 1975). Birds, such as various species of grouse, provide the most interesting examples of lek displays, but they are also seen in several other animal groups (Jarman, 1974; Wilson, 1975). In Southeast Asia, for example, the communal courtship displays of male fireflies at night provide such bright illumination that ship navigation along shore is facilitated (Lloyd, 1973).

Courtship behavior has been classified in somewhat different ways by other researchers. Lorenz (1935), for one, has recognized three types distinguished on the basis of the agonistic (agressive) relationship existing between mates during the courtship ceremony (1) In the "lizard" type of courtship, the female is completely quiescent while the male courts her (2) In the "labyrinth" type, both partners court, with the male being dominant and the female submissive (3) In the "cichlid" type of courtship, both partners are actively aggressive toward each other during the ceremony.

Courtship and the Mating System

The functional nature of a courtship display is generally associated with the type of mating system adopted by the species. Three mating systems have been recognized: monogamy, polygamy, and promiscuity (Brown, 1975). Each system creates a unique set of demands for courtship activities.

In the monogamous species an adult forms a pair bond or sexual bond with only one member of the opposite sex. Pair bonds are attachments between animals in which sexual behavior is

Figure 16.5. The mutual courtship display of the mute swan. Note that the swan on the left has a neck band on. (Photo By R.D. Van Deusen, Kellog Bird Sanctuary, Michigan State University, Augusta, Michigan.)

restricted exclusively to members of the bond. The pair bond may persist during the breeding season and break apart afterward (seasonal monogamy, as seen in most migrant birds), or it may last for many years, if not for a lifetime (perennial monogamy, as seen in swans, Canada geese, and some gibbons). It is apparent that when pair bonds exist for relatively long periods of time, the partners are precluded from using courtship displays to locate and identify the appropriate mate. Monogamy is very common in birds but rare in other animals.

A second type of mating system, polygamy, involves adults forming temporary pair bonds with two or more members of the opposite sex. Polygamy is common in mammals where it is generally the male of the species that mates with more than one female (polygyny). The opposite case where the female mates with more than one

male (polyandry) is rare in the animal kingdom, although it has been reported in some wading birds (Jenni, 1974). In either case, mating may occur with successive partners or it may occur simultaneously with several partners in a harem condition. Male sea lions, for example, band together a number of females into a harem and participate in successive matings (Bartholomew and Hoel, 1953). As a general rule, polygamous mates do not remain together for parental care, thus courtship activities are not needed to maintain the bond beyond the breeding season. Lek matings in various species of grouse provide good examples of polygynous systems (Wiley, 1974).

Promiscuous mating systems also involve multiple matings but without the establishment of pair bonds. Adults of both sexes mate with any number of the opposite sex without the "exclusivity" of the pair-bond arrangement. Such matings are not random matings as the term promiscuity seems to connote. Some promiscuous adults are highly selective in their choice of mates (Selander, 1972).

Function of Courtship

The complexity of any behavioral process, particularly courtship, is amenable to simplification by breaking the "whole" down into its "parts." This is historically one of the most frequently used strategies for understanding complex pheononema. One danger paramount in this process is that the "forest" may be lost sight of while the "trees" are being examined. With this danger in mind we discuss courtship in terms of its two most prominent features, the attracting of mates and the synchronizing of behaviors that lead up to fertilization. Breaking courtship down into two components is relatively easy on paper, but in reality the responses serving these functions blend into each other to such an extent that making a distinction between them is often impossible.

I. Broadcasting Availability to Potential Partners

In those species that remain paired throughout the year, such as the Canada goose, no special behaviors are generally required to locate and attract a mate since the mate is usually at hand. But in those species that do not maintain a pair-bond beyond the breeding season, elaborate behavioral displays involving long-range stimuli are generally employed to advertise the availability of the sexually receptive animal. This is true for such common and well-known animals as the dog, cat, and deer, as well as many others.

The stimuli produced by these attraction displays have been appropriately called "broadcast" stimuli (Schein and Hale, 1965). In most species, broadcasting is emitted by only one of the sexes, usually the male, on territories established for such purposes.

Mating and Territorial Behavior. Territories have traditionally been defined as areas of space which are patrolled and defended against intruders (Stokes, 1974). Territories are established for a variety of reasons, mating being a common one, although mating, feeding, nesting, and rearing of the young may be combined functions in so-called breeding or "all-purpose" territories (see also Chapters 2 and 3).

Breeding territories are usually established by the male of the species at the start of the breeding season. Their establishment often involves a considerable amount of aggressive behavior as competition ensues among the males for the more advantageous areas such as those offering the best food supplies. In some animals this aggression leads to death. For instance, three times as many bull fur seals die during the territorial breeding seasons as do females (Bartholomew, 1970). But once a territory is established, its resident "owner" may be nearly invincible (Nice, 1941). This is particularly true as the resident approaches the center of its territory (Tinbergen, 1951). Breeding territories provide the resident owner with an area that is relatively free from interference from other conspecific members during the mating process. In addition, social stimulation from neighboring territory holders may serve to regulate reproductive behavior. This phenomenon is called the Fraser-Darling effect (Darling, cited in Wilson, 1975).

The act of mating is generally a conspicuous activity that places the participating animals in a vulnerable position. In a variety of animals the act of mating attracts conspecifics as to the immediate area (e.g. birds, Armstrong, 1965; Scott, 1950; elephants, Douglas-Hamilton and Douglas-Hamilton, 1975), sometimes causing the mating process to end prematurely. In order for either internal or external fertilization to occur, however, the courtship chain must be emitted without interruption. Thus breeding territories, which provide this "free space," are highly advantageous for sexual reproduction. Some species, like the black-crowned night heron, will not even show pair formation until a territory has been established (Noble and Wurm, 1940).

Regardless of other functions it may have, a territory restricts the male's movement and represents an area to which females must be attracted. Eliot Howard (1948) was the first to point out that the territorial male's "freedom of action" was restricted by natural laws. He noted that adequate breeding areas are limited and that a male must remain on its territory in order to maintain it. The female, on the other hand, is "free" to move anywhere, searching for males that are the most "attractive." Although Howard's remarks centered on birds, his observations are known to apply generally to all vertebrate species that maintain breeding territories. Attraction displays in territorial owners are generally very elaborate and serve both to repel other males and attract potential mates from long distances away. Territorial behavior seems, for the most part, absent in invertebrates (Bastock, 1967).

Since a broadcast display also serves to identify the sex and species of the signaling animal, "broadcasters" must necessarily provide distinct species-specific signals. Hence, the variety of broadcast stimuli employed in the animal kingdom is as broad as the list of species that use them.

Broadcast Stimuli In Invertebrates. A wide variety of broadcast stimuli, called sex attractants because of their attracting function, have been reported in invertebrates. The great diversity in form of these displays across the invertebrates, and across the insects in particular (Carthy, 1965), is generally associated with differences in sense organs and sense physiology. For the most part, courtship displays are restricted to the arthropods. A general but by no means exhaustive sampling of these stimuli is presented below.

Visual broadcast stimuli are used by female cuttlefish, which become luminescent during the breeding season, thus creating a condition that attracts potential male mates (Tinbergen, 1951). Distinctive flight patterns serve as broadcast stimuli for many other invertebrates. For example, the male silver-washed fritillary (butterfly) chases females using a zigzag flight to attract them; and the receptive male Grayling butterfly pursues any female butterfly that happens along because of the pattern of visual stimuli (Tinbergen, 1972). The attraction is so strong that receptive male Graylings often pursue other male Graylings as well as males and females of other species. The sex flight is even elicited by falling leaves and the male's own shadow. The key stimulus is a combination of features that all stimuli share, for example, size, shade, "dancing" movements, and a certain proximity to the male.

The nocturnal male firefly locates females by giving species-specific light flashes and flight patterns. Some nine different species of the genus *Photinus* have been found to differ in these flash-flight patterns (Lloyd, 1969). The critical stimulus for female attraction seems to be the interflash interval. For example, males of *Photinus macdermotti* normally produce two flashes 2 seconds apart during attraction displays. The female only answers after the second flash if the interval between flashes falls within a certain range (Carlson et al., 1977). Thus when the male shifts from courtship to other behaviors, it changes the interflash interval.

Jumping spiders visually broadcast their availability by waving their legs up and down while approaching the female in a zigzag manner (Crane, 1943) and concomitantly exposing the more colorful features of their bodies. Since these species differ in body coloration, this difference may serve to promote reproductive isolation. Studies using models of spiders have found that the angle of the male's legs to its body is the critical stimulus in attracting mates; a similar visual display is used by female wolf spiders (Rovner, 1972) and by male fiddler crabs that "beckon" with their claws (Crane, 1943).

Tactual broadcast stimuli are used by web-building spiders (Argiopidae) with poor vision that rely on tactual stimuli to announce their availiabilty. Males of some species simply pluck the strands of webs containing females. If they give the appropriate "broadcast pluck," the female responds by remaining quiescent, allowing him to approach her; otherwise the male is treated as prey by the larger female. Males of at least one genus of spider (Ero) prey on females by imitating the species-specific broadcast pluck (Bristowe, 1958).

Auditory broadcast stimuli are used by many invertebrates (primarily insects) that produce mate-attracting sounds (songs) by vibrating certain body structures (e.g., wings). Male wolf spiders (Lycosa) strike their palps (appendages to the mouth area) together (Rovner, 1967), and crickets and grasshoppers rub their wings together or rub their legs against their wings (cf. Bailey, 1970). Male crickets produce a variety of sounds (called crepitations) in this way, each "song" serving a different function in the courtship sequence. For example, different songs are used for attracting mates, repelling intruders and synchronizing courtship at short range (Alexander, 1960). Different pulse frequencies across cricket species promote reproductive isolation (Bailey and Robinson, 1971).

Perhaps the most elaborate broadcast ceremonies are those seen in lek displays. Typically these provide spectacular auditory and visual signals. Accentuation of those signals appears to be the primary function of the communal display (Wilson, 1975). The group singing of male 13-year and 17-year locusts has been described by Wilson (1975) as "literally deafening to the human ear."

Chemical broadcast stimuli. These communication stimuli are called pheromones, especially for odors produced and received by insects (see also Chapters 13 and 20). The female silkworm moth attracts males by emitting a chemical attractant from the tip of the abdomen. The

chemical is called bombykol from the name of the moth, *Bombyx mori*. Receptor cells in the male's antennae respond only to this one specific chemical stimulus. Once activated by this sex attractant, "the male performs as little more than a sexual guided missile, programmed to home on an increasing gradient of bombykol centered on the tip of the female's abdomen" (Wilson, 1975, p. 182).

Similar sex attractants are used by females of some species of cockroach (Barth, 1964) and nocturnal moths (Birch, 1970). Some female nocturnal moths emit these pheromones from abdominal organs during species-specific receptive periods, usually around dawn or dusk (Butler, 1967). Wing movements are often used to disseminate these signals to potential male mates.

Broadcast stimuli in vertebrates. Male and female vertebrates are distinct in their reproductive behavior and often in appearance (sexual dimorphism). Even individuals that are hermaphroditic tend to function either as a male or a female but not both. Consequently, sexual discrimination during the reproductive process is aided by differences in appearance. As we will see, broadcast displays are frequently designed to emphasize these dimorphic features.

Broadcast stimuli in fish. These stimuli are typical of vertebrate sexual behavior in general and frequently involve the "donning" of special colorations (nuptial colors) at the beginning of the breeding season, as mentioned earlier for the three-spined stickleback. Associated with these colors or markings are behaviors that make these colorations more conspicuous during the courtship chain.

The red coloration of spawning salmon often turns the headwaters of Pacific Northwest rivers a vivid red as the fish migrate by the thousands to the areas where they originally hatched. In certain instances, nuptial colors change over time in the same fish. Some coral fishes exhibit as many as seven variations of the nuptial colors over a period of 24 hours (Ommanney, 1970).

In breeding territories, nuptial colors are displayed together with aggressive behaviors associated with territory defense. The male three-spined stickleback acquires a red belly and blue eyes, while the sexually receptive female has a silver belly distended with eggs. These differences in morphology between the two sexes are accentuated by the female's behavior in her attraction displays and thus serve to inhibit territorial aggression by the male (Tinbergen, 1951). The male jewelfish, after acquiring its nuptial colors and establishing a territory, attracts females simply by displaying its colors. Female jewelfish are attracted to the more brightly colored males; the brighter or "redder" the coloration, the greater the attraction (Noble and Curtis, 1939).

Special anatomical structures rather than nuptial coloration develop in some species at spawning time; these structures attract mates and differentiate the sexes. The male Atlantic salmon and brown trout develop a hook (called a kype) in their lower jaws; fantail darters, swordtails, and guppies show changes in fin structure, some of which directly facilitate the mating act. In sharks and rays, certain fins change into clasping structures that facilitate the transfer of sperm into the female's cloaca (*Larousse Encyclopedia*, 1967).

Some fish are known to attract mates using special sounds. Male satinfish shiners "purr" (Stout, 1963), male gobies give grunts (Tavolga, 1960), male toadfish give "boat-whistles" (Gray and Winn, 1961), and male blennies emit thumping sounds (Tavolga, 1958).

Chemical stimuli have been identified as sex attractants in a variety of fish species, including guppies (Gandolfi, 1969), catfish (Timms and Kleerekoper, 1972), and gobiids (Tavolga, 1956). How widespread the use of chemical sex attractants is among fish is not known. The goldfish has been one of the best-studied species. Male goldfish rely almost entirely on olfactory cues to discriminate ovulated from unovulated females (Partridge, Liley, and Stacey, 1976). The female appears to release this pheromone in her ovarian fluid shortly after ovulation, and the male may be sampling this fluid during the initial stage of courtship by repeatedly butting against her genital region.

Broadcast stimuli in amphibians and reptiles are often auditory. The din of mating calls by frogs in spring marshlands is a conspicuous event and a wide variety of species-specific calls have been identified. These calls probably attract other conspecific males as well as receptive females to the appropriate pond (Bogert, 1960). Male newts and salamanders, unlike frogs, are voiceless. They attract females by means of pheromones emitted from glands (called hedonic glands) on various parts of their bodies. These chemicals may also serve to identify the sender by sex and species as well as arouse the female (Organ, 1960).

Pair bonds are rare in reptiles: mates have to be brought together from considerable distances away. In some species (crocodile, tortoise) the sexes are similar in appearance, in others (snakes, lizards) sexual dimorphism is common. Most male lizards recognize females by visual cues while snakes recognize females by odors. Male alligators emit a characteristic roar and exude musk, either of which may serve to attract females (Beach, 1944).

Broadcast stimuli in birds have tremendous diversity, varying across both auditory and visual modalities. The form of presentation varies from the display of a single male in its territory to the highly elaborate communal lek display. Also, most birds are social during some periods of their lives, developing dominance relationships with group members, which, in turn, have a sizable influence on sexual habits (Schein, 1975); as a general rule, dominance status is positively correlated with mating behavior. All of these variables interact with the kind of mating system exhibited by the species. Where monogamous pair bonds exist for life, the broadcast display need only be directed at a particular mate. For a polygamous or promiscuous bird, on the other hand, its signal must be more attractive than any other signal in the area.

The most prominent feature of broadcast behavior in birds is the auditory display. Whether it be a vocal call or song, such as the "gobble" of the male turkey (Evans, 1961), or the "bob-white" of the bobwhite quail, or a nonvocal sound production like the "drumming" of wings by some species of grouse, such broadcast activity provides a more efficient means of attracting mates from long distances away than do chemical or visual stimili. Unlike visual displays, the auditory signal can be detected from afar even when the broadcaster is hidden behind foliage (Bastock, 1967).

There is great diversity among birds in the manner by which auditory displays are emitted. In its simplest form, the lone male emits the attraction song, usually from an elevated position in its territory (see Armstrong, 1965, for many examples). Almost everyone living in the northern regions of the United States has heard the broadcast song of the male robin and the male song sparrow in the spring. Moreover, the continuous tapping of woodpeckers is a commonly heard sound that is associated with the attraction of mates (Milne and Milne, 1954). The significance of song repertoires is described in the following extract (Krebs 1977).

Most song birds have song repertoires, that is, several forms of their broadcast song. All forms carry the same message and occur at the same time of the year. Some birds will sing one form of their song for awhile, then switch to a somewhat different form for awhile longer, and so on. These birds have been called "discontinuous singers" (Hartshorne, 1973).

All of this raises the intriguing question as to the adaptive significance of song redundancy. It has been suggested that song repertoires facilitate the females' individual recognition of neighboring males. A second theory proposes that males with repertoires tend to be more attractive to females, hence repertoires have evolved through natural selection. A related hypothesis suggests that repertoires aid in the establishment and maintenance of breeding territories. The mechanisms operating here may be of two types. First, neighboring territorial males often match each other's singing (i.e., they use the same song type) in what is called "countersinging." Bremond (in Armstrong, 1973) suggests that countersinging informs nearby potential intruders that they have been recognized. Thus a larger repertoire of song would enable matching with many more individuals, hence facilitating maintenance of territory. A second mechanism, proposed by Hartshorne (1956), emphasizes that a single song type would soon lose its signal effectiveness due to habituation. The larger the variety of song forms emitted, the less the habituation and consequently the territory is maintained.

After reviewing and noting weaknesses in the above theories, Krebs proposed what he calls the "Beau Geste" hypothesis. When territorial birds arrive in their spring breeding grounds, they must first assess the quality of the habitat in relation to the density of already established territories before establishing their own territories. This assessment is based on song displays by the already established residents. Since quality of habitat is highly dependent upon the density of those birds using this habitat, it seems advantageous to keep the density down by repelling possible residents. A bird with a variety of songs in its repertoire will give the impression of many more inhabitants in that area than are really there. A visitor is therefore likely to move to another area to establish a territory.

Males of many species cease their broadcast displays as soon as pairing occurs. The male Canada warbler, for example, gives broadcast songs at the rate of about six per minute while attracting a mate, but becomes quiet after pairing (Kendeigh, 1945). In other species, the broadcast display may continue throughout the breeding season. Ruffed grouse may "drum" the air with their wings, while standing on logs, for 7 or 8 months, but only during a brief 1 or 2-week period does this signal serve to attract females (Gullion, 1970). The rest of the time the "drumming" functions to ward off intruders from the territory and stimulate sexual receptivity in females.

Lek displays, as mentioned earlier, increase the attractiveness of the broadcast signal. Many males calling at the same time can obviously produce a louder signal than can a single male, enhancing mate attraction for a group member. There are other features of lek displays that enhance its signal value. Lek displays typically combine visual and auditory components into complex and highly conspicuous exhibitions, and the open areas where the lek display is performed make it possible for the signal to travel a long distance.

Lek displays have been reported in at least ten different families of birds (Wilson, 1975), but most studies have dealt with the grouse (Wiley, 1974). A study of a lek display in male sage grouse is summarized as follows (Wiley, 1973).

Each spring, male sage grouse gather on mating grounds (leks) in the sagebrush prairies of Montana and Colorado. A lek is divided into a large number of smaller continuous territories, each from 13 to 100 square meters in area, each "owned" by a single male. There tend to be certain areas in each lek where most of the copulation occurs. These areas are called "mating centers" and they tend to overlap a number of smaller territories. The larger the lek, the greater the number of these "centers" that exist. Younger males initially acquire territories around the periphery of the lek. As they mature over the years, they gradually acquire territories closer to the center and hence to the "mating

centers." Only the older, stronger males tend to control space in and around these mating areas.

Up to 400 males may combine to give spectacular attraction displays on a single lek. Each male exhibits a strutting display in which the white feathers on its neck are raised conspicuously, the head is held high, the wings are pulled against the body, and the chest sac is raised and lowered twice in quick succession. The combined movements of chest sac and wings causes a conspicuous acoustical output described as a "swish-swish-coo-oo-poink." This sound can be heard several hundred meters from the lek while the visual features are noticed by humans from more than one kilometer away.

The females, who are more drably colored than the males, usually arrive at the lek just before sunrise. They generally land near the periphery and proceed to walk directly to the nearest mating center. During this walk they are courted by males but rarely do they mate with any but those in the center. They eventually reach the center and congregate with the other females already there. Receptive females respond to male struts by adopting a solicitation posture, a crouched posture in which both wings are spread and the neck is extended. The male approaches, mounts, and copulation follows. Each female mates only once each year. Following copulation, the female leaves the lek and builds a nest on the ground, sometimes several miles away from the lek. The male is not involved with incubation or parenting.

The male great egret, a communal nester and native to the Gulf of Mexico area, attracts females with visual displays from its nest site (see Figure 16.6). These highly conspicuous displays consist of (1) stretches, in which the male thrusts its head and neck upward in a single stabbing motion (2) bowing, in which it reaches down with its bill, grabs a twig and laterally shakes its head and (3) snapping, in which it extends its head and neck downward while "snapping" its

(a)

(b)

(c)

Figure 16.6 Courtship displays in the great egret, including the primary components of (*a*) stretching (*b*) bowing, and (*c*) snapping. (From Wiese, 1976.)

mandibles together, causing a loud auditory signal (Wiese, 1976).

Bowerbirds of Australia and New Guinea provide the most elaborate of all visual displays by erecting brightly colored bowers, which are large hut-shaped ground nests. Coloration is achieved by attaching bright flower petals and shiny stones and colored berries to branches and twigs of the bower. During World War II, bowers were found to contain shiny pieces of metal dropped by soldiers. At least one species is known to mix a paint from fruit pulp and saliva and to dab this paint on the inside of the bower with a "brush" made from bark fibers (Eibl-Eibesfeldt, 1975).

Broadcast stimuli in mammals generally coincide with the period of time when the female is capable of reproduction (in estrus). Females in estrus are said to be in heat, and males that are potent are said to be in rut. Ovulation, or estrus, is a cyclically occurring event in most female mammals, while males are potent any time of the year, except for male deer, seals, and certain rodents that have a period of potency coinciding with that of the female of the species. These exceptions generally occur in animals that live in the colder climates where seasonal changes in food availability must be carefully timed with the reproduction and care of the young. In the warmer climates, where food is usually available all year around, breeding often occurs throughout the year (Carrington, 1970).

In some mammals estrus occurs at regular intervals during the year. Examples include many primates, bats, cats, whales, and squirrels. In others, estrus occurs during certain, often brief, periods just once or twice each year. During such breeding seasons there may be cyclical periods of estrus or just one estrus period lasting for a brief period of time, sometimes only for a few hours. All of this points to the necessity for precise timing of reproductive behaviors to match the time of ovulation. In fact, males of many species are attracted to the female sometime prior to the estrous period so as to ensure their presence during ovulation. Male wallabies, for one, are attracted to females several days before ovulation and frequently stay with her for one or two days afterwards. This is highly advantageous since the estrous period in wallabies lasts only for a very brief period of time (Kaufmann, 1974).

Sexual Behavior: Courtship and Mating

Chemical stimuli play a major role as broadcasting signals in mammals (see also Chapter 20). Since a scent remains relatively viable over a sizable distance, either when airborne or when deposited on a substrate, most mammals do not need to perform elaborate broadcasting behaviors in order to make these signals conspicuous. Sexual receptivity in female mammals is generally advertised through the odors she exudes. These odors are a by-product of the biochemical changes that occur before and during ovulation. These scents are secreted from various scent glands (sebaceous and sudoriferous) on the body, or they are given off in the urine. Most dog and cat owners are well aware of the long-distance attraction power of their female pet's odors. These sex attractants are released in the female's urine and readily elicit approach behavior of males. Once the males are in the area of these odors, they in turn may urine mark as a means of attracting females (Maier and Maier, 1970).

The vaginal discharge of female hamsters is primarily a male sex attractant. When a sample of these discharges is applied to glass bottles or objects near the female's burrow, it serves to attract the male to the vicinity. When applied to a male, the odor causes that male to be courted rather than attacked by other males (Murphy, 1973).

A prominent feature of the mammalian male's courtship is its tendency to approach and sample odors from the female's body, either by smelling or tasting [see Mochi and MacClintock's (1973) description of Flehmening summarized below; and Figure 16.7]. This is particularly true in social mammals (e.g., many primates) in which group living is the rule during the mating season. Group living generally eliminates the need for long-distance attraction displays, but the need for close-distance sexual communication remains. Odor marking and sampling serve this purpose (see also Chapter 20). Odor sampling also occurs as a greeting ceremony in many

(a)

(b)

Figure 16.7. Flehmening in the male giraffe. The male collects urine from the female in his mouth (a), then "samples" its olfactory characteristics by extending his head (b) curling his upper lip upwards. (From Mochi and MacClintock, 1973.)

mammals when they first encounter each other (Ewer, 1973).

Several mammalian species determine whether a female is in heat by sampling her urine in their mouths. This process which often involves a somewhat unusual set of facial responses, is called flehmening. Mochi and MacClintock (1973, pp. 77-79) aptly describe these movements in male giraffes. The male flehmens "by approaching a cow and pushing his nose against her hindquarters or licking her tail, inducing the cow to urinate. The bull collects some of the urine with his tongue, then extends his head and holds it motionless for a minute or two. His upper lip curls upward. This closes off his nostrils, trapping odors in the nasal cavity where they can be thoroughly assessed by the olfactory epithelium. The bull may eject the urine from his mouth in a long stream.

Flehmening has been reported in a wide variety of mammals, including some species of camels, cattle, rhinoceros and bats (Ewer, 1973). Flehmening in domestic barnyard animals, the bull in particular, is often called "lipping." This name stems from the conspicuous turning up of the upper lip during odor sampling.

Animals that flehm are known to have Jacobson's organ, an olfactory receptor located in the top part of the mouth, which is very likely stimulated when the chemicals are trapped by flehmening.

In many kangaroo and wallaby species, the male routinely smells the pouch or cloaca of any female with which he comes into contact. This usually includes a daily check of most of the females in his social group (called a mob). The female whiptail wallaby may even urinate in the male's mouth during his checking activities, a behavior not uncommon in mammals (Kaufmann, 1974)

Visual stimuli. The release of chemical sex attractants in mammals is often accompanied by visual modes of broadcasting. The examples are many and diverse. Distinctive tail movements serve as attractants in squirrels (Bakken, 1959). Certain seals give what may appear to be gymnastic displays in the water, including somersaulting and bobbing up and down (Mohr, cited in Ewer, 1973).

In primates, as in certain other mammals, the consort pair is frequently formed well before copulation occurs. The male is generally attracted to the female by chemical cues which he frequently samples on his own (Klein, 1971; Van Lawick-Goodall, 1968) While sampling these chemicals, the male spider monkey may lick or even drink the urine. Other primates will saturate their tails with urine as a sexual display (Lorenz, 1972). The genital areas of certain female primates will swell or grow in size and change color during estrus. The visual cues are enhanced by the female assuming the mating posture (called presenting) in front of a male (Wickler, 1967).

Auditory stimuli. The attraction sounds of many mammals are commonplace, conspicuous events in various parts of the northern hemisphere. These include the bugling of bull elk and the mating calls of tomcats as they seek out receptive females. Siamese tomcats are particularly well known for their mating calls. It is now known that some mice use ultrasonic calls to communicate with each other (Sales, 1972).

II. The Synchronization Function of Courtship

After two potential mates are drawn together by broadcast stimuli, the courtship chain proceeds in sequential order, bringing the two partners into close proximity so that each is identified according to appropriateness of sex, species, and sexual receptivity. Conspecific males that intrude are usually driven away. Aggressive tendencies on the part of both partners are inhibited and sexual responsiveness is increased. When internal fertilization is involved, proper orienting maneuvers occur to facilitate mounting and copulation. When external fertilization is involved, sperm and egg release are generally synchronized within close temporal and geographical limits (simultaneous spawning); on other occasions, sperm are released and collected by the female for future fertilization needs. All of these functions are facilitated by synchronized courting, of which a prominent feature is aggressive behavior.

Courtship and Aggression. When the "individual space" (Hediger, 1955) of any organism is encroached upon by another animal several natural behavioral tendencies come into play. These include the tendency to flee or fight and, if the contact is made during the mating period, there is also the tendency to approach and mate. Ethologists and comparative psychologists have studied these tendencies in many different species and formulated general theories regarding the phenomenon (Hinde, 1970). Most of these theorists have labeled the point of contact as a "conflict situation." In a conflict situation the animals exhibit one or another sequence of behavior depending on the motivational state and the presence or absence of critical stimuli. The strongest tendencies are to threaten, attack, or flee; initially these are the most frequently observed behaviors toward an intruder. It is not unusual for a receptive female to be attacked by a sexually motivated male; however, submissive behavior on her part and the presence of other stimuli associated with sexual behavior tend to inhibit attack behavior and lead to courtship.

To some extent, the close relationship between courtship and aggression has contributed to the difficulty in classifying them unambiguously. This is particularly true for courting displays and threat behavior. In many instances, the initial patterns are difficult to distinguish, and even the final components of copulation, spawning, and fighting are sometimes difficult to separate since some species exhibit fightinglike behavior during the copulatory act. The most extreme example is the praying mantis: the female devours the male during coitus (Roeder, 1935). There is some evidence that aggression during the courtship sequence serves to strengthen the pair bond that is established between mates.

Courtship and Secondary Sex Characteristics. Secondary sex characteristics are presumed to play a major role in identifying an animal by sex and species during the courtship process. Courtship behaviors generally accentuate those features of an animal that distinguish males from females and one species from another. It is further assumed that these identification signals are frequently, if not continuously, monitored by both partners during the courtship process. For example, the manes of male lions and the inflatable proboscis of the male elephant seal are difficult to hide during any sexual interaction.

Body size and coloration can also be secondary sex characteristics. Two good examples of a sex difference in body size are found in the Alaskan fur seal and polar bear. The female seal weighs 75 pounds to the male's 600 and the female bear weighs approximately 500 to the male's 1600 pounds. Although there is a general absence of color vision in mammals, primates have good color vision, with coloration serving as a secondary sex characteristic. In some primates, for example, the male mandrill baboon has a distinct purple muzzle, enormous blue cheek swellings, and multicolored hindquarters, while the female is dully colored.

Synchronized Courtship in Invertebrates. Courtship in invertebrates is primarily restricted to the arthropods and molluscs (Bastock, 1967). Complexity of courtship among these two animal groups varies considerably, reflecting different sensitivities to visual, auditory, and chemical signals. The heavy involvement of chemical communication during courtship is matched or exceeded only by that seen in mammals. The aggression that is a common component of courtship in male vertebrates is generally absent in invertebrates. Arthropod males, for instance, rarely attack their female mates. As a result, the submissive features of courtship in female vertebrates are usually absent in female arthropods.

Synchronized courtship displays serve to identify partners to each other and to coordinate movements leading up to copulation and internal fertilization. Since many arthropod females can store sperm for future fertilization use, there is no need for a precise coordination of sexual physiology between the two partners, as seen in vertebrates.

Fruit-fly courtship has been, perhaps, the best studied of all invertebrate patterns (Bastock, 1967; Bastock and Manning, 1955). Three component stages have been recognized, with each stage involving different behavioral elements. In the first stage, called orientation, the male moves to a position that is usually close behind the female. Here he orients his body toward her and often touches her with a fore-tarsus (called tapping). If she moves away, he follows, always keeping his body axis oriented toward her. The second stage, called wing vibration, is initiated during these orienting movements. The male begins to vibrate the wing that is closest to her head. These vibrations generate sound pulses, called courtship songs, which appear to be species specific: the songs seem to enable the female to discriminate males of her own species from males of other species (Ewing and Bennet-Clark, 1968). These songs also serve to increase receptivity in the female (von Schilcher, 1976).

The third stage, called licking, begins when the orienting male, still vibrating its wing, approaches the female from the rear and licks her genitalia with his proboscis. Licking, as well as tapping, may provide important chemical cues that synchronize the behavior chain and maintain responsiveness in the male (cf. Shorey and Bartell, 1970). Copulation follows licking except when the female terminates the chain either by escaping or actively rejecting the male by kicking or some similar response.

Courtship in the fruit fly illustrates that the passive courtship role played by a female may not be as "passive" as the term suggests. Although the female remains relatively quiescent during the courtship chain, she provides the visual, tactual, and chemical stimuli that maintin the behavioral sequence.

Butterfly courtship chains have been described in several species of butterfly. Tinbergen (1972), for example, has supplied an illustration of synchronized courtship in Grayling butterflies. The male's pursuit appears to stimulate the female to settle on the ground. The male usually lands behind the female, circles her with short jerky sideways movements, and stops when he is finally facing her. The male now proceeds to execute the courtship display in front of her, beginning with wing quivering and followed by antenna spinning and fanning, both of which develop out of the quivering movement. Antenna spinning involves both antenna moving synchronously in a circular pattern. Fanning involves a fast rhythmic opening and closing of the leading edge of the wings, which are held in the raised (vertical) position. Fanning and antenna spinning movements may last for several minutes.

Bowing is the last component in the courtship chain (See Figure 16.8). Here the male brings the forewings forward toward the female that is standing motionless throughout this sequence. The male's wings are then closed slowly, usually "capturing" the female's antennae between them

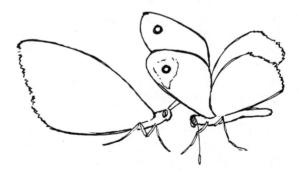

Figure 16.8 Grayling male (right) bowing so that the female's antennae come in contact with the scent organ of the male. (From Tinbergen, 1951.)

Sexual Behavior: Courtship and Mating

and followed by a drawing back of the wings, which releases the antennae. Bowing, fanning, and wing quivering probably provide chemical as well as visual cues. The male has scent glands in its wings that contact the female's antennae during bowing, and fanning and quivering both generate air currents that direct this scent toward the female's antennae. It is known that the tips of these antennae contain olfactory organs. As is true of the courtship chains in other animals, the Grayling butterfly's sequence may be repeated several times prior to copulation, with some of the components being reduced in intensity or omitted on repetition. The quiescence of the female is an important stimulus in the chain; a wing-flapping female prevents or terminates the courtship sequence.

Courtship in nocturnal moths, unlike that of diurnal butterflies, is primarily a chemical one. Both the male and female angel-shade moth, for example, emit scents, with the male's being emitted through an abdominal brush-organ. The sense organs for detection of these scents are located in the antennae of both sexes. When the brushes are removed from males, the females reject all attempts at mating by these brushless males. When the antennae are removed from either sex, courtship is inhibited in that animal. Mating is possible only when scents are produced and detected by both sexes (Birch, 1970).

Synchronized Courtship in Vertebrates.
Sexual dimorphism, when it occurs, is often emphasized in the courtship ceremony, presumably as an aid in sexual discrimination. As we will see, courtship ceremonies are often elaborate, frequently involving territorial aggressive behavior.

Synchronized courtship in fish. Some of the most spectacular courtship ceremonies occur in fish; among the vertebrate groups, the fishes' variety of signals and behavior patterns is exceeded only by those observed in birds. This fact was alluded to earlier in the description of the three-

spined stickle-back's courtship pattern (see Figures 16.1 and 16.2). Both external and internal fertilization occur in fish, adding to the complexity of the courtship sequences. When external fertilization is involved, precise coordination of egg and sperm release is critical for fertilization to occur. Even if the sperm are collected and stored externally by the female for future use, coordination between mates is important, for the water medium in which the sex cells are deposited is subject to continual change. The fish that fertilize internally include the sharks, rays, redfish, guppies and mollies, to name a few.

In the most common case, courtship consists of a series of movements that bring the two mates close together, causing egg release in the female followed immediately by sperm release from the male. If the courtship pattern is "successful," the sperm covers the eggs and fertilization occurs. Since many adult male fish have specific spawning grounds (or territories) which they defend, aggression is a common element in their courtship ceremonies as described earlier in the stickleback when the female exhibits appeasement in order to inhibit the male's aggression.

Courtship behavior in the European bitterling is different from that in most other fish, involving the location and protection of an object of critical importance to reproduction (Tinbergen, 1951). The female bitterling deposits her eggs inside the mantle cavity of mussels by lowering her long ovipositer down into the cavity. What is remarkable is that the mussel does not clamp down on the ovipositor while she is spawning. The male releases its sperm nearby. When the mussel begins to feed, it pumps in the sperm along with its regular food, and fertilization occurs (Ommanney, 1970).

Synchronized courtship in amphibians and reptiles. Most amphibians practice external fertilization, and mating generally occurs in the water in a particular breeding place during a particular season. Studies of frogs and toads reveal a relatively simple pattern of interaction that is heavily dependent on auditory calls. The female is attracted to the vicinity of the male by its broadcast call. The chorusing males, usually stationed a short distance apart from each other, clasp and mount any approaching frog, including other males. Vocal "release calls" given by any nonreceptive frog, regardless of sex, cause the courting male to unclasp and dismount (Bogert, 1960). Males of voiceless species are known to take longer to find the appropriate female mate.

Courtship patterns in most reptiles serve the function of discriminating sex, inhibiting escape, and stimulating receptivity. It is the male that usually plays the active role in courtship while the female tends to be passive. Some homosexual patterns in lizards are thought to be the result of a male remaining passive, a female signal in the presence of a courting male (*Larousse Encyclopedia*, 1967).

The kind of signals used to synchronize courtship in reptiles varies considerably. Lizards tend to rely on visual stimuli, snakes an olfactory stimuli, and alligators may use both olfactory and auditory stimuli. Since many reptiles are territorial during the breeding season, aggression is a common element in their courtship patterns. This is well illustrated in the four-stage courtship sequence of the side-blotched lizard, a native of the southwest states (see Figure 16.9; Ferguson, 1970). In the first stage, called Approaching, the male gives an aggressive display that probably dispels other males while attracting the female. Some males follow this by rushing the female and biting her. Most males, however, approach slowly, relaxing the aggressive display while giving what can be described as "head-bobbing" movements (called shuddering) and "push-ups." During the second stage, called Licking, the male licks the female's body, beginning with the tail region and moving anteriorly toward the head. These licks may be alternated with movements (circling) to the other side of the female. Push-

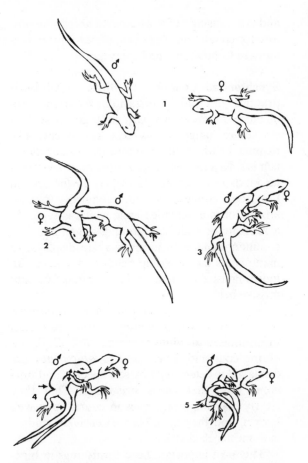

Figure 16.9 The mating sequence in the side-blotched lizard, showing (I) the male approaching, (II) licking, (III) neck-holding, (IV,V) and copulating with the female. (Modified from Ferguson, 1970.)

ups and shudder responses continue to be given during these circling movements. All of these responses probably pacify the female. Whether or not chemical stimuli are exchanged during licking is not known. Eventually the male's licks reach the loose skin in the neck region where it grabs on with its jaws. This initiates the third stage, Neckholding. Some males drag the female forward with this neckhold. More frequently they swing the female's head and shoulders from side to side in an arc. The male ultimately strokes the female's pelvic region with its hindleg and tail, causing her to assume an accessible posture for copulation. The chain of behavior culminates in Copulation, the final stage.

Synchronized Courtship in Birds. All birds practice internal fertilization. Courtship sequences bring the two partners together so that cloacal exchange of sex cells can occur. The manner in which this distance-decreasing problem is solved involves perhaps the most spectacular kinds of synchronized display in the animal kingdom. Since courtship generally occurs around or in a defended area, which is typically a nest-site or a display ground, aggression is a common component in many avian displays. In many cases the courtship behavior blends in an indistinguishable manner into dominance-submissive behavior.

Secondary sex characteristics in avian courtship are, for the most part, bodily features like head furnishings and plummage that are displayed during courtship. The extent to which they are displayed is determined by sex, species, and hormone level that varies seasonally. That they clearly play important roles in courtship is well known, and they have been extensively studied in domestic chickens.

The most important head furnishings in birds include the comb, wattles, bill, earlobes, skin color, caruncles (small growths), casque (helmet), crest, neck feathers, and ear tufts. Schoettle and Schein (1959) found that the head of a female turkey is all that is necessary to elicit courtship and copulatory movements in the male. By contrast, the domestic chicken requires both the head and body for similar stimulation (Carbaugh, Schein, and Hale, 1962). In the domestic chicken in which combs differ slightly across breeds, both size and shape of the comb influence mating behavior (Guhl and Ortman, 1953). The particular effect is related to genotype (Crawford and Smyth, 1965).

Male yellowthroats copulate with stuffed females (Noble and Vogt, 1935), yet attack this same model when a black mask is placed over its head. A black head adornment distinguishes males from females of this species. Similarly, Noble (1936) found that a previously courted female flicker was attacked when a malelike moustache was attached to her.

The male zebra finch sings continuously while

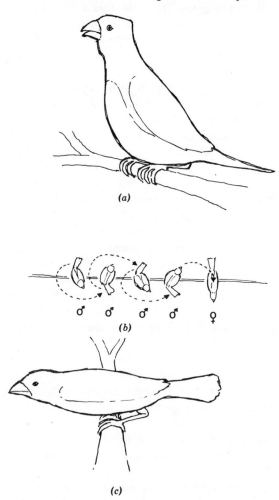

(a)

(b)

(c)

Figure 16.10. Courtship displays in the zebra finch, (A) the male assumes an upright posture and sings to the female, (B) approaches the female along the branch swinging his body from side to side (pivot courtship dance), (C) the female responds by assuming a flattened posture and giving a tail-vibration display. (Modified from Morris, 1970b.)

courting the female (Morris, 1970b). Each male gives a slightly different and unique version of the species-specific song. While singing, the male approaches the female along the branch, exhibiting an upright posture that clearly displays its male markings (see Figures 16.10). The approach consists of a rhythmical twisting, bodyswing from the left to the right. The tail, with its colorful black and white bands, is twisted around out of its normal position, clearly displaying the male-specific features. The female responds to this approach by assuming a lowered, horizontal posture on the branch. While in this posture, she gives rapid tail vibrations. Courtship proceeds in this manner, with the male eventually reaching the female and copulating.

The nuptial colors of the male wood duck play a role in his courtship. While courting, both sexes mutually bill-jerk, a display in which the bill is quickly thrust upward, exposing the white chin on the male. The female responds by adopting a prone position and copulation follows (Korschgen and Fredrickson, 1976).

The courtship sequence in the Japanese quail has been the subject of numerous studies, primarily because it is easily elicited under laboratory conditions (see also Chapter 5, pp. 71–72). The male courts the female by toe walking (strutting) in an arc around the female, exhibiting an extension of the neck and body and a puffing of the body feathers. The male's head is cocked inward toward the hen during the strut, and often times a hoarse call is given. A receptive female remains passive and assumes a crouched posture when the male attempts to mount her, otherwise she disrupts the chain by moving away (Farris, 1967).

Courtship in the Galapagos penguin includes mutual courtship displaying. Bill dueling is commonly seen, as the two mates stand face to face shaking their heads so that the tips of their bills contact each other. This behavior often leads to flipper patting: the male leans over the female, forcing her into a prone position, and the bills of both partners vibrate while the male pats her body with its flippers. Copulation may ensue while she is in this position (Boersma, 1976).

In most hummingbird species the male is dominant over the female and no long-term pair bonds are formed between mates. The male tends to acquire and defend the better food sources (territories), which, during times of food shortage, may be critical to the female's survival. Wolf (1975) has described one species of tropical hummingbird in which the female exhibits courtship behavior in order to gain access to a male's food supply during the nonbreeding season. Wolf refers to this as "prostitution behavior."

Courtship feeding [see the following summarized study (Stokes and Williams, 1971)] is an integral component of roadrunner courtship (Whitson, 1975). The roadrunner's ceremony usually begins with a ground chase that may last for several hours. The ensuing precopulatory interaction involves a complex synchrony of nine different vocal signals intermixed with a variety of behavioral displays (Figure 16.11). With the female in front of him, the male prances and tail wags. Food is usually held in the bill during tail wagging. The female reciprocates by rapidly flicking her tail, and typically mounting and copulation occur. During copulation, food is "exchanged for sex."

One of the more curious features of courtship in certain birds is the presentation of food or other object by one sexual partner to the other. It is usually the male that gives the gift to the female. Courtship feeding is usually accompanied by visual display and "food calls" in the ground-nesting species. Sometimes the combination of call and display has been called "tidbitting." These auditory calls are generally soft and have a signal capacity of less than 100 feet (Stokes, 1972).

Courtship feeding seems to serve two functions. First, it may occur early in the chain as a broadcast behavior, serving to attract the female to the male. A second function is to keep the

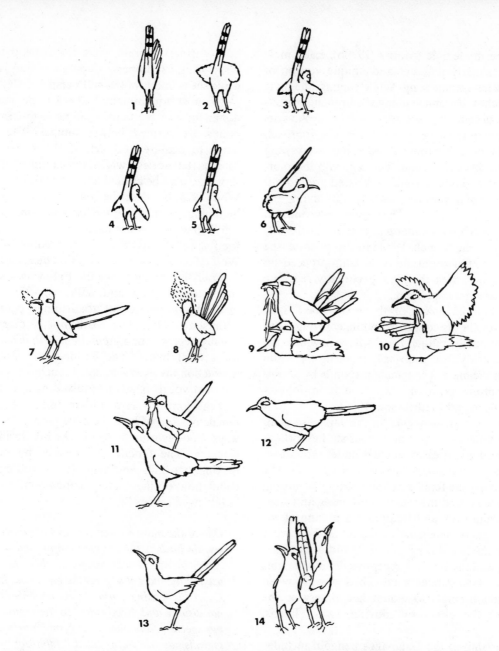

Figure 16.11. Courtship, copulation and post-copulation behavior in the road-runner. During the prance display, the male runs away from the female at first (1) holding the wings and tail in an upright position, (2-5) then lowering the wings down to the body, a side view of (3) is shown (6). The male's tail-wag display is characterized by side-to-side movements of the tail and (8) the tail may be elevated. The extremes of this lateral movement are indicated by the dotted line. (9, 10) Copulation may or may not involve food exchange. After dismounting, (11) the male circles the female, (12) bowing and (13 flicking the tail upwards and (14) mutual flick displays by both mates. (Adapted from Whitson, 1975.)

Some Major Classes of Behavior

female in close proximity to the male while he is displaying. Courtship feeding in this sense serves as an appeasement gesture.

The actual form in which the "food" is displayed varies from species to species. Four different forms of this display can be distinguished. (1) The most commonly seen form involves the male simply holding the food in his beak while moving near the female. (2) Males of some species, however, dabble with the food while in the presence of the female, repeatedly dropping it and picking it up over and over again. (3) Other males tend to remain frozen in an upright posture over the food when the female approaches to within a meter or so of them. (4) In still other species the courtship feeding display is integrated into the lateral courtship movements of the male in relation to the female. The lateral display is a common component of courtship in gallinaceous birds. Many species typically show more than one of these four forms of feeding displays during a mating ceremony.

Courtship and the breeding phase in birds. Some birds remain paired for long periods of time, both before and after nesting. The mallard duck, for one, may form a pair bond in the autumn that lasts until the nesting season in the spring, terminating when the female goes to her nesting territory to lay eggs. The roadrunner forms a pair bond at the beginning of the breeding season and remains paired until the young have matured sufficiently to feed independently. Courtship behaviors exhibited throughout this pair-bond period serve to maintain the bond. In some instances, then, courtship involves the whole reproductive sequence, including incubation, brooding, and rearing of the young. The question that arises here is whether or not there are differences in courtship behavior beteeen prefertilization and care of the young periods. Evidence from the roadrunner indicates that there are such differences.

Whitson (1975) divided the roadrunner's breeding season into six "breeding phases." These included pair formation, nest building, incubation, early and late nestling, and fledgling. Whitson's observations revealed quantitative differences in courtship behavior across these phases. For instance, copulation occurred in all but the pair-formation phase, and all courtship and copulation behaviors increased in frequency during the fledgling phase. These findings indicate that a full characterization of courtship in a long-pairing species must take into consideration which phase of the breeding cycle the observations are made.

Synchronized Courtship in Mammals. The synchronous courtship displays that are so commonly seen in birds are generally absent or kept at a minimum in mammals. In many cases the male, once he has found a mate, simply approaches her, mounts, and copulates. That courtship may not be needed at all for fertilization is attested to by the fact that artificial insemination is possible in many uncourted mammals (e.g., mink, cows, and horses).

As mentioned earlier, the main function of courtship in mammals is to ensure that mating will occur when the female is most capable of reproducing (Ewer, 1973). Males must be attracted and maintained in sexual readiness so that when the female's period of receptivity occurs, he will detect her signals and copulate. Often the sexual partners are attracted together a little while in advance of the female's receptive period; this is adaptive because the female's period of estrus is no more than a few hours long each year (e.g., in kangaroos).

Courtship in the dog begins several weeks before the female's estrus period begins. The female's scent attracts the male to her, but since she is not receptive at this time, she actively rejects him with aggressive behavior. The male continues to follow her, exhibiting playful stalking and pouncing behavior, and frequently smelling the genital area. Both partners mark their environment with urine and feces during this time. As the estrus period approaches, the female's rejecting behavior becomes less and less until her solicitng posture stimulates the male to mount and copulate (Ewer, 1973). There is fairly good evidence that the female is selective in her choice of mates: she does not invariably mate with every courting male she encounters.

Courtship in domestic cats rarely lasts for more than 4 or 5 days. It is not uncommon for several males to be attracted to a female by her odor and mating calls, particularly in urban areas. The excess of males usually causes fighting behavior among them. The male's initial approach to the female is usually rejected by spitting and clawing responses. Gradually over time he is allowed closer and closer to her. A low vocal call may be given by the male during this approach. Otherwise the female's actions generally inhibit his aggressive tendencies. She may respond by rolling on the ground in front of him or rubbing her head against objects. Ultimately the male is allowed close enough to mount when she assumes a mating posture (Ewer, 1973).

Odor sampling is a commonly seen courtship pattern in groups of elephants. The female (cow) is receptive for about 3 days a year and, if impregnated, she will not mate again for 3 or 4 years. The male's ability to detect sexual receptivity under these timetable conditions is obviously very important for the survival of the species. Odor sampling accomplishes this goal. Many males (sometimes up to ten) have been known to follow an estrus cow at the same time. Sexual chases may also occur. Eventually a male will catch up to a female, sometimes giving a soft trumpeting call in the approach. Pushing against her hindquarters with his trunk and laying his head on her back seem to be the signal for her to adopt a receptive posture (Douglas-Hamilton and Douglas-Hamilton, 1975).

The act of touching the female's hindquarters or sides is common in the courtship of other mammals as well. Male giraffes press or tap against the cow's hindleg and rest their head against her flank during the courtship sequence (Mochi and MacClintock, 1973). Male pigs give a specific grunt and touch the sides of the female with their snout, inducing her to allow him to mate (Ewer, 1973).

Aggression is a general feature of whiptail wallabie courtship (Kaufmann, 1974). Head bobbing and tail lashing, both common elements of the male's fighting display, are also exhibited during the male's courtship display. Penile erection often accompanies tail lashing. Penile erections are common in both males during male-male fights, the penile display ceases in the loser of the encounter. All of these findings suggest an association between dominance and courtship behavior, which can also be inferred from the fact that the female often exhibits defensive-threat behavior during a courtship ceremony. Courtship in male wallabies may serve as a dominance display, eliciting submission without escape in the female.

Male guinea pigs circle their mates, giving long trilling calls and frequently exposing their testes. The circling movements take him closer and closer to the female until she assumes the mating posture and mounting occurs. The male may enurinate (direct stream of urine at) the female if she fails to adopt the mating posture (Kunkel and Kunkel, cited in Ewer, 1973). Enurination occurs in a number of species, including the porcupine, chinchilla, and rabbit.

Infantile behaviors tend to inhibit aggressive behavior in adult animals (Eibl-Eibesfeldt, 1975). Infantile behaviors serve the same function when they occur as elements of the courtship display, as found in the golden hamster. The female golden hamster dominates the male during the courtship ceremony because the male has to enter her territory in order to mate with her (cf. Payne and Swanson, 1970). The male appeases her by giving a call that is similar to that of a nestling young in distress.

When a pair of gerbils are placed in a neutral

area, the female gerbil takes the lead by approaching the male, sniffing or "nosing" his face and genital area. If receptive, the male usually reciprocates by sniffing her back. More intensive sniffing usually follows by the male, causing threat behavior in the female. The male may break off at this point and exhibit foot stomping (rapid hindleg drumming movements) and ventral scent gland marking (flattening belly on the ground) and rolling completely over on its back. If courtship continues, however, the male may push into the female with his shoulder. Or, "boxing" behavior may occur in which both partners rise up on hind legs and strike out with their forepaws. Copulation ensues if the female adopts the mating posture (Swanson, 1974).

Ultrasonic calls are now suspected to play an important role in mouse courtship. The sexually aroused male domestic mouse gives ultrasonic calls almost continuously from the time it is first exposed to a female, through the courtship and mounting phase, and up until just before ejaculation (Sales, 1972). Since socially dominant males emit more calls than submissive males and since females usually do not call at all, it has been suggested that these calls serve to elicit subordination in the female (Whitney, et al. 1973). A pheromone from the female is thought to be partially responsible for eliciting these male calls (Nyby et al. 1977).

Courtship in Nonhuman Primates. Courtship here may be facilitated by a conspicuous anatomical change that occurs in females of many species during the estrus cycle. A patch of naked skin in the anal region gets brighter and swells during the receptive period. This skin is called the sexual skin because of its proximity to the genital area and reactivity to sex hormones (cf. Wickler, 1967).

Females in heat typically display their hindquarters (and sexual skins) to males. This display involves a four-legged stance made in front of a male with the rump directed towards the male. At times the female looks back over her shoulder at the male while in this posture. This display is called presenting, and in a sexual context it is generally regarded as an invitation to mate. Females with the most conspicuous colorations and swellings tend to be favored by males (Wickler, 1967). It is easy to surmise the signal value of a swollen, bright red rump of a female in heat. What is hard to understand, is this same context, is why these same females (e.g., rhesus monkeys, baboons, vervets) display even more conspicuous rumps (brighter and more swollen) when pregnant (Rowell, 1974).

Presenting also occurs in other social contexts, for example, by both sexes, young and old, as a sign of submissiveness. When presenting occurs to dominant members of the troop or to strangers, it serves as a greeting display. Its effect is to inhibit aggressive tendencies in the animal to which the presentation is made.

Sexual behavior ceases in female rhesus monkeys that have had their ovaries removed. An ovariectomy also causes a female's sexual skin to pale in color. However, when estrogen is externally applied to this skin, causing a restoration of the bright red coloration, male monkeys still do not mate with her. This finding indicates that the color of the sexual skin is not the sole stimulus for mate attraction; and when vaginal odors from other females in heat are applied to the sexual skin of the ovariectomized female, the males are highly attracted to her. Olfactory stimuli clearly play a major role in attracting mates among the primates (Rowell, 1974).

In summary, courtship displays (presenting, following, and grooming), while observed in nonhuman primates, are generally less elaborate than those observed in nonprimate species and in some instances are absent entirely (Ewer, 1973). For example, once a pair bond is formed between two troop members, mating occurs periodically without any conspicuous display ceremony. Courtship, although present, seems to play a minimal role in the sexual behavior of the apes. Schaller (1965) noted that copulation in lowland gorillas in a zoo was preceded by wrestling, chasing, and fondling behaviors but that these "courtship" behaviors were not seen in the wild. And, without prior courtship stimulation, female chimpanzees have been observed to invite copulation by crouching in front of a male. Goodall (1965) has reported that most of the copulations she observed in chimps were preceded only by the male swinging vigorously in trees for about one minute. The male then approached the female who in turn often assumed a receptive posture.

The Process of Fertilization

Fertilization in Invertebrates other than Arthropods

The ragworm, called the clam worm by many bait diggers, migrates to the surface of the sea to spawn. Eggs and sperm are shed into the water as a result of the male's "nuptial dance." The male swims around and around the female in a tightening circle. This circling "dance" causes the female to emit a chemical that stimulates the male to emit its sperm, causing the female to shed her eggs, and the chain is complete (Evans, 1968). The adults generally die soon after spawning.

Copulation in the hermaphroditic snail (Helix) involves a long-lasting sequence of movements (of one to several hours) which is performed in identical manner by each partner. After the two partners intertwine and become interconnected, they copulate by inserting each other's penis into the other's genital receptacle. Garden slugs (Limax) also copulate in an intertwined manner, while hanging from a cord of mucus attached to a tree branch or similar object. The penes unroll and twist together during sperm transfer. The earthworm is another common hermaphroditic animal. Sperm are mutually exchanged between sexual partners and stored in special receptacles called spermathecae until the time the eggs are laid. This procedure allows eggs to be fertilized when conditions are favorable for the raising of the young.

Fertilization in Arthropods

Internal fertilization is the general rule in arthropods. In most winged insects (e.g., mosquito and queen bee) the spermatophores or free sperm are transferred to the female via a vale copulatory organ. Once in the female they are stored in the spermatheca. Copulation in the desert locus and fruit fly (Bastock, 1967; Evans, 1968) occurs with the male on the back of the female (*Larousse Encyclopedia*, 1967), while the male of some cockroach species maneuver the female into a mating posture that begins with the female on its back (Roth and Willis, 1954). Once she is in this position, the male cockroach (*Nauphoeta*) grasps her genitalia, spins around so that he is facing away from her, and copulation occurs. This end-to-end copulation pattern is also observed in butterflies and moths. Generally the male approaches the female from behind, bending his abdomen and copulatory apparatus forward until contact (and hooking) is made with the female's genital area. The male then turns around, facing away from her, and copulation ensues.

Scorpions inseminate by means of a spermatophore. The male Parabuthus courts the female by grabbing and dragging her to a spot where the spermatophore is then deposited. He apparently quiets her by "juddering," administering a rapid series of fore-aft body movements. Ultimately the male pulls her across the deposited spermatophore, at which time she takes it into her genital system (Evans, 1968).

Copulation in spiders involves the insertion of the male's palpal organ into the female's genital opening on her abdomen. Following a period of foreleg "foreplay" with the female, the male wolf spider climbs on the female in such a way that they are facing in opposite directions. Palpal insertion follows (Rovner, 1972).

Fertilization in Fish

The majority of fish reproduce by spawning and the exact form that this act takes is species specific, being subject to such factors as the buoyancy of the eggs produced and the presence or absence of a nest site (Marshall, 1966). Buoyant eggs are subject to dispersal by water currents, necessitating immediate fertilization by the male. Oceanic fish tend to shed buoyant eggs.

Other fish (e.g., salmon) shed nonbuoyant eggs that sink to the bottom. Many of these kinds of eggs have a stickly substance on them that allows the eggs to adhere to the substratum: the fertilization process is facilitated when the eggs remain in one general area. Cod spawn eggs that float slowly to the surface where a better food supply (plankton) awaits the larvae when they hatch. The courtship of the male cod serves to entice the female as near as possible to the surface before she sheds her eggs. The act of spawning occurs with the male hanging below the female, clasping her with its pelvic fins (Marshall, 1966).

Some species of fish called mouth breeders, incubate and brood their eggs in their mouths. Denny and Ratner (1970) describe a species of mouth-breeding fish in which the male has a series of colored spots on its anal fin that are remarkably accurate replicas of the eggs she spawns. During mating, the female takes the unfertilized eggs into her mouth immediately after they are released. In order for the eggs to be fertilized she must snap up the male's sperm. She is stimulated to do this by the male's displaying the "egg lures" on its anal fin and releasing its sperm nearby. In her attempts to snap up these "egg dummies," she takes in the sperm and the eggs are fertilized.

Male labyrinthine fish make bubble nests. After an air bubble is blown, the male attracts a female and proceeds to court her by physically turning her upside down, releasing her, and moving below her to fertilize the nonbuoyant eggs that are shed. The male catches these eggs (from 3 to 7) in its mouth, covers them with a sticky substance, and then attaches them to the bubble that has floated to the surface. This courtship-spawning sequence is repeated until about 150 eggs are attached to the bubble (*Larousse Encyclopedia*, 1967).

When fertilization occurs out of the water, coordination between the mates takes on a new dimension. The characin, a fish that lives in the Amazon River, spawns in a highly unusual manner. The male stimulates the ripe female to come with him to a potential nest site, a leaf or branch that overhangs the water's surface by one or two inches. Here they lock their fins together and repeatedly leap together out of the water and over this leaf. Eggs are laid and fertilized when the fish make brief contact with this leaf. The male continues to splash water on these eggs during the 3 day incubation period, preventing them from drying out (Ommanney, 1970).

Perhaps the most extraordinary example of synchrony is that seen in the grunion, a small (7 inches long) fish that lives off the coast of Southern California. This fish spawns on shores of certain sandy beaches between late February and early September. Spawning in the grunion occurs only during the evenings and only during periods of high tide. These periods coincide with the new moon and the full moon, which is perhaps the critical visual stimulus for initiating spawning. Females wash up on shore and, at precise moments between waves, burrow into the sand and deposit their eggs. The nearest male promptly fertilize these eggs, and both mates move back into the water on the next high wave.

In the few fish that mate by copulation, the sperm are transmitted through a pair of stiff, cartilagenous projecting rods called "claspers." When erected, they direct the sperm into the female's genital opening.

Fertilization in Amphibians and Reptiles

Fertilization in this group varies greatly in kind and pattern. Male frogs sit on the backs of females and clasp them with their forearms. This clasping posture is called amphexux. The female sheds her eggs and at the same time stimulates the clasping male to release sperm by performing a series of shuffling movements. When spawning is completed, the female shuffles backward, causing the male to release her, thus ending the chain (Etkin, 1964). A similar pattern has been described in toads (Eibl-Eibesfeldt, 1975).

Some male newts and salamanders deposit a spermatophore in front of a female during the course of an elaborate courtship. The male then entices the female to follow him so as to find and pick up the sperm (Eibl-Eibesfeldt, 1975).

All reptiles exhibit internal fertilization by passing sperm into the female's cloacal opening. All male reptiles (except one, the Tuatara) have hollow copulatory organs, called hemipenes, which extend from the cloaca during copulation. Some hemipenes have spines on their surface which fix the organ in place during copulation. Snakes have two hemipenes but only one is used in copulation.

Copulatory behavior in snakes has been classified into two categories (Davis, as reported in *Larousse Encyclopedia*, 1967). In one type, common to boas and pythons, the male glides along the female's body scraping her with spines that are situated on his body. The tactual and auditory signals generated by this scraping cause the female to open her cloaca, thus facilitating cloacal contact between the two partners. In the second type of copulation, common to vipers, cobras, and rattlesnakes, the two partners intertwine so that their cloacae are brought into contact. Often the latter type is preceded by courtship dances of several hours duration.

Copulation in lizards generally depends on the female's assuming a passive posture during the male's aggressive advances. The male side-blotched lizard grabs on to the neck or shoulder of the female and often drags her around, swinging the anterior portion of her body back and forth much like "an automobile windshield wiper" (Ferguson, 1970). He then stimulates her tail to rise, making the cloaca accessible. By sliding his tail under hers, the cloacae make contact, and copulation begins with the insertion of the hemipenis.

Fertilization in Birds

All birds exhibit internal fertilization. Copulation involves cloacal contact and the exchange of free sperm from male to female. Only a few birds (e.g., ducks and ostriches) have a copulatory organ. Most birds copulate with the female assuming a relatively horizontal posture on the ground or on a perch. The male then mounts her dorsally, maintaining his balance with one or both feet on her body or wings. Sometimes the female will extend her wings to facilitate the mounting attempts. Cloacal contact is usually made by both sexes twisting their tails to one side. Birds mating on a perch often flap their wings in order to maintain balance. While there are sidespread variations of these postures across the avian species, the basic behavior pattern is the same: the male "treads" on the back of the female, maneuvering into a position adequate for contact of the cloacae.

Fertilization in Mammals

All mammals reproduce by internal fertilization. Copulation involves the male inserting its copulatory organ (penis) into the female's genital opening (vagina), with the male usually mounting the female. The male's mount is usually facilitated by the female adopting a crouched posture, called "lordosis". This posture and the male's mounting from the rear is relatively invariant across mammals, except in humans and in rare cases in nonhuman primates in which other copulatory positions have been observed (Maier and Maier, 1970). Neck grips are common in some mammals as a means of maintaining balance and perhaps for inducing ovulation. The neck grip is very common in the mustelidae group, which includes skunk, weasel and mink (Ewer, 1973).

Ovulation in domestic cats is induced or stimulated by the copulatory act itself. The male's penis has a number of spines on it. The tactual stimulation caused by these spines, in association with a neck grip (in his jaws) and a high number of copulations, induces the female to ovulate during the mating act.

Copulation in domestic dogs is frequently followed by the pair remaining joined together, with the penis "locked" inside the vagina of the female (Kleiman and Eisenberg, 1973). This lock or tie may last from 5 to 20 minutes. Generally the dogs remain in an end-to-end position during the lock. The lock is caused by the folds on the penis becoming turgid during copulation, preventing its retracting.

Copulation in the larger terrestrial mammals usually involves the male's climbing partially on to the female's back and straddling her with his four legs. This occurs in elephants (Douglas-Hamilton and Douglas-Hamilton, 1975) and giraffes (Mochi and MacClintock, 1973).

Postcopulatory Behavior

Although copulation appears to be the end of the sexual behavior sequence, in many instances postcopulatory patterns of behavior have been observed, particularly in birds and mammals. These responses appear to be regular, integral components of the sexual behavior chain. In this sense they are the terminating behavior in the chain. Many female birds, for example, exhibit fluffing or care of the body surface [e.g., mallards (Lorenz, 1971) hummingbirds (Wolf, 1975) and Japanese quail (Farris, 1967)]. Other female birds exhibit wingflapping immediately after copulation [e.g., striped goose, Eibl-Eibesfeldt (1975)].

Denny and Ratner (1970) propose that the prime function of these postcopulatory behaviors, as is also true of other postconsummatory behavior, is that of disengaging an animal from a consummatory response and allowing it to move toward other behaviors. The transitional status of postcopulatory behavior has also been recognized by Eibl-Eibesfeldt (1975) when he suggested that they have an inhibiting function. When sexual partners break apart following copulation, the danger exists that aggression will occur in one or both animals. The postcopulatory display can be postulated as serving an appeasement function, allowing the animal to move away without getting hurt.

Study Questions

1. Describe briefly hermaphroditism.
2. What are the advantages and disadvantages of sexual reproduction?
3. Define courtship and describe a specific courtship sequence in a particular species.
4. What is a lek display?
5. Discuss the two main functions or components of courtship.
6. Describe flehmening and its purpose.
7. Describe two unusual methods of copulation in invertebrates.
8. Do the same for fish or reptiles.

17

Parenting: Prenatal Behaviors

Louis E. Gardner

Creighton University

This chapter emphasizes behaviors involved in preparing for offspring that have not yet arrived; Chapter 18 emphasizes the actual care of the young. These behaviors are viewed across a wide range of animals, and both types of care are classed as parenting responses.

The idea of parenthood normally evokes images of an older member of a species strenuously providing for the safety and well-being of a developing member of that same species. Lott (1973) has defined parental behaviors as "Behavior that contributes directly to increasing the survival probability of fertilized eggs or offspring that have left the female's body". In Chapters 17 and 18, however, we take a somewhat broader approach, emphasizing the idea of interaction between young and adults.

The study of parent-offspring relations in a variety of animal species makes it obvious that diverse care systems have developed and that part of this diversity stems from parent-offspring interaction. For example, Etkin (1964) has extended the concept of trophallaxis (food exchange in ant colonies) to include a greater variety of responses than the exchange of food. That is, Etkin's idea of the trophallactic exchange phenomenon was to emphasize that " . . .

the relationship between parent and young is integrated by a mutual exchange rather than by a one-way giving."

Interactions between parent and young have also been recognized by J. P. Scott (1958) in his attempt to develop an all-inclusive system of behavior classification. In this system, Scott categorized the usual adult parental responses as *epimeletic* (care-giving) behaviors and care-soliciting behaviors by the young as *et-epimeletic*. In like manner, the parenting behaviors discussed in Chapter 18 include not only the usual adult-to-young responses, but also those young-to-adult responses that have evolved in some species to help increase the probability of survival for the young.

In the study of animal behavior, one is struck by the magnificent range of systems of parental care that have developed and with the manner in which each diverse system fits into an adaptive framework. For example, we find that the type of parent-offspring interaction varies along the following dimensions: present to a degree or totally absent, simple or complex, and of varied duration ranging from zero time to years. Let us briefly examine the meaning of these dimensions.

Some Dimensions of Parent-Offspring Interaction

Absence of Parenting

One of the determining factors with regard to the presence or absence of parent-offspring interaction is need. Whether there is need or not is dictated by the degree to which a sufficient number of offspring survive on their own. In some instances, the parents do nothing to insure the survival of eggs or offspring but only insure that large numbers will be given a chance to survive by themselves. For example, Wendt (1965) has described a variety of amazing phenomena related to reproduction in certain marine bristle worms. Among these are the segmented palolo worms that inhabit the reefs in the waters near the Samoan and Fiji islands. Each year, at dawn on the first day of the last quarter of the October-November moon, the posterior segments of the male and female palolo worms break off and rise to the surface carrying innumerable sex cells with them. As the detached segments writhe about, the sperm and eggs are released into the water where the eggs are fertilized and then sink to the bottom to develop into adult worms.

The success of this system is not dependent upon any kind of adult care giving or care seeking on the part of the young. Instead, success is a function of *timing*, which is controlled by a regular environmental event (lunar cycles), *internal conditions* of the worms, and large *numbers* of gametes. It is reported that the swarming of these segments is so thick that the seawater is discolored and that an oar stuck into the swarm will remain standing for quite some time. This is, of course, only one example of an absence of any real parent-offspring relation; there are many other different instances of absence of parenting among animals. Later, we discuss the possible reasons for absence of parenting, when examined from an adaptive viewpoint.

Temporal Dimension

Along the temporal dimension of the parent-offspring interaction, defined as the length of overall time the adult stays in proximity to the egg or offspring after it leaves the body of the parents, zero time refers to those cases in which animals increase the probability of survival of their egg or offspring by making certain responses prior to birth, hatching or laying, and then having no actual contact after the event. At the other end of the continuum are animals such as humans that provide for nearly every need of the offspring early in life and decrease the amount of care gradually over time.

Complexity Dimension

Complexity of the parent-offspring interaction can be viewed in several different ways. One aspect of complexity involves the nature of the interaction itself, that is, to what degree the adult is actually physically involved with the young. In the least complex situation, the adult animal never actually sees or comes into physical contact with the young, while the adult hovers nearby or remains in physical contact at all times in more complex interactions.

Another aspect of complexity involves the intricacies of the responses involved in the parent offspring interaction. At the lower end of this continuum would be an animal, such as a bird, that provides care of the egg and offspring by providing food and warmth directly. Food is provided by immediate transfer from adult to young, and warmth by proximity of the adult body. The other end of this continuum is well represented by the parental responses of the brush turkey.

There are several varieties of brush turkey found in such places as Indonesia and Australia. Wallace (1894) was the first to make detailed observation of the nest-building responses of these birds; and, much later, Frith (1962) filled in many of the details of the remarkably intricate system of egg care in the Australian variety (mallee-fowl). In some species, the male alone carries out the task of incubating the eggs, while in others it is a cooperative male-female endeavor. Although there are variations, the general theme of the egg care is similar. In the case of the South Australia brush turkey, the male prepares a large volcano-shaped hole within its territory and fills it with decomposing plant materials and sand to form a type of compost mound a little more than 1 meter high and 5 meters wide. Spring rains then begin a fermentation process within the mound of rotting material. When the fermentation process has produced a temperature of 90 to 96° F inside the sand mound, the brush turkey opens up a specially prepared egg chamber and the female lays several eggs in the chamber over a period of a few months.

Once the eggs are inside of the mound, they must be incubated within a narrow temperature range, and the parent or parents must maintain that range. In this case, the male measures the heat in the egg chamber by running the sand through its beak and out the sides. On a daily basis thereafter, the brush turkey either opens up the chamber to reduce the heat or, as the internal heat decreases, the male spreads sand in the hot sun to warm and then covers the mound with it. Each day, then, from early spring until fall, the brush turkey must move large amounts of sand in the rather involved task of keeping the incubation temperature optimal. It is interesting to note that all of the complexity here is found in the care of the egg. The brush turkeys pay no attention to their young after hatching.

Why the Diversity?

If one system of parental care works, why is there a need for a variety of methods? The answer to this must, of course, be shaped in the context of an evolutionary framework. One looks to the adaptive significance of a particular behavioral system, to the ways in which the behavior increases the chances for survival and reproduction, and thus to an increase in the genetic transmission of that characteristic. As we see from observing the various types of animal species that exist today, there is more than one successful method for ensuring survival of the young. Indeed, one could hypothesize that multiple means have been necessary due to variation in structural or environmental conditions for the different animal types. For example, what works in water would not necessarily work on land. Or, young animals that have evolved structural protection against predators would not need the degree of parental protection that vulnerable offspring would need.

Comparative Plan

Denny and Ratner (1970) define an area of study as comparative when the subject matter has *diversity*. Since as pointed out earlier, there is considerable diversity in parent-offspring interaction in animals, a comparative approach to this area is appropriate. As Denny and Ratner indicate, however, diversity is not always easy to handle in terms of a manageable analysis. When there is a great deal of diversity, it is impossible to present it in total, particularly in the space of two short chapters. The solution to this problem lies in starting with the assumption that the present effort is primarily a discussion of representative examples of the parental behaviors of different animals, related at times to their adaptive significance.

PRENATAL COMPONENTS OF PARENTAL BEHAVIORS

With this class of behavior, our concern is to touch only those prenatal responses that are directly related to the future welfare of the offspring. Generally, there are two types of changes occurring in relation to an organism's immediate preparation for offspring. One of these involves changes in the physical environment as a result of the parents' activities while the second involves changes in the parents themselves.

Environmental Preparation: Factors in Environmental Selection

Preparations by parents could be construed to include not only changes made in the environment preceding the coming of the egg or offspring but also those parental responses that result in the selection of a particular environment for the development of the progeny.

Parasitic Life-Style

Environmental selection is particularly important in the life cycle of many parasitic animals in which an appropriate host must be available for the eggs or young to develop. One such case is the bumblebee eelworm in which the fertilized female seeks out a specific host, the queen bumblebee, which winters in the ground. The eelworm penetrates the queen's body, and the eggs and young develop there until the fall of the year when they leave the bee's body to start the cycle over again.

In this case, as in most when the eggs or offspring are parasitic during development, the outstanding benefit to the developing organism lies in the ever-present source of nutrition. In the evolutionary history of the eelworm, the body of the queen bumblebee was available and constituted a suitable environment for development. Those worms that survived well in this host were those that produced succeeding generations that were genetically encoded in the same way and thus inclined to seek out the same host. Eelworms that did not seek out the bumblebee host would probably not survive or reproduce, unless of course a different but appropriate host was found.

Another interesting example of an animal's selecting the appropriate environment for the development of eggs or young is found in the behavior of the various types of cuckoo birds. The best known of these birds is the European cuckoo whose eggs and young are parasitic. The cuckoos have evolved an effortless and effective system of parental care in which they provide care for their eggs and young by laying the eggs in the nest of other species of birds that incubate the eggs and care for the young after hatching. Once again, the critical parental behavior here is the appropriate selection of an incubator and rearing site for the eggs and young birds. Because many birds will get rid of the strange eggs or birds in their nest, a variety of methods of keeping their kind in the nest of the host bird have evolved in the parasitic species. Selecting an environment consists of selecting a nest that will allow the young to survive.

Brood parasitism of this type was described in the early writings of Aristotle (*History of Animals*) and has been studied extensively in more recent times (e.g., Altrum, 1868; Baker, 1942; Friedmann, 1960; Gloger, 1865). The behavior of the cuckoo bird represents a peculiar situation among evolutionary trends in which nest building and care of young were presumably lost from the species (Brown, 1975). Welty (1962) describes two hypotheses to account for the loss of these behaviors. One hypothesis postulates that the development of polygamous or promiscuous mating behavior brought about a loss of territory defense by the male, which resulted in the gradual loss of its nest-building behavior. The females then began to lay eggs in strange nests, and a variety of characteristics that made them successful at it gradually evolved.

In a second hypothesis, originally suggested by Herrick (1935), interruption or delay of the reproductive cycle upsets the temporal sequence of nestbuilding and egg laying so that there is no nest available when the eggs are ready. The birds thus lay their eggs in any available nest and selection pressures work on the choice of strange nests to produce an efficient brood parasite.

Efficiency in a brood parasite requires that several different factors be present in the system. First, the parasite must be able to discriminate between the host and non-host nest. Second, the parasite must lay her eggs at the right stage of incubation of the host species. Third, the female must be able to mimic the size, coloration, and marking pattern of the host species. Fourth, the parasite's eggs must have a shorter incubation period than that of the host bird's egg. Fifth, the nestlings of the parasite must mimic in some fashion the host nestlings. Sixth, an accelerated rate of development in the parasite relative to that of the host nestlings must be present. How do all of these factors go together to make an efficient parasite? By way of illustration, let us describe the behavior of the European cuckoo.

The cuckoo, according to Welty (1962), parasitizes over 125 species of birds in the following way. The female cuckoo seeks out and watches the host bird building a nest or laying eggs and this stimulus apparently triggers physiological responses that ripen the egg follicle. After 4 to 5 days, the cuckoo lays an egg in the hosts's nest and does it in the very short time of about 5 seconds while the host is normally away from the nest (between 2:00 and 6:00 P.M.) The female parasite usually proceeds to remove one of the host eggs from the nest after laying her own in it. Since many birds react by throwing out strange eggs, egg mimicry must be achieved by the cuckoo and is done so with amazing accuracy. In cases where the host bird is much smaller, as with the wren, the cuckoo does not match the eggs since the wren is not strong enough to throw out the parasitic eggs and must brood them. In either case, due to accelerated development, the cuckoo hatches earlier than the host's young giving it a head start in posthatching development. At 10 hours posthatch time, another remarkable behavioral phenomenon appears. The cuckoo chick, which is blind and naked, throws any solid objects, including the eggs and young of the host, out of the nest. The host bird will then continue to feed the parasite even though the nestling sometimes grows two or three times larger than the parent host bird. In some parasites, such as the widow bird, the feeding targets or gaping mouths of the parasite match those of the host nestling in color and marking to further insure feeding.

Predators and Physical Hazards

Environmental selection is the end of parental care for parasitic animals while it is only the beginning of a long sequence of responses for nonparasites. Here choice of an environment is directly concerned with increasing the probability of survival of the eggs and young. The location of the incubation or rearing site is based on a high level of protection against predators and environmental hazards. For example, the kittiwake, a species of gull, selects small cliff ledges along coastal regions as nest sites. Such sites, according to Alcock (1975), provide protection against large predator birds because they cannot maneuver into the tiny ledges with the tricky air currents normal to such coastal cliff regions. And land predators, such as badgers, are not able to climb the cliffs to reach the eggs or young. Thus, environmental selection has solved many of the problems of survival of the young faced by other species of gulls that nest on the ground near the sea.

Resource Availability

Environmental selection as a form of parental care can also be based on the availability of resources in the area. The developing butterfly, or caterpillar, for example, feeds on plants, and each species feeds on a specific kind of plant. Thus, the adult female must select the appropriate plant for egg laying or the young will starve.

Territory Establishment

In the case of some animals, environmental selection for incubation or rearing is related to the establishment of a territory by the male or by both the male and its mate. Therefore, not only a specific nest site but also the surrounding area is chosen and defended. Territorial selection has the advantage of reducing interference from other members of the species in nest building, egg laying, and rearing of the young. In addition, the nearby foraging area is kept exclusive, helping to insure adequate food supplies for the young.

Favorable Environmental Variables

Another special case of environmental selection is found among animals that return to the site of their own birth or hatching in order to nest or rear young. In every case, one finds some advantage to the birthsite, and this advantage increases the probability of survival for that species. The green sea turtle will travel more than a thousand miles to deposit its eggs in a relatively predator-free area protected from Atlantic storms (Carr, 1967). In like manner, the salmon traverses the open seas to reach the cold freshwater river in which it was hatched. Once there, the conditions of the water and riverbed are ideal for the eggs and young salmon. Similar breeding migrations are seen in mammals such as whales and seals. In all cases, however, the adaptive significance of such behavior is readily apparent. If a particular environment favors survival of the offspring resulting from absence of predators or the presence of optimal levels of such variables as temperature, then selection pressure can operate on the behavior that gets the parent to a particular geographical spot.

Environmental Preparation: Construction of Special Structures

Nests

Another type of parental care that typically precedes the coming of eggs or offspring includes the parents' reshaping the environment to form a special structure for incubation and rearing purposes. Although we usually associate this activity most strongly with birds, nest building is a common behavior in both terrestial and aquatic animals. When we examine the range of behavioral complexity associated with nest building, we are once again reminded of the diversity of animal behavior. At the high end of complexity can be cited the activity of the Australian brush turkey in building an incubation mound, as described earlier in this chapter. At the low end of the complexity continuum would be the nests, or redds, of fish such as trout and salmon. These redds are merely shallow depressions at the bottom of the stream that are covered with gravel or sand after the eggs are deposited. In between are a variety of activities and resultant nest structures that we illustrate with the following examples.

Excavated Nests. Excavations (deep holes or burrows constructed solely for nesting purposes) that exceed the shallow depressions of the fish mentioned above, constitute one general class of nest types. A common characteristic of hole-digging animals is the practice of laying eggs in the hole and leaving enough food for the young to develop and emerge as self-sufficient organisms. A beetle, variously known as a sacred scarab, a tumblebug, or a dung roller, exemplifies this practice. This animal, which played a significant role in ancient Egyptian religious beliefs as a symbol of the sungod Ra, has been observed for centuries rolling dung balls or pills across the earth. The Egyptians, according to Wendt (1965), believed that the beetle was rolling the balls across the whole earth from sunset to sunrise just as Ra rolled the sun across the sky. Actually, the tumblebug rolls the dung balls in preparation for stuffing them into shafts that they have prepared underground. An egg is then layed in each dung ball; and, after hatching, the young beetle feeds on the dung, eventually emerging as a complete adult.

Another remarkable nest preparation accomplished by digging a hole of sorts, is done by the carrion beetle or, as it is sometimes called the burying beetle. In this case, after a group of adult animals locates the body of a dead animal such as a mouse or mole, they excavate underneath the carcass so that the body slowly sinks into the ground as the sand or earth piles up along the perimeter. Once the body is buried, it is shaped into a sphere with the top hollowed out to form a nest, and the adult females lay their eggs in the nest. Here, the eggs hatch and the larvae continue to develop in a medium rich in food supply.

Along similar lines to the burying beetle, is the behavior of various kinds of wasps. The sand wasps are unique in that they bury live animals to provide food for their developing larvae. The spider wasp, for example, constructs an underground burrow, then captures spiders by paralyzing them with a sting; the spider is then buried alive in the burrow with a wasp egg and continues to live there and provide fresh food for the larvae.

For many animals, like the dung beetle, parental care ends with the burying of nourishment with the egg. In such cases, selection pressures could work on the burrowing behavior and on the collecting and storing enough food for the complete development of the young. That is, if these two tasks are not performed adequately by the parent, there is no chance for correction since the parent leaves and does not return to the nest. Given this state of affairs, it is obvious that inadequate performance would result in the loss of the individual young and thus the eventual discontinuance of that trait in future generations.

A somewhat more refined version of parental care involving the burial of eggs is that in which the nutrients necessary for development are contained within the egg structure itself. This refinement, of course, insures a consistent amount of food supply through a much more reliable manner in which physiological processes in the mother determine the amount and kind of food that is made available to the developing organism. In this situation, then, the parent need only find a suitable burying spot and nutrition will be provided.

Nest Enclosures: Birds. Most of us harbor a strong association between nests and birds because bird nests are the kind we typically encounter, especially in an urban environment. In addition, as Welty (1962) indicates, of all the nest builders, birds are by far the most industrious and expert at the task. The diversity of materials, forms, and sites of nests is far greater for birds than any other animal. In light of this, we will try to represent that variety with several examples of site, form, and materials. Welty cites protection from predators and bad weather as a primary function of the bird nest and states that protection is gained through *location, camouflage, inaccessibility* and/or *colony nesting*. Which of these advantages is used by a particular species is a function of a number of variables. For example, ground-dwelling birds with limited flying ability, like pheasants, tend to build highly camouflaged nests that are readily accessible, while birds that are primarily airborne tend to build exposed nests in such inaccessible places as trees, cliff faces, or on water. Other birds build nests that are not only exposed but accessible, but in this case nesting is communal and protection comes from the number of animals present.

Some idea of the variety of nest-building behaviors that have evolved can be gleaned from examination of a comprehensive bird nest guide. Headstrom (1961) classifies nests according to location, material, and form. Nests found on the ground, in fields, or pastures or woods, such as those of the lark bunting, prairie chicken, meadowlark, or ovenbird, are typically constructed of the materials of the surrounding area (grasses, weeds, bark, etc.) and are thus well concealed. Descriptions of many of these nests indicate that they are somewhat loosely constructed so that this quality adds to the inconspicuous nature of the nest.

Bird nests built in marshes are frequently made of reeds and other materials of the marshland as with the American bittern. In other cases, however, the "nest" is merely a hollow in a decayed tree or stump as in the case of the black vulture. With some marsh-nesting birds, we find a degree of inaccessibility incorporated into their nesting sites. Inaccessibility is achieved by the bittern by building its nest as a platform above the water on a foundation of bent cattails. In another instance, the grebe uses the advantage of the water and solves the problem of water by constructing a floating nest in the marsh. Among the marsh nests, one finds the whole range of construction techniques from the mere hollow in a pile of reeds (Forster's tern) to the beautifully constructed grass and down nest of the fulvous tree duck.

Birds nesting on seashores or beaches tend to utilize materials from both land and water sources. For example, the common eider uses seaweed, mosses, sticks, grass, and its own down to construct a nest. Many of these shore nests are easily detected, but accessibility and visibility are counteracted by the protection that accompanies the colony-nesting behavior of birds such as herring gulls and laughing gulls. With solitary seashore nesters such as the common loon or American oyster catcher, the nests are usually inconspicuous, being little more than slight hollows in the sand lined with bits of grass, pebbles, or shells.

Another form of ground nesting is seen in those birds that construct their nest sites *in* the ground. That is, these species dig burrows in the

soil or simply move into an abandoned burrow of a skunk, prairie dog, fox, or badger. Another bird, Leach's petrel, digs ratlike burrows on sea islands off the northeast coast of the United States. These burrows, 1 to 3 feet long are dug downward and then horizontally to end in a rounded chamber that is used as a colony nesting site. In similar manner, the bank swallow burrows into the side of a bank or mud cliff to establish a colony nest. Birds such as the eastern belted kingfisher or the rough-winged swallow construct solitary nests by burrowing into clay or sandy banks.

Because of their inaccessibility, nests above ground are a common means of predator defense and are found in a variety of places. Bushes and trees are, of course, the best-known sites, but nests are also found on cliff ledges, rocks, bridges, and other man-made structures. In contrast to the many loosely constructed nests of the ground-nesting birds, those above ground are usually architecturally sound and built or located so as to withstand strong winds and provide protection from the weather.

The differences between the nests of ground and aboveground nesting birds are reflections of different behaviors that have evolved in response to selection pressures. That is, in the case of the aboveground nesting birds, selection favored those genes that were related to construction skills. One example of the evolution of nest-building behavior to produce a sturdy nest is seen in the jackdaw. Lorenz (1969), describes the inexperienced jackdaw as a collector of many unsuitable materials for nesting. However, as the jackdaw gains experience in gathering and putting together material into the nest, it becomes more selective using only those objects that would produce a strong weather-resistant nest. How does the jackdaw learn about suitable nest materials? Apparently, the jackdaw pushes each piece of material into the nest and, if there is resistance, it pushes yet harder and shakes the object until it is firmly seated in the nest. If the object offers no resistance it is discarded. This discarding behavior then has developed as a result of an apparent aversion to nonresistant material. On the other hand, approach tendencies to resistant material further strengthen the behavior. Lorenz makes the point that both acceptance and rejection of materials are the result of physiological events in the nervous system and that natural selection pressures would be involved in these physiological events.

As we indicated earlier, birds are the masters of environmental preparation by way of nest building. However, other kinds of animals have evolved nest construction behaviors that have been equally successful in providing an adequate environment for the developing offspring.

Nest Enclosure: Reptiles.   Most reptiles like birds lay eggs and must provide a protective nest for them. Bellairs (1970) provides brief accounts of nesting of various reptiles. The American alligator, for instance, builds a rather complicated nest. The female clears a patch of ground about 2.4 meters by 3 meters long by biting off the vegetation. Next she gathers the broken plants into a pile with her jaws and body and hollows out the middle of this pile with her hind feet while revolving the rest of the body around the nest. This hole is filled with mud and more plant material. From 15 to 80 eggs are then laid in this chamber and covered with mud and more plant materials brought from the water in her mouth. The female smooths the nest with her body and crawls around it many times molding it into a smooth conelike hill almost a meter tall. Fermentation of the plants in the nest provide heat for incubation of the eggs. Other species of crocodile use the simpler method of burying their eggs in sand holes.

The green turtle, as has been discussed, makes great efforts to reach a particular beach for purposes of egglaying. Once there and mated, the female selects a spot about 46 meters in from the high-tide line and digs a pit in the sand large enough to accommodate her body. At one end of the pit the female uses her hind paddles to dig a flask-shaped hole to serve as an egg chamber. This done, the green turtle can then lay concealed in the pit while dropping about 100 eggs in the chamber. Following the egg laying, the turtle goes to some lengths to conceal the nest. First, she fills in the egg chamber using her hind paddles; next, using her front paddles, she fills the larger pit and thrashes about the area to hide the excavated spot. Then she abruptly leaves and returns to the sea, leaving the eggs to develop and the young to hatch on their own.

Bellairs (1970) states that reptiles such as oviparous lizards and snakes are hardly deserving of the name nest builders, for the majority of them provide only token care in this regard. That is, they lay eggs in semiprotected spots under stones and logs, in crevices, or in piles of decaying vegetation. The grass snake in England lays its eggs in a manure heap where the heat provides adequate incubation conditions, and some snakes and lizards make a body nest by coiling their body around the clutch of eggs. The female king cobra snake, according to Bellairs, is the only snake known to make a nest of vegetation by piling the material that she has dragged to the site by using a body coil like a hook. After an egg chamber has been made by revolving her coiled body in the vegetation, the female lays eggs, covers them, and then coils on top of the mound (Oliver, 1956).

Nest Enclosures: Fish.   Nest-building activities among fish that do provide some structure for egg care vary widely in complexity and form. Fish such as trout and salmon simply scoop out a hollow in the stream bottom, lay the eggs, and then cover them with gravel. According to Marshall (1966), a great variety of freshwater fish construct rather formal nests for egg-laying purposes. The mormyroid, an electric fish, constructs a floating nest made up of a saclike arrangement of grasses. Another variation on the nest concept is seen in fishes that construct bubblenests. The task of building these bubblenests falls to the male member of the breeding pair. As each bubble is blown, it is covered with a mucous secretion from the mouth and one bubble is then stuck to the next until thousands of these form a substantial nest. After enticing a female to lay her eggs in the nest area, the male fertilizes them, gathers them in his mouth, and spits them into the bubblenest, which he guards thereafter.

Perhaps one of the best known and accomplished nest builders among fish is the male three-spined stickleback. After establishing a territory for breeding, the male stickleback digs a shallow pit in the sand bottom using its mouth as a shovel. Next, it collects bits of weeds and algae, which are placed in the prepared pit to form a loose pile. The male then repeatedly swims across this pile while secreting a sticky kidney fluid to glue the nest pieces together. This done, it then burrows through the nest creating a tun-

nel effect. It is in this tunnel that the females are enticed to lay their eggs to be fertilized (Tinbergen, 1951).

Nest Enclosures: Insects.   Some of the most fascinating aspects of nest building in preparation for offspring can be seen among the social insects. In many cases, of course, the nests of social insects serve a greater social purpose than brooding alone. Nevertheless, the care of the eggs and larvae are normally given top priority in social colonies. One interesting example of a colony-living insect that engages in unusual nest construction is the weaver ant, found in southern Asia. Its nest is made of live tree leaves held together in an oval shape by a thick silken web. This nest-building activity was thoroughly described in the words of Von Frisch in Chapter 13. Refer to this passage and to Figure 17.1, which shows how the larva are used to bind the leaves together. Aside from being cited as an in-

Fig. 17.1.   Weaver ants using larvae (bottom) to spin silken web used in the repair of a torn nest. (From Von Frisch, 1974, p. 113. Copyright 1974 by Turid Hölldobler. Redrawn from *Animal Architecture*, copyright 1974 by Karl von Frisch and Otto von Frisch; translation copyright 1974 by Harcourt Brace Jovanovich, Inc., by permission of the publishers.)

Parenting: Prenatal Behaviors

stance of tool usage by insects, this is a rare example of a situation in which the offspring actually assist in the building and maintenance of their own brooding nest.

Another of the insects known for its architectural skills is the termite. The more than 2,000 species of termite build a vareity of nests or termitaries. These termitaries range in complexity from a system of irregular underground passages to the highly organized and structured systems rising many feet above the ground. In the highly organized termite society such as *Macrotermes carbonarius*, environmental preparation for care of the egg and/or offspring consists of the construction of a special "royal cell" for the queen and king together with a nursery area of smaller chambers that surround the cell. It is in these brood chambers that the worker termites provide care for the eggs and larvae of the queen.

Among the arthropods, the European water spider provides an example of a unique brood nest. Wendt (1965) describes the nest as consisting of two linked underwater diving bells that are airtight. Both male and female weave the web material into the airtight chamber and then the eggs are hung from its roof where they are tended by the parents. The unique requirement of such a nest relates to the fact that the water spider and its young are airbreathers living underwater. Von Frisch (1974) describes the manner in which the parents provide oxygen in this nest, which is anchored by threads to plant and branches underneath the water. The water spider repeatedly ascends to the surface, turns over on her back, wraps her hind legs around an air bubble, carries it back under the nest, and then releases it up into the bell-shaped structure.

Nest Enclosures: Amphibians. Next, we turn to a group of animals that are at least partially aquatic, the amphibians. Amphibians typically lay their eggs in water either singly or in clusters. Very little, if any environmental preparation takes place, since eggs are normally left free floating or attached to some existing structure such as a rock or plant. If laid on land, the usual sites are cavities in logs and trees or under stones and vegetation. There are some amphibians, such as the salamander known as the Neetings dwarf siren, that lay their egg clusters in an excavation at the bottom of a pond or in mud (Oliver, 1955).

There are, of course, even more diverse exceptions to the general absence of nest building by amphibians and several of these are described by Wendt (1965). Tree frogs in Africa and Southeast Asia, for example, discharge a viscous fluid onto a twig hanging over water. Male and female proceed to beat his substance into a foam into which sperm and eggs are discharged. The first strong rain then washes the foam and tadpoles into the water below. Also, the maki frog makes a tree nest above water. In this case however, the male and female shape and glue a leaf into a funnel, which is filled with eggs and sperm.

An even more complex nest is constructed by the South American blacksmith frog as described by Frazer (1973). In order to isolate the eggs and tadpoles, the blacksmith frog builds a small brooding pond at the edge of a larger pool. This is accomplsihed by the male who carries mud from the bottom and molds a wall with its forelegs to enclose a small pool of water. The female then lays her eggs within this wall. Finally, a rather peculiar method of brood nesting is seen in the Surinam toad. This particular mode of providing a nest might better be discussed as a body change in parental care. Nevertheless, it still constitutes an environmental preparation of a nesting site. In this case, the male toad smears the fertilized eggs on the back of the female where a mobile nest is created by the growth of a layer of skin over the eggs. As the young toads become fully formed in 11 to 12 weeks, they "hatch" from these brood chambers on the mother's back.

Nest Enclosures: Infraprimate Mammals. In conclusion we look at some of the environmental preparations that take place among the various mammalian species below the primate level. The range of preparations among the mammals is extensive going from no preparation to building a complicated structure. However, as von Frisch (1974) indicated, nest building is not as important or widespread in mammals as it is in animals such as birds. He attributes this difference to the fact that the initial physical tie is stronger between mammalian parents and their offspring than birds. That is, since mammalians suckle their young and provide warmth, they have less need to leave the offspring alone to hunt food, and, thus generally have less need of a protective structure such as a nest. There are, however, some mammals that do make special environmental changes in preparation for the coming offspring, and we will look at examples of these.

A simple nest is constructed by some moles. These animals normally inhabit subterranean quarters made by burrowing into the gorund. As breeding time approaches, the female mole hollows out a special chamber in which she will give birth and rear the young. In addition to being set aside from the usual living and foraging burrows, the nursery chamber is lined with soft nesting materials.

Among the mammals, the rodents are one of the most extensive nest builders. The rodents, however, tend to live as adults in these nesting areas and care for their young there only incidentally. Our interest here is limited to those cases where the animals restructure the environment specifically for the purpose of providing a place to have and rear offspring. One particularly interesting example of this is cited by von Frisch (1974) in the case of the European harvest mouse. The female harvest mouse constructs a breeding nest that rivals some of the best constructed bird nests in form and durability. This rodent lives among cereal plants, long grasses, or reeds and builds a nest between ½ and 1 meter above ground on the stems of these plants. The small size of the harvest mouse (6 to 7 centimeters long) allows it to climb about on the stems or blades of the plants. It constructs the nest by shredding with its teeth the leaves or blades of a group of stems standing in close physical proximity. These shredded pieces are then woven together to form a base for the walls of the nest, which are built up with more shredded material. Finally, a domed roof is added and the inside of the nest is lined with seed down, flower petals, and shredded leaves. In some respects, the resultant globular nests of the harvest mouse resemble those of some birds nesting in marsh areas and building their nests among reeds and above the water.

Another rodent, the weed rat, makes special preparations for the young by including a nursery chamber among the multichambered nest of twigs built among thick undergrowth. The familiar sight of large nests of twigs and other plant materials high in the tops of trees can usually be attributed to another rodent, the squirrel. Actually, a squirrel may have several refuge nests within its territorial boundaries and one large "main" nest. The main nest or dray is conical in shape and better constructed than the rest. The squirrel may build the dray from scratch or simply take over a large bird nest, build up the sides, and add a roof. It is true that these nests serve as the usual living quarters of adults. However, just before the young are born, the female turns the dray into a nursery chamber by driving away the male and using it exclusively for the rearing of her offspring until they are weaned.

Environmental preparation for the young by members of the dog family is limited. Wolves and coyotes, for example, prepare a den just prior to the birth of the young. This den, however, is simply an enlarged burrow of a rabbit, squirrel, or badger (Orr, 1970.)

The largest of the carnivores, the bears, show relatively little special effort in preparation for the young. Among the bears, this behavior involves seeking out a den for winter hibernation and having the cubs in this winter den or cave.

The female polar bear does construct a special chamber where birth takes place (Wendt, 1965). She does this by digging into a snowbank and forming a bifurcated tunnel. One of these tunnel arms leads to a separate chamber in which she eventually gives birth. The walls of the tunnels and chambers are partially melted by her breath so that they refreeze and form a solid barrier against cold and drafts.

Nest Enclosures: Primate Mammals.   Carpenter (1964) states that the complex development of the nonhuman anthropoid brain, did not result in skills involved with building of shelters, dens or nests. Although we do find crude nests made by chimpanzees, orangutans, and gorillas, they are strictly to provide support for the builder and not related to rearing of the offspring.

The human primate shows one of the most extensive and complex systems of nestbuilding among the animals. Humans act in a cooperative manner to prepare environmental conditions for the birth and rearing of offspring. As a result, the parents usually need only to acquire the environmental preparations and not actually make them themselves. To begin, the human female usually goes to a special structure known as a hospital in order to give birth to her young. This structure has been built by other members of the species and space is shared with other females. The hospital is primarily intended to house sick members of the species; but, for some strange reason, women choose to have their babies there also. Therefore, we find that special chambers in this structure have been isolated for the birth and early care of the young. These preparations are actually carried out by the species, and the individual exchanges goods or labor for the use of the structure.

A similar exchange also takes place in the preparation of the long-term rearing site of the human offspring, called a home. There is extensive individual variability in the type and degree of special preparation that goes on prior to the birth of the human baby. Since most humans live in some kind of protective structure, the newborn is incorporated into that structure in one way or another. Some homes are single-chamber structures, and there is little preparation except to provide a special sleeping place for the young. Since human children stay with parents for long periods, this special sleeping spot, or bed, may be shared with older offspring.

In other homes, a multichambered design is found with the chambers separated according to function. In this case, we usually find the children isolated from the parents' sleeping quarters. Preparation of this special chamber normally begins long before the birth of the child, starting with the fixing of some kind of brightly colored substance to the walls of the chamber. This wall-covering might be a solid color or a repeated pattern usually showing pictures of other animals or human figures. Also, a soft, tightly knit cover may be placed on the floor or some part of it.

In addition, specially constructed objects will be gathered and brought into the sleeping chamber. First, a sleeping nest, known as a crib, provides protection from drafts and cold and a certain degree of softness and comfort. It is also a restraining device to keep the baby from falling or getting out of the nest while the parents are sleeping or away. Usually, we find objects attached to the edges of the crib or hanging over its center. The purpose of these objects is to provide visual or auditory stimulation for the young human. After 2 to 4 years, this crib is replaced by a larger sleeping nest which allows the more developed offspring freedom to enter or leave at anytime.

One might also find a special device for grooming and cleaning the human baby (a bassinet) and another article constructed to hold the parent in a sitting position and provide a rocking motion while feeding the baby.

Other environmental preparations might include special body coverings for the child and an assortment of objects for the child to manipulate, which typically provide auditory or moving visual stimuli when manipulated. As the human child matures, the objects and coverings are periodically changed to fit the developmental stage of the organism. When the young reach maturity, they either leave or are expelled from the nest at which time the parents may turn it over to a younger adult pair and environmental preparation of the nursery chamber begins anew.

Comparisons

In sifting through the range of examples of environmental preparations for approaching offspring, we become aware of pivotal questions. What are the reasons for this broad range of behaviors among the different types of organisms? That is, what factors are important in determining if a particular form of environmental preparation evolves, if any does at all? Several factors stand out as being related to the type and level of preparation. This does not imply, however, that there is necessarily a cause-and-effect relationship.

For example, nest constructions seem to be related to the amount of care that must be provided by the parent or parents or perhaps, more correctly, the degree of helplessness of the young. As a general rule among the animals that were considered, it seems as though the greater the amount of parental care needed for either eggs or young, the greater and more elaborate the nest building activity.

This is not, however, a simple relationship, but one dependent on interactions with other variables. That is, the bulk of parental care involves supplying nutritional needs and protection; and when the food supply can be left with the developing organism in a protected place, the nest tends to be simple, like the burrows of the dung beetle. When parents must forage for food for the young and leave them for periods of time, the nest design must be more elaborate in terms of keeping the young animals in the nest and

keeping the nest inaccessible to predators. This inaccessibility, of course, is provided by choice of location or camouflage.

In many mammals, where the food supply is self-contained in the female and the young are mobile shortly after birth, there is an absence of nest-building behavior. Or, in animals that have appropriate appendages and modes of locomotion, the female simply carries the young with her and there is no need for a nest. The marsupials and a number of primates are good examples of the latter.

There also appears to be a relationship of sorts between nest building and number of offspring or eggs produced. That is, where large numbers of progeny or eggs are produced, survival is based on probability and not parental care, which would demand a nest (as elaborated in Chapter 2). For example, most birds lay only a relatively few eggs, but provide in some way for protective nests while other animals such as the female Woodhouse's toad produce more than 25,000 eggs, most of which perish.

An overall view of the factors involved in nest building might be gained from considering the succession of changes in the evolution of nests. Makatsch (1950) proposes such a description of bird nest evolution as follows. The earliest nests consisted of depressions scraped or scratched from the ground. This was probably followed by a depression with vegetation. Turning movements of the incubating birds next molded the vegetation into a shallow cup, built up the walls, and produced a deep nest. The deep nest was next covered to provide a roof. As construction skills improved, the nests could be built in more precarious places such as trees and ledges or even suspended as hangnests.

Perhaps, in general, one could postulate a similar biological evolution of nest building, from the simpler depressions to the more complex construction. One could then hypothesize that the different degrees of sophistication of nest building result from different degrees of need dictated by selection pressures. That is, the nest for a particular species evolved as far as necessary to insure survival of the offspring and stopped there. Where it stopped depended possibly on such variables as the kind of parental care, the kind and number of predators, the kind of food required, and the number of offspring needed to insure the species' survival.

Physiological Changes

Here, we are interested only in those physiological changes that function in some way to contribute to the care of the eggs or offspring. Most of these are hormonal changes related to nest preparation or the provision of food for the young. Many of the cases of environmental preparation discussed earlier were initiated by hormonal factors, and we now examine some of the hormonal changes involved and how these hormonal changes interact to produce parental behaviors.

Hormonal Influence: Egg Production and Breeding

Evidence relating hormonal effects to parental behavior is abundant for birds and mammals, and our discussion is mainly drawn from these sources. An excellent illustration of the effects comes from the work of Hinde and his colleagues in their studies of domestic canaries (Hinde, Bell, and Steel, 1963; Hinde and Steel, 1964 (see the following summarized study); Steel and Hinde, 1964).

Just prior to egg laying, the female canary develops a brood patch; that is, the ventral surface of her body loses its feathers and becomes highly vascular and swollen. This brood patch is important for the transfer of heat during incubation and may serve as the site of stimulation by the nest cup to produce further reproductive behaviors. For this reason, the brood patch becomes more sensitive to tactile stimulation as the reproductive season advances.

The authors of this experiment hypothesized that this increased tactile sensitivity is a function of hormones and designed the study to assess the effects of three hormones, estrogen, progesterone, and prolactin, on tactile sensitivity. To do this, they injected canaries with a large (0.3 milligram) or small (0.05 milligram) dose of estrogen alone, progesterone alone, or prolactin alone, or in all possible combinations with each other. Tactile sensitivity was measured on the 4 days prior to injection to establish a threshold for the birds. This testing was done by using nylon filaments of various diameters to touch the breast of the canary. When a canary responded by moving its legs reliably, its threshold of sensitivity was established at that diameter. The smaller the diameter needed to elicit a response, the greater the tactile sensitivity. Then the same measurements were taken following the start of thrice-weekly injections of the hormones.

The results indicated that tactile sensitivity is increased by a low dosage of estrogen alone or in combination with prolactin. Thus, this particular influence of hormonal factors in the complex interaction of behavior, physiology, and environment was established.

Tinbergen (1965) has summarized the complex control system that coordinates changes in the canary so that appropriate behaviors occur at the appropriate time. This sequence involves eight steps, leading to successful parental care by the canary:

1. With longer springtime days, the sex glands are stimulated to produce hormones: androgen in the male and estrogen in the female.
2. The production of androgen in the male initiates courtship behaviors that increase the outpouring of estrogen in the female.
3. The continued stimulation by the male initiates the collection of nesting materials by the female and, at the same time, her eggs begin a rapid increase in size within the ovary.

4. The estrogen and secondary hormones (pro-lactin, androgen, and progesterone) cause the feathers to shed from the female's breast to form the sensitive brood patch. The contact of the brood patch with the nesting material serves as a further stimulus for nest building.

5. When nearing completion of the nest, the female behaviorally signals her readiness for copulation and completes the act several times prior to laying the first egg.

6. The continued stimulation from the nest cup results in the production of more estrogen and secondary hormones which enlarge the oviduct in preparation for egg-laying. At this time, the blood vessels in the skin enlarge and the brood patch becomes a bright red spot.

7. In the final stage of nest building, the female responds to the increased sensitivity of the brood patch and lines the nest with feathers. The stimulation of the soft nest, together with the various hormones now in the system, brings about ovulation at this time.

8. The female lays one egg a day for several days, and the stimulus due to contact of the eggs with the brood patch results in her incubating the eggs most of the time until hatching. The case of the canary shows the extensive involvement of hormonal factors in preparatory behaviors such as nest building and incubation.

Hormonal Influence: Nest Building

The effects of hormones on the nest-building behavior of rabbits have been studied extensively and are summarized by Zarrow, Denenberg, and Sachs (1972). Rabbits build nests of straw at any time in the reproductive cycle; but Zarrow et al. (1972) report that pregnancy initiates the building of what they have called the "maternal nest," which differs from the other nests in that it is lined with hair from the mother's body. A series of studies by Zarrow and others (Levine, 1972) determined the effects of hormones on the building of maternal nests either by removing the hormone-producing organs from the rabbit or by injecting hormones into nonpregnant females. From the results of these experiments, we know that maternal nest building requires the presence of two female sex hormones, estradiol and progesterone, and that a limited time exposure to these substances is necessary or else the progesterone will serve to inhibit maternal nest building. There is also an interesting relation between hormones and the female rabbit's use of rabbit hair to line the maternal nest. [Rabbit hair, as shown by Zarrow (1963), promotes survival of the young; only 5.7 percent of the young reared without hair in the nest survived while 87 percent reared with hair survived to weaning. Farooq et al. (1963) have demonstrated that the loosening of the female's hair so that she can pull it out, which normally occurs near the end of pregnancy, can be induced in ovariectomized females by injecting estradiol, progesterone, and prolactin for a period of 8 weeks.

Parenting in certain fishes also appears to be under hormonal influence. Smith and Hoar (1967), injected testosterone into castrated male stickleback fish and found that low doses initiated the early nesting behavior of sand digging. Also, Cohen (cited in Beach, 1961) found both nest building and the production of mucous materials used in nest building to be under the influence of gonadal hormones in some fish species.

Hormonal Influence: Feeding of Young

Rather spectacular physiological changes occur in certain animals preparatory to food production for their offspring after birth. Many animals simply go out in search of food for their young, but a significant number produce food within the body, reducing time away from the young and insuring food suplies close at hand.

The male and female ringdove feed their young in a manner which makes them somewhat unique among other birds (Hinde, 1970). These birds produce a specific food for their young out of the epithelial cells of the *crop* (a pouchlike enlargement of the gullet). This food, known as "crop milk," results from the enlargement of the crop and the subsequent peeling off of the epithelial layer of that organ. The enlargement of the crop precedes the hatching of the young and, according to Lehrman (1955), is stimulated in part by the hormone prolactin. Friedman (1966) later found that full development of the crop results from prolactin and stimulation from the act of incubating, plus stimulation from the mate. Lott and Comerford (1968) found yet another hormone, progesterone, to be involved in the feeding sequence. Inexperienced doves required injections of both prolactin and progesterone before any of them would complete the regurgitation-feeding response. Again, as with the canary, there is a complex interaction of hormoral output and environmental input that produces an efficient system of parenting.

One of the unique features of the mammal is the production of food for the young in the mammary glands. The presence of such food is the result of hormonal secretions and, in some cases, external stimulation. In the rabbit, for example, lactation (milk secretion) can be produced simply by injecting of estradiol, progesterone and prolactin into either castrated females or males (Ross *et al*, 1963).

There have been a number of studies in the past 40 years that attempted to delineate the effects of hormones and other factors on early maternal behavior in the female rat. Although initiation of lactation in the rat is brought about through the secretion of prolactin (Altman, 1966), other factors are apparently involved in the physiological changes that occur in preparation for providing an adequate milk supply. For example, self-licking of the nipples by the pregnant female rat is necessary for the full development of functional mammary tissue (Roth and Rosenblatt, 1967). Self-licking in turn is apparently activated by an increased need for salt during pregnancy (Barelare and Richter, 1938) and as elaborated as follows by Steinberg and Bindra (1962) and Roth and Rosenblatt (1967).

Genital licking has been observed frequently in rats, and this study attempted to determine the effects of pregnancy on this licking. Pregnant and nonpregnant females and males were observed twice a day for 30 minute periods on several consecutive days. As expected, there was significantly more genital licking in pregnant females than in either of the other two groups.

The hypothesis was also tested that there is a salt deficiency during pregnancy and that salt is obtained by genital licking. A 1.5 percent salt solution was made available to some of the animals in each groups. They found that salt availability decreased genital licking in the pregnant rats and that these females drank more of the salt solution than did the nonpregnant females or males.

The study by Roth & Rosenblatt was undertaken in an effort to understand the relationship of self-licking to parturitive and maternal behaviors. Self-licking was observed in both pregnant and nonpregnant female rats for 30 minutes a day during the pregnancy term of the mated rats.

These observations revealed two notable changes in self-licking during pregnancy. The first change involved a redistribution of self-licking times as pregnancy advanced. There was a shift in concentration of time spent licking certain areas so that critical regions were licked more and noncritical regions less. Critical regions were defined as those areas showing gestational changes, that is, the nipple lines, the genitals, and the pelvis. A second related finding indicated that the change in duration of licking the various regions was probably due to a change in the pattern of licking. The pregnant females departed from the usual pattern of licking the body in an anterior to posterior direction and went directly to the critical regions when licking.

In summary, we see that prenatal changes and responses are frequently a necessary component of a parental care system and that selection presssures can work just as easily on these factors as on those related to the postnatal care discussed in the next chapter.

Study Questions

1. Develop a detailed explanation for the fact that the Australian brush turkey does not incubate eggs in the same manner as most birds.

2. How does the European cuckoo select the appropriate nest in which to lay her eggs?

3. Discuss the evolution of egg mimicry by cuckoo birds.

4. What is one possible explanation for the widespread use of the brooding nest by birds as compared to mammals?

5. Frequently, we hear of pregnant women who seem to have a burst of activity just prior to delivery of their baby. Some refer to this behavior as a function of "maternal instinct." After defining instinct, defend or refute this idea.

6. What factors seem to be important in the success of a reproductive system that does not include parental care?

18

Parenting: Postnatal Behaviors

Louis E. Gardner

Creighton University

With some animals, prenatal preparations mark the end of the species' collective responsibility of caring for the
offspring. For a great number, however, there are
at least equally demanding tasks that follow the
birth or hatching of the young.[1] In this chapter,
we attempt to bring together a representative
sample of postnatal parental behaviors in order
to gain a comparative perspective. In doing so,
we consider parental behaviors ranging from
those involved in the birth process to those involved in the driving away or even destroying the
offspring.

Special Equipment for Parents

Before considering the parental responses specific to the care of offspring, we will describe
different ways in which special equipment for use
in parental activities have evolved. This equipment can be in the form of body colors, body
structures, or body configurations.

---

[1] The division of Gardner's two chapters on parenting into
prenatal and postnatal behaviors is admittedly arbitrary, and
the distinction can be difficult to maintain for egg-laying animals. Care of the egg is sometimes included in this chapter.

Color Markings

Color as a component of parental activity is
involved in different ways. One way is that a
color or spot of color may elicit feeding responses from either the parent or the offspring. This
situation occurs with the feeding responses of the
nesting herring gull (Tinbergen and Perdeck,
1950) in which a red spot on the parent's lower
bill elicits pecking from the young gulls. This
pecking acts as a stimulus for the parent to
regurgiate food, which is then eaten by the
young. In other birds, coloration or spots of
color in or around the mouth of the young serve
as releasing stimuli for the parental response. For
example, Tinbergen (1965) describes the open
mouth of the young parrot finch as having four
brightly colored blue spots on the mandibles,
which stimulte the parents to feed them.

Camouflage

Another use of color involves special coloration
or camouflage in the parent. Alcock (1975) refers
to hiding from one's enemies as the most common survival strategy and that hiding is generally achieved through coloration. We find that
same to be true in protecting the young. That is,

the parents of young animals that are highly subject to predation are often of a color pattern that blends with the surrounding environment. Since movement attracts predators, the surest means of survival for the parent and the young or eggs is for the parent to remain immobile and to cover or hide them with its body.

It is easy to understand how bright visible colors are selected against in many parents that care for the young. Two contrasting examples of this can be seen in the case of the cardinal and the common house sparrow. Recall the striking difference between the male and female cardinal, the male being a brilliant red and the female a very muted red, almost brown. The house sparrows, on the other hand, are almost indistinguishable by sex in their brown, dull coloration. In the first case, we say that the cardinals are dimorphic in coloration while the sparrows are monomorphic. Why this difference? At least part of the answer would seem to be natural selection; since both the male and female sparrow care for the young, it is adaptive for them to blend into the nest area. The male cardinal, however, does not normally feed and care for the young, and so its bright color could be selected for as a courtship simulus.

Color Patterns

Another way in which coloration acts as a protective device is within the young or eggs themselves. Many animals from insects to mammals are so colored or patterned during their juvenile stage of development that they are inconspicuous. In some cases, color and pattern combine to blend the young organism into its environment, as with young pheasants or deer. Others use color and pattern to mimic something unattractive to predators. An example of the latter is seen with the larvae of a swallow-tail butterfly, which looks like a bird dropping when resting on a leaf (Alcock 1975).

Feeding structures

Some more commonly known structures used in caring for offspring have already been alluded to in reference to the breasts, nipples, teats, and udders of mammals. In addition, special structures along with the feeding apparatus have evolved in some marsupials. Kangaroos deliver their young in such an undeveloped state (2 to 4 weeks after conception) that it would be considered a miscarriage for a placental animal such as a human. To help insure survival of the young, the female kangaroo has a pouch covering her teats and the newborn kangaroo travels there by wiggling along a path that the mother has licked into her fur. After doing so, the embryolike young search out a nipple, attach themselves, and remain in the pouch until they are mobile (Burton, 1950). Another interesting example of a special structure for parental care has been described by Wendt (1965). The octopus, *Argonauta argo*, secretes a substance from two of its arms to produce a silvery, paper-thin shell that is shaped into a cradle of sorts. This shell is held by the female in two arms and the young are pushed around the sea in it. This structure allows the female to keep the young enclosed while she forages for food to feed them.

Shape

Body configuration, like body color, can also be a factor in predator defense since certain configuration tend to hide an animal. Besides, configuration plays a further role in the parent-offspring relations of certain animals. In more than one instance, the configuration of the body and head of the parent serves as a specific stimulus to elicit care-seeking responses. The nestling thrush, for example, will gape for food toward a stimulus that has the appropriate size relationship between the head and body (Tinbergen, 1965); and young fish of the mouthbreeding *Tilpia mosambica* direct their approach responses to the female as a function of the configuration of the mother's face (Baerends, 1957).

In other species, the physical characteristics of the young elicit appropriate responses in the parent. In the fish, *Haplochromis wingatii*, the young fish must display horizontal stripes or the female parent will attack them rather than care for them (Albrecht, 1966). In fact, Lorenz, (1943) suggests that there is evidence that the configuration of the human baby's head (short face, prominent forehead, round eyes, plump cheeks) arouses parental responses and positive feelings in adults (see Figure 5.2, p. 67). Hall *et al.* (1977), in an extensive investigation, claim that their results support Lorenz's hypothesis.

Postnatal Parental Behaviors

Placentaphagia

Altman (1966) refers to the tendency to lick the young and eat the placenta, membranes, and umbilical cord as the first manifestation of nurturing behavior in some placental mammals. The behavior of eating the tissues remaining after birth is called *placentaphagia* and is not characteristic of all placental animals, but it does appear to be prevalant among those placental organisms that remain in some type of confinement with their young. Slijper (cited in Zarrow, Denenberg, and Sachs, 1972) offers several possible adaptation interpretations of placentaphagia. One hypothesis, without strong support according to Zarrow et al. (1972), holds that placental hormones act as a catalyst for further behavior. Other adaptive functions include the eating of the placenta as a hygienic measure to prevent disease or to prevent the placenta from serving as an attractant to predators. Both of these latter functions seem plausible in light of Fraser's (1968) observation that ungulates that eat the placenta are those that remain in some sort of nesting situation with their young and in light of Wendt's (1965) observation that aquatic placen-

tals do not eat the placenta but simply let it float away.

Licking, Cleaning, and Grooming

Cleaning the Young.   Licking of the young soon after delivery is illustrated by the rat. As soon as the rat pup is free of membranes, the mother (dam) begins to lick the head, body, and limbs of the pup, eventually concentrating her efforts on the anogenital region. These activities have the hygenic value of cleansing the young and at the same time stimulate the elimination processes for the young (Rosenblatt and Lehrman, 1963). A review of the maternal behavior of a variety of other mammals (mice, dogs, cats, sheep, langurs) indicates that this licking of the young is a widespread practice among mammals (Rheingold, 1963).

If one looks for analogous behaviors among lower animals, one finds some similarities. For example, a female cricket (Anurogryllus muticus) picks up her young and manipulates them in her mouthparts shortly after hatching (West and Alexander, 1963). Although no adaptive function has been offered for this behavior, it could function as generalized stimulation to arouse the young cricket.

Cleaning Nests.   Licking and cleaning of the young seem to be relatively rare except in the case of the mammals, but other kinds of cleaning as a part of the parental response are more common. That is, a variety of animal parents keep the nesting or brooding area free of contaminants and predator-attracting objects. One example of this is seen in passerine nesting birds that will not tolerate any foreign objects in their nest and will immediately throw any such objects out of the nest. As a result, the nests are kept clean of any fecal material of the young. Some parent birds eat the fecal material extracting any indigested materials to provide nourishment that they are often too busy to obtain for themselves

(Welty, 1965). Other young birds pass fecal material in a membranous sac and the parent bird is able to carry this away from the nest for disposal.

In the same way that the birth membranes and placenta can serve as cues for predators, the eggshells of birds can attract enemies. Therefore, many species of birds either eat the shells or carry them away from the nest area. It is interesting that some birds have such a strong tendency to throw out foreign objects that they do so even if their young are attached to them. According to Welty (1962), this is seen frequently when young have been banded for study. When the bands are ejected, out go the young.

Cleaning of the nest can be also observed in some insects. The female burrowing cricket seals herself into the brood chamber with her young. Being sealed in, she must defecate in a special chamber at the lower end of the tunnel. After filling that part of the burrow, she opens the burrow and carries out the fecal pellets

We have not as yet mentioned the parental cleaning responses of the human; but like other mammals that have a placenta, the human shows vigorous cleaning behaviors soon after birth and to a lesser extent thereafter. The initial cleaning is usually done by someone other than the mother, and tools of a sort have been substituted for a licking tongue. That is, a cloth dipped in warm water and a cleansing substance are normally used to clean away the fluids left from the birth process. The washing activity is continued on a schedule that is highly variable among parents, although many do it on a daily basis over the first 3 to 5 years. Also, the nest area of the human infant is usually kept very clean and hygenic. Products of elimination are not normally tolerated in the nest. Instead, the products are caught in a special cloth wrapping called a diaper, which is either washed or thrown away when soiled. Gradually, the human parent attempts to shift the responsibility of keeping the body and nest clean over to the offspring who normally resist this shift.

Retention and Retrieval of Young

One of the primary requisites of success in offspring care is to keep the offspring within the parents' jurisdiction. For those parents giving care, a variety of methods have evolved to ensure proximity of the young. One of the most obvious means is nest construction. In some nests, the young organism is in absolute confinement until it has developed beyond the stage of complete helplessness. This is the case with larvae of insects that are buried, with many birds, with some amphibians, and with humans. Even when the young are able to leave the immediate nest site, they are frequently not ready to be on their own and the parents must physically retrieve them.

Carrying. In its simplest form, retrieval involves picking the young organism up and carrying it back to the nest. Rosenblatt and Lehrman (1963) indicate that retrieval behavior in the female rat begins at the birth of her young and declines between the twelfth and sixteenth day after parturition. Also, the dam is not too discriminating at first in terms of objects retrieved, but is selective in choosing her own young pups after about a week. Apparently, maternal retrieval responses in rats are associated with lactation since lactating females retrieve more often and faster then males, virgin females, or pregnant females and since they are the only group able to discriminate between the retrieval of pups and inanimate objects.

Another example is the physical retrieval of eggs that have fallen from the bubble nests of anabantoid fishes. In this case, the male fish catches the egg in its mouth as it falls through the water and spits it back into the bubble nest.

Signals. A different form of retrieval is seen with animals that use some type of signal, resulting in the voluntary return of the young to the nest or parent. Harlow, Harlow and Hansen (1963) described two retrieval mechanisms used by rhesus moneky females in bringing back infants that have moved out of reach. One, a facial signal, they have dubbed the "silly grin response," the second retrieving signal observed was identical to the sexual presentation posture of the female rhesus. In both cases, these signals were frequently successful in bringing about the immediate return of the infant monkey.

A type of variation on retrieval is illustrated in the case of mouth breeding cichlid fish (Marshall, 1966). After hatching and for the next 4 to 5 days, the female fish shelters the young in her mouth at the sign of any trouble in the environment. When there is a disturbance, the female "calls" the young fish to her mouth by making backing movements.

Auditory as well as visual signals can be used to keep the young nearby. Many *precocial* birds (those having young that are mobile and able to follow parents shortly after hatching) emit an auditory signal that attracts the young and keeps the hatchling oriented to the parent (Armstrong, 1973). This calling behavior is useful in ground-living birds that must search over large areas for food since it allows the parent to forage visually keeping the chicks on an "auditory string."

Imprinting. Another mechanism that serves to keep parent and young together is an innate tendency called *imprinting*. This phenomenon is particularly noticeable among *nidifugous* birds (able to leave nest soon after hatching) that follow their parent or parents very closely. Hess (1973) defines imprinting as "a type of process in which there is an extremely rapid attachment, during a specific critical period, of an innate behavior pattern to specific objects which thereafter become important elicitors of that behavior pattern." The imprinting process appears to involve more than just the parent-offspring interaction and has long-term effects on the animal's relationship with its species in regard to recognition and reproduction. However, part of the process of attachment in birds such as ducks and chickens involves an inborn tendency to follow the first moving object encountered during a critical period after hatching. Usually this is the mother. Hess points out that not all following by the young constitutes imprinting and that all imprinting does not require following. Nevertheless, the following response, regardless of its relation to imprinting, serves to keep the young in physical proximity of the parent without the expenditure of effort on the part of the parent.

Tendencies toward responses that keep the young closeby are not restricted to birds nor are the eliciting stimuli restricted to the visual. Zippelius (1972) describes olfactory imprinting in the European shrew. The 8 to 14 day-old shrew is imprinted on the odor of the mother who can thereafter stimulate the young to form a line by each holding onto the fur of the one in front of it or onto the mother. With the mother leading, they move from place to place in this tandem arrangement. Ramsay and Hess (1954) demonstrated that auditory signals were effective in evoking the following response in mallard ducklings. A number of studies (cited in Hess, 1973) have demonstrated following tendencies in young guinea pigs; however, since the following of guinea pigs is only temporary, it may not be an instance of true imprinting. Even so, this simple following response of the guinea pig might still function on a short-term basis to keep the young close to the parent.

Among insects, one of the few instances of maternal retrieval and/or retention that does not involve physical confinement is seen in the behavior of a lace bug, *Gargaphia solani*. The female and her young migrate from leaf to leaf for feeding purposes and the mother keeps the nymphs close to herself and retrieves any stragglers by touching them with her long antennae. (Fink, cited in Wilson, 1971).

In human child rearing, the newborn infant is not very mobile and is thus physically confined by the environment. As development proceeds, however, the child wanders away from home and parent. At first, the child usually does not respond to signals in any modality and must be physically retrieved. In time, auditory and visual signals acquire meaning and the parents often retrieve the young without leaving the home. In addition humans have developed instruments of communication that make retrieval possible over long distances. These instruments are called telephones.

Supplying Physiological Needs.

As we saw earlier, some parents provide no care for young while others are occupied with the task for years. This, of course, also applies to providing for the physiological requirements of the young. We will consider several: *nourishment*, *oxygen*, and *temperature regulation*.

Feeding. Nourishment of the young is obviously one of the most important aspects of parental care. We have already seen how some organisms provide for the feeding of the young and then leave, never to return. This is typically accomplished by leaving food near the young or eggs or by depositing the young or eggs themselves in the source of food. We turn our attention now to parents more immediately involved in feeding the young and some of the diverse ways in which this is accomplished.

One of the most efficient forms of feeding that has evolved is the one in which the parent manufactures the food in the body, as has been well-developed in mammals and some birds. However, this mechanism of providing food is not limited to mammals and birds. According to West and Alexander (1963), the burrowing cricket female lays miniature eggs that are immediately eaten by the cricket nymphs. And social insects such as honeybees and ants feed their young with food manufactured in the body (Wilson, 1971). Worker bees produce a high-protein food called "royal jelly" and this is fed to the larvae. Ant workers feed the larvae various manu-

factured substances depending on the species. For some, the food consists of nutritious eggs laid by the queen while in other the nourishment comes from pellets of waste material produced by the workers.

The human female is a mammal and therefore capable of manufacturing milk for her offspring. Many human mothers do feed young infants from their breasts while others choose to use a commercially prepared liquid or cow's milk and feed the baby from a glass or plastic bottle tipped with a device resembling a human nipple. The latter method permits both male and female parents to make feeding responses and frees the mother from the need to be in almost constant attendance early in life. As the human child develops, feeding responses of the parents change in stages. The first stage, usually overlapping breast or bottle feeding, involves the provision of soft foods since the child has no teeth and is unable to chew. This is accomplished by grinding up meats and vegetables mechanically or, as in some cultures, in the mouth of the adult. In the next stage of development, the child eats the same foods as the adult, but the adult still supplies the food at regular time intervals or money that can be exchanged for food outside the home. The spectrum of human feeding responses is seen to include all the forms of feeding responses found in most other animals. That is, they manufacture food in the body, they change the nature of the food that they have gathered prior to feeding, and they simply provide adult-type foods. Let us turn to the latter two types of feeding behavior in other animal parents.

As seen earlier, some insects provide enough food at the time of egglaying to last until the young organism can find its own supply, some manufacture food in their bodies, but still others bring the food as needed. One insect, the burying beetle, combines the first and third means and represents an interesting parallel to the feeding responses of many birds. As described previously, the female burying beetle forms a cup nest out of the dead body of a small animal and lays eggs in the cup. After hatching, the larvae sit in the cup like young birds and exhibit a type of begging behavior at the approach of the mother by arching the anterior part of the body. Next, the female opens her mandibles and allows one of the larvae to put its head in her mouth where she transfers a brown liquid food that she has chewed and regurgitated. After a few hours, the larvae are able to eat directly from the carcass of the dead animal. (Pukowski cited in Wilson, 1971).

Spiders represent another insect that provide food for the young. In *Theridion saxatile*, spiderlings remain in the "nest" part of the web and the mother feeds them with captured prey until they are old enough to participate in the capture(Norgaard, 1956). Other females of the same species (*Theridion sysiphum*), first chew the prey and then feed the regurgitated material to the young (Kaston, 1965). One final example of food provision by insects is seen in the maternal behavior of the digger wasp (Evans and Eberhard, 1970). The larvae of the digger wasp develop in hidden burrows on a diet of caterpillars. The adult female, *Ammophila pubescens*, stocks as many as fifteen nests at one time with the number of caterpillars needed that day to nourish the larvae at their various stages of devepment. That is, the older larvae may need as many as seven caterpillars while the young larvae need only one to three per day.

The degree to which parents provide food for their young is quite varied among different kinds of birds. Newly hatched birds like ducks or chickens that are designated *precocial* can find and eat their own food with some direction from parents. *Altricial young*, which are hatched in a state of almost complete helplessness, may require up to months of attention. Welty (1962) excellently described the characteristics of feeding of the young by birds. In this account, he emphasized the variety existing among birds in regard to the different aspects of the feeding response.

One variation of feeding relates to which parent, if any, feeds the young. Here we find that every possible combination exists: neither male nor female parent feeds the young (cuckoos), both parents feed the young (most passerines and many shorebirds), the female alone feeds the young (European chiff-chaff), or the male alone feeds the young (English robin after the female has left to lay eggs for a second brood). Different species of the young show diversity in food preference, ranging from grain to insects and other larger animals. However, most species provide a high-protein diet for the young and, to accomplish this, may feed the young food that is entirely different from that eaten by the adults. There are many ways in which food is presented to young birds. The young of the precocial species simply find the food and eat it from the ground. Most other birds receive the food directly from the parent in its original form or, as in many cases, the food is swallowed and then regurgitated for the young. Welty points out that this latter method is more efficient since the parent can bring back more food and that it is partially digested for the young.

The elicitation of feeding responses involves one of those strong behavioral interactions mentioned in the previous chapter. A variety of stimuli (vibratory, auditory, tactile, and visual) will cause the young to make begging responses consisting of cries, head movement, and mouth gaping. These stimuli are targets for the parent and induce the adult bird to place the food in the mouth of the nestling. Equally important is the stimulus to stop feeding one particular bird so that none in the nest is neglected. This problem is taken care of by an instinctive cessation of the swallowing response for several moments after food is swallowed. When food is not immediately swallowed, the parent simply removes the food from the bird's mouth and gives it to another.

The frequency with which the feeding response is executed is a function of species, number of young, age of young, method of carrying food, the season, and the weather, according to Welty. Extreme examples cited are (1) the sooty shearwater birds that feed every other night but bring a meal that matches the weight of the nestling and (2) the great tit, which makes as many as 900 trips per day bringing small bits of food. As Welty points out, the energy expended in feeding young birds is tremendous in terms of distance travelled and hours worked by the parents. Some extreme examples of this can be seen in the white pelican that travels as far as 100 miles to provide one meal for the young and and in the male bluethroat of Lapland that works a 21-hour day to feed its young.

Oxygen Provision. For the young of some kinds of animals, there are other needs just at important as food. One of these is oxygen. Now, most organisms have built in automatic mechanisms for taking oxygen from the environment and using it. There are those, however, that have evolved in such a manner as to make it necessary for parental intervention in the provision of oxygen.

We have already encountered one instance of parental oxygen provision in the behavior of the European water spider carrying oxygen bubbles to its young in an underwater nest. Another insect, *Bleduis spectabilis*, provides oxygen in another manner. This female beetle has her brood nest in intertidal mud. The eggs and young larvae require continual oxygen, which is derived from the ventilating movements of the tidal waters. The mother's task is to keep the wide burrows leading to her brood chamber clear so that ventilation can occur. This she does by persistent digging activities (Bro Larsen, 1952).

Fanning the nest is frequently seen as part of the parental behavior of fish. The male stickleback uses its tail to fan fresh water into the entrance of the tunnel nest containing eggs and continues this activity at intervals for the entire week of incubation of the eggs. If necessary, the male stickleback also makes ventilation openings in the nest to insure proper oxygen levels for the eggs (von Frisch, 1974).

At least one instance of a parent supplying oxygen directly to its young exists among amphibians in the Darwin frog of Chile. In this species, the male frog broods the eggs and tadpoles in its vocal sac, a skin fold that expands like a balloon during croaking. Within this sac, the tadpoles are able to take oxygen from the father by means of a network of blood vessels in their thin-skinned tails (von Frisch, 1974).

Thermoregulation. A third major physiological need for many animals is that of temperature control. Although all animals have ranges of temperature in which they can exist, the range is more restricted and more important in some than in others. In addition, there are sometimes more rigid temperature requirements for the eggs and young than there are for the adult animal. Thus, we often find that parents exert control over the thermal environment of their eggs and offspring. There are two ways in which parents exert this kind of control. First, they can achieve optimal thermal conditions by seeking out the right temperature conditions and rearing their young in that particular environment. Second, they can exert some kind of influence on the environmental temperature so that it is kept within an optimal range.

Finding appropriate thermal conditions for brooding and rearing can be done by moving to a place where the tempurature is right or by breeding in a cycle that insures birth at the right time in a seasonal temperature cycle. The correct temperature range is one of the variables that any marine fish responds to in seeking a spawning ground according to Marshall (1966). The swordfish, for example, usually shows preference for waters as low as 12° to 13° C., but seeks a range of 25° to 29° C. for breeding. Gray whales make the longest migration of any living mammal in order to reach warm waters where they give birth to the young (Orr, 1970). Seasonal breeding is so common among animals that spring is generally associated with birth. In some cases such as with certain insects, the seasonal temperature variation is a catalyst that brings about the hatching of eggs laid earlier in the year. In animals such as squirrels, frogs, and many birds, temperature is partially responsible for initiating breeding activities, and a short gestation period insures that the young will be hatched at a time when the environmental temperature is optimal for survival. Animals with longer gestation periods like deer or many bears must time their mating to occur in the autumn or winter in order for birth to take place in the warmer spring climate.

The second method of thermal regulation by parents works just as efficiently for other animal types. For many parents, temparature control must start with incubation of the eggs. Incubation is, of course, a familiar activity in birds; and we have seen the extreme of this behavior in the Australian brush turkey. Most other birds use a simpler method of sitting on the eggs and letting their body heat keep them at optimal temperature. An exception to these two methods of incubation in birds is seen in the Egyptian plover which, according to Skutch (1976), buries three eggs in the sand along the Nile where the heat of the sun incubates them.

With birds that do incubate with their body, there are numerous behavioral variables involved, such as duration of incubation, optimal temperature, length of individual session, male-female involvment, and method of transferring heat. These patterns of behavior are summarized in a book by Skutch (1976). The brooding behaviors in those species that cover their young seems to develop from these incubation patterns. Skutch also points out that variation in method and duration of brooding is a function of such

factors as the type of nest, outside temperature, dampness, predation pressures, rate of maturity in the young. and body temperature of the young. These last two variables are concerned with the fact that most birds are warmblooded or *homeothermal*, which means that they can maintain a relatively constant body temperature amid variable environmental temperautres. However, homeothermy is not always present at hatching, and the rate of its development strongly influences the brooding responses of parents. At one extreme, in the megapodes or mound birds such as the Australian brush turkey, homeothermy is present at hatching and there is no brooding by parents. And, in precocial birds that leave the nest quickly to follow the parents, homeothermy develops much more rapidly than with the altricial species (Skutch, 1976).

In contrast to most birds, amphibians and reptiles are *poikilothermal* which means that their body temperature fluctuates with the temperature of their current environment. Perhaps this is one of the major reasons that we see little or no parental care among this type of animal. Even in terms of incubating the eggs at optimal temperatures, we find that most amphibians and reptiles put out little effort beyond burial. One exception to this generalization is the North American alligator, *Alligator mississippiensis* (Oliver, 1955). As mentioned earlier, the female alligator builds a mound-type nest that provides incubation in the form of energy given off by decaying vegetable material. Already standing out as a parent among reptiles, this alligator goes further and tends the nest during incubation. This nest tending takes the form of providing continued moisture for the rotting process, and this the female does by occasionally emptying her bladder over the nest.

As thermal regulators, many of the social insects excel. There is variation in the means employed by these insects to control the temperature of their brood chambers, which must be kept within an optimal range for brood development. Insects such as social bees, social wasps, and social ants must concern themselves with temperature regulation throughout the year. In some cases, this means providing heating in cold weather and cooling in the summer months. To do so, we find that the insects employ a variety of behavioral and physiological methods, some of which we present here by way of example.

The honeybee is particularly adept at keeping optimal temperature levels in the brood chambers. During spring, summer, and fall, the honeybee nest is kept within the range of 34.5° to 35.5° C (Wilson, 1971). To produce the heat necessary during cold weather, the bees utilize heat that is a by-product of their metabolism together with the behavioral tendency to cluster together as the temperature drops. As the temperature fails, the bees squeeze even closer together covering the brood combs. Wilson (1971) reports on findings that indicate that bees have been able to increase the temperature in the cluster as much as 59° C above the temperature outside of the hive.

Perhaps an even more serious problem for some social insects is that of keeping the nests from overheating during warmer periods. Both honeybees and a number of types of social wasp use a dual method of thermoregulation in cooling brood areas. The methods involve fanning and water evaporation, as described by Lindauer (1961). Fanning, or vigorous beating of the wings by worker bees, is used until the temperature in the hive begins to exceed 35° C. At this point, experienced foragers that know the surrounding environment begin to collect water and return it to the hive where the inexperienced young workers receive it and distribute the drops over the brood cells. Thus, the heat is dissipated as other bees continue to fan, carrying off the evaporated water. An interesting sidelight reported by Lindauer is that the young workers communicate the inside temperature to the older water bearers by their level of receptivity for water. Thus, as the temperature in the hive is brought near the optimal range, the foraging bees have difficulty

finding a worker to accept the water and return to their other tasks. The following account describes observations by Allen (1965) of "fanning" and "shiver dance" behavior in worker honeybees.

In the process of fanning, a worker bee remains stationary and moves its wings rapidly, thus creating an air current. This process inside of a hive seems to be in response to high humidity or temperature or to a need for increased gaseous exchange.

The "shiver dance" is a continuous vibration of the worker's body in a lateral plane, and its function is not understood at this point in time.

This and other studies by the author were carried out to determine the ages of the worker bees that engaged in these behaviors. This kind of investigation follows earlier studies, which found that there are divisions of labor based on the age of the worker bee. For instance, foraging is done only by older bees.

The method in these investigations consisted of marking workers and observing their behavior over a period of 2 to 3 months in the spring and summer.

In the case of fanning, it was found that the response is seen in all age groups, including 1 day old bees. Of the 104 observed, 26 were in the first week of life, 32 in the second week, 23 in the third, 12 in their fourth, 5 in their fifth and 6 were over 5 weeks old.

Results of similar observations of the shiver dance indicate a different outcome. In this case, it was found that only "older" bees performed the shiver dance. That is, none of these bees was less than two weeks old. The author points out that the age of the shiver dance corresponds to the age of foraging and thus suggests a relationship.

Like the bees and wasps, certain social ants must maintain a restricted range of temperature for brood development. As indicated by Wilson

(1971), however, the ants have no wings to use in fanning and are normally unable to acquire water quickly. Therefore, instead of attempting to change the temperature of the environment near the brood areas, the ants move their eggs or pupae to a different part of the nest if temperatures move out of the optimal range 25° to 40° C. Nesting underground has the advantage of minimal changes in temperatures; so for subterranean colonies, temperature regulation is not a major problem.

Turning next to mammals, we find that those that do nest tend to provide additional warmth for the young by lying on top of them with their fur-covered bodies. Most young fur bearers grow their own fur relatively soon after birth and become capable of regulating their own heat. The human infant, on the other hand, has very little body hair to help regulate heat and needs some external regulation, although able to survive in a fairly wide range of temperature. As the environmental temperature drops or rises, the human parent adds or subtracts layers of clothing. In extremely hot weather, the human parent may cool the baby by dipping it in water. In addition, the human may use mechanical devices to keep the entire nest within optimal temperature range.

Defense of the Eggs or Offspring

Many forms of defensive behavior in protection of the young are simply extensions of self-defensive responses. The subject of predator defense will be treated in some detail in a later chapter, and we are concerned only with those defensive responses that are specifically related to the potential predation of eggs or young. In some respects, we have already talked of predator defense by parents in other contexts. That is, such behaviors as nest building or seeking special places to give birth may function as antipredation devices in addition to those discussed as follows.

Covering and Immobility Responses. As

mentioned before, many animals have evolved specialized coloration that make them hard to spot; and they may have nests that blend into the environment. Along with these tactics, we often find that a parent's common form of defense of the young is simply to cover them with its body and then remain very still. If there is motion in a hiding animal, Edmunds (1974) indicates that it is a rocking from side to side so that the movements are similar to the movements of plants or leaves in the wind. This would seem to be the case with altricial (those having young that remain in the nest a comparatively long time) birds that nest in places accessible to predators. Even the young, after being able to discriminate the parents from the enemy, will crouch and remain still at the approach of any strange object (Skutch, 1976).

Since precocial birds move about with the parents, they are subject to detection, particularly from above. A common defensive device in this situation is exemplified by the behavior of the ruffed grouse (Edminister, 1947). The young birds innately respond to different calls made by the mother when a hawk is sighted. with one call, the young freeze; on the second call, they scatter and freeze; a third call keeps them motionless until all clear calls have been sounded.

Covering the young and signaling danger is also found among the insects, although it is relatively rare. Nymphs of some families of Nemiptera insects orient toward the mother and run to her to be covered by her body in time of threat. Or, as also cited by Wilson (1971), the mother of a semimarine insect, *Aepophilus bonnairei*, uses an alarm call in time of danger such as when the stone over them is lifted up at one corner. The call is tactile as the mother runs to each nymph and taps it on the head so that it runs to the other side of the rock where it again stands immobile.

Parental care in the form of predator defense is an almost universal trait among mammals. Covering of the young among smaller mammals is often an outgrowth of the nursing process and the thermal-regulation process. As a result, a freezing-covering response is frequently seen in the face of danger from a predator.

Diversion Responses.   A clear-cut parental protective behavior occurs when an animal distracts a predator from its nest or young. Edmunds (1974) reports that distraction display is found frequently in birds, especially waders and ducks, but also in some fish and mammals. Typically, the parent bird slips quietly from the nesting area and then makes herself conspicuous by flopping one wing as though it were injured. A similar behavior is found in a freshwater holostean fish, which thrashes around violently when a predator fish approaches the young, and in the female tiger, which makes itself known while moving away from the young when humans are approaching.

Aggressive Responses.   Although seldom used as a specific parental response, many animals seem to display a greater degree of aggression in the presence of their young than at other times. Edmunds (1974) states that aggressive retaliation with physical or chemical weapons is the final defense of a prey animal. Since aggressive behavior by the parent is risky, for it as well as the offspring, aggression is less common than other defenses as a first attempt to stave off predators. One circumstance, however, in which aggression seems to be the primary means of defense is in animals that have social nesting habits. In a communal nest of animals such as herring gulls or penguins, protection of the eggs and young is accomplished through the combined aggressive responses of many members. Such animals nest in open accessible places and must depend upon the group to protect the individual.

In most cases, the young animal's own defensive response to predator intrusion is the rather submissive one of crouching and remaining still. But, according to Skutch (1976), there are bird nestlings that aggressively defend themselves. For example, nestling red-billed tropic birds, ringed kingfishers, and night herons react fiercely by trying to bite nest intruders. Other forms of aggressive defense are seen in fulmer and hoopoe birds. Such nestlings attack with chemical repellents, which are ejected onto the intruder in the form of oil and a foul-smelling fluid. Even the parents of these chicks must perform some kind of appeasement or recognition behavior or they may be sprayed.

Alarm Signals and Flight.   Just as some parents emit signals to crouch and freeze at the sign of danger, others provide signals for the young to flee the area. As one might expect, this tendency is found in animals like deer whose young can usually out distance predators. The mother elk uses a rather different alarm call when the herd is moving; she emits continuous calls, and their cessation is an alarm signal for the young to be led away.

Up to this point, we have not mentioned the human parent as a defender against predation. In spite of the fact that most humans today have no natural predators, human parents do vigorously defend their offspring, mainly against inanimate threats created by the species itself. So, the human parent is concerned with dangers that other animals ignore or accept without defense, expending great effort in curing diseases of the young, making sure the child is not hit by mechanical devices, and warding off other humans who might physically or psychologically harm their young. In doing these kinds of things, human parents seem to use most forms of response discussed above: they may cover their young, signal them to freeze or run, and distract or fight an attacker.

Task Instruction

Many animals depend on the learning of certain skills for survival. Skills involved in hunting, food gathering, and sexual activities may have to be learned early in life even though they will not be used until later on. The learning of such skills is often called play because of its similarity to play behavior in human children. Often times, the learning goes on in the absence of parents or, at least, without their involvement. By this we mean that juvenile animals often interact with each other in such a way as to develop motor patterns necessary for future activities. Harlow and Harlow (1962) clearly indicate the importance of playlike behavior among young monkeys for the complete development of adult social interactions. In the present context, however, we are primarily concerned with those training experiences that are specifically initiated by the parent animal.

Models and Response Elicitation. The teaching of skills through initiating responses or providing a model is assumed to occur among both domestic and wild animals. The tendency of mother cats to lie on their sides and twitch the tips of their tails to entice their young to pounce is cited by Loizos (1969) as parental initiation of play with hunting characteristics. And according to Altmann (1963), elk mothers have been observed to initiate water splashing and running games with their young in shallow bodies of water. These games, which take place just prior to spring migration, are interpreted by Altmann as practice for the crossing of swollen streams during the migration of the herd.

Finally, as seen in the study summarized as follows (Krischik and Weber, 1975) male and female cichlid fish display a parental behavior called "fin digging," which stirs up the gravel and food particles for the young, and can thus be viewed as both food provision and task instruction.

The first part of this study undertook to determine that normal parental role of the male cichlid fish in caring for free-swimming young. A second aspect of the study attempted to determine if nonreproductive males could be induced to show parental behavior after a period of sensitization (familiarization).

Observing pairs of mated fish through the normal parental cycle yielded three components of parental behavior: (1) looking at the young, (i.e., parental attentiveness), (2) fin-digging,(i.e., stirring up gravel to make food available to young. and (3) attack (i.e., approaching and biting predator fish). Males exhibit the three components of parental care but usually at a lower level than the female.

In the second part of the investigation, five free-swimming young per day were introduced into the aquaria of nonreproductive males over a 50-day period. One half of the males had conspecific young placed in their aquaria while the other half had young of a different species of cichlid.

Results of this study indicated that the male cichlids gradually assume a parental role during a period of sensitization to the young of their own species. That is, the males progressed from making no response to chasing and eating their young and finally ended up herding them together and showing normal male parental responses. In contrast, the males living with young of another species never progressed beyond the stage of eating the young.

Hunting Skills. After leaving the nest, young birds still have many skills to develop in order to survive (Welty, 1962). Although many of the skills unfold as the bird matures, there are many circumstances in which parents are directly involved in the tuition process. Bent (1940), in describing the parental behavior of the eastern belted kingfisher, reports that they catch a fish, beat it against a branch into a state of semi consciousness, and drop it into the water. At first, the young bird dives awkwardly for the easy prey, but eventually sharpens it diving skills so that it can catch fully alert fish by itself.

Food Preference.　While some birds help teach their young how to catch food, others educate with regard to what to eat and what not to eat. Skutch (1967)mentions the peregrine falcon as an example of a bird whose food preferences are transmitted by parental behavior rather than genetic mechanisms. As evidence of this, he cites the occurrence of food preference in local populations being different from that of the species as a whole. Skutch also speculates that some parent birds warn their young away from bad tasting or poisonous foods such as certain kinds of insects or plants. Mother gorillas have also been reported to snatch poisonous leaves out of the mouths of their young (Schaller, 1963).

The Human Being.　In comparing parental involvement in the learning of skills by the offspring, we find that there is an apparent relationship between the duration of parental care and the amount of teaching that takes place. Also, it is apparent that animals that rely more heavily on parent education have few instinctive behavior patterns in their repertoire. The human being is at the extreme in terms of all of these characteristics. That is, parental care is extended, teaching is extensive, and instincts are minimal. The human child must be taught skills in nearly every area of its existence, especially the all-important skills involved in food gathering, communication, and social responses. With the evolution of the human species, the amount of needed teaching has become so extensive that specialization and division of labor has come about. Human parents generally involve themselves in the teaching of the basic behaviors necessary to produce a relatively self-sufficient child. At this point, about 5 or 6 years of age, surrogate parents join in the teaching process and, for an exchange of goods, attempt to impart training specific to successful survival in human culture. This kind of teaching by surrogates may continue well beyond parental involvement for the next 15 to 20 years.

Grooming

We have already discussed cleaning of the young earlier in this chapter, and Chapter 19 in this text concerns itself specifically with care of the body surface. In light of this, we cover grooming here only briefly and generally. Grooming is an important part of parental care for many animals. Eibl-Eibesfeldt (1970) points out that social grooming is a widespread behavior among those animals that seek body contact with other members of their species. We see such behavior in rats, mice, agoutis, monkeys, chimpanzees, and many other primates including humans. This is an adult behavior as well, but we find its origin in the grooming and cleaning of the young by the parent. Grooming, of course, has a function outside of helping to maintain close contact, and that is to help keep individuals and groups free of parasitic organisms and disease. With the human, grooming has taken on meaning beyond that of health care. That is, even though parents clean and groom the young child, they also teach the skill to the child since it is a necessary ingredient to being accepted by other members of the species.

Nest Expulsion

We are using the term nest expulsion to include those processes or events whereby a parent begins to free itself from its obligations toward the offspring. Since the concept of nest expulsion seems most familiar in regard to bird behavior, we start there. Among various birds, one finds considerable diversity in the amount of parental urging necessary to get the young out of the nest. Other factors involved in this process include weather, hunger, and accident. Some nestlings, such as the ringed kingfisher reported by Skutch (1976), might leave the nest spontaneously while the parent is gone. For those bird parents that use some form of urging, however, Welty (1962) cites a range of methods. Starvation is one means of enticement if the parent offers food at a distance from the nest. Calling the young out of the nest is effective in some birds (tree duck) while others (chachalaca) have to carry their young from the nest to the ground. And, finally, some species (pygmy nuthatch) use force in pulling the young out of the nest and pushing them off so that they must flutter to the ground. Of course, leaving the nest does not always signal the end of parental care, but it is the beginning of the process of acquiring independence by the young.

In the mammal, parental care is often extensive in time and effort, and the methods, of cutting off this care range from simply walking or running away to active aggression toward the young. In some herd-living animals such as elk or deer, maternal care weakens gradually since the young animal has simultaneously developed an attachment to other members of the group. There is no "shock" involved in the weaning process. The female elk will, however, become hostile toward her own yearling if it remains too close during the next calving season (Altmann, 1963).

The breaking of the parent-offspring bond in rhesus monkeys has been reported in detail by Harlow et al. (1963). Following the period of maternal attachment and protection, a two-stage sequence of behaviors results in establishing independence in the young monkey. In the first of these two stages, which they refer to as *maternal ambivalence*, the mother continues to nurture the young with cradling, grooming, and nursing responses while displaying an ever-increasing number of negative responses. These negative responses, including biting, slapping, fur pulling, and pushing away, eventually reach a frequency equal to positive responses.

The second stage, referred to as *maternal separation or rejection*, is characterized by physical separation of mother and juvenile and usually occurs when a new baby is born to the mother. However, there is still social contact between mother and offspring in terms of the young remaining in proximity to the mother for extended periods.

Jay (1963) has observed the occurrence of group care of young langurs, in the sense that adult females tend to treat all infants as their own. With these primates, there is a decline in this care when the 3 to 5-month-old infant changes from brown to a gray color. The natural mother, however, continues her care until about the eleventh month when she begins to show hostile and denying responses to her infant, as in the rhesus.

One can speculate on similar happenings with the human child, except that it is a more complicated process in humans and much more flexible. One extreme difference in humans arises from the typical parents' strong urge to socialize the child completely and their unwillingness to terminate training in this regard (McNeil, 1969). As a result, we find conflict between parent and child as the child makes a great effort toward achieving independence. Perhaps as a result of this kind of uncertainty and conflict, many human societies have specific ceremonies to mark the beginning of independence for the child. The transitional ritual is called a *rites de passage* and varies widely in structure and form. Where concrete rites of passage exist, they frequently involve some test of eligibility for adult status in the form of physical skills or endurance. In most contemporary urbanized cultures, however, there are only vestigial rituals, which are usually of a religious nature. The absence of any clear-cut separation procedure between parent and adolescent probably contributes to the conflict and hostility that so often exist between human parents and their adolescent offspring (McNeil, 1969).

Behavioral Anomalies in Parenting

Frequently, we see behavior by animals that seems to go against all the rules for good parenting. Indeed, some of these responses seem to make no sense at all when viewed in terms of evolutionary adaptation. There may be events in the rearing of young that do not go smoothly for a particular set of parents. For example, the nest is poorly constructed or the mother does a poor job of cleaning the young, but such individual differences could still allow for the survival of the young. King (1963) defined abnormal *maternal* behavior in mice as being any behavior resulting in the death or injury of the young. More generally, we would include as abnormal *parental* behaviors those that result in the destruction or injury of the young or egg by a parent that normally provides care for same.

There are three major classes of anomalous parental behavior: *prolicide*, *kronism*, and *abandonment*. Prolicide is a general term referring to the destruction of eggs or young by parent. Kronism refers to the act of eating one's own eggs or offspring, and abandonment means leaving dependent eggs or young to die from lack of care. Examples of these so called abnormal parental responses exist in many places in the animal kingdom. Wynne-Edwards (1962) reports studies depicting kronism and prolicide among insects (spiders), fish, birds, and mammals. Abandonment is less well documented but has been noted with some frequency among birds. What ever the label or method, the young in these situations ultimately die.

Why Do Animals Kill Their Young?   From an *anthropomorphic* stance (human perspective), the killing of one's young is an extremely aberrant behavior. However, if we take a close look at such behavior among non human animals, we may find that it is perfectly normal, given the conditions that exist. In regard to kronism and prolicide, Wynne-Edwards (1962) states ". . . these have to be regarded as very advanced adaptations, seemingly almost confined to the highest animals found in the arthropod and vertebrate

classes. That they are adaptations of homeostatic function cannot any longer be seriously doubted." How can killing the young be adaptive? This would hold when killing served a higher adaptive function than simply preserving the individual, that is, in the service of species preservation. Some examples illustrate this point.

Communal Nesting.   Penguins are communal nesters and will vigorously defend their specific nest site against any intruder. This is adaptive since communal nesting provides excellent protection against predators. And, should a young penguin be accidently knocked out of the nest area, the mother will probably kill it if it attempts to reenter: protection of the individual offspring is valued less than group protection.

Overcrowding.   In other instances of parents' killing or deserting the young or eggs, we find the "abnormal behavior" is adaptive in that it serves as a means of population control (see summarized study below). Wynne-Edwards (1962) cites ample laboratory evidence obtained from vertebrate animals to indicate that various forms of prolicide, kronism, or desertion are related to overcrowding and the resultant shortage of food.

Excessive Responsiveness.   On occasion, the killing of the young by the parent occurs as a result of the adult's failure to stop some ordinary parental function. For example, Fox (1968) includes a number of reports of mammals (swine, dogs, cats) that don't seem to respond to inhibiting stimuli when severing the umbilical cord. That is, the mother gnaws the cord down to the young and keeps going into the abdomen. Here, also, the adaptive behavior of removing the umbilical cord serves the species, but in this instance, kills the individual.

In most situations, then, acts that result in the death of the offspring are not really abnormal responses but normal responses under abnormal conditions, as illustrated in the following summarized study done by Langenau and Lerg (1976), which was in part supervised by the late Professor Ratner and dedicated to his memory.

This study was designed to determine the effect of winter nutritional stress on maternal and neonatal behavior during the first 3 days after parturition (birth). A total of forty-five penned deer were subjected to three levels of winter nutrition at 7 to 10, 19 to 22, and 31 to 34 months of age. Parturition occurred when does were about 24 and 36 months old. Maternal and fawn behaviors were observed during parturition and during random 1-hour periods up to 3 days after birth. The most common form of postnatal fawn mortality resulted from a maternal rejection syndrome, including failure to lick fawns at birth and failure to eat the afterbirth (which make the fawns vulnerable to predators), fear of neonates, and refusal to nurse fawns despite the presence of milk in the udder. Since winter nutritional stress is common for deer on northern ranges, this behavioral syndrome may function as an effective method of population control.

Study Questions

1. Are humans dimorphic or monomorphic? In evolutionary terms, explain how you think humans came to be dimorphic or monomorphic.

2. In 1943, Konrad Lorenz put forth a hypothesis concerning the attractive qualities of the human infant's head. This was discussed under special structures in this chapter. What kind of evidence can you find in support of this hypothesis simply by looking at commercial products in your environment?

3. What evidence can you find to indicate a phenomenon similar to imprinting in humans?

4. In the case of the digger wasp that stocks a number of nests with varying numbers of caterpillars, how does the female "know" how many are needed?

5. Speculate on the kinds of parental behaviors that you think are related to being homeothermal.

6. At the end of the discussion of parental defensive responses, it was suggested that human parents use a variety of defensive patterns in protecting their children. From your knowledge or experience, cite some examples of the use of these various defensive responses.

19

Care of the Body Surface (COBS)

Peter L. Borchelt

Animal Behavior Consultants, Inc.
Forest Hills, N.Y.

PART I

When people hear that my interest in research is the study of dustbathing in quail this usually evokes a blank stare or a quizzical "what?" When this happens I point out that many species of birds, particularly ground-nesting ones such as quail, grouse, and chickens, engage in a complicated sequence of behavior called dustbathing. The dustbathing sequence typically starts with the bird's pecking and scratching at the ground, usually in an area where the soil is dusty, or perhaps in a small pile of rotten wood. The bird then squats and may continue pecking and scratching. Shortly thereafter it ruffles the plumage slightly and makes a coordinated series of leg and wing movements that throws dust or soil onto the back and through the feathers. The bird also rubs the head and side of the body in the dust. After a variable number of such behaviors, the bird rises, ruffles the feathers again, and shakes out the dust. Some dustbathing bouts last only a few minutes whereas others go on for half an hour or more.

According to the literature, dustbathing behavior is a means of ridding the feathers of ectoparasites (lice, mites, and ticks). So in doing graduate research on the behavior of bobwhite quail (*Colinus virginianus*), I provided the birds with dried dirt and after the dust had settled their feathers were sleek rather than matted as before. However, an inspection of the feathers of the birds prior to any dustbathing indicated that *none* of the laboratory-raised birds had observable ectoparasites. My interests then focused on *why* quail dustbathe.

An exhaustive review of the literature in comparative psychology, zoology, animal behavior, ornithology, and natural history proved to be of little help. There was very little research on dustbathing. What was available included descriptions of dustbathing in various species, the hypothesis that it seemed to control ectoparasites, and the statement that the behavior was innate. The only thing I knew was that ectoparasites were *not* the only thing to elicit dustbathing, for my ectoparasiteless quail dustbathed every day. Relying heavily on this observation, I decided that, since the birds looked better after they dustbathed, the behavior might serve to keep the feathers clean. Of what?

Library research indicated that birds have a

uropygial gland located on the dorsal surface at the base of the tail feathers that secretes lipid in the form of a thin oil. The lipid is spread onto the feathers periodically by a behavior called oiling; this behavior involves mandibulation (nibbling) of the gland with the beak, followed by preening the lipid onto the feathers. Birds have no other secretory glands in the skin.

A hypothesis emerged. Perhaps birds dustbathed to remove the lipid on the feathers. Certainly, birds that were not allowed to dustbathe for long periods of time looked "oily." If this hypothesis was correct, then preventing birds from dustbathing should mean that they would have more lipid on the feathers than if they were allowed to dustbathe. So my colleagues and I predicted that if we deprived quail of the opportunity to dustbathe, they would show an increase in dustbathing when given the opportunity to do so, supporting our basic hypothesis. We did, they did, and the hypothesis was supported (Borchelt, Eyer and McHenry, 1973). This small, but successful, experiment convinced me to study dustbathing for my dissertation research.

Experiments on Dustbathing and Sandbathing

The dissertation consisted of three experiments. The first fully described the behavioral sequence in both male and female quail and replicated and extended our previous experiment by looking at the structure of the sequence under two levels of dust deprivation. Both sexes were observed because several studies had indicated that the uropygial gland is influenced by hormones, with androgens (male gonadal hormones) increasing the size and rate of secretion of the gland. Thus, if lipid on the feathers had anything to do with dustbathing, male birds should dustbathe more than females. The second experiment determined whether there really was an increase in feather lipid when birds were deprived of dust. This

experiment looked at feathers rather than behavior. The third experiment involved the surgical removal of the uropygial gland to see if there would be a decrease in dustbathing.

The results of the first experiment again showed that, following deprivation of dust, quail did more dustbathing than when not deprived. Dustbathing also appeared to be a rather predictable type of behavior. The sequence of dustbathing components, involving *dust toss* (the coordinated leg and wing movements that toss dust onto the back), *head rub, side rub,* and so on, was quite predictable when the focus was on the order of the first occurrence of each component. That is, it could be accurately predicted that a sequence of dustbathing would start with either pecking or scatching, although it was impossible to predict how many pecks or scratches would occur before the bird squatted in the dust. After that, it could be predicted accurately that the bird would continue pecking and scratching and would then exhibit one or more dust tosses. After an unpredictable number of dust tosses, it could be predicted that the bird would head rub, and that after an unpredictable number of additional dust tosses and head rubs, it would then side rub. Finally, the bird would rise to its feet and shake the dust out of the feathers. Figure 19.1 is a flowchart depicting the dustbathing sequence of one bird. The chart gives some idea of the way in which the various dustbathing behaviors are put together. The precise sequence of dustbathing behaviors differs among birds, but the stereotyped order in which the behaviors first occur is the same for all birds.

Thus, at one level of analysis, the dustbathing sequence is highly organized and predictable. At another level, it is quite unpredictable. This complex sequence of behavior poses some interesting questions about its particular organization. Is it necessary for a dust toss to occur prior to the first head rub, and a head rub to occur prior to the first side rub? If so, why? The answers to these questions are still unknown.

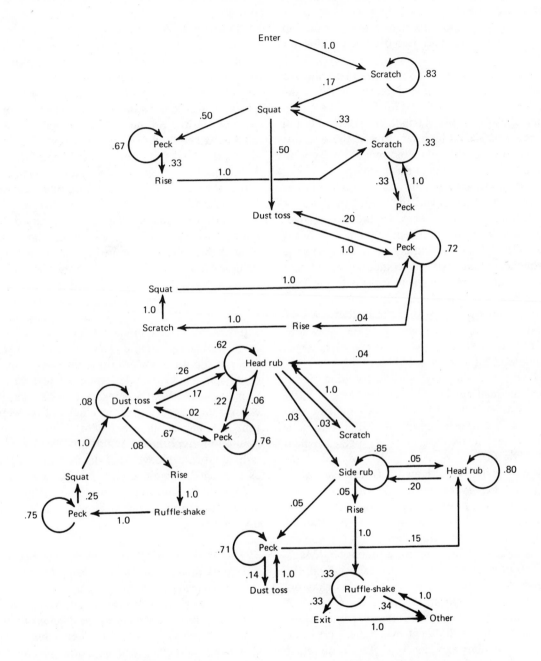

Figure 19.1. The sequence of occurrence of dustbathing components for a bobwhite quail. The numbers refer to the probability of various transitions from one component to another.

This first study also revealed that male birds did indeed show a higher frequency of some dustbathing components than female birds, but only after the birds had been deprived of dust for several days.

The results of the second experiment showed that the feathers contained more oil when the birds were deprived of dust for 5 or 15 days than after they had just dustbathed (Borchelt and Duncan, 1974). At least tentatively, these results provided support for the lipid regulation hypothesis about the function of dustbathing.

The third experiment was another matter. After surgically removing the uropygial glands of adult quail, waiting a week for them to recover from the operation, and testing them weekly for a month, I found absolutely no decrease in the frequency of dustbathing components. At first these results were thought to invalidate the budding hypothesis about why birds dustbathe, but it was soon recognized that the birds were very experienced dustbathers and perhaps were continuing to dustbathe for a variety of reasons, including an innate basis.

I was also studying how dustbathing developed in quail chicks, and on the basis of early results already had a hunch there might be several reasons for dustbathing. The literature indicated that dustbathing was a species-typical behavior for a variety of birds and was "unlearned" or innate. Although it is true that many complex behaviors are unlearned, the really interesting question is *how* do these behaviors develop. That is, how do they get from a state of not being there, or being there in an incomplete form, to a state of being fully functional. Many studies of a variety of behaviors, especially in the higher vertebrates, indicate that innate behaviors often do not occur in complete form the first time they appear. Instead, there is some degree of change or development over time, and some type of previous experience is often required. I hoped that the studies of the function of dustbathing in adults and of the development of

dustbathing in chicks would complement each other.

The first experiments conducted on the development of dustbathing were quite simple. The quail chicks were raised in small groups of ten to twelve. Since no quail parents were present, heat, as well as food and water, was provided. The chicks had a small box of dust presented once per day starting on the first day of age, and they all dustbathed by day 7. If dust was witheld until day 7, the chicks did not dustbathe until day 14. If the chicks were given finely ground dust, they dustbathed at an earlier age than if they received coarse dust.

After testing many groups under many different conditions, we discovered that the time when a quail chick first dustbathed is determined by a complex function of how old it was when it first received dust, the texture of the dust, how many daily experiences the chick had had with dust, and whether the chick was in the presence of experienced or inexperienced chicks when it was in the dust (Borchelt and Overmann, 1974, 1975). Clearly, the developmental process was complicated and could not be explained just by the term "innate." What was fascinating was that the entire sequence occurred in chicks prior to the time they began oiling behavior. Thus, the lipid regulation hypothesis could not explain why individual chicks developed dustbathing, at least as a learned phenomenon. The following is an account of regulation of dustbathing in Japanese quail. (Borchelt, Hoffman, Hurrell and McCarthy, 1979).

The results of these experiments further complicate the lipid regulation hypothesis. It was found that removing the uropygial gland from day-old chicks does not retard the development of dustbathing and that spraying large amounts of lipid on the feathers of adults does not increase dustbathing. However, spraying water on the plumage of adults, which presumably increases the amount of oiling behavior, does increase dustbathing. These results suggest that it is not the amount of lipid on the feathers that determines how much a bird will dustbathe, but rather the amount of oiling behavior that has occurred since it last dustbathed. Such results point the way to doing some interesting experiments in the near future on the relation between oiling behavior and dustbathing.

After graduate school, there was no longer an unlimited supply of bobwhite quail, but there was a small number of kangaroo rats available. Kangaroo rats sandbathe. This behavior involves two main movements or action patterns called *side rub* and *ventrum rub*. When side rubbing, an animal lowers its head to the sand and slides forward on either the left or the right side, while first flexing and then extending its torso. During ventrum rubs, the animal lowers its head to the sand and slides forward, rubbing the ventrum (chest and belly) in the sand. Perhaps kangaroo rats sandbathe for the same general reason that presumably quail dustbathe: to clean the body surface.

A search of the literature revealed that desert rodents (including kangaroo rats and gerbils) sandbathe frequently, and mark parts of their territories with secretions from specialized glands in the skin. These secretions seem to be related to the serious problem of retaining body water in a hot, dry environment. One means of retaining water for these animals was the evolution of highly active sebaceous glands in the skin. These glands deposit a hydrophobic lipid layer over the skin, which inhibits evaporative water loss. The secretory process from sebaceous glands is continuous, however, and within a few days the animal's fur is "greasy" and matted unless the rat sandbathes. From an adaptive point of view, a matted, disheveled pelage would not be a coat that retains heat; animals with such a coat would tend to become chilled during the cold desert nights, the time when they are usually most active.

Presumably, if kangaroo rats were deprived of a suitable sandbathing substrate for increasing periods of time, the fur would become increasingly greasy and, accordingly, the animals would exhibit increased sandbathing when sand became available. We tested kangaroo rats after either 1, 5, or 10 days of sand deprivation and found a systematic increase in the frequency of side and ventrum rubs (Borchelt, Griswold, and Branchek, 1976). We also found that grooming behavior (face washing and body grooming) accompanied sandbathing and also tended to increase in frequency when animals were sand deprived.

We concluded that sandbathing, grooming behavior, and secretions from sebaceous glands are integrated into a complex system. Secretions are deposited by a continuous, physiological process, one function of which is inhibition of evaporative water loss. The coordinaton of sandbathing and grooming behaviors cleans the fur of these secretions, maintaining the insulation properties of the pelage. Stating our hypothesis in this manner, as an integrated system composed of various parts or components, allowed us to pose a number of research questions that could help test this hypothesis.

A logical next step was to see if the experimental application of a "greasy" substance would lead to increases in sandbathing, even in animals that were not sand deprived. Since it is impossible to collect even moderate quantities of sebaceous gland secretions, we tried the next best substance, lanolin, and applied it to the fur of kangaroo rats that had recently sandbathed and had a clean pelage. We found that rats directed side and ventrum rubs, and grooming behavior, mostly to that part of the body to which lanolin was applied (Griswold, Borchelt, Branchek, and Bensko, 1977). For instance, applying lanolin to the left side of the body yielded a large number of left side rubs and left body grooms, but few, if any, right side rubs, right body grooms, or ventrum rubs. This meant that the rats *were* directing their behavior almost exclusively to the part of the body that was greasy.

After the accumulated evidence from the studies of dustbathing in quail and sandbathing and grooming in kangaroo rats and from the literature on a variety of similar behaviors in other species had been pondered, a general picture began to emerge about what these behaviors do for an animal and how they work. The next section briefly outlines a general model for care of the body surface (COBS) behavior.

A Model for COBS

Let us start by supposing that all COBS is divided into three parts. The first part includes behaviors or processes that involve the application or depositing of material onto the body surface. Perhaps the best illustration is oiling behavior in birds, which involves a behavioral process (the sequence of nibbling the nipple of the uropygial gland and preening the oil onto the feathers) and a physiological process (secretion of lipid from the gland). In other cases, there is no specific behavioral process involved, but only a physiological process of secretion of some material onto the body surface (e.g., from sebaceous glands), or, even more simply, the happenstance of substances coming from the environment (dirt, sticky material, etc.) and being deposited on the body surface.

The second part of COBS includes behaviors that remove materials from the body surface, for example, dustbathing, sandbathing, and grooming. Other such behaviors will be discussed shortly. The third part of COBS involves behaviors that realign integumentary structures, such as feathers and hairs. For instance, after dustbathing, quail ruffle their plumage to shake out the dust. In addition this behavior rearranges the structure of the feathers, which sometimes become disarranged after dustbathing. Quail often preen after dustbathing, which also helps rearrange the feathers. Perhaps some of the

grooming behavior exhibited by kangaroo rats after sandbathing serves to realign the hairs. This tripartite formulation of COBS is visualized in Figure 19.2a.

But things are not that simple. Some behaviors that seem clearly to be involved in cleaning the body surface of an animal appear to have additional functions, those of a social nature. Another three-part distinction seems appropriate. Care of the body surface behavior can be classified into *individual, social,* and *symbiotic* COBS.

Individual COBS occurs when a single animal "cares for" its body surface in some way. Social COBS involves two or more animals engaging in behavior patterns that appear to clean the body surface of one or more of them. Social COBS can be unilateral, with one animal cleaning the body surface of another, or bilateral, with reciprocal cleaning between animals. Some of the functions of social COBS, other than cleaning, are the establishment of social bonds or dominance. The distinction between behaviors that "care for" the body surface and those that have a social function is sometimes neither easy, nor desirable, to make. As we will see later, a single animal can engage in behavior that immediately cleans the body surface and at the same time deposits odors on the substrate, which can become a social signal for another animal passing by later. These two aspects of social COBS, and how they are integrated with individual COBS, are illustrated in Figure 19.2b.

Symbiotic COBS occurs when one animal has its body surface cleaned while the one that is doing the cleaning is engaging in another class of behavior, usually eating. Symbiotic COBS typically occurs between two different species, thereby making it less likely to have social functions. Figure 19.2c depicts how symbiotic COBS fits in with both individual and social COBS. This overall scheme of COBS behavior is a modification of one proposed by Denny and Ratner (1970).

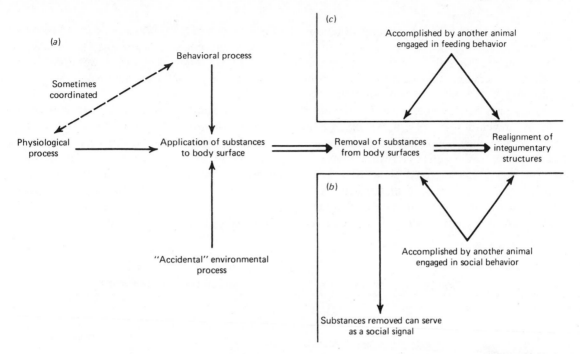

Figure 19.2. The coordination of processes involved in COBS. (*a*) Individual COBS. (*b*) Social COBS. (*c*) Symbiotic COBS.

PART II

Up to this point, the reader has been introduced to several behaviors that have been classified as COBS behavior. A general (and therefore incomplete) model for COBS behavior has been presented together with some experimental evidence from which it was derived. The rest of this chapter applies some of the early stages of the comparative method (see Chapter 9) to the study of COBS behavior. First, a brief review of the biology of the skin or integument is presented in order to provide background information about the possible function(s) of COBS behavior. Second, a description of COBS behavior in vertebrate and invertebrate species is presented. Here, the diversity of behavior patterns encompassed by COBS is highlighted. Third, the important variables affecting COBS are extracted from the literature. Finally, a brief summary indicates

where we are and where future research might go.

A Brief Introduction to the Integument

This outline of the comparative biology of the integument is based on an excellent review by Spearman (1973). The integument forms a barrier between the highly variable, often hostile conditions of the outside environment and the animal's living tissues with their stable physiological requirements. Two important functions of the integument, other than physical protection, are inhibiting the transport of water through the skin and inhibiting the loss of heat. In general, the skin is a highly active metabolic organ, with constant replacement of epidermal cells as an adaptation for withstanding the wear and tear from contact with the environment.

Table 19.1 presents the integumentary structures of both invertebrate and vertebrate species and points out some of the important functions these structures serve.

The main structures that aid in thermal regulation are feathers and hair, which occur only in homeothermic (warm blooded) animals that maintain a high body temperature. The problem of thermal regulation is not critical for aquatic species because they are buffered from extremes of temperature by the water. Terrestrial invertebrates and poikilothermic (cold blooded) animals (amphibians and reptiles) regulate their body temperature by choosing a suitable environment.

The problem of water transport through the skin is solved in terrestrial species by a hard cuticle that may contain waxes (insects), a layer of dead, keratin-filled cells called the horny layer (amphibia, reptiles, birds, mammals), or specialized lipid-secreting cells (birds, mammals). Water transport in aquatic species may occur either through diffusion or osmosis. Invertebrate marine species all have tissue fluids isotonic to seawater so only diffusion occurs. Fresh-water invertebrates and most fish have tissue fluids hypotonic to seawater and contend with osmosis by excreting water, while aquatic mammals are protected by a thick horny layer.

Table 19.1
A Comparison of Structures and Functions of the Integument

Structure of Integument	Thermal Insulation	Water barrier	Other
Invertebrates			
Generally, a single layer of specialized cells that secrete either (1) hard cuticle—replaced periodically, may contain waxes or (2) mucus—may help remove ectoparasites or detritus		Insects, decapod crustacea (lobster)	
Vertebrates			
Generally, a stratified epidermis several cells thick			
Fish—Cells secrete cuticle, mucus, or lipid		X	
Amphibians—Cells secrete mucus			Respiration
layer of dead cells filled with keratin (horny layer), periodically sloughed		X	
Reptiles—Keratinized horny layer periodically sloughed or flaked		X	
Birds—Keratinized horny layer		X	
Uropygial gland and skin secrete lipid		X	
Feathers	X	X	Flight, tactile appendages, used in visual signals, sound production, physical support
Mammals—Keratinized horny layer continuously flaked (dandruff)		X	
Sebaceous glands		X	
Eccrine and apocrine glands			Perspiration, scent production
Hair	X	X	Tactile appendages, used in visual signals

Care of the Body Surface — A Comparative View

We are now ready to look at a variety of COBS behavior patterns among many different species. All of the patterns subsumed under the terms COBS are clearly related to the animals' body surface. That is, the animal touches its body surface either with part of its own body or some other object or substance. However, it is not always clear how some of these behavior patterns "care" for the body surface. As mentioned earlier, COBS behavior not only cleans the body surface but many also serve to apply substances to the body surface or realign hairs or feathers. And there are other possible functions.

Individual COBS

Marine Invertebrates.   Sediment and other material settling on the surfaces of many marine animals, such as coral, anemones, and asteroids, become entangled in mucous and, in general, are carried off by ciliary currents produced by the animal. The caridean shrimp (*Pondalus danae*) spends a large proportion of its time grooming sediment, small sedentary animals, and small plants from the exoskeleton, gills, limbs, and antennae (Bauer, 1974). All external surfaces of the shrimp are cleaned by the use of stout, comblike setae on the appendages. Each thoracic appendage with grooming setae cleans a specific part of the body, with some areas of overlap; for example, certain "specialist" appendages groom only these areas that have high concentrations of sensory receptors, such as the antennae. There is little variability in the movements involved, and cleaning bouts are short but frequent.

Terrestrial invertebrates.   Many terrestrial invertebrates engage in some type of behavior to clean the body surface of substances such as dust, pollen, or bodily secretions. A general description of grooming behavior in 115 species of Hymenoptera (bees, ants, wasps and sawflies) reveals twenty-eight different grooming movements (Farish, 1972). This study focused mainly on the use of grooming behavior as an aid to the scientist in establishing phylogenetic relationships, rather than on the function(s) of the behavior.

Grooming behavior in the fruit fly (*Drosophila melanogaster*) includes two basic types of movements — sweeping and rubbing. Sweeping with the bristled legs cleans the body (head, thorax, abdomen, and wings), and rubbing the legs together cleans them. A grooming bout typically consists of a series of repeated alternations of these movements. Szebenyi (1969) has observed particles being removed by mutual leg rubbing and has suggested that grooming not only cleans but may also distribute a wax coating over the body surface. When fruit flies are dusted with fine chalk, the dust elicits grooming behavior, mostly of the head and eyes; and powdering specific parts of the body increases grooming only to the parts dusted.

Heinz (1949) described cleaning habits of flies, as summarized as follows.

> *The cleaning habits of true flies (Diptera), in particular the common house fly (**Musca domestica***) and the flesh fly (Sarcophaga carnaria), are described, and their "typical" behavior is compared with the behavior of other species. The typical behavior involves movements of the forelegs over the head, the forelegs and hindlegs rubbing each other, and the hindlegs sweeping over the wings. Both the top and the bottom sides of the wings are cleaned by the ipsilateral hindlegs. The middle legs do not clean each other, but are cleaned by the forelegs or hindlegs. The hindlegs also clean the abdomen.*

> *These same flies characteristically clean themselves after copulation; and an increase in ambient temperature, which increases general activity, increases the frequency of grooming movements, but changes in illumination have no*

effect. Dusting the fly, and applying acetic acid or a hot needle to the leg, elicits grooming. In general, amputation of one leg leads to another leg taking over, but with some limitations; for instance, the middle legs can take over for the forelegs, but not for the hindlegs. Experiments in which a wing was amputated while being cleaned showed little or not disruption of the cleaning behavior. The leg movements continued with the same coordination and orientation.

Ants exhibit many different grooming movements, generally clustered around three basic cleaning postures (Wilson, 1971). These postures include foreleg and antennal cleaning, leg cleaning, and abdominal cleaning. The cleaning "instruments" are the legs, which have comblike spurs for collecting material, and the lower mouthparts including the tongue. The antenna is always cleaned by the ipsilateral foreleg and each foreleg is cleaned by the ipsilateral maxilla (mouthpart). Cleaning the antennae is the most frequent of the cleaning movements, probably because antennae are important sensory organs. The limbs are cleaned more often than the body.

In addition to cleaning the animal, grooming movements in ants probably spread secretory materials over the body surface. Wallis (1962) has suggested that grooming in ants may spread a coat of saliva over the body, which could protect the surface from moisture and be sufficiently antiseptic to prevent the growth of lethal molds and bacteria.

Studies of insect grooming promise to yield interesting information about the way behavior is sequentially organized. Since insects have relatively simple nervous systems and groom under relatively constant environmental conditions, insect grooming is an excellent preparation for studying the relations between the nervous system and behavior.

Fish, Amphibians, and Reptiles. Few behavior patterns that could be described as COBS behavior occur in these animals. Specific movements of rubbing ("chafing") objects on the substrate aid in removing ectoparasites from fish and in sloughing of the skin during molting in amphibians and reptiles. Frogs and toads scratch or wipe the body with the legs and claws in response to tactile stimulation or to local irritants. Many amphibian and reptilian species "bask" in sunlight, but probably only as a means of behaviorally regulating body temperature.

Birds. Many elaborate COBS behaviors, also called maintenance and comfort behavior, have been described in birds.

Waterbathing, a common COBS behavior, consists of movements of head, wings, and sometimes the tail, together with ruffling of the body feathers, which wets the plumage. The method of bathing differs among groups of birds, particularly between water and land birds. Water birds bathe by ducking the head and shoulders under the water, sending water onto the back and beating the wings vigorously, splashing water over the plumage. Geese and swans occasionally even turn somersaults in the water.

Land birds use a number of methods to bathe, largely determined by anatomical structures and the habits of the species but to some extent modified by the local environmental situation. There are four main methods.

1. Some passerine (perching) birds *bathe by standing in the water* at a suitable depth, fluffing their feathers, flicking their wings, and ducking their head while rolling their bodies; this cycle is repeated until the bird is completely soaked.
2. Aerial birds such as swifts and swallows *bathe "on the wing"* by dropping repeatedly into the water and raising a spray of water on their backs.
3. Very active birds such as chickadees and wrens *dart into the water*, then perch and vibrate their wet fathers.

4. Other birds, such as the white breasted nuthatch and some woodpeckers, *expose their feathers to rain and dew.*

Bathing is longer in duration and more frequent during the summer and on sunny days. It is likely that one of the main functions of water-bathing is wetting the plumage so that efficient oiling and preening may be performed.

Birds also have specific movements for *drying* the feathers. These include "wing flapping," "ruffle and body shaking" (raising and lowering the contour feathers while relaxing and then jerking the body forward), "whirring" (vibration of the tail and wing tips), and "shuffling" the wings (drooping and vibrating them) and the tail.

Oiling almost always occurs after bathing; it involves the smearing of the lipid secretion of the uropygial gland onto the feathers, particularly the wings. Simmons (1964, p. 280) states: "The major (interrelated) functions of oiling probably include the water proofing and maintenance of the insulating character of the plumage, especially important in water birds: this includes keeping them supple, not over brittle, and hence reducing wear and the chances of breakage, a vital factor in the case of wing feathers."

The behaviors associated with oiling are transferring the oil from the uropygial gland to the plumage with the bill by "stroking" and "quivering" movements. The underparts of the wing pose problems for oiling. Most passerines get oil on the bill, transfer some of it to a foot, and then scratch their heads to get the head feathers oiled. The underside of the wing is then oiled mainly by the bill. Some species also rub the side of the head over the uropygial gland and then transfer oil to the body surface.

Preening, which almost always follows bathing and oiling, "is the basic and most important single activity in feather care" and "comprises the arrangement, cleaning, and general maintenance of the health and structure of the feathers by the bill, by direct contact between bill and feathers, and — in many species — by the dressing of the plumage with organic liquids (e.g., preen oil)" (Simmons, 1964, p. 280). The two main types of movements involved in preening are the use of both mandibles in "nibbling" or "drawing" and the use of the closed bill in "stroking" the feathers. When nibbling, the bird removes specks and other foreign material from the feather or skin by means of precise nibbling or digging action; drawing involves pulling feathers through the bill. Nibbling and drawing remove stale preen oil, feather exudates, dirt, and ectoparasites from the plumage.

Preening usually occurs in bouts. In many species (e.g., zebra finches, *Taeniopygia guttata*), bout lengths are distributed nonrandomly, with many short and many long ones. Long bouts seem to be due to general irritation and mainly involve cleaning of the plumage. Short bouts seem to be due to specific sources of irritation, but since they are often associated with disturbance of the bird, they could also be viewed at times as displacement activities, as will be discussed later.

Sunbathing involves exposing the plumage and the skin to the rays of the sun. The behavior varies in intensity, from a simple fluffing of the feathers and drooping of the wings to a more intense ruffling (especially the head feathers and the feathers around the uropygial gland) that is combined with fanning of the tail feathers, spreading of the wing feathers, and leaning away from the sun. Sometimes the drooped wing will be raised to expose the flank and undersurface of the bird to the sun. At very high behavioral intensity, a bird will lie on the ground with both wings and tail feathers completely spread out.

A number of functions have been proposed for sunbathing. One explanation is that birds are seeking warmth even though they are homeothermic and can regulate body temperature. Presumably they can reduce the energy expended for thermoregulation in cold air by taking sunbathing postures. Another explanation is that sunbathing increases the movement of ectoparasites, which makes them easier to remove by preening, but evidence for this function is not very convincing (Kennedy 1969).

Many birds sunbathe to dry their plumage after it has become wet. Mousebirds, which have soft, hairlike plumage, sunbathe most frequently after rain or dew. Cormorants and snakebirds, which do not have a waterproof plumage but chase and catch fish underwater, must dry themselves by perching in a tree or on a rock and by spreading their wings. It has also been proposed that sunbathing plays a role in molting and may increase the secretion of oil from the uropygial gland (Kennedy, 1969).

Dusting or dustbathing consists of squatting in fine dry earth or sand and forming hollows of dust by movements of the bill, scraping of the feet, and shuffling of the body. The dust is usually driven into the plumage by wing and feet movements. Afterward, the dust is removed by vigorous shaking. The movements involved in dusting differ between species; a unique example is the white winged chough, which stands up and applies dust to specific parts of its plumage with its bill. Dusting is not as widespread among avian species as bathing in water, and the behaviors are not identical in form. Data regarding the

sequence of movements of dustbathing are available for both bobwhite quail and Japanese quail (refs. in Table 19.2).

Care of feet and bill in many species involves lubricating the feet and bill with preen oil during oiling of the feathers, which probably prevents these parts from becoming dry and scaly. The bill is often cleaned by wiping it against the ground, branches, or any other firm object after bathing or eating. In some species, the bill is also cleaned by scratching it with the feet. Gulls plunge the bill into the ground, and many water birds dip the bill into water and shake it. During preening, the feet are usually examined and cleaned of dirt.

Anting is perhaps the most dramatic COBS behavior observed in birds. This behavior, which is typical of passerine birds, involves the application of fluids produced by ants to the bird's feathers. The fluids involved are formic acid produced by acid-ejecting formicine ants and a repugnant anal fluid produced by dolichoderine ants. The species of stinging ants are not used for anting.

The movements involved in anting are classified into "active" and "passive" anting. When a bird actively ants, it holds the ant in its bill and applies the fluid to specific parts of the body. In

Table 19.2
Studies on the Effects of Deprivation on COBS

Behavior	Stimulus Removed	Species	Reference
Dustbathing	Dust	Bobwhite quail	Borchelt, Eyer and McHenry, 1973; Borchelt, 1975
		Japanese quail	Benson, 1965; Borchelt, Hoffmann, Hurrell and McCarthy, 1979
Sandbathing	Sand	Kangaroo rat	Borchelt, Griswold and Brancheck, 1976
		Gerbil	Tortora, Eyer and Overmann, 1974
		Chinchilla	Stern and Merari, 1969
Posing for cleaning	The cleaner fish	Nine species of fish	Losey, 1971

Some Major Classes of Behavior

passive anting the bird permits ants to swarm over its body and into the plumage while ejecting their fluid. Interestingly, although anting is considered relatively stereotyped and "innate," birds have to learn which species of ants are correct for anting. Some individuals among anting species of birds never learn to ant, and others ant with inappropriate objects such as mothballs, cigarette butts, citrus fruits, and other pungent objects.

One of the functions of anting is the removal of ectoparasites; for formic acid and certain other ant secretions are insecticides (Dubinen, cited in Kelso and Nice, 1963). When anting, birds most often apply the fluids to the underside and tips of the wings.

Potter and Hauser (1974) described the relationship of anting and sandbathing to molting in wild birds.

> A relationship between the incidence of anting and sunbathing and the molting of specific feather tracts was noted. Sunning seems to occur when feather tracts are easily exposed to sunlight and hard to reach with an ant. Anting occurs when feather tracts are not easily exposed to sunlight but can be reached by anting. Since different feather tracts molt at different times, Potter and Hauser suggested that anting and sunning are coordinated comfort behaviors that apply heat to the skin.

Mammals. Individual COBS behavior is commonly observed in mammals. Such behaviors are referred to as grooming, maintenance, and comfort behavior; they remove ectoparasites, dirt, or other foreign substances from the hair and may also aid in wound healing.

Washing involves movements of the forelimbs and mouth (incisors and tongue) and is widespread among mammalian species. The tongue is used to lick the limbs and the teeth to nibble the fur. In rodents, washing typically follows a cephalocaudal or head-to-toe, pattern. Face

washing occurs first: the forepaws are licked repeatedly and rubbed over the face, head, and ears. Face washing is followed by body grooming, which consists of up and downward movements of the forelimbs and paws. The ventral part of the body is licked or nibbled, followed by licking of the genitalia and perineal regions; often the tail is grasped by the forepaws and licked from base to tip.

Face washing has functions other than cleaning. In a variety of rodents as well as marsupials, exposure to high temperature leads to saliva spreading. This behavior resembles partial face washing and serves to spread saliva over the face and body to aid the loss of body heat by evaporation. In gerbils, face washing also spreads a Harderian gland secretion over the face. The Harderian gland is located behind and under the eye, with ducts leading to the corners of the eyes and to the nose. Secretions from this gland elicit investigation and grooming from other gerbils. Thus, in gerbils, and probably other rodents as well, face washing plays a role in the regulation of social behavior. (see chapter 20).

Individual grooming, or autogrooming, is accomplished in lower primates such as tree shrews with the tongue and teeth, the lower incisors forming a "toothcomb." In higher primates like chimpanzees, the hands are also used for grooming (van Lawick-Goodall, 1968). Sometimes both hands are used, one for pushing or parting the hair and the other for picking at the exposed skin with the thumbs or fingers. The lower lip, and, in some species, the tail may also be used for parting the hair. Typically, any foreign material picked from the skin or fur is conveyed to the mouth and usually ingested.

Scratching involves the stroking of one limb (usually a hind limb) over a particular area of the body and is most often accomplished by a series of vigorous rhythmical movements. However, when scratching the inside of the ear, or the eye region, movements may be slower and more "cautious." Ground squirrels curl up their toes and scratch with the "knuckles" around the eye region.

Primates usually scratch using the hands. The body can also be rubbed against objects, such as branches or rocks, and ungulates may scratch using the horns of other animals. Chimpanzees scratch downward over the body while pulling the hair through the fingers to dry the hair (van Lawick-Goodall, 1968). Other drying movements include rubbing against trees, rubbing with leaves, or licking water from the hair.

Several studies have shown that scratching with the hind legs is important in controlling ectoparasites in mice. Amputating the toes (Weisbroth, Friedman, Powell and Scher, 1974) or placing collars on the animals (Murray, 1961) leads to increased numbers of ectoparasites.

Shaking is also common among mammals. Shaking removes dust, dirt, debris, or water from the hair. It may also realign hairs that have become disarranged by grooming behavior.

Waterbathing is observed in a variety of species, but probably functions as a means of losing heat rather than cleaning the body surface.

Sandbathing occurs in many rodents that inhabit arid, desert like environments. These mammals have evolved methods for reducing evaporative water loss, one of which is a copious sebaceous gland secretion. If the animal does not sandbathe the secretion eventually mats the fur. Sandbathing has been described in gerbils, deermice, bush mice, pocket mice, kangaroo rats and mice, chinchillas, and ground squirrels. The movements consist of side rubs, ventrum rubs, and writhing from side to side. The frequencies of the different movements vary among species. Chinchillas are unique in that they roll over on their backs and spin completely around.

In removing lipid materials from the body surface, sandbathing deposits them on the substrate, where they may be smelled by another animal. These odors may have communication value. Kangaroo rats repeatedly use certain sites for sandbathing, and the odors left there may be important for individual and social recognition. Laine and Griswold (1976) tested bannertail kangoroo rats (*Dipodomys spectabalis*) in the laboratory and found that both males and females are strongly attracted to sandbathing loci used by conspecifics, and that both sexes are able to distinguish the sex of an earlier user. Thus, sandbathing has both a cleaning and a communication function.

Sunbathing involves standing or lying in sunlight and is a common mammalian behavior. It is not usually a means of increasing body temperature since mammals are homeothermic, but is important in the biosynthesis of vitamin D. Many mammals do not obtain sufficient amounts of vitamin D from their food, but provitamin D in skin and sebaceous lipid is converted by sunlight to vitamin D, which is then absorbed into the circulatory system or is ingested by licking the fur.

Anting-like behavior has been reported in grey squirrels and domestic cats, but it consists only of rolling over ants or anthills rather than involving the more elaborate behaviors seen in birds. Its function is unknown. Cats and dogs also roll over and rub themselves with a variety of aromatic substances, including catnip and dung. Such behavior should probably be classified as scent marking.

One of the strangest examples of this type of behavior is "self-anointing" in hedgehogs. Various species have been observed to lick objects while accumulating saliva in the mouth and then "anointing" the spines with the saliva. Alternate licking of the object and then itself may continue for many minutes. In captivity, almost any object may be licked. Observations of wild hedgehogs (Brockie, 1976) suggest that the saliva gives off a sharp, rank odor. "Anointing" is observed in young hedgehogs removed from the mother and placed in novel environments and in adults during the breeding season. It probably functions only as a signaling device to advertise an animal's presence to another hedgehog. A similar behavior, possibly with a similar advertising function, has been observed in capuchin monkeys by Simmons (1966). These captive monkeys spread a mixture of onion juice and saliva over their bodies.

Social COBS

We have seen that COBS behaviors may also have social functions. Many of the behavior patterns of social COBS are similar to those of individual COBS, but social COBS immediately and intimately involves a social relationship.

Many social insects exhibit social COBS. For instance, ants lick one another, frequently around the mouthparts, abdomen, and limb joints. The use of the tongue to groom nestmates occurs in all ants, honeybees, termites, and in some social wasps and probably plays at least some role in the transfer of pheromones (Wilson, 1971). It is known, for instance, that the queen substance of the honeybee, 9-ketodecenoic acid, is transmitted from the queen to the workers by grooming.

Social COBS in birds, called allopreening, is most characteristic of species that are gregarious. Many cliff-nesting seabirds, such as gannets and guillemots, which are packed together on ledges, preen each other. Allopreening is most developed in, and plays a prominent role in the social life of, species that show "clumping" behavior (Sparks, 1965).

Sparks has described allopreening in the red avadavat (*Amandava amandava*), which may spend up to two-thirds of the daytime "clumping" — perching in body contact with one another. Ruffling of the head feathers serves as an "invitation" for a bird to be preened by another. Allopreening involves feather nibbling directed mainly at the feathers of the head. The bird being preened may move its head so as to present different surfaces to be preened.

Social preening of the head region in birds has an obvious function since birds cannot preen their own head feathers. In addition, however, allopreening tends to reduce aggression or fighting in the social group. The allopreening "invitation" posture appears to elicit nonaggressive preening rather than attack from other birds.

Allopreening also occurs in birds that are not particularly gregarious. Chickens allopreen the head regions of conspecifics, and the preened bird often adopts a characteristic posture. The specific behaviors of allopreening in chickens are not the same as those of autopreening. Pecking and feather pulling are commonly seen during allopreening, suggesting that feeding or aggression may be involved.

Allogrooming is widespread among mammals. Licking of the young occurs frequently as part of parental behavior, but decreases as the young become independent of the parents. Allogrooming among adult animals occurs frequently among rats and mice, ground squirrels, marmots, cats (both wild and domestic), and a variety of ungulate species.

In most mammals, allogrooming is elicited by a characteristic body posture on the part of the potential groomer. For instance, a marmot that approaches another marmot and rolls over on its back is likely to be groomed.

One of the functions of allogrooming is removing ectoparasites. Other functions of allogrooming include cleaning the fur of detritus, removal of dirt from wounds, identification of individuals, or transfer of scents. Allogrooming may also play a role in dominance relationships. In ground squirrels, prairie dogs, and domestic rats allogrooming is usually initiated or maintained by the dominant individual.

The dual cleaning and social function of allogrooming is most clearly seen among primates. Allogrooming starts with a "soliciting" posture by the potential groomer, which usually involves presenting the back to the groomer and looking away. The animal being groomed makes constant adjustments of body posture as the groomer works through the fur. Cleaning of the skin and fur in allogrooming is accomplished much as in autogrooming. The frequency of allogrooming in the higher primates is roughly correlated with the type of social structure of the species. A generalization is that species such as macaques (rhesus monkeys) and baboons, which have a rigidly maintained dominance hierarchy, show more allogrooming behavior than gorillas and chimpanzees, which have a less well-defined hierarchical organization (Marler, 1965). Allogrooming is predominately characteristic of mature females, and animals of lower status tend to allogroom those higher in the social hierarchy. Among rhesus monkeys and chimpanzees the relationship between allogrooming and rank is more complex; the age of an animal, kinship relations, and liasons between individuals determine which animal grooms another.

Social COBS sometimes occurs between members of different species. Morris (1955) observed Java sparrows, a species that shows "clumping" behavior, caged with a necklace dove. The Java sparrows were attracted to the dove, "clumped" with it, and preened it. According to Selander and LaRue (1961), the brown-headed cowbird is naturally adept at soliciting preening from many other species of birds, and van Lawick-Goodall (1968) describes interspecific grooming between chimpanzees and baboons. That chimpanzees will groom other species is clearly seen in a report by Falk (1958) who taught a chimpanzee a visual discrimination using as a reward the opportunity for the chimpanzee to groom the experimenter's arm.

Symbiotic Care of the Body Surface

An unusual form of care of the body surface occurs sometimes in symbiotic realtionships, whereby one species benefits by having its body surface cleaned and the other species benefits by obtaining food. Such relationships occur in many invertebrates and some species of fishes and birds. Ants, for instance, have parasitic mites that attach themselves to their legs and feed off the secretions that collect on the ant's legs when the ant cleans itself. Other parasitic species lick the surface of ants and feed on the cutaneous secretions and the coating of saliva with which ants cover themselves.

Cleaning symbioses in fish range from ones in which the cleaning relationship is constant and specific, as in the case of remoras (Echeneidae), which remain attached to one host for long periods of time, to species of shrimp and fish, which clean many individuals of a number of species. An example of the latter is the relationship between fishes of the genus Amphiprion and sea anemones. These fishes prefer certain species of sea anemone, frequently defend their anemone as their "territory" against other fishes, and remove organic and inorganic material from on and around their anemone, all without being injured by its poisonous tentacles. Another example are cleaner fish (*Labroides* species), which clean other host fish of parasites. These fish entice the host to permit itself to be cleaned by a "cleaner dance" consisting of butting the snout against the host's fins to spread them and against the host's mouth to open it so that the cleaner fish can enter. While cleaning the host, a cleaner fish continuously vibrates to signal the host it is being cleaned. The host fish may invite the cleaner fish to clean by opening its mouth. It signals the cleaner fish to leave by jerking movements of the body (Feder, 1966).

The significance of cleaning has been in part based on the hypothesis that cleaners are mutualistic symbionts that feed partially on ectoparasites. This hypothesis was supported by the observations of Limbaugh (1961) who removed all cleaning organisms from a reef and noted that there was both a decrease in the number of fish on the reef and an increase in the number of ectoparasites on the fish that remained. However, Losey (1972), in a more controlled experiment, failed to obtain the same results after removing cleaner fish (*Labroides*) from a reef in Hawaii. More recent field experiments by Losey (1974) in Puerto Rico indicate that, when the parasitic infection rate is high, effects such as reported by Limbaugh might be expected. It is probable that in some cases ectoparasites comprise only a small part of the diet of cleaners. In fact, Feder (1966) defined cleaning symbiosis in the marine environment as a relationship involving not only the removal of ectoparasites, but also removal of bacteria, diseased and injured tissue, mucus, and unwanted food particles from cooperating hosts.

Birds have symbiotic relationships with many other animals whose body surfaces they clean. For instance, when a crocodile rests with its mouth open, as a thermoregulatory mechanism, an Egyptian plover may enter the crocodile's mouth and feed on bits of food lodged between its teeth; the plover also picks parasites from the crocodile's skin. Oxpeckers obtain all their food by eating ticks and mites from the hides of large animals in Africa. They have sharp curved claws and a long stiff tail so that they can climb all over their hosts, up and down the legs, over their backs, and even under their bellies.

Variables Affecting COBS Behavior

Several categories of variables instigate or sustain the various classes of consummatory behavior. These categories include (1) deprivation and stimulation, (2) experiential factors, (3) temporal factors, (4) situational variables, (5) neural determinants, and (6) endocrine determinants. It will become obvious that COBS behavior has not been well studied at this stage of comparative analysis. Hopefully, this state of affairs will be seen as a challenge to budding students of animal behavior.

Deprivation and Stimulation Effects

Ideally, deprivation and stimulation techniques can be used together to help find out how a behavior works. For instance, *depriving* a kangaroo rat of the opportunity to sandbathe results in a subsequent increase in sandbathing behavior as well as an increase in lipid secretions on the pelage. These results suggest that the two phenomena are related, a hypothesis confirmed by *stimulating* the animal with artificial substances on the fur and nothing a subsequent increase in sandbathing. The deprivation experiment mimics a common occurrence in the natural environment and hints at one of the functions of sandbathing; the stimulation experiment tests this suggestion directly.

Deprivation. Only a few studies have investigated the effects of deprivation on COBS behavior. These are listed in Table 19.2. The general findings are that deprivation of relevant stimuli lead to a subsequent increase in behavior. Some of these studies show concomitant changes in conditions of the body surface, specifically lipid secretions and ectoparasite levels. It is possible that anting could be added to Table 19.2 since Goodwin (1951, p. 623) noted that for the Jay (*Garrulus glandarius*), "at least a week or more since the last session seems necessary for keen anting . . ." No mention was made here of changes in plumage condition.

Other studies have deprived animals of structures involved in COBS behavior. For instance, the ectoparasite levels increase in debeaked chickens (Brown, 1972) and the debris and settling organisms increase on shrimp with ablated cleaning legs (Bauer, 1974). Fentress (1973b) studied mice with the forelimbs amputated soon after birth and noted that they developed surprisingly normal coordination of facewashing movements, but no mention was made of the condition of the coat or pelage.

Stimulation. When an experiment suggests that body surface changes occur when an animal is deprived of COBS behavior or when an animal under natural conditions removes substances from the body surface, then a stimulation experiment is in order. Table 19.3 lists experiments in

Table 19.3
Experiments on the Stimulation of Body Surfaces

Behavior	Stimulus Applied	Species	Reference
Dustbathing	Uropygial lipid, water	Japanese quail	Borchelt, Hoffmann, Hurrell and McCarthy, 1979
Sandbathing	Lanolin, water	Kangaroo rat	Griswold, Borchelt, Branchek and Bensko, 1977
Grooming	Dust	Fruit fly, housefly, fleshfly	Connolly, 1968 Heinz, 1949
Bill wiping	Sticky syrup	Chaffinch	Rowell, 1961
Scratching	Touch, mild acid	Frog	Jacobson and Baker, 1969
Facewashing	Mild acid	Mouse	Fentress, 1972
Oiling	Water	Japanese quail	Borchelt, Hoffmann, Hurrell, and McCarthy, 1979
Sunbathing	Light	Chicken Hawk	Brown, 1974; Müeller, 1972
Preening	Water	Bunting Chaffinch Tern	Andrew, 1956 Rowell, 1961 van Iersel and Bol, 1958
	Lice	Chicken	Brown, 1974

which the body surface of animals has been stimulated by various substances. Often, the result is that a COBS behavior is elicited or increases in frequency when the relevant stimuli are applied to the body surface.

Experiential Factors

This category of variables refers to the effects of previous experience on COBS behavior when an animal is observed or tested under conditions similar to those it originally experienced.

Early Experience. Many reports on the natural history of various species contain information about the development of COBS behavior, but these reports are usually limited to the age when it first occurs. Very few studies have investigated the role of early experience on the development of COBS behavior. Early pecking experiences play an important role in the development of dustbathing in bobwhite quail chicks, as described in Part I of this chapter. Adolescent rhesus monkeys, restricted from social experiences since weaning, show fewer and less prolonged allogrooming bouts than monkeys captured in the field and allowed a variety of social experiences (Mason, 1960).

Learning. Learning theories that view reinforcement as the elicitation of consummatory sequences of behavior (Denny and Ratner, 1970; Glickman and Schiff, 1967) predict that an animal will learn an operant response in order to engage in a COBS behavior. Except for the aforementioned study by Falk with chimpanzees this question has apparently not been investigated. Several studies have tried to reinforce grooming or preening behavior with food, escape, and so on, (i.e., to make a COBS behavior into an operant), and have met with variable success (Hogan, 1964; Shettleworth, 1975; Thorndike, 1898). Usually the COBS behavior was not well learned, becoming increasingly abbreviated and incomplete over trials (see Chapter 5).

Temporal Factors

Many observations indicate either long-term (seasonal) or short-term (daily) cycles in the incidence or frequency of COBS behavior. Seasonal peaks have been reported for anting and sunbathing in birds (Potter and Hauser, 1974), with some indication for seasonal changes in the frequencies of dustbathing and waterbathing, and mutual preening in birds is definitely coordinated with the breeding cycle. Similarly, the amount of allo- and autogrooming in rhesus monkeys fluctuates throughout the course of the female's estrus cycle.

Field observations indicate that COBS behavior is often limited to particular times of the day. Many birds and mammals spend the time immediately after waking and before resting engaged in grooming or preening behavior. In domestic fowl, the peaks of preening occur in the morning and evening (Wood-Gush, 1959); but for quail, dustbathing is more prevalent in the afternoon (Schein, Borchelt, and Statkiewitz, 1977).

Grooming occupies over 60 percent of the nonsleeping, nonresting time of cats maintained in the laboratory and about 40 percent of the awake time of the laboratory rat. In rats, most of the grooming occurs during the morning hours prior to the diurnal sleep period. Different types of grooming occur along with other activities. Upon awakening, rats tend to scratch themselves whereas facewashing occurs mostly after eating and drinking (Bolles, 1960). Allogrooming in primates also appears to be coordinated with eating and drinking activities, but some species may start the day with grooming and others groom mostly during "leisure" hours of the afternoon.

Situational Variables.

Motivated behavior is generally influenced by the environmental setting in which the animal finds itself. Not surprisingly, then, some COBS behaviors occur only in specific situations. For instance, dustbathing and sandbathing are restricted to specific places where the substrate is appropriate, and allogrooming in primates is determined by who grooms whom.

The social setting is an important variable. An increase in COBS behavior when an animal is in the presence of other individuals engaged in COBS behavior has been commonly observed. Such social facilitation, for example, occurs for grooming in fruit flies. Here physical contact with other flies has been ruled out as the critical factor; for white-eyed mutants with severely impaired vision do *not* show the social facilitation effect. Social facilitation of sunbathing in birds is widespread (Kennedy, 1969). Social facilitation is a factor in the development of dustbathing in bobwhite quail chicks, as discussed in Part I of this chapter, and social facilitation of facewashing occurs in gerbils and perhaps other rodents.

COBS behavior frequently occurs in situations in which an animal is in conflict or is frustrated, as when the completion of a behavior sequence is thwarted by blocking or removing a goal stimulus. For example, rats placed on extinction in an alley (Miller and Stevenson, 1936) or on a partial reinforcement schedule (Bindra, 1963) show an increase in grooming; and Denny and Ratner (1970) describe unusual and excessive preening in a male Japanese quail that was unable to mount an unreceptive female that had not been adequately courted.

Grooming or preening that occur in situations in which an animal is in conflict is typically called "displacement" behavior. Displacement activities appear as irrelevant behaviors "out of context" to the ongoing behavior, and they are often characterized as incomplete or "frantic" in appearance (Tinbergen, 1952), as in the example of the quail mentioned above.

The original explanation for displacement behavior was that its causal factors were different from the same behavior shown in "normal" circumstances. A conflict, for example, between approach and withdrawal, prevented the expression of either fighting or fleeing, and the "energy" was then displaced into another behavior, such as preening. Subsequent research has suggested that ever-present peripheral (body surface) stimuli might be, at least in part, responsible for the expression of COBS behavior in conflict situations. Conflict could lead to autonomic (vasomotor or pilomotor) activity, which might provide stimulation to the skin, thereby eliciting COBS behavior (Andrew, 1956); or mutual incompatibility between two behaviors could also allow a third to be expressed through "disinhibition." The latter hypothesis states that preening and grooming that were inhibited by the ongoing behavior are disinhibited by a conflict situation so that they are now elicited by peripheral stimulation (material on fur; disarray of feathers, etc.). Some evidence in support of this hypothesis is provided by Andrew (1956), who studied preening in birds, and Fentress (1968), who studied grooming in voles.

Duncan and Wood-Gush (1972) have found topographic differences between normal and displacement preening. In conflict situations they found that preening movements tended to be shorter and occurred in different areas of the body as compared with normal preening. Displacement preening was directed mostly to the breast and wing areas whereas normal preening was to the entire body surface.

Additional evidence for the presence of overlapping causal factors in COBS and other consummatory behavior is the finding that water deprivation decreases grooming in rats (Bolles, 1960). Oral grooming (face washing and licking) account for about one third of the rat's normal evaporative water loss; thus, in situations where water is scarce, grooming behavior is less frequent.

These examples of situational variables influencing COBS behavior support the hypothesis that behavior in general is influenced by both "specific" and "non-specific" factors. For instance, a specific factor influencing COBS would be appropriate stimulation of the body surface; a non-specific factor would include those stimuli that are directly involved in another class of consummatory behavior (e.g., fleeing or drinking) but which, in some situations, influence COBS behavior. Thus, examples of displacement behavior show how multiple inhibitory, disinhibitory, and excitatory factors underlie the control of different behavior patterns.

Neural Determinants.

Understanding the neural mechanisms underlying any complex behavior involves detailed information concerning stimulus parameters, integration of sensorimotor systems, and interactions of these features with various central neural structures. Research on the neural determinants of COBS behaviors can best be characterized as scattered.

Electrical stimulation of the hypothalamus can induce grooming in a wide range of mammals (Roberts, 1970), probably through descending inputs to the lower brain stem. Stimulation of lower brain stem regions such as midbrain, pons, or medulla elicits grooming in cats and rats. Cerebellar stimulation can also induce grooming in cats, probably because of projections from the cerebellum to reticular formation systems. Studies of stimulation-induced grooming in cats (Berntson and Hughes, 1976) have shown that the behavior is not due to stimulation of simple motor mechanisms, since the topography of the grooming behavior is responsive to environmental changes such as foreign objects on the fur.

The brainstem loci responsible for grooming thus appear to involve complex organizations of sensorimotor systems sensitive to the external stimulus situation.

Electrical stimulation of some brain sites elicits occasional preening behavior in pigeons and in ring doves. Phillips and Youngren (1971) have obtained bill wiping, face and head scratching, body shaking, and preening in domestic chickens with electrical stimulation of certain sites. They also obtained prolonged oiling and preening sequences from a number of sites in mallard ducks.

Endocrine Effects

The effects of hormones on skin glands are well established, though few studies have investigated the effects of hormones on COBS behavior. The effect of gonadal and extragonadal hormones on sebaceous glands has been well clarified (Montagna, Ellis, and Silver, 1963). Androgens increase and estrogens decrease the size and secretion rate of sebaceous glands. Uropygial gland size and secretion rate are also influenced by gonadal and extragonadal hormones, but the complex relationships probably involved in its hormonal control in various species have yet to be worked out. Seasonal differences occur in uropygial gland size (Kennedy, 1971) and in amount of feather lipid (Dubinen, cited in Kelso and Nice, 1963).

Therefore, sex and seasonal differences might be expected to occur in COBS behaviors that are specifically involved in the regulation of skin gland secretions. Anting and sunbathing show seasonal differences coordinated with stage of molt, but the relative contribution of hormone levels and stimulation from feather tracts to the observed behavioral differences is presently unknown. Sex differences have been reported for dustbathing in quail, grooming in gerbils, and auto-and allogrooming in primates.

A Final Perspective

The term "care of the body surface" probably should be used in the same way as the term "reproduction" is used, that is, to refer to a broad class of behavior with a very general biological function. As reproduction in birds, for instance, may consist of courtship, nesting, mating, and so forth (each with its own particular function), so COBS may include dustbathing, preening, and oiling in birds or face washing, body grooming, and sandbathing in rodents. And each of these behavior patterns has its own set of controlling factors; or to use Fentress' (1973a) terminology, each probably has *both* "specific" and "nonspecific" causal factors.

The task of future research is to delineate the interrelationships among specific and nonspecific factors involved in each of the behaviors included in COBS. Perhaps the easiest strategy would be to investigate relatively specific factors first and then analyze the role of nonspecific ones. At some point in time, the term COBS may become less useful, especially if it becomes obvious that there is little overlap among the factors that affect the various behavior sequences included in COBS. At that point in the future, researchers will be ready to probe the later stages of comparative analysis. COBS behavior, as a widespread, diverse, multifunctional and multicausal class of behavior, should play an important role in the development of any lasting theory of behavior.

Study Questions

1. Describe the dustbathing sequence for bobwhite quail.
2. Why do animals dustbathe or sandbathe?
3. Describe an individual COBS behavior for some animal.
4. What is anting?

5. What are the functions of face washing?

6. What is displacement behavior and why may it occur?

7. What is allogrooming? Give an example.

8. Describe a specific symbiotic COBS behavior.

9. List the main groups of independent variables that affect COBS behavior.

20

Scent Marking in Mammals

Richard L. Doty

Department of Physiology and Department of Otorhinolaryngology and Human Communication, School of Medicine, University of Pennsylvania, Philadelphia, Pa., and Research Section, V.A. Hospital, Philadelphia, Pa.

Most organisms, from the simplest bacteria to the largest of the fishes and mammals, rely heavily on chemical signals for their survival. As human beings we can readily identify with our animal compatriots who follow aromas in their quests to find food, but their more seedy preoccupations with the smelling and licking of excrement and other foul things (to us) are often beyond everything but our wildest fantasies. As we all know, dogs spend considerable time and effort sniffing and urinating at selected spots throughout the neighborhood. While our own species demarcates its homes and buildings optically with signs and street numbers, many mammals use scents for similar purposes. Specialized scent glands have evolved in at least fifteen of the eighteen mammalian orders and have been classified into over forty different types on the basis of body location. Urine provides the most common source of chemicals used in scent marking, although feces, saliva, and general body secretions are also used in addition to scent gland products.

This chapter briefly examines the nature of mammalian scent marking and associated morphological adaptations and includes a discussion of several theories of the functions of these common behaviors. Since only limited data are available from different taxa within a given mammalian genus or family, a true comparative analysis of scent marking is not yet possible. Thus, of necessity, the present chapter focuses on widely divergent forms which exhibit scent marking, assuming, as has been done previously (cf. Ralls, 1971), that a likely similarity of function exists in many cases. Given the close relationship between scent marking activities and social processes, it is reasonable to assume that such behaviors are important for the survival of many species and should be viewed as having major evolutionary significance.[1]

---

[1] Since, of necessity, the present chapter is somewhat cursory, the interested student may wish to refer to other, more detailed, accounts of this topic (e.g., Bronson, 1976; Doty, 1974, 1976; Eisenberg and Kleiman, 1972; Ewer, 1968; Grau, 1976; Johnson, 1973; Muller-Schwarze and Mozell, 1977; Mykytowcz, 1970, 1974; Ralls, 1971; Thiessen and Rice, 1976; Wynne-Edwards, 1962).

Behavioral Descriptions and Definitions of Scent Marking

Mammals rarely leave excrement or other bodily secretions in random fashion within their home ranges. While it is true that some odorous chemicals are released into the environment passively (e.g., as we walk we leave chemical trails that are perceptible to bloodhounds and other macrosmatic animals), the majority of chemicals used in signaling are released in more deliberate ways. Most authorities appear to reserve the term "scent marking" for behaviors that facilitate the active transfer of bodily-produced chemicals to objects or specific sectors of the home range, although acts of spreading secretions or excretions from one animal to another, or from one sector of the body to another, are also placed in this classification. In this chapter, scent marking activities related to the deposition of odors on the substrate or on inanimate objects within the environment receive the major emphasis.

The exact form of scent marking behavior varies as a function of a number of factors, including the nature of the substance to be deposited, topographical aspects of the habitat, and the particular sex, species, and individual in question. Clearly, both internal and external factors influence the frequency and typology of such behaviors. Urine — the most ubiquitous of the chemicals used in scent communication — is deposited in a number of different ways by different species. For example, male housemice actively "spot" the substrate with urine using hairs at the end of the prepuce, which act like small paint brushes (Figures 20.1 and 20.2).

Male dogs commonly deposit urine on selected objects by elevating one of their hind legs in a characteristic fashion, although they sometimes use a few other postures as well. Female dogs, on the other hand, are more likely to use a wider variety of urination postures (Figure 20.3). Territorial male mountain gazelles, like many other artiodactyl (even-numbered toed) ungulates, perform a ritualized sequence of urination and defecation that deposits urine and feces at the same location on the substrate (Figure 20.4).

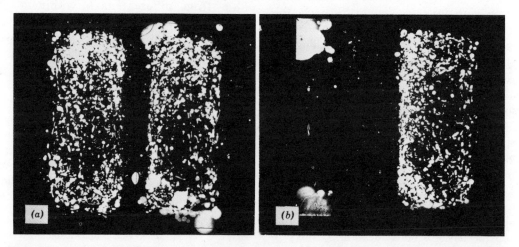

Figure 20.1. Ultraviolet visualizations of overnight urinary marking patterns of two male housemice housed in adjacent rectangular compartments separated by a screen partition before (a) and after (b) mice were permitted in the same compartment for the establishment of dominance. Note submissive mouse (b, left) urinated in large pools away from the wire partition and dominant mouse (b, right) concentrated marking activity near the wire mesh partition. (Photographs courtesy of Frank H. Bronson and Joel A. Maruniak, University of Texas.)

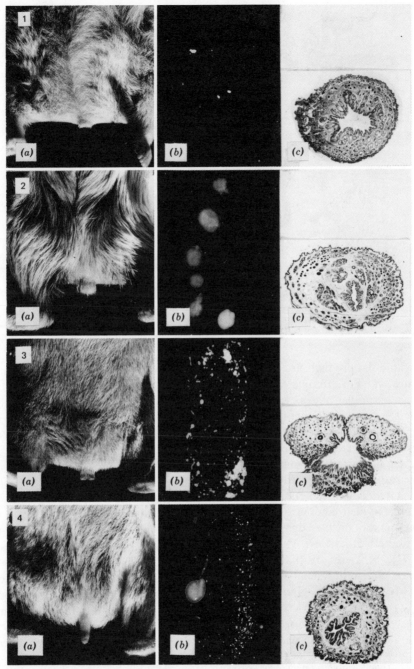

Figure 20.2. External appearance of the prepuce (*a*), typical patterns of open-field urination visualized by ultraviolet light (*b*), and cross sections of the distal regions of the prepuce (*c*), of four species of rodents: (1) golden hamster, *Mesocricetus auratus*; (2) Mongolian gerbil, *Meriones unguiculatus*; (3) housemouse, *Mus musculus*; and (4) deermouse, *Peromyscus maniculatus*. Note the length of the preputial sheath relative to the ankle. In general, a positive relation exists between the length of the prepuce and the number of urine spots deposited on the substrate. Magnifications: 1c, X11; 2c, X10; 3c, X14; 4c, X15. (Courtesy of Maruniak, Desjardins, and Bronson, 1975.)

Figure 20.3. Elimination postures exhibited by beagles. Males most commonly urinate using elevate and raise positions, whereas females most commonly urinate using squat and squat-raise positions. (Courtesy of Sprague and Anisko, 1973.)

Like urine, glandular products are also deposited in different ways.[2] For example, wild rabbits scent mark twigs and other objects with specialized chin glands, and deposit scent from anal glands on their fecal pellets while defecating. The odorized pellets are regularly deposited at "dunghills" within their home ranges, which serve as markers between adjacent group territories (Mykytowycz, 1970). Golden hamsters rub small flank glands on the sides of their laboratory cages and, in the wild, presumably on the edges of burrow entrances and tunnels (Drickamer, Vandenbergh, and Colby, 1973a, b; Tiefer, 1970). Wood rats, gerbils, deermice, and other small rodents rub specialized midventral scent glands on the

substrate or low-lying environmental protrusions, and ground squirrels and porcupines scent mark with glands located on the head (Doty and Kart, 1972; Ewer, 1966; Quay and Tomich, 1963; Thiessen and Rice, 1975). Yellow-cheeked voles and common water voles deposit scent from flank glands by scratching their feet on them and then stamping or walking on the ground (Frank, 1956; Wolfe and Johnson, personal communication).

The use of specialized glandular structures in scent marking is also noted in most of the larger mammals. For example, numerous ungulates rub glandular cephalic regions on objects, including soil, vegetation, and other conspecifics (Figure 20.5). Territorial male pronghorn antelope undertake regular walking journeys to renew old scent markings around their territory (Müller-Schwarze, 1972), as do various other artiodactyls (cf. Grau, 1976). A number of primates possess specialized scent glands that are used in a variety of marking behaviors (Figure 20.6), and wolves

---

[2]Specialized mammalian scent glands are usually aggregates of one or both of two general types of skin glands: sebaceous (holocrine, alveolar) and sudoriferous (apocrine, tubular, merocrine). The sebaceous holocrine glands (where the lipid secretion is formed by complete disintegration of the cells) are the most common skin glands of mammals, being dispersed throughout the hairy skin of all mammals except whales (Ebling, 1977).

Figure 20.4. Territorial male mountain gazelle (*Gazella gazella*) in the urination-defecation sequence at a dung pile. Starting in the urination posture (upper photo) the male steps forward with the hind legs only and assumes the defecation posture (bottom photo). Thus, the urine and feces are deposited at the same location. [Adapted from Grau (1976), with permission.]

Some Major Classes of Behavior

Figure 20.5. Territorial male Thomson's gazelle (*Gazella thomsoni*) marking vegetation with his preorbital gland. [Adapted from Grau (1976), with permission.]

Figure 20.6. Marmoset monkey (*Saguinus fuscicollis*) scent marking perch with sternal scent gland. This behavior is performed regularly on branches in the forest habitat. (Photograph courtesy of Giesla Epple, University of Pennsylvania.)

Scent Marking in Mammals

and other carnivores (including domestic cats and dogs) have several types of specialized scent structures (e.g., the anal sacs) that presumably play a role in scenting activity (Doty and Dunbar, 1974a, b). Even elephants possess specialized scent glands in several regions of the body, although the functions of such glands are poorly understood (Ewer, 1968).

Neuroendocrine Control of Scent Gland Proliferation and Scent Marking

In the majority of species for which data are available, the development of scent gland structures, as well as scent marking behaviors, is closely linked to gender and reproductive state. Thus, in most species, glandular development and associated scent depositing behaviors are sexually dimorphic, with males possessing larger glandular regions and marking more frequently than females (Doty and Kart, 1972; Ebling, 1977; Quay, 1968; Thiessen, Friend, and Lindzey, 1968). In many forms, variation in scent gland proliferation and marking follows seasonal patterns closely related to sexual recrudescence and abatement (cf. Müller-Schwarze, 1972; Stoddart, 1972). For example, the average size of the dorsal sebaceous glandular region of males of several species of kangaroo rats is largest from February to June (which coincides with their major breeding season), whereas the average size of the glands of females is relatively constant (Quay, 1953). Scent marking with forehead glands by male blacktailed deer is much more frequent during the Fall (preceding the climax of the rutting season) than during the Spring (Müller-Schwarze, 1972).

The strong relationship between scent gland development and reproductive hormones is demonstrated directly by castration and hormone replacement studies. Castration decreases the size and sebum production of both specialized and nonspecialized sebaceous skin glands of many male mammals, whereas testosterone replacement therapy does the opposite. Injection of testosterone increases cell mitoses — an activity that can be prevented by the simultaneous injection of antiandrogens such as cyproterone acetate (Ebling, 1973). Estradiol depresses sebaceous secretion in the skin glands of laboratory rats without significantly altering mitotic activity (Ebling, 1977).

Aside from being influenced by various metabolites of gonadal hormones (which, incidentally, can be formed in both human and rat skin), sebaceous activity is also affected by nongonadal hormones. Thus, pituitary or thyroid gland removal decreases the influence testosterone replacement has on skin gland sebaceous activity in castrated rats. Injections of growth hormone, prolactin, or synthetic d-MSH return the ability of testosterone to influence sebaceous gland activity (Ebling, 1977).

While one might intuitively expect that the neuroendocrine factors controlling scent marking behaviors would be the same as those controlling the production of scent gland secretion, separate, but coordinated, hormonal control mechanisms may be involved in a few instances. Thus, while certain testicular hormones can cause an increase in both scent marking frequency and sebum production from the midventral sebaceous gland region of Mongolian gerbils, other hormones can influence sebum production without influencing marking frequency (Yahr, 1976, 1977; Yahr and Thiessen, 1972). The neural target cells that mediate gerbil midventral marking respond to a narrower range of steroids than the sebaceous cells of the ventral gland. The more likely a steroid can be biochemically converted to testosterone, the more likely that it will stimulate marking in this species (Yahr and Thiessen, 1972).

In addition to being affected by levels of hormones present in adulthood, the scent marking patterns of many species are influenced by the presence of hormones during early development. For example, female gerbils, given neonatal testosterone injections, exhibit levels of scent marking behavior after testosterone treatment in adulthood similar to those observed in males (Turner, 1975). Female dogs, treated with testosterone prenatally during the second trimester of pregnancy and/or immediately after birth, show male-like urination postures when sexually mature. Unlike sexually dimorphic mating behaviors of dogs, such postures do not require hormone treatment in adulthood for their elicitation. Thus, the early neonatal hormone administrations permanently establish these behaviors in dogs (cf. Anisko, 1976). Postpubertal castration, which dramatically influences male mating behavior, has little or no influence upon the urination posture, although it does decrease the frequency of urination (Beach, 1974; Hart, 1974). Castration also reduces the frequency of urine spraying in most cats (Hart and Barrett, 1975). Interestingly, an apparent schism exists between the marking behavior and functional outcome of the elevated leg posture of male dogs, since the posture remains even after the surgical reconnection of the urethra near the anus for the elimination of kidney stone passage problems (personal observation).

Several investigators have sought to find specific brain regions where gonadal hormones operate to influence marking behaviors. Testosterone propionate, implanted into the preoptic region of the hypothalamus (a region that is also involved in mediating sexual behavior, among other things), reinstates scent marking in castrated male gerbils, whereas similar implants into the amygdala, hippocampus, reticular formation, septum, caudate nucleus or cortex do not (Thiessen, Yahr, and Owen, 1973). Estradiol implanted into the preoptic region also stimulates scent marking behavior in castrated males (Yahr and Thiessen, 1972), but implants of 5-dihydrotestoterone, a strong stimulant of sebaceous secretion in rat skin, do not (Thiessen, Yahr

and Owen, 1973). Lesions in the anterior hypothalamic-medial preoptic region of dogs generally decrease the scent marking frequency, although only rarely is the leg elevation posture *per se* eliminated (Hart, 1974).

Sensory Influences on Scent Marking Behaviors

Aside from hormonal influences on scent marking, sensory stimuli also play an important role in the initiation and maintenance of these behaviors. Thus, as dog owners know, certain odors and environmental objects (such as vertical protrusions) increase the likelihood of eliciting scent marking. In wolves, the primary stimulus for making a scent mark is believed to be the presence of an existing one, whether it is familiar or strange (Mech and Peters, 1977). Beavers reportedly mark when encountering alien castor (a strong smelling secretion from their perineal gland) placed in their territory (Aleksiuk, 1968), and objects already marked by tree shrews elicit intense marking in other shrews (Martin, 1968). Removal of the olfactory bulbs in gerbils nearly eliminates scent marking, suggesting that olfactory stimuli play an important role in eliciting or maintaining this behavior, although massive doses of androgen can partially reinstate the marking (Baran and Glickman, 1970; Thiessen, Lindzey, and Nyby, 1970). The perineal drag scent marking behavior of male guinea pigs is also nearly eliminated by olfactory bulbectomy (Beauchamp et al., 1977).

The role of cutaneous sensation in influencing scent marking has received little investigation, although in the case of the Mongolian gerbil neural feedback from the ventral region may be significant. Anesthetizing the midventral region with xylocaine decreases marking frequency, even though surgical excision of the glandular region does not (Blum and Thiessen, 1970; Goist, Twiggs, Schwartz, and Christenson, 1977).

Functions of Scent Marking

Although, as pointed out by Stoddart (1974) and Bronson (1976), natural selection has likely favored the proliferation of species with well-developed scent glands and scent marking behaviors in habitats that limit the use of visual and acoustic signals, species from less restricted habitats (which rely heavily on visual and auditory signals) also use scent in social communication. The unique property of olfactory signals — that they remain in the environment long after their depositors leave — means that they can be used in contexts where the communicating individuals are not simultaneously present. A consideration of the breadth of species that exhibit scent marking suggests that odor communication is not merely the domain of nocturnal, crepuscular (active in twilight), and fossorial (digging) forms, but of nearly all living mammalian species.

The diversity of forms exhibiting scent marking, along with the variety of types and locations of scent glands that have evolved, suggest that several functions are probably served by scent depositing behaviors. Although many informative studies have been published during the last few years on odor communication in mammals, definitive studies elucidating specific functions of scent marking per se are rare. In a gross way we know that sex, reproductive condition, age, individuality, species, dominance status, and group membership can be communicated via the odor medium in most social mammals. Furthermore, we have reasonably good evidence to indicate that odors are widely used, in a number of forms, in warning, defense, alarm, submission, attention seeking, greeting, and in encouraging approach or avoidance, as well as possibly regulating certain endocrine processes. However, which of these messages or processes are served in any particular scent marking context is difficult to establish. This is due, in part, to the flexible and frequently redundant nature of most mammalian chemical communication systems and the large individual differences in responsiveness exhibited by the respondents. The following is a description of experiments by Leon and Moltz (1971, 1972) and Moltz and Leon (1973) which illustrate the role of odors in infant-mother relationships:

> After about two weeks of age, rat pups approached the odor emitted by a lactating female rat in preference to that of a nonlactating female, regardless of whether it was their own mother or not. The preference was not displayed when the use of olfactory cues was eliminated by reversing the direction of airflow from the goal box containing the lactating female. The results indicated the existence of a maternal odor, which may function to synchronize mother-young relationships during lacation and may also explain how preweanling rats in the wild are often found reunited with their mothers in areas of the burrow system after long separations.

> The lactating female rat begins to emit this odor at about 14 days postpartum, when the young first become responsive to it, and the mother ceases to release the odor about 27 days after the birth of the pups — the age at which the young cease to be attracted to it.

> The production of this odor can be prevented if the female is exposed to a new set of one-day-old pups daily for a period of two weeks. The time of odor release cannot be speeded up, however, by the early substitution of pups of an advanced age for the mother's own litter.

While the responses of most mammals to scent deposits undoubtedly depend on underlying innate biological processes, learning is frequently important in establishing the meaning of particular marks and in influencing the behaviors of conspecifics to them. Thus, it is difficult to find simple stimulus-releaser situations to odors in mammals that cannot be modified by learning, even though it has become fashionable to label nearly all acts of odor communication as stereotyped responses that are minimally influenced by experience (e.g., "releasing pheromones" or, more commonly, simply "pheromones"). Such terminology was derived from insect odor communication studies where stereotypy was the norm, and implies to some investigators that external hormone-like messengers are passed from one individual to another in the external medium.[3] While the pheromone conceptualization may be appropriate in some circumscribed situations where specific odorants influence well-defined endocrine responses (e.g., the so-called "primer pheromones", cf. Bronson, 1976), the use of such terminology in other odor contexts has unfortunately led many scientists not well versed in mammalian behavior to think of chemical communication in mammals in terms of simple stimulus-releaser systems. Noting this and other difficulties, several authors have suggested modifying the "releaser pheromone" classification to "signaling pheromone" (Bronson, 1968, 1976) or informer pheromone" (Müller-Schwarze, 1977). Other investigators have suggested that the pheromone term be eliminated altogether from the mammalian chemosensory vocabulary (i.e., Beauchamp, Doty, Moulton, and Mugford, 1976). As evidenced by this chapter, such terminology is not needed to communicate essential details of chemical communication in mammals.

Examples of the influence of learning in mammalian chemical communication abound. For example, the preferences of male rats and dogs for estrus over diestrus conspecific female odors are enhanced by, if not dependent on, sexual or social experiences with the female (e.g., Carr,

Loeb, and Dissinger, 1965; Doty and Dunbar, 1974; Lydell and Doty, 1972; Stern, 1970). The ultrasonic vocalizing of adult male mice evoked by the odor of urine from adult female mice requires postpubertal exposure to females. Artificial odors (e.g., perfume) can elicit equivalent vocalizations in males following the males' exposure to them in social situations, suggesting that the specific components of the odorous signal are learned (Whitney and Nyby, 1977). Adult cotton rats, isolated from conspecifics since weaning, show no preference for traps containing cotton bedding soiled by other cotton rats over traps that are clean. However, following a social interaction in which subordination is produced, the same animals avoid the traps scented by conspecifics (Summerlin and Wolfe, 1973).

Early experiences with odors during the preweaning period can also influence subsequent behaviors in a number of species, although the majority of data come from rodents. For example, a single one-hour exposure of day-old Egyptian spiny mice to the odor of cinnamon results in a preference for this odor in subsequent tests (Porter and Etscorn, 1976). Neonatal rats as young as 2 days of age can acquire an illness-induced conditioned aversion to odor that can last several days (Rudy and Cheatle, 1977). Preference for conspecific or consubspecific odors may develop during the weaning and early post-weaning periods, as evidenced by the results of a number of experiments (cf. Doty, 1974).

A primary function of scent marking behavior in social animals relates to maintaining the orientation (or continued familiarization) of individuals to one another within the social community, or to orienting them to locations where conspecifics can be found. In many social animals, individual members of the clan, coterie, pack or colony learn to respond to and recognize one another, in part, on the basis of each other's odors. Indeed, there is little doubt that odors serve as discriminative stimuli for the elicitation of appropriate social behaviors following

---

[3]It is interesting to note that popular definitions of pheromones assume their hormone-like nature. For example, *Random House College Dictionary (revised edition) (New York): Random House, 1975) defines pheromone as follows:* "*Biochem.* Any of a class of hormonal substances secreted by an individual and stimulating a physiological or behavioral response from an individual of the same species."

encounters were dominance relations are established. From such continued experiences the dichotomy of strange vs. familiar is also formed, serving ultimately to define the membership of the group and insure its integrity. In many rodents, strange conspecifics from outside the social group are rebuffed by the adult group members if they intrude into the community, and are only rarely allowed to enter. Male strangers are viciously attacked and, in some cases, are killed. Juveniles and adult female strangers, in a few rare instances, gain admittance to the social group. Related to these processes is the tendency of the more dominant animals (typically males) to scent mark near or on strange conspecific scents. Thus, more scent marking activity occurs on the borders of overlap zones between adjacent colonies or on their peripheries than within the central sectors, although the degree to which this is true probably varies from species to species. The following extract describes experiments by Epple (1970, 1971, 1972, and 1974) dealing with the marmoset. (A New World monkey).

In a series of studies, Epple observed the behavior of three groups of marmosets in captivity. In the first study, the frequency of aggressive threats, attacks, fighting, and scent marking was recorded before and after the introduction of a strange male or a strange female into the group.

Before the introduction of the strangers, few aggressive interactions occurred although scent marking was frequent, with the dominant male and dominant female scent marking the most. When adult strangers were introduced, they were always attacked, with the dominant resident male attacking and scent marking the most. After removal of the stranger, fighting stopped; however the dominant male's scent marking activity remained higher than normal. Interestingly, when a strange female was introduced into the group, the dominant resident female was the one involved in the aggressive encounters, and she increased her marking

behavior after the strange animal was removed. In short, scent marking increases after aggressive encounters, and strangers of the opposite sex are more or less tolerated.

In a second series of experiments, a clean perch for the monkeys to rest upon was introduced into their home cages. The animals increased their scent marking activity after the presentation of this perch, with the dominant males showing the greatest increase. The introduction of a perch that had been scent marked by a strange group of marmosets showed an appreciable increase in scent marking activity.

Control perches that had been impregnated with mouse urine stimulated less scent marking than perches marked by strange marmosets and no greater scent marking activity than fresh perches, indicating that marmosets react to the odor of conspecifics in much the same way as they do to the introduction of a strange monkey.

It is tempting to hypothesize that some species use scent marking to cover up or minimize the influences of recently deposited scent marks of strangers, possibly decreasing the chance of a stranger's odor becoming familiar to most members of the group. If the dominant males of the colony cannot minimize the impact of the odor scent marks of a stranger in their home range, it is conceivable that the stranger's mark could, in time, become familiar to the group members, possibly allowing his assimilation into the colony. In a somewhat different context, Daly (1977) has suggested that the midventral scent marking of a male gerbil may mitigate the aggressiveness of a female, thereby increasing the likelihood of her mating with him. The tendency of an animal to cover up the scent marks of other conspecifics (or insure that its odor is alongside that of the strangers) may also provide an animal with an efficient way to keep track of the circulation of others within the home range, as has recently been suggested in the following extract from Barrette (1977) for the muntjac, a small Asian deer.

The scent marking behavior of four male and four female captive muntjacs was studied for 450 hours in a 2200 square meter enclosure at the Calgary Zoo. Males marked more than females, and subordinates of both sexes marked less than dominants. Experimental alterations of the composition of the herd revealed that dominants marked most when in the presence of their subordinate rival. Some muntjacs covered the scent of conspecifics with their own. This behavior was interpreted as a means of monitoring the circulation of conspecifics within the home range.

Where closely related forms live in the same region (sympatric species), scent markings may function to minimize interspecific mating, similar to the manner in which it apparently minimizes intercolonial mating (cf. Mykytowycz, 1974). As discussed in detail elsewhere (Doty, 1974), scent marking in some mammalian forms appears to be analogous to courtship behaviors seen in avian species. In most birds, characters that promote the reduction of interspecific mating have several general properties (Hinde, 1959). First, divergence is most marked in those characters that are important in pair formation (thus, in birds with long "engagement periods", early courtship displays differ more between species than those displays occurring immediately before copulation). Second, divergence is most marked in areas such as the overlap zones of partially sympatric species, where mating is otherwise possible. Third, species characters related to sexual isolation often disappear on islands where no closely related species occur. Finally, divergence is more marked in males than in females.

A number of studies support the notion that some specialized mammalian scent glands fulfill most of these general requirements. Thus, as noted earlier in this chapter, adult males from a wide variety of taxahomic categories possess sebaceous complexes that are excellent indicators of taxonomic relationships (e.g., Doty and Kart, 1972; Quay, 1968). These complexes are typically more variable in males than in females, being reduced or absent in the latter sex, and vary in size and sebum output in relation to the reproductive season. The limited comparative data available indicate that such complexes may be reduced or absent in species not having closely related species present (Doty and Kart, 1972). Interestingly, recent biochemical analyses of the components of mammalian scent glands demonstrate marked differences (possibly "olfactory dialects") between diverse populations of voles (Stoddart, Aplin, and Wood, 1975). It is conceivable, of course, that different diets may be responsible for such differences when they are found in wild populations (Beauchamp et al., 1976; Skeen and Thiessen, 1977).

Closely related to the group-defining functions of scent marking are functions variously described as those associated with reassurance, familiarity, increasing self-confidence, and so on (cf. Ewer, 1968). Making a living area more familiar by spreading one's own scent, or by spreading scents of others who are familiar to group members, serves a number of important functions, particularly those of minimizing novelty and (in an anthropomorphic sense) providing more comfort for the resident. Such a familiar refuge from predators, as well as from conspecific competitors of unknown abilities, may minimize the dangerous influences of stress that take a toll on the lives of members of many mammalian groups (cf. Archer, 1969; Christian, 1963; Christian, Lloyd, and Davis, 1965).

Another likely function of scent marking relates to the influences of the deposited odors on the reproductive states of the male and female conspecifics who encounter them frequently. As indicated by laboratory and animal husbandry studies, the odors from conspecific males of a number of species can facilitate the onset of estrus and other indicators of sexual maturation in females. For example, female mice exposed to males and their odors exhibit an earlier estrus than controls isolated from males (cf. Vandenbergh, 1967, 1969). Female swine exhibit an earlier than normal appearance of estrus following the introduction of a male pig into their pen, and female sheep and goats respond to the presence of a novel male before the end of seasonal anestrous by exhibiting estrus and ovulation (Hulet, 1966; Schinckel, 1954; Underwood, Shier, and Davenport, 1944). Such estrous induction does not occur in anosmic ewes (Morgan, Arnold, and Lindsay, 1972). A males' odor can produce estrous synchrony in grouped females of several types of wild and domestic mice (cf. Whitten, Bronson, and Greenstein, 1968), and the odor of a strange male conspecific mouse (i.e., not the stud) can block implantation of recently fertilized ova in the female. The effect does not require continuous exposure of the female to the male odor, since brief repeated exposures can produce the same outcome (Bruce, 1959; Chipman, Holt, and Fox, 1966).

In some natural circumstances, scent marking may provide odor cues that influence the endocrine processes of nearby female conspecifics in ways similar to those described above (cf. Rogers and Beauchamp, 1976). However, few data are available from wild populations of even rodents. Using housemice as an example, it would appear, *prima facie*, that a male who could control a breeding area by marking it regularly and thereby (1) accelerate the sexual maturation of resident females and (2) increase his probability of mating with them (by decreasing their antagonism and increasing his success in agonistic encounters with competing males), would hold an evolutionary advantage over less fortunate males. Similarly, if his scent marking produced estrous synchronization in a few resident females who were not pregnant, he may further optimize his ultimate contribution to the gene pool by minimizing total energy expenditure and exposure to predation likely associated with frequent courtship and copulation bouts. However, if another male (perhaps displaced from his own area by a more dominant male) is dominant enough to scent mark

over the resident's area and subsequently block ongoing pregnancies in some of the females, the resident male's reproductive advantage would be lessened. Unfortunately, such an idealized and simple picture is purely conjectural at the present time, since no empirical data on this point are available from field work. Such data are sorely needed to establish if male-odor induced endocrine phenomena occur in natural ecological settings, or if they are simply artifacts of the unnatural animal groupings observed in the laboratory. The following extract describes an experiment by Roper and Polioudakis (1977) dealing with marking behavior of Mongolian gerbils.

> *The behaviors of a colony of Mongolian gerbils (*Meriones unguiculatus*) were observed for 18 weeks in a seminatural environment provided with facilities for burrowing, nestbuilding, foraging, wheelrunning, and other behaviors. Initially, severe fighting reduced the number of animals rapidly to a stable level of two males and two females. Fighting was never observed between members of the opposite sex. Twenty-seven bouts of mutual marking were observed, most being directed by males to females. During the estrous periods, one male drove the other from the female's vicinity. Ventral marking by the males occurred mainly after encounters with one another. Ventral marking by the female and drumming by the male occurred at unusually high levels during mating. Although ventral marks were made throughout the enclosure, most occurred on the surface of the earth within the burrow area. Marks tended to be deposited in close spatial and temporal contiguity. There was a strong tendency for fresh marks to elicit countermarking by the same or another animal, but novel clean objects were also marked within a short time of being placed in the enclosure. There was no evidence that marked objects or areas were avoided by the other animals or defended by the marker, suggesting to these*

authors that such marking is not primarily territorial in nature. Mutual marking, mutual grooming, and sandbathing all occurred at the four most heavily marked sites near the burrow. This suggests that these activities, and the tendency for animals to countermark at specific sites, might distribute a colony odor consisting of the odors of the individuals, and that this may reduce intracolony aggression.

In addition to the influence of male odors on female reproduction, both male and female odors probably affect male reproductive processes. For example, male odors, as a result of serving as discriminative stimuli during social encounters, probably produce or reinforce stress responses in subordinate individuals. In subsequent exposures, this may reduce reproductive performance and androgen level (cf. Rose, Gordon, and Bernstein, 1972). In most species, dominant animals mark more frequently than submissive ones, particularly when in the presence of subordinate rivals (e.g., Barrette, 1977). Androgen level can directly influence odor preferences of some male rodents, conceivably influencing their responsiveness to or interest in receptive females. For example, castration eliminates the male rat's preference for estrous over diestrous urine odor (Carr and Caul, 1962). Conversely, exposure of males from a variety of species (e.g., rabbits, hamsters, mice, cattle, sheep, monkeys, and humans) to receptive females or their odors increases the plasma levels of testosterone (cf. Macrides, 1976).

In housemice, social subordination can completely inhibit scent marking behaviors independently of androgen level. Thus, subordinate mice bearing silastic implants that steadily release a physiological level of male hormone do not exhibit scent marking (Bronson, 1971). This inhibition is stable over long periods of time even when it is not routinely reinforced by exposure to the dominant animal. Apparently, in this case, psychological or learned factors can outweigh

endocrine ones in influencing scent marking.

As can be noted from the studies reviewed in this chapter, the home ranges of many mammals are constantly in odorous flux, perhaps somewhat akin to the visual flux of wall hangings and decorations within your own home. Just like the human residents, animal residents can produce sensorial artifacts lasting for varying periods of time, thereby communicating information about them to other members of the community on both spatial and temporal grounds. Time-released or time-dependent signals can facilitate the accurate communication of changing reproductive states, dominance hierarchies, and other information of social consequence. Estrous female rat urine loses its attractiveness to male rats in less than 24 hours (Lydell and Doty, 1972), as would be expected if it were to communicate the time of sexual receptivity accurately. Similarly, female guinea pig urine loses its attractiveness to conspecific males after 48 hours (Beauchamp and Beruter, 1973). A detailed discussion of chemical factors involved in the timed release of chemical signals is presented by Regnier and Goodwin (1977).

Conclusions

It is apparent from the preceding paragraphs that scent marking is a common mammalian behavior that is not confined solely to animals living in habitats devoid of other types of sensory communication. Furthermore, it is clear that most scent marking behaviors are closely related to reproductive, agonistic, territorial, and other social processes vital to species survival. Such behaviors are typically confined to the breeding season in those forms that do not breed year round, are closely correlated with gender and dominance status, mirror circulating levels of specific reproductive hormones, and are probably predictive of phylogenetic relationships.

While scent marking behaviors are important in facilitating mating between certain participants and discouraging mating between others, more work is needed to establish their other probable functions. For example, there is evidence that scents can be used to signify communal trails (e.g. Barnett, 1963) and to inform an animal of paths that it has just traversed (Ewer, 1968). Certain carnivores may even scent mark food caches in a way that provides a "bookkeeping system" for their scavenging activities (Henry, (1977).

Despite human preoccupations with the role of vision in the behavior of organisms (Doty, 1974), we should not ignore the fact that olfaction plays a dominant role in the lives of most mammals. Indeed, scent marking can be considered one of the primary behaviors of mammals, possibly on a par with foraging, eating, and copulation. As evidenced by this brief review, the field of mammalian chemical communication holds many interesting secrets yet to be uncovered by the refined eyes (and noses) of students of animal behavior.

Study Questions

1. What are the main sources of the chemicals used in scent marking in mammals and where are odors mainly deposited?

2. Describe the relationship between scent marking and reproductive hormones in dogs and rodents.

3. What are the various functions of scent marking?

4. Describe one bit of evidence indicating that learning plays a role in chemical communication.

5. Relate dominance in the male, together with situational variables, to scent marking activity.

6. Expand on the role scent marking plays in reproductive and maternal behavior.

21

Defense Against Predation

Jane Halonen

University of Wisconsin — Milwaukee

M. Ray Denny

Michigan State University

Practically every animal has another animal that serves as its predator. The network of predator-prey relationships represents a rather paradoxical system in which the immediate objective for a threatened prey animal is its survival, while the prey's failure to survive may confer group survival advantages to the predator as well as its conspecifics (Maier and Maier, 1970).

The complexities of predator-prey relationships are apparent from both ecological and evolutionary perspectives. Slobodkin (1974) has suggested that the most efficient systems are those in which the "prudent" predator attacks prey with the least reproductive value, including the very young, the old, the sick, and the sterile, thus encouraging the integrity of the prey species. Other researchers (e.g., Curio, 1976) have reported that odd or structurally conspicuous prey are also likely targets for predation, enhanced in fact by conspecific "hostility" directed toward atypical group members of the prey. Mueller (1974), however, has suggested that choice of prey may be unrelated to conspicuousness. Instead, he proposes that a predator is simply likely to continue past successful hunting strategies.

The size of the predator population is also an important consideration. An increase in predator density that leads to exaggerated efficiency of predation diminishes the food supply — to the predators' ultimate disadvantage. In an evolutionary framework, predator-prey systems are viewed as "coevolving" (Edmunds, 1954): as weapons of attack increase in efficiency, systems of defense evolve in kind as a form of evolutionary "arms race." In fact, increasing specialization of modes of attack and defense through evolution may inflate risks to survival.

Predators have traditionally been assumed to engage in hunting as a function of hunger (Lorenz, 1963). A review of the more recent literature (Polsky, 1975) suggests that hunger actually plays a fairly minor role in hunting activities, and Polsky cites several points of evidence: Predators may not consume "just-killed" prey and often kill more prey than necessary for survival; killing frequencies remain constant even when predators are denied eating access to their prey and are fed from other food sources; and non-killing species cannot be induced experimentally to kill even at the risk of starvation. Also, Polsky speculates that the separation of predation and hunger is consistent with the fact that different anatomical sites govern the behaviors of killing and eating. Polsky concludes that the act of predation is innate and initiated by hunger, but modified through experience to become secondarily reinforcing.

No definition of predation has met with uniform acceptance (Curio, 1976); however, O'Boyle's (1974) three-part definition seems appropriate here. O'Boyle specifies that predatory behavior (1) must involve interspecies conflict, (2) should be related in some manner to eating, and (3) should be topographically distinct from other behaviors. By contrast, Edmunds (1974) organized the components of defensive repertoires into (1) sensory mechanisms involved in the detection of prey (2) structural components comprised of relevant physical characteristics and (3) motor mechanisms representing defensive behaviors.

This chapter discusses defense mechanisms within a comparative framework. The first section classifies and describes various defense systems within the animal kingdom. The bulk of descriptive information is derived from the comprehensive work of Edmunds (1974), unless otherwise indicated. Next, tonic immobility (TI) is presented as one of the more extensively explored research preparations for examining predator-prey relationships. Within that context, species comparisons, variables affecting the tonic immobility response, and theoretical positions are presented.

Systems of Primary Defense

According to Edmunds, systems of "primary defense" consist of both structural systems that use protective coloration in various forms and behaviors or "life-styles" that afford protection. The primary systems, outlined in Table 21.1, are distinguished from "secondary defense" systems in that predators must be present for secondary defense behaviors to be initiated. Primary systems are mechanisms that occur regardless of whether the predator is in the vicinity, although the operation of primary systems may be enhanced in the presence of the predator through behavioral mechanisms.

Coloration

Specialized morphological characteristics have evolved, with the consequence of eluding prey or at least of decreasing the probability of capture (Denny and Ratner, 1970). In some cas-

Table 21.1
Primary Defense Systems

Coloration (structure)	Life-style (behavior)
Crypsis	Anachoresis
Aposematism	Association
	Own species
	Other species
Mimicry	
Batesian	
Mullerian	

Adapted from Edmunds (*Defence in Animals*, 1974).

es, prey behaviors can increase the effectiveness of structural components and thus increase the survival value of protective coloration.

Crypsis.   Edmunds defines crypsis as protection through camouflage. When an animal is cryptic, it is visible but not distinguishable against its background. Animals may resemble parts of their environment as in the sticklike apppearance of the praying mantis or they may change color appropriately against a variety of backdrops as demonstrated by the chameleon. The cuttlefish not only changes color but can also adopt different patterns for even better protection against a variety of backgrounds. Countershading in many species of fish provides enhanced protection merely through changing direction and exposing a different anatomical site. Partial crypsis also is possible. Eyestripes function in a variety of species to decrease predator detection of the prey's eyeball and thus prevent the elicitation of prey-capture responses on the part of the predator.

For maximum effectiveness, the cryptic animal must not move. This enforced immobility can cause conflict with other routine behaviors. For maximum protection, the cryptic must also be highly selective in choice of resting place. Crypsis depends on the predator's sense of vision; thus when predators can use other sensory modes, such as smell, the effectiveness of cryptic defense is lessened. Another threat to the effectiveness of crypsis is that the close spacing of prey members may promote a "search model" (or "search image") in the predator, helping it to find a camouflaged prey. Edmunds concludes that dependence on crypsis leads adaptively to variations in the form of the prey (polymorphism), and according to Curio (1976) rare phenotypes are apostatic (advantage conferring) not only because new variations escape the preditors' previously formed "search models," but also because polymorphism confers selection advantages in mating. The following extract describes visual detection of cryptic prey by blue jays (Pietrewicz and and Kamil, 1977).

Blue jays were trained to peck at slide pictures of Catocala *moths for food reinforcement and to inhibit pecking at the same scene minus the moth. Pecking at the negative stimulus was followed by a 60-second time-out. The jays were then tested on the ability to detect a moth as a function of background, orientation of moth (e.g. head down or head up), and distance (from camera to subject photographed).*

Background clearly affected detection of cryptic moth. The brown bark mimics were detected less frequently on the oak tree background than on a nonbark ground, and the birch mimic was detected less frequently on white birch bark. Both distance and orientation interacted with the background variable. Only when the moth was on the background that it matched did these variables matter; for example, greater distance reduced detection on a matching background, an effect that is in good agreement with observations of field-workers.

Aposematism.   Many animals have evolved structural warning features that signal a noxious consequence for the predator. Examples of noxious consequence include bad taste, painful sting, or the induction of vomiting. Aposematic signals are predominantly color based (bright colors, high contrast) even when the noxious consequence may not be directly related to color (e.g., some brightly colored caterpillars may have hairs that prevent or complicate ingestion although the color not the hair is the aposematic stimulus). Other examples of warning signals include distinctive noises or odors.

Aposematism can function in one of two ways according to Edmunds: (1) on the basis of innate predator avoidance of unusual stimuli and (2) on the basis of learned avoidance (obviously the noxious consequence cannot be lethal to the predator, although it may require the sacrifice of the sampled aposematic prey). Aposematic animals tend to move very slowly. Edmunds speculates that this slowness may serve to avoid initiating prey-catching mechanisms in the predator. One disadvantage to this system of defense is that in times of limited food supply the colors that usually warn may now attract predators that have developed a tolerance to the noxious consequences.

Mimicry. Two forms of mimicry are based on an animal's resemblance to an aposematic animal. Mullerian mimics not only resemble aposematics but are aposematic themselves. An example would be mimics of the coral snake, which are themselves poisonous. Batesian mimics are nonaposematic but resemble aposematics to some degree. Insects, which have birds or amphibians as predators, are frequently Batesian mimics. Even minor similarities to an aposematic confer a selective advantage to the mimic because most predators either do not discriminate well or do so on the basis of narrow criteria (Duncan and Shephard, 1965).

The best protection for the Batesian mimic occurs when the aposematic model is abundant, so that predator is frequently exposed to the noxious stimuli, or when the model elicits vomiting. Lea and Turner (1972) have demonstrated that artificially increasing the unpleasant taste of a model leads to poorer discrimination between models and their mimics on the part of the predator. If the predator is particularly destitute, both the model and the mimic may be consumed anyway. Another long-term disadvantage for the mimic is the possibility that the model may evolve away from the mimic's appearance. Van Brower (1960) studied the reactions of starlings to different proportions of models and mimics, summarized as follows.

This was an experimental study of Batesian mimicry — a phenomenon in which species that are not distasteful when eaten can closely resemble (mimic) an unpalatable species in appearance and behavior. Mimicry is adaptive because the predator cannot distinguish the mimic from the aversive stimulus (model). Starlings as predators were presented with highly palatable mealworms that had been banded with either green or orange paint. Some of the green-banded worms (models) were dipped in an aversive chemical solution. The rest of the green-banded worms were dipped only in distilled water and therefore remained palatable; these worms were the "mimics." None of the orange-banded worms were made distasteful. Each starling was given 10 trials per day for about 16 days, each trial consisting of two mealworms — one orange banded and one green banded. Of the green-banded worms, different groups of birds received a different proportion of "mimics" (palatable) to "models" (unpalatable). After a few aversive encounters with the "models," the birds learned to avoid them, with the result that the green-banded "mimics" also escaped predation, particularly when the percentage of "mimics" presented to the starlings was 60 percent or less. Even when the percentage of palatable "mimics" was as high as 90 percent, 17 percent of the "mimics" escaped predation. With one exception, all the starlings readily ate the orange-banded worms, demonstrating that the birds had not simply learned to avoid all mealworms. Note. It has been generally believed that, for Batesian mimicry to be effective, the model species must be more common than the mimic species. But the results of Van Brower's experiments showed that, if the model is distasteful enough, mimicry is still very effective when the ratio of mimics to models is as high as 60 to 40, and that mimics benefit to some degree even when the ratio is 90 to 10.

Life-styles

Anachoresis. Edmunds observes that some animals, such as worms, automatically escape predation by a life-style of routine concealment, as in living underground. Anachoretics may dig their own holes or live in holes dug by other animals. This type of defense does pose some problems. Concealment interferes with many functions, such as reproduction and feeding; thus, engaging in these functions above ground may alert predators. One successful encounter by the predator may help engender a search model, but ordinarily maximum protection for anachoretics is provided through their wide dispersion, which tends to prevent the formation of a search model.

Association. Individuals may live among members of their own or other species to form defensive groups. And Lorenz (1963) has specified that groups may form for other purposes than defense. A disadvantage to such association lifestyles is that the probability of detection is increased; an advantage is that group density may deter attack after detection. In contrast to the situation for anachoretics and cryptics, increased species density provides increased protection for the individual. Even when an attack does occur,

the scattering of the group may cause the predator to hesitate, thereby minimizing group losses. Mixed-species groups are somewhat more unusual and typically develop through feeding association (Lorenz, 1963). Some mixed-species groups consist of animals with good defensive systems and animals with limited defenses whose predators will avoid the former. Another advantage of mixed-species groups results from increasing the potential to detect the predator by expanding on the number of relevant sensory mechanisms that can effect detection. Also, the detection of a predator by one animal will typically be transmitted through some danger signal not only to conspecifics but other members of the group as well.

Secondary Defense Systems

Edmunds classifies secondary defense systems as those which are triggered in the prey animal by the presence of predators. These systems, which Bolles (1970) grouped as species-specific defense reactions, have traditionally been classified as

Table 21.2
Secondary Defense Systems

"Flight"	"Fight"	"Freeze"
Intraspecies warning	Individual retaliation Physical Chemical Implement use	Immobility
Retreat Destination Method		Tonic immobility
Diversion Autotomy Deflection Diematics Protean display Injury feigning Flash behavior "Pseudostructures"	Group retaliation Mobbing	

Adaptation from Edmund (1974).

Defense Against Predation

"flight, fight, or freeze." The classification of secondary defense systems is presented in Table 21.2. Note that the prey's reaction to predators can consist of one discrete response or several responses in a chain — responses that involve more than one form of secondary defense or that enhance primary defense systems.

Flight

Edmunds defines flight as "rapid locomotion away from a stimulus source." In lower forms of life, such as the coelenterates and planaria, avoidance responses are simply an exaggeration of ordinary locomotor responses; at higher levels, the form of escape is highly diversified (Cloudsley-Thompson, 1965). While predator detection is typically accomplished through vision, other sensory modes can be used. For example, Berg (1974) has observed that gastropods detect the presence of predators through chemical means.

The time at which flight responses occur varies in different species. Vertebrate prey maintain a "specific flight distance" or "reactive distance," and when a predator gets closer than this initial distance, an escape response is initiated (Hediger, 1969). The process is rather complex, however. For species like the Thomson gazelle, the mere sight of a predator is not enough to elicit escape and may even provoke approach responses; one species of prey may have different flight distances from different types of predators; predator size, predator density, and available ground cover can modify critical distances (Walther, 1969); and suddenness of predator appearance can elicit escape responses and in effect lengthen the critical distance (Blest, 1957).

Tinbergen (1951) suggested that, in birds, structural characteristics of the predator (e.g., neck shape of hawk versus goose) are critical to flight responses; however, later research (McNiven, 1960) indicated that in Tinbergen's study neck shape may have been confounded with speed of movement. In fact, McNiven concluded that speed of the predator may be more important than any other stimulus characteristic. For example, predators moving at slow speeds through herds of gazelle do not trigger escape until the predator abruptly stops (Walther, 1969); and, according to Cloudsley-Thompson (1965), antelopes can discriminate between a hungry and a well-fed lion and adjust their flight reactions accordingly, although this effect has not been well documented. One can speculate that speed differentials between "full" and "empty" predators could mediate this phenomenon, given that this effect is reliable.

Three main types of behaviors can be classified as escape or flight. These include intraspecies warnings that minimize group loss for animals involved in association life-styles, retreat with respect to both method and destination of escape, and a variety of diversionary tactics, including autotomy, deflection, and diematics, all of which are discussed below.

Intraspecies Warning. Intraspecies warnings, or distress signals, alert conspecifics to the presence of a predator. In some species, the warning may also provide qualitative information about the predator (Cully and Legon, 1976). The distress signal may take the form of vocalization as in birds, specific body movement as in rabbits, or alarm pheromones as released by fish and ants. From numerous observations, Curio (1974) has concluded that fear supresses vocalization, but his conclusion seems questionable when applied to distress signals.

Walther's (1969) studies of the Thomson gazelle provide a good scenario of intraspecies warning behavior. Typically, only one member of the herd is vigilant at any one time, and the vigilance is maintained for only a few seconds; the duties of predator "watching" are exchanged in apparent synchrony; alertness is increased by the detection of a predator; when the predator has surpassed the critical distance, an alert characterized by snorting and shaking the flanks is

Defense Against Predation

issued, at which point escape may be attempted; and finally when predatory invasion is imminent, the distress signals fade.

Retreat. Animals can retreat to three different destinations for protection. First, some animals can withdraw into their own protective structures, as with mollusks or turtles. Second, they can retreat into their own prepared hiding places, as represented by rabbits hiding in holes. Third, they can seek refuge in available ground cover by concealment or by taking advantage of the primary defense of crypsis. Withdrawal or hiding may protect but not always. Predators can follow, and some predators have developed effective means of cracking exoskeletons (Lorenz, 1963). In fact, ferrets are used professionally to follow rabbits down their escape holes, although prey can counter this by incorporating a second exit as a backup defense. There are other disadvantages. While in seclusion, the prey animal is unable to see and, worse still, unable to detect when predatory danger has passed. Habituation to phony warnings (e.g., shadows) rapidly occurs even though real predators are still in the area.

The specific pattern of retreat can also help afford protection. Retreat styles may include jumping, diving, flying, or dropping rapidly suspended by a thread (spiders). Retreats may be slow or fast and straight or protean (Proteus was a character in Greek mythology who frustrated his captors by constant transformation.), Protean retreats represent a systematic attempt to provide the predator with false information, thereby obscuring prediction and diminishing capture (Chance and Russell, 1974). Gazelles, for example, may double back across their own paths to obscure detection by scent. Predators may learn to rely on other forms of detection, such as chemoreception or sonar, to restore advantage.

Diversion. Dill (1974) has reported that predators avoid novel, high-intensity, or suddenly appearing stimuli; diversionary tactics exploit this response tendency of predators. *Autotomy* is one such diversion that involves the constriction and breaking off of a nonessential body part by reflex action (see also Chapter 13). Examples include loss of legs of grasshoppers, papillae of mollusks, and tails of lizards. In some cases, the body part regenerates. While the predator toys with the body part, which is often distasteful and compounds the predator's confusion, the prey escapes and is left with only a minor inconvenience.

In *deflection*, another kind of diversion, the prey animal rechannels a potentially deadly attack to a less-lethal part of its body, usually a part characterized by bad taste. Examples include the false antennae of butterflies and the false heads of snakes, both of which divert the predator to the wrong end.

Diematic ("I frighten") behaviors also stress structural features and are used to startle predators. Diematics may represent a real warning to the predator by indicating the prey's willingness to enter into conflict, or diematics may represent a bluff. Edmunds (1976) observed that the prey's successful use of diematics offers greater survival advantages than confrontation. Startling the enemy is effective because it elicits withdrawal or indecision, both of which facilitate the prey's escape.

Startle-inducing behaviors can be subdivided into more specific behaviors. *Protean display* is a diematic behavior in which the prey animal maintains its location but behaves in some atypical way (Chance and Russell, 1959). Because such displays differ across conspecifics, the unpredictability of the prey's behavior for the predator increases the power of the display as a defense mechanism. Chance and Russell describe convulsions or seizures, infrequently exhibited by frogs and small mammals, as an example of protean display. A specialized form of protean display is "injury feigning," a response characteristic of ground-nesting birds

(Armstrong, 1954). The parent conspicuously leaves the nest to divert predator attention from the young and then maintains an odd limb posture and circling behavior to simulate injury. Flash behavior is a diematic form in which brightly colored body parts are displayed briefly and rapidly and is typically followed by an escape response and crypsis in which flas colors are hidden. Eyespots are another structural feature that promotes hesitation in the predator. Some species of moths, toads, and frogs are characteristic. Edmunds noted that in some species of toads eyespots exist, but the animal may not use its structural oddity to its best advantage; that is, the toad may not orient the eyespots toward its predator. Other diematic "pseudostructures" involve the alteration of appearance to produce an apparent increase in body size, accomplished by erection of the hair, inflating the lungs, or rearing on back paws. Other alterations may be employed in addition to those eliciting a startle response; for example, to prevent consummation the pufferfish inflates beyond the capacity of its predator's throat size.

As a short-term defensive response, diematic displays have been demonstrated to habituate rapidly (Balderrama and Maldonado, 1971). When a stimulus is withheld for a short period of time, the diematic response will then show full recovery. If diematic prey behavior is successful, the prey escapes the predator; or in some cases, ironically, the predator escapes the prey. If the bluff fails to work, confrontation results.

Fight

Individual Retaliation. Hediger (1969) has indicated that there is frequently a "critical range" for fighting, one in which the presence of the predator induces an aggressive countering behavior. In such aggressive encounters, animals have been observed to employ parts of their own structure, chemical secretions, and even implements in their own defense. The weapons used are often the same as used in the capture or ingestion of food (e.g., biting or pecking), although some are specific to defense. Lorenz (1963) has reported that species use different types of weapons, depending on the nature of the conflict; deer use antlers in intraspecies conflict in which the objective is primarily territorial and reserve hooves for predator-prey confrontation. Quills, spines, and pincers represent typical tools of defense.

Three types of chemical secretions as tools of defense have been described: *oozing* secretions characteristic of millipedes, *airing* secretions produced by the evagination of glands in caterpillars and beetles, and *spraying* secretions characteristic of skunks, cockroaches, and earwigs. Regurgitation is another chemical weapon that has been reported by Edmunds (1976) as exhibited by vultures that regurgitate carrion as defense.

Implement use is restricted to higher phylogenetic levels. Primate use of implements, excluding humans, is usually limited to situations in which gravity can be exploited. For example, baboons loft stones over cliffs at predators, and monkeys drop excrement and twigs from overhead (Hamilton, Buskirk, and Buskirk, 1975).

Mobbing. Mobbing the predator represents group defense and appears to be especially characteristic of many species of birds (see also Chapter 8). Mobbing is initiated by distress calls which expose the predator and alert prey members (Cully and Legon, 1976; Hinde, 1954). The calls are followed by many individuals simultaneously assaulting the predator. If effective, the predator's enthusiasm for hunting may be reduced, resulting in the predator's changing its location or even the choice of prey. If not so effective, mobbing still serves to minimize group losses. An auxiliary function of mobbing is teaching the younger conspecifics to recognize the "eating enemy."

Cully and Legon have speculated from naturalistic observation of two species of gulls that social compatibility and spatial distance of conspecifics are important factors in the occurrence of mobbing. If members of a species are widely distributed, mobbing poses a threat to individual attackers. If group members are highly territorial, the close presence of conspecifics may cause them to attack each other, which then detracts from the effectiveness of mobbing. Hinde has also observed that the repeated presentation of a predatory stimulus induces rapid habituation of mobbing, as is true of other defense behaviors.

Freezing

Immobility and tonic immobility (TI) are two forms of "freeze" behaviors. TI can be distinguished from immobility on the basis of specific differences in posture and distance from the predator (Ratner, 1977). According to Ratner, immobility that occurs at some distance from the predator may simply be taking advantage of background color to avoid detection. However, Prestrude (1977) has observed that freezing as a camouflage, at least in higher species, is relatively rare and concluded that the adaptive value of freezing at a distance, as opposed to making an escape response, is unclear. TI, on the other hand, is a frequently observed and durable phenomenon and is elaborated below as illustrative of a particularly productive research preparation for the study of predator-prey relationships in the laboratory (see also Chapters 8 and 9).

Tonic Immobility

Tonic immobility was first described in 1643 by Kirchner under the label of "fascination" in chickens (Ratner, 1967). Since that time, TI has been variously described as catalepsy, thanatosis, enhancement, rho, akinesis, paroxysmal inhitibion, Totstell reflex, mesmerism, fright paralysis, monoidism, bewitchment, death feign or sham, animal hypnosis and immobility reaction (Gallup, 1974; Henning, Dunlap, and Gallup, 1976). As early as 1936, a review of the literature cited 240 articles about TI, including both Pavlov and Darwin among the contributors. More recently, Masur and Gallup (1977) compiled a "tricentennial" bibliography consisting of more than 800 articles. The list of entries included the use of TI to facilitate shoeing of horses and a reinterpretation of Moses' transforming a rod into a snake in terms of TI (Exodus 4:2-4).

Behavioral Description

A variety of species exhibit TI, from arthropods (Ratner, 1977) to humans (Crawford, 1977). Among invertebrates, TI appears to play a role in sexual rituals, in effect making the female of the species immobile for the duration of the act. Among vertebrates, TI has been observed in fish, frogs, reptiles, birds, guinea pigs, rabbits, rats, goats, coyotes, monkeys, dogs, fox, and cattle. Ratner (1967) has reported that birds are the best subjects for laboratory use because of their visual and aural acuity, responsiveness to a wide range of stimuli, and ease of handling.

Prestrude (1977) has conceptualized a functional cycle of TI which is presented in an adapted and expanded form in Figure 21.1.

TI can be induced by using one of the five techniques presented in Figure 21.1 or by using some combination of two or more (Ratner, 1967). Repeated, monotonous stroking or pressure on a particular body part can produce TI; however, inversion and manual restraint are perhaps the most frequently employed induction procedures in the laboratory. In birds, TI can be induced by hooding preceded by restraint, although the nature of the immobility response is slightly different and the response is less durable. Ratner (1967) observed that the exact posture exhibited in TI varies with both the method of induction and the orientation in which the animal is placed during immobility (e.g., upright versus supine). Induction of TI in humans has

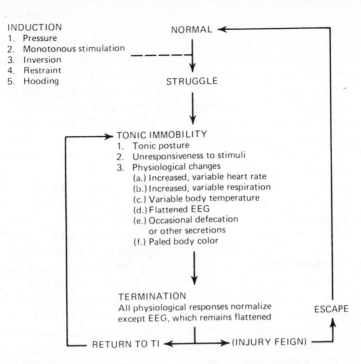

INDUCTION
1. Pressure
2. Monotonous stimulation
3. Inversion
4. Restraint
5. Hooding

NORMAL

STRUGGLE

TONIC IMMOBILITY
1. Tonic posture
2. Unresponsiveness to stimuli
3. Physiological changes
    (a.) Increased, variable heart rate
    (b.) Increased, variable respiration
    (c.) Variable body temperature
    (d.) Flattened EEG
    (e.) Occasional defecation
        or other secretions
    (f.) Paled body color

TERMINATION
All physiological responses normalize
except EEG, which remains flattened

ESCAPE

RETURN TO TI   (INJURY FEIGN)

Figure 21.1. An extension of Prestrude's functional cycle of tonic immobility.

been reported using two methods. Hoaglund (1928) described having a subject bend forward at a 90 degree angle and then thrown backward "violently," producing "vigorous muscle contractions" and immobility lasting several seconds. More recently, Crawford (1977) designed a movable chair that more safely permitted inversion and restraint while producing the immobility reaction. Crawford stated that following initial nausea human subjects began to report enjoying the sensations. On this basis, he questioned the comparability of the chair-induced response to other forms of TI.

With the use of the method of manual restraint, the subject typically contests restraint with a brief struggle followed by immobility that may last from a few seconds to several hours (Gallup, 1974). Gallup (1977) claims the TI record in the laboratory; one of his chickens remained immobile for 5 hours and 45 minutes.

Two observable changes mark the onset of

TI: a posture of waxy flexibility with occasional muscle tremor and an apparent unresponsiveness or analgesia to external stimuli that include pinpricks, cutting, and electric shock. Sometimes there is protrusion of the eyeball with sporadic eye closure during TI. Physiological changes include heightened autonomic responsiveness (heart, rate, respiration, body temperature), flattened electroencephalogram (EEG) patterns that are characteristic of extreme alertness, occasional defecation, and altered body color in some species (Gallup, 1974). These physiological measures indicate that stimuli are having some sort of effect during TI.

Behaviors that signal the usually abrupt termination of TI are vocalization, small bodily movements, and return of color (Ratner, 1967); at this time physiological systems normalize with the exception of the EEG, which maintains a flattened pattern. This indication in the EEG record of continued alertness probably relates to

Defense Against Predation

the fact the animal coming out of TI may attempt to escape, with or without the feigning of injury, or may revert to the tonic posture, depending on the surrounding stimuli.

The most frequently used dependent variable in TI research is duration of the tonic response from point of inversion to uprighting by the animal (Gallup, 1977; Ratner, 1977). Other measures that have been used to assess TI effects include the proportion of the subject population achieving a viable immobility response and the stimulus duration or intensity required to produce immobility.

Variables Influencing TI

Ontogeny. The TI response appears to develop in a "piecemeal" fashion (Ratner, 1977). Laboratory induction of TI cannot be accomplished immediately after birth (or hatching), although certain species exhibit TI very early. For example, chickens exhibit TI 8 days posthatching, as do rat pups 5 days after birth. Bronstein and Hirsch (1976) found that Norway rats are unresponsive to cats at 20 days of age but are sufficiently responsive at 30 days of age to exhibit TI in their presence. Borchelt and Ratner (1973) observed that both frequency and duration of TI increase with age in bobwhite quail. That this occurred with both measures reaffirms Maier and Schneirla's (1935) notion that vertebrate ontogeny is characterized by both recruitment and differentiation of response in the strengthening of withdrawal tendencies.

Environmental Variables. A recent study (Henning, Dunlap, and Gallup, 1976) contrasts TI production in laboratory settings with and without ground cover. When cover is available, anoles (lizards) attempt to escape significantly more often than they exhibit immobility responses, while the reverse is true when ground cover is absent. In an open area, attempting to escape may initiate recapture because movement elicits attack responses in the predator. Placement of a subject over a visual cliff also prolongs TI (Ratner, 1977).

For beetles, higher light intensities increase TI while darker environments diminish immobility (Ratner, 1977). Ratner speculated that dark environments may cue animals to escape — that escape in a dark environment is more adaptive than TI.

The maintenance of TI is not strictly a function of the intensity of environmental stimulation (Halton and Thompson, 1975). These authors discovered a curvilinear relationship between stimulus intensity and immobility duration: low decibel sounds have little, if any, effect on TI; midrange auditory stimuli prolong TI; and extremely loud stimuli startle the animal, in effect creating an "override" that jolts the animal from its immobile posture.

Studies that incorporate noise have often lost subjects through incapacitating audiogenic seizures that are produced readily in rodents in an enclosed space by a continuous high frequency noise like the vigorous jingling of keys (Gallup, 1977); for this reason, Gallup paired a light with noise for many trials (a type of emotional conditioning) and found that responses to the conditioned light signal were five times the duration of TI responses of control groups without this pairing. Edson and Gallup (1972) also found that loud, brief noises produce more enduring TI, but suggested that suddenness of onset may be just as critical a factor as intensity.

Response Variability. The finding that some members of a species do not exhibit TI under any condition (Ratner, 1967) is evidence for intraspecies variability, ranging from immunity to exaggerated vulnerability when TI lasts as long as 5 hours and 45 minutes. Interspecies variability also exists. European wrens have never been observed to show immobility, which Armstrong (1954) attributes to the agility and energy of the species, speculating that such energy makes active escape responses more appropriate. Smith (1966) compared two species of gulls and found ground-dwelling species exhibit direct forms of escape while cliff-dwellers often exhibit immobility. Using other kinds of comparisons, including nest construction and egg size, Smith concluded that cliff dwellers are evolutionarily more advanced than ground dwellers. From this he inferred, perhaps somewhat questionably, that immobility responses are more sophisticated than escape responses.

Internal Variables. The results of investigations of TI in relation to the circadian rhythm suggest that there are two peaks of susceptibility per day, at least for one species of toad and one species of tarantula (Ternes, 1977). Ternes speculated that circadian susceptibility may bear some relation to predation cycles so that greatest susceptibility occurs when predators are most likely to be in hot pursuit.

Studies involving brain ablation have produced inconsistent results, although such operations have never resulted in prolonging TI (Ratner, 1967). Gallup (1977) reviewed drug intervention studies and concluded that both adrenalin and chlorpromizine (an antipsychotic drug) increase TI while imipramine (a tranquilizer) reduces TI.

Experiential Variables. Crawford (1977) found that position within a pecking order has an inverse relationship to amount of TI a bird exhibits. In general, the higher the position a bird maintains, the less it exhibits TI. Ratner (1967) claims that pets tend to be immune to TI primarily because of the familiarity of surroundings and the amount of handling they receive. After one TI response has been induced in the laboratory, familiarity with the situation often results in habituation of the immobility reaction; however, with a change in the mode of induction the response typically recovers to full strength. Gallup (1977) has reported that not all species exhibit

habituation of TI, citing the quail and iguana as examples; among anoles, TI remains at full strength for as long as a year beyond the first induction. Exposure to a preinduction electric shock is another variable, that prolongs TI (Gallup, 1974).

Predator Characteristics. In laboratory research on the predator variable, investigators have used live predators and stuffed predators, or the experimenter has served the same purpose. When the experimenter served as the predator, Ginsburg (1975) found that the magnitude of TI was an inverse function of the distance the chicken was from the experimenter's hand. The presence of a human was also enough to induce TI in anoles (Edson and Gallup, 1972).

Blanchard, Mast, and Blanchard (1975) concluded that stimulus movement is a necessary and sufficient condition to produce immobility. These investigators presented albino rats with a variety of predatory stimuli and found that neither the smell or sound of a live cat nor the sight of a dead cat induced immobility, but that a moving cat, dog, or inanimate card produced freezing. Blanchard et al. identified movement as the initiating stimulus for TI and suggested that maintenance of immobility may be due to other factors.

The importance of predator distance has been elaborated by Ratner (1967) in his application of the comparative method to the analysis of TI. This analysis, an example of Stage V comparisons resulted in conceptualizing TI as the "terminal defense reaction in a sequential series of distance dependent predator defenses." The sequence of responses, the description of distances, and the mode of detection by the prey are presented in Table 21.3.

Gallup (1977) recently elaborated on an earlier finding from his laboratory (Gallup, Nash, and Ellison, 1971) that eye contact prolongs immobility in chickens and lizards by demonstrating that TI increased when detached glass eyes were sus-

Table 21.3

Ratner's Conception of the Variable of Distance in the Elicitation of Tonic Immobility as a Defense Against Predation

Distance of Predator	Type of Predator Stimulus	Elicited Prey Response
Great	Vision, audition	Freeze
Reduced	Movement—vision	Escape
Zero	Movement—vision, tactile	Fight
Prolonged zero	Prolonged tactile	TI

Adapted from Ratner (1967).

pended over a chick or when a mirror was arranged so as to produce a constant self-reflection. By contrast, there was no increase in immobility in control groups presented with dead, bloodsmeared predators or with live predators whose eyes had been sutured closed. Gallup concluded that the eye behaviors of both predator and prey are significant factors in the initiation and maintenance of tonic immobility responses.

Theoretical Approaches To Tonic Immobility

Both Ratner (1967) and Gallup (1977) outline six theoretical positions that attempt to explain TI. Three of the positions have generally been dismissed in light of contradictory evidence. Of the three surviving approaches, two of them stem from original discussions of Pavlov and Darwin.

The first antiquated position is that TI is a form of hypnosis. Both Gallup and Ratner agree that there is no evidence to support the notion that hypnosis in human beings is related to TI. Ratner comments that the cataleptic feature shared by both phenomena is only one minor component of hypnosis in humans. Gallup adds that creating a connection between the two is anthropomorphizing. A second unpopular notion is viewing TI as sleep related. Gallup suggests that EEG recordings reflecting an alert state undermine this position; and Ratner points out that sleep is invoked to explain both hypnosis and TI and does not adequately explain

either. A third hypothesis is based on spatial disorientation effects. Two bits of data counter this view. First, subjects placed horizontally during TI immediately assume an upright position upon termination of TI, which is not in keeping with the idea that orientation is disturbed. Second, hooding produces TI and does not involve any change in vestibular orientation.

A fourth explanation, which still has some advocates (e.g., Prestrude, 1977), maintains that TI is a reflexive response produced through cerebral inhibition mechanisms. Pavlov is credited with the inhibition notion, which assumes that some sort of stimulus releases a behavioral inhibitor. Hoaglund (1928) proposed central mediation through an adrenalin agent. Prestude's advocacy is based on the idea that TI is a parasympathetic "rebound" effect from high levels of initial sympathetic arousal created by the inducing conditions. Ratner (1967) proposed that there are more parsimonious explanations without involving inhibition. The research finding that TI habituates and recovers (Gallup, 1977) suggests that greater sophistication than that found in reflexive behavior is required.

The fear hypothesis has been attributed to Preyer's writings in 1878 (Gallup, 1977) and suggests that animals freeze when a threatening stimulus becomes apparent. Prestrude anthropomorphized that animals are "scared stiff." This view is supported by a variety of research findings in which variables that might elevate fear (preinduction shock, loud noises, etc.) do prolong TI (Edson and Gallup, 1972).

Tonic immobility as a "death feign" was proposed by Darwin and appears to fit the data for all species (Ratner, 1967 and 1977). This view maintains that predators elicit a complex unlearned response that does not necessitate past experience of any kind. The Darwinian tradition was favored by Ratner when he proposed that TI is a last-ditch effort of survival on the part of the prey. This adaptation interpretation comments minimally about underlying processes; however, it is predicated on the idea that immobility is more likely to lead to survival than an alternative escape or fight response. As examples, ducks in their natural habitat have been observed to feign death to avoid capture by their predator, the red fox (Sargeant and Eberhart, 1974), and the Thomson gazelle sometimes falls into a submissive posture, which results in the gazelle's completely eluding the predator (Walther, 1969). Gallup (1977) concluded that the adaptiveness of immobility is dependent on the predator's ignoring immobile prey.

Ratner, just before he died in 1975, suggested that the catatonic stupor seen in certain schizophrenic patients might be an example of an adaptive immobility reaction at the human level. Where all else has failed, a defense that throughout evolution has been at least partially sucessful comes into play. The catatonic stupor could be such an emergency reaction for human beings under excessive stress.

While most contributors to the special *Psychological Record* commemorative issue to the memory of Professor Ratner (1977) align themselves with one of the three hypotheses described above, two authors recommend a reanalysis of the concept of TI which could potentially incorporate all three positions. Lefebvre and Sabourin (1977) stress that the distinct differences in posture and duration of responses produced by the various induction methods argue against homogeneity of TI. They list many phenomena that represent or resemble immobility, including (1) immobility by inversion and restraint methods, (2) skin pressure by clipping or pinching to produce immobility, (3) TI produced through hooding, (4) death feigning in natural habitats, (5) photogenic catalepsy from repeated light stimulation, (6) inhibited behaviors induced by experimental "neurosis," and (7) attention fixation demonstrated by predatory snakes. Predatory snakes appear to use immobility for predation instead of defense. The immobile image of the snake apparently signals "safeness" to the frog. Also, the snake's tongue flicker seems to activate the frog's "bug-catching" mechanisms, and this stimulus overrides all other information. The frog appears to jump right into the snake' mouth (Zhuralev, 1969). Lefebvre and Sabourin (1977) conclude that different types of stimulation are needed to produce these responses and that the variety of behaviors argues for the concept of heterogeneity among immobility responses — a view that is not easily handled by one theoretical position.

Study Questions

1. Distinguish between "primary defense" and "secondary defense" and list at least four types of primary defense.

2. List and briefly describe at least three types of secondary defense under the major category of *flight*.

3. What is mobbing and when does it occur?

4. Define tonic immobility (TI) and describe when and how it occurs.

5. Briefly discuss two theories of TI.

6. Criticize the label of animal hypnosis for the TI effect.

22

Feeding Behaviors

Stephen R. Overmann[1]

Department of Animal Physiology
University of California, Davis

Animals maintain themselves through the intake of nutrients. Essential to all animal life are water, inorganic salts, and a variety of organic compounds including proteins, vitamins, lipids, and carbohydrates. Ingestion is the process of obtaining these materials from the external environment.

The precise pattern of nutrient requirements varies among species and depends largely on the capacity of the organism to synthesize certain substances. For example, animals use approximately twenty different amino acids; those that cannot be internally synthesized by a species must be ingested. Similarly, vitamins must by synthesized, ingested, or obtained from beneficial microorganisms internal to the host. There is a weak inverse relationship between capability to synthesize and phylogenetic position. That is, more complex forms tend to have less capacity for synthesis and therefore must rely on ingestive behaviors for a greater proportion of their nutrients. Lipids and carbohydrates serve primarily as energy sources for animals and also as raw materials for synthesis. All animals convert car-

bohydrates from one form to another, but *de novo* synthesis of carbohydrates from carbon dioxide and water occurs in only a few species. Green plants via photosynthesis are the primary source of carbohydrates. Inorganic salts must, of course, be ingested.

Diversity of Ingestion Mechanisms

A wondrous array of means of procuring required nutrients has evolved in animals, and an examination of ingestion mechanisms fails to reveal a consistent relationship with phylogeny. Species of the same taxonomic class may use different ingestive mechanisms, and, conversely, the same feeding mechanism may be used by species quite different in complexity and lineage. For example, sponges, some mollusks and tunicates (microscopic marine animals), and the great baleen whales all feed through filtration of particles from their aqueous environment. Classification of feeding mechanisms along classical taxonomic lines is clearly impossible. Yonge (1954) proposed a classification scheme based on the nature of the ingesta (objects ingested) and the morphological adaptations for obtaining

[1]Written during the tenure of a NIEHS postdoctural fellowship ES05057.

Table 22.1
Animal Feeding Mechanisms[a]

A.	Mechanisms for dealing with small particles	
	1. Pseudopodial	4. Tentacular
	2. Flagellate	5. Mucoid
	3. Ciliary	6. Setous
B.	Mechanisms for dealing with large particles	
	1. Mechanisms for swallowing of food and substrate	
	2. Mechanisms for scraping and boring	
	3. Mechanisms for seizing food	
	(a) For seizing and smallowing only	
	(b) For seizing and masticating before swallowing	
	(c) For seizing and achieving external digestion before swallowing	
C.	Mechanisms for taking in fluids or soft tissues	
	1. Mechanisms for piercing and sucking	
	2. Mechanisms for sucking only	
	3. Mechanisms for absorbing through general body surface	

[a]Adapted from Yonge, 1954.

food (Table 22.1). Although intended for invertebrates, the scheme is sufficiently comprehensive for extension to vertebrates (Jennings, 1972).

Mechanisms for Dealing with Small Particles

Small particles (microscopic animals, plants, and organic material) serve as food for many animals. With the exception of the action by pseudopodia which engulf food bits, small particles are usually filtered from the surrounding fluid. Flexible and moving broomlike processes such as flagella, cilia, or tentacles are used to facilitate the direction and rate of flow of the particle-bearing fluid medium; mucus and threadlike processes, or setae, are used to trap the small particles. Filter feeding is relatively more rare among chordates, although examples among sharks, fish, birds, and mammals can be cited. The use of small particles as food stuffs is restricted to aquatic forms.

Mechanisms for Dealing with Large Particles

Feeding mechanisms for exploitation of large particles have evolved in aquatic and nonaquatic species throughout the phyla. A few species appear nonselectively to ingest earth, silt, or mud, relying on alimentary processes to extract the usable material. For example, a terrestrial annelid, the familiar earthworm, swallows and digests the substrate that it burrows through; nutrients are absorbed as the material passes slowly through the gut.

A less familiar feeding mechanism is the act of scraping or boring into large food masses. The molluscan radula, a series of fine, horny teeth worked in a sawing motion, provides an excellent example of a structural adaptation for such a behavior. In various species the radula may be used to scrape algae from a stone, to rasp off pieces of plants or animals, or to bore or drill through the protective shell of molluscan or crustacean prey. An example of boring into food masses is also seen in the behavior of larvae of many insects.

At all phyletic levels species can be found that seize and swallow their food intact. The feeding apparatus and behavior of many snakes provide excellent illustrations of this class of feeding mechanism: their spikelike teeth are suited for seizing and holding prey and in some species are specialized for the injection of powerful toxins into the prey, and morphological modificaions of the skull and jaw often allow swallowing intact prey larger in diameter than the snake's head.

Instead of swallowing food items intact many species rend off smaller pieces or partially pulverize their food before swallowing it. The structures accompanying these feeding behaviors consist of mandibles and other mouth parts of Crustacea and Insecta, the horny beak of birds and some reptiles, and specialized dentition in rays, sharks, fish, reptiles, and mammals. The relation between feeding habit and mammalian teeth is well established. Briefly put, incisors are used for cutting or gnawing, canines for cutting or piercing, and premolars and molars for crushing and grinding. The relation between teeth and jaw structure on the one hand and feeding habit on the other is useful in inferring the nature of the food eaten by animals that are now extinct, including early humans. Instead of having structures to reduce the size of large food items by grinding or tearing, a few invertabrate species secrete enzymatic digestive juices over their solid food and then suck up the resultant semiliquid material.

Mechanisms for Taking in Fluids or Soft Tissues

Feeding mechanisms for taking in fluid and soft tissues are largely limited to invertebrates, with only a few species of lampreys and bloodsucking bats as chordate representatives. Animals feeding in this manner are typically ecto- or endoparasitic. Ectoparasitic species, those that live external to their host, have evolved accessory feeding structures for piercing the external layers of plants or animals. Animals that rely on absorbtion of nutrients through the general body surface are typically endoparasites that live inside their host.

The Chemical Senses and Feeding

Of the various modalities for gathering external information about food, the chemosensory receptors are the most common. Foodstuffs, after all, are nothing more than mixtures of chemicals. Chemoreception may be considered the most primitive biological sense since all organisms exhibit chemosensitivity. Among invertebrates, chemical stimuli are often of prime importance in both appetitive and consummatory components of ingestion sequences. Vertebrates rely relatively little on chemical cues for the appetitive components, but for many species chemosensory stimuli retain control of the consummatory portion of ingestive behavior.

The role of chemicals as releasing stimuli in the feeding sequences of animals can be highly complex. Originally proposed by Dethier, Barton-Browne, and Smith (1960), Table 22.2 presents a terminology intended to clarify the stimulus-response relationships involved. Originally proposed by Dethier, Barton-Brown, and Smith (1960) the scheme was modified by Beck (1965) and then by Lindstedt (1971). Reception of dispersed attractant or repellent chemicals lead respectively to orientation toward or away

Table 22.2[a]
Classification of Role of Chemical Stimuli in Feeding Behaviors

	Eliciting stimulus	
Response	Positive	Negative
Orientation (distant)	Attractant	Repellent
Orientation (close)	Arrestant	Repellent
Initiation of feeding	Incitant	Suppressant
Continuation of feeding	Stimulant	Deterrent

[a]Adapted from Lindstedt, (1971).

from the source. Animals cease locomotion on contact with an arrestant stimulus. Incitant stimuli elicit feeding responses, and suppressant stimuli inhibit feeding behaviors. Once feeding has begun, chemicals may act as stimulants to further ingestion or as deterrents that bring about a cessation of ingestion. Often several different chemical stimuli are involved in feeding sequences: one or more compounds acting as attractants, others as incitants, and still other as stimulants. Some insect species have separate sense receptors for the different classs of chemicals.

Chemoreceptors may be divided into two types. One type responds to stimuli in a medium (e.g., air or water), often in very low concentrations; the second type requires direct contact with the food source. Typically, the former is termed olfaction and the latter gustation, although these distinction are not always clear. In addition, chemoreceptors may function as specialists — responding to a very few closely related compounds — or as generalists responsive to a wide variety of chemical stimuli.

Specialized sensory cells for chemoreception first appear in the coelenterates. For example, Hydra, have nematocysts, stinging cells and spikes found singly or in arrays around the mouth and on the tentacles. The combined chemical and mechanical stimulation of these organs by prey produces an explosive reaction. Depending on the species, the nematocysts, may act simply as an adhesive to trap and hold the prey or may pierce the prey's body surface (even through chitinous armor) to release a paralytic toxin. The ensnared or immobilized prey is then brought to the mouth by the tentacles and ingested.

The platyhelminthes (flatworms) show more complex neural and sensory structures than the coelenterates. The evolutionary trend toward encephalization appears here in the form of the first centralized nervous systems. In Turbellaria, the free-living flatworms, chemoreceptors mediate complex orientation behaviors toward food from a distance. The chemoreceptors are localized in ciliated grooves or pits largely on the head region. Ablation of these sensory areas results in a loss in the ability to orient toward or detect food stimuli. In marine and freshwater species these structures are termed the auricular groove or auricular sense organ. An investigation of the effects of different chemical stimuli on the orientation of a freshwater planarian is abstracted as follows and illustrated in Table 22.3 (Mason, 1975).

Previous work had demonstrated that planaria can orient toward and locate a food source. Pilot work had indicated that fatty acids are the

Table 22.3[a]
Group Mean Values ($\pm$ SE) for Four Measures of Planarian Movement in Eight Solutions

	Angle Turned ($°$)	Straight Path (cm)	Speed (cm/min)	Rate of Turning ($°$/min)
Doionized water	41 $\pm$ 9	2.4 $\pm$ 0.6	10.0 $\pm$ 1.6	150 $\pm$ 194[b]
Phosphate buffer	38 $\pm$ 9	2.7 $\pm$ 0.7	10.4 $\pm$ 1.6	157 $\pm$ 52
Pentamoic acid	44 $\pm$ 9	2.3 $\pm$ 0.5	9.6 $\pm$ 1.0	206 $\pm$ 51
Hexanoic acid	48 $\pm$ 8	2.0 $\pm$ 0.4	9.1 $\pm$ 1.2	229 $\pm$ 39
Heptanoic acid	55 $\pm$ 10	1.9 $\pm$ 0.3	8.8 $\pm$ 1.1	265 $\pm$ 52
Octanoic acid	63 $\pm$ 13	1.8 $\pm$ 0.3	8.1 $\pm$ 0.8	307 $\pm$ 61
Nonanoic acid	62 $\pm$ 19	1.7 $\pm$ 0.3	7.9 $\pm$ 0.9	312 $\pm$ 61
Decanoic acid	70 $\pm$ 10	1.5 $\pm$ 0.1	7.7 $\pm$ 0.8	385 $\pm$ 62

[a]Adapted from Mason, 1975.
[b]Range of pretest control means for seven succeeding solutions.

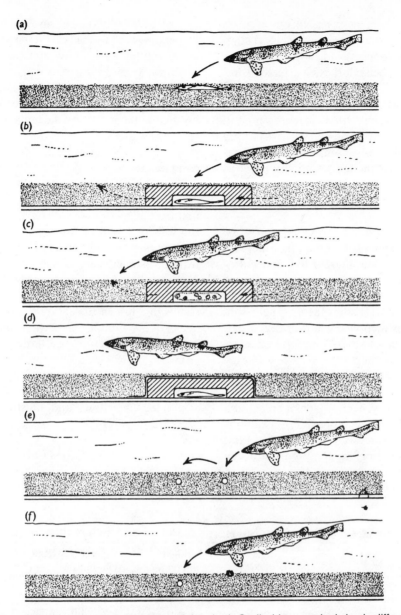

Figure 22.1. Illustration of the feeding responses of the shark *Scyliorhinus canicula* in six different experimental conditions. (A) Small flatfish are the natural foods of this shark species. When a plaice (*Pleuronectes platessa*), a weakly electric flatfish, was released in the tank the fish would hide itself in the sand. Hungry sharks would orient toward the buried plaice, uncover it by sucking up and expelling sand through their gill slits, and then capture and ingest the smaller fish. (B) An agar chamber with inlet and outlet pipes (arrows indicate water flow) was constructed around a live plaice and also buried. The sharks continued to orient toward the plaice and attempted to unbury it. Chemical and vibratory cues of the fish's location were attenuated by the agar chamber but it was essentially transparent to weak electric fields. (C) When bits of fish were placed in the agar chamber the sharks oriented toward chemical stimuli emanating from the outlet. (D) When the agar chamber with a live fish was wrapped in polyethylene film the sharks did not orient or show feeding behaviors. The plastic sheet had high resistance and prevented passage of dc and low frequency ac electric fields. (E) A one Hz sine wave current with an amplitude of 120 micro amperes fed into the water through two buried electrodes also elicited orienting and digging by the sharks. (F) The sharks would preferentially direct feeding responses to the buried electrodes even when bits of fish were readily available on the surface. (Adapted from Kalmijn, 1971).

chemical stimuli most effectively located. Previous procedures have used a point-source technique in which a single central chemical source was allowed to diffuse through the still-water medium. This method establishes a concentration gradient within the test chamber, but maintenance of a stable gradient over a period of time is impossible. Consequently, this study used instead a homogeneous concentration of the test chemical, established by constant flow of the solution through intake and outlet manifolds of the experimental tank. The effect of each chemical used on planarian orientation was assessed thirty times using a fresh animal on each trial.

A subject was adapted to the tank, and recording began after the inlet control valve had been switched from deionized water to the test solution for at least 10 minutes. A grid of 1.0 square centimeter under the translucent tank was used to note the planarian's position at 10-second intervals. The mean angle turned, the mean distance of straight paths between turns, the speed of movement, and the rate of change of direction were calculated for each animal. Group means for these measures for each solution are presented in Table 22.3

The results showed several relationships between planarian behavior and the number of carbon atoms in the fatty acid molecules. As carbon chain length increased the speed of movement decreased, the length of straight paths decreased, and the rate of turning, as well as the angle turned, increased. The net effect of increasing carbon chain length was to stimulate the angular velocity of planarian movement. According to the classification of orientation movements by Fraenkel and Gunn (1961, p. 45), an undirected response involving a change in turning rate or angular velocity is termed klinokinesis. Since chemical stimuli elicited this turning pattern it can be called a chemoklinokinetic orientation. Without much doubt, such orientation responses facilitate food localization by planaria.

The chemical senses reach their zenith in elaboration and specialization in the terrestrial arthropods. Correspondingly, a large literature exists on the varied roles of chemical stimuli and chemoreceptors in arthropod ingestion (Chapman, 1974; Schoonhaven and Derksen-Koppers, 1973), The excellent research of Vincent Dethier (see for example 1976), and his colleagues has served as a model for the work in this area. A taste of Dethier's extensive work on the feeding of the blowfly is presented in Chapter 13.

Among chordates, chemosensory control of ingestion is of greatest importance in the fishes. Bardach (1967) presented data on the orientation of bullheads to chemical food stimuli and reviewed other studies on chemosensory control of feeding in fish. Within the class *Amphibia*, some salamanders have long been known to use chemosensory orientation to food but the feeding of anurans (frogs and toads) was thought to be controlled solely by visual cues. Recent studies with frogs and toads confirm the predominance of vision but indicate that olfactory cues are also used (Sternthal, 1974). The chemical senses are involved in the food getting of many reptiles, particularly snakes (Burghardt and Pruitt, 1975). Chemoreceptors in snakes are located in the olfactory epithelium and also in Jacobson's organ in the roof of the mouth. Like reptiles, taste is relatively less important in birds than in mammals. The olfactory capabilities of birds are recognized; but the use of olfaction in feeding in these highly visual species has not been sufficiently studied, although Stager (1964) did demonstrate the importance of chemoreception in the location of food by turkey vultures. The roles of taste and olfaction in mammalian feeding has received considerable attention (Kare and Maller, 1967), but we are only beginning to appreciate the complexity of the chemical senses (Erickson and Schiffman, 1975); rapid development of this area should be anticipated.

Other Senses and Feeding

Sound Localization and Echolocation in Ingestive Behavior

Invertebrates are often very good at accurate localization of sounds (Burtt, 1974), but many vertebrates are also quite competent in using sound to locate prey. Owls, relative to other birds, have enlarged and asymmetrically placed eardrums, elongated cochlea, and facilitative facial plumage. These adaptations contribute to the ability of owl species to pinpoint the minute sounds of their prey's movement (Konishi, 1973).

Several species of birds and mammals emit vocalizations that are used in echolocation to detect prey. Animal sonar has been most extensively studied in cetaceans (whales and porpoises) and chiropterans (bats). In related species of bats, of the subfamily *Glossophaginae*, the bats range from insectivores to nectar and pollen feeders. In an experiment by Howell (1974) that was concerned with echolocation and feeding preferences, individuals from the different species were blindfolded and flown through an obstacle course (a darkened room with many floor-to-ceiling wires), and the bats' navigation behaviors were recorded by audiotape and stroboscopic photography. Also, the sensitivities of the auditory receptor in each species were determined by electro-physiological recording of cochlear potentials evoked by 5000 to 10,000 Hertz tones. The results showed that insectivorous species were superior in the flying test. Receptor sensitivity differed little across species, but the pattern of sound production did. Navigation performance was positively related to echolocation ability, reflecting adaptation by insectivores to the pressure for highly accurate localization of small objects.

Daly (1973) investigated the stimuli involved in the appetitive and consummatory components of feeding in *Harmothoë imbricata*, a carnivorous marine annelid. These worms use water-borne vibrations from a prey's movements to locate it. Four sensory appendages are involved in this type of mechanoreception, but as long as any one of these appendages is intact, the animal can locate food. If all appendages are removed, then responses to food stimuli cease until the structures have regenerated. Upon contact, prey items are examined via chemoreceptors on the palps (also one of the mechano- receptors). The appropriate chemical stimuli release an attack response that consists of a rapid outward thrust of the proboscis. The prey is seized between chitinous jaws, and the proboscis and prey are withdrawn into the mouth.

Exotic Senses

Snakes of the family Crotalidae, the pit vipers, have interesting means for detecting and killing prey. Their fangs fold into skin sheaths in the roof of the mouth; that is, fang length is not restricted by mouth size. "Coupled with a powerful toxin, the mobile, elongated, and easily replaced fangs of the vipers are terrible weapons. More than that, however, they are highly efficient food-getting tools" (Caras, 1974, p. 247). Pit vipers have a pair of facial pits that are richly endowed with receptors for radiant heat, each pit containing many more thermoreceptors than are contained in the entire skin of a human. The pit leads into a small chamber with a membranous floor that is densely innervated with branching nerve fibers. The sensitivity of the pit receptor is limited to detection of warm-blooded prey at a few feet. The initial appetitive orientation toward prey appears to be guided by olfactory and visual cues. Once within effective range, however, the snake attacks with the deadly accuracy of a heat-seeking missile armed with a venomous warhead. Temperature receptors are also important in the location of warm-blooded hosts by some ectoparasites.

Animals are not limited to sensing chemical, visual, vibratory or thermal stimuli. Many species use more exotic sensory signals in their ingestive behaviors, with which we cannot empathize. The electroreception of fish provides an excellent example. Species of approximately a dozen families of fish are able to produce and sense electrical pulses. Massive cerebellar enlargement accompanies well-developed electrolocation abilities (Burtt, 1974, P. 129). The electric organs are modified muscles by which these fish establish a dipole electrical field in the water surrounding their bodies. Objects such as food that differ in conductivity from the surrounding water distort the electrical field and are thereby detected (Harder, 1972). Lissman (1963), who is recognized as a pioneer in the study of electroreception, has observed that the electrical discharge rate of some species is too fast (as high as 1600 per second) for sensory nerves to follow and speculates that these fish may be sensing the average value of electrical current over some unit of time. This averaging process is familiar in electronics as a method of increasing the signal-to-noise ratio.

That certain fish, like some catfish, possess electroreceptors but do not generate an electrical field might be considered surprising. However, electroreceptive abilities are more widely distributed among fish than are electrogenerative abilities. A study of Kalmijn (1971) outlines the use of electric signals in food location by two non-electric species, the shark *Scyliorhinus canicula* (Figure 22.1, see p. 418), and the ray *Raja clavata*.

The electrical generating abilities of some fish, eels, and rays are so strong that their electrical discharges are used for defense and prey capture. A South American freshwater species, *Electrophorus electrius*, can deliver a 2-millisecond jolt of 600 volts at 1000 watts, certainly not a character that you would want in your swimming pool.

Selection and Avoidance of Ingesta — The Problem of Selectivity

Animals have exploited every conceivable food source, and it is not an overstatement to say that any organic matter may be used as food by at least one animal species in the world. The factors that determine what an animal will ingest as food is the problem of selectivity (Rozin, 1976; see also Chapter 13).

Simple organisms have simple nutrient requirements, and many are dietary specialists. Their selectivity of ingesta is under the tight control of external stimuli: the initiation or inhibition of feeding is typically an innate response to specific chemosensory cues. In a few instances, however, early food experiences determine the food choice of specialists. For example, in some insects the food stuff in which the eggs were deposited may become the food of choice because of early larval ingestive experience. Generalists face more severe problems: the wired-in system of the specialists assures adequate nutrition while the absence of such a system in the generalists means an adequate diet must come through a balanced intake of different food stuffs.

Among the carnivores, herbivores, and omnivores, the omnivores face the most difficult selection problems, for they ingest a variety of materials that differ widely in nutritional content and adequacy. Herbivores have opted for easily available and well-distributed foods of low nutrient content. They rely on bulk intake and selection of plant parts with the most favorable nutrient content. Carnivores maintain themselves on widely dispersed foods of high nutrient content that are selected on the basis of prey size, conspicuousness, and availability.

Ecologists have developed numerous models of selectivity, often based on carnivorous feeding, although much of their work may be generalized to other feeding habits. The basic assumption of these models is that natural selection favors maximization of energy-intake per unit of time and the minimization of energy spent in food acquisition (Pulliam, 1974; Rappaport, 1971).

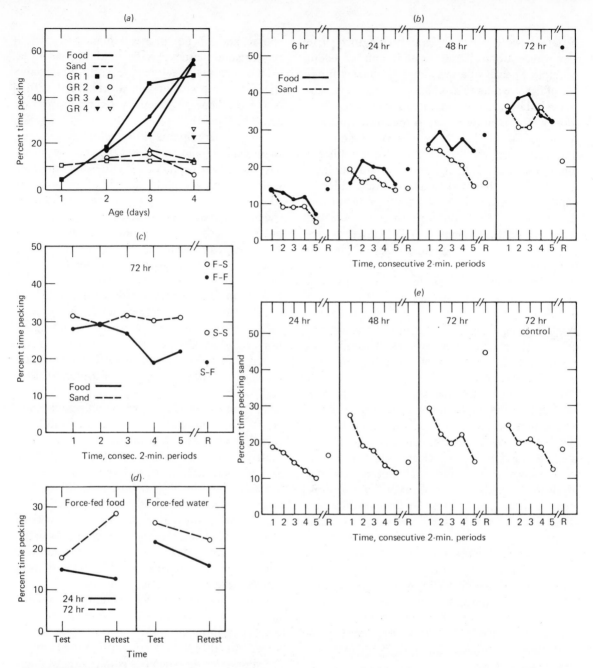

Figure 22.2. Mean percent time spent pecking sand or food by junglefowl chicks in five experimental conditions. (A) Four grops of chicks were individually tested in a simultaneous-choice situation. Birds of each group were exposed to the stimuli for the first time at the age indicated and were subsequently retested at 24 hr intervals. (B) Eight Experimental groups are shown. In this experiment each chick was exposed to only one stimulus (sand or food) and was tested and retested only once at one age. The retest (R) occurred 1½ hr. after the original 10 min. test. (C) Chicks were tested at 3 days of age on food or sand and rested 1½ hr. later. F-S indicates food (F) experience on test and sand (S) experience on retest, etc. (D) Chicks of 24 or 72 hr of age were allowed to peck at sand for 5 min. and were then immediately force-fed either a liquid diet or water. 1½ hr later the chicks were retested on sand for 5 min. (E) Chicks of 24, 48, or 72 hr of age were force-fed a liquid diet immediately after a 10 min exposure to sand and were retested with sand 1½ hr later. Chicks in the control group were force-fed 2 hr after the original test and were retested 1½ hr after force-feeding. (Adapted from Hogan, 1973 a).

The Role of Early Experience in Food Selection

A different approach, often adopted by psychologists, is to examine the role of experience in food selection. For example, food selection by the weanling rat appears to be influenced by cues transmitted through the mother's milk (Galef and Sherry, 1973), and rats and chicks imitate parental food choices (Cowan and Evans, 1974; Galef, 1971). Also, many species prefer those foods that were experienced during early development.

In chickens and other birds, pecking accuracy, feeding success, and feeding efficiency improve with age (Dunn, 1972; Recher and Recher, 1969). In a series of experiments Hogan (1973a, b) has examined how chicks learn to recognize food; one of these studies is abstracted as follows and the results illustrated in Figure 22.2.

Under natural conditions, the first food normally eaten by a newly hatched chick is food offered to it by the mother hen. However, as shown in this experiment, socially isolated chicks do learn to recognize food.

"My dear, I owe it entirely to my strict protein diet."

Figure 22.3. "(There) are times when the female fly has a hunger for protein. It can be demonstrated . . . (by) measuring food intake. For the present demonstration, one of the J-shaped pipettes contains protein and the other, sugar . . . If you have the fortitude to measure a fly's daily consumption of sugar and protein over a three-week period, you will doscover that the males always prefer sugar. The females, on the other hand, prefer protein to sugar during the first six or eight days of life; thereafter, they, too, prefer sugar. A series of simple dissections will reveal that it is during the first week of life that a female is building her eggs. The development of a fly's eggs cannot proceed to completion without protein any more than a hen's eggs can be packaged in a shell by a hen that lacks calcium in her diet." (Adapted from Dethier, 1962, pp. 67-69).

Some Major Classes of Behavior

The subjects were Burmese red junglefowl chicks (Gallus gallus spadecius), individually housed on a solid floor with water available. The basic design was to provide chicks of different ages test and retest experiences with sand and/or food. The data are reported as percent of total time spent pecking sand or food.

In the first experiment chicks of several ages were offered a choice between sand and food at both test and retest (Figure 22.2a). There was no indication of preference for either stimulus on the first test at any age. When retested, the amount of pecking at sand remained relatively constant, while pecking at food tended to increase over days. One-day-old chicks, however, showed no preference for food on day 2, while both 2 and 3-day-old chicks showed a marked preference for food on retest on the following day. Equivalent experiences clearly have different effects on chicks of different ages.

In experiment 2 chicks were tested on food or sand and retested later on the same material (Figure 22.2b). The amount of time spent pecking increased as the chicks increased in age from 6 to 72 hours. Following a food test, the changes in pecking levels in the retest were of small magnitude for chicks of 6, 24, and 48 hours old. The 72 hour chicks, however, showed a large increase in pecking at food. For chicks initially tested with sand, pecking at sand in the retest increased at 6 hours and progressively declined as the chicks became older.

Experiment 3 determined if 3-day-old chicks discriminted between food and sand when they had been exposed to food or sand 1½ hours earlier (Figure 22.2c). Chicks initially exposed to food showed increased pecking on retest regardless of whether sand or food was presented on retest. Conversely, chicks first exposed to sand showed decreased pecking to both sand and food on retest.

Experiments 4 and 5 investigated the possibility that the lack of effect of food exposure prior to day 3 might be due to a failure of the chicks to ingest sufficient food at the earlier ages via pecking. The results of experiment 4 (Figure 22.2d) showed that 1-day-old chicks force fed a liquid food immediately after the pecking test showed no increase in pecking during the retest. Similarly treated 3-day-old chicks, however, showed a large increase. Neither age group that was force fed water showed increased pecking in the retest. The results of experiment 5 (Figure 22.2e) substantiate the results of experiment 4 and indicate that the increase in pecking by 72-hour chicks does not occur without temporal contiguity of pecking and food ingestion.

Taken together, the results indicate that the critical period for learning about food peaks around three days of age in the chick. Also, rather than a particular stimulus being associated with reinforcement at this age, the act of pecking itself seems to be reinforced or punished (the results of experiment 3).

Among primates, early food experiences may lead to a learned fixation for certain foods as an adult. It is often difficult to persuade primates captured as adults to take strange or new foods (Lang, 1970)). Young animals are more likely to accept new foods.

Learning also seems to be involved in the preparation of food. Extended study of troops of *Macca fuscata* by Japanese primatologists have yielded fascinating observations of cultural transmission of food habits (Itani, 1958 Kawai, 1965). In 1953 the first instance of sweet potato washing was observed in a young female. Sweet potato washing spread slowly through the monkey troop, primarily along lines of playmate relationships among young monkeys. Within 5 years most monkeys under 7 years of age, but only one-fifth of the adults, washed their potatoes prior to ingestion. This "tradition" subsequently shifted from the use of freshwater to using salt water and from peer transmission primarily to mother-child transmission.

In humans, of course, a vast array of cultural

food habits have evolved. Examine the yellow pages for any large city and find restaurants specializing in Armenian, Cantonese, Danish, German, Kosher, Polynesian, or Sicilian fare. Rozin (1976) presents an interesting discussion of human food cultures or cuisines. He argues that distinctive cuisines are among the most conservative and dearly preserved characteristics of one's ethnic identity.

Dietary Selection for Nutrients

Adequate intake of essential nutrients is assured for those animals that are dietary specialists; their nutrient requirements are attuned to the food ingested. Elaborate physiological mechanisms have evolved to conserve and mobilize available stores of nutrients when nutrient intake is inadequate. In addition, many species of generalists adjust their nutrient intake in accordance with bodily needs.

The clearest example of such physiological and behavioral regulation is seen with sodium. In the intact mammal, sodium levels are regulated by adrenal activity. Richter (1936) demonstrated that adrenalectomy, which leads to excessive sodium loss, results in a marked appetite for sodium. Adrenalectomized rats without a source of sodium perish within a few days of operation, whereas if access to sodium is provided adrenalictomized animals can maintain themselves in good condition indefinitely. Inadequate dietary intake of sodium also results in an increased appetite for foods or liquids that contain sodium (Stricker and Wilson, 1970).

The behavioral response to sodium deficiency clearly seems to be innately organized; deficient animals show immediate recognition and avid ingestion of sodium solutions on initial contact (Bolles, Sulzbacher, and Arant, 1964). This appetite for sodium appears to be mediated by deficiency-induced changes in the gustatory response to sodium salts (Contreras and Hatton, 1975). Sodium is the most important ionic constituent

of the internal environment and an adequate intake is essential to all terrestrial vertebrates. In fact men have fought wars over the control of localized salt deposits (Denton, 1967).

Salt appetite seems to be unique with respect to its genetic determination. The selection of other nutrients seems to be largely mediated by the association of the stimulus properties of a food with the consequences of its ingestion. The role of learning in dietary selection has been carefully described in an excellent series of studies by Paul Rozin and colleagues (eg. Rozin and Kalat, 1971).

The bulk of the literature on dietary selection consists of laboratory studies, most often conducted with rat subjects (Overmann, 1976). However, the phenomenon is not a laboratory artifact and is not peculiar to *Rattus norvegicus*. Among the more interesting nonrat, nonlaboratory demonstrations of behavioral regulation of nutrient intake is the work of Clara Davis (1934, 1939) with young children. Davis, a physician, maintained children in a hospital setting on a total self-selection regime for periods of several years. At no time was any effort made to control the children's intake of the thirty unseasoned and unmixed foods that were used. Refined products such as sugar or flour were excluded. Nutrient intake, as well as physical status of the children, was continually monitored. The selected diets were consistent with nutrient requirements, and the children were judged to be exceptionally healthy.

Another extraordinary example of dietary selection exists in the phenomenon of pica. The term pica refers to an unusual or "perverted" appetite for nonfood, usually inorganic materials. Green (1925) has reported a particularly striking example of this phenomenon: cattle pastured on phosphorus-poor grazing land became oestophagic or bone eaters. When bones were unavailable, the normally herbivorous cattle consumed live turtles! Addition of phosphorous to the cattle's ration caused a cessation of the pica.

The phenomenon of pica is well documented in animals and has often become a culturally accepted behavior in humans. Such abnormal feeding behaviors may result in the ingestion of toxic materials, and pica may be responsible for cases of lead poisoning in children (de la Burde and Reames, 1973).

The increased mineral demands of pregnancy, lactation, or hard- shell egg production have also been observed to result in increased ingestion of inorganic materials by wild species (Korschgen, 1964; Moss, 1972). The ability to select a diet in accordance with bodily needs is not limited to vertebrates. Lobsters increase their calcium intake prior to periodic exoskeleton moults (Ennis, 1973). Also, Dethier (1976, pp. 299-335) discusses at length the relationship between egg production and the specific hunger for protein in gravid female blowflies (see Figure 22.3, p. 423).

Learned Effects: Avoidance of Ingesta Based on Postingestional Consequences

Ingestion sequences may be halted by the lack of appropriate stimuli or by the presence of inhibitory stimuli. Some foods are avoided on the basis of external cues up to and including stimuli immediately preceding ingestion. But taste or contact chemoreceptors are the final deciding stimuli for many species (cf Table 22.3) Bitter-tasting compounds, for example, quinine in sufficient concentrations, are avoided by a broad range of phyla. Of those foods that are ingested some will be unpleasant or harmful. Natural selection pressures favor mechanisms that lead to avoidance of foodstuffs with deleterious post-ingestional consequences (Rozin and Kalat, 1971).

Taste Aversion Learning. Psychologists have focused on learning mechanisms involved in tastes becoming associated with unfavorable internal events, as mentioned in Chapters 5, 14, and 15 under the heading of bait shyness and conditioned taste aversions. Interest in this area

was spurred by the work of Garcia and colleagues (eg. Garcia, Erwin, and Koelling, 1966). They demonstrated, first, that a rat can learn to avoid a substance with a neutral taste cue even if the rat were made sick several hours later by x-rays. This procedure became the paradigm for typical taste aversion learning studies, with injected drugs such as lithium chloride (LiCl) most often used as the noxious agent. Second, they found that different stimuli were preferentially associated with different aversive consequences (the Garcia effect). Rats can easily learn to avoid a taste that is followed by nausea but have great difficulty learning to avoid a taste that is followed by painful electric shock; conversely, auditory or visual cues are easily conditioned to shock avoidance, but not to food aversion. These results were considered surprising in light of two accepted learning principles: (1) that temporal contiguity of only a few seconds or less between CS (taste) and UCS (nausea) is necessary for learning to take place, and (2) that all CS's are equally good for all US's (equipotentiality assumption).

Exceptions to equipotentiality — that certain stimuli are preferentially associated with other events — has been attributed to belongingness (Garcia and Koelling, 1966), preparedness (Seligman, 1970) or stimulus relevance (Capretta, 1961; McFarland, 1973). Attempts to account for taste aversion learning with long CS-UCS intervals by persistence of oral cues or by lack of subsequent stimulus interference by other stimuli (Kalat and Rozin, 1970) have not been successful: effective CS-UCS intervals of up to 24 hours have been reported (Etscorn and Stephens, 1973), and although it has been reported that anesthesia during the CS-US interval facilitates conditioning, this facilitory effect is apparently due to the aversive effects of the anesthetic (Buresova and Bureš, 1975). (A possible resolution of this problem is discussed in Chapter 14).

That rats reject foodstuffs associated with illness should have been no surprise to psycholo-

Figure 22.4. Scale drawings of the seven common wader species on the Gann Flat. Bill and tarsus length were estimated for each species by measurement of representative animals. Mean bill lengths (cm) were: C = 11.5; O = 7.3; G = 5.5; R = 4.1; D = 3.1; RP = 1.4; T = 2.2. Mean tarsus lengths (cm) were: C = 8.0; O = 4.5; G = 5.6; R = 4.8; D = 2.4; RP = 2.6; T = 2.6. (Adapted from Edington, Morgan, and Morgan, 1973).

gists. Folklore has long been rich with tales of rat colonies that withstand attempts at extermination by poisoning. In addition, Franke and Potter (1936) demonstrated that rats would invariably select the diet with lowest available content of toxic seleniferous wheat and that sublethal injections of sodium selenite result in voluntary starvation in the presence of unadulterated food. Subsequent studies repeatedly demonstrated that rats tend to avoid new food (neophobia) as well as avoiding poisoned diets (Chitty, 1954; Richter, 1953). Like all dietary generalists, rats are faced with the potential ingestion of many toxic materials. Unlike many species, the rat lacks the ability to regurgitate, which means that unfavorable materials once ingested cannot be expelled. As mentioned earlier, young rats learn what foods to eat and what

not to eat from imitating the food choices of older animals (Galef and Clark, 1972); and rats sample food in a way that helps identify the consequences of its ingestion (Barnett, 1956; Rozin 1969).

The relative novelty of the CS has been found to be an important determinant of the strength of a learned taste aversion. Tastes that have been experienced often, for a long period of time, or without aversive consequences are not likely to be associated with illness (Kalat, 1974; Kalat and Rozin, 1970) while highly salient or nonpreferred taste stimuli are most likely to be associated with illness. Weaker conditioned aversions are reported if the material is only tasted and not ingested. Prior experience with the UCS (the same or similar drugs) has also been shown to reduce the strength of conditioned taste aversion

Some Major Classes of Behavior

(Braveman, 1975), and the extinction of taste aversions may be hastened by forced exposure to the CS.

The known generality of taste avoidance conditioning is considerable and the specific references for the many statements in the next five paragraphs can be found in the comprehensive bibliography by Riley and Baril (1976). Mammals other than rats that form aversions include mice, hamsters, guinea pigs, gerbils, coyotes, wolves, deer, cats, and monkeys. Quail and chickens form aversions on the basis of visual rather than chemical cues, and guinea pigs form aversions to both visual and taste cues. Learned food avoidance has been shown in garter snakes, Atlantic cod, and a terrestrial slug. The slug (*Limax maximus*) would not learn to avoid highly palatable dog food poisoned by metaldehyde but did learn to avoid mushrooms or potatoes when paired with blasts of CO_2. Interestingly, the poisoning of mice prevented mouse ingestion but not mouse killing by rats.

The list of noxious agents that induce taste aversion learning grows steadily longer since irradiation was originally used by Garcia. Mechanical stimulation via rapid rotation is effective; and LiCl, the drug most widely used, has been extensively investigated for effects of dose route and concentration on taste aversion learning. Other chemicals reported to be effective when injected include: ethanol, d-amphetamine and methamphetamine, mescaline, chlorpromazine, scopolamine, lorazepam, methylscopolamine, methylatropi, Emorphine or naloxone-induced morphine withdrawl, formalin, tetraethyl lead, and hypertonic saline. With repeated exposure to LiCl injections, rats may show taste aversions following placebo injections of isotonic saline.

A practical study by Nachman and Hartley (1975) compared the taste aversions formed by strong, near lethal doses of LiCl with several rodenticides given in sublethal doses. LiCl produced strong aversions while rodenticides like warfarin, cyanide, or strychnine produced weak aversions or no aversions at all.

Although injections are aversive both to humans and rats, the injection itself does not seem to mediate food aversion learning. The studies cited above have typically used placebo injected control animals, and taste aversions have been demonstrated following intubation of a histidine-free amino acid load directly into the stomach of rats.

Several studies have investigated whether taste aversions develop in animals in which a bodily need for the CS has first been induced. The answer seems to be a slightly qualified "no." When either a sucrose or saline solution is used as the CS and one of the following, X-rays, formalin, or insulin injections, is used as the UCS, the irradiated rats without any induced needs learned to avoid both solutions, formalin-injected animals avoided sucrose but not the needed saline solution, and insulin-injected rats avoided saline but not the needed sucrose solution. But multiple LiCl pairings with saline solution prior to adrenalectomy or formalin injections did prevent increased salt intake in the treated animals when they needed the extra salt.

Natural Toxins and Feeding

Laboratory studies of taste aversion learning have natural analogues in the avoidance of toxic foods by animals in the wild. Blue jays, for example, need only one aversive experience to learn to avoid monarch butterflies, as discussed in Chapter 5. Not all monarchs in a wild population are poisonous. However, the presence of a proportion of toxin-containing individuals not only protects them from predators but also confers an advantage on all members of monarch species.

The poisonous chemicals sequestered within the butterflies' body are representative of a large number of plant secondary compounds. These compounds are nonessential to the plant's life, and one of their principal functions appears to be defense against animal ingestion. One of the evolutionary counter strategies of animals was to develop detoxification mechanisms (Krieger, Feeny, and Wilkinson, 1971). Detoxification of a plant's secondary compounds by mammals occurs primarily in the gut, liver, and kidney. Cooking also serves to detoxify many secondary plant compounds and represents a recent advance that allows a human being to ingest a wide range of plants. For humans and other animals many plants remain toxic because of the absence of any biological or technological adaptation to their secondary compounds.

The study of the effects of plant poisons is known as phytotoxicology. There is an enormous literature in the area; an excellent source for further study is the *USDA Bibliography of Agriculture*. Popular interest in plant poisoning has increased in the United Sates. The increase seems to be due to naive foragers' use of wild foods or foods with psychoactive properties. An increased incidence of poisoning in America's pets seems to be attributable to the boom in houseplants. As many owners sadly learn, various ornamental or exotic plants are very toxic to pets. Historically, the area of greatest concern has been the effect of poisonous plants on grazing livestock, especially in the Western United States. The problem has been partially improved by better range management, but such poisoning still accounts for significant livestock loss.

The literature indicates that cattle and sheep are the most often poisoned. Horses are a distant third with goats and pigs comprising only a small fraction of affected animals. Ruminants and simple-stomached animals seem to differ in susceptibility to plant poisoning. The feeding strategy of ruminants involves the intake of a large amount of food material and a long period of digestion. Both of these factors probably increase the incidence of plant poisoning in cattle and sheep.

The deleterious effects of toxic plants on livestock are threefold. First, and most obviously, ingestion can result in fatality. Secondly, those animals that are not poisoned severely enough to die are often rendered useless to their owner; the poisoned cattle and sheep may remain emaciated and generally unmarketable. Third, many of the poisonous plants have serious effects on reproduction, acting to abort the embryo or fetus or as teratogens that result in the birth of abnormal offspring (Keeler, 1975).

Although there are literally hundreds of toxic plants, approximately forty account for the bulk of livestock poisoning. Methods of reducing livestock losses from these plants have been developed from years of painful experience. The methods are summarized as follows.

Practice Good Range and Pasture Management

Avoid overgrazing — because most toxic plants are less palatable than safe ones, animals will ingest many poisonous plants only when other forage is unavailable.

Increase desirable forage — many toxic plants can be exterminated through land cultivation; this will simultaneously decrease the availability of toxic plants along with increasing the availability of safe forage.

Decrease toxic plants — in addition to cultivation, toxic plants may be decreased through (1) mechanical means — digging out the plants or mowing prior to seed development, (2) chemical means — application of herbicides.

Feed Supplementation to Decrease Ingestion of Toxic Plants

Provide supplemental feed during times of low forage availability — that is, during droughts or early frost.

Provide salt and mineral blocks, which tend to decrease the incidence of poisoning.

Reduce Access of Livestock to Toxic Plants

Graze infested pastures with livestock species which are not poisoned by available plants.

Avoid turning stock to pasture in early spring

— many toxic plants begin spring growth prior to the growth of safe forage.

Avoid turning stock to infested pastures when they are very hungry — that is, after long periods of confinement or shipping: poisoning may be frequent because of indiscriminate grazing.

Graze infested areas at times when the plants are least toxic — some plants are relatively harmless during certain periods of their growth.

Avoid putting up hay or silage from infested areas — the mixing will make it difficult for animals to avoid the toxic plants.

In addition to advocating preventative measures, several authors have speculated on why livestock ingest poisonous plants. From these discussions, it appears that there are three classes of toxic plants: unpalatable, palatable, and "addictive." Most toxic plants seem to be unpalatable to livestock. There is virtual unanimity in stating that plants in this group are ingested only under conditions of hunger induced by insufficient forage or restricted food access. Preference for these plants is low and they are taken only as an alternative to starvation.

The larkspurs, of delphiniums, are the principal exceptions to the general unpalatability of toxic plants to livestock. They are among the more toxic of poisonous plants and are thought to be responsible for more cattle losses than any other poisonous plant (Cronin, 1971). Sheep can graze with impunity on these plants, being markedly less affected by the plant's toxicity. While larkspurs seem to be palatable to cattle and other livestock, they are definitely not preferred over good forage.

The many species of locoweed appear to be the only toxic plants that livestock prefer to safe forage. The etiology of this preference is quite interesting. If sufficient good forage is available, locoweeds will not be taken because of their initial unpalatability. However, if a considerable quantity is taken, animals develop "loco-habit," or marked appetite for loco plants. Affected stock will, in fact, seek out loco plants to the exclusion of all other forage. All types of livestock, including cattle, sheep, horses, goats and pigs may develop loco habit; and, if allowed, all will ingest fatal quantities (James, 1972). Because of their apparent addictiveness, many authors have speculated that loco plants contain some powerful "narcotic." However, despite considerable research effort, neither the toxic principle nor the addictive principle has been unquestionably identified (James and VanKampen, 1976).

Of those plants of the United States known to be poisonous to man and domestic animals (Kingsbury 1964), many are ingested by our wildlife (Martin, Zim, and Nelson, 1951). As Freeland and Janzen (1974) note, it is easy to find examples of wildlife's ingestion of plants known to be toxic to man or domestic species. The more difficult problem is assessing whether a particular species of wildlife uses or avoids plants that are toxic to the particular species. Scattered reports in this area have appeared, but our current knowledge is relatively scant. A study abstracted as follows (Glander, 1977) illustrates the danger of plant toxins to wildlife, as well as selective feeding behaviors that facilitate avoidance of plant toxins.

This report relates a 14-month study of the ecology of mantled howling monkeys (Alouatta paliata) in a Costa Rican forest. The life-style and habitat of the monkeys requires them to excute precise movements high in the forest canopy, including leaps into space between trees. Shortly after the study began a number of monkeys exhibited bizzare behavior, convulsions, and then fatal plummets from the trees. Autopsy of these animals failed to reveal disease or apparent pathology. These events prompted the author to investigate the use of toxic plants as foodstuffs by the monkeys. The deaths appeared to be attributable to the monkeys' sampling of toxic leaves of the carne asada (Andira inermis) tree.

Further study indicated that the howlers were

very successful in avoiding the toxic secondary compounds of some tree species. Identification of the 1699 trees in the study area was made. The howlers were observed to take their food from 331 trees or fewer than 20 percent of the available trees. Seventy-five percent of their feeding occurred in only 88 trees. The animals were highly selective, showing consistent preference for certain species and even for individual trees within a species.

In the forest were 149 madera negra (Gliricidia sepium) trees. The leaves of this tree are known to be toxic to dogs, rats, mice, and horses. The howlers used only three of these trees for food. The remaining 146 madera negra trees were visited but not used for food. Chemical analysis revealed that the leaves of these three scattered trees were free of alkaloids, while the leaves of adjacent trees of this species were quite high in toxic chemicals. From other trees the monkeys also ingested the leaf stalks, the plant part lowest in alkaloids, while discarding the more highly toxic mature leaves.

Behavioral Interactions and Ingestion — Intraspecific Influences

Many organisms are responsive to the ingestive behavior of conspecifics. Social effects on ingestion appear to run a continuum from competition to cooperation. Measures of intraspecific dominance have often been based on competition for food or water. For example, frogs and toads, considered by traditional herpetologists to be without social awareness except during breeding season, have been shown to form stable, size-related dominance hierarchies in competition for insect prey (Boice and Boice, 1970; Tracy, 1973).

For many species foraging and feeding are social activities. In studying the effects of group activity on ingestion, psychologists have focused on the role actively eating conspecifics play in the ingestion behavior of the target animal. Presumably ingestion can be facilitated by an ani-

mal's imitating its conspecifics or through having its attention directed to relevant enviromental stimuli (Hughes, 1971). Zoologists, on the other hand, have been concerned with the adaptive value of social feeding activities. For zoologists there is a basic question: What are the selective advantages of feeding in large numbers rather than individually? Sociality *per se* has been proposed as one advantage; social species may simply find the company of conspecifics attractive (Turner, 1964). Also, there is speculation that feeding in groups confers greater protection from predators: in large groups, not all animals will be feeding simultaneously; hence collective eyes and ears will be more effective in detecting predators and in warning the group; also, multi directional flight could confuse potential predators. (See also Chapter 21, p. 404.) Finally, Cody (1971) has propsed that social feeding may lead to more efficient exploitation of food resources: animals feeding in groups probably consume all available food in an area before moving on.

Food sharing occurs between conspecifics; and the practice finds its greatest expression in the social insects. Trophallaxis, or liquid food exchange, occurs in social wasps, bees, termites and ants (Wilson, 1971). Trophallaxis varies directly with the amount of liquid in the species' diet and typically occurs between nestmates of all castes; in some species it also occurs between adult and larval forms. In one species of wasp (*Vespa orientalis*), the adults feed the larvae frequently and receive a drop of larval salivary secretion in return. The adults, but not the larvae, of this species are incapable of protein digestion and gluconeogenesis; thus, the larvae receive protein essential for their growth, and the adults receive a needed carbohydrate-rich salivary secretion.

Certain species of ants have expandable crops that allow individual foragers to carry home large loads of liquid food. This social stomach has been carried to an extreme in some species found in arid areas. Individual animals, called repletes, are essentially prevented from movement by their hugely distended abdomen filled with carbohydrate-rich liquid. During cool, moist weather they become living storage tanks to be tapped during hot, dry weather when the metabolism and food demands of the colony increase. A colony may contain hundreds or even thousands of repletes, and Australian aborigines have been reported to eat them like candy.

Several ant species show adaptations for the social transport of foods back to the colony. In *Formica obsovripes*, the smaller workers milk the colony's "cattle" for honeydew, while the larger forms with greater crop capacity act as tankers to gather and transport the solution home. One of the most curious forms of chain transport, as these behaviors are known, is exhibited by *Lasios fuliginosos*. Workers of this species forage individual areas with which they become highly familiar. When an insect prey is captured, an ant begins a return trip to the nest until it reaches a worker foraging an adjacent area. The food is transferred to the second ant, which similarly carries the food homeward until encountering the next adjacent forager.

Interspecific Behavioral Interactions and Feeding

Interaction between different species in relation to ingestion behavior may take several forms. One animal may be killed and consumed by another species (predator-prey relations). Second, food may be gained through symbiotic relationships as discussed below. Third, animals of one species may interfere with the food getting of another through competition for similar food resources.

Symbiosis, literally translated from the Greek, means "life together" and refers to a nonlethal, intimate physical relationship between two species (see also Chapter 19). Typically, the larger animal is termed the host and the smaller organism the symbiote. The smaller animal always

benefits from the association, but the host is usually not so lucky. Symbiotic relationships are of three types. In parasitism, the most common from of symbiosis, the symbiote benefits at the expense of the host. Common examples include humans as host for endoparasitic tapeworms and ectoparasitic ticks. In commensalism, the symbiotic benefits but the host is neither benefited nor harmed. A classic example of commensalism is between sea urchins and small tropical fish. The fish obtain safe shelter among the urchin's protective spines without affecting the sea urchin for better or worse. In mutualism, perhaps the least common form of symbiosis, both host and symbiote benefit from the relationship.

Excellent examples of mutualism are seen in cleaning symbiosis. Galàpagos tortoises are freed of ticks by two species of Darwin's finches (MacFarland and Reeder, 1974). The bird symbiotes gain high-protein tidbits by removing ectoparasitic symbiotes feeding on the blood of the tortoise! A cleaning bout is initiated by a hopping display by the birds. In response, the tortoise assumes a raised posture, with head and legs fully extended to maximize the area of skin exposure. The finches busily inspect the tortoise, including under the carapace and around the eyes; the tortoise remains motionless until the birds have finished their work and departed.

Equally fascinating are the cleaning symbiosis of fish and the fish that mimic the cleaners (Wickler, 1968, pp. 157-176). Cleaning customers, as Wickler terms the host, may seek out their small symbiotic cleaners. Characteristically, the cleaner approaches the customer with distinctive display movements (a dancelike swim), and the customer assumes a motionless posture extending and exposing those parts to be cleaned. Fish from a different family than the cleaners have become mimics as a means of obtaining food. According to Wickler's colorful description:

(The mimic) is similar in size, coloration, and swimming behavior and even exhibits the same dance as the cleaner. Fish which have had experience with the cleaner will also position themselves unsuspectingly in front of the mimic, showing the invitation posture for cleaning described above. They than receive a nasty surprise. The mimic approaches carefully and bites off a semicircular piece of the victim's fin and eats it. The fish immediately jerks around after the jab, but the mock cleaner calmly stays put as if knowing nothing about it, and remains unmolested because of its cleaner's costume.

Food Allocation in Species Occupying the Same Region

It is axiomatic in biology that two coexisting, or sympatric, species cannot occupy precisely the same niche; competitive exclusion of the less successful species will eventually occur. Ecologists have demonstrated that differences in the use of food resources are necessary for stable coexistence of interspecific communities. The differential use of limited food supplies by sympatric species has been termed resource allocation.

Among sympatric seed-eating rodents of the Southwestern Deserts, resource allocation has been shown to be related to several factors. Differences in seasonal activity levels among species contribute to reduced competition. The areas foraged for seeds may differ because of differences in preference for ground cover or because of the exclusion of some species from certain areas by the aggressive behavior of other species (Brown and Lieberman, 1973; Cameron, 1971). Resource partitioning by seed size may also take place, with size of seed selected being positively correlated with body size, though this relation appears to be controversial (Brown and Lieberman, 1973; Smigel and Rosenzweig, 1974).

Food resource allocation by sympatric species is described in the study abstracted as follows (Edington, Morgan, and Morgan, 1973) and illustrated in Figure 22.4, p. 427 and Figures 22.5a and b.

In autumn flocks of mixed species of wading birds congregate in a system of coastal habitats near Dale (Wales). The Gann Flat, a muddy beach, is the major feeding area for all the common species (Figure 22.4). During high tide, all species stayed at various sites adjacent to the shore; as the tide receded the majority of birds moved to the beach to feed and reversed their movements as the tide returned. Teams of observers stationed along the beach recorded the birds' feeding location and the depth of their feeding probes into mud or water during daylight from 3 hours before low tide to 3 hours after low tide; the main feeding period of all species. Every 20 minutes the entire beach was scanned and the location and behavior of the feeding birds scored.

The results showed that the long-legged and short-legged species had different feeding zones (Figure 22.5a). Depth of feeding seemed to separate species which overlapped in use of feeding zones (Figure 22.5b). For example, among the short waders frequenting the top of the beach, the Ringed Plover was distinguished by being predominantly a surface picker, while the Turnstone was distinguished by stone turning and the Dunlin by probes into the thin layer of sand and mud. Oystercatchers and Curlews had the same feeding sites and probing depth but took different foods. Curlews most often took shore crabs and were never seen to take bivalves; Oystercatchers, as implied by their name, relied on bivalves including cockles and mussels.

Applied Aspects of Feeding — A Concluding Statement

Ingestive behaviors are not only interesting they are also important. We all must eat. Unfortunately, a large proportion of the world's population is undernourished. Malnutrition during development often leads to profound and lasting impairment of the individual. The plight of the hungry world must touch the human compassion

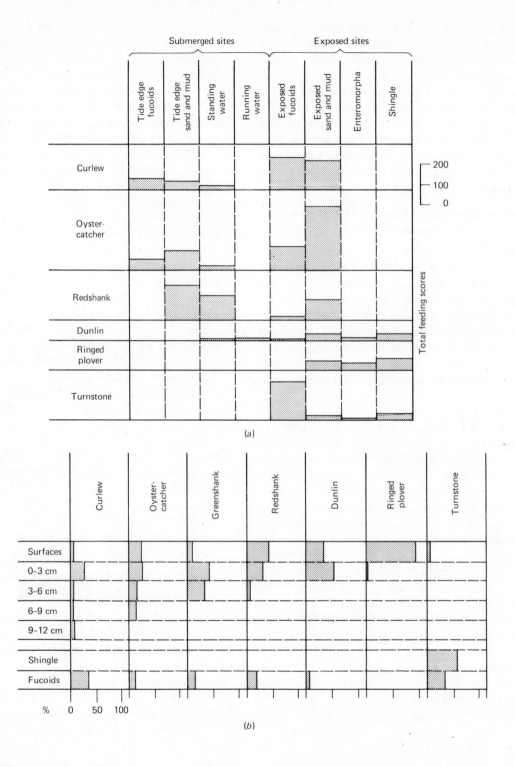

within each of us. Moreover, students of feeding behaviors should contribute toward understanding and amelioration of these problems whenever possible.

Humans beings are locked in a perpetual struggle with other species for foodstuffs. Insects in particular consume or foul many tons of food intended for us. Further understanding of the ingestive behaviors of agricultural pests may assist in their control. Additional areas of applied investigation currently being conducted by psychologists include the ingestive behaviors of economically important species, feeding patterns and obesity in humans, and the behavioral effects of natural toxins and artificial food additives in our diet.

Study Questions

1. Briefly discuss the lack of relation between phylogeny and feeding mechanisms.

2. Summarize the role of chemical stimuli in eliciting feeding behaviors.

3. Design an experiment to investigate the sensory stimuli involved in the feeding of an animal. Designate a species and describe its feeding behavior. Identify the sensory modality to be studied and discuss your methods of investigation.

4. How do the following factors affect food selection?
   (a) Early experience of an animal
   (b) Nutritional status of an animal
   (c) Aversive post ingestional consequences of a food.

5. A person eats oysters for the first time and later that evening feels ill. Explain the person's subsequent dislike of oysters.

6. Briefly discuss the relations between plant secondary compounds and the selection and ingestion of plants by animals.

7. Discuss the concept of resource allocation among sympatric species.

Figure 22.5 (Facing page) (a) Horizontal feeding patterns showing use of eight habitat categories by six species. Very few Greenshanks were present during the single observation period shown here and their data are not presented. Fucoids and *Enteromorpha* are types of seaweed, and shingle is coarse gravel. Only the long-legged waders made use of the deepwater habitat at the tide edge. The *Enteromorpha* and shingle areas on the upper parts of the beach were likewise used by only a limited range of species. The remaining habitat categories were used to some degree by all the species although the actual amount of overlap across species was somewhat less than the diagram suggests. For example, when feeding in sand and mud, Dunlin and Ringed Plover concentrated on the upper parts of the beach, whereas the long-legged waders consistently used the lower parts of the beach. (b) Vertical feeding patterns are shown as percentage of feeding activity. The figure represents cumulative data from two years of observation. The category "surfaces" included bird's pecking at any surface, whether sand, mud, shingle, or the surface of fucoid mound. Shingle and fucoid categories indicate penetration or overturning by the birds. There is a general correlation between bill length and depth of probing. However, for the five species probing frequently in sand and mud, the 0-3 cm depth was most often used. (Adapted from Edington, Morgan, and Morgan, 1973.)

References

Abler, R., Adams, J. S., and Gould, P. *Spatial organization: The geographer's view of the world.* Englewood Cliffs, N.J.: Prentice-Hall, 1971.

Adler, N., and Hogan, J. A. Classical conditioning and punishment of an instinctive response in *Betta splendens. Animal Behaviour,* 1963, *11,* 351–354.

Agricola, G. *De re metallica.* Translated by H. C. Hoover and L. H. Hoover. New York: Dover, 1950. Originally published 1556.

Albrecht, F. O., Verdier, M., and Blackith, R. E. Determination de la fertilite par l'effet de groupe chez le Criquet migrateur (*Locusta migratoria migratoriodes* R. et F.). *Bulletin Biologie,* 1958, *92,* 350–427.

Albrecht, H. Zur stammesgeschichte einer bewegungsweisen bei fischen: untersucht am verhalten von *Haplochromis (Pisces, Cichlidae). Zeitschrift für Tierpsychologie,* 1966, *23,* 270–302.

Alcock, J. *Animal behavior: An evolutionary approach.* Sunderland, Mass.: Sinauer Associates, 1975.

Aleksiuk, M. Scent mound communication, territoriality, and population regulation in the beaver. *Journal of Mammalogy,* 1968, *49,* 759–762.

Alexander, R. D. Sound communication in Orthoptera and Cicadidae. In W. E. Lanyon and W. E. Tavolga (Eds.), *Animal sounds and communication.* Washington, D.C.: AIBS, 1960.

Allen, A. A. The shore birds, cranes and rails, willets, plovers, sandpipers and their relatives deserve protection. In G. Grosvenor, and A. Wetmore, (Eds.), *The book of birds.* Vol. I. Washington, D.C.: Nat. Geog. Soc., 1939.

Allen, D. M. The ages of worker honeybees (*Apis mellifera L.*) engaged in "fanning" and in "shiver dances." *Animal Behaviour,* 1965, *13,* 347.

Alloway, T. M. Learning and memory in insects. *Annual Review of Entomology,* 1972, *17,* 43–56.

Altman, J. *Organic foundations of animal behavior.* New York: Holt, Rinehart and Winston, 1966.

Altmann, M. Naturalistic studies of maternal care in moose and elk. In H. Rheingold, (Ed.), *Maternal behavior in mammals.* New York: Wiley, 1963.

Altrum, B. *Der vogel und sein leben.* Munster: W. Nieman, 1868.

Anderson, J. K. *Ancient Greek horsemanship.* Berkeley and Los Angeles: University of California Press, 1961.

Andrew, R. J. Some remarks on behaviour in conflict situations with special reference to *Emberiza* sp. *British Journal of Animal Behaviour,* 1956, *4,* 41–45.

Anisko, J. J. Communication by chemical signals in Canidae. In R. L. Doty (Ed.), *Mammalian olfaction, reproductive processes, and behavior.* New York: Academic Press, 1976.

Applewhite, P. B., and Morowitz, H. J. The micrometazoa as model systems for studying the physiology of memory. *Yale Journal of Biology and Medicine,* 1966, *39,* 90–105.

Archer, J. Effects of social stimuli on the adrenal cortex in male mice. *Psychonomic Science,* 1969, *14,* 17–18.

Ardrey, R. *The territorial imperative.* New York: Atheneum, 1966.

Armstrong, E. A. The ecology of the distraction display. *British Journal of Animal Behaviour,* 1954, *2,* 121–135.

Armstrong, E. A. *Bird display and behavior.* (Rev. ed.). New York: Dover, 1965.

Armstrong, E. A. *A study of birdsong.* (2nd ed.) New York: Dover, 1973.

Arrianus. fl. second century *Cynegeticus.* Translated by D. B. Hull, *Hounds and hunting in ancient greece.* Chicago: The University of Chicago Press, 1964.

Ashmole, N. P. The regulation of numbers of tropical oceanic birds. *Ibis,* 1963, *103,* 458–473.

Ashmole, N. P. Adaptive variation in the breeding regime of a tropical sea bird. *Proceedings National Academy of Science, Washington, D.C.,* 1965, *53,* 311–318.

Askew, H. R., and Kurtz, P. J. Studies on the function of the abdominal rotation response in pupae of *tenebrio molitor. Behavior* 1974, 47, 152–172.

Austin, O. L., Jr. Site tenacity, a behavior trait of the Common Tern (*Sterna hirundo* Linn.). *Bird Banding,* 1949, *20,* 1–39.

Azrin, N. H., Hutchinson, R. R., and Sallery, R. D. Pain-elicited aggression toward inanimate objects. *Journal of Experimental Analysis of Behavior,* 1964, *7,* 9–11.

Bachelder, B. L., and Denny, M. R. A theory of intelligence: I. Span and the complexity of stimulus control. *Intelligence*, 1977, *1*, 127–150. (a)

Bachelder, B. L., and Denny, M. R. A theory of intelligence: II. The role of span in a variety of intellectual tasks. *Intelligence*, 1977, *1*, 237–256. (b)

Baerends, G. P. The ethological analysis of fish behavior. In M. E. Brown, (Ed.), *The physiology of fishes.* New York: Academic Press, 1957.

Baerends, G. P. The functional organization of behaviour. *Animal Behaviour*, 1976, *24*, 726–738.

Bagné, C. A. *The role of fear-withdrawal and relaxation-approach in avoidance responding.* Unpublished doctoral dissertation, Michigan State University, 1974.

Bailey, W. J. The mechanics of stridulation in bush crickets (Tettigonioidea, Orthoptera). I. the terminal generator. *Journal of Experimental Biology*, 1970, *52*, 495–505.

Bailey, W. J., and Robinson, D. Song as a possible isolating mechanism in the genus *Homorocoryphus*, (Tettigonoidea, Orthoptera). *Animal Behaviour*, 1971, *19*, 390–397, 1971.

Baillie-Grohman, W. A. *Sport in art.* (2nd ed.) London: Simpkin, Marshall, Hamilton, Kent & Co., 1919.

Baker, E. C. S. *Cuckoo problems.* London: Witherby, 1942.

Baker, T. C., and Cardé, R. T. Courtship behavior of the oriental fruit moth (*Grapholitha molesta*): Experimental analysis and consideration of the role of sexual selection in the evolution of courtship pheromones in the Lepidoptera. *Annals of the Entomological Society of America*, 1978, 72, 173–188.

Bakken, A. Behavior of gray squirrels. *Symposium on gray squirrel*, Contr. 162, Maryland Dept. Res. Ed. 1959, 393–407.

Balderrama, N., and Maldonado, H. Habituation of the diematic response in the mantid (stagmatoptera biccellata). *Journal of Comparative and Physiological Psychology*, 1971, *75*, 98–106.

Baldwin, F. M. Diurnal activity of the earthworm. *Journal of Animal Behavior*, 1917, *7*, 187–190.

Bamber, R. T., and Boice, R. The labyrinth method of comparing wild and domestic rats: History revisited. *Psychonomic Science*, 1972, *29*, 161–163.

Baran, D., and Glickman, S. E. 'Territorial marking' in the Mongolian gerbil: A study of sensory control and function. *Journal of Comparative and Physiological Psychology*, 1970, *71*, 237–245.

Barash, D. P. *Sociobiology and behavior.* New York: Elsevier, 1977.

Bardach, J. E. The sensitivity of the goldfish (*Carassius auratus* L.) to point heat stimulation. *American Naturalist,* 1956, *90*, 309–317.

Bardach, J. E. The temperature sensitivity of some American freshwater fishes. *American Naturalist*, 1957, *91*, 233–251.

Bardach, J. E. The chemical senses and food intake in the lower vertebrates. In M. Kare and O. Maller (Eds.), *The chemical senses and nutrition.* Baltimore: Johns Hopkins Press, 1967.

Barelare, B., and Richter, C. P. Increased sodium chloride appetite in pregnant rats, *American Journal of Physiology.* 1938, *121*, 185–188.

Barnett, S. A. Behavior components in the feeding of wild and laboratory rats. *Behaviour*, 1956, *9*, 24–43.

Barnett, S. A. *A study in behaviour.* London: Methuen, 1963.

Barnhart, P. S. The spawning of the little-smelt, *Leuresthes tenuis* (Ayres). *California Fish and Game*, 1918, *18*, 181–182.

Barrass, R. A quantitative study of the behaviour of the male *Mormoniella vitripennis* (Walker) (Hymenoptera, Pteromalldae) towards two constant stimulus situations. *Behaviour*, 1961, 18, 288–312.

Barrette, C. Scent-marking in captive muntjacs, *Muntiacus reevesi. Animal Behaviour*, 1977, *25*, 236–241.

Barth, R. H., Jr. The mating behavior of *Byrsotria fumigata* (Guerin) (Blattidae, Blaberinae). *Behaviour*, 1964, *23*, 1–30.

Bartholomew, G. A. A model for the evolution of pinniped polygyny. *Evolution*, 24, 546–559, 1970.

Bartholomew, G. A., and Hoel, P. G. Reproductive behavior of the Alaska fur seal, *Callorhinus ursinus. Journal of Mammalology*, 1953, *34*, 417–436.

Bass, B. M., and Bass, R. Concern for the environment: Implications for industrial and organizational psychology. *American Psychologist*, 1976, *31*, 158–166.

Bastock, M. *Courtship: An ethological study.* Chicago: Aldine Publishing Co., 1967.

Bastock, M., and Manning, A. The courtship of *Drosophila melanogaster. Behaviour*, 1955, *8*, 85–111.

Bateson, P. P. G. Internal influences on early learning in birds. In R. Hinde and J. Stevenson-Hinde (Eds.), *Constraints on learning.* New York: Academic Press, 1973.

Bauer, R. T. Grooming behaviour and morphology of the caridean shrimp *Pandalus danae* Stimpson (Decapoda: natantia: Pandalidae). *Zoological Journal of Linnaeus Society*, 1974, *56*(1), 45–71.

Baum, A., Harpin, R. E., and Valins, S. The role of group phenomena in the experience of crowding. *Environment and Behavior*, 1975, *7*, 185–198.

Baxter, J. *Component dependent interruptability in the sexual behavior sequence of the house cricket.* Paper presented at the meeting of the Midwestern Psychological Association, Chicago, 1977.

Beach, F. A. Responses of captive alligators to auditory stimulation. *American Naturalist*, 1944, *78*, 481–505.

Beach, F. A. The snark was a boojum. *American Psychologist,* 1950, *5*, 115–124.

Beach, F. A. *Hormones and behavior.* New York: Cooper Square Publishers, Inc., 1961.

Beach, F. A. Frank A. Beach. In G. Lindzey (Ed.), *A history of psychology in autobiography.* Vol. VI. Englewood Cliffs, N.J.: Prentice-Hall, 1974.

Beach, F. A. Effects of gonadal hormones on urinary behavior in dogs. *Physiology and Behavior*, 1974, *12*, 1005–1013.

Beauchamp, G. K., and Beruter, J. Source and stability of attractive components of guinea pig (*Cavia porcellus*) urine. *Behavioral Biology*, 1973, *9*, 43–47.

Beauchamp, G. K., Doty, R. L., Moulton, D. G., and Mugford, R. A. The pheromone concept in mammalian chemical communication: A critique. In R. L. Doty (Ed.), *Mammalian olfaction, reproductive processes, and behavior.* New York: Academic Press, 1976.

Beauchamp, G. K., Magnus, J. G., Shmunes, N. T. and Durham, T. Effects of olfactory bulbectomy on social behavior of male guinea pigs (*Cavia porcellus*). *Journal of Comparative and Physiological Psychology*, 1977, *91*, 336–346.

Beck, A. M. *The ecology of stray dogs: A study of free ranging urban animals.* Baltimore: York Press, 1973.

Beck, S. Resistance of plants to insects, *Annual Review of Animology,* 1965, 10, 207–232.

Beebe, F. L., and Webster, H. M. *North American falconry & hunting hawks.* Denver, Colo.: Privately printed, 1964.

Beebe, F. L. *Hawks, falcons & falconry.* Saanichton, B.C., Canada: Hancock House, 1976.

Bellairs, A. *The life of reptiles.* Vol. II. New York: Universe Books, 1970.

Benson, B. N. Dustbathing in Japanese quail. Unpublished master's thesis, Pennsylvania State University, 1965.

Bent, A. C. Life histories of North American birds. *United States Natural Museum Bulletin.* Washington, D. C.: 1940.

Bentley, D., and Hoy, R. R. The neurobiology of cricket song. *Scientific American*, 1974, *231*, 34–44.

Berg, C. J. A comparative ethological study of strombid gastropods. *Behaviour,* 1974, *5*, 274–322.

Beritoff, I. S. Phylogeny of memory development in vertebrates. In A. G. Karczmar, and J. C. Eccles, (Eds.), *Brain and human behavior.* New York: Springer Verlag, 1972.

Berkson, G. Food motivation and delayed response in gibbons. *Journal of Comparative and Physiological Psychology*, 1962, *55*, 1040–1043.

Berntson, G. G., and Hughes, H. C. Behavioral characteristics of grooming induced by hindbrain stimulation in the cat. *Physiology and Behaviour*, 1976, *17*, 165–168.

Billings, S. M. Homing in Leach's petrel *Auk*, 1968, *85*, 36–43.

Bindra, D. Temporal analysis of relevant and irrelevant behavior components in partial reinforcement and extinction. *Psychological Reports*, 1963, *13*(2), 551–563.

Bintz, J. Between and within-subject effect of shock intensity on avoidance in goldfish (*Carassius Auratus*). *Journal of Comparative and Physiological Psychology*, 1971, *75*, 92–97.

Birch, L. C. The role of weather in determining the distribution and abundance of animals. *Cold Spring*

References

Harbor Symposium on Quantitative Biology, 1957, *22*, 203–218.

Birch, M. Pre-courtship use of abdominal brushes by the nocturnal moth, *Phlogophora Meticulosa* (L.) (Lepidotera: Noctuidae). *Animal Behaviour*, 1970, *18*, 310–316.

Bitterman, M. E. Toward a comparative psychology of learning. *American Psychologist*, 1960, *15*, 704–712.

Bitterman, M. E. The comparative analysis of learning. *Science*, 1975, *188*, 699–709.

Blake, M. O., Meyer, D. R., and Meyer, P. M. Enforced observation in delayed response learning by frontal monkeys. *Journal of Comparative and Physiological Psychology*, 1966, *61*, 374–379.

Blanchard, R. J., Mast, M., and Blanchard, D. C. Stimulus control of defense reactions in the albino rat. *Journal of Comparative and Physiological Psychology*, 1975, *88*, 81–88.

Blest, A. D. The function of eyespot patterns in the Lepidoptera. *Behaviour*, 1957, *11*, 209–256.

Blum, S. L., and Thiessen, D. D. Effect of ventral gland excision on scent marking in the male Mongolian gerbil. *Journal of Comparative and Physiological Psychology*, 1970, *73*, 461–464.

Boersma, P. D. An ecological and behavioral study of the Galapagos penguin. *Living Bird*, 1976, 15:43–93.

Bogert, C. M. The influence of sound on the behavior of amphibians and reptiles. In W. E. Lanyon and W. N. Tavolga (Eds.), *Animal sounds and communication*, American Inst. Biol. Sciences, Pub. No. 7, 137–320, 1960.

Boice, R. *The problem of domestication in the laboratory rat and a comparison of partially reinforced "discriminatory" and anticipatory licking in domestic and wild strains of* Rattus norvegicus. Unpublished doctoral dissertation, Michigan State University, 1966.

Boice, R. Animalizing. *The Journal of Biological Psychology*, 1976, 18, 5–15.

Boice, R. Conditioned licking in wild F_1 and domestic Norway rats. *Journal of Comparative and Physiological Psychology*, 1968, *66*, 796–799.

Boice, R. Avoidance learning in active and passive frogs and toads. *Journal of Comparative and Physiological Psychology*, 1970, *70*, 154–156. (a)

Boice, R. Effect of domestication on avoidance learn-

ing in the wild rat. *Psychonomic Science*, 1970, *18*, 13–14. (b)

Boice, R. Excessive water intake in captive Norway rats with scar-markings. *Physiology & Behavior*, 1971, *7*, 723–725. (a)

Boice, R. Laboratorizing the wild rat (*Rattus norvegicus*). *Behavior Research Methods and Instrumentation*, 1971, *3*, 177–182. (b)

Boice, R. Some behavioral tests of domestication in Norway rats. *Behaviour*, 1972, *42*, 198–231.

Boice, R. Domestication. *Psychological Bulletin*, 1973, *80*, 215–230.

Boice, R. A test of the Daly hypothesis with burrows and albino rats. Paper presented at Animal Behavior Society, Boulder, 1976. (a)

Boice, R. In the shadow of Darwin. In R. G. Green and E. O'Neal (Eds.), *Perspectives on aggression*. New York: Academic Press, 1976. (b)

Boice, R. Animalizing. *Journal of Biological Psychology*, 1977, (a)

Boice, R. Burrows of wild and domestic rats: Effects of domestication, outdoor raising, age, experience, and maternal state. *Journal of Comparative and Physiological Psychology*, 1977, *91*, 649–661. (b)

Boice, R. Heroes as teachers. *Teaching of Psychology*, 1977, *4*, 55–58. (c)

Boice, R. Surplusage. *Bulletin of the Psychonomic Society*, 1977, *9* 452–454. (d)

Boice, C., and Boice, R. Precedence in feeding and mounting in captive toads. *Psychonomic Science*, 1970, *20*, 259–260.

Boice, R., Denny, M. R., and Evans, T. A. A comparison of albino and wild rats in shuttlebox avoidance. *Psychonomic Science*, 1967, *8*, 271–272.

Bolles, R. C. Grooming behavior in the rat. *Journal of comparative Physiological Psychology*, 1960, *53*(3), 306–310.

Bolles, R. C. Species-specific defense reactions and avoidance learning. *Psychological Review*, 1970, *71*, 32–48

Bolles, R., Sulzbacher, S., and Arant, H. Innateness of the adrenalectomized rats' acceptance of salt. *Psychonomic Science*, 1964, *1*, 21–22.

Borchelt, P. L. The organization of dustbathing components in bobwhite quail (*Colinus virginianus*). *Behaviour*, 1975, *53*, 217–237.

Borchelt, P. L., and Duncan, L. Dustbathing and feather lipid in bobwhite quail (*Colinus virginianus*). *The Condor*, 1974, *76*, 471.

Borchelt, P. L., Eyer, J. and McHenry, D. S., Jr. Dustbathing in bobwhite quail (*Colinus virginianus*) as a function of dust deprivation. *Behavioral Biology*, 1973, *8*(1), 109–114.

Borchelt, P. L., Griswold, J. G., and Branchek, R. S. An analysis of sandbathing and grooming in the kangaroo rat (*Dipodomys merriami*). *Animal Behaviour*, 1976, *24*, 347–353.

Borchelt, P. L., Hoffman, R., Hurrell, R. M., and McCarthy, R. Regulation of dustbathing in Japanese quail. *Journal of Comparative and Physiological Psychology*, 1979, 93, 134–139.

Borchelt, P. L., & Overmann, S. R. Development of dustbathing in bobwhite quail. I. Effects of age, experience, texture of dust, strain, and social facilitation. *Developmental Psychobiology*, 1974, *7*, 305–313.

Borchelt, P. L., and Overmann, S. R. Development of dustbathing in bobwhite quail. II. Effects of early pecking experiences. *Developmental Psychobiology*, 1975, *8*(5), 417–423.

Borchelt, P. L., and Ratner, S. C. Development of freezing and immobility, predator defenses in the Bobwhite quail. *Behavioral Biology*, 1973, *8*, 83–92.

Borror, D. J., and DeLong, D. M. *An introduction to the study of insects.* (3rd ed.) New York: Holt, Rinehart and Winston, 1971.

Borror, D. J., Delong, D. M., and Triplehorn, C. A. *An introduction to the study of insects.* (4th ed.) New York: Holt, Rinehart and Winston, 1976.

Boulding, K. *Economics as a science.* New York: McGraw-Hill, 1970.

Bovet, D., Bovet-Nitti, F., and Oliverio, A. Genetic aspects of learning and memory in mice. *Science*, 1969, *163*, 139–149.

Braveman, N. Formation of taste aversions in rats following prior exposure to sickness. *Learning and Motivation*, 1975, *6*, 512–534.

Brehm, J. W. *A theory of psychological reactance.* New York: Academic Press, 1966.

Breland, K., and Breland, M. A field of applied animal psychology. *American Psychologist*, 1951, *6*, 202–204.

Breland, K., and Breland, M. The misbehavior of organisms. *American Psychologist*, 1961, *16*, 681–684.

Breland, K., and Breland, M. *Animal behavior.* New York: The Macmillan Co., 1966.

Brett, J. R. Some principles in the thermal requirements of fishes. *Quarterly Review of Biology*, 1956, *31*, 75–87.

Bristowe, W. S. *The world of spiders.* London: William Collins, 1958.

Brockie, R. Self-annointing by wild hedgehogs, *Erinaceus europaeus*, in New Zealand. 1976, *24*(1), 68–71.

Bro. Larsen, E. On subsocial beetles from the salt-marsh, their care of progeny, and adaptation to salt and tide. *Transactions of the Eleventh International Congress of Entomology*, Amsterdam, 1972, *1*, 502–506.

Bronson, F. H. Pheromonal influences on mammalian reproduction. In M. Diamond (Ed.), *Reproduction and social behavior.* Bloomington: Indiana University Press, 1968.

Bronson, F. H. Rodent pheromones. *Biology of Reproduction*, 1971, *4*, 344–357.

Bronson, F. H. Urine marking in mice: Causes and effects. In R. L. Doty (Ed.), *Mammalian olfaction, reproductive processes, and behavior.* New York: Academic Press, 1976.

Bronstein, P. M., and Hirsch, S. M. Ontogeny of defense reactions in Norway rats. *Journal of Comparative and Physiological Psychology*, 1976, *90*, 620–629.

Brookshire, K. H. Comparative psychology of learning. In M. H. Marx (Ed.), *Learning Interactions.* Canada: The Macmillan Co., 1970.

Brookshire, K. H., and Rieser, T. C. Temporal course of exploratory activity in three inbred strains of mice. *Journal of Comparative and Physiological Psychology*, 1967, *63*, 549–551.

Brousse-Gaury, P. Contribution a L'etude de L'autotomie chez Acheta domestica L. *Bulletin Biologique de La France et de la Belgique*, 1958, *92*, 55–85.

Brower, L. P. Ecological chemistry. *Scientific American*, 1969, *220*, 22–29.

Brown, F. A., Jr. Responses of the planarian, *Dugesia*, and the protozoan *Paramecium* to very weak horizontal magnetic fields. *Biological Bulletin*, 1962, *123*, 264–281.

Brown, F. A., Jr. Some orientational influences of nonvisual terrestrial electromagnetic fields. *Annals of New York Academy of Science*, 1971, *188*, 224–241.

Brown, F. A., Jr., Barnwell, F. H., and Webb, H. M. Adaptation of the magneto-receptive mechanism of mudsnails to geomagnetic strength. *Biological Bulletin*, 1964, *127*, 221–231.

Brown, F. A., Jr., Brett, W. J., Bennett, M. E., and Barnwell, F. H. Magnetic response of an organism and its solar relationships. *Biological Bulletin*, 1960, *118*, 367–381.

Brown, F. A., Jr., and Chow, C. S. Differentiation between clockwise and counterclockwise magnetic rotation by the planarian, *Dugesia dorotacephala*. *Physiological Zoology*, 1975, *48*, 168–176.

Brown, J. H. Acquisition and retention of nystagmic habituation in cats with distributed acceleration experience. *Journal of Comparative and Physiological Psychology*, 1965, *60*, 340–343.

Brown, J. L. Territorial behavior and population regulation in birds: A review and re-evaluation. *Wilson Bulletin*, 1969, *81*, 293–329.

Brown, J. L. *The evolution of behavior*. New York: Norton, 1975.

Brown, J., and Lieberman, G. Resource utilization and coexistence of seed-eating desert rodents in sand dune habitats. *Ecology*, 1973, *54*, 788–797.

Brown, L. H., and Watson, A. The Golden Eagle in relation to its food supply. *Ibis*, 1964, *106*, 78–100.

Brown, N. A. The effect of host beak condition on the size of *Mencanthus* stramineus populations of domestic chickens. *Poultry Science*, 1972, *51*, 162–164.

Brown, N. S. The effect of louse infestation, wet feathers, and relative humidity on the grooming behavior of the domestic chicken. *Poultry Science*, 1974, *53*, 1717–1719.

Brown, P. J. *Selected Results, Colorado deer survey*, 1975. Unpublished report to Colorado Division of Wildlife, 1975.

Brown, W. L., McDowell, A. A., and Robinson, E. M. Discrimination learning of mirrored cues by rhesus monkeys. *Journal of Genetic Psychology*, 1965, *106*, 123–128.

Browne, D. J. *The American bird fancier*. New York: C. M. Sexton, 1850.

Bruce, H. M. An exteroceptive block to pregnancy in the mouse. *Nature* (London), 1959, *184*, 105.

Brusewitz, T. *Hunting*. New York: Stein and Day, 1969.

Bull, H. O. Studies on the conditioned responses in fishes. 7. Temperature perception in teleosts. *Journal Marine Biological Association, United Kingdom*, 1936, *21*, 1–27.

Buresova, O., and Bureš, J. The antagonistic influence of anesthesia and functional decortication on conditioned taste aversion. *Activas Nervosa Superior* (Praha), 1975, *17*, 58.

Burghardt, G., and Pruitt, C. Role of the tongue and senses in feeding of naive and experienced garter snakes. *Physiology and Behavior*, 1975, *14*, 185–194.

Burton, M. *Infancy in animals*. New York: Roy Publishers, 1950.

Burtt, E. *The senses of animals*. London: Wykeham, 1974.

Butler, C. G. Insect pheromones. *Biological Review*, 1967, *42*, 42–87.

Cade, T. J. Ecology of the Peregrine and Gyrfalcon population in Alaska. *University California Publications in Zoology*, 1960, *63*, 151–290.

Carpenter, C. R. *Naturalistic behavior of non-human primates*. University Park, Pa.: Pennsylvania State University Press, 1964.

Calhoun, J. B. *The ecology and sociology of the Norway rat*. Bethesda, Md.: U.S. Department of Health, Education and Welfare, 1962. (a)

Calhoun, J. B. Population density and social pathology. *Scientific American*, 1962, *206*, 139–146. (b)

Calhoun, J. B. From mice to men. *Transaction and Studies of the College of Physicians of Philadelphia*, 1973, *41*, 92–118.

Calhoun, J. B. Scientific quest for a path to the future. *Populi*, 1976, *3*, 1–7.

Cameron, G. Niche overlap and competition in woodrats. *Journal of Mammalogy*, 1971, *52*, 289–296.

Capretta, P. An experimental modification of food preference in chickens. *Journal of Comparative and Physiological Psychology,* 1961, *54*, 238–242.

Caras, R. *Venomous animals of the world.* Englewood Cliffs, N.J.: Prentice-Hall, 1974.

Carbaugh, B. T., Schein, M. W., and Hale, E. B. Effects of morphological variations of chicken models on sexual responses of cocks. *Animal Behaviour*, 1962, *10*, 235–238.

Cardé, R. T. Utilization of pheromones in the population management of moth pests. *Environmental Health Perspectives*, 1976, *14*, 133–144.

Cardé, R. T., Baker, T. C., and Roelofs, W. C. Ethological function of components of a sex attractant system for Oriental fruit moth males, *Grapholitha molesta* (Lepidoptera: Tortricidae). *Journal of Chemical Ecology*, 1975, *1*, 475–491.

Cardé, R. T., and Hagaman, T. E. Behavioral responses of the gypsy moth in a wind tunnel to air-borne enantiomers of Disparlure. *Environmental Entomology*, 1979, 8, 475–484.

Carlson, A. D., Copeland, J., Raderman, R., and Bulloch, A. G. M. Response patterns of female *Photinus macdermotti* firefly to artificial flashes. *Animal Behaviour*, 1977, *25*, 407–413.

Carr, A. Adaptive aspects of the scheduled travel of *Chelonia.* In R. M. Storm, (Ed.), *Animal orientation and navigation.* Corvallis, Ore.: Oregon State University Press, 1967.

Carr, W. J., and Caul, W. F. The effect of castration in rat upon the discrimination of sex odours. *Animal Behaviour*, 1962, *10*, 20–27.

Carr, W. J., Loeb, L. S., and Dissinger, M. L. Responses of rats to sex odors. *Journal of Comparative and Physiological Psychology*, 1965, *59*, 370–377.

Carrington, R. and Editors of Time-Life Books. *The mammals.* New York: Time-Life Books, 1970.

Carthy, J. D. *The behavior of arthropods.* Oliver and Boyd, 1965.

Caton, J. D. *The antelope and deer of America.* New York: Hurd and Houghton, 1877.

Cesario, F. J. Operations research in outdoor recreation. *Journal of Leisure Research*, 1969, *1*, 33–52.

Chance, M. R. A., and Russell, W. M. S. Protean display: A form of allasthetic behavior. *Proceedings of Zoological Society of London*, 1959, *132*, 65–70.

Chapman, R. The chemical inhibition of feeding by photophagous insects: A review. *Bulletin of Entomological Research*, 1974, *64*, 339–363.

Chipman, R. K., Holt, J. A., and Fox, K. A. Pregnancy failure in laboratory mice after multiple short-term exposure to strange males. *Nature* (London), 1966, *216*, 653.

Chisholm, A. H. The history of anting. *Emu*, 1959, *59*, 101–130.

Chitty, D. *The control of rats and mice.* (Vols. 1 and 2). Oxford: Clarendon Press, 1954.

Christian, J. J. Endocrine adaptive mechanisms and the physiologic regulation of population growth. In W. V. Mayer and R. G. van Gelder (Eds.), *Physiological mammalogy.* New York: Academic Press, 1963.

Christian, J. J., Lloyd, J. A., and Davis, D. E. The role of endocrines in the self-regulation of mammalian populations. *Recent Progress in Hormone Research*, 1965, *21*, 501–578.

Clark, R. B. Habituation of the polychaete *Nereis* to sudden stimuli. 2. Biological significance of habituation. *Animal Behaviour*, 1960, *8*, 92–103.

Clark, M. M., and Galef, B. G. The role of physical rearing environment in the domestication of the Mongolian gerbil. (*Meriones unquiculates*). *Animal Behaviour*, 1977, 25, 298–316.

Clarke, E., and Dewhurst, K. *An illustrated history of brain function.* Berkeley: University California Press, 1972.

Clarke, G. L. Quantitative aspects of the change of phototropic sign in Daphnia. *Journal of Experimental Biology*, 1932, *9*, 180–211.

Clarke, W. E., and Penman, G. G. The projection of the retina in the lateral geniculate body. *Proceedings of the Royal Society of Britain*, 1934, *114*, 291–313.

Cloudsley-Thompson, J. L. *Animal conflict and adaptation.* Chester Springs, Penn.: Dufour Editions, 1965.

Cody, M. Finch flocks in the mojave desert. *Theoretical Population Biology*, 1971, *2*, 142–158.

Committee on tourism and outdoor recreation plan, Province of Ontario. *Tourism and Recreation in Ontario: Concepts of a Systems Model*, 1970.

Connolly, K. The social facilitation of preening behavior in *Drosophila melanogaster. Animal Behaviour*, 1968, *16*, 385–391.

Contreras, R., and Hatton, G. Gustatory adaptation

as an explanation for dietary-induced sodium appetite. *Physiology and Behavior*, 1975, *15*, 569–576.

Cope, O. B. Some migration patterns in cutthroat trout. *Proceedings of Utah Academy of Science*, 1956, *33*, 113–118.

Copp, J. D. Why hunters like to hunt. *Psychology Today*, 1975, *9*, 60–67.

Cornwall, I. W. *Prehistoric animals and their hunters.* New York: Praeger, 1968.

Cousins, L. S., Zamble, E., Tait, R. W., and Suboski, M. D. Sensory preconditioning in curarized rats. *Journal of Comparative and Physiological Psychology*, 1971, *77*, 152–154.

Cowan, P., and Evans, R. Calls of different individual hens and the parental control of feeding behavior in young *Gallus gallus. Journal of Experimental Zoology*, 1974, *188*, 353–360.

Craig, W. Appetites and aversions as constituents of instincts. *Biological Bulletin*, 1918, *34*, 275.

Crane, J. Display breeding and relationship of fiddler crabs (Genus *Uca*) in the Northeastern United States. *Zoology*, 1943, *28*, 217–223.

Crane, J. Comparative biology of salticid spiders at Rancho Grande Venezuela. Part IV. An analysis of display. *Zoologica*, 1949, *34*, 159–214.

Crawford, F. T. Induction and duration of TI. *Psychological Record*, 1977, *1*, 89–107 (special issue).

Crawford, F. T., and Prestrude, A. M. (Eds.) Animal hypnosis. *The Psychological Record*, 1977, *27*, ii + 218, (special issue).

Crawford, R. S., and Smyth, J. R., Jr. The influence of comb genotypes on mating behavior in the domestic fowl. *Poultry Science*, 1965, *44*, 115–122.

Cronin, E. Tall larkspur: Some reasons for its continuing preeminence as a poisonous plant. *Journal of Range Management*, 1971, *24*, 258–263.

Cully, J. F., and Legon, J. D. Comparative mobbing behavior of scrub and Mexican jays. *Auk*, 1976, *93*, 116–125.

Cummings, W. W. A bird's eye glimpse of men and machines. In R. Ulrich, T. Stachnik, and J. Mabry (Eds.), *Control of human behavior.* Vol. 1. Glenview, Ill.: Scott, Foresman, 1966.

Curio, E. *Zoophysiology and ecology: The ethology of predation.* Vol. 7. New York: Springer-Verlag, 1976.

Daly, J. The ability to locate a source of vibrations as a prey-capture mechanism in *Harmothoë imbricata* (Annelida Polychaeta). *Marine Behavior and Physiology*, 1973, *1*, 305–322.

Daly, M. Early stimulation of rodents: A critical view of present interpretations. *British Journal of Psychology*, 1973, *65*, 435–460.

Daly, M. Some experimental tests of the functional significance of scent-marking by gerbils (*Meriones unguiculatus*). *Journal of Comparative and Physiological Psychology*, 1977, *91*, 1082–1094.

Danguir, J., and Nicolaidis, S. Lack of reacquisition in learned taste aversions. *Animal Learning and Behavior*, 1977, *5*, 395–397.

Darwin, C. *Origin of species.* (6th ed.) New York: Appleton, 1872.

Darwin, C. *The expression of the emotions in man and animals.* New York: D. Appleton, 1920.

Darwin, C. *The origin of species by means of natural selection.* London: Penguin Books, 1968. Originally published 1859.

D'Atri, D. Psychophysiological responses to crowding. *Environment and Behavior*, 1975, *7*, 237–252.

Davis, C. Studies in the self-selection of diet by young children. *Journal of the American Dental Association*, 1934, *21*, 636–640.

Davis, C. Results of the self-selection of diets by young children. *Canadian Medical Association Journal*, 1939, *41*, 257–261.

Davis, H. and Hubbard, J. Conditioned vocalization in rats. *Journal of Comparative and Physiological Psychology*, 1973, *82*, 152–158.

Davis, M. Effects of interstimulus interval length and variability on startle-response habituation in the rat. *Journal of Comparative and Physiological Psychology*, 1970, *72*, 177–193. (a)

Davis, M. Interstimulus interval and startle response habituation with a "control" for total time during training. *Psychonomic Science*, 1970, *20*, 39–40. (b)

Davis, M., and Sollberger, A. Twenty-four-hour periodicity of the startle response in rats. *Psychonomic Science*, 1971, *25*, 37–39.

Davis, P. Recoveries of swallows ringed in Britain and Ireland. *Bird Study*, 1965, *12*, 151–169.

Dawkins, R. Hierarchical organization: A candidate

principle for ethology. In P. P. G. Bateson, and R. A. Hinde, (Eds.), *Growing points in ethology.* Cambridge: Cambridge University Press, 1976.

Dawkins, R. *The selfish gene.* New York: Oxford University Press, 1976.

Day, A. T., and Day, L. H. Cross-national comparison of population density. *Science,* 1973, *181,* 1016–1023.

Deal, R. E., and Halbert, M. H. *The application of value theory to water resources planning and management.* Report for the Office of Water Resources Research, United States Department of the Interior, Contract No. 14-13-0001-3373; C-2154, 1971.

de la Burdé, B., and Reames, B. Prevention of pica, the major cause of lead poisoning in children. *American Journal of Public Health,* 1973, *63,* 737–743.

Delius, J. D. A population study of skylarks, *Alauda arvensis. Ibis,* 1965, *107,* 466–492.

Dember, W. N. Response by the rat to environmental change. *Journal of Comparative and Physiological Psychology,* 1956, *49,* 93–95.

Denny, M. R. Research in learning and performance. In H. Stevens, and R. Heber, (Eds.), *Mental retardation.* Chicago, Ill.: University of Chicago Press, 1964.

Denny, M. R. Relaxation theory and experiments. In F. R. Brush, (Ed.) *Aversive conditioning and learning.* New York: Academic Press, 1971. (a)

Denny, M. R. A theory of experimental extinction and its relation to a general theory. In H. H. Kendler and J. T. Spence (Eds.), *Essays in neobehaviorism.* A memorial volume to Kenneth W. Spence. New York: Academic Press, 1971. (b)

Denny, M. R., and Adelman, H. M. Elicition theory: I. An analysis of two typical learning situations. *Psychological Review,* 1955, *62,* 290–296.

Denny, M. R., and Ratner, S. C. *Comparative psychology. (Rev. ed.) Homewood, Ill. Dorsey, 1970.*

Denny, M. R., and Weisman, R. G. Avoidance behavior as a function of length of nonshock confinement. *Journal of Comparative and Physiological Psychology,* 1964, *58,* 252–257.

Denton, D. Salt appetite. In C. Code (Ed.), *Handbook of physiology* (Sec. 6), *Alimentary Canal* (Vol. 1). Washington, D.C.: American Physiological Society, 1967.

Desjardins, D., Maruniak, J. A., and Bronson, F. H. Social rank in housemice: Differentiation by ultraviolet visualization of urinary marking patterns. *Science,* 1973, *182,* 939–941.

Desor, J. A. Toward a psychological theory of crowding. *Journal of Personality and Social Psychology,* 1972, *21,* 79–83.

Dethier, V. G. *To know a fly.* San Francisco, Calif.: Holden-Day, 1962.

Dethier, V. G. *The hungry fly.* Cambridge, Mass.: Harvard University Press, 1976.

Dethier, V., Barton-Browne, L., and Smith, C. The designation of chemicals in terms of the responses they elicit from insects. *Journal of Economic Entomology,* 1960, *53,* 134–136.

Dethier, V. G., and Stellar, E. *Animal behavior.* New York: Prentice-Hall, 1961.

Diamond, L. The effect of training procedures on the double alternation-behavior of laboratory rats in a temporal maze. *American Journal of Psychology,* 1967, *80,* 594–601.

Dill, L. M. The escape response of the zebra danio: The stimulus for escape (Part I): The effect of experience (Part II). *Animal Behavior,* 1974, *22,* 711–730.

Dingle, H. Turn alternation by bugs on causeways as a delayed compensatory response and the effects of varying visual inputs and length of straight path. *Animal Behaviour,* 1965, *13,* 171–177.

Dolan, E. G. *TANSTAAFL: The economic strategy for environmental crisis.* New York: Holt, Rinehart and Winston, 1969.

Dolnik, V. R., and Blyumental, T. I. Autumnal, premigratory and migratory periods in the Chaffinch (*Fringilla coelobs coelobs*) and some other temperate-zone passerine birds. *Condor,* 1967, *69,* 435–468.

Donaldson, R., and Allen, G. H. Return of silver salmon, *Oncorhynchus kisutch* (Walbaum) to point of release. *Transactions of American Fisheries Society,* 1957, *87,* 13–82.

Doty, R. L. A cry for the liberation of the female rodent: Courtship and copulation in *Rodentia. Psychological Bulletin,* 1974, *81,* 159–172.

Doty, R. L. (Ed.), *Mammalian olfaction, reproductive processes, and behavior.* New York: Academic Press, 1976.

Doty, R. L., and Dunbar, I. Attraction of Beagles to

conspecific urine, vaginal, and anal sac secretion odors. *Physiology and Behavior*, 1974, *12*, 825–833. (a)

Doty, R. L., and Dunbar, I. Color, odor, consistency, and secretion rate of anal sac secretions from male, female, and early-androgenized female Beagles. *American Journal of Veterinary Research*, 1974, *35*, 729–731. (b)

Doty, R. L., and Kart, R. A comparative and developmental analysis of the midventral sebaceous glands in 18 taxa of *Peromyscus*, with an examination of gonadal steroid influences in *Peromyscus maniculatus bairdii. Journal of Mammalogy*, 1972, *53*, 83–99.

Douglas-Hamilton, I., and Douglas-Hamilton, O. *Among the elephants.* New York: Viking Press, 1975.

Draper, W. A. Cue dominance in oddity discriminations by rhesus monkeys. *Journal of Comparative Physiological Psychology*, 1965, *60*, 140–141.

Drickamer, L. C., Vandenbergh, J. G., and Colby, D. R. Predictors of dominance in the male golden hamster (Mesocricetus auratus). *Animal Behaviour*, 1973, *21*, 557–563. (a)

Drickamer, L. C., Vandenbergh, J. G., and Colby, D. R. Predictors of social dominance in the adult female golden hamster (*Mesocricetus auratus*). *Animal Behaviour*, 1973, *21*, 564-570. (b)

Duncan, C. J., and Shephard, P. M. Sensory discrimination and its role in the evolution of Batesian mimicry. *Behaviour*, 1965, *24*, 269-282.

Duncan, I. J. H., and Wood-Gush, D. G. M. An analysis of displacement preening in the domestic fowl. *Animal Behaviour,* 1972, *20,* 68-71.

Duncan, N. C., Grossen, N. E., and Hunt, E. B. Apparent memory differences in inbred mice produced by differential reaction to stress. *Journal of Comparative Physiological Psychology*, 1971, *74*, 383–389.

Dunn, E. Effect of age on the fishing ability of sandwich terns (*Sterna sandvicensis*). *Ibis*, 1972, *114*, 360–366.

Eastwood, E. *Radar ornithology.* London: Methuen, 1967.

Ebling, F. J. The effects of cyproterone acetate and estradiol upon testosterone stimulated sebaceous activity in the rat. *Acta Endocrinologica*, 1973, *72*, 361–365.

Ebling, F. J. Hormonal control of mammalian skin glands. In D. Müller-Schwarze and M. M. Mozell (Eds.), *Chemical signals in vertebrates.* New York: Plenum, 1977.

Edgerton, F. (Trns.) *The elephant lore of the Hindus.* New Haven, Conn.: Yale University Press, 1931.

Edington, J., Morgan, P. and Morgan, R. Feeding patterns of wading birds on the Gann Flat and river estuary at Dale. *Field Studies*, 1973, *3*, 783–800.

Edminister, F. C. *The ruffed grouse.* New York: Macmillan, 1947.

Edmunds, M. *Defence in animals.* New York: Longman; Inc., 1975.

Edney, J. J. Human territoriality. *Psychological Bulletin,* 1974, *81*, 959–975.

Edson, P. H., & Gallup, G. G. TI as a fear response in lizards (anolis carolinensis). *Psychonomic Science*, 1972, *26*, 27–8.

Edward, 2nd Duke of York. *The master of game.* W. A. Baillie-Grohman and F. Baillie-Grohman (Trns. and Eds.), New York: AMS Press, 1974. Originally published 1406.

Egan, G. *The skilled helper: A model for systematic helping and interpersonal relating.* Belmont, Calif.: Wadsworth Publishing Co., 1975.

Eibl-Eibesfeldt, I. *Ethology: The biology of behavior.* New York: Holt, Rinehart and Winston, 1970.

Eibl-Eibesfeldt, I. *Ethology: The biology of behavior.* (2nd ed.) New York: Holt, Rinehart and Winston, 1975.

Eisenberg, J. F., and Kleiman, D. G. Olfactory communication in mammals. *Annual Review of Ecology and Systematics*, 1972, *3*, 1–32.

Eisenstein, E. M., and Peretz, B. Comparative aspects of habituation in invertebrates. In H. V. S. Peeke and M. J. Herz (Eds.), *Habituation.* Vol. II. *Physiological substrates.* New York: Academic Press, 1973.

Ellis, J. B., and Van Doren, C. S. A comparative evaluation of gravity and system theory models for statewide recreational travel. *Journal of Regional Science*, 1966, *6*, 57–70.

Ennis, G. Food, feeding, and condition of lobsters, *Homarus Americanus*, throughout the seasonal cycle in Bonavista Bay, Newfoundland. *Journal of the Fisheries Research Board of Canada*, 1973, *30*, 1905–1909.

References

Epple, G. Quantitative studies on scent marking in the marmoset. *Folia Primatologica*, 1970, 13 48–62.

Epple, G. Discrimination of the odor of males and females by the marmoset. *Proceedings of the 3rd International Congress of Primatology, 1970*, 1971, *3*, 166–171.

Epple, G. Social communication by olfactory signals in marmosets. *International Zoo Yearbook*, 1972, 12, 36–42.

Epple, G. Olfactory communication in South American primates. Annals of the New York Academy of Sciences, 1974, 237, 261–278.

Erickson, R., and Schiffman, S. The chemical senses: A systematic approach. In M. Gazzaniga and C. Blakemore (Eds.), *Handbook of psychobiology*. New York: Academic Press, 1975.

Estes, W. K., and Skinner, B. F. Some quantitative properties of anxiety. *Journal of Experimental Psychology*, 1941, *29*, 390–400.

Etkin, W. Reproductive behaviors. In W. Etkin (Ed.), *Social behavior and organization among vertebrates.* Chicago: University of Chicago Press, 1964.

Etscorn, F. and Stephens, R. Establishment of conditioned taste aversions with a 24-hour CS-US interval. *Physiological Psychology*, 1973, *1*, 251–253.

Evans, A. C. Studies on the relationship between earthworms and soil fertility. III. Some effect of earthworms on soil structure. *Annals of Applied Biology*, 1948, *35*, 1–13.

Evans, H. E., and Eberhard, M. J. W. *The wasps.* Ann Arbor, Mich.: University of Michigan Press, 1970.

Evans, L. N. An interpretation of turkey courtship. *American Zoologist*, 1961, *1*, 353–354 (abstract).

Evans, S. M., *Studies in invertebrate behavior.* London: Heinemann Educational Books Ltd., 1968.

Evans, S. M. Habituation of the withdrawal response in Nereid polychaetes: II. Rates of habituation in intact and decerebrate worms. *Biological Bulletin*, 1969, *137*, 105–117.

Ewer, R. F. *Ethology of mammals.* New York: Plenum, 1968.

Ewer, R. F., *Ethology of mammals.* London: Elek Science 1973.

Ewing, A. W. Attempts to select for spontaneous activity in *Drosophila melanogaster. Animal Behaviour*, 1963, *11*, 369–378.

Ewing, A. W., and Bennet-Clark, H. C., The courtship songs of *Drosophila.* Behaviour, 1968, *31*, 288–301.

Falk, J. L. The grooming behavior of the chimpanzee as a reinforcer. *Journal of Experimental Analysis of Behavior*, 1958, *1*, 83–85.

Farish, D. J. The evolutionary implications of qualitative variation in the grooming behavior of the hymenoptera (insecta). *Animal Behaviour*, 1972, *20*(4), 662–676.

Farner, D. S. Predictive functions in the control of annual cycles. *Environmental Research*, 1970, *3*, 119–130.

Farooq, A., Denenberg, V. H., Ross, S., Sawin, P. B., and Zarrow, M. X. Maternal behavior in the rabbits: Endocrine factors involved in hair-loosening. *American Journal of Physiology*, 1963, *204*, 271–274.

Farris, H. E. *Behavioral development, social organization, and conditioning of courting behavior in Japanese quail,* Coturnix coturnix japonica. Unpublished doctoral dissertation, Michigan State University, 1964.

Farris, H. E. Classical conditioning of courting behavior in the Japanese quail, *Coturnix coturnix japonica. Journal of the Experimental Analysis of Behavior*, 1967, *10*, 213–17.

Feather, N. T. *Values in education and society.* New York: The Free Press, 1975.

Feder, H. M. Cleaning symbiosis in the marine environment. In J. M. Henry, (Ed.), *Symbiosis.* Vol. 1. New York: Academic Press, 1966.

Fentress, J. C. Interrupted ongoing behavior in two species of vole (*Microtus agrestis* and *Clethrionomys britannicus*). I. Response as a function of preceding activity and the context of an apparently "irrelevant" motor pattern. *Animal Behaviour*, 1968, *16*, 135–153.

Fentress, J. C. Development and patterning of movement sequences in inbred mice. In J. A. Kiger, Jr. (Ed.),*The biology of behavior.* Corvallis, Ore.: Oregon State University Press, 1972.

Fentress, J. C. Specific and nonspecific factors in the causation of behavior. In P. P. G. Bateson and P. H. Klopfer (Eds.), *Perspectives in ethnology.* New York: Plenum Press, 1973 (a).

Fentress, J. C. Development of grooming in mice with amputated forelimbs. *Science*, 1973, *179*, 704–705. (b)

Ferguson, W. Mating behavior of the side-blotched lizards of the genus *Uta* (Sauria: Iquandidae). *Animal Behaviour*, 1970, *18*, 65–72.

Ferrier, D. *The functions of the brain.* London: Smith, Elder & Co., 1886.

Fidura, F. G. *The role of selective attention and the distinctiveness of cues in simple and complex discrimination learning.* Doctoral dissertation, Michigan State University, 1966.

Figler, M. H. The relation between eliciting stimulus strength and habituation of the threat display in male Siamese fighting fish, *Betta splendens. Behaviour*, 1972, *42*, 63–96.

Finch, G. Delayed matching-from-sample and non-spatial delayed response in chimpanzees. *Journal of Comparative Psychology*, 1942, *34*, 315–319.

Fischer, G. J., and Kitchener, S. L. Comparative learning in young gorillas and orangutans: II. Spatial and non-spatial delayed response. *Journal of Genetic Psychology*, 1965, *107*, 337–348.

Fisher, J. C. *Energy crises in perspective.* New York: Wiley-Interscience, 1974.

Fowler, H. *Curiosity and exploratory behavior.* New York: Macmillan, 1965.

Fox, M. W. *Abnormal behavior in animals.* Philadelphia: W. B. Saunders, 1968.

Fox, M. W. A comparative study of the development of facial expressions in canids; wolf, coyote, and foxes. *Behavior*, 1970, *36*, 49–73.

Fox, M. W. *Behavior of wolves, dogs, and related canids.* New York: Harper and Row, 1971.

Fox, M. W. *The wild canids.* New York: Van Nostrand Reinhold, 1975.

Fox, S. S. Evoked potential habituation rate and sensory pattern preference as determined by stimulus information. *Journal of Comparative and Physiological Psychology*, 1964, *58*, 225–232.

Fraenkel, G. S., and Gunn, D. D. *The orientation of animals.* New York: Dover, 1961.

Frank, F. Das Duftmarkieren der grossen Wühlmaus, *Arvicola terrestris* (L.). *Zeitschrift für Säugertierkunde*, 1956, *21*, 172–175.

Franke, K., and Potter, V. The ability of rats to discriminate between diets of varying degrees of toxicity. *Science*, 1936, *83*, 330–332.

Fraser, A. F. *Reproductive behavior in ungulates.* New York: Academic Press, 1968.

Frazer, J. F. *Amphibians.* London: Wykeham Publications, 1973.

Frederick II, Holy Roman Emperor. *The art of falconry.* C. A. Wood, and Majorie Fyfe (Trns. and Eds.), Stanford: Stanford University Press, 1943. Originally published 1250.

Freedman, J. L., *Crowding and behavior: The psychology of high density living.* New York: Viking Press, 1975.

Freedman, J. L., Heshka, S., and Levy, A. Population density and pathology: Is there a relationship? *Journal of Experimental Social Psychology*, 1975, *11*, 539–552.

Freedman, J. L., Levy, A., Buchanan, R. W., and Price, J. Crowding and human aggressiveness. *Journal of Experimental Social Psychology*, 1972, *8* 528–548.

Freeland, W., and Janzen, D. Strategies in herbivory by mammals: The role of plant secondary compounds. *American Naturalist*, 1974, *108*, 269–289.

Freud, S. *Standard edition of the complete psychological works of Sigmund Freud.* Translated by James Starchey. Vol. 1. London: Hogarth, 1909.

Fried, R., Korn, S. J., and Welch, L. Effect of change in sequential visual stimuli on GSR adaptation. *Journal of Experimental Psychology*, 1966, *72*, 325–327.

Friedman, M. C. Physiological conditions for the stimulation of prolactin secretion by external stimuli in the ring dove. *Dissertation Abstracts*, 1966, *27*, 312-B.

Friedmann, H. The parasitic weaverbirds. *Bulletin of the United States Natural Museum*, 1960, *223*, 1–196.

Friedrich II, Holy Roman Emperor. *De art venandi cum avibus.* Introduction and elucidative description of the Facsimile edition by C. A. Willemsen, Graz, Austria: Akademische Druk-u. Verlagsanstalt, 1969. Originally published 1250.

Frith, H. J. *The Mallee-fowl.* London: Angus and Robertson, 1962.

Galef, B. Aggression and timidity: Response to novelty in feral Norway rats. *Journal of Comparative and Physiological Psychology*, 1970, *70*, 370–381.

Galef, B. Social effects in the weaning of domestic rat pups. *Journal of Comparative and Physiological Psychology*, 1971, *75*, 358–362.

Galef, B., and Clark, M. Mother's milk and adult presence: Two factors determining initial dietary selection by weanling rats. *Journal of Comparative and Physiological Psychology*, 1972, *78*, 220–225.

Galef, B., and Sherry, D. Mother's milk: A medium for transmission of cues reflecting the flavor of the mother's diet. *Journal of Comparative and Physiological Psychology*, 1973, *83*, 374–378.

Gallon, R. L. Spatial location of a visual signal and shuttle box avoidance acquisition by goldfish (*Carassius auratus*). *Journal of Comparative and Physiological Psychology*, 1974, *86*, 316–321.

Gallup, G. G. Animal hypnosis: Factual status of a fictional concept. *Psychological Bulletin*, 1974, *81*, 836–853.

Gallup, G. G. Self recognition in primates: A comparative approach to the bidirectional properties of consciousness. *American Psychologist*, 1977, *32*, 329–338. (a)

Gallup, G. G. TI: The role of fear and predation. *Psychological Record*, 1977, *1*, 41–62. (b)

Gallup, G. G., Nash, R. D., Donegan, N. H., and McGuire, M. K. The immobility response: A predator-induced reaction in chicks. *Psychological Record*, 1971, *21*, 513–519.

Gallup, G. G., Nash, K. F., and Ellison, A. L. TI as a reaction to predation: Artificial eyes as a fear stimulus for chickens. *Psychonomic Science*, 1971, *23*, 79–80.

Gallwey, Sir R. Payne. *The book of duck decoys*. London: John Van Voorst, 1886.

Gandolfi, G. A chemical sex attractant in the guppy *Poecilia reticulata Peters* (Pisces: Poeciliidae). *Monitors Zoology*. 1969, Ital. (N.S.), *3*, 89–98.

Gantt, W. H. Experimental basis of neurotic behavior. *Psychosomatic Medicine Monographs*, 1944, *3*(3 and 4).

Garcia, J., Erwin, F. R., and Koelling, R. A. Learning with prolonged delay of reinforcement. *Psychonomic Science*, 1966, *5*, 121–122.

Garcia, J., and Koelling, R. Relation of cue to consequence in avoidance learning. *Psychonomic Science*, 1966, *4*, 123–124.

Garcia, J., and Koelling, R. A. A comparison of aversions induced by x-rays, drugs and toxins. *Radiation Research*, 1967, Suppl. 7, 439–450.

Garcia, J., McGowan, B. K., and Green, K. F. Biological constraints on conditioning. In A. H. Black and W. F. Prokasy (Eds.), *Classical conditioning II: Current research and theory*. New York: Appleton-Century-Crofts, 1972.

Garcia, J., Rusiniak, K. W., and Brett, L. P. Conditioning food-illness aversions in wild animals: Caveant canonici. In H. Davis and H. M. B. Hurwitz, (Eds.), Operant-Pavlovian interactions. Hillsdale, N.J.: Lawrence Erlbaum Assoc., 1977.

Gardiner, Mary S. *The biology of invertebrates*. New York: McGraw-Hill, 1972.

Gardner, B. T., and Gardner, R. A. Two way communications with an infant chimpanzee. In A. M. Schrier and F. Stollnitz (Eds.), *Behavior of nonhuman primates*. Vol. 4. New York: Academic Press, 1971.

Gardner, L. E. Retention and overhabituation of a dual-component response in *Lumbricus terrestris*. *Journal of Comparative and Physiological psychology*, 1968, *66*, 315–319.

Gardner, L. E., and Ratner, S. C. In-burrow behavior of earthworms. *Psychological Record*, 1970, *20*, 387–394.

Geer, J. H. Generalization off inhibition in the orienting response. *Psychophysiology*, 1969, *6*, 197–201.

Gillett, J. D. *The mosquito*. Garden City, N.Y.: Doubleday, 1972.

Gilman, T. T., and Marcuse, F. L. Animal hypnosis. *Psychological Bulletin*, 1949, *56*, 141–165.

Ginsburg, H. J. Defensive distance and immobility in young precocial birds. *Developmental Psychology*, 1975, *8* 281–285.

Ghiselin, M. T. The evolution of hermaphroditism among animals. *Quarterly Review of Biology*, 1969, *44*(2), 189–208.

Glander, K. Poison in a monkey's garden of Eden. *Natural History*, 1977, *86*, 34–41.

Glickman, S. E., and Hartz, K. E. Exploratory behavior in several species of rodents. *Journal of Comparative and Physiological Psychology*, 1964, *58*, 101–104.

References

Glickman, S. E., and Schiff, B. A biological theory of reinforcement. *Psychological Review*, 1967, *74*, 81–109.

Gloger, C. L. *Die hegung der hohlenbruter.* Berlin: Allgemeine Deutsch verlags-anstalt, 1865.

Goist, K. C., Twiggs, D. G., Schwartz, B. D., and Christenson, T. E. Role of cutaneous feedback in ventral rubbing in the male Mongolian gerbil. *Phsiology and Behavior*, 1977, *19*, 581–583.

Goodall, J. Chimpanzees of the Gombe stream reserve. In I. DeVore (Ed.), *Primate behavior: Field studies of monkeys and apes.* New York: Holt, Rinehart and Winston, 1965.

Goodwin, D. Some aspects of the bahavior of the Jay, *Garrulus glandarius. Ibis,* 1951, *93.* 602–625.

Goodman, D. A., and Weinberger, N. M. Habituation in "lower" tetrapod vertebrates: Amphibia as vertebrate model systems. In H. V. S. Peeke and M. J. Herz (Eds.), *Habituation* Vol I. *Behavioral studies.* New York: Academic Press, 1973.

Gormezano, I. Yoked comparisons of classical and instrumental conditioning of the eyelid response: And an addendum on "voluntary responders." In W. F. Prokasy (Ed.), *Classical conditioning: A symposium.* New York: Appleton-Century-Crofts, 1965.

Gossette, R. L. Successive discrimination reversal (SDR) performance of four avian species on a brightness discrimination task. *Psychonomic Science,* 1967, *8*, 17–18.

Graham, F. K. Habituation and dishabituation of responses innervated by the autonomic nervous system. In H. V. S. Peeke and M. J. Herz (Eds.), *Habituation.* Vol. I. *Behavioral studies.* New York: Academic Press, 1973.

Grau, G. A. Olfaction and reproduction in ungulates. In R. L. Doty (Ed.), *Mammalian olfaction, reproductive processes, and behavior.* New York: Academic Press, 1976.

Graves, W. The imperiled giants. *National Geographic,* 1976, *150*, 722–751.

Gray, G. A. and Winn, H. E. Reproductive ecology and sound production of the toadfish, *Opsanus tay. Ecology,* 1961, *42*, 274–282.

Gray, J. *Animal locomotion.* London: Weidenfeld and Nicolson, 1968.

Graziano, A. M. *A gestalt versus a stimulus-response analysis of reasoning in the rat.* Unpublished master's thesis, Michigan State University, 1956.

Green, H. Perverted appetites. *Physiological Review,* 1925, *5*, 336–348.

Greenwood, J. *Wild sports of the world.* London: Ward, Lock, and Tyler, 1865.

Grice, G. R. An experimental test of the expectation theory of learning. *Journal of Comparative physiological Psychology,* 1948b, *41*, 137–143.

Griswold, J. G., Borchelt, P. L., Branchek, R. S., and Bensko, J. A. Condition of the pelage regulates sandbathing and grooming behavior in the kangaroo rat (*Dipodomys merriami*). *Animal Behaviour,* 1977, *25*, 602–608.

Gross, C. G. Effect of deprivation on delayed response and delayed alternation performance by normal and brain operated monkeys. *Journal of Comparative Physiological Psychology,* 1963, *56*, 48–51.

Groves, P. M., and Thompson, R. F. Habituation: A dual-process theory. *Psychological Review,* 1970, *77*, 419–450.

Guedry, F. E., Jr. Habituation to complex vestibular stimulation in man: Transfer and retention of effects from twelve days of rotation at 10 rpm. *Perceptual and Motor Skills,* 1965, *21*, 459–481.

Guhl, A. M., and Ortman, L. L. Visual patterns in the recognition of individuals among chickens. *Condor,* 1953, *55*, 287–298.

Gullion, G. W. Factors influencing Ruffed Grouse populations. *Trans. North American Wildlife National Resources Conference.* 1970, *35*, 93–105.

Gurdjian, E. S. Head injury from antiquity to the present with special reference to penetrating head wounds. Springfield, Ill.: Charles C. Thomas, 1973.

Gustavson, C. R., Garcia, J., Hankins, W. G., and Rusiniak, K. W. Coyote predation control by aversive conditioning. *Science,* 1974, *184*, 581–583.

Guthrie, E. R. *The psychology of learning.* (Rev. ed.) New York: Harper, 1952.

Hagaman, T. E. *Sequence effects in the antipredator behavior of the house cricket (Acheta domesticus L.).* Unpublished doctoral dissertation, Michigan State University, 1977.

Hakluyt, R. *Voyages.* Eight Vols. London: J. M. Dent & Sons, 1907. Originally published 1859.

Hall-Sternglanz, Sarah, Gray, J. L., and Murakami, M. Adult preferences for infantile facial features; An ethological approach. *Animal Behaviour.* 1977, *25*, 108–115.

Hallett, J. P. *Animal Kitabu.* New York: Random House, 1968.

Halton, D. C., and Thompson, R. W. Termination of TI in chickens by loud stimulation. *Bulletin of the Psychonomic Society*, 1975, *75*, 61–62.

Hamblin, R. L., Jacobsen, R. B., and Miller, J. L. *A mathematical theory of social change. New York: Wiley-Interscience, 1973.*

Hamilton, D. I., and Hamilton, D. O. *Among the elephants.* New York: Viking Press, 1975.

Hamilton, G., and Robbins, M. Applied clinical psychology: An immodest reply. *American Psychologists*, 1975, *30*, 712–713.

Hamilton, W. J., Buskirk, R. E., and Buskirk, W. H. Defensive stoning of baboons. *Nature*, 1975, *256*, 488–489.

Hands, Rachel. *English hawking and hunting in the boke of St. Albans.* London: Oxford University Press, 1975.

Hara, T. J. An electrophysiological basis for olfactory discrimination in homing salmon: A review. Journal of Fisheries Research Board of Canada, 1970, *27*, 563–586.

Harden-Jones, F. R. *Fish migration.* London: E. Arnold, 1968.

Harder, W. Proof of active (electric) localization in Mormyridae (Teleostei, Pisces). *Zeitschrift für Tierpsychologie*, 1972, *30*, 94–102.

Harlow, H. F. The formation of learning sets. *Psychological Review*, 1949, *56*, 51–65.

Harlow, H., and Harlow M. Social deprivation in monkeys. *Scientific American*, 1962, *207*, 136–146.

Harlow, H. F., Harlow, M., and Hansen, E. The maternal affectional system of rhesus monkeys. In H. Rheingold, (Ed.), *Maternal behavior in mammals.* New York: Wiley, 1963.

Harlow, H. F., and Settlage, P. H. Comparative behavior of primates: VII. Capacity of monkeys to solve patterned strings tests. *Journal of Comparative Physiological Psychology*, 1934, *18*, 423–435.

Harris, D., Imperato, P. J., and Oken, B. Dog bites—An unrecognized epidemic. *Bulletin of the New York Academy of Medicine*, 1974, *50*(9), 981–1000.

Harris, J. D. Habituatory response decrement in the intact organism. *Psychological Bulletin*, 1943, *40*, 385–423.

Hart, B. L. Environmental and hormonal influences on urine marking behavior in the adult male dog. *Behavioral Biology*, 1974, *11*, 167–176.

Hart, B. L., and Barrett, R. E. Effects of castration on fighting, roaming, and urine spraying in adult male cats. *Journal of the American Veterinary Medical Association*, 1975, *163*, 290–292.

Hartshorne, C. The monotony-threshold in singing birds. Auk, 1956, *83*, 176–192.

Hartshorne, C. *Born to Sing.* Bloomington, Ind.: Indiana University Press, 1973.

Harwood, D., and Vowles, D. M. Forebrain stimulation and feeding behavior in the ring dove (Streptopelia risoria). *Journal of Comparative and Physiological Psychology*, 1966, *62*, 388–396.

Haskins, C. H. *Studies in the history of medieval science.* New York: Frederick Ungar Publishing Co., 1960. Originally published 1924.

Hasler, A. D. *Underwater guideposts.* Madison: University of Wisconsin Press, 1966.

Hasler, A. D., and Wisby, W. J. Discrimination of stream odors by fishes and its relation to parent stream behavior. *American Naturalist*, 1951, *85*, 223–228.

Hauser, D. C. Anting by gray squirrels. *Journal of Mammalogy*, 1964, *45*, 136–138.

Hawn, L. J. *1975 deer season kill rate in Michigan.* Michigan Department of Natural Resources Surveys and Statistical Services Report, N. 158, 1976.

Hearst, E., and Franklin, S. R. Positive and negative relations between a signal and food: Approach-withdrawal behavior to the signal. *Journal of Experimental Psychology: Animal Behavior Processes*, 1977, *3*, 37–52.

Hearst, E., and Jenkins, H. M. *Sign-tracking: The stimulus reinforcer relation and directed action.* Austin, Tex.: Psychonomic Society, 1974.

Hediger, H. *Studies of the Psychology and Behavior of Captive Animals in Zoos and Circuses.* Butterworths, London, 1955.

Hediger, H. Zur biologie und psychologie der flucht

bie tieren. In F. R. Walther (Ed.), Flight behavior and avoidance of predators in Thomson gazelles. *Behavior*, 1969, *34*, 184–221.

Heinz, H. J. Beobachtungen uber die Putzhandlungen bei Dipteran in allgemeinen und bei *Sarcophaga carnaria* L. im besonderen. *Zeitshrift Tierpsychology*, 1949, *6*, 652–664.

Heise, D. R. *Causal analysis.* New York: Wiley-Interscience, 1975.

Hendee, J. C. Appreciative vs. consumptive uses of wildlife refugees: Studies of who gets what and trends in use. *Transactions of the 34th North American Wildlife and Natural Resources Conference*, 1969, *34*, 252–264.

Hendee, J. C. and Potter, D. R. Human behavior and wildlife management: Needed research. *Transactions of the 36th North American Wildlife and Natural Resources Conference*, 1971, *36*, 383–396.

Hendee, J. C., and Potter, D. R. *Hunters and hunting: Management implications of research.* U.S.D.A. Forest Service General Technical Report SE-9:137-161, 1976.

Henderson, N. D. Genetic influences on the behavior of mice can be obscured by laboratory rearing. *Journal of Comparative Physiological Psychology*, 1970, *72*, 505–511.

Henning, C. W., Dunlap, W. P., and Gallup, G. G. The effects of distance between prey and predator and the opportunity to escape TI in anolis carolinensis. *Psychological Record*, 1976, *26*, 313–320.

Henry, J. D. The use of urine marking in the scavenging behaviour of red fox (*Vulpes vulpes*). *Behaviour*, 1977, 61, 82–106.

Herrick, F. H. *Wild birds at home.* New York: Appleton-Century-Crofts, 1935.

Hess, E. H. *Imprinting.* New York: Van Nostrand Reinhold Co., 1973.

Hilgard, E. R., and Marquis, D. G. *Conditioning and learning.* New York: Appleton, 1940.

Hinde, R. A. Factors governing the changes in strength of a partially inborn response, as shown by the mobbing behaviour of the chaffinch (*Fringilla coelebs*). II. The waning of the response. *Proceedings of the Royal Society of London, Series B*, 1954, *142*, 306–359.

Hinde, R. A. Behaviour and speciation in birds and lower vertebrates. *Biological Reviews*, 1959, *34*, 85–128.

Hinde, R. A. Behavioural habituation. In G. Horn and R. A. Hinde (Eds.), *Short-term changes in neural activity and behaviour.* New York: Cambridge University Press, 1970. (a)

Hinde, R. A. *Animal Behavior: A systhesis of the ethology and comparative psychology.* (2nd ed.) New York: McGraw-Hill Book Co., 1970. (b)

Hinde, R. A., Bell, R. Q., & Steel, E. A. Changes in sensitivity of the canary brood patch during the natural breeding season. *Animal Behavior*, 1963, *11*, 553–560.

Hinde, R. A. and Stevenson-Hinde, J. (Eds.), *Constraints on learning.* New York: Academic Press, 1973.

Hinde, R. A., and Tinbergen, N. The comparative study of species-specific behavior. In A. Roe and C. G. Simpson (Eds.), *Evolution and behavior.* New Haven: Yale University Press, 1958.

Hirsch, J., and Boudreau, J. C. Studies in experimental behavior genetics: 1. The heritability of phototaxis in a population of *Drosophila melanogaster. Journal of Comparative and Physiological Psychology*, 1958, *51*, 647–651.

Hoaglund, H. The mechanisms of Tonic I ("animal hypnosis"). *Journal of General Psychology*, 1928, *1*, 426–477.

Hodgkin, A. L. Presidential address, *Proceedings of the Royal Society of Britain*, 1973, *183*, 1–19.

Hodjat, S. H. Effects of sublethal doses of insecticides and of diet and crowding on *Dysdercus fasciatus* Sign. (Hem., Pyrrhocoridae). *Bulletin of Entomological Research*, 1969, *60*, 367–378.

Hodjat, S. H. Effects of crowding on colour, size and larval activity of *Spodoptera littoralis* (Lepidoptera, Noctuidae). *Entomology, Experimental and Applied*, 1970, *13*, 97–106.

Hodos, W., and Campbell, C. B. G. Scala naturae: Why there is no theory in comparative psychology. *Psychological Review*, 1969, *76*, 337–350.

Hogan, J. Operant control of preening in pigeons. *Journal of Experimental Analysis of Behavior*, 1964, *7*, 351–352.

Hogan, J. Development of food recognition in young

chicks: I. Maturation and nutrition *Journal of Comparative and Physiological Psychology*, 1973, *83*, 355–366. (a)

Hogan, J. Development of food recognition in young chicks: II. Learned associations over long delays. *Journal of Comparative and Physiological Psychology*, 1973, *83*, 367–373.

Honzik, C. H. Delayed reaction in rats. *University of California Publication of Psychology*, 1931, *4*, 307–318.

Horner, J. L., Longo, N., and Bitterman, M. E. A classical conditioning technique for small aquatic animals. *American Journal of Psychology*, 1960, *73*, 623–626.

Horner, J. L., Longo, N., and Bitterman, M. E. A shuttlebox for the fish and a control circuit of general applicability. *American Journal of Psychology*, 1961, *74*, 114–120.

House, B. J., and Zeaman, D. Visual discrimination learning in imbeciles. *American Journal of Mental Deficiency*, 1958, *63*, 447–452.

Howard, E. *Territory in bird life.* London: Collins, 1948.

Howell, D. Acoustic behavior and feeding in glossophagine bats. *Journal of Mammalogy*, 1974, *55*, 293–308.

Howse, P. E. Design and function in the insect brain. In L. B. Browne (Ed.), *Experimental analysis of insect behaviour.* New York: Springer-Verlag, 1974.

Howse, P. E. Brain structure and behavior in insects. *Annual Review of Entomology*, 1975, *20*, 359–379.

Hubbert, H. B. The effect of age on habit formation in the albino rat. *Behavior Monographs*, 1915, *2*, 1–55.

Hubbert, M. K. The energy resources of the earth. *Scientific American*, 1971, *224*, 61–70.

Huff, D. L. A probabalistic analysis of shopping center trade areas. *Land Economics*, 1963, *39*, 81–90.

Hughes, B. Allelomimetic feeding in the domestic fowl. *British Poultry Science*, 1971, *12*, 359–366.

Hughes, C. W. Early experience in domestication. *Journal of Comparative and Physiological Psychology*, 1975, *88*, 407–417.

Hughes, C. W., and Boice, R. Domestication, sophistication, and avoidance in Norway rats. *Journal of Comparative and Physiological Psychology*, 1973, *84*, 408–413.

Hughes, R. N. Exploration in three laboratory rodents. *Perceptual and Motor Skills*, 1969, *28*, 90.

Hulet, C. V. Behavioral, social and psychological factors affecting mating time and breeding efficiency in sheep. *Journal of Animal Science*, 1966, *25*, Supplement, 5–20.

Hull, C. L. *A behavior system.* New Haven: Yale University Press, 1952.

Hull, D. B. *Hounds and hunting in ancient Greece.* Chicago: The University of Chicago Press. 1964. (Also contains Xenophon's *Cynegeticus*.)

Humphrey, G. *The nature of learning in its relation to the living system.* New York: Harcourt, Brace and Co., 1933.

Hunter, W. S. The delayed reaction in animals and children. *Behavioral Monographs*, 1912, *2*, 1–85.

Hunter, W. S. A kinesthetically controlled maze habit in the rat. *Science*, 1940, *91*, 267–269.

Hupka, R. B., Massero, D. W., and Moore, J. W. Yoked comparisons of instrumental-avoidance and classical conditioning of the rabbit nictitating membrane response as a function of interstimulus interval and number of trials per day. *Psychonomic Science*, 1968, *12*, 93–94.

Hurlbut, C. S., Jr. (Ed.) *The planet we live on.* New York: H. N. Abrams, 1976.

Hurst, M. E. *A geography of economic behavior, an introduction.* North Scituate, Mass.: Duxbury Press, 1972.

Hyman, L. *The invertebrates.* New York: McGraw-Hill, 1940.

Idyll, C. P. (Ed.) *Exploring the ocean world.* New York: T. Y. Crowell, 1969.

Ikeshoji, T., and Mulla, M. S. Overcrowding factors of mosquito larvae. *Journal of Economic Entomology*, 1970a, *63*, 90–96.

Ikeshoji, T., and Mulla, M. S. Overcrowding factors of mosquito larvae. 2. Growth-retarding and bacteriostatic effects of the overcrowding factors of mosquito larvae. *Journal of Economic Entomology*, 1970b, *63*, 1737–1743.

Isaacson, R. L. Experimental brain lesions and memory. In *Neural mechanisms of learning and memory.* Cambridge: MIT Press, 1976.

Itani, J. On the acquisition and propogation of a new

food habit in the natural group of the Japanese monkey at Takasaki-Yama. *Primates*, 1958, *1*, 84–98.

Izquierdo, I. Orsingher, O., and Ogura, A. Hippocampal facilitation and RNA build-up in response to stimulation in rats with a low inborn learning ability. *Behavioral Biology*, 1972, *7*, 699–707.

Jack, R. W., and Williams, W. L. The effect of temperature on the reaction of Glossina morsitans Westw. to light. A preliminary note. *Bulletin of Entomological Research*, 1937, *28*, 499–503.

Jacobson, M., and Baker, R. E. Development of neuronal connections with skin grafts in frogs: Behavioral and electrophysiological studies. *Journal of Comparative Neurology,* 1969, *137*, 121–142.

Jakway, J. S. The inheritance of patterns of mating behavior in the male guinea pig. *Animal Behaviour*, 1959, *7*, 150–162.

James, L. Syndromes of locoweed poisoning in livestock. *Clinical Toxicology*, 1972, *5*, 567–573.

James, L. & VanKampen, K. Effects of locoweed toxin on rats. *American Journal Veterinary Research*, 1976, *37*, 845–846.

Jarman, C. *Atlas of animal migration.* London: Heinemann, 1970.

Jarman, P. J. The social organization of antelope in relation to their ecology. Behavior, 1974, *58*(3, 4), 215–267.

Jay, P. Mother-infant relation in langurs. In H. Rheingold, (Ed.), *Maternal behavior in mammals.* New York: Wiley, 1963.

Jenkins, D. W. Population control in Red Grouse (*Lagopus lagopus scoticus*). *Proceedings 13th International Ornithology Congress*, 1963, 690–697.

Jenkins, D. W., Watson, A., and Miller, G. R. Population studies on Red Grouse, *Lagopus lagopus scoticus* (Lath.) in north-east Scotland. *Journal of Animal Ecology*, 1963, *32*, 317–376.

Jenkins, H. M., and Moore, B. R. The form of the autoshaped response with food or water reinforcers. *Journal of the Experimental Analysis of Behavior*, 1973, *20*, 163–181.

Jenni, D. A. Evolution of polyandry in birds. *American Zoologist*, 1974, *14*, 129–144.

Jennings, H. S. *Behavior of the lower organisms.* New York: Columbia University Press, 1906.

Jennings, J. *Feeding, digestion and assimilation in animals.* (2nd ed.) London: Macmillan, 1972.

Jensen, D. D. Operationism and the question "Is this behavior learned or innate?" *Behaviour*, 1961, *17*, 1–8.

Jensen, D. D. Polythetic operationism and the phylogeny of learning. In W. C. Corning and S. C. Ratner (Eds.), *Chemistry of learning.* New York: Plenum, 1967.

Jensen, D. D. Foreword to the 1962 edition. In H. S. Jennings, *Behavior of the lower organisms.* Bloomington, Ind.: Indiana University Press, 1976.

Jobe, J. B., Mellgren, R. L., Feinberg, R. A., Littlejohn, R. L., and Rigby, R. L. Patterning, partial reinforcement, and N-length effects at spaced trials as a function of reinstatement of retrieval cues. *Learning and Motivation*, 1977, *8*, 77–97.

Johnsgard, P. A. *Handbook of waterfowl behavior.* Ithaca, N.Y.: Cornell University Press, 1965.

Johnson, C. G. *Migration and dispersal of insects by flight.* London: Methuen, 1969.

Johnson, L. K., and Hubbell, S. P. Contrasting foraging strategies and coexistence of two bee species on a single resource. *Ecology*, 1975, *56*, 1398–1406.

Johnson, R. P. Scent marking in mammals. *Animal Behaviour*, 1973, *21*, 521–535.

Jones, M. C. The elimination of children's fears. *Journal of Experimental Psychology*, 1924, *7*, 282–390.

Kalat, J. Taste-aversion learning in infant guinea pigs. *Developmental Psychobiology*, 1975, *8*, 383–287.

Kalat, J., and Rozin, P. "Salience": A factor which can override temporal contiguity in taste-aversion learning. *Journal of Comparative and Physiological Psychology*, 1970, *71*, 192–197.

Kalmijn, A. The electric sense of sharks and rays. *Journal of Experimental Biology*, 1971, *55*, 371–383.

Kanfer, F. H. and Phillips, J. S. *Learning foundations of behavior therapy.* New York: Wiley, 1970.

Kantor, J. R. *Principles of psychology.* (2nd ed.) Chicago: Principia Press, 1959. Originally published 1924, 1926.

Kantor, J. R. *The scientific evolution of psychology.* Two vols. Chicago: Principia Press, 1963, 1969.

Kantor, J. R. History of psychology: What benefits? *The Psychological Record*, 1964, *14*, 433–443.

Kammenhuber, Annelies. *Hippologia Hethitica.* Wiesbaden: Otto Harrassowitz, 1961.

Karczmar, A. G., and Scudder, C. L. Behavioral responses to drug and brain catecholamine levels in mice of different strains and genera. *Federal Proceedings,* 1967, *26,* 1186–1191.

Kare, M., and Maller, O. (Eds.) *The Chemical Senses and Nutrition.* Baltimore: Johns Hopkins Press, 1967.

Karn, H. W. A case of experimentally induced neurosis in the cat. *Journal of Experimental Psychology,* 1938, *22,* 589.

Karn, H. W. The experimental study of neurotic behavior in infra-human animals. *Journal of General Psychology,* 1940, *22,* 431.

Karnopp, D., and Rosenberg, R. *Systems dynamics: A unified approach.* New York: Wiley-Interscience, 1975.

Kaston, B. J. Some little known aspects of spider behavior. *American Midland Naturalist,* 1965, *73*(2), 336–356.

Kaufman, J. H. Social ethology of the whiptail wallaby, *Macropus parryi,* in northeastern New South Wales. *Animal Behaviour,* 1974, *22,* 281–369.

Kaufman, M. E., & Peterson, W. M. Acquisition of learning set by normal and mentally retarded children. *Journal of Comparative Physiological Psychology,* 1958, *51,* 619–621.

Kawai, M. Newly acquired precultural behavior of the natural troop of Japanese monkeys on Koshima islet. *Primates,* 1965, *6,* 1–30.

Kawanabe, H. The significance of social structure in production of the "Ayu", *Plecoglossus altivelus.* In T. G. Northcote, (Ed.), *Symposium on salmon and trout in streams.* H. R. MacMillan Lectures in Fisheries. Vancouver: University of British Columbia Press, 1968.

Keeler, R. Toxins and teratogens of higher plants. *Lloydia Journal of Natural Products,* 1975, *38,* 56–86.

Keeton, W. T. Magnets interfere with pigeon homing. *Proceedings National Academy of Science, Washington, D.C.,* 1971, *68,* 102–106.

Kelleher, R. T. Concept formation in chimpanzees. *Science,* 1958, *128,* 777–778.

Kelso, L., and Nice, M. M. A Russian contribution to anting and feather mites. *Wilson Bulletin,* 1963, *75*(1), 23–26.

Kendall, S. B., and Thompson, R. F. Effect of stimulus similarity on sensory preconditioning within a single stimulus dimension. *Journal of Comparative and Physiological Psychology,* 1960, *53,* 439–442.

Kendeigh, S. C. Nesting behavior of wood warblers. *Wilson Bulletin,* 1945, *57,* 145–164.

Kenk, R. Species differentiation and ecological relations of planarians. In W. C. Corning and S. C. Ratner (Eds.), *Chemistry of learning.* New York: Plenum, 1967.

Kennedy, J. S., and Marsh, D. Pheromone-regulated anemotaxil in flying moths. *Science,* 1974, *184,* 999–1001.

Kennedy, R. J. Sunbathing behavior of birds. *British Birds,* 1969, *62,* 249–258.

Kennedy, R. J. Preen gland weights. *Ibis,* 1971, *113,* 369–372.

Kessel, B. Distribution and migration of the European Starling in North America. *Condor,* 1953, *55,* 49–67.

Khalaf El-Duweini, A., and Ghabbour, S. I. Observations on the burrowing activities of Allolubuphora caliquosa f. trapazoidas. *Bulletin Zoological Society of Egypt,* 1964, *19* 60–63.

Khalifa, A. Sexual behavior in *Gryllus domesticus* L. *Behaviour,* 1949, *2,* 264–274.

Kimble, D. P., and Ray, R. S. Reflex habituation and potentiation in *Rana pipiens. Animal Behaviour,* 1965, *13,* 530–533.

Kimble, G. A. *Hilgard & Marquis' conditioning and learning.* (2nd ed.) New York; Appleton-Century-Crofts, 1961.

Kimble, G. A. *Foundations of conditioning and learning.* New York: Appleton-Century-Crofts, 1967.

Kimmel, H. D. Habituation, habituability, and conditioning. In H. V. S. Peeke and M. J. Herz (Eds.), *Habituation.* Vol I. *Behavioral studies.* New York: Academic Press, 1973.

Kinastowski, W. (The problem of "learning" in *Spirostomum ambiguum.*) *Acta Protozoologica,* 1963, 1, 223–236. (In German.)

King, J. A. Maternal behavior in *Peromyscus.* In H. Rheingold, (Ed.), *Maternal behavior in mammals.* New York: Wiley, 1963.

King, J. E., and Witt, E. D. The learning of patterned strings problems by rock squirrels. *Psychonomic Science,* 1966, *4,* 319–320.

References

Kingsbury, J. *Poisonous plants of the United States and Canada.* Englewood-Cliffs, N.J.: Prentice Hall, 1964.

Kipling, C., and Frost, W. E. Variations in the fecundity of pike *Esox lucius* L. in Windermere. *Journal of Fish Biology*, 1969, *1*, 221–237.

Kleiman, D. G., and Eisenberg, J. F. Comparisons of canid and felid social systems from an evolutionary perspective. *Animal Behaviour*, 1973, *21*(4), 637–659.

Klein, L. L. Observations on copulations and seasonal reproduction of two species of spider monkeys, *Ateles Belzebuth* and *A. geoffrogi. Folia. Primat.*, 1971, *15*, 233–248.

Klessig, L. L. *Hunting in Wisconsin: Initiation, desertion, activity patterns, and attitudes as influenced by social class and residence.* Masters thesis, University of Wisconsin, 1970.

Kling, J. W., and Riggs, L. A. (Eds.) *Woodworth & Schlosberg's experimental psychology.* (3rd ed.) New York: Holt, Rinehart and Winston, 1971.

Kluckhohn, C. Values and value orientations in the theory of action. In T. Parsons and E. A. Shils (Eds.), *Toward a general theory of action.* Cambridge: Harvard University Press, 1951.

Koenig, H. E., and Edens, T. C. Resource management in a changing environment: With applications to the rural sector. Report to National Science Foundation, Grant No. GI–20, 1976.

Kolb, L. C. Curt P. Richter. In J. Zubin and H. F. Hunt (Eds.), *Comparative psychopathology: Animal and human.* New York: Grune & Stratton, 1967.

Konishi, M. How the owl tracks its prey. *American Scientist*, 1973, *61*, 414–424.

Korschgen, C. E. and Fredrickson, L. H. Comparative displays of yearling and adult male wood ducks. *Auk*, 1976, *93*, 793–807.

Korschgen, L. Foods and nutrition of Missouri and midwestern pheasants. *Transactions of the North American Wildlife and Natural Resources Conference*, 1964 *29*, 159–181.

Kozak, W., and Westerman, R. Basic patterns of plastic change in the mammalian nervous systen. *Symposia of the Society for Experimental Biology*, 1966, *20*, 509–544.

Kramer, G. Weitere Analyse der Faktoren die Zugaktivitat des Gekafigten Vogels orientieren. *Naturwiss Chaften*, 1950, *37*, 377–378.

Kramer, S. N. *From the tablets of Sumer.* Indian Hills, Colo.: The Falcon's Wing Press, 1956.

Kramer, S. N. *The Sumerians.* Chicago: The University of Chicago Press, 1963.

Krebs, C. J. *Ecology. The experimental analysis of distribution and abundance.* New York: Harper & Row, 1972

Krebs, J. R. Regulation of numbers in the Great Tit (Aves: Passeriformes). *Journal of Zoology*, 1970, *162*, 317–333.

Krebs, J. R. Territory and breeding density in the Great Tit, *Parus major. Ecology*, 1971, *52*, 1–22.

Krebs, J. R. The significance of song repertoires: The Beau Gests hypothesis. *Animal Behaviour*, 1977, *25*, 475–478.

Krecker, F. H. *General zoology.* New York; Henry Holt, 1934.

Krieger, R., Feeny, P., and Wilkinson, C. Detoxication enzymes in the guts of caterpillars: An evolutionary answer to plant defenses. *Science*, 1971, *172*, 579–581.

Krischic, V. A. and Weber, P. G. Induced parental care in male convict cichlid fish. *Developmental Psychobiology*, 1975, *8*, 1–11.

Kristof, E. The last U.S. whale hunters. *National Geographic*, 1973, *143*, 346–353.

Laine, H., & Griswold, J. G. Sandbathing in kangaroo rats (*Dipodomys spectabilis*). *Journal of Mammalogy*, 1976, *57*(2), 408–410.

Lang, C. Organoleptic and other characteristics of diet which influence acceptance by nonhuman primates. In R. Harris (Ed.), *Feeding and nutrition of nonhuman primates.* New York: Academic Press, 1970.

Langenau Jr, E. E. and Lerg, J. M. The effects of winter nutritional stress on maternal and neonatal behavior in penned white-tailed deer. *Applied Animal Ethology,* 1976, *2* 207–223.

Langenau, E. E., Levine, R. L., Jamsen, G. C., and Lange, P. M. *Attitudes of forest recreationists, other than firearm deer hunters, using experimental clearcuttings.* Michigan Department of Natural Resources, Wildlife Division Report No. 2748, 1975.

Larkin, P. A. Interspecific competition and population

control in freshwater fish. *Journal Fisheries Research Board of Canada*, 1956, 13, 327–342.

Larousse encyclopedia of animal life. New York: McGraw-Hill, 1967.

Lashley, K. L. In search of the engram. In F. Beach, D. Hebb, C. Morgan, and H. Nissen (Eds.), *The neuropsychology of Lashley.* New York: McGraw-Hill, 1960.

Laughlin, W. S. Hunting: An integrating biobehavior system and its evolutionary importance. In R. B. Lee and I. Devore (Eds.), *Man the hunter.* Chicago: Aldine Publishing Co., 1968.

Lazarus, A. A. *Behavior therapy and beyond.* New York: McGraw-Hill, 1971.

Lea, R. G., and Turner, J. R. Experiment on mimicry (Part II): The effect of a Batesian mimic on its model. *Behaviour*, 1972, *42*, 131–151.

Lefebvre, L., & Sabourin, M. Response differences in animal hypnosis: A hypothesis. *Psychological Record*, 1977, *27*, 77–88.

Legault, J. In the jaws of the white bear. *Outdoor Life*, April 1976, *157*(4), 68–69 and 150–156.

Lehner, G. F. J. A study of the extinction of unconditioned reflexes. *Journal of Experimental Psychology*, 1941, *29*, 435–456.

Lehrman, D. S. The physiological basis of parental feeding behavior in the ring dove (*Streptopelia risoria*). Behaviour, 1955, *7*, 241–286.

Leibrecht, B. C. Habituation, 1940–1970: Bibliography and key word index. *Psychonomic Monograph Supplements*, 1972, *4*, 189–217.

Leibrecht, B. C. Habituation: Supplemental bibliography. *Physiological Psychology*, 1974, *2*, 401–419.

Leibrecht, B. C., and Askew, H. R. Habituation of the head-shake response in the rat: Recovery, transfer, and changes in topography. *Journal of Comparative and Physiological Psychology*, 1969, *69*, 699–708.

Leibrecht, B. C., and Kemmerer, W. S. Varieties of habituation in the chinchilla (*Chinchilla lanigera*). *Journal of Comparative and Physiological Psychology*, 1974, *86*, 124–132.

Leon, M. and Moltz, H. Maternal phenomena: Discrimination by preweanling albino rats. *Physiology and Behavior*, 1971, *7*, 265–267.

Leon, M. and Moltz H. The development of the phenomenal bond in the albino rat. *Physiology and Behavior*, 1972, *8*, 683–686.

Leonard, C., Schneider, G. E., and Gross, C. J. Performance on learning set and delayed-response tasks by three shrews (Tupaia glis). *Journal of Comparative Physiological Psychology*, 1966, *62*, 501–504.

Leonard, D. E. Recent developments in ecology and control of the gypsy moth. *Annual Review of Entomology*, 1974, *19*, 197–229.

Leslie, J. C., and Garrud, P. Conditioned suppression of a positively reinforced shuttle response. *Animal Learning and Behavior*, 1976, *4*, 99–104.

Lett, B. T. Delayed reward learning: Disproof of the traditional theory. *Learning and Motivation*, 1973, *4*, 237–246.

Levine, R. L., Boling, R. H., and Higgs, G. K. Toward understanding the role of environmental variables on attractivity and recreational choice: A model for evaluating activity bundles. Unpublished report, Michigan State University, 1973.

Levine, R. L., Boling, R. H., and Higgs, G. K. Bundle theory and its application to recreational choice: A geographic model. *Man-Environment Systems*, 1975, *5*, 245–246.

Levine, S. (Ed.) *Hormones and behavior.* New York: Academic Press, 1972.

Lewontin, R. C. *The genetic basis of evolutionary change.* New York: Columbia University Press, 1974.

Leyhausen, P. The communal organization of solitary animals. *Symposium Zoological Society*, London, 1965, *14*, 249–263.

Leyhausen, P. *Verhaltensstudien an zatzen.* Berlin: Paul Parey, 1973.

Leyhausen, P. On the function of the relative hierarchy of moods (1965). Reprinted in K. Lorenz and P. Leyhausen, *Motivation of human and animal behavior: An ethological view* (translated by B. A. Tonkin). New York: Van Nostrand Reinhold, 1973.

Limbaugh, C. Cleaning symbiosis. *Scientific American*, 1961, *205*, 42–49.

Lincoln, F. C. *Migration of American birds.* New York; Doubleday, Doran, 1939.

Lindauer, M. *Communication among social bees.* Cambridge, Mass.: Harvard University Press, 1961.

Lindauer, M., and Martin, H. Die Schwerorientierung der Bienen unter dem Einfluss des Erdmagnetfeldes. *Zeitschrift vergleichend Physiologie*, 1968, *60*, 219–243.

Lindner, K. *The hunting book of Wolfgang Birkner*. A. Havlu and I. T. Havlu (Trns.) New York: Winchester Press, 1969.

Lindstedt, K. Chemical control of feeding Behavior. *Journal of Comparative Biochemistry & Physiology*, 1971, 39, 553–581.

Lipsitt, L. P., and Kaye, H. Change in neonatal response to optimizing and non-optimizing sucking stimulation. *Psychonomic Science*, 1965, *2*, 221–222.

Lissman, H. Electric location by fishes. *Scientific American*, 1963, *208*, 50–59.

Lloyd, J. E. Flashes, behavior and additional species of nearctic Photinus fireflies (Coleoptera: Lampyridae), *Coleoptera Bulletin*, 1969, *23*, 29–40.

Lloyd, J. E. Fireflies of Melanesia: bioluminescence, mating behavior, and synchronous flashing (Coleoptera: Lampyridae). *Anals of the Entomological Society of America*, 1973, *2*(6), 991–1008.

Lockard, R. B. The albino rat: A defensible choice or a bad habit? *American Psychologist*, 1968, *23*, 734–742.

Loizos, C. Play behavior in higher primates: A review. In Morris, D. (Ed.) *Primate ethology*. New York: Doubleday, 1969.

Lorenz, K. Der Kumpan in der Umwelt des Vogels. *Journal of Ornithology*, 1935, *83*, 137–213, 289–413.

Lorenz, K. Ueber die Bildung des Instiuktbegriffes. *Naturwissenschaften*, 1937, *25*, 289–300, 307–318, 324–331. English transl.: Studies in Animal and Human Behaviour, I. Cambridge, Mass.: Harvard University Press, 1970.

Lorenz, K. The comparative study of behavior (1939). In K. Lorenz and P. Leyhausen (Eds.), *Motivation of human and animal behavior: An ethological view* (translated by B. A. Tonkin) New York: Van Nostrand Reinhold, 1973.

Lorenz, K. Die angeborenen formen möglicher erfahrung. *Zeitschrift für Tierpsychologie*. 1943, *5*, 235–409.

Lorenz, K. The comparative method in studying innate behavior patterns. In Symposium of the Society for Experimental Biology. Vol. IV. *Physiological mechanisms in animal behavior*. London and New York: Cambridge University Press, 1950.

Lorenz, K. The nature of instinct. In C. E. Schiller (Ed.), *Instinctive behavior*. New York: International Universities Press, 1957.

Lorenz, K. *On aggression*. New York: Bantam Books, 1963.

Lorenz, K. *Evolution and modification of behavior*. Chicago: University of Chicago, 1965.

Lorenz, K. Innate bases of learning. In K. Pribram, (Ed.), *On the biology of learning*. New York: Harcourt, Brace, Jovanovich, 1969.

Lorenz, K. Comparative studies of the motor patterns of Anatinae. In K. Lorenz (Ed.), *Studies in animal and human behavior*. Vol. II. Cambridge, Mass., Harvard University Press, 1971.

Lorenz, R. Management and reproduction of the Goeldi's monkey *Callimico goeldii* (Thomas, 1904). Callimiconi dae, Primates, 1972. In D. D. Bridgewater (Ed.), *Saving the lion marmoset, proceedings of WAPT golden lion marmoset conference.*

Losey, G. S. Communication between fishes in cleaning symbiosis. In T. C. Cheng (Ed.), *Aspects of the biology of symbiosis*. Baltimore: University Park Press, 1971.

Losey, G. S. The ecological importance of cleaning symbiosis. *Copeia*, 1972, *4*, 820–833.

Losey, G. S. Cleaning symbiosis in Puerto Rico with comparison to the tropical Pacific. *Copeia*, 1974, *4*, 960–979.

Lott, D. F. Parental behavior. In G. Bermant, (Ed.), *Perspectives on animal behavior*. Glenville, Ill.: Scott, Foresman, 1973.

Lott, D. F., and Comerford, S. Hormonal initiation of parental behavior in inexperienced ring doves, *Zeitschrift für Tierpsychologie*. 1968, *25*, 71–75.

Lubow, R. E. Latent inhibition: Effects of frequency of nonreinforced preexposure of the CS. *Journal of Comparative and Physiological Psychology*, 1965, *66*, 688–694.

Lydell, K., and Doty, R. L. Male rat odor preferences for female urine as a function of sexual experience, urine age, and urine source. *Hormones and Behavior*, 1972, *3*, 205–212.

Lynn, R. *Attention, arousal and the orientation reaction*. New York: Pergamon Press, 1966.

Macan, T. *Freshwater ecology*. London; Longmans, 1963.

MacFarland, C., and Reeder, W. Cleaning symbiosis involving Galápagos tortoises and two species of Darwin's finches. *Zeitschrift für Tierpsychologie*, 1974, *34*, 464–483.

McFarland, D. J. *Feedback Mechanisms in Animal Behaviour*. New York: Academic Press, 1971.

McFarland, D. J. Stimulus relevance and homeostasis. In R. Hinde and J. Stevenson-Hinde (Eds.), *Constraints on learning*. New York: Academic Press, 1973.

McFarland, D. J. *Motivational control systems analysis*. New York: Academic Press, 1974.

Mackintosh, N. J. Stimulus selection: Learning to ignore stimuli that predict no change in reinforcement. In R. A. Hinde and J. Stevenson-Hinde (Eds.), *Constraints on learning*. London: Academic Press, 1973.

Mackintosh, N. J. *The psychology of animal learning*, New York; Academic Press, 1974.

McNamara, H. J. Long, J. B., and Wike, E. L. Learning without response under two conditions of external cues. *Journal of Comparative Physiological Psychology*, 1956, *49*, 477–480.

McNeil, E. R. *Human socialization*. Belmont, Calif.: Brooks/Cole, 1969.

McNiven, M. A. Social releaser mechanisms in birds. *Psychological Record*, 1960, *10*, 259–265.

Macrides, F. Olfactory influences on neuroendocrine function in mammals. In R. L. Doty (Ed.), *Mammalian olfaction, reproductive processes, and behavior*. New York: Academic Press, 1976.

Maier, N. R. F. Reasoning in white rats. *Comparative Psychological Monographs*, 1929, *6*, 1–93.

Maier, N. R. F., and Schneirla, R. C. *Principles of animal behavior*. New York: McGraw-Hill, 1935.

Maier, R. A., and Maier, B. M. *Comparative Animal Behavior*. Belmont, Calif. Brooks/Cole, 1970.

Makatsch, W. Der vogel und sein nest. *Akademische Verlagsgesellschaft*, Liepzig: Geest and Portig, 1950.

Markham, G. *Cavelarice; or the English horseman*. London: E. White, 1607.

Markham, G. *Hungers prevention: Or the whole art of fowling by water and land*. London: A. Mathewes, 1621.

Marler, P. Communication in monkeys and apes. In I. DeVore (Ed.), *Primate behavior*. Holt, Rinehart and Winston: New York, 1965.

Marshall, N. B. *The life of fishes*. World Publishing Co., Cleveland, 1966.

Martin, A., Zim, H, and Nelson, A. *American Wildlife and Plants: A Guide to Wildlife Food Habits*, New York, Dover Press, 1951.

Martin, P. S. and Wright, H. E., Jr. (Eds.) *Pleistocene extinctions*. New Haven: Yale University Press, 1967.

Martin, R. D. Reproduction and ontogeny in three shrews (*Tupaia belangeri*) with reference to their general behaviour and taxonomic relationships. *Zeitschrift für Tierpsychologie*, 1968, *25*, 409–495, 505–532.

Maruniak, J. A., Desjardins, C., and Bronson, F. H. Adaptations for urinary marking in rodents: Prepuce length and morphology. *Journal of Reproduction and Fertility*, 1975, *44*, 567–570.

Mason, P. R. Chemo-klino-kinesis in planarian food locations. *Animal Behaviour*, 1975, *23*, and 460–469.

Mason, W. A. The effects of social restriction on the behavior of rhesus monkeys: I. Free social behavior. *Journal of Comparative and Physiological Psychology*, 1960, *53*, 582–589.

Masserman, J. H. *Behavior and neurosis*. Chicago: University of Chicago Press, 1943.

Masters, W. H. and Johnson, V. E. *Human sexual inadequacy*. Boston: Little, Brown and Co., 1970.

Masur, J. D. Sex differences in "emotionality" and behavior of rats in the open-field. *Behavioral Biology*, 1972, *7*, 749–754.

Masur, J. D., and Gallup, G. G. TI and related phenomena: A partially annotated tricentennial bibliography (1636–1976). *Psychological Record*, 1977, *1*, 177–216.

Matthews, G. U. T. The orientation of pigeons as affected by the learning of landmarks and by the distance of displacement. *Animal Behaviour*, 1963, *11*, 310–317.

Maynard-Smith, J. The evolution of behavior. *Scientific American*, 1978, *239*(3), 176–192.

Mayr, E. *Population, species, and evolution*. Massachusetts: The Belknap Press of Harvard University Press, 1970.

Mech, L. D., & Peters, R. P. The study of chemical communication in free-ranging mammals. In D. Müller-Schwarze and M. M. Mozell (Eds.), *Chemical signals in vertebrates.* New York: Plenum, 1977.

Mewaldt, L. R. California sparrows return from displacement to Maryland. *Science,* 1964, *146,* 941–942.

Mewaldt, L. R., Morton, M. L., and Brown, I. L. Orientation of migratory restlessness in *Zonotrichia. Condor,* 1964, *66,* 377–417.

Meyer, D. R., Yutzey, D. A., and Meyer, P. M. Effects of neocortical ablations on relearning of a black white discrimination habit by two strains of rats. Unpublished manuscript, Ohio State University.

Meyers, W. J., McQuiston, M. D., and Miles, R. C. Delayed-response and learning set performance of cats. *Journal of Comparative and Physiological Psychology,* 1962, *55,* 515–517.

Michels, K. M., and Brown, D. R. The delayed-response performance of raccoons. *Journal of Comparative Physiological Psychology,* 1959, *52,* 737.

Michels, K. M., Pustek, J. J., Jr., and Johnson, J. I., Jr. The solution of patterned string problems by raccoons. *Journal of Comparative and Physiological Psychology,* 1961, *54,* 439–441.

Michener, Charles D. *The social behavior of the bees: A comparative study.* Cambridge, Mass.: Belknap Press of Harvard University, 1974.

Milgram, S. The experience of living in cities. *Science,* 1970, *167,* 146–1486.

Millar, R. D. Free-operant comparisons of wild and domestic Norway rats. *Journal of Comparative and Physiological Psychology,* 1975, *89,* 913–922.

Miller, N. E., and Stevenson, S. S. Agitated behavior of rats during experimental extinction and a curve of spontaneous recovery. *Journal of Comparative Psychology,* 1936, *21,* 205–231.

Milne, L., and Milne, M. *The mating insect.* New York: New American Library, Inc., 1954.

Mitchell, E. V. *The horse & buggy age in New England.* Ann Arbor, Mich.: Gryphon Books, 1971. Originally published 1937.

Mochi, U. and MacClintock D. *A natural hystory of giraffes.* New York: Charles Scribner's Sons, 1973.

Moisimann, J. E., and Martin, P. S. Simulating overkill by paleoindians. *American Scientist,* 1975, *63,* 304–313.

Moltz, H. Contemporary instinct theory and the fixed action pattern. *Psychological Review,* 1965, *72* 27–47.

Moltz, H. and Leon M. Stimulus control of the maternal pheromone in the lactating rat. *Physiology and Behavior,* 1973, *10,* 69–71.

Montagna, W., Ellis, R. A., and Silver, A. F. *Advances in biology of skin.* Vol. 4. Oxford: Pergamon Press, 1963.

Montgomery, D. J. Making the "quality of life" an operational concept. *Phi Kappa Phi Journal,* 1975, *55,* 46–51.

Moore, B. R. The role of directed Pavlovian reactions in simple instrumental learning in the pigeon. In R. A. Hinde and J. Stevenson-Hinde (Eds.), *Constraints on learning.* London: Academic Press, 1973.

Moos, R. H. *Evaluating correctional and community settings.* New York: Wiley-Interscience, 1975.

Moos, R. H. *The human context: Environmental determinants of behavior.* New York: Wiley-Interscience, 1976.

Morgan, C. L. *Introduction to comparative psychology.* London, England: Methuen, 1894.

Morgan, C. L. *Animal behaviour.* (2nd ed.) New York: Longmans, Green, 1908.

Morgan, P. D., Arnold, G. W. and Lindsay, D. R. A note on the mating behaviour of ewes with various senses impaired. *Journal of Reproduction and Fertility,* 1972, *30,* 151–152.

Morrell, L., and Morrell, F. Non-random oscillation in the response-duration curve of electrographic activation. *Electroencephalography and Clinical Neurophysiology,* 1962, *14,* 724–730.

Morris, D. The feather postures of birds and the problem of the origin of social signals. *Behaviour,* 1955, *9,* 75–112.

Morris, D. The function and causation of courtship ceremonies. In D. Morris (Ed.), *Patterns of reproductive behavior: Collected papers by Desmond Morris,* New York: McGraw-Hill Book Co., 1970(a).

Morris, D. The reproductive behavior of the zebra

finch. In D. Morris (Ed.). *Patterns of Reproductive Behavior: Collected Papers by Desmond Morris*, New York: McGraw-Hill Book Co., 1970(b).

Moss, F. A. (Ed.) Comparative psychology. New York: Prentice-Hall, 1942.

Moss, R. Food selection by red grouse (*Lagopus lagopus scoticus* (Lath.)) in relation to chemical composition. *Journal of Animal Ecology*, 1972, *41*, 411–428.

Mountjoy, P. T. Some early attempts to modify penile erection in horse and human; An historical analysis. *The Psychological Record*, 1974, *24*, 291–308.

Mountjoy, P. T. *The De arte venandi cum avibus* of Frederick II: A precursor of twentieth century behavioral psychology. *Studies in Medieval Culture*, 1976, VI and VII, 107–115.

Mountjoy, P. T., Bos, J. H., Duncan, M. O., and Verplank, R. B. Falconry: Neglected aspect of the history of psychology. *Journal of the History of the Behavioral Sciences*, 1969, *5*, 59–67.

Mowrer, O. H. *Learning theory and behavior.* New York: Wiley, 1960.

Mueller, H. C. Factors influencing prey selection in the American kestril. *Auk*, 1974, *91*, 705–921.

Mueller, H. C. Sunbathing in birds. *Zeitshrift Tierpsychology*, 1972, *30* 253–258.

Muller, K. Diurnal rhythms in "organic drift" of *Gammarus pulex. Nature*, 1963, *198*, 806–807.

Müller-Schwarze, D. Social significance of forehead rubbing in blacktailed deer (*Odocoileus hemionus columbianus*). *Animal Behaviour*, 1972, *20*, 788–797.

Müller-Schwarze, D. Complex mammalian behavior and pheromone bioassay in the field. In D. Müller-Schwarze and M. M. Mozell (Eds.), *Chemical signals in vertebrates*. New York: Plenum, 1977.

Müller-Schwarze, D., and Mozell, M. M. (Eds.) *Chemical signals in vertebrates.* New York: Plenum, 1977.

Murphy, M. R. Effects of female hamster vaginal discharge on the behavior of male hamsters. *Behavioral Biology*, 1973, *9*, 367–375.

Murray, M. D. The ecology of the louse *Polyplax serrata* (Blum) on the mouse mus musculus L. *Australian Journal of Zoology*, 1961, *9*, 1–13.

Mykytowycz, R. The role of skin glands in mammalian communication. In J. W. Johnston, Jr., D. G. Moulton, and A. Turk (Eds.), *Advances in chemoreception.* Vol. 1. *Communication by chemical signals.* N.Y.: Appleton-Century-Crofts, 1970.

Mykytowycz, R. Odor in the spacing behavior of mammals. In M. C. Birch (Ed.), *Pheromones.* Amsterdam: North-Holland Publishing Co., 1974.

Nachman, M. and Hartley, P. Role of illness in producing learned taste aversions in rats: A comparison of several rodenticides. *Journal of Comparative and Physiological Psychology*, 1975, *89*, 1010–1018.

Nelson, R. K. *Hunters of the northern ice.* Chicago: University of Chicago Press, 1969.

Nero, R. W. A behavior study of the red-winged blackbird. I. Mating and nesting activities. *Wilson Bulletin*, 1956, *68*, 4–37.

Nice, M. M. The role of territory in bird life. *American Midland Naturalist*, 1941, *26*, 441–87.

Nicholson, A. J. Experimental demonstrations of balance in populations. *Nature*, 1954, *173*, 862–863.

Nisbet, I. C. T. Studying migration by moon-watching. *Bird Migration*, 1961, *1*, 38–42.

Nisbet, I. C. T. Study on migration across the face of the moon. *Ardeola*, 1963, *8*, 5–17.

Nisbet, I. C. T., and Drury, W. H., Jr. A migration wave observed by moonwatching and at banding stations. *Bird-Banding*, 1969, *40*, 243–252.

Noble, G. K. Courtship and sexual selection of the flicker (*Colaptes auratus lutus*). *Auk*, 1936, *53*, 269–82.

Noble, G. K., and Curtis, B. The social behavior of the jewelfish, *Hemichromis bimaculatus. Bulletin American Museum National History*, 1939, *76*, 1–48.

Noble, G. K., and Vogt, W. An experimental study of sex recognition in birds. *Awk, 52*, 278–86, 1935.

Noble, G. K. & Wurm, M. The effect of testosterone propionate on the blackcrowned night heron. *Endocrinology*, 1940, *26*, 837–850.

Noirot, E. Changes in responsiveness to young in the adult mouse. I. The problematical effect of hormones. *Animal Behaviour*, 1964, *12*, 42–58.

Norgaard, E. Environment and behavior of *Theridion saxatile. Oikos* (Acta Oecologica Scandinavica) 1956, *7*(2), 159–192.

Nyby, J., Wysocki, C. J., Whitney, G., and Dizinno, G. Pheromonal regulation of male mouse ultrasonic courtship. (*Mus musculus*). *Animal Behaviour*, 1977, *25*, 333–341.

O'Boyle, M. Rats and mice together: The predatory nature of rats' mousekilling response. *Psychological Bulletin*, 1974, *81*, 261–269.

Odum, H. T. *Environment, power, and society*. New York: Wiley-Interscience, 1971.

Odum, H. T., and Odum, E. C. *Energy bases for man and nature*. New York: McGraw-Hill, 1976.

Oliver, J. A. *North American amphibians and reptiles*. New York: Van Nostrand, 1955.

Oliver, J. A. Reproduction in the king cobra, *Ophiophagus hanna*. *Zoologica*, 1956, *41*, 145–152.

Ommanney, F. D. and The Editors of Life. *The fishes*. New York: Life Nature Library, Time-Life Books, 1970.

Oppian of Corycos. fl. second century. *Cynegetica. Oppian: Colluthus, Tryphiodorus*. Translated by A. W. Mair. Cambridge, Mass.: Harvard University Press, 1958. Contains both *Cynegetica* and *Halieutica*.

Organ, J. Studies on the life history of the salamander, *Plethodon welleri*. *Copeia*, 1960, (4), 287–297.

Orr, R. T. *Mammals of North America*. New York: Doubleday & Co., 1970.

Overmann, S. Dietary self-selection by animals. *Psychological Bulletin*, 1976, *83*, 218–235.

Palmer, R. S. *The mammal guide*. New York: Doubleday, 1954.

Papi, F., and Tongiorgi, P. Innate and learned components in the astronomical orientation of the wolf spider. *Ergebnisse Biologische*, 1963, *26*, 259–280.

Partridge, B., Liley, N., and Stacey, N. The role of pheromones in the sexual behavior of the goldfish. *Animal Behaviour*, 1976, *24*, 291–299.

Pascal, G. R., Stolurow, L. M., Zabarenko, R. N., and Chambers, K. S. The delayed reaction in mental defectives. *American Journal of Mental Deficiency*, 1951, *56*, 152–160.

Pavlov, I. P. *Conditioned reflexes*. New York: Oxford University Press, 1927.

Payne, A. P., and Swanson, H. H. Agonistic behavior between pairs of hamsters of the same and opposite sex in a neutral observation area. *Behaviour*, 1970, *36*, 259–269.

Peek, F. W. An experimental study of the territorial function of vocal and visual displays in the male red-winged blackbird (*Agelaius phoeniceus*). *Animal Behaviour*, 1972 *20*, 112–118.

Peeke, H. V. S., and Herz, M. J. (Eds.) *Habituation*. Vol. I. *Behavioral studies*. New York: Academic Press, 1973.

Peeke, H. V. S., and Herz, M. J. (Eds.) *Habituation*. Vol. II. *Physiological substrates*. New York: Academic Press, 1973.

Peeke, H. V. S., and Peeke, S.C. Habituation, reinstatement and recovery of predatory responses in two species of teleosts, *Carassius auratus* and *Macropodus opercularis*. *Animal Behaviour*, 1972, *20*, 268–273.

Peeke, H. V. S., and Peeke, S. C. Habituation in fish with special reference to intraspecific aggressive behavior. In H. V. S. Peeke and M. J. Herz (Eds.), *Habituation*. Vol. I. *Behavioral Studies*. New York: Academic Press, 1973.

Pelkwijk, J. J., and Tinbergen, N. Eine reizbiologische Analyse einiger Verhaltensweisen von *Gasterosteus aculeatus* L. *Zeits Tierpsychol*, 1937, *1*, 193–204.

Pendergrass, V. E., and Kimmel, H. D. UCR diminution in temporal conditioning and habituation. *Journal of Experimental Psychology*, 1968, *77*, 1–7.

Pennak, R. W. An effective method of diagramming diurnal movement of zooplankton organisms. *Ecology*, 1943, *24*, 405–407.

Perkins, C. C., Jr. The relations of secondary reward to gradients of reinforcement. *Journal of Experimental Psychology*, 1947, *37*, 377–392.

Petrinovich, L. A species-meaningful analysis of habituation. In H. V. S. Peeke and M. J. Herz (Eds.), *Habituation*. Vol I. *Behavioral studies*. New York: Academic Press, 1973.

Pfungst, O. 1911. *Clever Hans*. Translated by C. L. Rahn. New York: Henry Holt and Co. Reissued: New York: Holt, Rinehart and Winston, 1965.

Phillips, R. E. Sexual and agonistic behavior in the kildeer (*charadrius vociferus*). *Animal Behaviour*, 1972, *20*, 1–9.

Phillips, R. E., and Youngren, O. M. Brain stimulation and species-typical behavior: activities evoked by electrical stimulation of the brains of chickens (*Gallus gallus*). *Animal Behaviour*, 1971, *19*, 757–779.

References

Pietrewicz, A. T. and Kamil, A. C. Visual detection of cryptic prey by blue jays (*Cyanocitta cristata*). *Science*, 1977, *195*, 580–582.

Pinchbeck, W. F. *The expositor: Or many mysteries unravelled*. Boston: Printed for the author, 1805.

Pinckney, G. A. The effect of intertrial interval on avoidance learning in fish. *Psychonomic Science*, 1966, *6*, 497–498.

Platt, J. Social traps, *American Psychologist*, 1973, *28*, 641–651.

Plomin, R., DeFries, J. C., and Roberts, M. K. Assortative mating by unwed biological parents of adopted children. *Science*, 1977. *196*. 449–450.

Polsky, R. H. Hunger, prey feeding, and prey aggression. *Behavioral Biology*, 1975, *13*, 81–93.

Pomerantz, G. A. *Young peoples attitudes towards wildlife*. Michigan Department of Natural Resources, Wildlife Division Report No. 2781, 1977.

Porter, R. H., and Etscorn, F. A sensitive period for the development of olfactory preferences in *Acomys cahirinus*. *Physiology and behavior*, 1976, *17*, 127–130.

Potratz, H. A. *Das Pferd in der Fruehzeit*. Rostock: Carl Hinstorffs Verlag, 1938.

Potter, E. F., and Hauser, D. C. Relationship of anting and sandbathing to molting in wild birds. *The Auk*, 1974, *91*, 537–563.

Precht, H., and Freytag, G. (On the aspects of fatigue and inhibition of innate behavior in jumping spiders (Salticidae). Also a contribution to the problem of instinct.) *Behaviour*, 1958, *13*, 143–211. (In German.)

Prechtl, H. F. R. The directed head turning response and allied movements of the human baby. *Behaviour*, 1958, *13*, 212–240.

Premack, D. *Intelligence in ape and man*. Hillsdale, New Jersey: Erlbaum, 1976.

Premack, D. Reinforcement theory. In D. Levine (Ed.), *Nebraska symposium on motivation*. Lincoln, Neb.: University of Nebraska Press, 1965.

Pressman, I., and Carol, A. Crime as a diseconomy of scale. *Review of Social Economy*, 1971, *29*, 227–236.

Prestrude, A. M. Some phylogenetic comparisons to TI with special reference to habituation and fear. *Psychological Record*, 19771, 21–40.

Prewitt, E. P. Number of preconditioning trials in sensory preconditioning using CER training. *Journal of Comparative and Physiological Psychology*, 1967, *64*, 360–62.

Price, E. O. The laboratory animal and its environment. In T. McSheeny (Ed.), *Control of the animal house environment* (Laboratory Animal Handbook No. 7). London: Laboratory Animals Ltd., 1976.

Price, P. W. *Insect ecology*. New York; Wiley, 1975.

Prosser, C. L., and Hunter, W. S. The extinction of startle responses and spinal reflexes in the white rat. *American Journal of Physiology*, 1936, *117*, 609–618.

Prosser, C. L., and Nagai, J. Effects of low temperature on conditioning in goldfish. In D. Ingle (Ed.), *The Central Nervous System and Fish Behavior*, Chicago: University of Chicago Press, 1968.

Pulliam, H. On the theory of optimal diets. *American Naturalist*, 1974, *108*, 59–74.

Quay, W. B. Seasonal and sexual differences in the dorsal skin gland of the kangaroo rat (*Dipodomys*). *Journal of Mammalogy*, 1953, *34*, 1–14.

Quay, W. B. The specialized posterolateral sebaceous glandular regions in microtine rodents. *Journal of Mammalogy*, 1968, *49*, 427–445.

Quay, W. B., and Tomich, P. Q. A specialized midventral sebaceous glandular area in *Rattus exulans*. *Journal of Mammalogy*, 1963, *44*, 537–542.

Rachman, S. Sexual fetishism: An experimental analogue. *Psychological Record*, 1966, 16, 293–296.

Rackmam, D. W. *Conditioning of the pigeon's courtship and aggressive behavior*. Unpublished master's thesis, Dalhousie University, 1971.

Radcliffe, W. *Fishing from the earliest times*. Chicago: Ares Publishers, 1974. Originally published 1921.

Ralls, K. Mammalian scent marking. *Science*, 1971, *171*, 443–449.

Ramsay, O. A., and Hess, E. H. A laboratory approach to the study of imprinting. *Wilson Bulletin*, 1954, *66*, 196–206.

Rapoport, A. Toward a redefinition of density. *Environment and Behavior*, 1975, *7*, 133–158.

Rappaport, D. An optimization model of food selection. *American Naturalist*, 1971, *105*, 575–587.

Raths, L. *Values and teaching*. Columbus, Ohio: Charles Merrill, 1966.

Ratner, S. C. Comparative aspects of hypnosis. In J. E.

Gordon (Ed.), *Handbook of clinical and experimental hypnosis*. New York: Macmillan, 1967.

Ratner, S. C. Reliability of indexes of worm learning. *Psychological Report*, 1968, *22*, 130.

Ratner, S. C. Habituation: Research and theory. In J. H. Reynierse (Ed.), *Current issues in animal learning*. Lincoln, Neb.: University of Nebraska Press, 1970.

Ratner, S. C. Kinetic movements in magnetic fields of chitons with ferro-magnetic structures. *Behavioral Biology*, 1976, *17*, 573–578.

Ratner, S. C. Immobility of invertebrates: What can we learn? *Psychological Record*, 1977, *1*, 1–14.

Ratner, S. C., and Boice, R. Effects of domestication on behaviour. In E. S. E. Hafez (Ed.), *Behaviour of domestic animals*. (3rd ed.) Baltimore: Williams & Wilkins, 1975.

Ratner, S. C., and Denny, M. R. *Comparative psychology*. Homewood, Ill. Dorsey, 1964.

Ratner, S. C., and VanDeventer, J. M. Effects of water current on responses of planaria to light. *Journal of comparative and physiological Psychology*, 1965, *60*, 138–140.

Razran, G. Raphael's "Idealess" behavior. *Journal of Comparative Physiological Psychology*, 1961, *54*, 366–367.

Recher, H., and Recher, J. Comparative foraging efficiency of adult and immature little blue herons (*Florida caerulea*). *Animal Behavior*, 1969, *17*, 320–322.

Reilly, W. J. *The law of retail gravitation*. New York: W. J. Reilly, 1931.

Regnier, F. E., and Goodwin, M. On the chemical and environmental modulation of pheromone release from vertebrate scent marks. In D. Müller-Schwarze and M. M. Mozell (Eds.), *Chemical signals in vertebrates*. New York: Plenum, 1977.

Rescorla, R. A. Pavlovian conditioning and its proper control procedures. *Psychological Review*, 1967, *74*, 71–80.

Rescorla, R. A. Conditioned inhibition of fear. In N. J. Mackintosh and W. K. Honig (Eds.), *Fundamental issues in associative learning*. Halifax: Dalhousie University Press, 1969.

Revusky, S., and Bedarf, E. Association of illness with prior ingestion of novel foods. *Science*, 1967, *155*, 219–220.

Revusky, S., and Garcia, J. Learned associations over long delays. In G. Bower (Ed.), *The psychology of learning and motivation: Advances in research and theory*. Vol. 4. New York: Academic Press, 1970.

Rheingold, H. *Maternal behavior in mammals*. New York: Wiley, 1963.

Rheinwald, G., and Gutscher, H. Dispersion and Ortstreue der Mehlschwalbe (*Delichon urbica*). *Vogelwelt*, 1969, *90*, 121–140.

Richardson, H. M. The growth of adaptive behavior in infants. *Genetic Psychology Monographs*, 1932, *12*, 195–357.

Richter, C. Increased salt appetite in adrenalectomized rats. *American Journal of Physiology*, 1936, *115*, 155–161.

Richter, C. Domestication of the Norway rat and its implications for the problems of stress. *Proceedings of the Association for Research in Nervous and Mental Diseases*, 1949, *29*, 19–47.

Richter, C. Experimentally produced reactions to food poisoning in wild and domesticated rats. *Annals of the New York Academy of Science*, 1953, *56*, 225–239.

Richter, C. Rats, man and the welfare state. *American Psychologist*, 1959, *14*, 18–28.

Richter, C. Experiences of a reluctant rat-catcher: The common Norway rat — friend or enemy? *Proceedings of the American Philosophical Society*, 1968, *112*, 403–415.

Richter, C., and Mosier, H. D. Maximum sodium chloride intake and thirst in domesticated and wild Norway rats. *American Journal of Physiology*, 1954, *176*, 213–222.

Riege, W. H., and Cherkin, A. One trial learning in goldfish: Temperature dependence. *Communications in Behavioral Biology*, 1971, *7*, 255–263.

Riesen, A. H., Greenberg, B., Granston, A. H., and Fantz, R. L. Solutions of patterned strings problems by young gorillas. *Journal of Comparative Physiological Psychology*, 1953, *46*, 19–22.

Riley, A. L., and Baril, L. L. Conditioned taste aversions: A bibliography. *Animal Learning and Behavior*, 1976, *4*(1B), 1S–13S.

Rilling, M., and Caplan, H. J. Extinction induced aggression during errorless discrimination learning.

Journal of the Experimental Analysis of Behavior, 1973, *20*, 85–92.

Rizley, R. C., and Rescorla, R. A. Associations in second-order conditioning and sensory preconditioning. *Journal of Comparative and Physiological Psychology*, 1972, *81*, 1–11.

Roberts, W. W. Hypothalamic mechanisms for motivational and species-typical behavior. In R. E. Whalen, R. F. Thompson, M. Verzano, and N. M. Weinberger (Eds.), *The neural control of behavior*. New York: Academic Press, 1970.

Rodgers, W. L., Melzack, R., and Segal, J. R. "Tail flip response" in goldfish. *Journal of Comparative and Physiological Psychology*, 1963, *56*, 917–923.

Roeder, K. D. An experimental analysis of the sexual behavior of the praying mantis. *Biological Bulletin*, 1935, *69*, 203–220.

Rogers, C. R. *On becoming a person*. Boston: Houghton Mifflin Co., 1961.

Rogers, J. G., and Beauchamp, G. K. Some ecological implications of primer chemical stimuli in rodents. In R. L. Doty (Ed.), *Mammalian olfaction, reproductive processes, and behavior*. New York: Academic Press, 1976.

Rohles, F. H., Jr., and Devine, J. V. Chimpanzee performance on a problem involving the concept of middleness. *Animal Behaviour*, 1966, *14*, 159–162.

Rohrmann, G. P. Misleading mantids. *Natural History*, 1977, *86*(3) 66–71.

Rokeach, M. *Beliefs, attitudes and values*. San Francisco: Jossey-Bass, 1968.

Rokeach, M. *The nature of human values*. New York: The Free Press, 1974.

Romanes, G. J. *Animal intelligence*. New York: Appleton, 1912.

Roper, T. J. and Polioudakis, E. The behaviour of Mongolian gerbils in a semi-natural environment, with special reference to ventral marking, dominance, and sociability. *Behaviour*, 1977, *LXI*, 207–237.

Root, A. I. *The ABC of bee culture*. Medina, Ohio: The A. I. Root Company, 1901.

Roots, Betty. The water relations of earthworms. II. Resistance to desiccation and immersion, and behavior when submerged and when allowed a choice of environment. *Journal of Experimental Biology*, 1956, *33*, 29–43.

Rose, R. M., Gordon, T. P., and Bernstein, I. S. Plasma testosterone levels in the male rhesus: Influences of sexual and social stimuli. *Science*, 1972, *178*, 643–645.

Rosenblatt, J. & Lehrman, S. Maternal behavior of the laboratory rat. In H. Rheingold, (Ed.), *Maternal behavior in mammals*. New York: Wiley, 1963.

Ross, M., Layton, B., Erickson, B., and Schopler, J. Affect, facial regard and reactions to crowding. *Journal of Personality and Social Psychology*, 1973, *28*, 68–76.

Ross, S., Sawin, P. B., Zarrow, M. X., & Denenberg, V. H. Maternal behavior in the rabbit. In H. Rheingold (Ed.), *Maternal behavior in mammals*. New York: Wiley, 1963.

Ross, W. D. *The student's Oxford Aristotle*. Vol. III. *Psychology*, London, England: Oxford University Press, 1942.

Roth, L. L., and Rosenblatt, J. S. Changes in self-licking during pregnancy in the rat. *Journal of Comparative and Physiological Psychology*, 1967, *63*, 97–400.

Roth, L. M., and Willis, E. R. The reproduction of cockroaches. *Smithsonian Miscellaneous Collection*, 1954, *122*, 1–49.

Rovner, J. S. Copulation by sperm induction by normal and palpless male linyphiic spiders. *Science*, 1967, *157*, 835.

Rovner, J. S. Copulation in the lycosid spider (*Lycosa rabida* walckenaer). *Animal Behaviour*, 1972, *20*, 133–138.

Rowell, C. H. F. Displacement grooming in the chaffinch. *Animal Behaviour*, 1961, *9*, 38–63.

Rowell, T. *Social behavior of monkeys*. Baltimore: Penguin Books, 1974.

Rozin, P. The use of poikilothermy in the analysis of behavior. In D. Ingle (Ed.), *The central nervous system and fish behavior*, Chicago: University of Chicago Press, 1968.

Rozin, P. Adaptive food sampling patterns in vitamin deficient rats. *Journal of Comparative and Physiological Psychology*, 1969, *69*, 126–132.

Rozin, P. The selection of foods by rats, humans, and

other animals. *Advances in the Study of Behavior*, 1976, *6*, 21–76.

Rozin, P., and Kalat, J. Specific hungers and poison avoidance as adaptive specializations of learning. *Psychological Review*, 1971, *78*, 459–486.

Rudy, J. W., and Cheatle, D. Ontogeny of associat learning: Acquisition of odor aversions by neonatal rats. In N. E. Spear and B. A. Campbell (Eds.), *Ontogeny of learning and memory*. Hillsdale, N.J. Laurence Erlbaum Assoc., 1977.

Ruhen, O. *Harpoon*. New York: Norden Publications, 1966.

Rumbaugh, D. M. *Language learning by a chimpanzee*. New York: Academic Press, 1977.

Rushforth, N. B. Behavioral studies of the coelenterate *Hydra pirardi* Brien. *Animal Behaviour Supplement*, 1965, *1*, 30–42.

Russell, E. M. Changes in the behaviour of *Lebistes reticulatus* upon a repeated shadow stimulus. *Animal Behaviour*, 1967, *15*, 574–585.

Saegert S., Mackintosh, E., and West, S. Two studies of crowding in urban public places. *Environment and Behavior*, 1975, *7*, 159–184.

Sales, G. D., Ultrasound and mating behavior in rodents with some observations on other behavioral situations. *Journal Zoological Society London*. 1972. *168*, 149–164.

Salonen, A. *Hippologica Accadia*. Helsinki: Suomalainen Tiedeakatema, 1955.

Sargeant, A. B., & Eberhardt, L. E. Death feigning in ducks in response to predation by red foxes. *American Midland Naturalist*, 1975, *94*, 108–119.

Sa: Rid. *The art of jugling or legerdemine*. London: 1612.

Sato, R., Hiyama, Y., and Kajihara, T. The role of olfaction in return of chum salmon, *Oncorhynchus keta* (Walbaum) to its parent stream. *Proceedings 11th Pacific Science Congress, Tokyo*, 1966.

Schaller, G. B. *The mountain gorilla*. Chicago: University of Chicago Press, 1963.

Schaller, G. B. The behavior of the mountain gorilla. In I. DeVore (Ed.), *Primate behavior: Field studies of monkeys and apes*. New York: Holt, Rinehart and Winston, 1965.

Schaller, G. B. *The deer and the tiger*. Chicago: University of Chicago Press, 1967.

Schaller, G. B. *Serengeti lions: A study of predator-prey relations*. Chicago: University of Chicago Press, 1972.

Schalock, R. L., and Klopfer, F. D. Phenylketonuria: Enduring behavioral deficits in phenylketonuric rats. *Science*, 1967, *155*, 1033–1035.

Schein, M. W. (Ed.) *Social hierarchy and dominance*. Benchmark Papers in Animal Behavior. Vol. 3. Stroudsburg, Penn.: Dowden, Hutchinson & Ross, Inc., 1975.

Schein, M. W. Borchelt, P. L., and Statkiewitz, W. Paper presented at XVth International Ethological Conference, Bielefeld, Germany, 1977.

Schein, M. W., and Hale, E. B. Stimuli eliciting sexual behavior. In F. A. Beach (Ed.), *Sex and behavior*. New York: John Wiley & Sons, Inc., 1965.

Schilcher, F. von The role of auditory stimuli in the courtship of Drosophila *melanogaster*. *Animal Behaviour*, 1976, *24*, 18–26.

Schiller, C. H. *Instinctive behavior*. New York: International Universities Press, 1957.

Schinckel, P. G. The effect of the ram on the incidence and occurrence of oestrus in ewes. *Australian Veterinary Journal*, 1954, *30*, 189–195.

Schlosberg, H., and Katz, A. Double alternation leverpressing in the white rat. *American Journal of Psychology*, 1943; *56*, 274–282.

Schneider, B. *The grizzly: Is he villian or victim? Outdoor Life*, January 1977; 159, 53–54, 128–129.

Schneirla, T. C. Learning and orientation in ants. *Comparative Psychological Monographs*, 1929, *6*, 143.

Schoettle, H. F. T., and Schein, M. W. Sexual reactions of male turkeys to deviations from a normal female head model. *Anatomical Record*, 1959, *134*, 635 (abstract).

Schole, B. J., Glover, T., Sjogren, D., and Decker, E. Colorado hunter behavior, attitudes and philosophies. In J. C. Hendee and C. Schoenfeld (Eds.), *Human dimensions in wildlife programs*. Washington, D.C.: Wildlife Management Institute, 1973.

Schoonhaven, L., and Derksen-Koppers, L. Effects of secondary plant substances on drinking behavior in some heteroptera. *Entomolgia Experimentalis et Applicata*, 1973, *16*, 141–145.

References

Schrier, A. M., and Povar, M. L. Eye-movements of monkeys during learning-set formation. *Science*, 1978, *199*, 1362–1364.

Scott, J. W. A study of the phylogenetic or comparative behavior of three species of grouse. *Annals of the New York Academy of Sciences*, 1950, *51*(6), 1062–1073.

Scott, J. P. *Animal behavior*. Chicago: University of Chicago Press, 1958.

Scott, J. P., and Fuller, J. L. *Genetics of the social behavior of the dog.* Chicago: University of Chicago Press, 1965.

Selander, R. K., Sexual selection and dimorphism in birds. In B. Campbell (Ed.), *Sexual selection and the descent of man, 1871–1971*. Chicago: Aldine Publishing Co., 1972.

Selander, R. K., and LaRue, C. J. Interspecific preening invitation display of parasitic cowbirds. *The Auk*, 1961, *78*, 473–504.

Seidel, R. J. A review of sensory preconditioning. *Psychological Bulletin*, 1959, *56*, 58–73.

Seligman, M. E. On the generality of the laws of learning. *Psychological Review*, 1970, *77*, 406–418.

Seligman, M. E. *Helplessness: On depression, development and death*, San Francisco: W. H. Freeman, 1975.

Seligman, M. E. P., and Hager, J. L. (Eds.) *Biological boundaries of learning*. Englewood Cliffs, N.J.: Prentice-Hall, 1972.

Seligman, M. E. P., and Maier, S. F. Failure to escape traumatic shock. *Journal of Experimental Psychology*, 1967, *74*, 1–9.

Shaler, N. S. *Domesticated animals*. New York: Charles Scribner's Sons, (1895).

Shaw, W. W. *Attitudes toward hunting: A study of some social and psychological determinants*. Michigan Department of Natural Resources, Wildlife Division Report No. 2740, 1975.

Shepard, J. F. An unexpected cue in maze learning. *Psychological Bulletin*, 1929, *26*, 164–165.

Shepard, J. F. More learning. *Psychological Bulletin*, 1931, *28*, 240–241.

Sherif, M., and Sherif, C. W. (Eds.) *Interdisciplinary relationships in the social sciences*. Chicago: Aldine, 1969.

Shettleworth, S. J. Reinforcement and the organization of behavior in Golden Hamsters: Hunger, environment and food reinforcement. *Journal of Experimental Psychology: Animal Behavior Processes*, 1975, *104*(1), 56–87.

Shinn, A. M. An application of psychophysical scaling techniques to the measurement of national power. *Journal of Politics*, 1969, *31*, 932–951.

Shorey, H. H., and Bartell, R. J. Role of a volatile female sex pheromone in stimulating male courtship behavior in *Drosophila melanogaster*. *Animal Behaviour*, 1970, *18*, 159–164.

Siegel, S. Effect of CS habituation on eyelid conditioning. *Journal of Comparative and Physiological Psychology*, 1969, *68*, 245–248.

Simmons, K. E. L. Feather maintenance. In A. L. Thomson, (Ed.), *A new dictionary of birds*. London: Nelson, 1964.

Simmons, K. E. L. Anting and the problem of self-stimulation. *Journal of Zoology*, 1966, *149*, 145–162.

Simons, L. A., Dunlop, C. W., Webster, W. R., and Aitkin, L. M. Acoustic habituation in cats as a function of stimulus rate and the role of temporal conditioning of the middle ear muscles. *Electroencephalography and Clinical Neurophysiology*, 1966, *20*, 485–493.

Skeen, J. T., and Thiessen, D. D. Scent of gerbil cuisine. *Physiology and Behavior*, 1977, *19*, 11–14.

Skinner, B. F. *The behavior of organisms*. New York: Appleton, 1938.

Skinner, B. F. *Science and human behavior*. New York: Macmillan, 1953.

Skinner, B. F. Pigeons in a pelican. *American Psychologist*, 1960, *15*, 28–37.

Skinner, B. F. The phylogeny and ontogeny of behavior. *Science*, 1966. *153*, 1205–1213.

Skinner, B. F. The shaping of phylogenetic behavior. *Journal of the Experimental Analysis of Behavior*, 1975, *24*, 117–120.

Skutch, A. F. *Parent birds and their young*. Austin, Texas: University of Texas Press, 1976.

Slobodkin, L. B. Prudent predation does not require group selection. *American Naturalist*, 1974, *10*, 665–678.

Small, W. S. Experimental study of the mental processes of the rat. II. *American Journal of Psychology*, 1901, *12*, 206–239.

Smigel, B., and Rosenzweig, M. Seed selection in *Dipodomys merriami* and *Perognathus penicillatus*. *Ecology*, 1974, *55*, 329–339.

Smith, D. G. The role of the epaulets in the red-winged blackbird (*Agelaius phoeniceus*) social system. *Behaviour*, 1972, *41*, 251–268.

Smith, N. G. Adaptation to cliff-nesting in some artic gulls. *Ibis*, 1966, *108*, 68–83.

Smith, R. J., and Hoar, W. S. The effects of prolactin and testosterone on the parental behavior of the male stickleback *Gasterosteus aculiatus*. *Animal Behavior*, 1967, *15*, 342–352.

Sokal, R. R., and Sneath, P. H. A. *Principles of numerical taxonomy*. San Francisco: Freeman, 1963.

Southern, W. E. Homing of Purple Martins. *Wilson Bulletin*, 1959, *71*, 254–261.

Sparks, J. H. On the role of allopreening invitation behaviour in reducing aggression among red adadavats, with comments on its evolution in the Spermestidae. *Proceedings Zoological Society of London*, 1965, *145*(3), 387–403.

Spearman, R. I. C. *The integument: A textbook of skin biology*. London: Cambridge University Press, 1973.

Spence, K. W. *Behavior theory and conditioning*. New Haven: Yale University Press, 1956.

Spragg, S. D. S. Anticipation as a factor in maze errors. *Journal of Comparative Psychology*, 1933, *15*, 313–329.

Sprague, R. H., & Anisko, J. J. Elimination patterns in the laboratory beagle. *Behaviour*, 1973, *XLVII*, 257–267.

Stager, K. The role of olfaction in food location by the turkey vulture (*Cathartes aura*). *Los Angeles County Museum Contributions in Science*, No. 81, 1964.

Stahl, J. M., and Ellen, P. Septal lesions and reasoning performance in the rat. *Journal of Comparative and Physiological Psychology*, 1973, *84*, 629–638.

Stahl, J. M., and Ellen, P. Factors in the reasoning performance of the rat. *Journal of Comparative and Physiological Psychology*, 1974, *87*, 598–604.

Steel, E. A., and Hinde, R. A. Effects of exogenous oestrogen on brood patch development of intact and ovariectomized canaries. *Nature*, 1964, *202*, 718–719.

Steinberg, J. and Bindra, D. Effects of pregnancy and salt-intake on genital licking. Journal of Comparative and Physiological Psychology, 1962, *55*(1), 103–106.

Steiner, A. Etude du comportement predateur d'an Hyménoptère Sphégien, *Liris nigra* V. d. L. *Annales des Sciences Naturelles Zoologie et Biologie Animale*, 1962, 12, *4*, 1–126.

Steiner, A. L. Body-rubbing, marking and other scent-related behavior in some ground squirrels (Sciuridae), A descriptive study. *Canadian Journal of Zoology*, 1974, *52*, 889–906.

Stern, J. J. Responses of male rats to sex odors. *Physiology and Behavior*, 1970, *5*, 519–524.

Stern, J. J., and Merari, A. The bathing behavior of the chinchilla: Effects of deprivation. *Psychonomic Science*, 1969, *14*, 115.

Sternthal, D. Olfactory and visual cues in the feeding behavior of the leopard frog (*Rana pipiens*). *Zeitschrift für Tierpsychologie*, 1974, *34*, 239–246.

Stewart, J. S. Clarifying values clarification; A critique. *Phi Delta Kappan*, 1975, *56*, 684–688.

Stoddart, D. M. The lateral scent organs of *Arvicola terrestris* (Rodentia: Microtinae). *Journal of Zoology* (London), 1972, *166*, 49–54.

Stoddart, D. M. The role of odor in the social biology of small mammals. In M. C. Birch (Ed.), *Pheromones*. New York: American Elsevier, 1974.

Stoddart, D. M., Aplin, R. T., and Wood, M. J. Evidence for social difference in the flank organ secretion of *Arvicola terrestris* (Rodentia: Microtinae). *Journal of Zoology* (London), 1975, *177*, 529–540.

Stokes, A. W., Courtship feeding calls in Gallinaceous birds. *Auk*, 1972, *89*, 177–180.

Stokes, A. W., (Ed.) *Territory*. Stroudsburg, Penn.: Dowden, Hutchinson & Ross, Inc., 1974.

Stokes, A. W., and Williams, H. W., Courtship feeding in gallinaceous birds. *Auk*, 1971, *88*, 543–559.

Stokols, D. On the distinction between density and crowding: Some implications for future research. *Psychological Review*, 1972, *79*, 275–277.

Stone, C. P. Wildness and savageness in rats of different strains. In K. S. Lashley (Ed.), *Studies in the dynamics of behavior*. Chicago: University of Chicago Press, 1932.

Stone, C. P. Introduction. In C. P. Stone (Ed.),

References

Comparative psychology. (3rd ed.) Englewood Cliffs, N.J.: Prentice-Hall, 1951.

Stout, J. F., The significance of sound production during the reproductive behavior of *Notorpis analostanus* (Family Cyprinidae). *Animal Behaviour*, 1963, *11*, 83–92.

Stricker, E. & Wilson, N. Salt-seeking behavior in rats following acute sodium deficiency. *Journal of Comparative and Physiological Psychology*, 1970, *72*, 416–420.

Strong, P. N., Jr. Comparative studies in simple oddity learning: II Children, adults and seniles. *Psychonomic Science*, 1966 *6*, 459–460.

Sullivan, C. M. Temperature recognition and response in fish. *Journal of Fisheries Research Board of Canada*, 1954, *11*, 153–170.

Summerlin, C. T., and Wolfe, J. L. Social influences on trap responses of the cotton rat, *Sigmodon hispidus*. *Ecology*, 1973, *54*, 1156–1159.

Swanson, H. Sex differences in behavior of the Mongolian gerbil (*Meriones unguiculatus*) in encounters between pairs of same or opposite sex. *Animal* Behaviour, 1974, *22*, 638–644.

Szebenyi, A. L. Cleaning behaviour in Drosophila melanogaster. *Animal Behaviour*, 1969, *17*, 641–651.

Szlep, R. Change in the response of spiders to repeated web vibrations. *Behaviour*, 1964, *23*, 203–238.

Taylor, J. *Pondoro: Last of the ivory hunters.* New York: Simon and Schuster, 1955.

Tavolga, W. N. Visual, chemical and sound stimuli as cues in the sex discriminatory behavior of the gobiid fish, *Bathygobius soporator, Zoologica*, 1956, *41*, 49–64.

Tavolga, W. N. Underwater sounds produced by males of the blenniid fish, *Chasmodes bosquianus*. *Ecology*, 1958, *39*, 759–760.

Tavolga, W. N. Sound production and underwater communication in fishes. In W. E. Lanyon and W. M. Tavolga (Eds.), *Animal sounds and communication*, Washington, D.C.: AIBS, 1960.

Teale, E. W. (Ed.). *The insect world of J. Henri Fabré* New York: Dodd, Mead, and Co., 1949.

Ternes, J. W. Circadian susceptibility of animal hypnosis. *Psychological Record*, 1977, *1*, 15–20.

Thiessen, D. D. The relation of social position and wounding to exploratory behavior and organ weights in house mice. *Journal of Mammalogy*, 1966, *47*, 28–34.

Thiessen, D. D., Friend, H. C., and Lindzey, G. Androgen control of territorial marking in the Mongolian gerbil. *Science*, 1968, *160*, 432–433.

Thiessen, D. D., Lindzey, G., and Nyby, J. The effects of olfactory deprivation and hormones on territorial marking in the male Mongolian gerbil. (*Meriones unguiculatus*). *Hormones and Behavior*, 1970, *1*, 315–325.

Thiessen, D. D., and Rice, M. Mammalian scent gland marking and social behavior. *Psychological Bulletin*, 1976, *83*, 505–539.

Thiessen, D. D., and Rodgers, D. A. Population density and endocrine function *Psychological Bulletin*, 1961, *58*, 441–451.

Thiessen, D. D., Yahr, P., and Owen, K. Regulatory mechanisms of territorial marking in the Mongolian gerbil. *Journal of Comparative and Physiological Psychology*, 1973, *82*, 382–393.

Thompson, R. F., and Spencer, W. A. Habituation: A model phenomenon for the study of neuronal substrates of behavior. *Psychological Review*, 1966, *73*, 16–43.

Thompson, R. K. R., & Herman, L. M. Memory for lists of sounds by the bottle-nosed dolphin: Convergence of memory processes with humans? *Science*, 1977, *195*, 501–502.

Thompson, T., and Sturm, T. Classical conditioning of aggressive display in Siamese fighting fish. *Journal of the Experimental Analysis of Behavior*, 1965, *8*, 397–403.

Thorndike, E. L. *Animal intelligence: An experimental study of the associative powers in animals.* New York: Columbia University Press, 1898.

Thorndike, E. L. *The psychology of learning.* New York: Teachers College, 1913.

Thorpe, W. H. Bird song: The biology of vocal communication and expression in birds. *Cambridge Monographs in Experimental Biology*, 1961, *12*, 129–136.

Thorpe, W. H. *Learning and instinct in animals.* Cambridge, Mass.: Harvard University Press, 1963. Originally published 1956 (Methuen).

Tiefer, L. Gonadal hormones and mating behavior in the adult golden hamster. *Hormones and Behavior*, 1970, *1*, 189–202.

Timms, A. M., and Kleerekoper, H. The locomotor

References

response of male *Ictalurus punctatus*, the channel catfish, to a pheromone released by the ripe female of the species. *Transaction American Fish Society*, 1972, *102*(2), 302–310.

Tinbergen, N. *The Study of Instinct*. Oxford: Clarendon Press, 1951.

Tinbergen, N. *Social Behavior in Animals*. New York: John Wiley & Sons, 1953.

Tinbergen, N. "Derived" activities: their causation, biological significance, origin and emancipation during evolution. *Quarterly Review of Biology*, 1952, *27*, 1–32.

Tinbergen, N. *Animal behavior*. New York: Time, 1965.

Tinbergen, N. *Curious naturalists*. New York: Doubleday and Co., 1968.

Tinbergen, N. The courtship of the Grayling *Eumenis* (*Satyrus*) *semele* L., In N. Tinbergen (Ed.), *The animal in its world*, Vol. 1 *Field studies*, Cambridge, Mass.: Harvard University Press, 1972.

Tinbergen, N. Ethology and stress disease. *Science*, 1974, *185*, 20–27.

Tinbergen, N., Broekhuysen, G. J., Feekes, F., Houghton, J. C. W., Kruuk, H., and Szulc, E. Egg shell removal by the black-headed gull. *Larus ridibundus*, L.; a behaviour component of camouflage. *Behaviour*, 1962, *19*, 74–117.

Tinbergen, N., and Perdeck, A. C. On the stimulus situation releasing the begging response in the newly hatched herring gull chick (*Larus argentatus*). *Behaviour*, 1950, *3*, 1–38.

Tinkelpaugh, O. L. Multiple delayed reaction with chimpanzees and monkeys. *Journal of Comparative Psychology*, 1932, *13*, 197–236.

Tolman, E. C. Principles of performance. *Psychological Review*, 1955 *62*, 315–326.

Tolman, E. C., & Honzik, C. H. "Insight" in rats. *University of California Publication of Psychology*, 1930, *4*, 215–232.

Tompa, F. S. Territorial behavior: the main controlling factor of a local Song Sparrow population. *Auk*, 1962, *79*, 687–697.

Tompa, F. S. Factors determining the number of Song Sparrows, *Melospiza melodia* (Wilson) on Mandarte

Island, B.C., Canada. *Acta Zoologica Fennae*, 1964, *109*, 1–73.

Topsell, E. *The history of four-footed beasts and serpents and insects*. Three vols. New York: Da Capo Press, 1967. Originally published 1658.

Tortora, D. F. *Help! This animal is driving me crazy*. New York: Playboy Press, 1977.

Tortora, D. F., Eyer, J. C., and Overmann, S. R. The effect of sand deprivation on sandbathing and marking in mongolian gerbils. (*Meriones unguiculatus*). *Behavioral Biology*, 1974, *11*, 403–407.

Tourism and recreation in Ontario. Report for the Committee on Tourism and Outdoor Recreation Plan, Province of Ontario, Canada, 1970.

Toynbee, Jocelyn M. C. *Animals in roman life and art*. London: Thames and Hudson, 1973.

Tracy, C. Observations on social behavior in immature California toads (*Bufo boreas*) during feeding. *Copeia*, 1973 2, 342–345.

Trivers, R. L., and Hare, H. Haplodiploidy and the evolution of social insects. *Science*, 1976. *191*, 249–263.

Trueblood, C. K., & Smith, K. U. String pulling behavior of the cat. *Journal of Genetic Psychology*, 1934, *44*, 413–427.

Truman, J. W. The physiology of insect ecdysis. 1. The eclosion behaviour of saturniid moths and its hormonal release. *Journal of Experimental Biology*, 1971, *54*, 804–814.

Tuber, D. S., Hothersall, D., and Voith, V. L. Animal clinical psychology: A modest proposal. *American Psychologist*, 1974, *29*, 762–766.

Turner, E. Social feeding in birds. *Behaviour*, 1964, *24*, 1–46.

Turner, J. W. Influence of neonatal androgens on the display of territorial marking behavior in the gerbil. *Physiology and Behavior*, 1975, *15*, 265–270.

Turner, L. H., and Solomon, R. L. Human traumatic avoidance learning: Theory and experiments on the operant-respondent distinction and failure to learn. *Psychological Monographs*, 1962, *76*(40, Whole No. 559).

Ueda, K., Hara, T. J., and Gorbman, A. Electroencephalographic studies on olfactory discrimination in adult spawning salmon. *Comparative Biochemistry and Physiology*, 1967, *21*, 133–143.

References

Ulrich, R. E., and Azrin, N. H. Reflexive fighting in response to aversive stimulation. *Journal of the Experimental Analysis of Behavior*, 1962, *5*, 511–520.

Underwood, E. J., Shier, F. L., and Davenport, N. Studies in sheep husbandry in western Australia. V. The breeding season in merino, crossbred and British ewes in the agricultural districts. *Journal of Agriculture Western Australia*, 1944, *21*, 135–143.

Uno, T., and Grings, W. Autonomic components of orienting behavior. *Psychophysiology*, 1965, *1*, 311–321.

Uzzell, T. Meiotic mechanisms of naturally occurring unisexual vertebrates. *American Naturalist*, 1970, *104*(939), 433–445.

Valle, F. P. Rats' performance on repeated tests in the open field as a function of age. *Psychonomic Science*, 1971, *23*, 333–335.

Van Brower, Jane Z. The reactions of starlings to different proportions of models and mimics. *American Naturalist*, 1960, *94*, 271–282.

Vandenbergh, J. G. Effect of the presence of a male on the sexual maturation of female mice. *Endocrinology*, 1967, *81*, 345–349.

Vandenbergh, J. G. Male odor accelerates female sexual maturation in mice. *Endocrinology*, 1969, *84*, 658–660.

Van Iersel, J. J. A., and Bol, A. C. A. Preening of two tern species. A study on displacement activities. *Behaviour*, 1958, *13*, 1–88.

Van Lawick-Goodall, J. The behavior of free-living chimpanzees in the Gombe Stream Reserve. *Animal Behavior Monographs*, 1968, *1*(3), 161–311.

Van Riper, W., and Kalmbach, E. R. Homing is not hindered by wing magnets. *Science*, 1952, *115*, 577–578.

Verhave, T. The pigeon as a quality-control inspector. *American Psychologist*, 1966, *21*, 109–115.

Vernon, W., and Ulrich, R. Classical conditioning of pain-elicited aggression. *Science*, 1966, *152*, 668.

Volgyesi, F. A. *Hypnosis of man and animals.* (2nd ed.) Baltimore: Williams & Wilkins, 1966.

von Frisch, K. *The dancing bees.* New York: Harcourt Brace Jovanovich, 1953.

von Frisch, K. *The dance language and orientation of bees.* Cambridge: Harvard Univ. Press, 1967.

von Frisch, K. *Animal architecture.* New York: Harcourt, Brace, Jovanovich, 1974.

Walcott, C., and Green, R. P. Orientation in homing pigeons altered by a change in the direction of an applied magnetic field. *Science*, 1973, *184*, 180–182.

Wallace, A. R. *The Malay Archipelago, the land of the Orang utan and the Bird of Paradise.* New York: Macmillan Co., 1894.

Wallis, D. I. Behaviour patterns of the ant *Formica fusca. Animal Behaviour*, 1962, *10*, 105–112.

Wallraff, H. G. Ortlich und zeitlich bedingte Variabilitat Heimkehr Verhaltens von Brieftauben. *Zertschrift Tierpsychologie*, 1959, *16*, 513–544.

Walther, F. R. Flight behavior and avoidance of predators in Thomson's gazelles. *Behaviour*, 1969, *34*, 184–221.

Warden, C. J. The historical development of comparative psychology. *Psychological Review*, 1927, *34*, 57–85, 135–168.

Warden, C. J., & Hamilton, E. L. The effect of variations in length of maze pattern upon the rate of fixation in the white rat. *Journal of Genetic Psychology*, 1929, *36*, 229–237.

Warden, C. J., Koch, A. M., and Fjeld, H. A. Solution of pattenred string problems by monkeys. *Journal of Genetic Psychology*, 1940, *56*, 283–295.

Warden, C. J., and Reiss, B. F. The relative difficulty of mazes of different lengths for the chick. *Journal of Psychology*, 1941, *11*, 411–419.

Warren, E. W. Modification of the response to high density conditions in the guppy. *Poecilia reticulata* (Peters). *Journal of Fish Biology*, 1973a, *5*, 737–752.

Warren, E. W. The effects of relative density upon some aspects of the behavior of the guppy — *Poecilia reticulata* (Peters). *Journal of Fish Biology*, 1973b, *5*, 753–765.

Warren, E. W. The establishment of a "normal" population and its behavioral maintenance in the guppy — *Poecilia reticulata* (Peters). *Journal of Fish Biology*, 1973c, *5*, 285–304.

Warren, J. M. Effect of geometrical regularity on visual form discrimination by monkeys. *Journal of Comparative and Physiological Psychology*, 1953, *46*, 237–40.

Warren, J. M. Primate learning in comparative

perspective. In A. M. Schrier, H. F. Harlow, and F. Stollnitz, (Eds.), *Behavior of nonhuman primates*. New York: Academic Press, 1965.

Waters, R. H. The nature of comparative psychology. In R. H. Waters, D. A. Rethlingshafer, and W. E. Caldwell (Eds.), *Principles of comparative psychology*. New York: McGraw-Hill, 1960.

Watson, A. Aggression and population regulation in Red Grouse. *Nature*, 1964, *202*, 506–507.

Watson, A. Population control by territorial behaviour in the Red Grouse. *Nature*, 1967, *215*, 1274–1275.

Watson, A., and Jenkins, D. Experiments on population control by territorial behaviour in Red Grouse. *Journal of Animal Ecology*, 1968, *37*, 595–614.

Watson, A., and Miller, G. R. Territory size and aggression in a fluctuating Red Grouse population. *Journal of Animal Ecology*, 1971, *40*, 367–383.

Watson, J. B. *Behavior: An Introduction to Comparative Psychology*. New York: Holt, 1914.

Webb, E. J., Campbell, D. T., Schwartz, R. D., and Seechrest, L. *Unobtrusive measures: Nonreactive research in the social sciences*. Chicago: Rand McNally, 1966.

Wehner, R., and Labhart, T. Perception of the geomagnetic field in the fly *Drosophila melanogaster*. *Experientia*, 1970, *26*, 967–968.

Weidmann, U. and Darley, J. The role of the female in the social display of mallards. Animal Behaviour, 1971, *19*, 287–298.

Weinstein, B. The evolution of intelligent behavior in rhesus monkeys. *Genetic Psychological Monographs*, 1945, *31*, 3–48.

Weisbroth, S. H., Friedman, S., Powell, M., and Scher S. The parasitic ecology of the rodent mite Myobia musculi. I. Grooming factors. *Laboratory of Animal Science*, 1974, *24*(3), 510–516.

Weiskrantz, L. Encephalization and the scotoma. In W. H. Thorpe, and O. L. Zangwill, (Eds.), *Current problems in animal behavior*. Cambridge: Cambridge University Press, 1961.

Weisman, R. G. *A new method of classical conditioning in the rat: Comparisons with an instrumental conditioning technique using the same response*.

Unpublished doctoral dissertation, Michigan State University, 1964.

Weisman, R. G. Experimental comparison of classical and instrumental appetitive conditioning. *American Journal of Psychology*, 1965, *78*, 423–431.

Wells, H. G., Huxley, J. S., and Wells, G. P. *The science of life*. Garden City, N.Y.: The Literary Guild, Country Life Press, 1934.

Welty, J. C. *The life of the birds*. Philadelphia: Saunders Co., 1962.

Wendt, H. *The sex life of the animals*. New York: Simon and Schuster, 1965.

Werth, I. The tendency of Blackbirds and Song Thrushes to breed in their birthplaces. *British Birds*, 1947, *40*, 328–330.

West, J. J., and Alexander, R. D. Sub-social behavior in a burrowing cricket *Anurogryllus muticus* (DeGeer) Orthoptera: Gryllidae. *Ohio Journal of Science*, 1963, *1*, 19–24.

Westerman, R. A. Somatic inheritance of habituation of responses to light in planarians. *Science*, 1963, *140*, 676–677.

White, T. H. *The book of beasts*. New York: G. P. Putnam's Sons, 1954.

Whitney, G., Coble, J. R., Stockton, M. D. and Tilson, E. F. Ultrasonic emissions: Do they facilitate courtship of mice? *Journal of Comparative Physiological Psychology*, 1973, *84*, 445–452.

Whitney, G., and Nyby, J. Ontogeny of mammalian pheromone function: Adult experience is crucial for mice. Paper presented at the 15th International Ethological Congress, Bielefeld, West Germany, 23-31 August, 1977.

Whitson, M. Courtship behavior of the greater roadrunner. *The living bird*, 1975, *14*, 215–255.

Whitten, W. K., Bronson, F. H., & Greenstein, J. A. Estrus-inducing pheromone of male mice: Transport by movement of air. *Science*, 1968, *161*, 584–585.

Wickens, D. D., Nield, A. F., and Wickens, C. D. Habituation of the GSR and of breathing disturbances in the cat. *Psychonomic Science*, 1966, *6*, 325–326.

Wickler, W. Socio-sexual signals and their intra-specific imitation among primates. In D. Morris (Ed.), *Primate ethology*, Chicago: Aldine Publishing Co., 1967.

Wicklund, R. A. *Freedom and reactance.* New York: Halsted Press, 1974.

Wickstra, L. L., and Zerbolio, D. J. Jr. Spatially located visual CS effects in Conditioned Avoidance Shuttle Response (CASR) acquisition in goldfish (*Carassius auratus*): Training over days. *Bulletin of the Psychonomic Society,* 1976, *8,* 124–126.

Wiese, J. H. Courtship and pair formation in the great egret. *AUK,* 1976, *93,* 709–724.

Wigglesworth, V. B. *The principles of insect physiology.* (7th ed.) London: Chapman and Hall, 1974.

Wilcoxon, H. C., Dragoin, W. B., and Kral, P. A. Illness-induced aversions in rat and quail: relative salience of visual and gustatory cues. *Science,* 1971, *171,* 826–826.

Wiley, R. H. Territoriality and non-random mating in sage grouse, *Centrocercus urophasianus. Animal Behaviour Monographs,* 1973, *6*(2), 85–169.

Wiley, R. H. Evolution of social organization and life history patterns among grouse (Aves: tetraonidae). *Quarterly Review of Biology,* 1974, *49*(3): 201–227.

Williams, G. C. *Adaptation and natural selection.* Princeton, N.J.: Princeton University Press, 1966.

Wilson, E. O. *The insect societies.* Cambridge, Mass.: Belknap Press of Harvard University, 1971.

Wilson, E. O. *Sociobiology.* Cambridge, Mass.: Belknap Press of Harvard University, 1975.

Wilson, M. M., and Fowler, H. Variables affecting alternation behavior in the cockroach, Blatta orientalis. *Animal Learning and Behavior,* 1976, *4,* 490–494.

Wilson, R. A., and Collins, G. D. Establishment of a classically conditioned response and transfer of training via cannibalism in planaria. *Perceptual and Motor Skills,* 1967, *24,* 727–730.

Wilz, K. Causal and functional analysis of dorsal picking and nest activity in the courtship of the three-spinned stickleback *Gasterosteus aculeatus. Animal Behaviour,* 1970, *18,* 115–124.

Wimer, C. C., Wimer, R. E., and Roderick, T. H. Some behavioral differences associated with relative size of hippocampus in the mouse. *Journal of Comparative Physiological Psychology,* 1971, *76,* 57–65.

Wimer, R. E., Wimer, C. C., and Roderick, T. H. Genetic variability in forebrain structures between inbred strains of mice. *Brain Research,* 1969, *16,* 257–264.

Wisby, W. J., and Hasler, A. D. The effect of olfactory occlusion on migrating silver salmon (*Oncorhynchus kisutch*). *Journal of Fisheries Research Board of Canada,* 1954, *11,* 472–478.

Wolf, C. P. (Ed.) Social impact assessment — a special issue of *Environment and Behavior,* 1975, *7,* 259–404.

Wolf, L. "Prostitution" behavior in a tropical hummingbird. *Condor,* 1975, *77,* 140–144.

Wolfe, J. B., and Spragg, S. D. S. Some experimental tests of "reasoning" in white rats. *Journal of Comparative and Physiological Psychology,* 1934, *18,* 455–469.

Wolpe, J. *Psychotherapy by reciprocal inhibition,* Stanford, Calif.: Stanford University Press, 1958.

Wolpe, J. *The practice of behavior therapy.* New York: Pergamon, 1969.

Wolpe, J., and Lazarus, A. A. *Behavior therapy techniques.* New York: Pergamon, 1966.

Wood, D. C. Parametric studies of the response decrement produced by mechanical stimuli in the protozoan, *Stentor coeruleus. Journal of Neurobiology,* 1970, *1,* 345–360.

Woodard, W. T., and Bitterman, M. E. Classical conditioning of goldfish in the shuttlebox. *Behavior Research Methods and Instrumentation,* 1971, 3, 192–194.

Woodard, W. T., and Bitterman, M. E. Pavlovian analysis of avoidance conditioning in the goldfish (*Carassium Auratus*). *Journal of Comparative and Physiological Psychology,* 1973, *82* 123–129.

Wood-gush, D. G. M. Time lapse photography: A technique for studying diurnal rhythms. *Physiological Zoology,* 1959, *32,* 273–283.

Wyers, E. J., Peeke, H. V. S., and Herz, M. J. Behavioral habituation in invertebrates. In H. V. S. Peeke and M. J. Herz (Eds.), *Habituation.* Vol I. *Behavioral studies.* New York: Academic Press, 1973.

Wynne-Edwards, V. C. *Regulation of animal numbers by social behaviour.* Edinburgh & London: Oliver & Boyd, 1962(a)

Wynne-Edwards, V. C. *Animal dispersion in relation to social behavior.* New York: Hafner Publishing Co., 1962(b)

Xenophon. fourth century B.C. *Cynegeticus.* Xeno-

References

phon: Scripta minora. Translated by E. C. Marchant. Cambridge, Mass.: Harvard University Press, 1956, Contains both *Cynegeticus* and *Hippike*.

Yager, D. Behavioral analysis of color sensitivities in goldfish. In D. Ingle (Ed.), *The central nervous system and fish behavior*. Chicago: University of Chicago Press, 1968.

Yahr, P. The role of aromization in androgen stimulation of gerbil scent marking. *Hormones and Behavior*, 1976, 7, 259–265.

Yahr, P. Central control of scent marking. In D. Müller-Schwarze and M. M. Mozell (Eds.), *Chemical signals in vertebrates*. New York: Plenum, 1977.

Yahr, P., and Thiessen, D. D. Steroid regulation of territorial scent marking in the Mongolian gerbil (*Meriones unguiculatus*). *Hormones and Behavior*, 1972, 3, 359–368.

Yerkes, R. M. The heredity of savageness and wildness in rats. *Journal of Animal Behaviour*, 1913, 3, 286–296.

Yonge, C. Feeding mechanisms in the invertebrata. *Tabulae Biologicae*, 1954, 21, 46–68.

Young, C. L., and Stephen, W. P. The acoustical behavior of *Acheta domesticus* L. (Orthoptera: Gryllidae) following sublethal doses of Parathion, Dieldrin, and Sevin. *Oecologia*, 1970, 4, 143–162.

Zanich, M. L., and Fowler, H. Primary and secondary reinforcers as distinctive cues which acquire information value in partial-reinforcement discrimination training. *Learning and Motivation*, 1975, 6, 299–313.

Zarrow, M. X. Denenberg, V. H., and Sachs, B. B. Hormones and maternal behavior in mammals. In S. Levine, (Ed.), *Hormones and behavior*. New York: Academic Press, 1972.

Zarrow, M. X., Farooq, A., Denenberg, V. H., Sawin; P. B., and Ross, S. Maternal behavior in the rabbits: Endocrine control of maternal nest-building. *Journal of Reproduction and Fertility*, 1963, 6(3), 375–383.

Zarrow, M. X., Sawin, P. B., Ross, S., and Denenberg, V. H. In E. L. Bliss (Ed.), *Roots of behavior*. New York: Harper (Hoeber), 1962.

Zener, K. The significance of behavior accompanying conditioned salivary secretion for theories of the conditioned response. *American Journal of Psychology*, 1937, 50, 384–403.

Zerbolio, D. J. Temperature-dependent learning in goldfish: a multi-trial active avoidance situation. *Behavioral Biology*, 1973, 8, 775–761.

Zerbolio, D. J. Spatially located visual CS effects in conditioned shuttlebox avoidance in goldfish: A phototactic explanation. *Bulletin of the Psychonomic Society*, 1976, 8, 359–361.

Zerbolio, D. J., Reynierse, J. H., Weisman, R. G., and Denny, M. R. Discriminated learning and reversal in the wheel-turn avoidence situation. *Canadian Journal of Psychology*, 1967, 21, 185–195.

Zerbolio, D. J., and Wickstra, L. L. The effect of power (US intensity X US duration) on shuttlebox avoidance acquisition in goldfish. *Bulletin of the Psychonomic Society*, 1975, 4, 345–347.

Zerbolio, D. J., and Wickstra, L. L. Spatially-located visual CS effects on conditioned shuttlebox avoidance in goldfish (*Carassius auratus*): Further analysis. *Bulletin of the Psychonomic Society*, 1976, 7, 503–505.(a)

Zerbolio, D. J., and Wickstra, L. L. Spatially-located visual CS effects in conditioned avoidance shuttle acquisition in goldfish: Conditioned aversion or phototaxis. *Bulletin of the Psychonomic Society*, 1976, 8, 156–158.(b)

Zerbolio, D. J., and Wickstra, L. L. Discriminated active/passive avoidance conditioning in goldfish (*Carassius auratus*). Paper read before the Psychonomic Society, St. Louis, Mo., November 1976.(c)

Zhuralev, G. E. O. Concerning the hypnotic gaze of snakes. *Voprosy Psikhologii*, 1969, 15, 156–157. (Abstract).

Zimny, G. H., and Schwabe, L. W. Stimulus change and habituation of the orienting response. *Psychophysiology*, 1965, 2, 103–115.

Zippelius, H. Die karawanenbildung bei feld — und hausspitzmaus. *Zeitschrift für Tierpsychologie*, 1972, 30, 305–320.

Zutz, D. Walk up your own grouse. *The American Hunter*, February, 1977, 5(2), 28–31.

References

Additional References

Askew, H. R. Effects of stimulus intensity and inter-trial interval on habituation of the head-shake response in the rat. *Journal of Comparative and Physiological Psychology*, 1970, *72*, 492–497.

Askew, H.R., Leibreckt, B. C., and Ratner, S. C. Effects of stimulus duration and repeated sessions on habituation of the head-shake response in the rat. *Journal of Comparative and Physiological Psychology*, 1969, *67*, 497–503.

Bartoshuk, A. K. Response decrement with repeated elicitations of human neonatal cardiac acceleration sound. *Journal of Comparative and Physiological Psychology*, 1962, *55*, 9–13.

Headstrom, B. R. *Birds' nests; a field guide; identification manual to the nests of birds of the United States east of the hundreth meridian.* New York: I. Washburn, 1961.

Laurence, S., and Stein, D. G. Recovery after brain damage and the concept of localization of function. In S. Finger (Ed.) *Recovery from brain damage: Research and theory*. New York: Plenum Press, 1978.

AUTHOR INDEX

Gray, J. L., 66
Graziano, A. M., 257
Green, H., 425
Green, K. F., 271
Green, R. P., 57
Greenberg, B., 259
Greenstein, J. A., 397
Greenwood, J., 150
Grice, G. R., 256
Grings, W., 219
Griswold, J. G., 367, 374, 376, 380
Gross, C. G., 254
Gross, C. J., 260
Grossen, N. E., 204
Groves, P. M., 213, 220
Guedry, F. E., Jr., 223
Guhl, A. M., 318
Gullion, G. W., 310
Gunn, D. D., 157, 419
Gursbian, E. S., 191
Gustavson, C. R., 271
Guthrie, E. R., 274
Gutscher, H., 61

Hagaman, T. E., 245, 247
Hager, J. L., 281
Hailman, J., 166
Hakluyt, R., 141
Halbert, M. H., 115, 119
Hale, E. B., 305, 318
Hall, Marshall, 4
Hallett, J. P., 159
Hall-Sternglanz, S., 348
Halton, D. C., 410
Hamblin, R. L., 124
Hamilton, D. I., 268
Hamilton, D. O., 268
Hamilton, E. L., 251
Hamilton, G., 271
Hamilton, W. J., 407
Hands, R., 135, 136
Hankins, W. G., 271
Hansen, E., 349, 360
Hara, T. J., 60
Harder, W., 421
Hare, H., 26
Harlow, H. F., 91-92, 259, 349, 358, 360
Harlow, M., 349, 358, 360
Harpin, R. E., 113
Harris, D., 268
Harris, J. D., 208, 221, 225
Hart, B. L., 392

Hartley, P., 428
Hartshorne, C., 309
Hartz, K. E., 211, 226
Haskins, C. H., 139
Hasler, A. D., 60
Hatton, G., 425
Hauser, D. C., 375, 381
Hawn, L. J., 118
Headstrom, B. R., 334
Hearst, E., 75, 78
Hediger, H., 314, 405, 407
Heinz, H. J., 371, 380
Heise, D. R., 102
Hendee, J. C., 115, 118
Henderson, N. D., 204
Henning, C. W., 360, 362, 408, 410
Henry, J. D., 399
Herman, L. M., 261
Herrick, F. H., 331
Herz, M. J., 228
Heshka, S., 111
Hess, E. H., 350
Higgs, G. K., 116
Hilgard, E. R., 166
Hinde, R. A., 64, 143, 154, 166, 209, 211, 214, 216, 219, 222, 225, 281, 298, 299, 314, 342, 344, 396, 407
Hirsch, J., 6, 234
Hirsch, S. M., 362
Hiyama, Y., 60
Hoaglund, H., 409, 412
Hoar, W. S., 343
Hobbes, T., 3
Hodgkin, A. L., 194
Hodjat, S. H., 37
Hodos, W., 201-202
Hoel, P. G., 304
Hoffman, R., 366, 374, 380
Hogan, J., 72, 381, 422, 423
Holt, J. A., 397
Honzik, C. H., 254, 256, 257
Horner, J. L., 168
Hothersall, D., 271, 290
Houghton, J. C. W., 16
House, B. J., 260
Howard, E., 306
Howell, D., 420
Howse, P. E., 231, 235
Hoy, R. R., 19
Hubbard, J., 74
Hubbell, S. P., 12
Hubbert, H. B., 91
Hubbert, M. K., 122

Huff, D. L., 115
Hughes, B., 431
Hughes, C. W., 92, 93
Hughes, H. C., 382
Hughes, R. N., 226
Hulet, C. V., 397
Hull, C. L., 282
Hull, D. B., 132
Humphrey, G., 220, 221
Hunt, E. B., 204
Hunter, W. S., 223, 252, 254
Hupka, R. B., 222
Hurlbut, C. S., Jr., 35
Hurrell, R. M., 366, 374, 380
Hurst, M. E., 115
Hutchinson, R. R., 276
Huxley, A. F., 194
Huxley, J. S., 156
Hyman, L., 298

Idyll, C. P., 58
Ikeshoji, T., 38
Imperato, P. J., 268
Isaacson, R. L., 198-199
Itani, J., 424
Izquierdo, I., 205

Jack, R. W., 43
Jacobsen, R. B., 124
Jacobson, M., 380
Jakway, J. S., 6
James, L., 430
Jamsen, G. C., 118
Janzen, D., 430
Jarman, C., 53
Jarman, P. J., 303
Jay, P., 360
Jenkins, D. W., 37, 38
Jenkins, H. M., 70, 71, 75
Jenni, D. A., 304
Jennings, H. S., 5, 41, 232
Jennings, J., 415
Jensen, D. D., 162, 164, 179, 189, 232
Jobe, J. B., 262
Johnsgard, P. A., 301
Johnson, C. D., 264
Johnson, C. G., 46
Johnson, J. I. Jr., 259
Johnson, L. K., 12
Johnson, R. P., 385
Johnson, V. E., 148
Jones, M. C., 283

Marcuse, F. L., 166
Markham, G., 141, 142
Marler, P., 378
Marquis, D. G., 166
Marsh, D., 247
Marshall, N. B., 293, 325, 336, 350,
  353
Martin, A., 430
Martin, H., 58
Martin, P. S., 130
Martin, R. D., 392
Maruniak, J. A., 386, 387
Mason, P. R., 417
Masserman, J. H., 293, 294
Massero, D. W., 222
Mast, M., 411
Masters, W. H., 148
Masur, J. D., 211, 408
Matthews, G. U. T., 56, 282
Maynard-Smith, J., 27
Mayr, E., 202, 268
Mech, L. D., 392
Mellgren, R. L., 262
Melzack, R., 222, 223
Merari, A., 374
Mewaldt, L. R., 56
Meyer, D. R., 206, 254
Meyer, P. M., 206, 254
Meyers, W. J., 255
Michels, K. M., 255, 259
Michener, D., 297
Miles, R. C., 255
Milgram, S., 112
Millar, R. D., 82
Miller, G. R., 38
Miller, J. L., 124
Miller, N. E., 381
Milne, L., 309
Milne, M., 309
Mitchell, E. V., 145
Mochi, U., 312-313, 322, 327
Moisimann, J. E., 130
Moltz, H., 18, 393
Montagna, W., 383
Montgomery, D. J., 123
Moore, B. R., 66, 68, 70-71, 75, 78
Moore, J. W., 222
Moos, R. H., 113, 116
Morgan, C. L., 1, 4, 5
Morgan, P. D., 397, 427, 433, 434-
  435
Morgan, R., 427, 433, 434-435
Morowitz, H. J., 225, 226

Morrell, F., 215
Morrell, L., 215
Morris, D., 299, 318-319, 378
Morton, M. L., 57
Mosier, H. D., 89
Moss, R., 426
Moulton, D. G., 394
Mountjoy, P. T., 139, 147
Mowrer, O. H., 172
Mozell, M. M., 385
Mueller, H. C., 400
Mugford, R. A., 394
Mulla, M. S., 38
Müller-Schwarze, D., 385, 388, 391,
  394
Murakami, M., 348
Murphy, M. R., 312
Murray, M. D., 376
Mykytowycz, R., 340, 341, 348,
  385, 388, 396

Nachman, M., 428
Nagai, J., 171
Nash, K. F., 411
Nelson, A., 430
Nelson, R. K., 130
Nero, R. W., 20
Nice, M. M., 305, 375, 383
Nicolaidis, S., 263
Nield, A. F., 220
Nisbet, I. C. T., 52
Noble, G. K., 306, 308, 318
Noirot, E., 223
Norgaard, E., 352
Nyby, J., 323, 392, 394

O'Boyle, M., 401
Odum, E. C., 101
Odum, H. T., 101
Oken, B., 268
Oliver, J. A., 293, 295, 338,
  354
Olivierio, A., 203, 204
Ommanney, F. D., 308, 316, 325
Oppian of Corycus, 133
Organ, J., 308
Orr, R. T., 296, 339, 354
Orsingher, O., 205
Ortman, L. L., 318
Overmann, S. R., 366, 374, 425
Owen, K., 392

Palmer, R. S., 40

Papi, F., 57
Partridge, B., 308
Pascal, G. R., 255
Pavlov, I. P., 69, 70, 80, 166, 172,
  293, 294, 408, 412
Payne, A. P., 322
Peek, F. W., 15
Peeke, H. V. S., 216, 219, 221, 222,
  223, 225, 228
Peeke, S. C., 216, 219, 221, 222,
  223, 225
Pelkwijk, J. J., 299
Pendergrass, V. E., 219
Penman, G. G., 201
Pennak, R. W., 46
Perdeck, A. C., 346
Peretz, B., 225
Perkins, C. C., Jr., 256
Peters, R. P., 392, 344
Peterson, W. M., 260
Petrinovich, L., 221, 222, 224
Pfungst, O., 149
Phillips, J. S., 273, 278
Phillips, R. E., 383
Pietrewicz, A. T., 402
Pinchbeck, W. F., 148
Pinckney, G. A., 170
Platt, J., 282
Plomin, R., 264
Polioudakis, E., 397
Polsky, R. H., 400-401
Pomerantz, G. A., 119
Porter, R. H., 394
Potratz, H., 131
Potter, D. R., 115, 118
Potter, E. F., 115, 118, 375, 381
Potter, V., 427
Povar, M. L., 260
Powell, M., 376
Precht, H., 223
Prechtl, H. F. R., 217
Premack, D., 265, 274, 282
Pressman, I., 111
Prestrude, A. M., 149, 364, 408,
  409, 412
Prewitt, E. P., 77
Price, E. O., 85
Price, J., 112
Price, P. W., 37
Prosser, C. L., 171, 223
Pruitt, C., 419
Ptolemy II, 133, 138
Pulliam, H., 421

Sollberger, A., 214
Solomon, R. L., 172
Southern, W. E., 55
Sparks, J. H., 377
Spearman, R. I. C., 369
Spence, K. W., 282
Spencer, W. A., 209-210, 213, 214, 215, 220, 221, 223
Spinoza, 3
Spragg, S. D. S., 252, 257
Sprague, R. H., 388
Stacey, N., 308
Stager, K., 419
Stahl, J. M., 258
Statkiewtitz, W., 381
Steel, E. A., 298-299, 342
Stein, D. G., 202
Steinberg, J., 301
Steiner, A. L., 231
Stellar, E., 42
Stephen, W. P., 240
Stephens, R., 426
Stern, J. J., 374, 394
Sternthal, D., 419
Stevenson, S. S., 381
Stevenson-Hinde, J., 281
Stewart, J. S., 124
Stockton, M. D., 323
Stoddart, D. M., 391, 393, 396
Stokes, A. W., 305, 319
Stokols, D., 113
Stolurow, L. M., 255
Stone, C. P., 85, 91, 98, 159
Stout, J. F., 308
Stricker, E., 425
Strong, P. N., Jr., 261
Sturm, T., 72
Suboski, M. D., 77
Sullivan, C. M., 36
Sulzbacher, S., 425
Summerlin, C. T., 394
Swanson, H. H., 322
Szebenyi, A. L., 371
Szlep, R., 223
Szulc, E., 16

Tait, R. W., 77
Tavolga, W. N., 308
Taylor, J., 150
Teale, E. W., 230-231
Ternes, J. W., 411
Thiessen, D. D., 88, 110, 385, 388, 391, 392, 396

Thompson, R. F., 77, 209-210, 213, 214, 215, 220, 221
Thompson, R. K. R., 261
Thompson, R. W., 410
Thompson, T., 72
Thorndike, E. L., 5, 280-281, 381
Thorpe, W. H., 79, 143, 156, 209, 211, 220, 221, 225
Tiefer, L., 388
Tilson, E. F., 323
Timms, A. M., 308
Tinbergen, N., 16, 43, 66-67, 90, 154, 155, 166, 236, 284, 298, 299, 305, 306, 308, 315, 316, 337, 342, 346, 347, 382, 405
Tinkelpaugh, O. L., 255
Tolman, E. C., 65, 80, 257
Tomich, P. Q., 388
Tompa, F. S., 38
Tongiorgi, P., 57
Topsell, E., 135
Tortora, D. F., 273, 374
Toynbee, J. M. C., 133
Tracy, C., 431
Triplehorn, C. A., 237
Trivers, R. L., 26
Trueblood, C. K., 259
Truman, J. W., 235
Tryon, R. C., 6
Tuber, D. S., 271, 291
Turner, E., 431
Turner, J. R., 403
Turner, J. W., 392
Turner, L. H., 172
Twiggs, D. G., 392

Ueda, K., 60
Ulrich, R., 72, 222-223
Underwood, E. J., 397
Uno, T., 219
Uzzell, T., 297

Valins, S., 113
Valle, F. P., 211, 223
Van Brower, J. Z., 403, 428
Vandenbergh, J. G., 388, 397
VanDeventer, J. M., 157
Van Doren, D. S., 116
Van Iersel, J. J. A., 380
Van Kampen, K., 430
Van Lawick-Goodall, J., 313, 324, 375, 376, 378
Van Riper, W., 57

Verdier, M., 38
Verhave, T., 270
Vernon, W., 72
Verplank, R. B., 139
Vogt, W., 318
Voith, V. L., 271, 290
Volygyesi, F. A., 166
von Frisch, K., 44, 236, 242-243, 294, 295, 296, 337, 338, 339, 353
von Schilcher, F., 315

Walcott, C., 57
Wallace, A. R., 329
Wallis, D. I., 372
Wallraff, H. G., 56
Walther, F. R., 358, 405, 413
Warden, C. J., 234, 251, 259
Warren, E. W., 38
Warren, J. M., 265
Waters, R. H., 159
Watson, A., 37-38, 54, 61
Watson, J. B., 5, 232
Webb, E. J., 164
Weber, P. G., 358
Webster, H. M., 135
Webster, W. R., 219
Wehner, R., 58
Weidmann, U., 301
Weinberger, N. M., 214
Weinstein, B., 262
Weisbroth, S. H., 376
Weiskrantz, L., 200-201
Weisman, R. G., 70, 79, 189
Welch, L., 220
Wells, H. G., 156
Wells, G. P., 156
Welty, J. C., 288, 289, 291, 331, 332, 334, 349, 352, 353, 358, 359
Wendt, H., 329, 333, 338, 340, 347, 348
Werth, I., 60
West, J. J., 351
West, S., 112
Westerman, R., 223, 225
White, T. H., 135
Whitney, G., 323, 394
Whitson, M., 319, 320, 321
Whitten, W. K., 397
Wickens, C. D., 220
Wickens, D. D., 220
Wickler, W., 313, 323, 432
Wicklund, R. A., 124

Wickstra, L. L., 170, 171, 176, 187
Wiese, J. H., 311
Wigglesworth, V. B., 240, 244
Wike, E. L., 257
Wilcoxon, H. C., 74
Wiley, R. H., 304, 310
Wilkinson, C., 429
Williams, G. C., 13
Williams, H. W., 319
Williams, W. L., 43
Willis, E. R., 324
Wilson, E. O., 25, 232, 242, 243,
244, 303, 305, 307, 310, 350,
351, 352, 355, 356, 372, 377,
431
Wilson, M. M., 239
Wilson, N., 425
Wilson, R. A., 164
Wilz, K., 300
Wimer, C. C., 206
Wimer, R. E., 206
Winn, H. E., 24, 25, 308

Wisby, W. J., 60
Witt, E. D., 259
Wolf, C. P., 123
Wolf, L., 319, 327
Wolfe, J. B., 257
Wolfe, J. L., 394
Wolpe, J., 278, 283, 293,
294
Wood, D. C., 225
Wood, M. J., 396
Woodard, W. T., 171, 172, 175,
176, 182
Wood-Gush, D. G. M., 381, 382
Wright, H. E., Jr., 130
Wurm, M., 306
Wyers, E. J., 211, 221, 223,
225
Wynne-Edwards, V. C., 25, 26,
361, 385
Wysocki, C. J., 323

Xenophon, 132, 149

Yager, D., 171
Yahr, P., 391, 392
Yerkes, R. M., 5, 85
Yonge, C., 414, 415
Young, C. L., 240
Young, J. Z., 194
Youngren, O. M., 383
Yutzey, D. A., 206

Zabarenko, R. N., 255
Zamble, E., 77
Zanich, M. L., 250
Zarrow, M. X., 300, 343, 348
Zeaman, D., 260
Zener, K., 70
Zerbolio, D. J., 87, 170, 171, 176,
179, 187, 189
Zhuralev, G. E. O., 413
Zim, H., 430
Zimny, G. H., 220
Zippelius, H., 350
Zutz, D., 149

SUBJECT INDEX

Defense systems: primary, 401-404
    secondary, 404-408
Defensive or antipredator behavior
    in insects, 246
Defensive behavior, conditioning
    of, 73
Deflection, type of diversion, 406
Degeneracy, 84, 85, 86, 87, 91
Delayed compensatory response,
    239
Delayed response, 253-255
    and deprivation level, 254-255
    direct method, 253
    frontal lesions, 254
    and incentive magnitude, 254
    indirect method, 253
    one-trial learning interpretation
        of, 254
    and orienting, 253
    time to forget after one learning
        trial, 253
Delayed-response performance,
    rank order of species, 255
Denny, Thomas, and Elliott, 252
Density (population): and design
    of buildings, 112-113
    experimental manipulations, 112
    systems perspective, 114
Density-intensity theories (for
    populations), 113
Density level, of populations, 116
Deprivation, 141, 142, 254, 364,
    374, 379
Detoxification mechanisms, 429
Diematic behaviors or displays,
    406
Dietary selection, 425-426
Differential reinforcement contin-
    gencies, 69
Differential reinforcement of other
    behavior (DRO), 274, 277,
    287
Differential selection contingencies,
    69
Discriminated avoidance, 186
Discrimination learning: conditional,
    250, 261
    simple, 250
    special methodology of, 259-260
Dishabituation, 214, 219-220
Disinhibition and displacement
    behavior, 382
Dispersal of animals, 30, 33, 39

barriers to, 35
directional factors, 41
and sensory capacities, 41
Displacement behavior, 381-382
Displays as instincts, 18, 19
Distractability to external stimuli,
    255
Distribution of animals, 30, 32, 33
    determinants, 36
    environmental variables, 37
Distribution of human populations,
    109
Disruption of behavioral sequence,
    199
Diversion as a flight mechanism,
    406
Diversity, 2, 330
    of behavior, 30, 128, 167
    of subject matter, 153
DNA, 28
Dog bites, incidence of, 268
Domestication, 84, 85, 86, 87, 91,
    131
    and learning, 93-94
Dominance biting, 274, 276-277
Dominance relations, 277, 278
    modification of, 287-289
    and scent marking, 395-396
Double alternation problem, 255-
    256
Dray (main nest), 339
Dressing out "grolloching", 141
Drug effects, class, genus, and spe-
    cies differences, 204
Dualism, 3, 4
Duck decoy (endekooy), 142-143
Dung ball rolling, 334
Dustbathing, 363-367, 374, 380
    effects of early experience, 366-
        367, 380
    experiments on, 364-366
    sequence of component occur-
        rence, 364-365

Echolocation: in bats, 420
    and feeding, 420
Ecological interactional problems,
    271
Ecological knowledge of hunters,
    119
Ecological niche, 12, 205
Ecological relevance of laboratory
    experiments, 94-95

Ecology, 31
    of species, 66
Ecosystems, natural, 105
Educated pig, 148
Effector fatigue, 214
Electric fish, 418, 421
Electroreception and feeding, 418,
    421
Elephant behavior, 134
Elicitation theory or framework,
    254, 380
Emotion, 21, 22
Emotionality in rats, 89, 93
Encephalization, 200-201
Encyclopedias of animal behavior,
    141
Energy and increased population
    density, 123
Energy conversion, 105
Energy resources, scarcity of, 122
Energy sources and environmental
    values, 122
Enrichment, early, 93
Entomologists, 18
Environment: definition, 31
    external, 32
    internal, 31, 33
    source of variation, 10
Environmental selection, parenting,
    331-333
Epimeletic (care giving) behaviors,
    328
Equipotentiality assumption, 426
Escape, 409, 412
    from fear provoking CS, 170,
        189
    from US, 170
Estrous synchronization, 397
Et-epimeletic (care seeking) behav-
    iors, 328
Ethologists, 66, 68, 154
Ethology, 4, 154
Evolution, 10-12, 68
    and conditioning, 81
    theory of, 10-12, 144, 154
Evolutionary adaptation and behav-
    ior, 32
Evolutionary biology, 64
Evolutionary changes, 11
Evolutionary history (of migratory
    species), 61
Evolutionary mechanisms,
    105

Intelligence, 266
"Intelligence" in insects, 235
Interaction between environment
    and individual, 100
Interactive behavior in crickets, 240
Interbreeding, 11
Interorganism interactions, 281
Intraorganism interactions, 280
Intraspecies warnings and flight,
    405
Intrinsic density of populations,
    111
Isolation of species, 11
Invertebrate behavior, study of,
    230, 232

Jacobson's organ, 419

Kineses, 157, 417
Kinesthesis: complex maze-learning,
    252
    perseverative, 256
    unit-alike maze, 252-253
Kinetic reaction, 57. *See also*
    Kineses

Laboratorization in domestic rats,
    94
Lana, 265
Landowners and hunting, 119-120
Language: in chimpanzees, 265
    functions in brain, 194
Lark mirror, 141
Latent inhibition, 222
Lateral geniculate, differentiation
    of, 201
Laws of learning, generality of, 95
Learned irrelevance, 80
Learned release, of innate behavior,
    80-81
Learning, 14, 69
    and animal dispersal, 44
    as associative mechanism, 65
    biochemistry of, 171
    and color vision, 19
    complex maze, 250-251
    demonstration of, 172
    differences between strains,
        genus, and species, 197
    and early enrichment, 93
    in evolutionary context, 69
    and fixed action patterns, 19
    genetic factors in, 202-203

in goldfish, 170-172
and habituation, 221-222
in insects, 235-237
with long-delay, 263
in mazes, 91
as the modification of innate be-
    havior, 158, 162
nicotine, effects of, 204
operant, 158
respondent, 158
in wild and laboratory rats, 90-96
Learning history of the horse, 132
Learning to ignore, 80
Learning to inhibit, 80
Learning to learn, 92
Learning the meaning of scents,
    394
Learning set, 259-269
Legislature and hunting, 119
Lek displays, 303, 310-311
Licking, conditioned, 70, 90
Life-styles for defense, 356
Life-support systems, 105, 106,
    107, 109, 122
Lithium chloride (LiCl) as a UCS,
    271, 426
Localization of function in brain,
    198
Loco-habit, 430
Locomotor behavior, 67, 68, 75
Long CS-US interval and condition-
    ing, 263

Magnetic field, earth, 57
Maier's three-table "reasoning"
    problem, 257-258
Makafeke (octopus lure), 130-131
Mapping of knowledge, 65, 81
Mass-energy processes in human
    ecology, 108
Mass-energy systems, 101
Mass-energy and control systems,
    coupling of, 102-103
Masturbation in horse and human,
    147-148
Matching theories, 113
Maternal care, 27, 44
Mating: and territorial behavior,
    305
    systems, 303
Maturational changes and habitua-
    tion, 215
Maze learning in wild rats, 91

Medieval bestiary, 135, 141
Meme, 28
Memory, 249-250, 262
    consolidation, mechanisms of,
        205
    and forebrain, 199
    genetic factors in, 202-203
    for images, after brain damage,
        200
    immediate, 249
    for minor disasters (humans), 125
    short term, in mice, 204
    and span, 250
    in vertebrates and invertebrates,
        44, 199-200, 204
Metabolic changes during premigra-
    tory period, 49
Migration, 45, 54, 55
    as consummatory behavior, 61
    defined, 46
    diurnal, 46
    in eels, 59
    "flyways," 52
    in golden plover, 47
    "half-distance," 54
    initiation of, 48
    IRM (innate releasing mechanism)
        of, 51
    in insects, 59
    orientation and navigation in, 45,
        54, 55
    physiological mechanisms of, 47
    predisposing factors for, 49
    releasing factors for, 45, 46
    and reproductive cycle, 49
    route description, 51
    route selection, 48
    site specificity, 60
    as species specific, 48
    species-specific releasing mechan-
        ism for, 50, 51
    "traffic counts," 48
    vertical or horizontal, 46, 62
Migratory cycle, 61
Migratory flights, 49
Migratory routes, genetic determi-
    nation of, 54
Military use of animals, 270
Mimicry, 355
Mirror image stimulation of chim-
    panzees, 264
Mobbing behavior of birds, 127,
    143, 144, 360

Subject Index